300 CREATIVE PHYSICS PROBLEMS
with Solutions

László Holics

A

ANTHEM PRESS
LONDON · NEW YORK · DELHI

Anthem Press
An imprint of Wimbledon Publishing Company
www.anthempress.com

This edition first published in UK and USA 2011
by ANTHEM PRESS
75-76 Blackfriars Road, London SE1 8HA, UK
or PO Box 9779, London SW19 7ZG, UK
and
244 Madison Ave. #116, New York, NY 10016, USA

Sponsored by Graphisoft Foundation

British Library Cataloguing in Publication Data
A catalogue record for this book is available from the British Library.

Library of Congress Cataloging in Publication Data
A catalog record for this book has been requested.

ISBN-13: 978 0 85728 402 0 (Pbk)
ISBN-10: 0 85728 402 9 (Pbk)

TABLE OF CONTENTS

How to Use This Book

The best way of understanding the laws of physics and learning how to solve physics problems is through practice. This book features almost three hundred problems and solutions worked out in detail. In Part I, *Problems* are arranged thematically, starting in Chapter 1 with problems about **mechanics**, the branch of physics concerned with the behaviour of physical bodies when subjected to forces or displacements, and the subsequent effect of the bodies on their environment. Chapter 2 offers problems in **thermodynamics**, the study of energy conversion between heat and mechanical work, while the **electrodynamics** problems in Chapter 3 deal with the phenomena associated with moving electrical charges and their interaction with electric and magnetic fields. Chapter 4's problems on **magnetism** seek to understand how materials respond on the microscopic level to an applied magnetic field. Lastly, the **optics** problems in Chapter 5 address the branch of physics that studies the behaviour and physical properties of light.

While the problems are arranged by topic, the problems within a single topic are often arranged by increasing level of difficulty. Indeed, many of these physics problems are difficult – yet we encourage students to try and solve the problems on their own, and to only consult the *Solutions* section in order to compare their own attempts with the correct results. We encourage creativity in problem-solving, and these physics problems are intended as a means of developing the student's knowledge of physics by applying them to concrete problems.

Physical Constants and Other Data

Gravitational constant	G	6.673×10^{-11} $\mathrm{Nm^2kg^{-2}}$
Speed of light (in vacuum)	c	2.998×10^8 $\mathrm{ms^{-1}}$
Elementary charge	e	1.602×10^{-19} C
Electron mass	m_e	9.109×10^{-31} kg (511.0 keV)
Proton mass	m_p	1.673×10^{-27} kg (938.3 MeV)
Neutron mass	m_n	1.675×10^{-27} kg (939.6 MeV)
Charge-to-mass ratio of electron	e/m_e	1.759×10^{11} $\mathrm{Ckg^{-1}}$
Unified atomic mass constant	m_u	1.661×10^{-27} kg
Boltzmann constant	k	1.381×10^{-23} $\mathrm{JK^{-1}}$
Plank constant	h	6.626×10^{-34} Js
Avogadro constant	N_A	6.022×10^{23} $\mathrm{mol^{-1}}$
Gas constant	R	8.315 $\mathrm{Jmol^{-1}\,K^{-1}}$
Permittivity of free space	ε_0	8.854×10^{-12} $\mathrm{CV^{-1}}m^{-1}$
Permeability of free space	μ_0	$4\pi \times 10^{-7}$ $\mathrm{Vs^2}C^{-1}m^{-1}$
Coulomb constant	$k = 1/4\pi\varepsilon_0$	8.987×10^9 $\mathrm{VmC^{-1}}$
Compton wavelength of electron	λ_c	2.426×10^{-12} m
Mean radius of the Earth	R	6371 km
Sun-Earth distance (Astronomical Unit, AU)		1.49×10^8 km
Mean density of the Earth	ρ	5520 $\mathrm{kgm^{-3}}$
Acceleration due to gravity	g	9.807 $\mathrm{ms^{-2}}$
Mass of the Earth		5.978×10^{24} kg
Mass of the Sun		1.989×10^{30} kg
1 light year		9.461×10^{15} m
Surface tension of water	γ	0.073 $\mathrm{Nm^{-1}}$
Heat of vaporisation of water	L	2256 $\mathrm{kJkg^{-1}} = 40.6$ $\mathrm{kJmol^{-1}}$
Tensile strength of steel	σ	500–2000 MPa

Part I

PROBLEMS

Chapter 1

Mechanics Problems

1.1 Kinematics

Problem 1. A train is moving at a speed of v towards the railwayman next to the rails. The train whistles for a time of T. How long does the railwayman hear the whistle? The speed of sound is $c = 330\,\text{m/s}$; $v = 108\,\text{km/hour} = 30\,\text{m/s}$, $T = 3\,\text{s}$; the train does not reach the railwayman until the end of the whistle.

Problem 2. The speed of a motorboat in still water is four times the speed of a river. Normally, the motorboat takes one minute to cross the river to the port straight across on the other bank. One time, due to a motor problem, it was not able to run at full power, and it took four minutes to cross the river along the same path. By what factor was the speed of the boat in still water reduced? (Assume that the speed of the water is uniform throughout the whole width of the river.)

Problem 3. Consider a trough of a semicircular cross section, and an inclined plane in it that leads from a point A to point B lying lower than A. Prove that wherever point C is chosen on the arc AB, an object will always get from A to B faster along the slopes ACB than along the original slope AB. The change of direction at C does not involve a change in speed. The effects of friction are negligible.

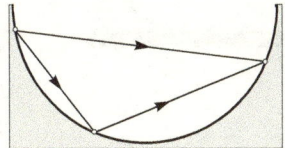

Problem 4. The acceleration of an object is uniformly increasing, and it is $a_0 = 2\,\text{m/s}^2$ at $t_0 = 0\,\text{s}$ and $a_1 = 3\,\text{m/s}^2$ at $t_1 = 1\,\text{s}$. The speed of the object at $t_0 = 0\,\text{s}$ is $v_0 = 1\,\text{m/s}$.

a) Determine the speed of the object at $t_2 = 10\,\text{s}$.

b) Determine the $v-t$ function of the motion, and then plot it in the $v-t$ coordinate system.

c) Estimate the distance covered by the object in the first and last second of the time interval $0 < t < 10\,\text{s}$.

Problem 5. An object moves on a circular path such that its distance covered is given by the function: $s = 0.5t^2$ m $+ 2t$ m. The ratio of the magnitudes of its accelerations at times $t_1 = 2$ s and $t_2 = 5$ s is $1 : 2$. Find the radius of the circle.

Problem 6. The radius of the tire of a car is R. The valve cap is at distance r from the axis of the wheel. The car starts from rest without skidding, at constant acceleration. Is it possible, in some way, that the valve cap has no acceleration

a) in the $\dfrac{1}{8}$ turn following the bottom position,

b) in the $\dfrac{1}{8}$ turn preceding the bottom position?

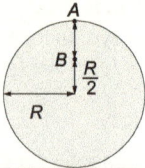

Problem 7. A disc of diameter 20 cm is rolling at a speed of 4 m/s on the ground, without slipping. How long does it take until the speed of point A first becomes equal to the present value of the speed of point B?

Problem 8. A disc of radius $R = 1$ m rolls uniformly, without skidding on horizontal ground. The speed of its centre is $v = 0.5$ m/s. Let A stand for the topmost point at $t = 0$ and B for the mid-point of the corresponding radius.

a) At what time will the speed of point A first equal the speed of point B?

b) Following on from part a) above, when the speed of point A first equals the speed of point B, what is this speed?

c) Following on from part a) above, find the distance travelled by the centre of the disk up to the time when the speed of point A first equals the speed of point B.

Problem 9. A cart moves on a muddy road. The radius of its wheels is $R = 0.6$ m. A small bit of mud detaches from the rim at a height $h = \frac{3}{2}R$ from the ground.

a) Find the speed of the cart if the bit of mud falls back on the wheel at the same height.

b) Find the length of the arc on the rim that connects the points of detaching and falling back.

c) Find the distance covered by the car in the meantime.

Problem 10. A balloon is rising vertically from the ground in such a way that with high accuracy its acceleration is a linearly decreasing function of its altitude above the ground level. At the moment of release the velocity of the balloon is zero, and its acceleration is a_0.

a) Determine the speed of the balloon at the height H, where its acceleration becomes zero.

b) What is the speed of the balloon at half of the altitude H?

c) How long does it take the balloon to reach the altitude H?

Problem 11. A massive ball is falling down from an initial height of $h = 20$ m. With a gun held horizontally, $d = 50$ m far from the trajectory of the falling ball, at the height of $h' = 10$ m, we are going to shoot at the falling ball. The bullet leaves the gun at a speed of $v = 100$ m/s. At what time after the start of the fall should the gun be fired in order to hit the falling ball with the bullet? (The air resistance is negligible.)

Problem 12. Two objects, one sliding down from rest on a smooth (frictionless) slope, the other being thrown from the point O, start their motion at the same instant. Both get to the point P at the same time and at the same speed. Determine the initial angle of the throw.

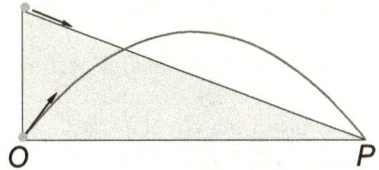

Problem 13. A projectile is projected on the level ground at an angle of $30°$ with an initial speed of 400 m/s. At one point during its trajectory the projectile explodes into two pieces. The two pieces reach the ground at the same moment; one of them hits the ground at exactly where it was projected with a speed of 250 m/s. At what height did the explosion occur? (Air drag and the mass of the explosive material is negligible, the acceleration due to gravity can be considered as 10 m/s^2.)

Problem 14. The bullet of a poacher flying at a speed of $v = 680$ m/s passes the gamekeeper at a distance $d = 1$ m. What was the distance of the bullet from the gamekeeper when he began to sense its shrieking sound? The speed of propagation of sound is $c = 340$ m/s.

1.2 Dynamics

Problem 15. A frictionless track consists of a horizontal part of unknown length, which connects to a vertical semicircle of radius r as shown. An object, which is given an initial velocity v, is to move along the track in such a way that after leaving the semicircle at the top it is to fall back to its initial position. What should the minimum length of the horizontal part be?

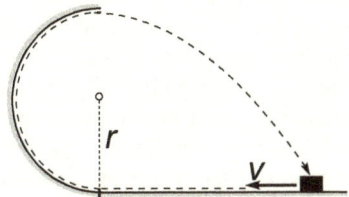

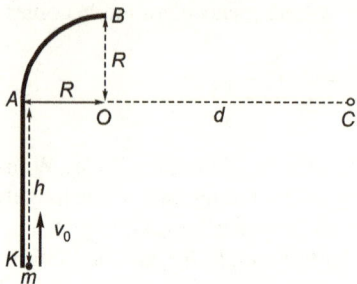

Problem 16. A pointlike object of mass m starts from point K in the figure. It slides along the full length of the smooth track of radius R, and then moves freely and travels to point C.

a) Determine the vertical initial velocity of the pointlike object.

b) What is the minimum possible distance $OC = d$, necessary for the object to slide along the entire length of the track?

c) Find the normal forces exerted by the track at points A and B.

(Let $R = 1\,\text{m}$, $h = 2\,\text{m}$, $d = 3\,\text{m}$, $m = 0.5\,\text{kg}$, use $g = 10\,\text{m/s}^2$)

Problem 17. A small object starts with a speed of $v_0 = 20\,\text{m/s}$ at the lowest point of a circular track of radius $R = 8.16\,\text{m}$. The small object moves along the track. How big a part of the circular track can be removed, if you want to carry out the same trick? (Neglect friction, $g = 9.8\,\text{m/s}^2$.)

Problem 18. A small object of mass $m = 0.5$ kg that hangs on a string of length $L = 5.6$ m is given a horizontal velocity of $v_0 = 14\,\text{m/s}$. The string can withstand a maximum tension of $40\,\text{N}$ without breaking. Where is the stone when the string breaks? Use $g = 10\,\text{m/s}^2$.

Problem 19. An object slips down the frictionless surface of a cylinder of radius R.

a) Find the position in which the acceleration of the object is two thirds of the gravitational acceleration G.

b) Find the direction of the object's acceleration in that position.

Problem 20. Two horizontal tracks are connected through two circular slopes the radii of which are equal and $R = 5$ m. The tracks and the slopes are in a vertical plane and they join without a break or sharp corner. The height difference between the horizontal tracks is $h = 2\,\text{m}$. An object moves from the track at the top onto the bottom one without friction. What is the maximum initial speed of the object when it starts, in order for it to touch the path at all times during its motion?

Problem 21. A small object is moving on a special slope consisting of a concave and a convex circular arc, both of which have a right angle at the centre and radius $R = 0.5$ m, and they join smoothly, with horizontal common tangent, as it is shown in the figure. Determine the distance covered by the object on the slope, provided that it started from rest and it detaches from the slope at the altitude $\dfrac{3}{4}R$. (The friction is negligibly small.)

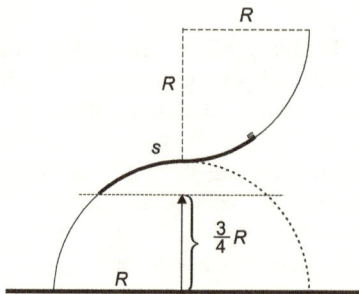

Problem 22. A pendulum, whose cord makes an angle $45°$ with the vertical is released. Where will the bob reach its minimum acceleration?

Problem 23. Two blocks, each of mass 3 kg, are connected by a spring, whose spring constant is 200 N/m. They are placed onto an inclined plane of angle $15°$. The coefficient of friction between the upper block and the inclined plane is 0.3, while between the lower block and the inclined plane it is 0.1. After a while, the two blocks move together with the same acceleration. Use $g = 10 \, \text{m/s}^2$.
a) Find the value of their acceleration.
b) Find the extension of the spring.

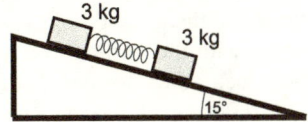

Problem 24. A solid cylinder of mass M and radius R, rolling without sliding on a rough horizontal plane, is pulled at its axis with a horizontal velocity of v_0. By means of a string of length $2R$ attached to its axis, the cylinder is dragging a thin plate of mass $m = 2M$ lying on the plane. If the system is released, how long does it take to stop, and what is the stopping distance?
($\mu = 0.4$; $v_0 = 2$ m/s; $R = 0.5$ m, use $g = 10 \, \text{m/s}^2$)

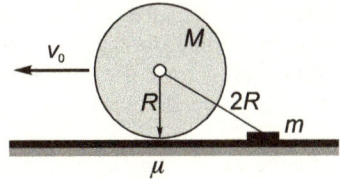

Problem 25. A rigid surface consists of a rough horizontal plane and an inclined plane connecting to it without an edge. A thin hoop of radius $r = 0.1$ m is rolling towards the slope without slipping, at a velocity of $v_0 = 3.5 \, \dfrac{\text{m}}{\text{s}}$, perpendicular to the base of the slope.
a) In which case will the hoop get higher up the slope: if there is friction on the slope or if there is not?
b) Assume that the slope is ideally smooth. At a time $t = 2.4$ s after arriving at the slope, what will be the speed of the hoop returning from the slope?
(The coefficients of both static and kinetic friction between the horizontal plane and the hoop are $\mu = 0.2$. The slope connects to the horizontal plane with a smooth curve of radius $R > r$, which is considered part of the slope. The hoop does not fall on its side during the motion.)

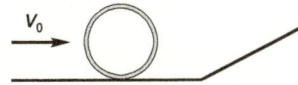

Problem 26. A block of mass $M = 5$ kg is moving on a horizontal plane. An object of mass $m = 1$ kg is dropped onto the block, hitting it with a vertical velocity of $v_1 = 10$ m/s. The speed of the block at the same time instant is $v_2 = 2$ m/s. The object sticks to the block. The collision is momentary. What will be the speed of the block after the collision if the coefficient of friction between the block and the horizontal plane is $\mu = 0.4$?

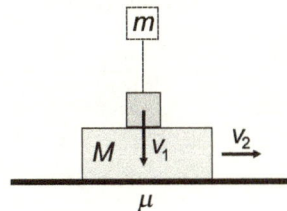

Problem 27. A pointlike ball of mass m is tied to the end of a string, which is attached to the top of a thin vertical rod. The rod is fixed to the middle of a block of mass M lying at rest on a horizontal plane. The pendulum is displaced to a horizontal position and released from rest.

If the coefficient of static friction between the block and the ground is μ_s, what angle will the string create with the vertical rod at the time instant when the block starts to slide? ($M = 2$ kg, $m = 1$ kg, $\mu_s = 0.2$.)

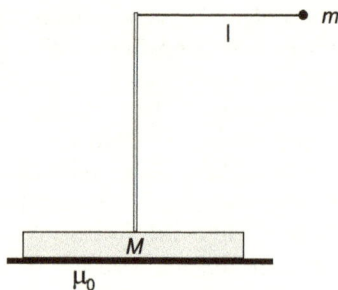

Problem 28. Two small cylinders of equal radius are rotating quickly in opposite directions. Their spindles are parallel and lie on the same horizontal plane. The distance between the spindles is 2L. Place a batten of uniform density onto the top of the two cylinders so that the batten is perpendicular to the spindles, and its centre of mass is at a distance of x from the perpendicular bisector of the segment between the two spindles, which is perpendicular to the spindles. What type of motion does the batten undergo?

Problem 29. An object is pulled up uniformly along an inclined plane which makes an angle of α with the horizontal. The angle between the force with which it is pulled up and the plane of the incline is β. The coefficient of friction between the plane and the object is μ. In what interval can the angle β vary to allow the force to pull up the object?

Problem 30. A coin is placed onto a phonograph turntable at a distance of $r = 10$ cm from the centre. The coefficient of static friction between the coin and the turntable is $\mu = 0.05$. The turntable, which is initially at rest, starts to rotate with a constant angular acceleration of $\beta = 2 \text{ s}^{-2}$. How much time elapses before the coin slips on the turntable?

Problem 31. A rigid rod of length $L = 3$ m and mass $M = 3$ kg, whose mass is distributed uniformly, is placed on two identical thin-walled cylinders resting on a horizontal table. The axes of the two cylinders are $d = 2$ m from each other. As for the rod, one of its endpoints is directly above the axis of one cylinder, while its trisector point (closer to its other end) is directly above the axis of the other cylinder. The mass of the cylinders is $m = 1$ kg each. A constant horizontal pulling force $F = 12$ N acts on the rod. Both cylinders roll without friction.

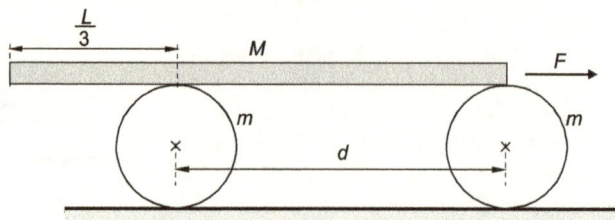

a) Find the final speed of the rod, when its leftmost end is exactly above the axis of the left cylinder.

b) Find the friction force and the minimum coefficient of friction required between the cylinders and the rod for pure rolling.

c) Find the minimum coefficient of friction between the table and the cylinders.

Problem 32. A cart of mass 3 kg is pulled by a 5 kg object as shown. The cart, whose length is 40 cm moves along the table without friction. There is a brick of mass 2 kg on the cart, which falls from it 0.8 s after the start of the motion. Find the coefficient of kinetic friction between the cart and the brick. Use $g = 10\,\text{m/s}^2$.

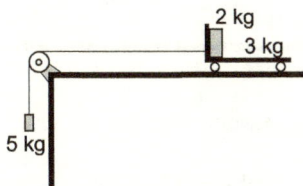

Problem 33. A small solid sphere of mass $m = 8\,\text{kg}$ is placed inside a rigid hollow sphere of mass $M = 8\,\text{kg}$. The hollow sphere is then dropped from a great height. Air drag is in direct proportion to the square velocity: $F = kv^2$. If speed and force are measured in m/s and Newton respectively, then $k = 0.1$. Draw a graph that represents the force exerted by the small sphere on the hollow sphere in terms of velocity. Use $g = 10\,\text{m/s}^2$.

Problem 34. A small body that is fixed to the end of a string of length $l = 20\,\text{cm}$ is forced to move along a circle on a slope whose angle of inclination is $\alpha = 30°$. The body starts from the lowest position in such a way that its speed at the topmost position is $v = 3\,\text{m/s}$.

a) Find the initial velocity, if at the topmost point, the tension in the string is half of what it is at the moment of starting.

b) Find the coefficient of friction.

c) Find the distance travelled by the body until stopping, if after 5/4 turns the string is released and the body remains on the slope throughout its motion.

Problem 35. The inner radius of a frictionless spherical shell is $OA = 0.8\,\text{m}$. One end of a spring of relaxed length $L = 0.32\,\text{m}$ and spring constant $D = 75\,\text{N/m}$ is fixed to point B, which is 0.48 m below the centre of the sphere. A ball of mass $m = 3.2\,\text{kg}$ is attached to the other end of the spring, while the spring is extended in a horizontal position to reach point C. Then the ball is released. ($g = 10\,\text{m/s}^2$)

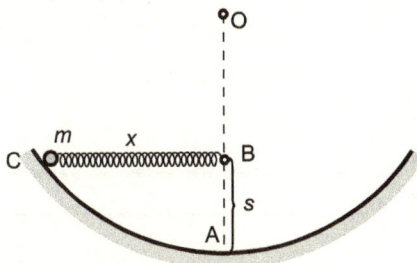

a) Find the speed of the ball when it has traveled furthest down the cylinder.

b) Find the force exerted by the ball on the spherical shell at that point.

9

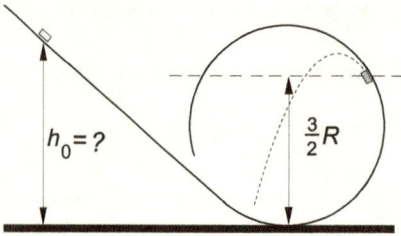

Problem 36. A tangentially attached slope leads to a circular match-box track with radius $R = 32$ cm set in a vertical plane. The toy car starts from rest at the top of the slope, runs down the slope and detaches from the track at height $h = \dfrac{3}{2}R$ measured from the bottom.

a) Find the height the car starts from.

b) Find the maximum height reached by it after it reaches the bottom of the track.

(Assume that the toy car is point-like, neglect drag and friction.)

Problem 37. A small wheel, initially at rest, rolls down a ramp in the shape of a quarter circle without slipping. The radius of the circle is $R = 1$ m and $\alpha = 60°$, $\beta = 30°$. Find the height x reached by the wheel after leaving the track.

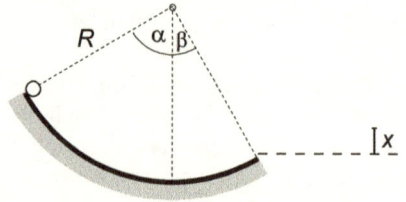

Problem 38. Two banks of a river whose width is $d = 100$ m are connected by a bridge whose longitudinal section is a parabola arc. The highest point of the path is $h = 5$ m above the level of the banks (see the figure). A car with mass $m = 1000$ kg traverses the bridge at a constant speed of $v = 20$ m/s. Find the magnitude of the force that the car exerts on the bridge

a) at the highest point of the bridge,

b) at 3/4 of the distance between the two banks.

(Drag can be neglected. Calculate with $g = 10$ m/s^2.)

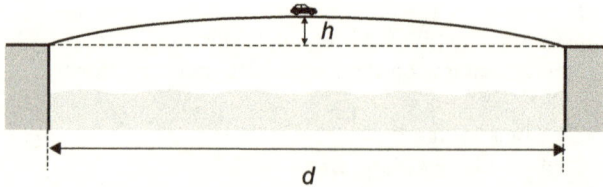

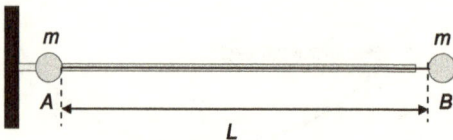

Problem 39. An iron ball (A) of mass $m = 2$ kg can slide without friction on a fixed horizontal rod, which is led through a diametric hole across the ball. There is another ball (B) of the same mass m attached to the first ball by a thin thread of length $L = 1.6$ m. Initially the balls are at rest, the thread is horizontally stretched to its total length and coincides with the rod, as is shown in the figure. Then the ball B is released with zero initial velocity.

a) Determine the velocity and acceleration of the balls (A) and (B) at the time when the thread is vertical.

b) Determine the force exerted by the rod on the ball (A) and the tension in the thread at this instant. (In the calculations take the gravitational acceleration to be $g = 10 \text{ m/s}^2$.)

Problem 40. A plane inclined at an angle of $30°$ ends in a circular loop of radius $R = 2 \text{ m}$. The plane and the loop join smoothly. A marble of radius $r = 1 \text{ cm}$ and of mass $m = 20 \text{ g}$ is released from the slope at a height of $h = 3R$. What is the lowest value of the coefficient of friction if the marble rolls along the path without sliding?

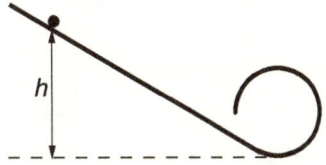

Problem 41. The vertical and horizontal parts of a track are connected by a quarter of a circular arc whose radius is $R = 0.2 \text{ m}$. A ball slides on the track with negligible friction; it is pulled through a slit along the track by a stretched spring as is shown in the figure. The length of the unstretched spring is 0.2 m, the spring constant is 100 N/m. The sliding ball starts from a point that is higher than $\alpha = 45°$ above the horizontal part of the track when viewed from the centre of the arc and reaches the maximum velocity at angle $\beta = 34°$ below the horizontal part of the track.

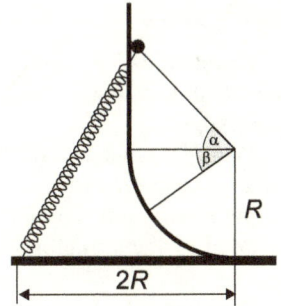

a) Find the mass of the ball.

b) Find the maximum speed of the ball.

Problem 42. A horizontal disk of radius $r = 0.2 \text{ m}$ is fixed onto a horizontal frictionless table. One end of a massless string of length $L = 0.8 \text{ m}$ is fixed to the perimeter of the disk, while the other end is attached to an object of mass $m = 0.6 \text{ kg}$, which stands on the table as shown. The object is then given a velocity of magnitude $v = 0.4 \text{ m/s}$ in a direction perpendicular to the string.

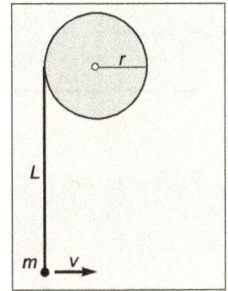

a) At what time will the object hit the disk?

b) Find the tension in the string as a function of time.

Problem 43. A semi-cylinder of radius $r = 0.5 \text{ metres}$ is fixed in horizontal position. A string of length L is attached to its edge. The object tied to the end of the string is released from a horizontal position. When the object at the end of the string is rising, at a certain point the string becomes slack. When the string becomes slack, the length of the free part of the string is $s = 0.96r = 0.48 \text{ metres}$. What is the total length of the string?

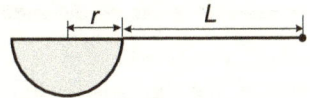

Problem 44. On a horizontal table with the height $h = 1$ m there is a block of mass $m_1 = 4$ kg at rest. The block is connected by a long massless string to a second block of mass $m_2 = 1$ kg which hangs from the edge of the table. The blocks are then released. Find the distance between the points where the two blocks hit the ground. Neglect friction.

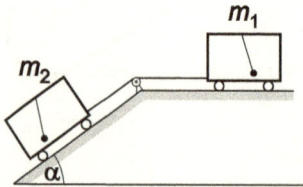

Problem 45. Two carts of masses $m_1 = 8$ kg and $m_2 = 17$ kg are connected by a cord that passes over a pulley as shown. Cart m_2 stands on an incline with an angle $\alpha = 36°52'$. If the system is released, what would be the positions of the pendulums inside the two carts? Neglect friction.

Problem 46. A solid cube of mass $m = 8$ kg and edge $l = 20$ cm is lying at rest on a smooth horizontal plane. A string of length l is attached to the midpoint of one of its base edges.

With the other end of the string kept on the plane, the cube is pulled with the string at an acceleration of $a = 3g$. The string stays perpendicular to the edge of the cube that it pulls on. Find the constant force exerted by the cube on the ground and the force exerted by the string on the cube.

Problem 47. A uniform solid disc of radius R and mass m is pulled by a cart on a horizontal plane with a string of length $2R$ attached to its perimeter. The other end of the string is attached to the cart at a height R above the ground. In the case of equilibrium, what angle does the string create with the horizontal plane if

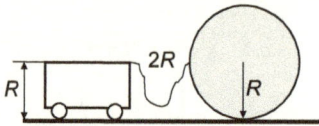

a) there is no friction,
b) there is friction?
The axis of the disc is perpendicular to both the string and the velocity.

Problem 48. The system shown in the figure undergoes uniformly accelerated motion. Data: $m_1 = 10$ kg, $F_1 = 20$ N, $m_2 = 2$ kg, $F_2 = 10$ N. Find the reading on the spring scale:

a) in this arrangement,
b) if the forces F_1 and F_2 are swapped,
c) if $m_1 = m_2 = 6$ kg. How does the result change in cases a) and b) if m_2 is negligibly small in comparison to m_1, for example $m_2 = 10$ g? Friction is negligible and the mass of the spring is negligible as well.

Problem 49. A block of mass $m = 3\,\text{kg}$ is connected to a spring and held on top of an inclined plane of angle $\alpha = = 30°$ as shown. The spring, whose spring constant is $D = = 80\,\text{N/m}$ is in its relaxed state when the block is released. The coefficient of friction is very small. Use $g = 10\,\text{m/s}^2$.
  a) What is the greatest depth reached by the block?
  b) Where will the very small friction make the block stop?

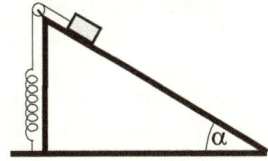

Problem 50. A body of mass m is placed on a wedge whose angle of inclination is α and whose mass is M. Find the horizontal force F that should be applied on the wedge in order for the body of mass to slide from the top to the bottom of the wedge in twice as much time as it would if the wedge were stationary. The friction between the wedge and the horizontal ground can be neglected, the coefficient of friction between the wedge and the body is μ. Initially both bodies are at rest. ($M = 1\,\text{kg}$, $m = 1\,\text{kg}$, $\alpha = 30°$, $\mu = 0.2$, $g = 9.81\,\text{m/s}^2$)

Problem 51. A block of mass $m_1 = 7$ kg is placed on top of a $h = 1$ m high inclined plane with an angle $\alpha = 36.87°$ and mass $M = 2\,\text{kg}$ which is connected by a cord of length h over a massless, frictionless pulley to a second block of mass $m_2 = 1$ kg hanging vertically as shown. The inclined plane can move without friction in the horizontal direction. The blocks are then released. After how long will the two blocks be nearest to each other? Neglect friction and use $g = 10\,\text{m/s}^2$.

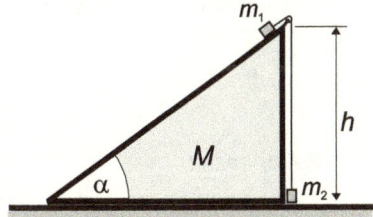

Problem 52. A sphere of mass m is placed between a vertical wall and a wedge of mass M and angle α, in such a way that the sphere touches the wedge tangentially at the topmost point of the wedge, as is shown in the figure. The wedge is standing on a horizontal plane, and both the sphere and the wedge move without friction.
  a) How should the mass ratio M/m and the angle α be chosen so that the wedge does not tilt after releasing the sphere?
  b) Determine the speed reached by the sphere by the time it slides along a segment of length $l = 20$ cm of the wedge, provided that $\alpha = 60°$ and $M/m = 12$.

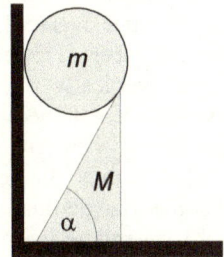

Problem 53. A large, closed box slides down on a very long, inclined plane. An observer inside the box wants to determine the angle of the inclined plane (α) and the coefficient of kinetic friction. What experiments should he do and what should he measure in order to be able to calculate the above quantities?

Problem 54. A thin, rigid wooden rod of height h is fixed to the ground and is standing vertically. A simple pendulum of length $l < h$ and mass m is attached to its upper end. The pendulum is moved to a horizontal position and released. Determine the torque that the fixed lower end must bear to keep the rod in position. (Let $h = 1.2\,\text{m}$, $m = 0.5\,\text{kg}$, use $g = 10\,\text{m/s}^2$)

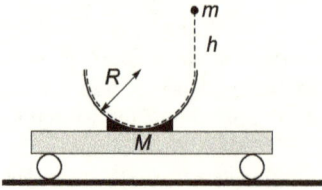

Problem 55. As shown in the figure, a smooth hemisphere of radius R is fixed to the top of a cart that can roll smoothly on a horizontal ground. The total mass of the cart is M, and it is initially at rest. A pointlike ball of mass m is dropped into the hemisphere tangentially, from a point $h = R$ above its edge. The ball slides all the way along the hemisphere with negligible friction.

a) Where will the ball be when it reaches the maximum height during its motion?

b) With what force will the ball press on the hemisphere at its lowermost point?

(Let $R = 0.5\,\text{m}$, $M = 2\,\text{kg}$, $m = 0.5\,\text{kg}$, use $g = 10\,\text{m/s}^2$)

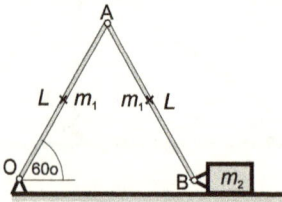

Problem 56. Two rods, each of length $L = 0.5\,\text{m}$ and mass $m_1 = 1\,\text{kg}$, are joined together by hinges as shown. The bottom end of the left rod is connected to the ground, while the bottom end of the right one is connected to a block of mass $m_2 = 2\,\text{kg}$. The block is then released to a position where the rods form a $60°$ angle with the horizontal plane. Friction is negligible.

a) Find the velocity of point A as it hits the ground.

b) Find the acceleration of mass m_2 at that moment.

Problem 57. A right triangle of side lengths a, b and c is formed using three thin rods of the same material, which are firmly fixed to each other. The triangle, which is initially placed vertically onto a horizontal plane on its edge b, tumbles down from this unstable position. $a = 30$ cm, $c = 50$ cm.

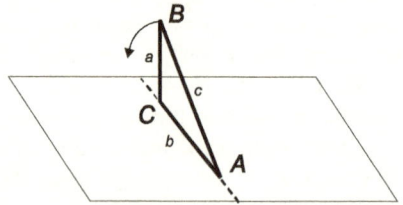

a) Determine the velocity of the vertex B when it hits the horizontal plane, provided that the triangle does not slide along ground.

b) Determine the position and velocity of the vertex B when it hits the horizontal plane, provided that the friction is negligible!

Problem 58. Two thin rods of identical material and cross-section with lengths $l_1 = 0.6$ m and $l_2 = 1$ m are connected by a frictionless joint. The structure slides from its unstable equilibrium position in such a way that the rods remain on a vertical plane and the angle enclosed by them decreases. Find the place where the joint reaches the ground and find its speed upon impact.

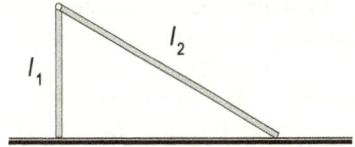

Problem 59. As shown in the figure, a thin and solid rod of length $L = 2R$ is leaning against a smooth semi-cylinder of radius $R = 1$ m that is fixed to a horizontal plane. The lower end of the rod A is held on the ground and then released from rest. The rod falls, sliding along the side of the cylinder. What will be the speed of its upper end B at the time instant when it reaches the surface of the cylinder? (Neglect all friction.)

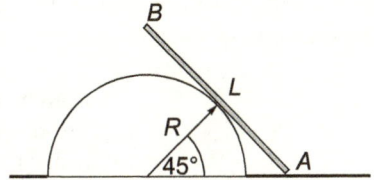

Problem 60. A rod with length L stands on the edge of a table in such a way that its bottom is propped against a smooth (frictionless) peg. Then the rod tilts and falls. Find the height of the table if the rod reaches the floor in a vertical position, with its top end hitting the floor first.

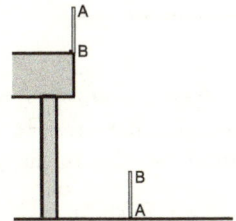

Problem 61. The following forces act on a body, which is initially at rest: $F_1 = 10$ N for $t_1 = 4$ s, then $F_2 = 4$ N acting in the same direction for $t_2 = 14$ s, then $F_3 = 15$ N acting in the opposite direction for $t_3 = 2$ s.

Find the magnitude of the constant force that causes the same final velocity of the body:

a) at the same time,

b) at the same distance.

Problem 62. A block of mass m with a spring fastened to it rests on a horizontal frictionless surface. The spring constant is D_0, the relaxed length of the spring is L and the spring's mass is negligible. A second block of mass m moves along the line of axis of the spring with constant velocity v_0 and collides with the spring as shown.

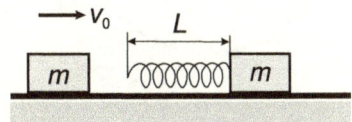

a) What is the shortest length of the spring during the collision?

b) The second block then sticks to the left end of the spring. What is the frequency of oscillation of the system?

Values: $m = 1$ kg, $L = 0.2$ m, $D_0 = 250$ N/m, $v_0 = 0.8$ m/s.

Problem 63. Our model rocket is a trolley on which several spring launchers are installed. Each spring is compressed and therefore stores $E = 100$ J of elastic energy. The system, whose total mass is $M = 100$ kg is initially at rest. Find the velocity of the trolley if the structure shoots out three balls with mass $m = 5$ kg in succession and in the same direction along the longitudinal axis.

Problem 64. A ball of mass m and of speed v collides with a stationary ball of mass M. The collision was head-on but not totally elastic. Determine the kinetic energy which is lost during the collision as a function of the speeds as well as the given masses before and after the collision. Based on the result, define a quantity which characterizes the elasticity of the collision.

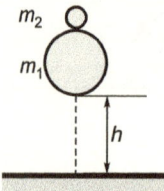

Problem 65. An object of mass m_1 and another of mass m_2 are dropped from a height h, the second one immediately following the first one. All collisions are perfectly elastic and occur along a vertical line.

a) For what ratio of the masses will the object of mass m_1 remain at rest after the collisions?

b) According to a), how high will the object of mass m_2 rise?

Problem 66. Two blocks of masses $m_1 = 5$ kg and $m_2 = 3$ kg are at rest on a table at a distance of $s_1 = 0.5$ m from each other. Block m_2 is at a distance of $s_2 = 0.5$ m from the edge of the table as shown. The coefficient of friction is $\mu = 0.102 = 1/9.8$.

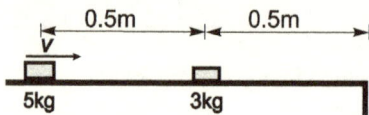

Find the velocity that should be given to block m_1 if after the elastic collision of the two blocks

a) block m_1,

b) block m_2 is to reach the edge of the table and stop there.

Problem 67. At the rim of a hollow hemisphere of diameter 4 metres two objects of masses $m_1 = 3$ kg and $m_2 = 2$ kg are released at

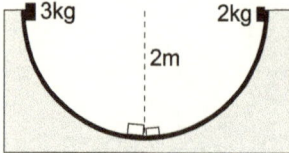

the same moment. Initially the two objects are at the two endpoints of a diameter of the hemisphere. They collide totally elastically. After the first collision what are the greatest heights the blocks can reach? The friction is negligible.

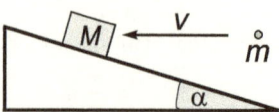

Problem 68. A block of mass $M = 1.6$ kg is lying on a plane inclined at an angle of $\alpha = 16.25°$ to the horizontal. The coefficient of friction is $\mu = 0.2$. At the same time that the block on the inclined plane is released, a shell of mass $m = 0.4$ kg is fired into it horizontally with a speed of $v = 12$ m/s. How much will the block of mass and the shell of mass slide up the incline? ($g = 10$ m/s^2)

Problem 69. A block of mass M, supported by a buffer, stays at rest on a plane inclined at an angle α to the horizontal. From below, parallel to the inclined plane, a bullet of mass m is shot into the block at a speed of v. How long does it take for the block to reach the buffer again? The coefficient of friction between the block and the plane is μ. The bullet penetrates into the block. During the penetration the displacement of the block is negligible. The coefficients of static and kinetic friction can be considered equal.

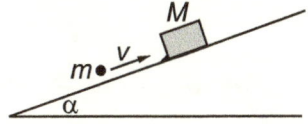

Problem 70. A ball made of a totally inelastic material is hung between two heavy iron rods, which are also hung as pendulums. The mass of the ball is negligible with respect to that of the rods. The masses of the rods are: m_1 and m_2, $(m_1 > m_2)$. One of the rods is pulled out, so that its centre of mass rises to a height of h, and then it is released. The plastically deformable ball becomes flat due to the collision. Which rod should be raised in order to cause the greater compression of the ball if h is the same in both cases. Based on the result, draw a conclusion about the efficiency of deforming an object by hammering it.

Problem 71. A projectile thrown upwards explodes at the top of its path into two parts of masses $m_1 = 3$ kg and $m_2 = 6$ kg. The two parts reached the ground at equal distances from the position of the projection, and with a time difference of $T = 4$ seconds. At what height did the projectile explode? (Neglect air resistance.)

Problem 72. From a horizontal ground a projectile is shot at an initial speed of $v_0 = 150$ m/s and at an angle of $\alpha = 60°$ from the horizontal ground. After a time of $t_1 = 10$ s the projectile explodes and breaks up into two pieces of masses m and $2m$. At the moment $\Delta t = 10$ s after the explosion the piece of mass m hits the ground at a distance of $d = 500$ m behind the place of shooting, in the plane of the trajectory of the unexploded projectile. At this instant how far is the other piece of mass $2m$ from the cannon?

Problem 73. A trolley of mass $M = 20$ kg is travelling at a speed of $V = 10$ m/s. A spring, initially compressed, launches an object of mass $m = 2$ kg off the trolley in a forward direction in such a way that after the launch the speed of the object is $v = 2$ m/s relative to the trolley. Determine the kinetic energy of the object relative to the ground.

Problem 74. Two elastic balls are suspended at the same height; one has mass $m_1 = 0.2$ kg, the other has mass m_2. If the system is left alone in the position shown in the figure, we find that – after an elastic and central collision – both balls rise to the same height.

a) Find the mass of the other ball.

b) At what fraction is height h reached by the balls after the collision of H?

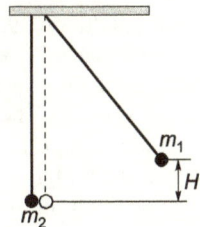

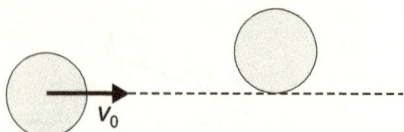

Problem 75. There are two thin, homogeneous disks of the same radius and mass lying on a horizontal air cushion table. One of the disks is at rest, while the other is moving at a speed of $v_0 = 1$ m/s. The line going through the centre of the moving disk, which follows the direction of its velocity, touches the other disk tangentially. The two disks collide elastically. Determine the velocities of the disks after the collision. The directions of the velocities can be described by angles relative to the initial velocity $\vec{v}_0$. In the process investigated friction is negligible everwhere.

Problem 76. There are three thin disks of identical mass ($m_A = m_B = m_C = m$) and radius lying at rest on a smooth horizontal plane. The disks B and C are connected by a thin thread of length $l = 1$ m. Initially the thread is straight, but not stretched, and it makes an angle of $45°$ with the line going through the midpoints of the disks A and B. Now we push the disk A at a speed $v = 2$ m/s in such a way that it centrally collides with the disk B. The collisions are elastic and instantaneous. At what time after the collision of the disks A and B will the line connecting the centres of the disks B and C be parallel to the trajectory of the disk A? At this instance, determine the distance of the disk A from B and C. (The disks can be considered pointlike.)

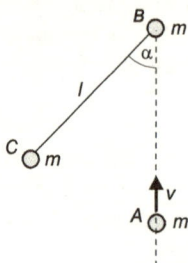

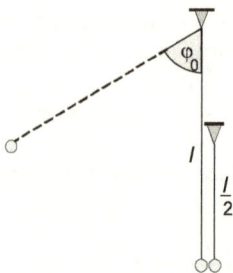

Problem 77. There are two identical balls of mass $m = = 0.2$ kg suspended on two threads of lengths $l = 1$ m and $l/2$. The threads are made of the same material, and in their vertical position the two balls touch each other. If the ball hanging on the longer thread is released from an initial angle of $\varphi_0 = 60°$ with respect to the vertical, then the thread breaks just before the collision.

What is the maximum initial angle from which this ball can be released, so that none of the threads break after the totally elastic collision?

Problem 78. A mathematical pendulum of length l and mass m is suspended on a smoothly running trolley of mass M. Another pendulum, also of length l and mass m is suspended from the ceiling, displaced through angle α and then released without initial velocity. The two pendulums collide centrally and perfectly elastically. Find the angle φ through which the pendulum suspended from the trolley swings out. ($M = 3$ kg, $m = 2$ kg, $\alpha = 60°$.)

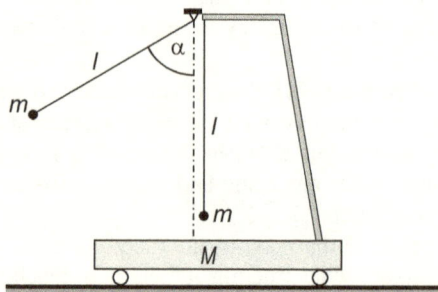

18

Problem 79. A small cart of mass m is at rest on a horizontal track. A vertical column of length $L = 2$ m and the same mass m is fixed to the cart. A rod of the same mass m and length $L = 2$ m is attached to its upper end with a hinge, and released from a horizontal position. At what speed will the end of the rod hit the base of the column? ($g = 10\,\mathrm{m/s^2}$.)

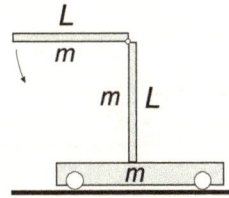

Problem 80. A cylinder of mass M and radius R can rotate freely about its horizontal axis. A thread is wound around its lateral surface, and a weight of mass m is attached to the free end of the thread. Initially the thread below the cylinder is vertical, and unstrained. Then the weight is lifted to a height h, and released from that position at zero initial speed. At what time after its release does the weight cover the distance $2h$?

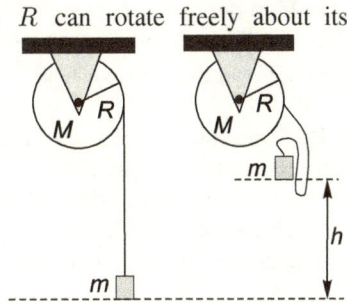

(The thread is unstretchable, and the interaction is instantaneous and totally inelastic.

Data: $M = 2$ kg, $R = 0.2$ m, $m = 3$ kg, $h = 1.2$ m.)

Problem 81. An inclined plane of angle α and mass M can move on the ground without friction. A small object of mass m and vertical velocity v collides with the stationary inclined plane. Assuming that the collision is elastic, find the velocity of the object (u) after the collision, the angle (φ) formed by this velocity and the horizontal ground. Find the speed (c) of the inclined plane after the collision. Data: $\alpha = 36.87°$, $m = 6$ kg, $M = 18$ kg, $v = 14\,\mathrm{m/s}$.

Problem 82. A big chest of mass $M = 50$ kg is sliding on the horizontal ground, and a sand bag of the same mass is falling into it. The bag was projected from the initial height of $h = 3$ m at certain a horizontal speed, and when it hits the chest, the speed of the chest is $v_1 = 5$ m/s. The velocity of the chest is in the plane of the trajectory of the bag, and the bag hits the chest in such a way, that its velocity makes an angle of $60°$ with the velocity of the chest. The coefficient of kinetic friction between the chest and the ground is $\mu = 0.4$. The collision of the bag is instantaneous. Determine the distance covered by the chest from the collision until it stops. What would the distance be if the bag was not thrown into the chest?

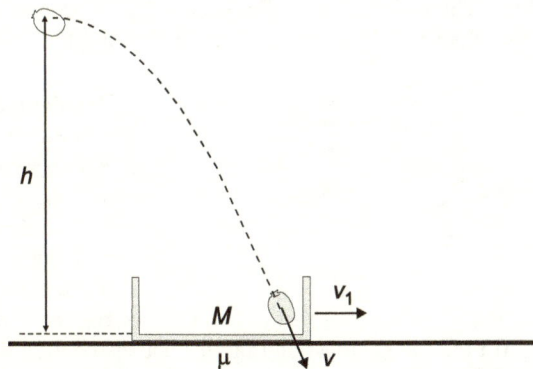

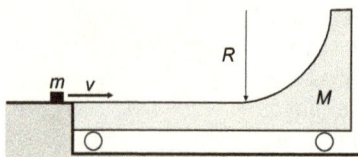

Problem 83. A quarter-round slope of radius $R = 0.5$ m is attached tangentially to a freely rolling trolley of mass $M = 3$ kg, originally at rest. A small-sized body of mass $m = 2$ kg slides onto the trolley at velocity $v = 15$ m/s.

a) Find the velocity of the trolley when the small body leaves it.

b) Find the distance travelled by the trolley from parting to reunion with the body.

c) Find the velocities of the trolley and the body when they part from each other again. (Friction and drag can be neglected. Calculate with $g = 10 \, \text{m/s}^2$.)

Problem 84. A small object of mass $m = 1$ kg is released from rest at the top of an inclined plane that connects to a horizontal plane without an edge. It slides onto a cart of mass M that has a semi-cylindrical surface of radius $R = 0.36$ m fixed to the middle of it, as shown in the figure.

The small object reaches the topmost point of the semi-cylinder and stops there.

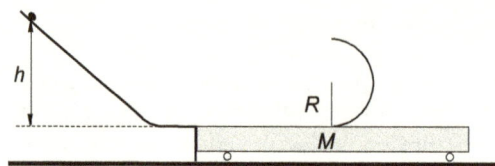

In continues to move vertically with free fall and hits the cart exactly at the edge. All friction can be neglected.

a) What is the minimum possible length of the cart?

b) What is the mass of the cart?

c) At what height h was the small object released?

Problem 85. An 80 kg man stands on the rim of a 300 kg rotating disk with radius 5 m. The disk initially rotates at $0.1 \, \text{s}^{-1}$ around a vertical axis. Then the man walks from the rim to the centre of the disk. Find the change in the energy of the system.

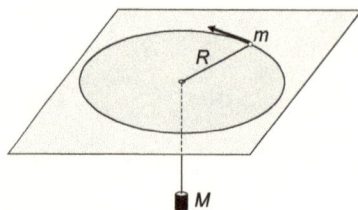

Problem 86. An object of mass $m = 1$ kg attached to a string is moving in a circle of radius $R = 40$ cm on a horizontal surface. The other end of the string is threaded through a hole at the centre of the circle and a mass of $M = 2$ kg is hung from it.

If the mass M is released, the closest approach of the mass m to the centre will be $r = 10$ cm.

a) Find the smallest and largest speeds of the mass m.

b) What is the speed of each object when the mass m is at a distance of $R/2$ from the centre?

c) Find the accelerations of the mass M at the highest and lowest points. (Neglect all friction, use $g = 10 \, \text{m/s}^2$.)

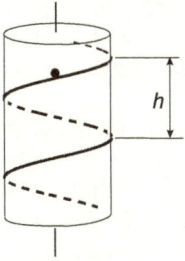

Problem 87. A solid cylinder of radius $R = 0.2$ metres is supported at the endpoints of its axis by frictionless pin bearings. An object slides down a frictionless helical track threaded around the cylindrical surface. The mass of the object is one fifth of the mass of the cylinder. The pitch of the track is $h = 0.2$ metres. $g = 10 \, \text{m/s}^2$.

a) What will be the speed of the object when it has descended through a height of $h = 0.2$ metres below the starting point?

b) How long will it take to attain that speed?

Problem 88. A disc of mass $2 \, \text{kg}$ and radius $R = 0.5 \, \text{m}$ can rotate freely around a vertical axis supported by bearings at a height $h = 1 \, \text{m}$ from the ground. A constraining vertical surface of negligible mass, whose shape is a semicircular arc of radius $r = R/2$, is fixed on the disc as shown in the figure. A small ball of mass $m = 1 \, \text{kg}$ is placed on the stationary disc and is bowled at a speed $v = 3 \, \text{m/s}$ in such a way that it reaches the internal side of the constraining surface tangentially.

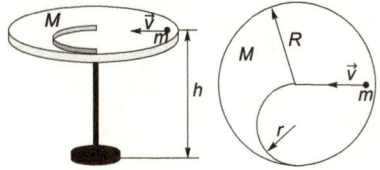

a) Find the distance from the rim of the disc where the ball reaches the ground.

b) How far is the ball at the moment of reaching the ground from the point of leaving on the disc? (Every type of friction can be neglected.)

Problem 89. A pointmass moves on the frictionless inner surface of a spherical shell, whose inner radius is $R = 1.4 \, \text{m}$. Its velocity reaches its maximum and minimum at heights $h_1 = 0.1 \, \text{m}$ and $h_2 = 0.3 \, \text{m}$ respectively. Find the maximum and minimum values of the velocity.

Problem 90. A $2 \, \text{m}$ long rod of negligible mass is free to rotate about its centre. An object of mass $3 \, \text{kg}$ is threaded into the rod at a distance of $0.5 \, \text{m}$ from its end in such a way that the object can move on the rod without friction. The rod is then released from its horizontal position. Find the speed of the rod's end in the rod's vertical position. Use $g = 10 \, \text{m/s}^2$.

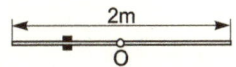

Problem 91. A board of length $L = 3.06 \, \text{m}$ and mass $M = 12 \, \text{kg}$ hangs vertically on a hinge that is connected to one of its ends. A bullet of mass $m = 0.25 \, \text{kg}$ is fired into the bottom end of the board, making the board swing up. What should the velocity of the bullet be if the board is to swing up to the horizontal position?

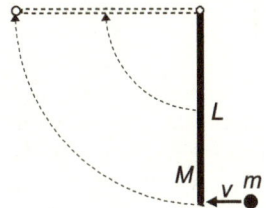

21

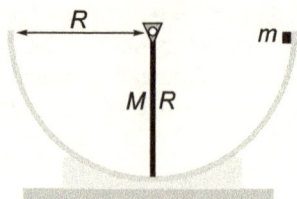

Problem 92. A rod of mass M and length R is fixed to a horizontal axis of rotation above a track with a semicircular cross section and a radius R, as is shown in the figure.

a) Find the mass of the rod relative to the mass of a point-like body that starts on the track at a height of R if it stops after an elastic collision with the rod.

b) Find the angular displacement of the rod after the collision. (Friction is negligible everywhere.)

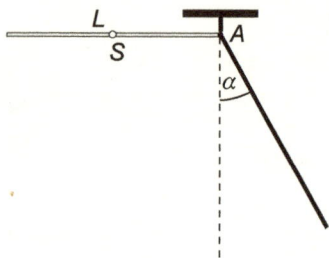

Problem 93. A thin, homogeneous stick has a length $L = 1$ m. An axis perpendicular to this stick is fixed at one end (A) of the stick; the stick is hung on the axis by a hook. The stick is sent into a horizontal position and then released without an initial velocity. The hook forms a (small) arc which allows the stick to leave it when it encloses an angle of $\alpha = 30°$ with the vertical plane.

Find the angle enclosed by the stick and the horizontal at the moment when its centre of mass (S) is at the highest point after detachment from the hook.

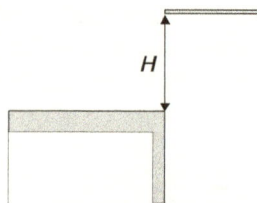

Problem 94. A thin rod of length L is falling freely in horizontal position from a height H above the surface of the table, in such a way that the end of the rod just hits the edge of the table. This collision is instantaneous and totally elastic. At what time after the collision does the rod perform a whole revolution? Where is its centre at that moment?

($H = 80$ cm, $L = 40$ cm, calculate with free fall acceleration $g = 10$ m/s.)

Problem 95. One end of a thin and heavy rod of length $L = 1$ m is attached to a horizontal axis at a height of $2L$ above the ground, and the rod is held in a horizontal position. One of two pointlike objects of negligible mass is placed on the free end of the rod and another is held against it from below, as shown in the figure. The coefficient of friction between the small objects and the rod is $\mu = 0.841$. The system is released from rest. At what distance from each other will the small objects hit the ground?

Problem 96. A thin, homogeneous rod of length L and mass m is suspended on a hinge at one end and then displaced into a horizontal position as is shown in the figure. The rod is released without an initial velocity. Find the magnitude and the direction of the force exerted by one half of length $L/2$ of the rod on the other half of $L/2$ when the angular displacement is $\varphi = 60°$.

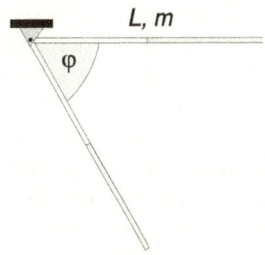

Problem 97. A disk rotates at constant angular velocity around its vertical axis of symmetry. A rod of length $L = = 1$ m is placed onto the disk in a way that its one end touches the disk at a distance of $r = 0.8$ m from the centre, while its other end is above the centre as shown. The rod is then released and rotates together with the disk in this position. Find the angular velocity of the disk. Use $g = = 10 \, \text{m/s}^2$.

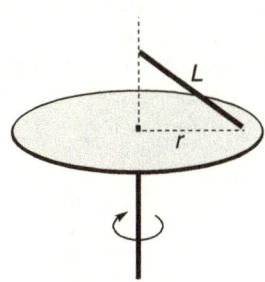

Problem 98. There is a rod of length l, mass m lying on a horizontal table. A cord is led through a pulley, and its horizontal part is attached perpendicularly to one end of the rod, while its vertical part is attached to a weight of mass m_1. The mass of the pulley and the friction are negligible.

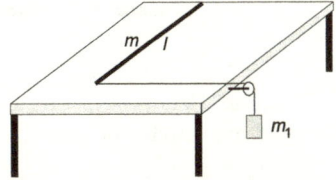

a) Which point of the rod has zero acceleration at the moment of releasing the weight?

b) At what mass ratio is the acceleration of the centre of the rod maximal at the moment of releasing the weight? Determine this acceleration.

Problem 99. A thin rod of length l, mass m and uniform mass distribution is lying on a smooth tabletop. One end is given a sudden horizontal impulse in a direction perpendicular to the length of the rod. How long will the rod slide along the table as it makes two complete revolutions?

Problem 100. Two discs of radius $R = 4$ cm rotating in the same direction at angular velocity $\omega = 2 \, \text{s}^{-1}$ move in opposite directions at velocity $v = 10 \, \text{cm/s}$ on an air-cushioned table as shown in the figure. The discs collide along the spikes that are located on their circumferences and whose dimensions are negligible. Determine the velocities after the collision if the discs

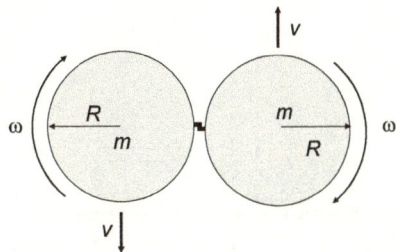

a) stick together firmly after a perfectly inelastic collision,

b) part after a perfectly elastic, instantaneous collision.

23

Problem 101. There are two homogeneous, solid disks of radius $R = 10$ cm and mass $m = 4$ kg mounted by two parallel, horizontal axes at the ends of a horizontal rod of negligible mass. The distance between these axes is $d = 25$ cm and the disks can freely rotate around them. The rod itself, with the disks mounted on it, can also freely rotate around a horizontal axis in its midpoint. (See the figures. All the three axes are perpendicular to the rod.) On the rim of each disk there is a small pin, and between them there is a spring of spring constant $D = 1800$ N/m, which is initially compressed by $\Delta l = 5$ cm. Determine the angular velocity of the disks after we burn the thread that holds the spring in its compressed position, provided that its initial position corresponds to figure a) or figure b). (The spring is in contact with the pins until it extends to its unstretched position, and then falls down.)

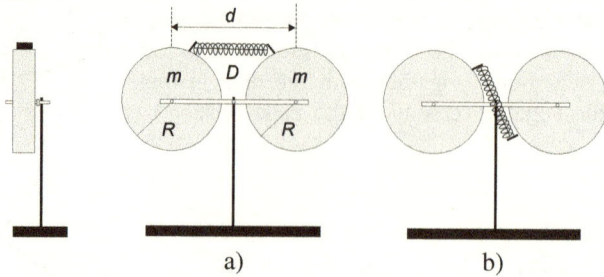

a)   b)

Problem 102. A thin ring of radius $r = 10$ cm, rotating in a horizontal plane, is dropped onto a tabletop from a height of $h = 20$ cm. At the instant when it starts to fall, the angular speed of the ring is $\omega_0 = 2\,\text{s}^{-1}$ around its vertical axis. The collision is inelastic and takes a very short time. The coefficient of friction between the ring and the tabletop is $\mu = 0.3$. $g = 10\,\text{m}\,\text{s}^{-2}$. How many revolutions will the ring make from the start of its fall until it finally stops?

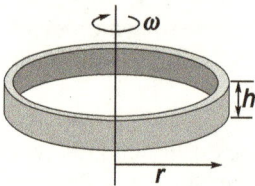

Problem 103. A solid and rigid sphere of mass $m = 80$ kg and radius $R = 0.2$ m is spun about a horizontal axis at an angular speed of ω, and then dropped without an initial speed onto a stationary cart of mass $M = 200$ kg from a height of $h = 1.25$ m. It hits the cart exactly at the centre. (The longitudinal axis of the cart lies in the plane of the rotation.) The cart can roll smoothly, its deformation in the collision is perfectly elastic, and the collision is momentary. The sphere keeps sliding throughout the entire duration of the collision. The coefficient of kinetic friction between the sphere and the cart is $\mu = 0.1$. The sphere rebounds from the cart and falls back onto it again.

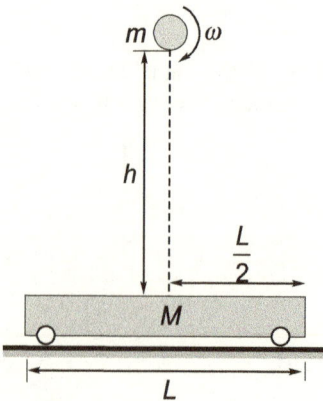

a) What is the minimum possible length of the cart?

b) What is the minimum possible initial angular speed of the sphere?

c) Provided that the sphere is started at the minimum angular speed as in question b), how much mechanical energy is dissipated in each of the first and second collisions?

d) Find the total work done by the friction force and the works done by the sphere on the cart and by the cart on the sphere.

e) How much translational kinetic energy does each object gain? What is the change of the rotational kinetic energy?

Problem 104. A small ball of mass $M = 4$ kg is attached to a solid cylinder of radius $r = 3$ dm and mass $m = 40$ kg by a massless rod as shown. The ball is at a distance of $R = 5$ dm above the centre of the cylinder. The system is then tipped from its unstable equilibrium position. Find the speed of the ball when it hits the ground. The cylinder rolls without slipping. Use $g = = 10$ m/s^2.

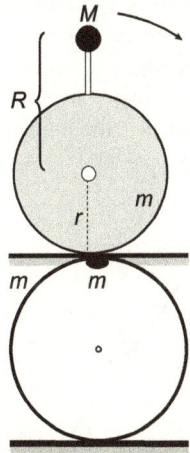

Problem 105. A weight of mass $m = 5$ kg is fixed to the perimeter of a hoop of the same mass $m = 5$ kg and radius $r = 1$ m. The hoop is placed on a horizontal plane. Friction is negligible. $g = 10$ m/s^2. Initially, the weight is at the top. Then the hoop is released.

a) Find the acceleration of the centre of the hoop when the weight is level with the centre.

b) With what force does the hoop press on the ground at that time instant?

Problem 106. A horizontal rod is fastened to a vertical axis as shown. There are two identical particles beaded onto the rod, each of mass 1 kg. The particles are connected to each other and to the axis by two springs, each of which have a length of $L = 0.1$ m in their relaxed states. The particles can move on the rod without friction. What should the angular velocity of the system be if the distance of the outer particle from the axis is to be $3L$? The spring constant is $D = 10 \dfrac{M}{m}$.

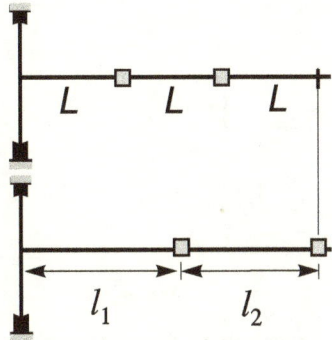

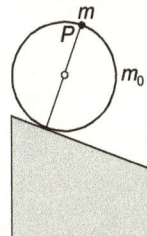

Problem 107. A ring of mass m_0 rolls along a slope with angle of inclination α without sliding. When it begins, a beetle of mass m lands at point P. Find the force with which the beetle should hang on to the ring after $5/4$ turns in order to remain on the ring. ($\alpha = 20°$, $m = 1$ g, $m_0 \gg m$.)

Problem 108. A hoop of radius r and of mass m is thrown above the ground in such a way that the plane of the hoop is vertical. The hoop is rotating backwards, about its centre with an angular speed of ω_0 and the velocity of its centre is v_0 in the forward direction. What must the angular speed of the hoop be if after reaching the ground during the course of its motion the hoop turns back (moves backward)? At what angular speed of ω_0 will the speed of the hoop moving backward be v_0?

Problem 109. A ping-pong ball of mass $m = 3$ g is hit back in such a way that it gains a horizontal velocity at a height of $h = 20$ cm above the table. There is a spin put on the ball causing it to rotate about a horizontal axis that is perpendicular to its velocity. After hitting the table the ball bounces back in the vertical direction without rotation. The collision is elastic, and due to the unevenness of the surfaces the coefficient of kinetic friction between the ball and the table is not zero, but $\mu = 0.25$. Therefore, what is the maximum heat produced during the collision of the ball with the table? (Use $g = 10$ m/s^2.)

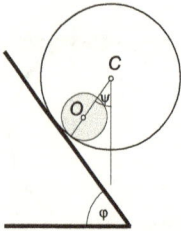

Problem 110. A hollow rim of radius $r_1 = 1$ m and mass $m_1 = 670$ g rolls down an inclined plane of angle $\varphi = 53^0 08'$. Inside the rim there is a solid cylinder of radius $r_2 = 0.3$ m and mass m_2. The centre of mass of the cylinder remains at rest relative to the centre of mass of the rim so that the line connecting the two centres (points O and C) forms an angle $\psi = 36^\circ 52'$ with the vertical throughout the motion. Find the mass of the cylinder if both objects roll without slipping.

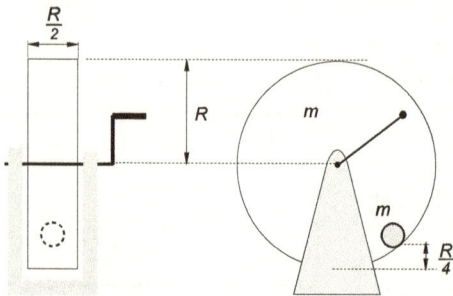

Problem 111. For a freely rotating wheel of fortune of mass m, the base and the nappe of the cylinder, whose radius is R and height is $R/2$, are made of a plate of uniform width and material. Within the originally stationary wheel there is a solid ball of radius $r = R/6$ and the same mass m, which is in touch with the surface of the cylinder at a height $R/4$ and is initially at rest.

a) Find the torque that should be applied on the wheel of fortune in order to have the centre of mass of the ball in it stay at rest.

b) Find the work done this way in 2 s.

c) Find the angular acceleration of the ball and the wheel of fortune.

(The ball rolls without skidding. Let $R = 0.54$ m and $m = 2$ kg. The mass of the driving rod is negligible.)

Problem 112. A cylinder of mass $m_1 = 30$ kg and radius $r = 8$ cm lies on a board of mass $m_2 = 60$ kg. The ground is frictionless and the coefficient of friction (both static and kinetic) between the board and the cylinder is $\mu = 0.1$. The centre of mass of the cylinder is pulled with a force of $F = 44.15$ N for two seconds. Find the work done by force F.

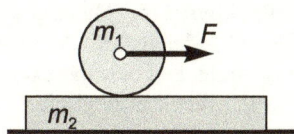

Problem 113. A solid sphere is rolling down, without sliding, on an incline of angle $30°$. The angle of the incline is variable.

a) The experiment is repeated with a hollow sphere, containing a concentric, spherical hole of half radius inside. Determine the slope of the incline so that the time of the motion is the same as in the previous experiment, provided that the two spheres are started from the same point on the incline.

b) In which case is larger the minimal static friction coefficient necessary for the slide free rolling?

Problem 114. One half of a semi-cylinder of radius $R = 1$ m has a rough inner surface, while the other half of the surface is frictionless. A solid sphere of radius $r = 0.2$ m is released from the position described by the initial angle $\varphi = 60°$ on the rough part of the semi-cylinder. Determine how high the centre of the sphere gets on the other, frictionless part of the semi-cylinder, in respect to the lowest point of the circular ramp. (On the rough part of the surface the static friction is strong enough for rolling without slipping, and the rolling friction is negligible.)

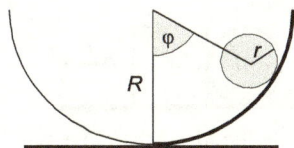

Problem 115. A disk of mass $m = 10$ kg and radius $r = 0.2$ m is placed on top of a cart of mass $M = 5$ kg that stands on a frictionless surface. A massless string is wrapped around the disk.

a) Find the accelerations of the disk and the cart, if the free end of the string is pulled with a constant horizontal force of magnitude $F = 100$ N. The coefficient of friction between the cart and the disk is $\mu = 0.1$.

b) Find the kinetic energies of the two objects at the instant when the length of the unwound string is $L = 2$ m.

c) Find the work done by force F until that moment.

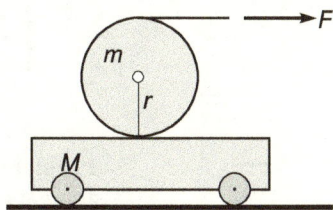

Problem 116. There is a ball of mass m at the middle of the top of a block of mass M and of length $2l$. A constant force of F is exerted on the block from the initial time 0 till time t. Then the exerted force is ceased. Friction between the horizontal surface and the block is negligible. The static friction between the ball and the block ensures that the ball rolls without sliding. Find the time T which elapses until the ball falls off the block. (When will the ball reach the end of the block?) The rolling resistance exerted on the ball is negligible.

Problem 117. A cylinder of mass M and radius R lies in a corner so that it touches both the wall and the ground as shown. A massless chord passes around the cylinder, over a pulley, and is attached to a small object of mass m. The coefficient of kinetic friction is μ for all surfaces. Find the acceleration of the object attached to the string. Data: $\mu = 0.5$, $m = 11\,\text{kg}$, $M = 8\,\text{kg}$, $R = 0.4\,\text{m}$, $g = 10\,\text{m/s}^2$.

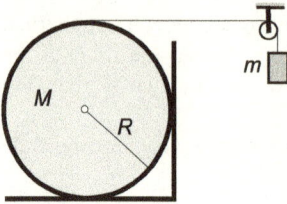

Problem 118. A cube and a cylinder are placed on a horizontal surface such that a generator of the cylinder touches the side of the cube as shown. The radius of the cylinder is equal to the side length of the cube and the masses of the two objects are also equal. For all surfaces the coefficients of static and kinetic friction are μ_0 and μ respectively ($\mu_0 > \mu$). With what force should the cube be pushed if the two objects are to move together in such a way that the cylinder's motion remains purely translational? Data: $m = 12\,\text{kg}$, $\mu = 0.2$, $\mu_0 = 0.6$, $g = 10\,\text{m/s}^2$.

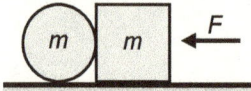

Problem 119. Describe the motion of the system shown in the figure. The coefficient of friction between the board of mass m_1 and the table is μ_1, while the coefficient of friction between the board and the brick of mass m_2 is μ_2. (The coefficients of static and kinetic friction are the same.) Data: $m_1 = 2\,\text{kg}$, $m_2 = 2\,\text{kg}$, $m_3 = 1\,\text{kg}$, $\mu_1 = 0.1$, $\mu_2 = 0.35$.

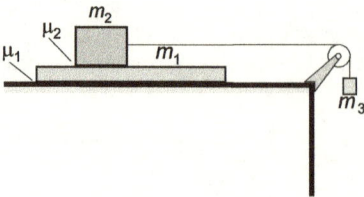

Problem 120. A homogeneous full hemisphere is suspended by a string at a point on its edge is such a way that it touches but does not push the ragged surface beneath it. Find the minimum value of the coefficient of friction at which the hemisphere will not slip after burning the string. The centre of mass of a hemisphere is at $3/8$th of its radius.

Problem 121. A massless cord that has one of its ends attached to a peg on the ground passes below a cylinder, over a pulley, and is attached to a small object of mass $m = 8$ kg as shown. The rotating part of the pulley is identical to the cylinder on the ground, both having a radius of $r = 25$ cm and a mass of $m = 8$ kg. The cord between the pulley and the cylinder (that are at a great distance from each other) forms $60°$ with the horizontal. Find the acceleration of the hanging object at the moment when it is released. (The cord does not slip on the pulley.)

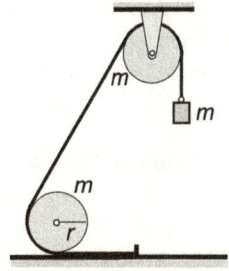

Problem 122. Two coaxial pulleys of the same thickness and of the same material have radii 10 cm and 20 cm respectively. The total mass of the pulley-system is 5 kg. The blocks hanging from the pulleys have a mass of 9 kg each. Find the times the hanging blocks need to travel down to a depth of 4.9 m from their original positions.

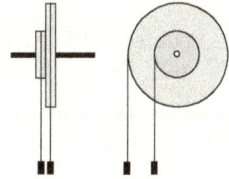

Problem 123. Two disks with radii $r_1 = 0.3$ m and $r_2 = 0.2$ m are fixed together so that their centres are above each other. The rotational inertia of the disk-system is $\Theta = 0.25$ kgm^2. The greater disk stands on a frictionless table. Massless chords that are wrapped around the greater and the smaller disks pass over pulleys and are attached to small objects of masses $m_1 = 5$ kg and m_2 respectively as shown. Find the value of m_2 at which the axis of symmetry of the disk-system remains stationary. Use $g = 10$ m/s^2.

Problem 124. A cylinder of radius R has two disks, both of radius $r = R/3$ fixed onto its two base surfaces. The system is suspended on two massless chords that are wrapped around the disks. There are inked letters placed all around the cylindrical surface. With what acceleration should the end of the cords be moved if our task is to print the letters clearly onto a vertical wall? Neglect the mass of the disks.

Problem 125. A loosely hanging thread of length l is attached to a freely rolling trolley of mass m; the other end of it is attached to a cylindrical spring with spring constant k whose other end is attached to a trolley of mass $2m$ as shown in the figure. The spring can also be compressed and its axis always remains straight. The cart of mass $2m$ is pushed at velocity v_0.

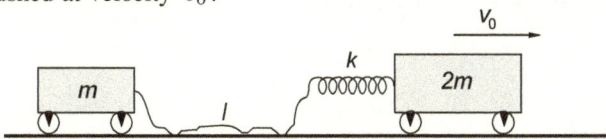

a) Find the time elapsed from the stretching of the thread to the rear trolley reaching the spring.

b) Find the time after which the thread stretches again.

$(m = 8\,\text{kg}, \; k = 23.3\,\text{N/m}, \; l = 1\,\text{m}, \; v_0 = 2\,\text{m/s}.)$

Problem 126. A spring balances a disc of radius R and of moment of inertia Q, which is able to rotate about a horizontal axle, so that the torque exerted by the spring is proportional to the angle turned. A thread which is attached to the spring is wound around the disc and a small body of mass m is hung from its other end. What type of motion will this system undergo if it is moved a little bit out of its equilibrium position? Neglect friction and air resistance.

Problem 127. An axle is attached to a disk at its centre perpendicularly to the plane of the disc. Then two pieces of thread are wound round the two ends of the axle. The ends of the threads are kept vertically and attached to the ceiling, while the disc is held at rest. Symmetrically to the disc two frictionless rings are placed on the axle, and two springs are attached to the rings. The other ends of the springs are fixed to the ceiling so that they hang vertically. The springs are not extended at this position.

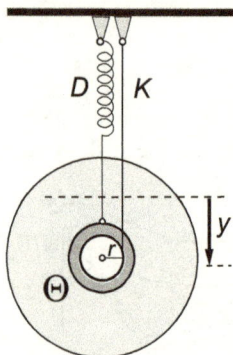

Then the system is released. How much time elapses until the disc reaches its lowest position?

(Numerical data: the mass of the disc is $m = 2$ kg, its moment of inertia $\Theta = 0.01$ kgm^2, radius of the axle $r = 2$ cm, spring constant of one spring (the springs are alike) $D = 1.5$ N/m, $g = 10$ m/s^2.)

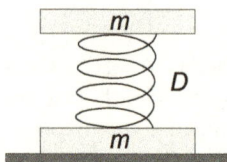

Problem 128. Two slabs of mass $m = 0.1$ kg are connected by a spring of spring constant $k = 20$ N/m, whose unstretched length is $l_0 = 0.3$ m as shown in the figure. The upper slab is pushed down by 0.15 m and then released. Find the maximum distance between the two slabs.

(The mass of the spring is negligible. Calculate with $g = 10$ m/s^2.)

Problem 129. An object hangs from a spring in the cockpit of a truck and causes an elongation of $\Delta l = 0.1$ m of the spring. The truck arrives at a highway that was built from concrete plates of length $x = 20$ m fitted next to each other, but the fittings are not perfect. When the truck runs at speed v, the hanging body oscillates with very high amplitude. What is the speed of the truck?

Problem 130. An object of mass $m = 1$ kg moving on a horizontal ground is given an initial speed of $v_0 = 2$ m/s. Initially, the distance of the object from the wall is $s = 1$ metre. A spring of length $L = 8$ cm and spring constant $D = 100$ N/m is attached to the object. The coefficient of friction is $\mu = 0.2$. $g = 10$ m/s^2.
a) Where will the block stop?
b) When will the block stop?

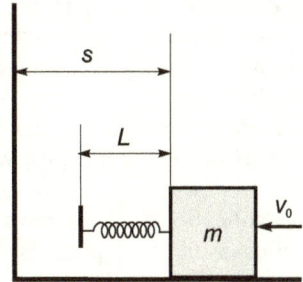

Problem 131. The unstretched length of a spring is $L_0 = 0.6$ metres and the spring constant is $D = 80$ N/m. The lower end of the spring is attached to an object of mass $m = 2$ kg lying on the ground, and the upper end is held at a height of 0.6 metres vertically above the object. Initially, the spring is unstretched. Then the upper end is lifted at a uniform speed of $v_0 = 0.5$ m/s. $g = 10$ m/s^2.
a) How high will the object be lifted in 1.75 seconds?
b) What is the work done by the lifting force?
c) Describe the variation of power as a function of time.

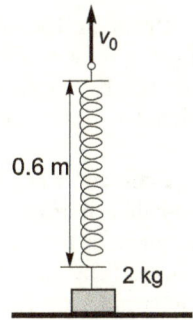

Problem 132. A body of mass $m = 1.25$ kg is suspended vertically by a spring of spring constant $D = 250$ N/m and unstretched length $l = 1$ m. It is released at zero initial speed from the unstretched position of the spring. Determine the time when the speed of the body reaches the value $v = 0.5$ m/s first.

Problem 133. A body of mass $m = 1$ kg is at rest on a horizontal, frictionless ground. A thin rubber thread is attached to the side of the body at the point A. The unstretched length of the thread is $L_0 = 50$ cm. Initially the other end of the thread (point B) is at a distance L_0 from A in horizontal direction. When the rubber thread is stretched, it behaves as if it had a spring constant $D = 100$ N/m, but it is impossible to "compress" the thread, since then it loosens and exerts no force.

At a given moment we start to pull the end B of the rubber thread horizontally, at a constant speed $v_0 = 1$ m/s to the right (see the figure), and continuously maintain this uniform pull.
a) Determine the longest distance between the points A and B.
b) How long does it take for the body to catch up with point B?

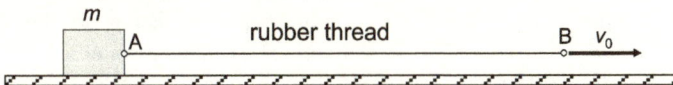

Problem 134. A pipe produces a tone of frequency 440 Hz. (This is the frequency of the normal a' above middle c'.) We sound the pipe twice, first normally, by blowing air into it, then by breathing pure helium, and blowing it into the pipe. In both cases the gas flows in the same way in the pipe.

a) Determine the frequency ratio of the two sounds. What is the musical interval?

b) How long is this pipe when it is open and when it is closed?

Problem 135. For a wave travelling along a straight line, the difference between two points in the same phase is 5 m, while the distance between two points that are in the opposite phase is 1.5 m. Find the possible values of the wavelength.

Problem 136. During an earthquake the ground is observed to move horizontally. First it moves suddenly 5 cm to the right, then after 1 second it moves suddenly to the left by 5 cm. A chandelier hangs on a $4m$ long cord. Find the amplitude of the chandelier after the earthquake.

Problem 137. A pipe produces sound whose frequency is 440 Hz. (This is the so-called normal sound.) The pipe is sounded twice in such a way that first the gas originating from a container of air, then the gas from a container of helium is 'blown' into it. (The gas flows out of both containers under the same conditions.)

Determine the ratio of the frequencies of the sounds produced by the pipe and the frequency of the sound produced by the pipe "blown" with helium.

Problem 138. Somebody intends to determine the moment of inertia of the first wheel of a bicycle so that a) he totally balances the wheel at its axle (so the wheel stays at rest at any position when its is held at its axle), b) he fixes a point-like lead weight of mass m to the spoke of the wheel at a distance of l from the centre of the rotation, c) he makes the wheel swing, and measures the period of swinging T. Using this data can he find the moment of inertia of the wheel? What is this moment of inertia if $m = 0.5\,\text{kg}$, $l = 0.2\,\text{m}$ and $T = 1.2\,\text{s}$?

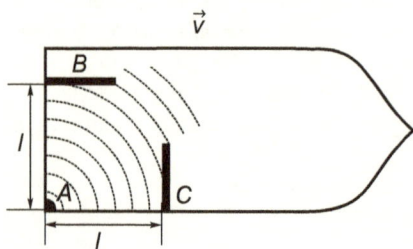

Problem 139. A ship swims at constant velocity $\vec{v}$ on a windless ocean. A short sound pulse is emitted from a sound source located at point A of the open deck of the ship. The sound is reflected from wall B that is at distance l from point A and is parallel to the direction of travel. The sound is also reflected from wall C that is also at distance l but is perpendicular to the direction of travel. The reflected sounds arrive back at the sound source with time difference Δt. (This time difference is measured by a timepiece that is connected to a microphone placed next to the sound source.)

Find the speed of the ship if distance l, the speed of propagation of sound (c) and the measured time difference (Δt) are given.

($l = 15\,\text{m}$, $c = 320\dfrac{\text{m}}{\text{s}}$, $\Delta t = 40\mu\,\text{s}$.)

Problem 140. Underneath the topmost, homogeneous covering rock layer which covers the ground and has a horizontal surface, there is another inclined rock plate of different density and composition. The seismic waves generated by an explosion on the surface of the ground are detected at three different places with the help of geophones. The first geophone is at the place of the explosion, and it detected the reflected seismic waves 0.2 s after the explosion. The second geophone is at 50 m east, the third is at 50 m west from the place of the explosion. The second geophone detected the reflected waves with a time delay of 0.26 s, while the third seismic detector measured a delay of 0.34 s.

a) Determine the propagation speed of seismic waves in the topmost, covering rock layer.

b) Determine the distance of the inclined rock plate from the place of the explosion.

c) Determine the angle of inclination of the rock plate in east–west direction.

Problem 141. With what speed can a vehicle move on a planet of uniform density, which is equal to the average density of the Earth, and of radius 500 times greater than that of the Earth. The planet does not rotate. (The radius of the Earth is 6370 km.)

Problem 142. A spaceship moves in a circular orbit of radius r_1 around the Earth with period T_1. Then, with the help of two separate course corrections, the spaceship is put into a new circular orbit of radius $2r_1$. In the first correction only the magnitude of the spaceship's velocity is changed keeping its direction unchanged. In the second correction, which is carried out in the first appropriate moment, only the direction of the spaceship's velocity is changed while its magnitude remains unchanged.

a) By what percentage is the kinetic energy increased during the first course correction?

b) By what angle is the direction of velocity changed during the second correction?

c) Find the time that elapses between the two course corrections. (Assume that the course corrections are carried out instantaneously.)

Problem 143. At what height, measured from the surface of the Earth, does the satellite complete its ninety minute orbit? The Earth is considered to be a sphere with a radius of 3670 km. Assume that the acceleration due to gravity at the surface of the Earth is known ($g = 9.81\,\text{m/s}^2$). The orbit of the satellite is circular.

Problem 144. A spy satellite, travelling above the equator of the Earth, is taking pictures. Assuming that in six hours the satellite is ready with pictures around the whole equator, determine the altitude of the orbit.

Problem 145. An astronaut revolves around the Earth along a circular path while facing the same point of the Earth all the time. For which points on the Earth can this condition hold true? What is the speed of the revolving spaceship?

Problem 146. How can the mass of an object be determined in a spaceship orbiting the Earth? The engines of the spaceship are shut off and air resistance is negligible. Find as many different ways as you can and describe the methods and equipment used. Which of these equipments need to be calibrated in advance?

Problem 147. A satellite follows a circular orbit around a planet, whose period of revolution is $T_1 = 8$ h. As it wishes to change over to another circular orbit whose period of revolution is $T_2 = 27$ h, it makes a course correction. First it changes the magnitude of its velocity by switching on the rockets for a short period of time and orbiting on a transitional elliptical orbit. When it reaches the desired altitude, it switches on the propulsion again and changes over the circular orbit with period of revolution T_2 solely by changing the magnitude of its velocity.

a) Find the time required for the course correction.

b) Find the percentage change in the magnitude of the velocity of the satellite caused by the switching on of the rockets in the first and second steps within the context of the non-rotating reference frame fixed to the planet.

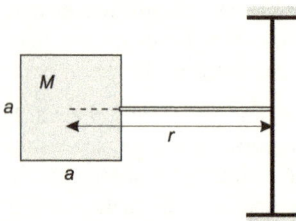

Problem 148. A 100%-reflexive square mirror is attached to a horizontal massless rod that is attached to an axis of rotation supported in the vertical position by bearings as shown in the figure. The mass of the mirror is $M = 20$ g, the side of the square is $a = 10$ cm. The centre of the square is $r = 20$ cm from the axis of rotation. Intense sunlight shines on the mirror at right angles, which delivers 0.125 J energy on each cm^2 of the surface of the mirror in 1 s.

The apparatus starts rotating due to the light pressure. Find the angular displacement which takes place in 1 minute, if the system can move freely, and if it is ensured that light propagates at a right angle to the mirror in each phase of the rotation. (The relationship between the energy and the momentum of the photon is $E = p \cdot c$, where c is the speed of light.)

Problem 149. A double-armed lever has equal arms on both sides. One end of the lever has a pulley of negligible mass fixed on it by a hinge, while the other end has a block of mass m_0 suspended from it. Two blocks of masses m_0 and m are attached to each end of a string that runs around the pulley. Find the value of m at which the lever remains in its horizontal position.

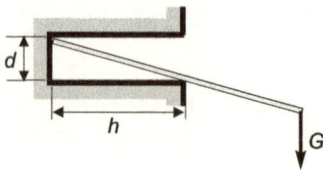

Problem 150. A $h = 6$ cm deep hole of diameter $d = 2$ cm is drilled into a wall. A thin rod of negligible mass is then placed into the hole as shown. The coefficient of friction is $\mu = 0.2$. What is the shortest possible length of the rod if it is to be used as a coat-hanger?

1.3 Statics

Problem 151. One end of a rod of mass 1 kg and of length 1 m can freely rotate about a fixed horizontal axis. Initially the rod makes an angle of 30° to the horizontal. A thread of length 1.3 m is attached to the two ends of the rod. A small pulley can run without friction along the thread, and a weight of mass 0.2 kg is suspended on the axis of the pulley.

Determine the work needed to lift the rod to a horizontal position. (Use the value $g = 10$ m/s^2 for the acceleration due to gravity.)

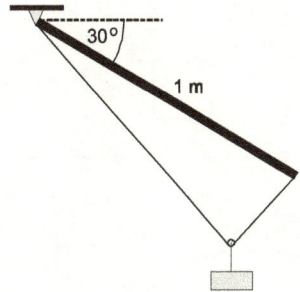

Problem 152. Two beads of masses m and $2m$ can move on a circular vertical loop of radius $r = 0.5$ m. The beads are connected by a massless string, and if the string is taut, it keeps the beads on the ends of a quarter-circle as shown. The coefficient of friction is 0.15. Find the positions in which the beads are in equilibrium with the string being taut.

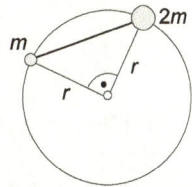

Problem 153. An analytical balance is used with brass weights. Find the mass of a body made of Plexiglas, whose two measurements result in a difference of at least one mark if one measurement is performed in dry weather and the other in wet weather? In both cases the room temperature is $23\,°C$ and the atmospheric pressure is 10^5 Pa. In wet weather the pressure of the water vapour in the air is $2 \cdot 10^3$ Pa. The sensitivity of the balance is 0.1 mg/scalemark. ($\varrho_{Cu} = 8.5 \cdot 10^3$ kg/m^3; $\varrho_{Plexiglas} = 1.18 \cdot 10^3$ kg/m^3.)

Problem 154. The two ends of a homogeneous chain of mass 2 kg are fixed to columns of height 1 m as shown in the figure. The chain is clutched in the middle and is pulled down until it becomes tight. In the meantime 0.5 J of work is done. The lowest point of the chain is then 0.5 m from the ground then. Where was the centre of mass of the chain initially?

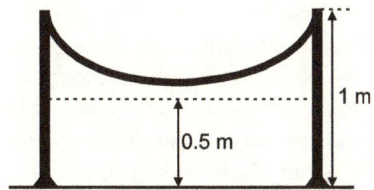

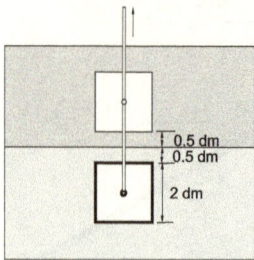

Problem 155. A thick layer of oil with density $0.8 \, \text{g/cm}^3$ is placed at the top of the water in a tank. The area of the base of the tank is very big. A cube made of magnesium is placed in the tank in such a way that its top face is $0.5 \, \text{dm}$ below the boundary. The edge of the cube is $2 \, \text{dm}$ and its density is $1.7 \, \text{g/cm}^3$. The cube is then pulled up so that its bottom face is $0.5 \, \text{dm}$ above the boundary. How much work was performed?

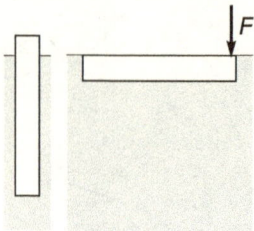

Problem 156. A cuboid shaped piece of wood of base area $1 \, \text{dm}^2$ and height $4 \, \text{m}$ is floating vertically in a pond, because its centre of mass is not in its geometric centre. To make the wood submerge and float in a horizontal position as shown, we need to exert a downward force of $F = 80 \, \text{N}$ at its end. Where is the centre of mass of the wood? Find the work done to the wood by moving it from its first to its second position.

Problem 157. A container is filled with water, and a plank of width $10 \, \text{cm}$ and of density $\varrho_0 = 0.5 \, \text{g/cm}^3$ floats on the surface of the water. Through the tube air at a pressure of 100 atmosphere is compressed into the container. What is the height of that part of the plank which is submerged into the water. (Assume that water is incompressible.) The density of air at a pressure of 1 atmosphere is $0.0013 \, \text{g/cm}^3$.

1.4 Fluids

Problem 158. a) A solid sphere of radius $R = 0.2 \, \text{m}$ and of negligible mass is swimming on the surface of a lake of depth $h = 1 \, \text{m}$. The sphere is slowly pushed under the water, down to the bottom of the lake. Determine the work done by the external pushing force in the process.

b) Now the sphere investigated in question a) is swimming in a water tank of base surface area $A = 0.5 \, \text{m}^2$. The depth of the water in the tank is $h = 1 \, \text{m}$. Determine the work needed to push the sphere down to the bottom of the tank. (Assume that no water flows out of the tank. The density of water is $\varrho = 1000 \, \text{kg/m}^3$, and $g = 9.81 \, \text{m/s}^2$.)

Problem 159. A square based cuboid shaped metal container, whose mass is $13 \, \text{kg}$, has a height of $6 \, \text{dm}$, a base edge of $2 \, \text{dm}$, and is half full of water. The container is laid on its side at the bottom of a cuboid shaped tank, whose base area is $20 \, \text{dm}^2$ and in which the level of water is at a height of $4 \, \text{dm}$. Find the total work that is required to stand the metal container upright on its square base.

Problem 160. One end of a thin rod of length $L = 1$ m and density ϱ connects to a hinge at a depth of $h = 0.8$ m below water level. Find the equilibrium positions of the rod and state whether the equilibrium is stable or unstable if

a) $\varrho = 500\,\text{kg/m}^3$,

b) $\varrho = 853\,\text{kg/m}^3$.

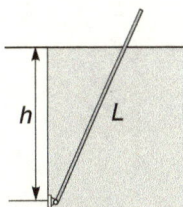

Problem 161. A cuboid shaped container has two wheels attached to its bottom and a massless string connected to its side so that it passes over a pulley and attaches to a small object of mass 1.2 kg as shown. The length, height and width of the container are 20 cm, 10 cm and 10 cm respectively, and the height of the water in the container is 9 cm. The mass of the cart and water is 2 kg. Describe the motion of the system. Neglect friction.

Problem 162. A closed cylindrical container with a vertical axis is completely filled with water. A plastic bead of density $\varrho = 0.5$ kg/dm^3 and radius $r = 1$ cm is placed at distance $R = 20$ cm from the axis and is anchored to the bottom of the container by a thin thread of length $l = 16$ cm. If as a result of the containers revolutions, the beads sink by $h = 4$ cm, how many revolutions around its axis of symmetry does the container have to make? (In the final state the total content of the container rotates at the same angular speed. Calculate with $g = 10$ m/s^2.)

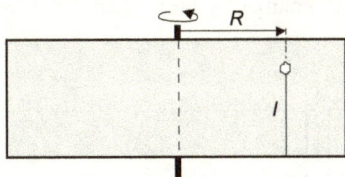

Problem 163. A cylindrical container whose base area is $A = 10$ cm^2 contains a $h = 60$ cm high water column.

a) Find the increase in the hydrostatic pressure at a height of $h_1 = 20$ cm above the bottom of the container if the temperature of the water column is increased by $\Delta t = 80\,°\text{C}$.

b) Give the value of pressure increase as function of distance x measured from the bottom of the container.

(For water the mean coefficient of expansion is $\beta = 0.00013\ 1/°\text{C}$, the density of cold water is $\varrho = 10^3\ \dfrac{\text{kg}}{\text{m}^3}$, the expansion of the container is negligible.)

Chapter 2

Thermodynamics Problems

2.1 Thermal expansion

Problem 164. The upthrust exerted on a steel ball which is immersed in paraffin of temperature 20 °C is 0.2145 N, and 0.200 N when the temperature of the paraffin is 100 °C. Based on this measurement, find the volumetric thermal expansion coefficient of paraffin if the coefficient of linear thermal expansion of steel is $1.2 \cdot 10^{-5}$ 1/°C.

Problem 165. A solid brass sphere rotates freely around an axis which goes through its centre. By how much may its temperature change provided that its frequency does not change by more than 1%? (All frictional effects are negligible.)

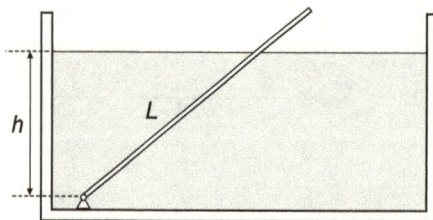

Problem 166. A rectangular glass tank of large base area contains water to a height of $h_0 = 0.6$ m. The closed lower end of an aluminium tube of length $L_0 = 1$ m, exterior cross-sectional area $A_e = 1.2$ cm^2 and interior cross-sectional area $A_i = 1$ cm^2 is fixed to the bottom of the tank by a hinge. The initial temperature of the whole system is $t = 4$ °C.

How much will the angle enclosed by the tube and the horizontal change if the temperature of the whole system is raised to 94 °C? (Further data: the coefficient of linear expansion of aluminium and its density are $\alpha_{Al} = 2.4 \cdot 10^{-5}$ °C^{-1} and $\varrho_{0Al} = 2.7 \cdot 10^3$ kg/m^3, the coefficient of linear expansion of glass is $\alpha_{glass} = 8 \cdot 10^{-6}$ °C^{-1}. The mean coefficient of volume expansion of water in this temperature interval is $\beta_w = 4.4 \cdot 10^{-4}$ °C^{-1}. The buoyancy of air is negligible.)

Problem 167. Air at a pressure of 1 atmosphere is confined within a syringe of volume 20 cm^3. Formerly a sample of porous material was placed into the syringe. Find the volume of the porous material if the pressure inside the syringe increases to 2.2 atmospheres when the piston of the syringe is pushed till the mark of 10 cm^3.

2.2 Ideal gas processes

Problem 168. For an experiment a mixture of gases containing 50 volume percents hydrogen and 50 volume percents nitrogen should be continuously provided at a speed of 0.5 kg/min. The cross section of the gas tubes is 10 cm^2. Determine the speed of gas flow in the tubes, provided that the pressure is 10^5 Pa and the temperature is 27 °C in the tubes.

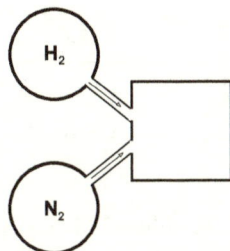

Problem 169. A cylinder with base area 1 dm^2 lies on its side on a horizontal surface and is divided into two parts of volumes 0.8 litre and 4.2 litre by a frictionless vertical piston as shown. The pressure in each part is 0.02 N/cm^2. The masses of the cylinder and piston are 0.8 kg and 0.2 kg respectively. The cylinder is then pushed by a constant horizontal force of magnitude 2.5 N to the left. What will be the new position of the piston be? (Assume constant temperature.)

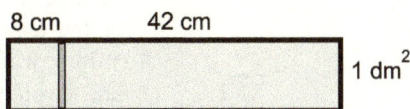

Problem 170. A cylinder of base area 10 cm^2 in which a 47 cm high air column is enclosed by a piston is floating upside down in a container. The piston is connected by a cord to the bottom of the container, which is filled with mercury and has a base area of 20 cm^2. The closed end of the cylinder is 10 cm below mercury level.

a) Find the new position of the cylinder if the cord is shortened by 6 cm.

b) Find the volume of mercury that should be poured into the container to set the mercury level back into its original height.

Problem 171. The cylindrical vessel shown in the figure has two pistons in it. The piston on the left touches a spring attached to the wall of the vessel. The wall has a hole in it. The volume of the air between the pistons is 2000 cm^3 and its pressure is initially equal to the external atmospheric pressure of 10^5 N/m^2. The piston on the right is slowly pressed inwards, maintaining constant temperature, until its inner surface is at the position where the inner surface of the piston on the left was initially. What will be the final volume of the air between the pistons?

The cross-sectional area of the cylinder is 100 cm^2, and a force of 10 N compresses the spring by 1 cm.

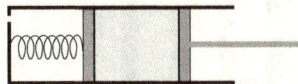

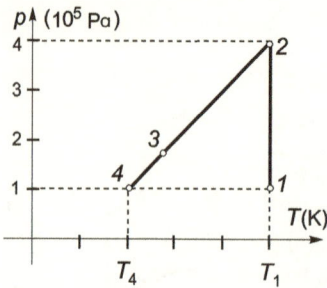

Problem 172. An ideal gas undergoes the process shown in the figure. $T_1 = 500$ K, $T_4 = 200$ K, $p_1 = 10^5$ Pa and $p_2 = 4 \cdot 10^5$ Pa. In state 3, $3V_3 = V_1$. What is the pressure of the ideal gas in state 3?

Problem 173. Using ideal gas we perform the thermal cyclic process $ABCA$, shown in the figure. Found on the volume-temperature plane of the graph $(V;T)$ is a right triangle with legs parallel to the V and T axes. In the state A the temperature of the gas is 373 K and its volume is 5 dm^3, while in the state C the gas has a temperature 273 K and a volume 12 dm^3.

At which volume on the subprocess $C \to A$ does the gas have the same pressure as in the state B?

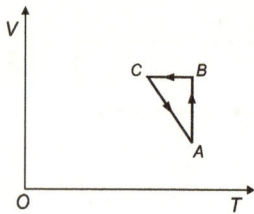

Problem 174. One arm of a communicating vessel containing mercury is closed by a piston 20 cm above the mercury. The other arm is open. The mercury level is the same in both arms, whose cross-sectional areas are 2 cm^2. In an isothermal process the piston is pushed down by 10 cm.

a) Find the difference of the mercury levels in the new position of the piston.

b) Find the change in the energy of the mercury.

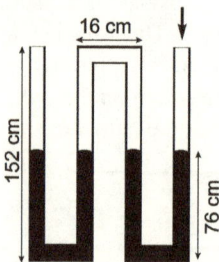

Problem 175. Initially, the height of the mercury column is the same in each branch of the narrow glass tube. Atmospheric pressure balances 76 cm of mercury. Then air pressure is increased over the right end until it equals the pressure of 232.8 cm-height of mercury. What is the height of the mercury now in each branch?

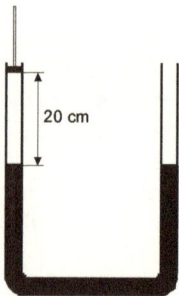

Problem 176. A glass tube is closed at one end and has a cross-sectional area of 0.2 cm^2. The tube is held in a vertical position with its open end facing upwards. It contains a 0.25-cm column of liquid ether that is closed off by a 19-cm column of mercury. The temperature is 35 °C (the boiling point of ether). What will be the position of the mercury column if the tube is inverted? The density of liquid ether is 0.7 g/cm^3 and its relative molar mass is 74.

Problem 177. The cross-sectional areas of all three branches of a device for the electrolysis of water are $A = 4\,\mathrm{cm}^2$. Initially, the height of the water column is the same in every branch, and there is no air above the water in the branches on the sides. How long does it take for the water level to rise by $\Delta h = 1\,\mathrm{m}$ in the middle tube if the device extracts 0.6 mg of hydrogen per minute? What is the (average) speed of the rising water level? The temperature is $27\,^\circ\mathrm{C}$. ($g = 9.8\,\mathrm{m/s}^2$, external air pressure is $p_0 = 10^5\,\mathrm{Pa}$, $\varrho = 10^3\,\mathrm{kg/m}^3$.)

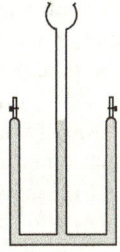

Problem 178. A glass balloon of volume $V = 1\,\mathrm{dm}^3$ is attached to a thin-walled tube of length $l = 40$ cm and cross-sectional area $A = 1\,\mathrm{cm}^2$. The glass tube is immersed into mercury to half of its length as shown in the figure. The container containing the mercury is a square prism with base edges of $a = 3$ cm. At the initial temperature $t_1 = 10\,^\circ\mathrm{C}$ the level of mercury in the tube is the same as the level of the external mercury.

Find the temperature at which the enclosed air should be heated in order to push out the mercury from the tube? (The external atmospheric pressure is $p_0 = 10^5$ Pa, the thermal expansion of the mercury and the glass can be neglected.)

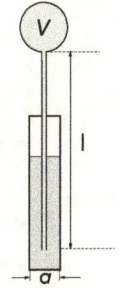

Problem 179. In a container with heat insulator walls a heat insulator piston encloses a diatomic gas at pressure $p_1 = 139.2$ kPa. We turn on an electric heater inside the container, and slowly let the piston extend in such a way that the pressure inside the container remains constant. After some time the temperature of the gas is increased by $\Delta T_1 = 29.3\,^\circ\mathrm{C}$, while its volume is increased by $\Delta V_1 = 5\,\mathrm{dm}^3$. Then we turn off the heater and let $\Delta m = 5$ g gas stream out of the container. Thus, the pressure decreases to $p_2 = 130.5$ kPa, but the temperature of the gas remains unchanged.

Now we turn on the heater, and again maintaining constant pressure by the piston we let the volume grow by $\Delta V_2 = 8\,\mathrm{dm}^3$, while the temperature increases by $\Delta T_2 = 46.88\,^\circ\mathrm{C}$.

a) Determine the initial mass of the gas in the container.

b) What kind of gas is in the container?

c) How much energy did the heater transfer to the gas during the first extension process?

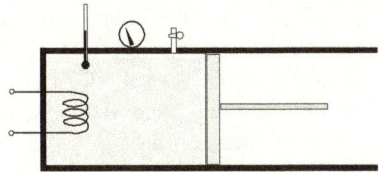

Problem 180. A long glass pipe of cross section $A = 3$ cm^2, which is closed at one end, is partially submerged into the water of a lake in such a way that the open end of the pipe points vertically downwards. When the length of the air column in the pipe is $l_0 = 60$ cm, the levels of the water in the pipe and in the lake coincide. Then the pipe is slowly pulled out of the water until the water level inside it rises by $h = 50$ cm. At that time the length of the air column is $l_1 = 63$ cm.

a) Determine the external air pressure.

b) Now the pipe is held fixed at its last position, and the initial temperature of the air in it is $5°$C. By how many degrees $°$C should this temperature be increased in order for the water level in the pipe to decrease by 16 cm?

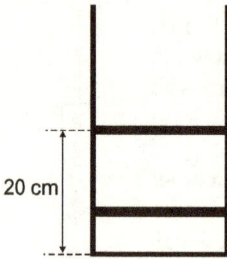

Problem 181. In a cylindrical container of height 40 cm two pistons enclose certain amounts of gas, as is shown in the figure. The upper piston is at a height of 20 cm from the bottom of the cylinder. If the upper piston is slowly lifted by 10 cm, then the lower piston rises by 4 cm. Determine the position of the lower piston if the upper one is removed from the cylinder. The external air pressure is 10^5 Pa, the cross section of the cylinder is 10 cm^2 and each piston has a mass of 1 kg. (Assume that the temperature is constant during the process.)

20 cm

Problem 182. Determine the specific heat of air at constant volume, given the information that 75.5% of air is nitrogen, 23.2% is oxygen and 1.3% is argon, and the atomic masses of nitrogen, oxygen and argon are 14 u, 16 u and 40 u respectively.

Problem 183. There was a block of ice in an isolated container at temperature $0\,°$C. We wanted to determine its mass, therefore we let some steam with a temperature of $100\,°$C into the container, but we could not determine the exact amount of the steam. After re-closing the container all the ice melted, and the new equilibrium temperature became $10\,°$C. Then, once more we let some steam of temperature $100\,°$C into the container, but again, we could not determine its exact amount. The temperature in the container became $15\,°$C. Finally, we let again some steam into the container, and this time we could determine its mass, which was 0.3 kg. The new equilibrium temperature in the container became $23\,°$C. Determine the mass of the ice block.

Problem 184. In an isolated container, which has cooling tubes built in the walls, an amount of $m = 18$ kg of clean water is very carefully cooled down to the temperature of $t_1 = -9\,°$C. After this a small ice crystal of negligible mass is thrown into the water, which starts to freeze the super cooled water. Determine the amount of ice produced.

(The necessary material constants should be looked up in a table.)

Problem 185. A vertical cylinder with cross-sectional area $A = 1$ dm^2 contains $h_1 = 25$ cm of water at the bottom. The space above it is filled with the saturated vapour of the water, which is separated from the external space by a piston. The bottom of the piston is $h_2 = 75$ cm above the water level. The density of water at this temperature is $n = 2$ times the density of saturated vapour.

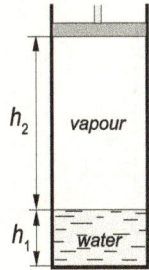

a) If temperature is held constant, by how much should the piston be pushed down in order to decrease the volume of vapour to $V = 4.5$ dm^3?

b) If temperature is held constant, by how much should the piston be pushed down in order to have the vapour condense completely?

(The sum of the masses of water and vapour is constant throughout the process.)

Problem 186. Helium gas whose volume is $V_1 = 3$ litres, pressure is $p_1 = 4 \cdot 10^5$ Pa and temperature is $T_1 = 1092$ K is separated from helium gas whose volume is $V_2 = 2$ litres, pressure is $p_2 = 2.5 \cdot 10^5$ Pa and temperature is $T_2 = 1365$ K by a highly insulated wall of mass $m = 2$ kg in an insulated cylinder. The partition wall is released, it can move without friction. Find the maximum speed acquired by the partition wall.

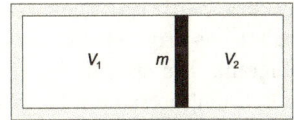

Problem 187. 4 grams of helium and 16 grams of oxygen are enclosed by a piston in a cylinder. The a temperature of the gas is $0\ °C$ and its pressure is 10^5 Pa. The cylinder walls and the piston are good thermal insulators. The pressure is increased to $2 \cdot 10^5$ Pa. What will be the final temperature and volume of the gas? The molar specific heats of helium are $C_{vh} = 12.3$ J/(mod·K), $C_{ph} = 20.5$ J/(mol· K); and those of oxygen are $C_{vo} = 20.5$ J/(mol· K), $C_{po} = 28.7$ J/(mod·K).

Problem 188. A smoothly moving, fixed piston made of good insulating material separates two gases in an insulated cylinder whose cross-sectional area is $A = 1$ dm^2. One part contains helium, the other part contains hydrogen. The initial data of helium is: its pressure is $p_1 = 2 \cdot 10^5$ Pa, its volume is $V_1 = 4$ dm^3, its temperature is $T_1 = 350$ K, the corresponding data of hydrogen are: $p_2 = 3 \cdot 10^5$ Pa, $V_2 = 5$ dm^3 and $T_2 = 280$ K. Find the displacement of the piston when it is released and it reaches an equilibrium

a) if the piston does not allow the gases to mix,

b) if the piston is permeable and particles can diffuse through it slowly,

c) if the piston allows only the helium to diffuse through it.

Problem 189. Three identical containers, each containing 32 g of oxygen gas at a temperature of $200\ °C$ and pressure of 10 N/cm^2 are connected by thin tubes. The container on the left is then cooled down to $100\ °C$, the one on the right is heated to $300\ °C$, while the temperature of the middle one remains $200\ °C$.

a) Find the new pressure of the system.

b) Find the change in the total internal energy of the oxygen gas. The specific heat of oxygen is $c_v = 670$ J/(kg·K).

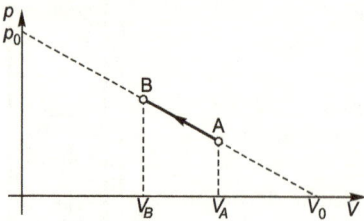

Problem 190. The figure shows the $p(V)$ diagram of a process carried out with a certain quantity of oxygen gas. The values of the volume V_0 and pressure p_0 in the figure are $V_0 = 12\,dm^3$, $p_0 = 1.2 \cdot 10^5$ Pa. In the initial state (A), the volume of the gas is $V_A = \frac{2}{3}V_0$ and its temperature is $T_A = 300$ K. In the final state (B), $V_B = \frac{5}{12}V_0$.

Determine the heat absorbed and, separately, the heat given off by the gas during the process.

Problem 191. 2 g of hydrogen gas of volume 22.4 litre at 0 °C and 10^5 Pa is taken through a cyclic process. First, it is slowly heated at constant volume until its pressure reaches $2 \cdot 10^5$ Pa. Then, it is heated to 546 °C at constant pressure. Finally, it is taken back to its original state along a path whose graph is a straight line segment on the p-V diagram. The specific heat of hydrogen is 10.1 kJ/(kg·K) at constant volume, while at constant pressure it is 14.28 kJ/(kg·K).

a) Find the efficiency of this cycle.

b) How does the temperature change in terms of the volume and in terms of the pressure through one complete cycle?

Problem 192. The cyclic process shown in the figure is carried out with 1 mole of diatomic gas. Find the percentage of the heat absorbed by the gas that is converted into useful work.

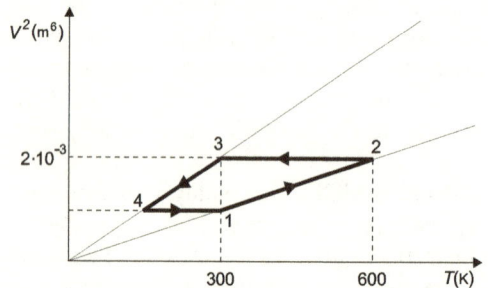

Problem 193. A closed container contains diatomic gas at temperature T_1 and pressure p_1. The gas is then heated to temperature T_2, during which 20% of the molecules are broken into atoms.

a) Find the final pressure of the gas.

b) Find the ratio of the final and initial internal energies of the gas. (Neglect the oscillation of the molecules.)

Problem 194. 1 mol of He is enclosed by a piston in a heatable and coolable container at an initial volume of 30 dm^3 and an initial temperature of 5 °C. From this initial state the gas is compressed in such a way that ratio $\Delta p/\Delta V$ remains constant during the process. Find this ratio if during the compression process the maximum temperature of the gas is 71 °C.

Problem 195. Let us model the atmosphere of the Earth, which has a radius $R_E =$ $= 6370$ km, in the following way: the temperature of the atmosphere is the same everywhere. The air molecules have 5 thermodynamical degrees of freedom, and their average molar mass is $M = 29$ g/mol. The air pressure at the surface of the Earth is $p_0 = 100$ kPa. Furthermore, the acceleration due to gravity is $g = 10$ m/s^2 in the region of the atmosphere. Now let us assume that for some reason the temperature of the atmosphere increases everywhere, uniformly by $\Delta T = 1°C$, but the total mass and the composition of the atmosphere remains unaltered. Determine the increase of the (gravitational) potential energy of the atmosphere due to the temperature change.

Problem 196. A piston of cross section $A = 100$ cm^2 and of mass $m = 0.5$ kg moves freely (without friction) in vertical direction in an isolated cylinder with negligible heat capacity. The specific heat of the material of the piston is $c = 210$ J/(kg °C). Initially the temperature of the piston is $t_0 = 100°C$, and there is an amount of $n_1 = 0.05$ mol noble gas at temperature $t_1 = -90$ °C above the piston, and an amount of $n_2 = 0.03$ mol air at temperature $t_2 = 46$ °C under the piston. The initial volumes of the gases are just equal.

a) Determine the final temperature of the piston.

b) Determine the displacement of the piston.

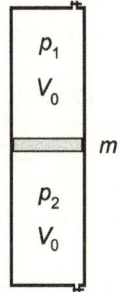

Problem 197. The closed cabin of a space station orbiting around the Earth is filled with artificial atmosphere that contains oxygen gas at pressure $p = 50$ kPa and temperature $T = 295$ K. The internal volume of the cabin is $V = 80$ m^3. A tiny hole of area $A = 0.1$ mm^2 appears on the wall of the cabin and the oxygen starts to escape. Estimate the time required for the pressure to decrease by 1 % in the cabin.

(The heating system maintains a constant temperature inside the cabin.)

Problem 198. A cylinder of mass 25 kg contains helium gas, which is enclosed by a well-fitted piston of mass 25 kg. The cross-sectional area of the cylinder is 0.4 dm^2 and the piston is at a height of 8.96 dm from the base of the cylinder. The piston is attached to a massless string that is wrapped around a pulley of radius 0.2 m and rotational inertia $3 \cdot$ kg $\cdot$ m^2. The container and piston move downwards with the same constant acceleration. The atmospheric pressure is $p_0 =$ $= 10$ N/cm^2, the temperature is $0°$ C and $g = 10$ m/s^2. Find the mass of the helium gas. (Neglect friction)

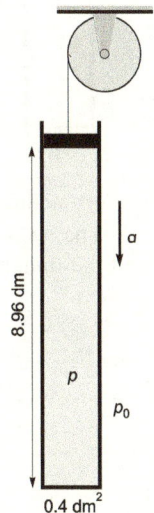

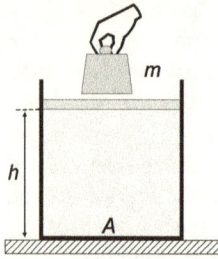

Problem 199. A certain amount of air is enclosed into a vertical cylinder of base surface $A = 1 \text{ dm}^2$ by a frictionless piston of negligible mass. The height of the air column in the cylinder is $h = 5$ dm. We carefully put a weight of mass $m = 14$ kg onto the piston, and release it. The piston and the weight on it start an oscillating motion with small amplitude, which can be regarded as harmonic. Determine the amplitude and the frequency of the oscillation, as well as the maximal speed of the piston.

(The wall of the cylinder can be considered a heat insulator. The external air pressure is $p_0 = 100$ kPa. If necessary, the approximation $(1 \pm x)^n \approx 1 \pm nx$ can be used, which is valid if x is close to zero, i.e., if $|x| \ll 1$.)

Problem 200. A gas, enclosed in a cylinder by a piston, is given a heat energy of $Q = 3988$ kJ, and as a consequence of this, the gas expands at constant pressure. The ratio of the specific heats measured at constant pressure and constant volume is $\gamma = 1.4$ for the gas. Determine how much of the absorbed heat increases the internal energy of the gas, and how much is given off in the form of work during the expansion.

2.3 First law of thermodynamics

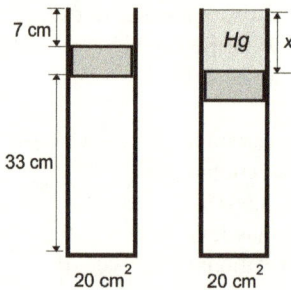

Problem 201. In a cylinder, whose cross-sectional area is 20 cm^2, a frictionless piston of mass 7.2 kg encloses a 33 cm high air column at $0\,°C$ so that there is a 7 cm high empty part above the piston as shown. The atmospheric pressure is 10 N/cm^2, the densities of mercury and air in its initial state are 13.6 g/cm^3 and 1.8 g/dm^3 respectively, the specific heat of the air at constant volume is 0.7 J/(g K). Use $g = 10 \text{ m/s}^2$.

a) Mercury is poured into the empty part above the piston until the cylinder is full. Find the mass of the mercury column. (Assume constant temperature.)

b) The air is then heated very slowly until all the mercury runs out from the cylinder. Find the minimum heat transferred to the air in this process.

46

Problem 202. A cylinder of mass 8 kg and cross-sectional area 20 cm^2 is hanging, suspended on its piston. The cylinder contains helium of temperature 27 °C. The temperature is slowly decreasing. How much heat is necessary to extract from the helium so that the initial length 11.2 dm of the gas column decreases to 8.96 dm? The external air pressure is 10^5 Pa, $g = 10$ m/s^2. The molar specific heat of helium at constant volume is $C_v = 12300$ J/(kmol· K).

Problem 203. A cylindrical container of base area 0.5 m^2 contains helium gas at 218.4 K. The gas is enclosed by a frictionless piston of mass 600 kg that is connected to the base of the container by a spring, whose spring constant is $2.67 \cdot 10^5$ N/m. Initially the piston is at a height of 0.32 m, which is the relaxed length of the spring. Atmospheric pressure is 10^5 Pa, the molar specific heat of helium is $C_v = 12.3$ joule/(mol K), $g = 10$ m/s^2. The wall of the container is a good thermal conductor causing the temperature of the gas to change until it reaches the external temperature. The work done by the gas is found to be 1800 joules.
a) Find the external temperature.
b) Find the heat given to the helium gas.

11.2 dm

0.32 m

0.5 m^2

Problem 204. In an 11.2 dm high cylindrical container, whose base area is 1 dm^2, a frictionless piston of mass 8 kg is held at a height of 5.6 dm. The piston encloses 1 mol of helium at 273 °C. The wall of the container is insulated. Find the maximum height reached by the piston after being released. The molar specific heat of helium at constant volume is $C_v = 12.6$ J/(molK), while at constant pressure it is $C_p = 21$ J/(molK). The atmospheric pressure is 10.12 N/cm^2.

Problem 205. A piston encloses some air in the cylindrical vessel with horizontal longitudinal axis as shown in the drawing. The initial pressure of the air is equal to the external atmospheric pressure of 10^5 Pa. The cross-sectional area of the piston is 0.03 m^2. An originally unstretched spring with spring constant 2000 N/m is attached to the piston. The walls of the vessel and the piston are perfectly insulated. The initial volume of the enclosed air is 0.024 m^3, its initial temperature is 300 K. The air is heated to 360 K with a heating filament built into the vessel.
a) Find the displacement of the piston caused by the heating.
b) Find the energy delivered by the heating filament.

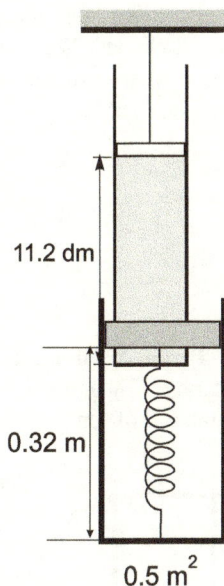

Problem 206. Ideal gas at pressure 10^5 Pa and volume 1 m^3 is enclosed by a piston in a cylinder. We start to move the piston outwards at a constant velocity of 1 cm/s. The cross-sectional area of the piston is 0.1 m^2. While the piston is moving, we can deliver heat to the gas through a heating filament.

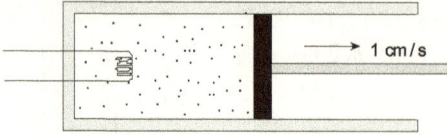

How should the heating power change as a function of time if we keep the temperature of the gas constant? (Apart from the heat transfer between the gas and the heating filament all other heat exchange can be neglected.)

Problem 207. Ideal gas which has degrees of freedom f, is part of a process that starts at T_0 and ends at $2T_0$ $V = aT^2$ ($a =$ constant). Give the molar heat capacity as function of temperature.

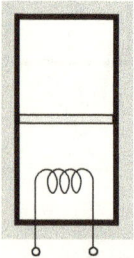

Problem 208. A cylindrical container of volume 44.8 litres is divided into two equal parts by a horizontal frictionless piston. Each half of the cylinder contains 4 g of helium at 0 °C. The walls of the container and the piston are perfect insulators. There is a 220 V heater of resistance 242 Ω in the lower part. For how long should the heater be switched on to make the temperature of the helium in the upper part rise to 136.5 °C? The specific heats of helium are $c_p = 5230$ J/(kg·K) and $c_v = 3140$ J/(kg·K).

Problem 209. For a given amount of nitrogen gas the initial, minimum temperature is T_0, while the maximum temperature is $4T_0$. The gas is first heated at constant volume, then it is allowed to expand at constant pressure. Then it is cooled at constant volume and finally it is compressed at constant pressure. This way the gas returns to its initial state. Find the maximum possible efficiency of the cyclic process.

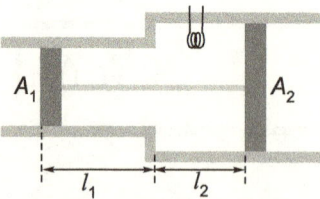

Problem 210. The walls of the two connecting cylinders shown in the figure are adiabatic (thermally insulating). The cross-sectional areas of the parts are $A_1 = 10$ dm^2 and $A_2 = 40$ dm^2. There is a well-fitting but freely moving, thermally insulating piston in each cylinder, at a distance $l_1 = l_2 = l = 1.5$ dm from the point where the cross-sectional area changes.

The pistons are fixed to each other by a thin and rigid rod. The enclosed volume contains air. The temperature and air pressure are $T_0 = 300$ K and $p_0 = 10^5$ Pa both inside and outside. The heater filament inside is operated for $t = 2$ minutes at a power of $P = 36$ W.

a) How much, and in what direction, will the pistons move until the new equilibrium position is reached?

b) What will the temperature of the enclosed air be?

Problem 211. Consider the system of two pistons in two cylinders shown in the Figure. The cylinder walls and the pistons are good thermal insulators. Initially, the pressure of the air in all three compartments is 20 N/cmn^2, and the temperature is $0 \,^\circ\text{C}$. The filament in the leftmost compartment is heated for a short time. As a result, the pistons move 5 cm to the right.

a) What are the resulting pressures?

b) How much heat is given off by the filament?

The density of air at $0 \,^\circ\text{C}$ and normal atmospheric pressure is 1.3 g/dm^3, and its specific heat is $0.7 \text{ J/(g} \cdot \text{ K)}$ at constant volume and $0.98 \text{ J/(g} \cdot \text{ K)}$ at constant pressure.

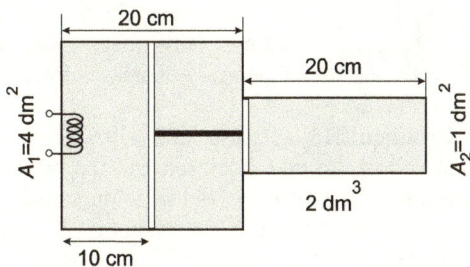

Problem 212. In a closed container, there is a mixture of helium and oxygen gases of a total mass of 2.2 kg at a temperature of $0 \,^\circ\text{C}$. 143 500 joules of heat is added to the gas mixture. As a result, its temperature rises by $50 \,^\circ\text{C}$ and its pressure increases by 13 740 pascals.

a) Find the mass of each gas.

b) Find the initial pressure of the mixture.

c) Find the volume of the container.

At constant volume, the molar specific heat of helium is $12\ 300 \text{ J/(kmol} \cdot \text{K)}$ and the molar specific heat of oxygen is $20\ 500 \text{ J/(kmol} \cdot \text{K)}$.

Problem 213. Hydrogen gas of mass $m = 20 \text{ g}$ undergoes the processs $1-2-3-4-5$ shown in the figure. The following data are given: $p_1 = p_2 = 5 \cdot 10^5 \text{ Pa}$, $p_3 = p_4 = 7 \cdot 10^5 \text{ Pa}$, $T_1 = T_5 = 200 \text{ K}$, $T_2 = T_4 = 500 \text{ K}$. (In the stages $2-3$ and $4-5$ of the process, pressure is directly proportional to temperature.)

a) Find the values of the volume in the states 1, 2, 3, 4, and 5, and the values of pressure and temperature not given.

b) Represent the process in both p-V and T-V diagrams.

c) Determine the net heat absorbed by the gas and the net work done on the gas during the whole process.

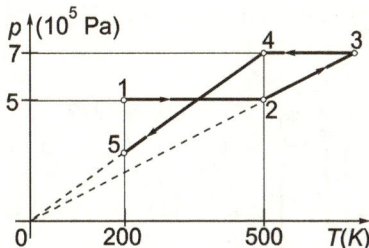

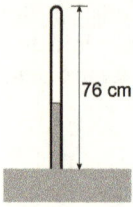

Problem 214. The upper end of a 76-cm-long glass tube is closed and the open lower end is submerged in mercury. The tube is partly filled with mercury, with 0.001 moles of air enclosed in the upper end. External atmospheric pressure can balance a mercury column of 76 cm. The molar specific heat of air is $C_v = 20.5$ J/(mol·K) at constant volume. How much heat is given off by the enclosed air while its temperature decreases by 10 °C?

76 cm

Problem 215. A glass tube with thin walls is placed in a chamber of rarefied air. One end of the tube is closed and the other is covered by a stretched liquid film. The pressure of the air is p_0 and its temperature is T_0 both inside and outside the tube. The length of the tube is h, its radius is R. The surface tension of the liquid is α. The temperature in the tube starts to rise slowly.

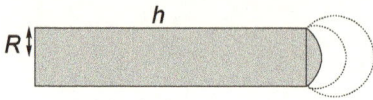

h

R

a) At what temperature will the enclosed air have a maximum pressure?

b) How much heat is absorbed by the enclosed air until the state of maximum pressure is reached?

$R = 5\,\text{mm}$, $h = 25\,\text{mm}$, $T_0 = 250\,\text{K}$, $p_0 = 1000\,\text{Pa}$, $\alpha = 5 \cdot 10^{-2}\,\text{J/m}^2$.
Assume that, in the pressure and temperature ranges investigated, the liquid is far away from its boiling point.

Problem 216. A piston of mass m encloses air with a pressure greater than the external atmospheric pressure in a horizontal cylinder whose walls are thermally insulated. If the piston is released, it can move in the cylinder without friction. In the adiabatic change that takes place, the maximum volume of the enclosed gas is twice as much as the original. Determine

a) the ratio of the minimum and maximum pressures of the gas,

b) the magnitude of the initial pressure.

(The pressure of the external air is $p_{\text{ext}} = 10^5$ Pa. The air can be considered as a gas with 5 degrees of freedom, therefore the ratio of its two specific heat capacities is $\gamma = c_p/c_v = 1.4$.)

80 kg

Problem 217. A 2.24 m high cylinder, whose base area is 1 dm^2 contains 4 g of helium gas at a temperature of 0 °C and pressure of 10 N/cm^2. An 80 kg piston is then dropped into the cylinder. Find the maximum speed of the piston if it moves without friction. There is no heat transfer between the gas, the cylinder and the piston because of the rapidity of the process. Use $g = 10\,\text{m/s}^2$. The specific heats of helium are: $c_v = 3150$ J/(kg·K), $c_p = 5250$ J/(kg·K).

2.24 m

1 dm^2

Problem 218. Initially $n = 10$ mol of an ideal gas has the pressure $p_1 = 10^5$ Pa, volume $V_1 = 249.42$ dm^3 and temperature $T_1 = 300$ K. Then the gas is heated, and in an isobaric process it reaches the temperature T_2. During this process the work done by the gas is 68% of the increase of its internal energy. If, however, from the same initial state an adiabatic compression is used to increase the temperature of the gas to T_2, then $W = 36.85$ kJ has to be done on the gas.
   a) What type of gas is the experiment performed with?
   b) Determine the final temperature T_2.

Problem 219. There is 5 g of a certain diatomic gas in a container closed with a frictionless piston. The gas is heated for 25 seconds by an electric resistor of 50 Ω built in the container, applying a voltage of 220 V. While the gas expands at constant pressure, its temperature increases by 250 °C. The efficiency of the electric heater is 75%. What kind of gas can be found in the container?

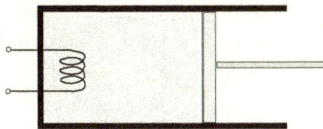

Problem 220. A container, closed by a freely moving piston, contains a mixture of hydrogene and helium gas of total mass $m = 180$ g. A heat of $Q = 156$ kJ is transferred to the gas at constant pressure. Due to this the gas performs 56 kJ work. Determine the mass of hydrogene in the mixture. Determine the temperature change of the system.

Problem 221. The state of helium gas is changed in such a way that its graph is a straight line segment on the pressure–volume plane. During this process the total heat transferred to the gas is equal to the heat necessary to double the absolute temperature of the gas at constant volume. By what ratio may the volume of the gas most increase? (The expression "total heat" refers to the signed sum of heat absorbed and heat released during the process.)

Problem 222. A small ball of mass $m = 1$ g and charge Q is attached to the end of a string of length $R = 10$ cm. Level with the suspension point of the pendulum, at a distance of $R = 10$ cm there is a small fixed object of the same charge Q. If the pendulum is released from a position $\alpha = 60°$ below the horizontal, the string will become slack when the pendulum bob has covered a semicircle exactly. Find the magnitude of the charge Q.

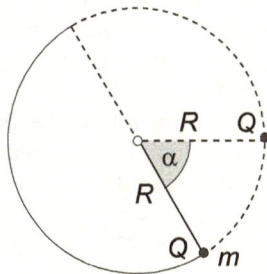

Chapter 3

Electrodynamics Problems

3.1 Electrostatics

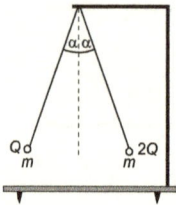

Problem 223. Two small metal balls of mass $m = 0.1$ g are suspended at the same point by insulating threads of length $l = 30$ cm. One of the balls is loaded with twice as much electric charge as the other. Pushing the balls towards each other by insulating materials, we move them to a position where both threads make an angle of $\alpha = 20°$ with the vertical, and the threads remain in a common vertical plane. After releasing the two balls from this position at the same time, the angle between the two threads reaches the largest value of $\beta = 84°$.

Determine the charge of the balls.

Problem 224. In free space, far from all celestial objects, two particles, one of mass $m_1 = 6 \cdot 10^{-12}$ kg and of charge $Q_1 = 2.43 \cdot 10^{-13}$ C and the other of mass $m_2 = 1.2 \cdot 10^{-11}$ kg and of charge $Q_2 = -2.43 \cdot 10^{-13}$ C move at a constant speed in such a way that the distance $d = 1.5$ cm between them is also constant. How is this possible? Determine the speed of the particles.

Problem 225. In free space two specks of dust, one of mass $m_1 = 1.7 \cdot 10^{-11}$ kg and of electric charge $Q_1 = 10^{-9}$ C and the other of mass $m_2 = 1.3 \cdot 10^{-11}$ kg and charge $Q_2 = -5 \cdot 10^{-9}$ C are released at a distance $d_1 = 6$ cm from each other with zero initial speed.

a) Where will the two specks of dust meet?

b) Determine the speed at which the specks approach each other, when they are at the distance $d_2 = 1$ cm.

Problem 226. A capacitor has plates of large area separated by $d = 3$ cm. The potential difference between the plates is $V = 60\,000$ V. What should be the speed of a small object of charge $Q = 4 \cdot 10^{-3}$ C and mass $m = 5 \cdot 10^{-6}$ kg shot horizontally into the uniform field at the height of half the plate separation d, so that it reaches one of the plates at a distance of $h = 12$ cm?

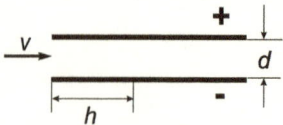

Problem 227. A potential difference V is applied between two finely woven parallel wire meshes D_1–D_2 with the polarity shown in the figure. Electrons originating from electron source E arrive at mesh D_1 at velocity v.

a) Show that for the angle of incidence α and the angle of refraction β Snell's law is valid (ratio $\sin\alpha/\sin\beta$ is independent of the angle of incidence and has the same value for every electron).

b) Determine the value of the refractive index.
(You can assume that the electric field between the meshes is homogenous and everywhere else the electric field is zero. $v = 3\cdot10^6$ m/s, $V = 25$ V.)

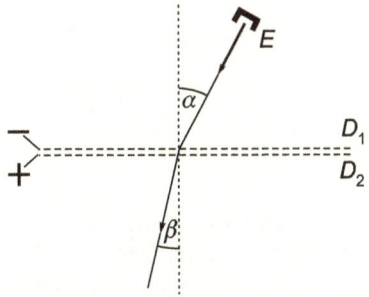

Problem 228. In a vacuum tube electrons accelerated through a potential difference V_0 leave the anode with beam angle α. A metal lattice pair is then placed in the way of the beam. What potential difference should be applied to the lattices if we want the electron beam to form an angle of 2α after leaving the lattice-pair? Values: $V_0 = 60000$ V, $\alpha = 30°$.

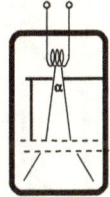

Problem 229. A particle of charge $Q = +10^{-5}$ C is fixed. A second particle of mass $m = 0.01$ g and charge $q = +10^{-7}$ C standing at infinity is given a velocity of $v_0 = 200$ m/s in a direction whose line passes at a distance of $d = 0.1$ m from the fixed charge.

a) Find the smallest separation between the two charges.

b) What should the value of d be if the final velocity of the moving charge is now perpendicular to its initial velocity v_0?

Problem 230. If the cathode of a photocell is illuminated with a light of increasing frequency, the anode current will start at a frequency of $3\cdot10^{14}$ $\frac{1}{\text{s}}$. A capacitor with capacitance 1 pF is connected between the anode and the cathode of this photocell, and the cathode is illuminated with light of wavelength 425 nm. Assuming that the illumination is long enough, find the number of electrons arriving on the anode.

Problem 231. Two metal spheres of equal mass and radius are suspended from a common point, with two insulating threads of equal length. If the spheres are loaded with equal electric charges, and submerged into paraffin, the angle between the two threads is $2\alpha_P = 60°$. If the paraffin bath is removed, i.e., the charged spheres are in the air, then the angle between the threads is $2\alpha_A = 70°$. Determine the density of the spheres. (Paraffin is an electric insulator, its relative permittivity is $\varepsilon_r = 2$, and its density is $\varrho_p = 800$ kg/m^3. The diameter of the spheres is much less than the length of the threads.)

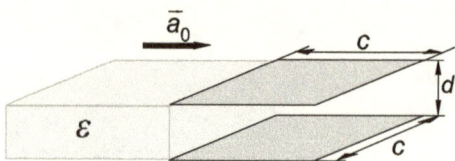

Problem 232. A parallel plate capacitor consists of a pair of square plates with sides c that are at distance d apart. The capacitor is connected to a generator of constant voltage U. The space between the plates is originally filled with air. A plate with relative dielectric constant ε_r is inserted between the plates at a constant acceleration a_0 as shown in the figure. The insulator starts from the edge of the plate, from stationary position. Determine the charge-time function of the capacitor and the charging current-time function. Sketch the shape of the functions. Calculate the maximum value of the charge on the capacitor and of the charging current.

($c = 20\,\text{cm}$, $d = 2\,\text{mm}$, $U = 100\,\text{V}$, $a_0 = 2\,\text{m/s}^2$, $\varepsilon_r = 101$.)

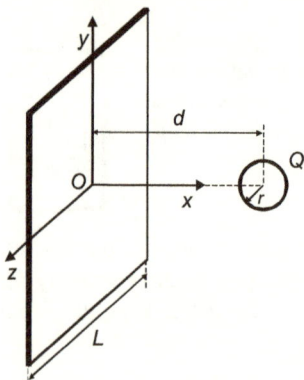

Problem 233. A big insulating square plate of size L and negligible width is uniformly charged with a charge of $100\,Q$. Let the plane of the plate be the $y - z$ coordinate plane. There is a hollow insulating sphere of radius r with centre at the point $(d,0,0)$ in front of the plate. The sphere has a thin wall, and is uniformly charged with charge Q. Determine the electric field at the interior points of the sphere, and at the point $(d/2,d/2,0)$, provided that $L = 100d$ and $r = d/5$. Express these results in terms of Q, d and the dielectric constant ε_0.

Problem 234. Two identical air capacitors with capacitance C are connected in series to a battery with constant voltage V. Find the change in the energy of the capacitors, of the battery and of the surroundings

a) if the distance between the plates of one of the capacitors is increased to twice the original distance using an insulating handle,

b) an insulator with dielectric constant $\varepsilon = 2\varepsilon_0$ is inserted between the plates of one of the capacitors.

Problem 235. A parallel-plate capacitor is connected to a battery which builds up an electric field of $600\,\text{V/m}$ between the plates.

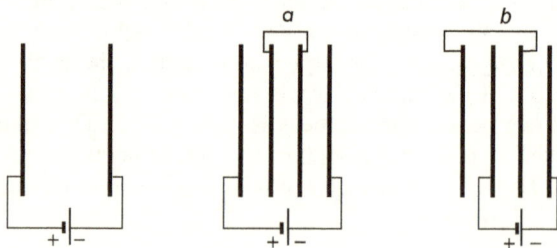

a) In the first part, two plates are placed into the capacitor as shown. The plates, that are initially neutral, are connected by a wire and are positioned such that the four plates are at equal distance from each other. Find the electric field strengths between the plates.

b) In the second part, the two initially neutral plates that are connected are positioned as shown in figure b). The plates are at equal distances from each other in this case as well. Find the electric field strengths between the plates.

Problem 236. One plate of a $2\text{-}\mu\text{F}$ capacitor charged to 150 volts is connected to the oppositely charged plate of a $3\text{-}\mu\text{F}$ capacitor charged to 120 volts. The other plate of each capacitor ends in a free wire. An uncharged capacitor of $1.5\text{-}\mu\text{F}$ is dropped onto the free ends.

a) What will be the potential difference across each capacitor?

b) How much charge will pass through point A and in what direction?

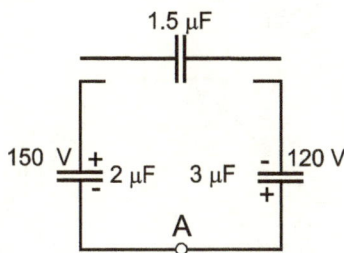

Problem 237. In ancient times, people believed that the Earth was a big, flat disc. Let us imagine that the Earth is not actually sphere with radius R but a flat disc with a very large radius and a thickness of H. What thickness H is needed to experience the same gravitational acceleration on the surface of the disc (far from its rim) as on the surface of the spherical Earth? ($R = 6370\,\text{km}$. Let us consider the densities in the two 'Earth' models to be constant and equal to each other.)

Problem 238. A long insulating cylinder of radius R has a cylindrical bore of radius r in it. The axes of the cylinder and the bore are parallel, separated by a distance d. The insulator carries a positive charge of uniform distribution with a charge density of ϱ. The relative dielectric constant of the material is 1. Find the electric field inside the bore.

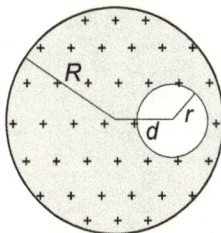

Problem 239. If the values of the resistance of the resistors shown in the figure are equal then the current in the main branch is I. By what factor does this current change if the resistance of the two resistors, which are diagonally opposite each other, is doubled?

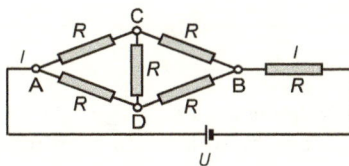

3.2 Direct current

Problem 240. We have two rechargeable batteries available, their electromotive forces and their internal resistances are the following: $U_{01} = 12.6$ v, $R_1 = 0.05$ ohm, $U_{02} = 12.2$ V, $R_2 = 5$ ohm. What will happen if the two rechargeable batteries are connected in parallel and the circuit is closed through a resistor of resistance $R_k = 2$ ohm?

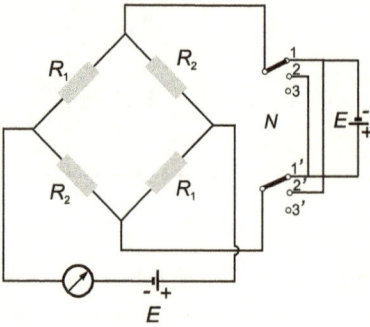

Problem 241. The figure shows an electric circuit which contains a double switch labelled by S. When the switch is in the position $11'$ the ammeter reads $I_I = 6$ A, and when the switch is in position $22'$ the reading is $I_{II} = 3$ A. What is the reading on the ammeter when the switch is in position $33'$? The electromotive forces E of the two batteries are equal, their internal resistances and the internal resistance of the ammeter are negligible.

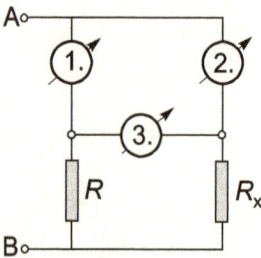

Problem 242. In the circuit shown the three ammeters are identical, each have a resistance $R_0 = 2\,\Omega$. Between points A and B there is a constant potential difference of 19 V. The first and second ammeter read $I_1 = 2.5$ A-t and $I_2 = 1.5$ A respectively.

a) What does the third ammeter read?

b) Investigate what happens to current I_3 if the value of R_x is changed.

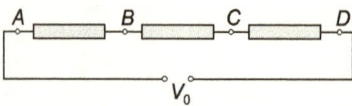

Problem 243. Three resistors are connected in series with a battery of internal voltage $V_0 = 62$ V and internal resistance $R_b \approx 0$ as shown in the figure, then measurements are carried out with a single voltmeter. The results of the first three measurements are: $V_{AB} = V_{BC} = V_{CD} = 20$ V. What does the instrument show when it is connected between point pairs AC and AD?

Problem 244. In the circuit shown in the figure switch K is kept closed for a long time and then it is opened. The constant voltage across the terminals of the battery is $V_0 = 9$ V, the capacitance of the capacitor is $C = 50$ μF, the values of resistances R_1 and R_2 are equal, $R_1 = R_2 = 100$ Ω.

a) Find the charge that flows through resistor R_3 after the switch is opened if the value of resistance R_3 is 400 Ω.

b) Find the maximum charge that can flow through resistor R_3 after the switch is opened, if the value of resistance R_3 is chosen suitably.

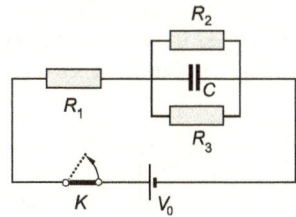

Problem 245. We have N identical cells whose no-load voltage is V_0 and internal resistance is R. We create a battery from these in the following way: first we connect a given number of cells with the same polarity in series into a chain, and then connect these chains containing the same number of cells in parallel with the same polarity. Then we connect a consumer whose resistance is optimal for maximum power output to the acquired battery.

a) Find the number of batteries that should be connected into a chain, that is, find the arrangement of the cells in order to acquire the maximum power output on the consumer.

b) Find this power if $N = 64$, $V_0 = 12$ V, $R = 2$ Ω.

Problem 246. A $100 - \Omega$, $2 - $W resistor is to be operated from a variable voltage supply. A variable resistor of resistance $1000\,\Omega$, which has three terminals, and which can be loaded by 15 W, and a voltage supply of 48 V, whose internal resistance is negligible, are given. In what interval can the voltage across the resistor be varied?

Problem 247. The range of voltage of a meter used as a voltmeter can be changed to n times its original value with the help of a $27\,\Omega$ multiplier. Using the same meter as an ammeter, its range of current can be changed to n times its original value using a $3\,\Omega$ shunt.

a) Find the internal resistance of the meter.

b) The power dissipated by the moving-coil of the meter when giving a full-scale reading is $9 \cdot 10^{-4}$ W. Find the voltage and current across the moving-coil.

Problem 248. The circuit diagram shows an emf source with an electromotive force V_0 and an internal resistance R_0 between points A and B. The total resistance of the variable resistor is R, which is greater than $4/3$ times the internal resistance of the emf source. The resistance of the ammeter and the other wires can be neglected. If the sliding contact is moved along the variable resistor, the ammeter shows a changing current.

Show that the minimum current that can be measured is smaller then $3/4$ times the maximum current.

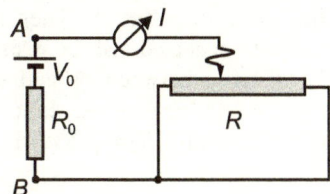

Problem 249. The stator and the rotor of our direct-current electromotor are connected in series and have a total resistance of 62 Ω. The motor is connected to a dc voltage of 220 V. Can this motor produce a mechanical power of 200 W?

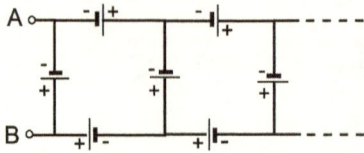

Problem 250. All batteries in the infinite chain shown in the figure have emf ε and internal resistance r. Find the resultant emf and internal resistance across A and B.

Problem 251. The resistor chain shown in figure 2 contains n "quadrupoles" shown in figure 1. $R_1 = 1\ \Omega$ and $R_2 = 6\ \Omega$. The resistor chain is terminated by a resistor R_x.

a) Find the resistance of resistor R_x in order to ensure that the resistance measured between points A and B is independent of number n of the included quadrupoles.

b) The resistor chain is terminated by the resistor R_x determined in part a) and a battery of terminal voltage $U_{AB} = 3$ V is connected between points A and B. The chain contains $n = 21$ quadrupoles now. Find the potential difference across resistor R_x in this case.

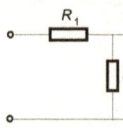
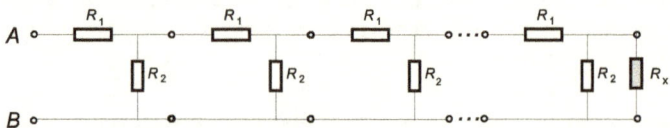

figure 1.   figure 2.

Problem 252. Between the two ends of a broken conductor the charges are carried by a metal sphere mounted on an insulating handle. The radius of the metal sphere is 1 cm, and it touches one end and then the other end of the conductor 54 times in one minute. Find the resistance of the break, which is "bridged" in the way described above. (The capacitance of the metal sphere can be calculated as the capacitance of a single sphere standing in space.)

Problem 253. In a cable, which is under the ground, there are two wires, and somewhere between the points A and B a conducting path has been developed between the wires. The cable can be reached at positions A and B. In order to find the position of the conducting path is, first the two wires are connected at B and the resistance (R_1) is measured at A. Then the measurement is repeated so that at A the points at 1-$1'$ are connected and the resistance (R_2) at B between the points 2-$2'$ is measured. The distance between A and B is known (L). The resistance of the wire of unit length is r ohm/metre. Find the position of the conducting path. Numerical data: $R_1 = 3.75$ ohm, $R_2 = 2.5$ ohm, $L = 200$ metre, $r = 0.01$ ohm/metre.

Chapter 4

Magnetism Problems

4.1 Magnetic field

Problem 254. In a mass spectrometer the Cl^- ions, after passing through the diaphragm A_1 at different speeds, first travel in perpendicular (homogeneous) electric and magnetic fields. Then, after passing diaphragm A_2, they move further in a magnetic field only. The ^{35}Cl and ^{37}Cl isotopes hit the photo plate at points $\Delta x = 4$ cm apart from each other. The magnetic induction is $B = 0.02$ T (in both regions).

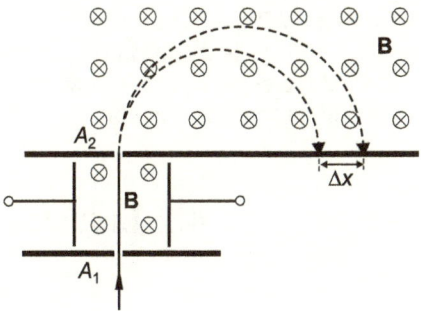

a) Determine the speed of the Cl isotopes when they pass through the diaphragm A_2.

b) Determine the magnitude and the direction of the electric field between the two diaphragms A_1 and A_2.

Problem 255. Two points lying on the same field line are separated by a distance $\overline{XY} = L = 10$ cm in vacuum, in a uniform magnetic field where the magnitude of the magnetic induction vector is $B = 0.02$ tesla. An electron accelerated by a potential difference of 800 volts passes through the point X. Its velocity encloses an angle α with the field lines. What should be the measure of the angle α so that the electron also passes through the point Y? The charge of an electron is $1.6 \cdot 10^{-19}$ coulombs, and its mass is $9 \cdot 10^{-31}$ kg.

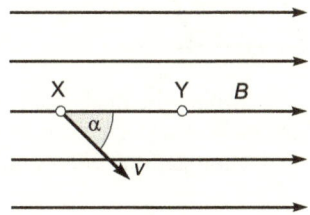

Problem 256. A sphere of radius 1 cm is charged to a voltage of 900 V. The sphere is mounted to a 30 cm long insulating handle and is rotated, the number of revolutions is 18000/minute. Determine the magnetic induction which can be observed at the position of the axis of the rotation. (Consider the rotating small sphere as a pointlike charge.)

The magnetic field at the centre of a current carrying single loop is: $H = \dfrac{I}{2r} \left(\dfrac{A}{m} \right)$.

Problem 257. The density of turns of a very long solenoid of diameter 1 cm is 2000 m^{-1}. The coil is wound in one layer. The strength of the magnetic field, produced by the coil, at a distance of 5 cm from the axis of the solenoid is $4 \cdot 10^{-4}$ T. Determine the strength of the magnetic field inside the solenoid. What would be the magnetic field strength at a distance of 5 cm from the axis, if the solenoid was wound in two layers?

Problem 258. The density of turns in a very long solenoid of diameter 1 cm is 2000 m^{-1}. The magnetic field produced by the solenoid, inside the coil is 0.251 T. There is a straight wire, carrying a current of 40 A, parallel to the axis of the solenoid, at a distance of 5 cm from it. Determine the magnetic Lorentz force acting on 1 m of the solenoid, provided that the solenoid is wound in two layers.

Problem 259. A small ball of mass $m = 0.003$ g carrying a charge of $Q = +0.5 \cdot 10^{-5}$ C is dropped in a uniform horizontal magnetic field $B = 0.4$ T.
a) Find the depth of the deepest point of its path.
b) Find its speed at that point.

4.2 Induction (motional emf)

Problem 260. Two parallel metal rails, lying at a distance L from each other, are

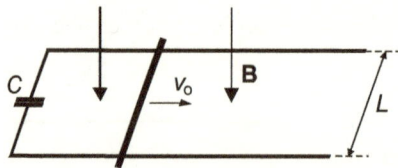

connected by a capacitor of capacitance C at one end. The capacitor is initially uncharged. The arrangement is in a vertical, homogeneous magnetic field **B**, which is constant in time. A conducting rod of resistance R and mass m is laid perpendicularly onto the rails, and it is given an initial speed v_0.

Determine the final speed of the rod, provided that the rails are long enough, and the homogeneous magnetic field extends far enough. (The electric resistance of the rails, the friction and the effects of self induction are negligible.)

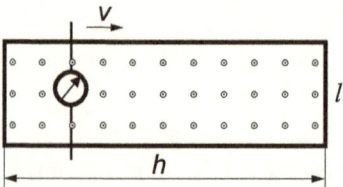

Problem 261. A rectangular conducting frame is in a uniform magnetic field which is perpendicular to the plane of the frame. A straight wire of length l is placed onto two parallel sides of the frame and is moved back and forth with a uniform speed of v so that it remains parallel to the side labelled by l. The direction of the motion is parallel to h. An ammeter of resistance R is inserted into the moving wire. The resistances of the other wires are negligible with respect to that of the ammeter. What is the reading on the ammeter? Explain the phenomenon.

Problem 262. A closed rectangular conducting frame with homogeneous mass distribution and negligible resistance can rotate around one of its axes of symmetry. The frame rests in a homogeneous magnetic field whose induction B is perpendicular to its plane, is constant in time and has no current flowing though it. One side of the frame is pushed and the frame starts to rotate. The area of the frame is A, its inductance is L. The friction of the axis is negligible.

a) How does the current in the frame change as a function of angular displacement?

b) Find the position of the frame where the magnetic field of the frame is the greatest.

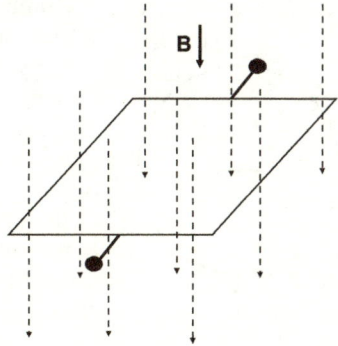

Problem 263. A disc of radius r is made of a material of negligible resistance and can rotate about a horizontal shaft. A smaller disc of radius ϱ is fixed onto the same shaft and has a massless cord wrapped around it, which is attached to a small object of mass m as shown. Two ends of a resistor of resistance R are connected to the perimeter of the disc and to the shaft by wiping contacts. The system is then placed into a uniform horizontal magnetic field B and mass m is released. Find the constant angular velocity with which the disc will rotate after a certain time. Data: $r = 10\,\text{cm}$, $\varrho = 2\,\text{cm}$, $R = 0.01\,\Omega$, $B = 0.2\,\text{T}$, $m = 50\,\text{g}$.

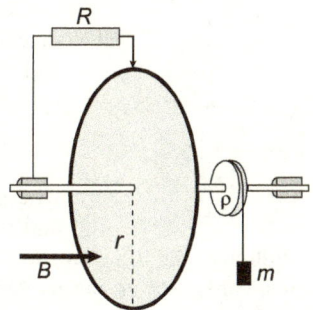

Problem 264. A straight horizontal conductor of length l can rotate frictionless about a vertical axle, which goes through its centre. The two ends of the conductor are immersed to mercury, in which the total drag force exerted on the ends of the wire is $k_1 v^2$, so the drag force is proportional to the square of the speed v. The system is in a uniform vertical magnetic field. Current flows through the mercury tank and the axle. The current is kept at a constant value of I with the help of a variable resistor. All ohmic resistances and air drag are negligible. What is the angular speed of the wire? What is the voltage between the axle and the mercury tank? Data: $l = 20\,\text{cm}$, $k_1 = 6.25 \cdot 10^{-3}\,\text{kg/m}$, $I = 4\,\text{A}$, the magnetic induction is $B = 5 \cdot 10^{-2}\,\text{Vs/m}^2$.

Problem 265. A metal cylinder is rotating at an angular velocity ω around its axis of symmetry. The cylinder is in a uniform magnetic field with the induction vector $\vec{B}$ parallel to its axis.

a) Determine the charge density in the interior of the cylinder.

b) At what angular speed will the charge density be zero?

Problem 266. A circular metal ring whose radius is 0.1 m rotates in the magnetic field of the Earth at uniform angular velocity around a vertical axis that passes through the centre of the ring.

A small magnetic needle is located in the centre of the metal ring, which can rotate freely around a vertical axis. If the metal ring does not rotate, the magnetic needle points in the direction of the horizontal component of the magnetic field of the Earth. If the ring completes 10 revolutions per second, the magnetic needle diverts by $2°$ from this direction in average. Find the electric resistance of the ring.

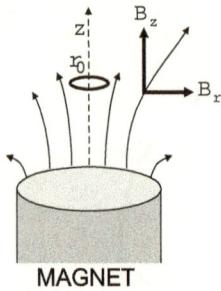

MAGNET

Problem 267. A thin ring of negligible resistance ($R=0$) is held over a cylindrical bar magnet that is in vertical position. The axis of the ring coincides with the axis of the magnet. The magnetic field surrounding the ring has a cylindrical symmetry, and the coordinates of the magnetic induction vector are given by the following equations:

$$B_z = B_0(1 - \alpha z) \qquad \text{and} \qquad B_r = B_0 \beta r,$$

where B_0, α, β are constants, and z and r denote the vertical and radial coordinates of position.

Initially, the ring carries no current. The ring is released, and it starts to move downwards, preserving its vertical axis.

a) Investigate whether the magnetic flux inside the ring is constant during its motion.

b) Describe the motion of the ring. Express the vertical coordinate of the ring as a function of time.

c) Express the current flowing in the ring as a function of time. Find the maximum value of the current.

Let the initial coordinates of the centre of the ring be $z=0$ and $r=0$. In describing the motion, neglect air resistance. Data: $B_0 = 0.01$ T, $\alpha = 2\beta = 32 \text{ m}^{-1}$, the mass of the ring is $m = 50$ mg, the inductance of the ring is $L = 1.3 \cdot 10^{-8}$ H, the radius of the ring is $r_0 = 0.5$ cm, the acceleration of gravity is $g = 9.8 \text{ m/s}^2$.

4.3 Induction (transformer emf)

Problem 268. A solid copper ring of square cross section has an internal radius $R_i = 5$ cm and an external radius $R_e = 7$ cm. The ring is in a uniform magnetic field parallel to its axis. The magnetic induction $B = 0.2$ T of the field changes uniformly to its reverse in a time interval $\Delta t = 2$ s. Express the drift speed v and angular speed ω of the conduction electrons in the ring in terms of the distance r from the axis if
a) the uniform field only fills the interior of radius R_i of the ring,
b) the entire ring is in the magnetic field.

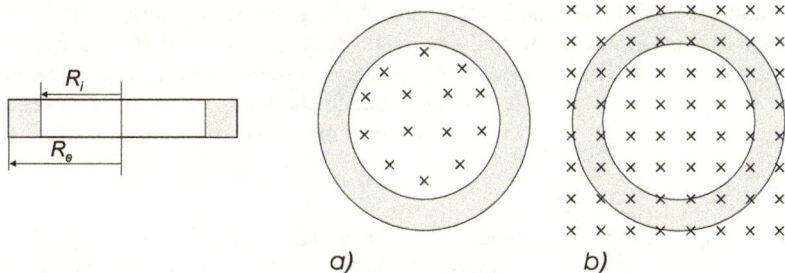

a)   b)

Problem 269. A copper ring of radius $R = 8$ cm and circular cross-sectional area $A = 2$ mm^2 is in a homogeneous magnetic field whose induction is perpendicular to its plane and changes uniformly. At $t = 0$ the induction is $B_0 = 0$ and in $t = 0.2$ s it increases to $B = 2$ T. Find the angular velocity ω at which the ring should be rotated uniformly in order not to have tensile stress in it at time instant $t_1 = 0.1$ s. Can this problem be solved if magnetic induction changes from 2 T to 0? (Self induction can be neglected.)

Problem 270. The resistance of one third of a circular conducting loop is 5 ohms, and the resistance of the remaining two thirds is 2 ohms. The area of the circle is 0.3 m^2. The points where the two parts join are connected with radial wires to an ammeter of small size placed at the centre of the circle. The resistance of the ammeter is 0.5 ohms. The loop is in a uniform magnetic field perpendicular to its plane. The magnitude of the magnetic induction vector changes uniformly with time:

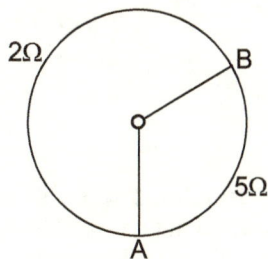

$$\frac{B}{t} = 0.4 \ \frac{T}{s}.$$

a) What current does the ammeter read?
b) The ammeter is replaced by an ideal voltmeter. What voltage does it read?

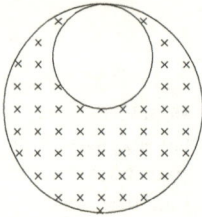

Problem 271. Inside a long cylinder of radius $R = 10$ cm there is a smaller cylinder of radius $R/2$. These are arranged in such a way that the two cylinders touch each other along a common generatrix. There is no magnetic field inside the small cylinder, and in the remaining part of the big cylinder there is homogeneous magnetic field which is changing uniformly in time. The speed of change of the magnetic field is $\Delta B / \Delta t = 80$ V/m^2, and the magnetic field is parallel to the axis of the cylinder. Determine the induced electric field inside the small cylinder.

Problem 272. A small bead of mass m and charge q is threaded on a thin horizontal ring of radius R made of insulating material. The bead can move on the circular track without friction and is initially at rest. A magnetic field that is cylindrically symmetric (about axis t) is created, in which the component of magnetic induction that is perpendicular to the plane of the track depends only on the distance r measured from the centre and time t:

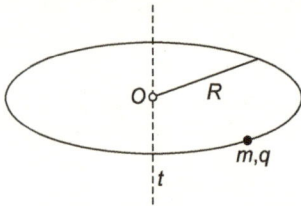

$$B(r,t) = \frac{E_0}{r} \cdot t,$$

where E_0 is a given constant. (In a negligibly small neighbourhood of $r = 0$ the induction has some finite value.)

a) Determine the velocity–time function of the bead.

b) How does the radial component of the normal force between the bead and the track change as function of time?

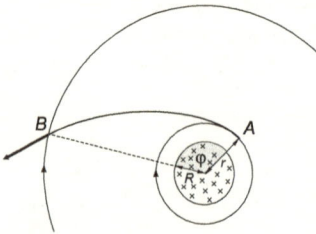

Problem 273. In the interior of a long straight coil of radius $R = 2$ cm, the magnitude of the magnetic induction decreases uniformly from $B = 0.8$ Vs/m^2 to zero in a time interval of $\Delta t = 10^{-1}$ s.

a) Find the initial acceleration of an electron at rest at a distance of $r_A = 3$ cm from the axis of the coil.

b) Calculate the speed gained by the electron as it gets to point B while covering an angular displacement of $\varphi = 120°$ as seen from the common point of its plane of orbit and the axis of the coil.

Problem 274. On an iron wire of cross-sectional area $A = 10$ mm^2 and with relative permeability $\mu = 200$ $N = 2000$ coils of insulated copper wire are wound up closely and this one-layer coil is bent into a circle with a radius of $R = 10$ cm. In the acquired round coil a current of $I_1 = 10$ A is started, which is changed uniformly to $I_2 = -10$ A in time $\Delta t = 1$ s. Find the magnitude and the direction of the acceleration of the electron that is in the centre of the circle at the very moment and is moving in the plane of the circle at velocity $v = 100$ m/s when

a) the current in the coil is exactly zero,

b) $t_1 = 0.6$ s has elapsed since the beginning of the decreasing of the current.

4.4 Alternating current

Problem 275. Two metal spheres of radius R are placed at a very large distance from each other, and they are connected by a coil of inductance L, as it is shown in the figure. One of the spheres is loaded with electric charge. At what time, after closing the switch S, does the charge on this sphere decrease to the half? At what time will the charge reach the original value again?

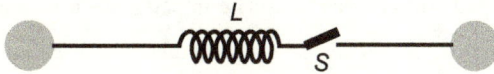

Problem 276. A capacitor that has a capacitance of $C_1 = 10 \ \mu F$ and a breakdown voltage of 130 V is filled with a dielectric whose ohmic resistance is $10^9 \ \Omega$. A second capacitor with a capacitance of $C_2 = 12.5 \ \mu F$ and a breakdown voltage of 170 V is filled with a dielectric whose ohmic resistance is $4 \cdot 10^9 \ \Omega$.

a) What happens if a 220 V direct potential is applied across AB?
b) What happens if a 220 V alternating potential is applied across AB?

Problem 277. A series R–L–C circuit is connected to a voltage described by function $V = 200 \text{ V} \cdot \sin(628\frac{1}{s} \cdot t)$. The current changes according to function $I = 7.07 \text{ A} \cdot \sin\left(628\frac{1}{s} \cdot t - \frac{\pi}{4}\right)$. The inductance is $L = 143 \text{ mH}$.

a) Find the values of R and C.
b) Determine the potential difference-time functions across the coil and the capacitor.

Problem 278. In the electric circuit shown in the figure the inductance of the coil is $L = 10 \text{ mH}$ and the capacitance of the capacitor is $C = 0.2 \text{ mF}$. The circuit is powered by an alternating current. Determine the frequency of the alternating current, provided that the current value measured by the ideal ammeter in the main branch does not depend on the resistance of the resistor!

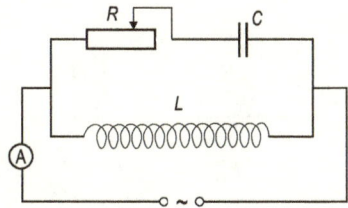

Problem 279. A coil of inductance $L = 2 \text{ H}$ and a capacitor of capacitance $C = 5 \text{ mF}$ are connected in a series to the terminals AB of a power supply. Ohmic resistance is negligible. At a certain point in time instant, the current flowing in the circuit is $I = 1 \text{ A}$ and the potential difference across the capacitor is $V_C = 1 \text{ V}$, with the direction and polarity shown in the figure.

How long does it take the potential difference between terminals A and B to become zero if the current

a) varies sinusoidally with a frequency of 50 Hz?

b) decreases uniformly at a rate of 0.8 A/s?

c) varies sinusoidally as in a), and decreases uniformly as in b), but moves in the opposite direction.

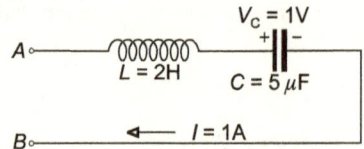

Problem 280. Alternating voltages of various angular frequencies are connected between the two terminals of a closed box. The impedances are measured and tabulated below:

$\omega \ [\text{s}^{-1}]$	20	200	250	300	325	350	400	1000	5000
$Z \ [\Omega]$	782	53.2	34.0	25.4	25.2	27.2	34.9	145.5	792

What does the box contain?

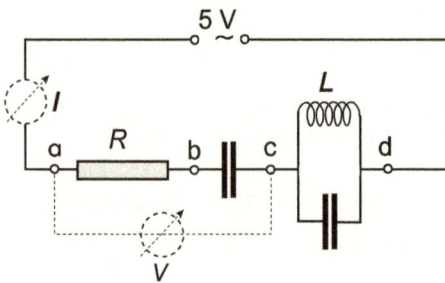

Problem 281. The circuit shown in the figure is connected to an AC generator that supplies 5 V. $R = 5 \ \text{k}\Omega$ and the two capacitors are identical. The ammeter reads 1 mA while the voltmeter reads 13 V. What will the meters read if the angular frequency of the generator is changed from ω to $\omega/\sqrt{2}$? Assume the meters to be ideal. (The voltmeter's impedance is infinitely large, the impedance of the ammeter is negligible.)

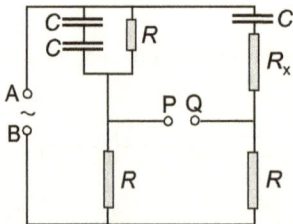

Problem 282. In the circuit shown $C = 2\mu\text{F}$, $R = 1 \ \text{k}\Omega$ and R_x is a resistor of unknown resistance. An alternating potential is applied across AB. Under what conditions will we not hear any sign of a potential difference in a sensitive headphone connected across points PQ?

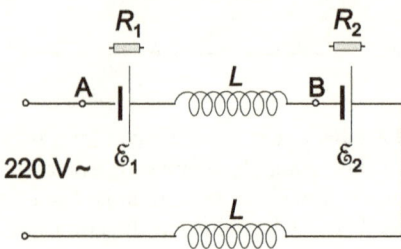

Problem 283. Two coils of equal inductance and two gavlanic cells of emfs $\mathcal{E}_1 = 50$ V and $\mathcal{E}_2 = 100$ V are connected to a 220 V AC outlet as shown. The internal resistances of the cells are not negligible. In the circuit the current lags the potential difference by $45°$. A DC voltmeter connected across points A and B reads zero. What will an AC voltmeter read when connected across points A and B?

Chapter 5

Optics Problems

Problem 284. Two power supplies with the same output voltage U are connected in a series. We then gain a power supply whose output voltage is also U. Can it happen?

Problem 285. Four layers of glass plates are placed on top of each other in such a way that the bottom one has thickness a_1 and refractive index $n_1 = 2.7$, the next one has thickness a_2 and refractive index $n_2 = 2.43$, and the third one and the top one have thicknesses a_3 and a_4 and refractive indices n_3 and n_4 respectively. Three rays of light starting simultaneously from points A_1, A_2, A_3 reach points B_2, B_3, B_4 at the same time, with their angles of incidence being the critical angles as shown. $A_2B_2 = A_3B_3 = A_4B_4 = b = 10$ mm. Find thicknesses a_1, a_2, a_3 and refractive indices n_3, n_4.

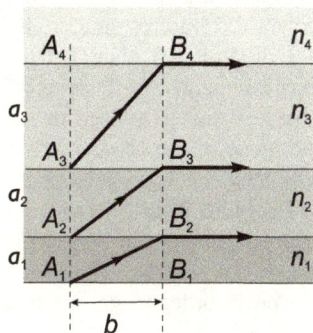

Problem 286. A glass spherical shell with an outer radius of $R = 7.5$ cm and an inner radius of $r = 6.5$ cm has a refractive index $n_2 = 1.5$. The inside of the shell is filled with carbon disulphide, whose refractive index is $n_1 = 1.6$. A source of light is placed at a distance of $a = 6$ cm from the centre. What percent of the energy of the light source leaves the system?

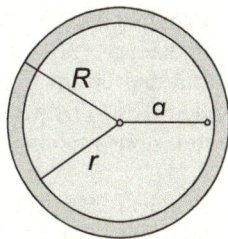

Problem 287. The optical model of an endoscope is an optical fibre of refractive index n_1, which is covered by a cladding of refractive index n_2. The end of the fibre is flat and it is in contact with the surrounding material of refractive index n_3. (The refractive indices are with respect to air.) How should the value of n_1 be chosen if through the fibre the whole half-space below the end of the fibre is to be visible

   a) $n_2 = n_3 = 1$,
   b) $n_2 = 1$ and $n_3 = 4/3$?

Problem 288. We have three equal lenses of focal length f. By placing these lenses at distances d_a and d_b from each other we build an optical system. With this optical system the image of an object is detected on a screen, which is at distance A from the object. We observe that when moving the optical system along the optical axis back and forth the image on the screen remains sharp. By what values of the geometric data is this possible?

Problem 289. If we accommodate our eye to infinity and look into a telescope the image of the Sun would be clear. If a sharp image of the sun is to be created on a screen which is 16 cm from the telescope, how far a distance must the image of the telescope be moved? The absolute value of the focal length of the eyepiece is 2 cm.

Problem 290. You have three converging lenses. Their focal lengths are 90 cm, 10 cm and 8 cm. How can you build a telescope from them, with the with the greatest magnification, if the maximum length of the telescope is 150 cm? (The lenses are all thin lenses and lens aberrations can be neglected.)

Problem 291. At one end of a 50 cm long tube there is a converging lens of optical power 2 dioptres and at the other end there is a diverging lens of optical power -2 dioptres. A plane mirror is placed behind the diverging lens at a distance of x, perpendicularly to the axis of the tube. For which distance of x can the real image of object, which is placed in front of the converging lens at a distance of 100 cm, be in the plane of the object? What is the magnification, and is the image inverted or erect?

Problem 292. There is a hole in the middle of small thin circular converging lens of focal length $f = 4$ cm. The diameter of the hole is half of the diameter of the lens. There is a pointlike light-source $A = 9$ cm away from a wall. Where should the lens be placed in order to get a single, circular illuminated spot on the wall, which also has a sharp edge?

Problem 293. A 20 cm long light tube lies on the principal axis of a converging lens with diameter $2R = 4$ cm and focal length 40 cm. The ends of the tube are at distances 60 cm and 80 cm from the lens. Where should a screen (which is perpendicular to the principal axis) be put on the other side of the lens, if the diameter of the light spot on it is to take its minimum value? Find the minimum diameter of the light spot.

Problem 294. The following objects are placed after each other onto a central axis with a separation of 4 dm each, a point source of light (O), a diverging lens of focal length -4 dm, a converging lens of focal length $+4$ dm and a concave mirror of focal length 8 dm. The diameter of the lenses and mirror is $d = 2$ dm. The point source of light is then moved perpendicular to the central axis. What should its perpendicular displacement (x) be if the image is to be captured on a screen?

Part II

SOLUTIONS

Chapter 6

Mechanics Solutions

6.1 Kinematics

Solution of Problem 1. The railwayman hears the signal during the time which elapses between the moments when the beginning and the end of the signal reach him. The time is measured from the initial moment when the sound is emitted. The beginning of the whistle reaches the railwayman after a time of $t_1 = d/c$. Time T elapses between the moments when the beginning and the end of the whistle are emitted, and the end of the whistle covers a distance of $d - vT$, thus $(d - vT)/c$ time elapses. So, the total time which elapses until the railway man hears the end of the whistle is $t_2 = T + (d - vT)/c$. The railwayman hears the signal for a time of $\Delta t = t_2 - t_1$, which is

$$\Delta t = t_2 - t_1 = T + \frac{d - vT}{c} - \frac{d}{c} = \frac{c - v}{c} T = \frac{330 - 30}{330} \cdot 3\,\text{s} = 2.727\,\text{s}.$$

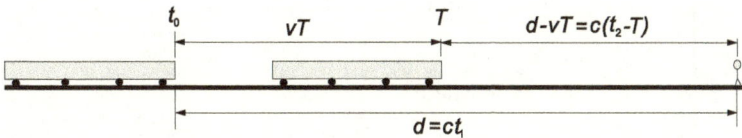

Solution of Problem 2. Let d and c denote the width and speed of the river. Let v_1 and v_2 be the speeds of the boat relative to the ground in the two cases, and let $4c = v_{1_{\text{rel}}}$ and $v_{2_{\text{rel}}}$ denote its speeds relative to the water. The task is to find the ratio $v_{2_{\text{rel}}}/v_{1_{\text{rel}}}$.

In both cases, the component parallel to the riverbanks is equal to c. The speeds of the boat relative to the ground in the two cases are

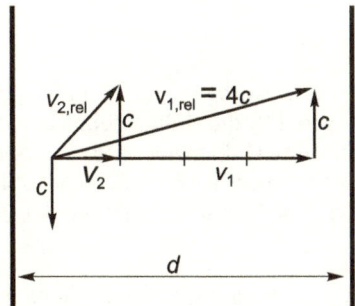

$$v_1 = \frac{d}{t_1}, \quad \text{and} \quad v_2 = \frac{d}{t_2} = \frac{d}{4t_1} = \frac{v_1}{4}.$$

As shown in the figure, the speeds are related as follows:

$$v_{2_{\text{rel}}}^2 = c^2 + v_2^2 = c^2 + \frac{v_1^2}{16}. \tag{1}$$

71

Since $v_{1_{\text{rel}}}^2 = c^2 + v_1^2 = (4c)^2 = 16c^2$, it follows that $v_1^2 = 15c^2$. Thus, from (1), the speed relative to the water, of the boat with its motor broken down is

$$v_{2_{\text{rel}}}^2 = c^2 + \frac{15}{16}c^2 = \frac{31}{16}c^2,$$

and the ratio in question is

$$\frac{v_{2_{\text{rel}}}}{v_{1_{\text{rel}}}} = \sqrt{\frac{31c^2/16}{16c^2}} = \frac{1}{16}\sqrt{31} = 0.348.$$

Solution of Problem 3. To prove the statement, we will use a subsidiary theorem: pointlike objects released simultaneously from rest on frictionless planes of various angles of inclination starting at the uppermost point of a vertical circle will all reach the circle simultaneously. (In other words: particles starting simultaneously from a point of a horizontal line on frictionless planes all containing the line will always be on a circle of increasing radius.)

Proof of the subsidiary theorem:

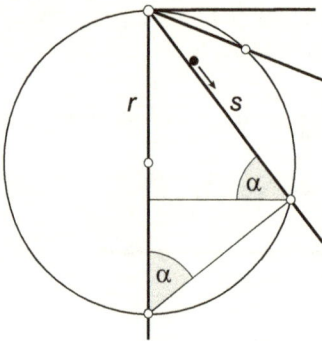

Draw a circle of arbitrary radius passing through the common horizontal line of the inclined planes, and draw some of the planes inclined at arbitrary angles α to the horizontal. Select one of the planes and consider the point that started from rest and is just reaching the circle along the selected plane. The sliding time of the point is

$$t = \sqrt{2s/a},$$

where

$$a = g\sin\alpha.$$

The sliding time is therefore

$$t = \sqrt{\frac{2s}{g\sin\alpha}}.$$

To express the length of the slope from the starting point to the circle (i.e. the distance covered by the sliding point) in terms of the radius of the circle, connect the lower end of the vertical diameter to the intersection point of the slope and the circle. The connecting line segment is perpendicular to the slope (Thales' theorem). The length of the slope is expressed from the right-angled triangle obtained:

$$s = 2r\sin\alpha,$$

where, because of angles with pairwise perpendicular arms, α equals the angle of inclination of the slope. By substituting this expression in the formula for sliding time, the following value of t is obtained:

$$t = \sqrt{\frac{2 \cdot 2r\sin\alpha}{g\sin\alpha}} = 2 \cdot \sqrt{\frac{r}{g}},$$

which is independent of α, as stated by the subsidiary theorem to be proved.

The result can be used to prove the original statement.

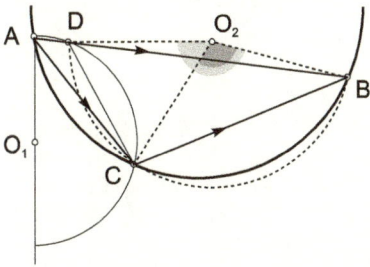

Draw the circle that passes through the points A and C in a plane perpendicular to the inclined planes so that the point A lies on its vertical diameter. The circle intersects the original slope at D. Since it follows from the subsidiary theorem proved before that the sliding times are equal along the slopes AD and AC, there remains to compare the times needed to cover the slopes DB and CB. Draw the circle passing through the points DCB. The chord DB of the circle subtends a greater central angle than chord CB, so the path DB is longer than the path CB. Furthermore, since every point of the path CB lies lower than any point of the path DB, it follows from the conservation of energy that the speed is greater at every point of the path CB than anywhere on the path DB. Therefore, the sliding time along the path CB is shorter than the sliding time along DB, which proves the original statement.

Solution of Problem 4. The acceleration–time graph can be seen in the figure.

Proportionally, the acceleration change in time t_2 is:

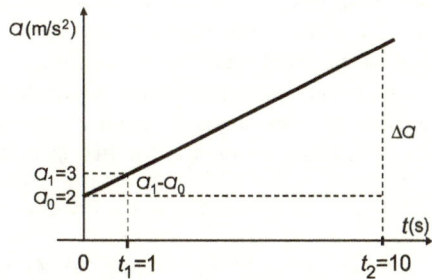

$$\frac{\Delta a}{\Delta t} = \frac{a_1 - a_0}{t_1} \ \rightarrow \ \Delta a = (a_1 - a_0)\frac{t_2}{t_1}. \quad (1)$$

The speed change is equal to the area under the graph. (E.g., the sum of the area of a rectangle and a right triangle.)

$$\Delta v = a_0 t_2 + \frac{1}{2}(a_1 - a_0)\frac{t_2}{t_1}t_2 = a_0 t_2 + \frac{1}{2}(a_1 - a_0)\frac{t_2^2}{t_1}. \quad (2)$$

Since the object had an initial speed v_0 at $t_0 = 0$, the speed acquired by t_2 is:

$$v = v_0 + a_0 t_2 + \frac{1}{2}(a_1 - a_0)\frac{t_2^2}{t_1}. \quad (3)$$

a) Substituting into equation (3) the known numerical data, the speed of the object after 10 s is:

$$v = 1\,\frac{\text{m}}{\text{s}} + 2\,\frac{\text{m}}{\text{s}^2} \cdot 10\text{ s} + \frac{1}{2}\left(3\,\frac{\text{m}}{\text{s}^2} - 2\,\frac{\text{m}}{\text{s}^2}\right) \cdot \frac{10^2\text{ s}^2}{1\text{ s}} = 71\,\frac{\text{m}}{\text{s}}. \quad (4)$$

b) Using the equation (3) and the known data, the $v-t$ function of the motion is:

$$v = 1\,\frac{\text{m}}{\text{s}} + 2\,\frac{\text{m}}{\text{s}^2}t + \frac{1}{2}(3-2)\,\frac{\text{m}}{\text{s}^2} \cdot \frac{t^2}{1\text{ s}},$$

and in dimensionless form:

$$v = 1 + 2t + 0.5t^2. \tag{5}$$

In order to plot the v–t diagram, let us complete the square in the function (5).

$$v = \frac{1}{2}(t^2 + 4t) + 1,$$

$$v = \frac{1}{2}[(t+2)^2 - 4] + 1,$$

$$v = \frac{1}{2}(t+2)^2 - 1. \tag{6}$$

The function (6) is obtained by transforming the simple parabola $v = t^2$, and its graph is plotted in the figure.

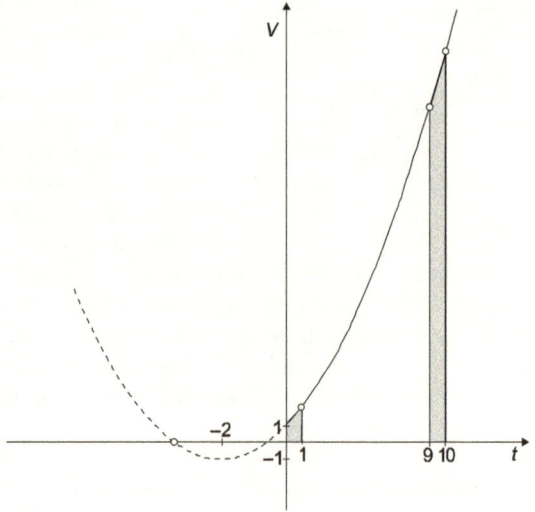

c) The distances covered in the time intervals $0 < t < 1$ s and 9 s $< t < 10$ s are equal to the appropriate areas under v–t diagram. Since the time intervals are short, the diagrams can be approximated by linear segments, and the problem can then be simplified to the calculation of the areas of two trapeziums.

The distance covered in the first second is:

$$s_1 = \frac{v_0 + v_1}{2} t_1 = \frac{1\,\frac{m}{s} + 3.5\,\frac{m}{s}}{2} \cdot 1\,s = 2.25\ m,$$

where, according to the formula (6), v_1 is:

$$v_1 = \left[\frac{1}{2}(1+2)^2 - 1\right]\frac{m}{s} = 3.5\,\frac{m}{s}.$$

Similarly, the speeds at the 9 and 10 second marks are:

$$v_9 = \left[\frac{1}{2}(9+2)^2 - 1\right]\frac{m}{s} = 59.5\,\frac{m}{s},$$

and

$$v_{10} = \left[\frac{1}{2}(10+2)^2 - 1\right]\frac{m}{s} = 71\,\frac{m}{s}.$$

Using these values, the approximate value of the distance in question is:

$$s_2 = \frac{v_9 + v_{10}}{2}\Delta t = \frac{59.5\,\frac{m}{s} + 71\,\frac{m}{s}}{2} \cdot 1\,s = 65.25\ m.$$

74

Remark: The legitimacy of the approximations can be checked by comparing the previous results with the exact ones obtained by integration. The exact values of the two distances are, by integration:

$$s_1 = \int_0^1 \left(\frac{1}{2}t^2 + 2t + 1 \right) dt = \left[\frac{1}{2} \cdot \frac{t^3}{3} + 2 \cdot \frac{t^2}{2} + t \right]_0^1 = 2.17 \text{ m},$$

and

$$s_2 = \int_9^{10} \left(\frac{1}{2}t^2 + 2t + 1 \right) dt = \left[\frac{1}{2} \cdot \frac{t^3}{3} + 2 \cdot \frac{t^2}{2} + t \right]_9^{10} = 65.17 \text{ m}.$$

The relative errors in the two cases are:

$$\frac{\Delta s_1}{s_1} = \frac{2.25 - 2.17}{2.17} = 0.0369 = 3.69\%,$$

and

$$\frac{\Delta s_2}{s_2} = \frac{65.25 - 65.17}{65.17} = 0.00123 = 0.123\%.$$

(The second error is smaller, since the curvature of the parabola is less.)

Solution of Problem 5. Since the distance covered is a quadratic function of time, velocity must be a linear function of time. In general, if the distance covered can be written in the form of

$$s = \frac{1}{2}a_t t^2 + v_0 t,$$

then

$$v = v_0 + a_t t,$$

where v_0 is the initial velocity, a_t is the tangential acceleration and t is the time elapsed. Comparing the parametric equation with the one given in this case:

$$s = 0.5t^2 + 2t$$

it follows that $a_t/2 = 0.5 \text{ m/s}^2$ so $a_t = 1 \text{ m/s}^2$ and $v_0 = 2 \text{ m/s}$.

The accelerations at times $t_1 = 2$ s and $t_2 = 5$ s can be calculated as the resultant vector of the tangential and normal (centripetal) accelerations, whose magnitude is:

$$a = \sqrt{a_t^2 + a_n^2} = \sqrt{a_t^2 + \left(\frac{v^2}{R} \right)^2},$$

where $v = v_0 + a_t t$.

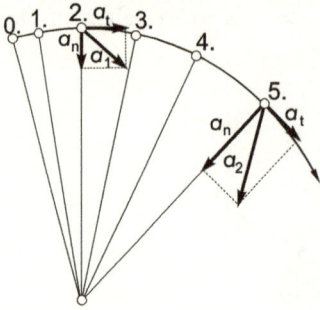

Substituting this into the expression for acceleration, we obtain:

$$a_1 = \sqrt{a_t^2 + \frac{(v_0 + a_t t_1)^4}{R^2}} = \frac{1}{R} \cdot \sqrt{R^2 a_t^2 + (v_0 + a_t t_1)^4},$$

$$a_2 = \sqrt{a_t^2 + \frac{(v_0 + a_t t_2)^4}{R^2}} = \frac{1}{R} \cdot \sqrt{R^2 a_t^2 + (v_0 + a_t t_2)^4}.$$

The ratio of the accelerations is given:

$$\frac{a_1}{a_2} = \frac{1}{2} = \sqrt{\frac{R^2 a_t^2 + (v_0 + a_t t_1)^4}{R^2 a_t^2 + (v_0 + a_t t_2)^4}}.$$

Squaring the equation and isolating the radius give:

$$R = \frac{1}{a_t} \sqrt{\frac{(v_0 + a_t t_2)^4 - 4(v_0 + a_t t_1)^4}{3}}.$$

Substituting known values, we find:

$$R = \frac{1}{1\,\text{m/s}^2} \sqrt{\frac{(2\,\text{m/s} + 1\,\text{m/s}^2 \cdot 5\,\text{s})^4 - 4(2\,\text{m/s} + 1\,\text{m/s}^2 \cdot 2\,\text{s})^4}{3}} =$$

$$= \frac{\text{s}^2}{\text{m}} \sqrt{\frac{2401\,\text{m}^4/\text{s}^4 - 1024\,\text{m}^4/\text{s}^4}{3}} = \sqrt{\frac{1377}{3}\,\text{m}^2} = \sqrt{459\,\text{m}^2} = 3\,\text{m} \cdot \sqrt{51} = 21.42\,\text{m}$$

So the radius of the circle is $R = 21.42\,\text{m}$

First solution of Problem 6. In order to achieve the required acceleration-free state, the acceleration of the car's tire axle (**a**), the normal acceleration of the valve cap (**a_n**), and the tangential acceleration of the valve cap (**a_t**) should produce a resultant of zero at the given moment.

a) From the figure it is clear that this condition cannot be fulfilled at point A (the other two acceleration components point into the same half-plane determined by the line that fits on vector **a**).

b) At point B the conditions for the horizontal and vertical components of the accelerations are

$$a_n \cdot \sin\alpha + a_t \cdot \cos\alpha = a \tag{1}$$

$$a_n \cdot \cos\alpha - a_t \cdot \sin\alpha = 0. \tag{2}$$

Because of the required $1/8$ turn $\alpha = 45°$, so $\sin\alpha\cos\alpha = \dfrac{\sqrt{2}}{2}$. With it in detail:

$$r\cdot\left(\frac{a}{R}\cdot t\right)^2\cdot\frac{\sqrt{2}}{2} + r\cdot\frac{a}{R}\cdot\frac{\sqrt{2}}{2} = a \qquad (1')$$

$$r\cdot\left(\frac{a}{R}\cdot t\right)^2\cdot\frac{\sqrt{2}}{2} = r\cdot\frac{a}{R}\cdot\frac{\sqrt{2}}{2}. \qquad (2')$$

If the first term of $(1')$ is replaced by the right side of $(2')$:

$$r\cdot\frac{a}{R}\cdot\frac{\sqrt{2}}{2} + r\cdot\frac{a}{R}\cdot\frac{\sqrt{2}}{2} = a,$$

after combining the like terms and simplifying by a:
$R = r\cdot\sqrt{2}$.

So the valve cap can be only at a certain distance ($r = R/\sqrt{2} \approx 0.71R$) from the axle. Substituting the result for time $t = \sqrt{R/a}$ from $(2')$ into the relationship for angular displacement $\varphi = \dfrac{1}{2}\beta t^2 = \dfrac{a}{2R}\cdot t^2$ gives

$$\varphi = \frac{1}{2} = 28.65°$$

for φ, so we should start from a given position preceding point B (at the moment of starting, the radius drawn to the valve cap should enclose an angle of $\alpha + \varphi = 3.65°$ with the vertical).

Second solution of Problem 6. In case b) the problem requests an acceleration-free state in a position where the normal acceleration and the tangential acceleration encloses the same ($45°$) angle with the vertical. Their resultant should be the opposite of the (horizontal) acceleration of the car, which is only possible if the tangential and the normal accelerations have the same magnitude and the vector parallelogram formed by them is a square whose diagonal has the same magnitude as the acceleration of the car:

$$a_t = a_n = a/\sqrt{2},$$

that is,

$$\frac{a}{\sqrt{2}} = r\cdot\frac{a}{R},$$

from which

$$R = r\cdot\sqrt{2}.$$

As the normal acceleration is

$$a_n = a_t \qquad \rightarrow \qquad r\cdot\left(\frac{a}{R}t\right)^2 = r\cdot\frac{a}{R},$$

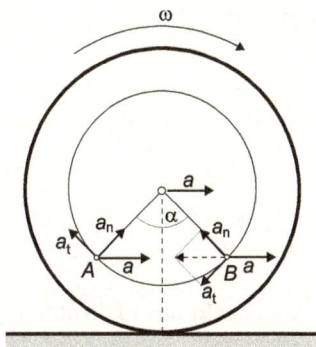

from here

$$t = \sqrt{\frac{R}{a}},$$

and with this the angular displacement required after starting is

$$\varphi = \frac{1}{2} \cdot \frac{a}{R} \cdot \left(\sqrt{\frac{R}{a}} \right)^2 = \frac{1}{2} \ \text{rad} = 28.65°.$$

First solution of Problem 7. *With superposition of velocities (coordinate transformation).*

The "absolute" velocity $\vec{v}_a$ of the point with respect to the ground is the sum of its relative velocity $\vec{v}_{rel}$ with respect to the coordinate frame travelling along with the centre of the disc and the translational velocity $\vec{v}_{tr}$ of the coordinate frame:

$$\vec{v}_a = \vec{v}_{tr} + \vec{v}_{rel}. \tag{1}$$

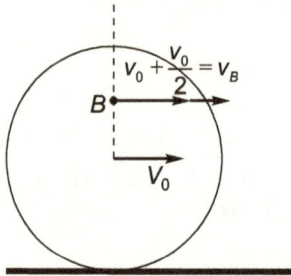

At point B, this is also true for the magnitudes of the velocities (since initially the velocity vectors are parallel):

$$v_B = v_0 + \frac{R}{2}\omega,$$

where $R\omega = v_0$ since the disc rolls without slipping. Thus the speed of point B is

$$v_B = \frac{3}{2}v_0.$$

Let us apply (1) to point A. As seen from the figure, the magnitudes of the absolute velocity and the translational velocity are equal, $v_{A_{rel}} = R\omega = v_0 = v_{tr}$, and they enclose an angle φ, equal to the angular displacement of the radius. From the isosceles triangle,

$$v_A = 2v_0 \cos\frac{\varphi}{2} = 2v_0 \cos\left(\frac{v_0}{2R} \cdot t\right). \tag{2}$$

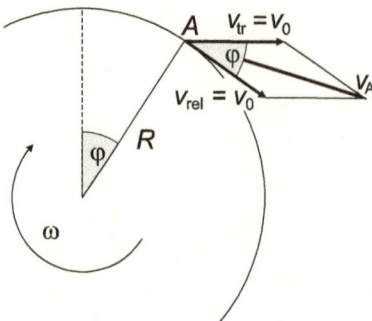

At the time instant in question,

$$2v_0 \cos\left(\frac{v_0}{2R} \cdot t\right) = \frac{3}{2}v_0.$$

Hence

$$\cos\left(\frac{v_0}{2R} \cdot t\right) = \frac{3}{4},$$

and the time in question is

$$t = \frac{2R}{v_0} \cdot \arccos\frac{3}{4} = \frac{0.2\,\text{m}}{4\,\text{m/s}} \cdot \arccos 0.75 = 0.36\,\text{s}.$$

Second solution of Problem 7. *With an instantaneous axis of rotation.*

The figure shows that the instantaneous axis of rotation is the point P where the disc touches the ground. The speed of point A is thus

$$v_A = r_A \omega,$$

where

$$r_A = 2R\cos\left(\frac{\varphi}{2}\right) \quad \text{and} \quad \omega = \frac{v_0}{R}.$$

The expression (2) is obtained again by substituting $\varphi = \omega t = \frac{v_0}{R} t$:

$$v_A = 2R\cos\left(\frac{v_0}{2R}\cdot t\right)\cdot \frac{v_0}{R} = 2v_0 \cos\left(\frac{v_0}{2R}\cdot t\right),$$

and hence the requirement of the problem leads to the same result as above.

Solution of Problem 8. a) According to the condition $v_A = v_B$. Since the magnitude of the velocity for a point on the circumference $0 \leq v_A \leq 2v$, there will be momentary instants when it is equal to v_B, which is always greater than zero and always less than $2v$ (its direction will obviously be different). This requirement is fulfilled when $r_A \omega = r_B \omega$, where r_A and r_B are the momentary radii of rotation drawn to A and B respectively, which are the distances of A resp. B measured from the point that is stationary at the moment (the point that is exactly touching the ground). Since the angular speed is the same for each point of a rigid disc, in order to fulfil the condition

$$r_A = r_B = r$$

should be true.

From the figure it can be seen where the points should be to fulfil this condition. (From the figure it is clear that this state is reached in the second quarter of the angular displacement first.) Triangles OAP and PAB are similar because they are isosceles and their angles on the base are common.

Let φ stand for the angular displacement of the radius belonging to point A and α for its supplementary angle. The momentary radius of rotation from the big triangle is

$$r = 2R\sin\frac{\alpha}{2}.$$

and from the small triangle

$$r = \frac{R}{4\sin\frac{\alpha}{2}}.$$

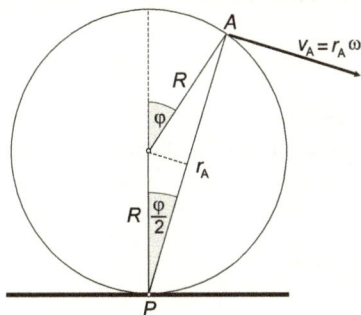

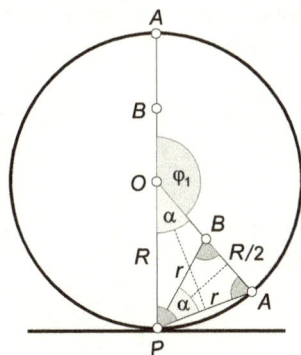

Therefore the right sides are equal:

$$2R\sin\frac{\alpha}{2} = \frac{R}{4\sin\frac{\alpha}{2}}.$$

From here – independently of the radius – the following value is acquired for the sine of the half of the angular position:

$$\sin^2\frac{\alpha}{2} = \frac{1}{8},$$

from which

$$\sin\frac{\alpha}{2} = \frac{1}{\sqrt{8}} = \frac{\sqrt{2}}{4}.$$

From this

$$\alpha = 2\cdot\arcsin\frac{\sqrt{2}}{4} = 41.41°.$$

So the first angular displacement that fulfils the requirements of the problem is

$$\varphi_1 = \pi - \alpha = 180° - 41.41° = 138.59° = 2.42 \text{ rad}.$$

The time elapsed in the meantime is

$$t_1 = \frac{\varphi_1}{\omega} = \frac{\varphi_1 R}{v} = 4.84 \text{ s}.$$

b) The requested speed is

$$v_A = v_B = r\omega = 2R\sin\frac{\alpha}{2}\cdot\frac{v}{R} = 2\sin\frac{\alpha}{2}\cdot v = \frac{2}{\sqrt{8}}\cdot 0.5\,\frac{\text{m}}{\text{s}} = 0.354\,\frac{\text{m}}{\text{s}}.$$

c) The distance travelled by the centre is

$$s_1 = R\varphi_1 = 1\,\text{m}\cdot 2.42\,\text{rad} = 2.42\,\text{m}.$$

Solution of Problem 9. a) Let us examine the phenomenon from a reference frame fixed to the uniformly moving cart. At this frame the bit of mud leaves the rim in the direction of the tangent, that is, in this system the initial velocity of the projection encloses an angle of $\alpha = 60°$ with the horizontal. As the bit of mud falls back at the same height as it starts from, the distance between these points is the distance of the projection:

$$x_{\text{max}} = 2R\sin\alpha.$$

So in the reference frame of the cart:

$$\frac{2v_0^2\sin\alpha\cos\alpha}{g} = 2R\sin\alpha,$$

where v_0 is the peripheral velocity of the rim and the travelling velocity of the cart as well. From here

$$v_0 = \sqrt{\frac{Rg}{\cos\alpha}} = \sqrt{\frac{0.6\,\text{m}\cdot 9.81\,\text{m/s}^2}{0.5}} = \sqrt{11.772\,\text{m}^2/\text{s}^2} \approx 3.43\,\frac{\text{m}}{\text{s}}.$$

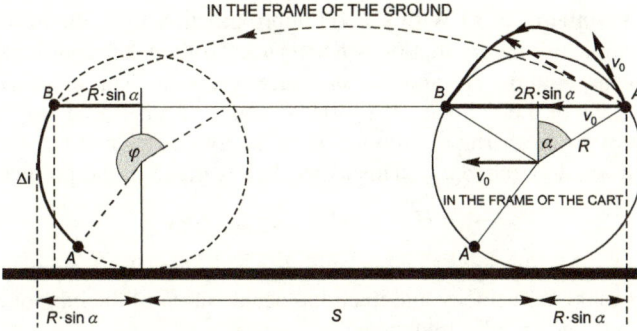

IN THE FRAME OF THE GROUND

b) The time of the oblique projection of the bit of mud is

$$t = \frac{2v_0 \sin\alpha}{g} = \frac{2 \cdot 3.43 \text{ m/s} \cdot 0.866}{9.81 \text{ m/s}^2} = 0.61 \text{ s}.$$

In this time the point of the rim where the bit of mud detaches from travels through an arc of

$$i = v_0 t = 3.43 \text{ m/s} \cdot 0.61 \text{ s} = 2.09 \text{ m} \approx 2.1 \text{ m}$$

due to the skid-free rolling motion, from this arc i' that the bit of mud flew along, that is,

$$i' = R \cdot \frac{2\pi}{3} = 1.257 \text{ metres},$$

should be subtracted, so the length of the requested arc is

$$\Delta i = i - i' = 2.09 \text{ m} - 1.257 \text{ m} = 0.833 \text{ m} \approx 0.8 \text{ m}.$$

c) The motion of the cart is skid-free rolling, the axles of its wheels move exactly at velocity $v_0 = 3.43$ m/s, so the in the time between the detachment and the falling back of the bit of mud the cart travels a distance of

$$s = v_0 t = 3.43 \text{ m/s} \cdot 0.61 \text{ s} = 2.09 \text{ m} \approx 2.1 \text{ m},$$

which is obviously equal to i.

(The special angle of projection enables us to reach the conclusion faster. Namely, in the coordinate system fixed to the ground the bit of mud travels exactly at velocity $v_x = v_0 \cos 60° + {} + v_0 = 3v_0/2$ in the horizontal direction, which is 3/2 times the velocity of the cart. Therefore the horizontal displacement of the bit of mud is 3/2 times that of the cart, that is,

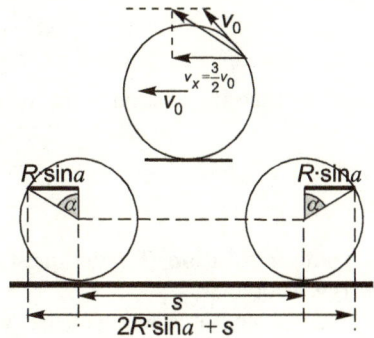

$$2R\sin\alpha + s = \frac{3}{2}s.$$

From this, the distance travelled by the cart is:

$$s = 4R\sin\alpha = 4 \cdot 0.6 \text{ m} \cdot 0.866 = 2.1 \text{ m.})$$

Solution of Problem 10. a) With a good approximation the balloon in the problem performs a harmonic oscillatory motion, since its acceleration is proportional to its height measured from the altitude H, and has opposite direction. Through this analogy the kinematic equations of the balloon are similar to those of a harmonic motion.

The kinematics of the harmonic motion is uniquely determined by its amplitude A and its maximal acceleration a_{max}. This exact data is given in the problem:

$$A = H \qquad \text{and} \qquad a_{max} = a_0.$$

In the first question the speed at the altitude H is just the maximal speed of the oscillation. The maximal velocity and maximal acceleration of the harmonic motion can be expressed using the angular frequency:

$$v_{max} = A\omega,$$

$$a_{max} = A\omega^2.$$

From here, the angular frequency can be expressed using the known data:

$$\omega = \sqrt{\frac{a_{max}}{A}}.$$

So, using the previous notations, the unknown speed at altitude H is:

$$v(H) = v_{max} = A\sqrt{\frac{a_{max}}{A}} = \sqrt{a_{max}A} = \sqrt{a_0 H}.$$

b) The speed at altitude $H/2$ can be determined by the known formula:

$$v = \omega\sqrt{A^2 - y^2},$$

so

$$v = \sqrt{\frac{a_0}{H}}\sqrt{H^2 - \left(\frac{H}{2}\right)^2} = \sqrt{0.75 a_0 H}.$$

c) The time in question is one quarter of the period of the harmonic oscillation, so:

$$t = \frac{T}{4} = \frac{2\pi}{4\omega} = \frac{\pi}{2}\sqrt{\frac{H}{a_0}}.$$

Another solution (for the questions concerning the speed) is based on the work-energy theorem.

Since the net force acting on the balloon is linearly decreasing to zero with the altitude, the force averaged over the altitude is just half of the maximal force.

The change of the kinetic energy is equal to the work done by this force:

$$\frac{ma_0}{2}H = \frac{1}{2}mv^2,$$

thus, the speed at height H is:

$$v(H) = \sqrt{a_0 H}.$$

From ground level to $H/2$ the average force is:

$$\frac{ma_0 + \frac{ma_0}{2}}{2} = 0.75ma_0,$$

so the speed at height $H/2$ is

$$v = \sqrt{0.75a_0 H}.$$

The simplest, most elementary way to determine the time needed for the balloon to rise is to apply the analogy to the harmonic oscillation.

Solution of Problem 11. First we have to determine the time it takes the bullet, moving at a constant horizontal velocity component, to arrive at the trajectory of the falling ball. During this time, in a vertical direction, the bullet performs a free fall and loses its height of h_1. However, because the bullet hits the ball, the ball covers the distance $(h - h') + h_1$. The time in question is therefore simply the difference between the time of the free fall of the ball and the time of the flight of the bullet.

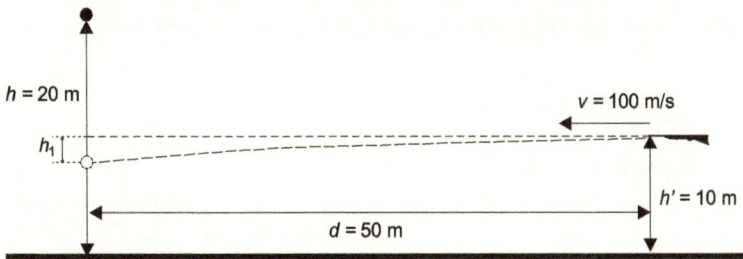

It takes the bullet

$$t_1 = \frac{d}{v} = \frac{50 \text{ m}}{100 \frac{\text{m}}{\text{s}}} = 0.5 \text{ s}$$

to reach the trajectory of the falling ball. During this time it loses a height of

$$h_1 = \frac{1}{2}g \cdot t_1^2 = \frac{1}{2} \cdot 9.81 \frac{\text{m}}{\text{s}^2} \cdot 0.25 \text{ s}^2 \approx 1.23 \text{ m}.$$

The time of the free fall of the ball, until being hit by the bullet, is:

$$t = \sqrt{\frac{2(h - h' + h_1)}{g}} = \sqrt{\frac{2 \cdot 11.23 \text{ m}}{9.81 \frac{\text{m}}{\text{s}^2}}} = 1.51 \text{ s}.$$

83

So the time difference in question is:

$$\Delta t = t - t_1 = 1.51 \text{ s} - 0.5 \text{ s} = 1.01 \text{ s} \approx 1 \text{ s}.$$

The *parametric solution* of the problem can be significantly simplified by considering the fact that $h - h' = h/2$. With this in mind, the time of the fall of the ball is:

$$t = \sqrt{\frac{2 \cdot \left(\frac{h}{2} + h_1\right)}{g}} = \sqrt{\frac{2 \cdot \left(\frac{h}{2} + \frac{1}{2}g\frac{d^2}{v^2}\right)}{g}} = \sqrt{\frac{h}{g} + \frac{d^2}{v^2}},$$

and the time difference between the start of the fall and the gun fire is:

$$\Delta t = t - t_1 = \sqrt{\frac{h}{g} + \frac{d^2}{v^2}} - \frac{d}{v}.$$

Solution of Problem 12. Let us write down all the requirements for the two motions. The projectile and the object sliding on the slope arrive at point P at the same instant. Thus, the vertical velocity component of the projectile is equal to the vertical component of the average velocity of the other object. Since the object on the slope performs uniformly accelerated motion, its average velocity is half of its final velocity, so

$$v_0 \cos\varphi = \frac{v}{2}\cos\alpha,$$

where φ is the angle of the throw (above the horizontal), and α is the angle of the slope. The two objects arrive at P at the same speed, i.e., $v_0 = v$, so we can simplify using the initial speed of the throw and the final speed of the sliding:

$$\cos\varphi = \frac{\cos\alpha}{2}. \tag{1}$$

The two angles should certainly obey this relation, but it does not mean that any α could solve the problem.

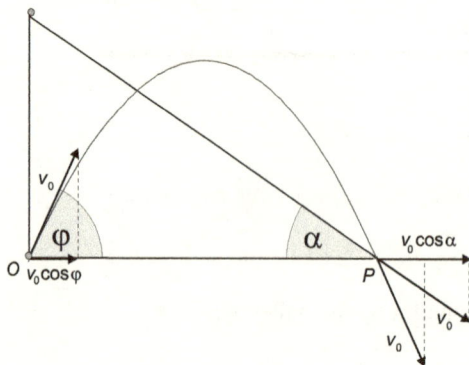

A further requirement should also be satisfied: the total time of the throw should be equal to the time of the sliding. (Indeed, if only equation (1) was satisfied then the x coordinates of the two objects would be equal at the instant when the object on the slope gets to P, but the y coordinate of the projectile would not be 0.) From this requirement we get that $t_{\text{throw}} = t_{\text{slide}}$, so:

$$\frac{2v_0 \sin\varphi}{g} = \frac{v_0}{g\sin\alpha},$$

which means that the angles obey another relation as well. Only one pair of angles can satisfy all the requirements of the problem. After simplification:

$$2\sin\varphi = \frac{1}{\sin\alpha}. \tag{2}$$

Now we solve the system of equations (1–2). Taking the square of equation (2), and using a trigonometric equation to change the sine functions to cosines, which appear in (1), we get that:

$$4\cdot(1-\cos^2\varphi) = \frac{1}{1-\cos^2\alpha}.$$

Using (1) to substitute $\cos\alpha = 2\cdot\cos\varphi$:

$$4\cdot(1-\cos^2\varphi) = \frac{1}{1-4\cos^2\varphi}.$$

After multiplying with the denominator:

$$4\cdot(1-\cos^2\varphi)(1-4\cos^2\varphi) = 1.$$

Then performing the multiplications:

$$4-4\cos^2\varphi-16\cos^2\varphi+16\cos^4\varphi = 1$$

After arranging the terms:

$$16\cos^4\varphi-20\cos^2\varphi+3 = 0.$$

The solution of this equation for $\cos^2\varphi$ is:

$$\cos^2\varphi = \frac{20\pm\sqrt{400-4\cdot16\cdot3}}{2\cdot16} = \begin{cases} 1.07569 \\ 0.17431 \end{cases}$$

Only the second root is meaningful, and since φ is an acute angle in this problem, we obtain that:

$$\cos\varphi = +\sqrt{0.17431} = 0.41750 \quad \rightarrow \quad \varphi = \arccos 0.41750 = 65.32°.$$

From equation (1) the angle of the slope can also be determined:

$$\cos\alpha = 2\cos\varphi = 2\cdot0.4175 = 0.835,$$

so the angle of the slope is

$$\alpha = \arccos 0.835 = 33.38°.$$

The phenomenon described in the problem occurs only at this value.

First solution of Problem 13. We can start by using the two conditions which state that the the two pieces reach the ground at the same moment, and that one of them falls back to the place at which it was projected. From the first condition it can be concluded that only the horizontal components of their velocitis change, thus the heights of the trajectories of both pieces are the same as the height of the path of the projectile if it does not explode, from the second we can draw the conclusion that the two pieces always move in the same plane, which is the plane of the trajectory of the original projectile motion.

The centre of mass of the system of splinters — according to the theorem of the motion of the centre of mass — moves along the trajectory of the original imaginary projectile which does not explode, and reaches the ground at the range of the original projectile, at the moment when the splinters reach the ground. Let us describe the motion of the projectile which does not explode. The vertical component of the initial velocity is $v_y = v_0 \sin \alpha = 200$ m/s, and its horizontal component is $v_x = v_0 \cos \alpha = 346.4$ m/s. The time while the projectile ascends is $t_{asc} = v_y/g = 20$ s, thus the time of the projectile motion is $t_{pro} = 2t_{asc} = 40$ s. The total range of the projectile motion is $x_{max} = v_x t_{pro} = 13856$ m, and the height to which the projectile ascends is $v_y^2/2g = 2000$ m.

The vertical component u_{1y} of the new velocity u_1 of the splinter which goes back to the place of the projection after the explosion does not change, and its horizontal component u_{1x} can be calculated from the final speeds given in the problem. Because the vertical motion is not influenced by the explosion the magnitude of the vertical component of the final velocity of the splinter which hits the ground at the original position is the same as the magnitude of the vertical component of the initial velocity of the projectile, which is: $v_0 \sin \alpha = 200 \, \dfrac{\text{m}}{\text{s}}$.

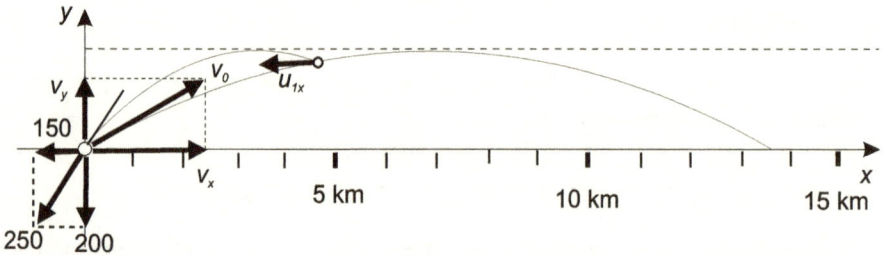

The speed of the impact is given: $v_{imp} = 250$ m/s, from these data using the Pythagorean theorem the constant horizontal component of the velocity can be calculated:

$$u_{1x} = \sqrt{v_{imp}^2 - v_{0y}^2} = \sqrt{250^2 \text{m}^2/\text{s}^2 - 200^2 \text{m}^2/\text{s}^2} = 150 \, \frac{\text{m}}{\text{s}}.$$

Let us denote the time elapsed between the moment of the projection and the explosion by t_1. The time elapsed between the explosion and the impact is $t = t_{pro} - t_1$. During this time the splinter which goes back to the place of projection covers a distance of $x_1 = u_{1x}(t_{pro} - t_1)$ along the horizontal, while the common centre of mass covers a horizontal distance of $x_2 = v_{0x}(t_{pro} - t_1)$. The sum of these distances is exactly the total range of the projectile motion, thus:

$$x_{max} = x_1 + x_2 = u_x(t_{pro} - t_1) + v_{0x}(t_{pro} - t_1) =$$
$$= 150 \, \frac{\text{m}}{\text{s}}(40\,\text{s} - t_1) + 346.4 \, \frac{\text{m}}{\text{s}}(40\,\text{s} - t_1) = 346.4 \, \frac{\text{m}}{\text{s}} \cdot 40\,\text{s} \ (= 13856\,\text{m}).$$

The solution of the equation gives the time between the projection and the explosion: $t_1 = 12.087\,\text{s}$.

Thus the height of the explosion is:

$$h_1 = v_{0y}t_1 - \frac{1}{2}gt_1^2 = 200\,\frac{\text{m}}{\text{s}} \cdot 12.087\,\text{s} - \frac{1}{2} \cdot 10\,\frac{\text{m}}{\text{s}^2} \cdot 12.087^2\,\text{s}^2 = 1686.9\,\text{m}.$$

Second solution of Problem 13. The problem can be easily solved if we use the fact that phenomena in mechanics are reversible. If the velocity of the impact was reflected, that is, if the splinter was projected with the velocity opposite to the the velocity at which the splinter hits the ground then the splinter, which falls back to the initial position, would move from the place of the projection to the place of the expolosion along the same trajectory upon which it moves when it falls back to the place of the projection from the position of the explosion. Thus the paths of the projectile, which does not explode, and the splinter which falls back, intersect each other at the place where the projectile explodes. Therefore, we only have to write the equations of both paths and to solve the equation system to y.

The equation of the path (of the centre of mass) of the original projectile is

$$y = \tan\alpha_1 \cdot x - \frac{g}{2v_0^2\cos\alpha_1^2} \cdot x^2,$$

The equation of the path of the splinter which falls back to the place of the projection, and which is "projected back", is

$$y = \tan\alpha_2 \cdot x - \frac{g}{2v_{imp}^2\cos\alpha_2^2} \cdot x^2,$$

where $\alpha_1 = 30°$, $\tan\alpha_2 = 200/150$, $\cos\alpha_2 = 150/250$.

The trivial solution of the equation system is $x = 0$, which is the initial point of both paths, and the solution which we would like to find when $x \neq 0$ can be calculated from the linear equation, which we gain if x is cancelled.

$$\tan\alpha_1 - \frac{g}{2v_0^2\cos^2\alpha_1}x = \tan\alpha_2 - \frac{g}{2v_{imp}^2\cos^2\alpha_2}x.$$

Substituting the numerical data:

$$\tan 30° - \frac{1}{2 \cdot 400^2\cos^2 30°}x = \frac{200}{150} - \frac{10}{2\cdot 250^2\left(\frac{150}{250}\right)^2}x.$$

The solution for x:

$$x = 4187\,\text{m},$$

and substituting this result into the first equation the height at which the explosion occurred is:

$$h_1 = y_1 = \tan 30° \cdot 4187\,\text{m} - \frac{10}{2\cdot 400^2\cos^2 30°} \cdot 4187^2\,\text{m} = 1686.9\,\text{m}.$$

(The velocity of the splinter which moves forward and the ratio of the masses of the splinters cannot be calculated from the given data.)

Solution of Problem 14. Let line a be the path of the bullet, point A is the lair of the gamekeeper. (The descent of the bullet can be neglected in this phase of the motion.) $AB = d = 1$ m.

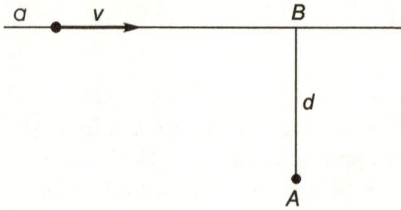

During its flight, the bullet produces spherically propagating sound waves at each point of the path. The enveloping surface to these at a given moment is a conical surface whose generatrices mark the maximum distance reached at the moment in concern. After time t, when the spherical wave of the bullet is at distance ct from point C, then the bullet itself is at a distance of vt from this place (point D shown in the figure). Point D is the apex of the enveloping conical surface (because the spherical wave starts from this point exactly now).

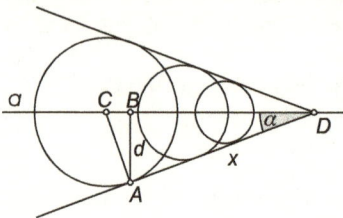

The sound can be sensed when the enveloping conical surface reaches A. Then for the semi-apex angle of the cone on one hand:

$$\sin\alpha = \frac{CA}{CD} = \frac{ct}{vt} = \frac{c}{v},$$

on the other hand

$$\sin\alpha = \frac{AB}{AD} = \frac{d}{x},$$

where x is the unknown distance. From these

$$x = \frac{v}{c} \cdot d = \frac{680 \text{ m/s}}{340 \text{ m/s}} \cdot 1 \text{ m} = 2 \text{ m}.$$

6.2 Dynamics

Solution of Problem 15. Let us assume that the object is pointlike. The object should reach the top of the semicircle, after which its motion will be a horizontal projection. If the object is to reach the top of the semicircle, the normal force $\vec{K}$ exerted by the track should not become zero anywhere other than at the top.

According to Newton's second law:

$$m\vec{g} + \vec{K} = m\vec{a},$$

which at the top of the semicircle takes the form of:

$$mg + K = m\frac{v^2}{r}, \tag{1}$$

where v^2/r is the centripetal acceleration of the object. (As the vectors are all vertical, their magnitudes can be used in the equation.) The object will reach the top of the semicircle if the normal force remains positive or becomes zero there. Since the extreme case should be investigated (because that is when the velocity v_0 and therefore the distance of horizontal projection is minimum) let us substitute $K=0$ into equation (1):

$$mg = m\frac{v_0^2}{r},$$

from which

$$v_0 = \sqrt{rg}. \tag{2}$$

This horizontal velocity is maintained throughout the horizontal projection until the object hits the track in its original position. The time of fall equals the time of a freefall from a height of $h=2r$:

$$t = \sqrt{\frac{2h}{g}} = \sqrt{\frac{4r}{g}}.$$

The horizontal component of the object's displacement during the fall is:

$$x = v_0 t = \sqrt{rg}\sqrt{\frac{4r}{g}} = 2r$$

It is interesting to see that the horizontal displacement equals the height from which the object falls. This distance is the shortest possible distance of the horizontal track that we wanted to find. The velocity given to the object in its initial position in the extreme case can be calculated using the conservation of energy:

$$\frac{1}{2}mv^2 = mg2r + \frac{1}{2}mv_0^2,$$

hence

$$v = \sqrt{rg + v_0^2} = \sqrt{4rg + rg} = \sqrt{5rg} \quad (= \sqrt{5}v_0).$$

Solution of Problem 16. a) Considering the requirements of the problem, let us start the reasoning at the end. The object leaving the track at B becomes a projectile with a horizontal initial velocity of v_B. Since it is to travel through C, it needs to cover a horizontal distance of d while falling through a vertical distance of R below the point B. The equations for the displacement of the projectile are

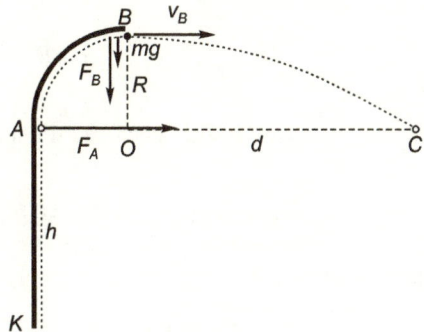

$$v_B t = d$$

and

$$R = \frac{g}{2}t^2.$$

Hence, with the elimination of t,

$$v_B = d \cdot \sqrt{\frac{g}{2R}}.$$

Given the speed at B, the law of energy conservation can be used to determine the speed at K:

$$\frac{1}{2}mv_K^2 = mg(h+R) + \frac{1}{2}mv_B^2.$$

With the substitution of the above expression for v_B, the speed at K is

$$v_K = \sqrt{2g(h+R) + \frac{d^2 g}{2R}} = \sqrt{2 \cdot 10\,\frac{m}{s^2}(2\,m+1\,m) + \frac{9\,m^2 \cdot 10\,\frac{m}{s^2}}{2 \cdot 1\,m}} = 10.25\,\frac{m}{s}.$$

b) Since the object must slide all the way along the track to get to point B, the normal force cannot decrease to zero anywhere along the track. That imposes a lower limit on the initial speed of the projectile motion. Thus the horizontal distance d has to be long enough to be reached during the time of the fall. The normal force F_B exerted by the track at point B is obtained from the equation for the centripetal force:

$$F_B + mg = m\frac{v^2}{R}$$

$$F_B = m\frac{v^2}{R} - mg = mg\left(\frac{d^2}{2R^2} - 1\right) \geq 0. \tag{1}$$

The value of zero corresponds to the minimum value of d, thus $d_{min} = R\sqrt{2} = 1.41\,m$.

c) At the point A, the normal force of the track changes suddenly from the value of zero along the line segment $\overline{KA}$ to the value F_A required by circular motion. At point A of the circular arc,

$$F_A = m\frac{v_A^2}{R}.$$

The value of v_A is obtained from the law of energy conservation again, applied between the points A and B separated by a vertical distance of R:

$$mgR + \frac{mv_B^2}{2} = \frac{mv_A^2}{2}.$$

Hence the square of the speed and the normal force at A are $v_A^2 = 2Rg + \frac{d^2 g}{2R}$,

$$F_A = mg\left(\frac{d^2}{2R^2} + 2\right) = 0.5\,kg \cdot 10\,\frac{m}{s^2}\left(\frac{9\,m^2}{2 \cdot 1\,m^2} + 2\right) = 32.5\,N. \tag{2}$$

From (1) and (2),

$$F_B = F_A - 3mg = 32.5\,N - 0.5\,kg \cdot 10\,\frac{m}{s^2} = 27.5\,N.$$

Solution of Problem 17. Let us describe the instantaneous position of the object with the angle α between the vertical and the radius drawn to the small object. Where the wall ends, the object undergoes projectile motion with an initial angle of α as well. The omission of some part of the wall does not lead to the failure of the trick if the downward part of the parabola smoothly fits to the circle again.

From this, it is derived that the missing part of the circular track must be symmetrical along the vertical diameter of the circle. This condition can be considered as the horizontal component of the displacement of the object during the time of the ascent of the object (half of the range of the projectile motion) and is the same as the half of the chord which belongs to the arc cut off the circle. Let us determine the central angle subtended by the arc cut off. Let the magnitude of this angle be 2α.

The time of the ascent of the projectile motion is:

$$t_{\mathrm{a}} = \frac{v\sin\alpha}{g}.$$

The distance covered during this time is:

$$v\cos\alpha\cdot t_{\mathrm{a}} = \frac{v\cos\alpha\cdot v\sin\alpha}{g} = R\sin\alpha$$

From this $\cos\alpha = \dfrac{Rg}{v^2}$.

The initial speed of the projectile motion can be calculated using the work-energy theorem:

$$-mgR(1+\cos\alpha) = \frac{1}{2}mv^2 - \frac{1}{2}mv_0^2,$$

from which: $v^2 = v_0^2 - 2gR(1+\cos\alpha)$, and $\cos\alpha = \dfrac{Rg}{v_0^2 - 2Rg(1+\cos\alpha)}$.

This is a quadratic equation for the cosine of half of the asked angle:

$$\cos^2\alpha + \left(1 - \frac{v_0^2}{2Rg}\right)\cos\alpha + \frac{1}{2} = 0.$$

In our case $\dfrac{v_0^2}{2Rg} = \dfrac{400}{2\cdot 8.16\cdot 9.8} = 2.5$, which can be substituted into our equation, such that:

$$\cos^2\alpha - 1.5\cos\alpha + \frac{1}{2} = 0,$$

from which 2 solutions are gained for $\cos\alpha$:

$$\cos\alpha_1 = 1, \quad \text{and} \quad \cos\alpha_2 = 0.5.$$

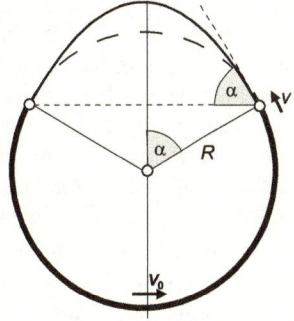

The solutions for the central angle of the arc which is to cut off are: $\varphi_1 = 2\alpha_1 = 0^0$ and $\varphi_2 = 2\alpha_2 = 120^0$, so the length of the circular path is: $i = R\varphi = \dfrac{2\pi}{3}R = 17.15\,\text{m}$.

Solution of Problem 18. The object moves on a vertical circular path, during which the tension in the string decreases. The maximum tension occurs at the bottom of the circle, i.e. at the start of the motion. If the string does not break at the start, there are two possibilities: 1. If the initial velocity is enough to make the object to move around the circle without the string becoming slack, the string will never break. 2. If, however, the object leaves the circular path at a given point (where the string becomes slack), it will undergo projectile motion until it reaches the circular path again, where the string will become tense. In this case, assuming that the string is not stretchable, the tension in the string will be extremely high (well above the maximum $40N$) and because it is pulled suddenly, the string will break. In this case, the solution becomes the point of intersection of the parabolic path and the circle.

1. The tension acting at the start can be determined using Newton's second law:

$$K - mg = m\frac{v^2}{L},$$

which yields

$$K = m\left(\frac{v_0^2}{L} + g\right) = 0.5\,\text{kg}\left(\frac{196\,\text{m}^2/\text{s}^2}{5.6\,\text{m}} + 10\,\frac{\text{m}}{\text{s}^2}\right) =$$
$$= 22.5\,\text{N} < 40\,\text{N},$$

so the string does not break at the start of the motion.

2. The point in which the projectile motion of the object starts is the point where the string becomes slack, i.e. tension K becomes zero.

Let φ be the angle formed by the string and the vertical in the above point. Applying Newton's second law to the object in that point, we obtain:

$$mg\cos\varphi + K = m\frac{v^2}{L}, \tag{1}$$

where $K = 0$. The velocity (v) of the object in that point can be determined using the work-kinetic energy theorem:

$$-mgL(1+\cos\varphi) = \frac{1}{2}mv^2 - \frac{1}{2}mv_0^2$$

(the work of the tension is zero), hence

$$v^2 = v_0^2 - 2gL(1+\cos\varphi). \tag{2}$$

Substituting equation (2) and $K = 0$ into equation (1) and dividing by m give:

$$g\cos\varphi = \frac{v_0^2}{L} - 2g(1+\cos\varphi),$$

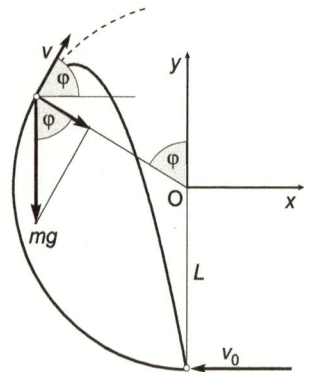

which yields

$$3\cos\varphi = \frac{v_0^2}{gL} - 2,$$

hence the cosine of the angle that gives the position in which the object leaves the circle is:

$$\cos\varphi = \frac{v_0^2}{3gL} - \frac{2}{3} = \frac{14^2\,\mathrm{m^2/s^2}}{3\cdot 10\,\mathrm{m/s^2}\cdot 5.6\,\mathrm{m}} - \frac{2}{3} = 0.5, \tag{3}$$

so the angle formed by the string and the vertical turns out to be:

$$\varphi = 60°.$$

The launch speed of the projectile motion can be calculated by substituting the value of $\cos\varphi$ into equation (2):

$$v = \sqrt{v_0^2 - 2gL(1+0.5)} = \sqrt{14^2\,\mathrm{m^2/s^2} - 2\cdot 10\,\mathrm{m/s^2}\cdot 5.6\,\mathrm{m}\cdot 1.5} = \sqrt{28}\,\frac{\mathrm{m}}{\mathrm{s}} = 5.29\,\frac{\mathrm{m}}{\mathrm{s}}. \tag{4}$$

According to the figure, the coordinates of the point where the object leaves the circle are:

$$x_0 = -L\sin\varphi,$$
$$y_0 = L\cos\varphi,$$

because the angle above the horizontal at which the object is launched equals the angle formed by the string and the vertical.

The equation of the circle in the coordinate-system defined in the figure is:

$$x^2 + y^2 = L^2.$$

The coordinates of the object during its projectile motion as a function of time are:

$$x = x_0 + v\cos\varphi\cdot t = -L\sin\varphi + v\cos\varphi\cdot t, \tag{5}$$
$$y = y_0 + v\sin\varphi\cdot t - \frac{1}{2}gt^2 = L\cos\varphi + v\sin\varphi\cdot t - \frac{1}{2}gt^2. \tag{6}$$

Inserting these coordinates into the equation of the circle, we get:

$$L^2\sin^2\varphi - 2Lv\sin\varphi\cos\varphi t + v^2\cos^2\varphi t^2 + L^2\cos^2\varphi + v^2\sin^2\varphi t^2 + \frac{1}{4}g^2t^4 +$$

$$+ 2Lv\cos\varphi\sin\varphi\cdot t - 2L\cos\varphi\cdot\frac{1}{2}gt^2 - 2v\sin\varphi\frac{1}{2}gt^3 = L^2.$$

Using that $L^2\sin^2\varphi + L^2\cos^2\varphi = L^2$, $v^2t^2\sin^2\varphi + v^2t^2\cos^2\varphi = v^2t^2$ and that the sum of the second and seventh term equals zero, our equation simplifies to:

$$v^2t^2 + \frac{1}{4}g^2t^4 - L\cos\varphi gt^2 - v\sin\varphi gt^3 = 0.$$

Dividing by $t^2 \neq 0$, we obtain:

$$\frac{1}{4}g^2t^2 - v\sin\varphi gt + (v^2 - L\cos\varphi g) = 0.$$

This is a quadratic equation for t, whose solution is:

$$t = \frac{v\sin\varphi g \pm \sqrt{v^2\sin^2\varphi g^2 + g^2(L\cos\varphi g - v^2)}}{\frac{1}{2}g^2}.$$

after simplifying the fraction by g, part of the expression under the square root can be written as:

$$v^2\sin^2\varphi - v^2 = -v^2(1 - \sin^2\varphi) = -v^2\cos^2\varphi$$

thus

$$t = 2 \cdot \frac{v\sin\varphi \pm \sqrt{(Lg - v^2\cos\varphi)\cos\varphi}}{g}.$$

Substituting known values and using equations (3) and (4), we get:

$$t = 2 \cdot \frac{5.29\,\frac{\mathrm{m}}{\mathrm{s}} \cdot 0.866 \pm \sqrt{(5.6\,\mathrm{m} \cdot 10\,\frac{\mathrm{m}}{\mathrm{s}^2} - 28\,\frac{\mathrm{m}^2}{\mathrm{s}^2} \cdot 0.5) \cdot 0.5}}{10\,\frac{\mathrm{m}}{\mathrm{s}^2}},$$

hence

$$t_1 = 1.833\,\mathrm{s} \quad \text{and} \quad t_2 \approx 0.$$

Substituting the value of t_1 into the x and y coordinates of the object as given in equations (5) and (6) gives the position of the object at the moment when the string breaks:

$$x = (-5.6\,\mathrm{m} \cdot 0.866 + 5.292 \cdot 1.833 \cdot 0.5)\,\mathrm{m} = -(4.8496 + 4.850)\,\mathrm{m} \approx 0,$$

$$y = (5.6 \cdot 0.5 + 5.292 \cdot 0.866 \cdot 1.833 - 5 \cdot 1.833^2)\,\mathrm{m} = -5.6\,\mathrm{m} = -L,$$

which means that the object comes back into its initial position (at distance L below the point of suspension) when the string break.

Solution of Problem 19. The position of the object can be described by angle α, which is the angle enclosed by the vertical and the radius connecting the centre of the semicircle and the object as shown on the figure. The acceleration of the object can be resolved into tangential and normal components, which are $a_t = g\sin\alpha$ and $a_n = v^2/R$, where v is the instantaneous velocity of the object in the given position. As the two components are perpendicular, the net acceleration of the object can be calculated as:

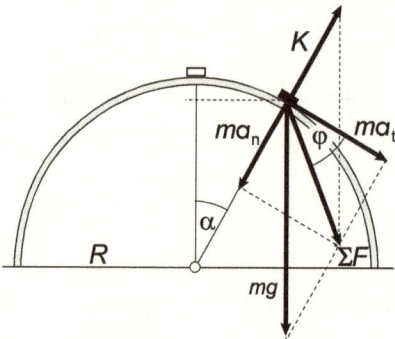

$$a = \sqrt{a_t^2 + a_n^2} = \sqrt{(g\sin\alpha)^2 + (v^2/R)^2}.$$

Using the conservation of energy, we can express the velocity of the object in terms of angle α:

$$mgR(1 - \cos\alpha) = \frac{1}{2}mv^2,$$

which yields

$$v^2 = 2gR(1 - \cos\alpha).$$

Substituting this into the formula for acceleration and assuming that the acceleration should be two thirds of g, we get:

$$a = g\sqrt{\sin^2\alpha + 4(1 - \cos\alpha)^2} = \frac{2}{3} \cdot g.$$

after some algebra, we get a quadratic equation for $\cos\alpha$:

$$27\cos^2\alpha - 72\cos\alpha + 41 = 0,$$

the only solution to the equation that has a physical meaning is:

$$\cos\alpha = \frac{12 - \sqrt{21}}{9} = 0.8242, \qquad \rightarrow \qquad \alpha = 34.5°.$$

The net acceleration and the tangent line form an angle φ, for which we get:

$$\cos\varphi = \frac{g\sin\alpha}{2g/3} = 1.5\sin\alpha = 0.8496, \qquad \rightarrow \qquad \varphi = 31.8°.$$

The angle enclosed by the acceleration and the horizontal is $\varepsilon = \varphi + \alpha = 66.3°$.

Solution of Problem 20. The object leaves the slope when the normal reaction becomes zero. In our case this may happen along the part of the path which is concave downward, with the chance of it happening being greatest at the lowest points. Let us assume that the object is a point-like one. The critical position is the inflexion point of the path, so if the normal reaction becomes zero there for a moment, then it will increase abruptly to a high value because of the opposite curvature. Let us consider this case as the critical case, because if the object reaches this point at a greater speed than the speed which belongs to the critical case then it will surely leave a finite segment of the path.

The question can be stated in the following way as well: What should the initial speed of an object which slides down on a smooth circular path of radius R be, so that it it leaves the path just as it descends from a height of $h/2$?

Let the speed of the object at the top of the path be v_1, and v_2 after descending a height of $h/2$. During the motion of the object the resultant force is the vector sum of the normal reaction and the gravitational force. At the moment when the normal reaction ceases the resultant force is equal too the gravitational force. At this moment

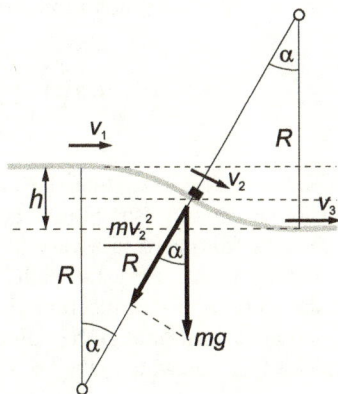

the object moves along the circular path of radius R making the centripetal force equal to the radial component of the gravitational force. Thus for this position:

$$mg\cos\alpha = m\frac{v_2^2}{R}.$$

After calculating the speed the law of conservation of energy is applied:

$$mg\Delta h = \frac{1}{2}mv_2^2 - \frac{1}{2}mv_1^2,$$

where $\Delta h = h/2$. From this

$$v_2 = \sqrt{gh + v_1^2}, \quad \text{and} \quad v_1 = \sqrt{v_2^2 - gh}.$$

Expressing v_2 from the first equation and substituting it into the last one:

$$v_1 = \sqrt{Rg\cos\alpha - gh}.$$

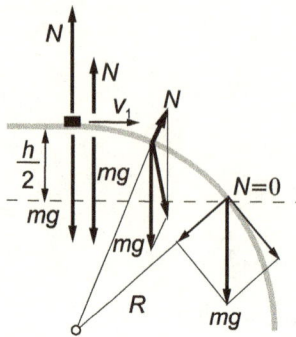

Reading from the figure

$$\cos\alpha = \frac{R - h/2}{R} = 1 - \frac{h}{2R}.$$

using the value of $\cos\alpha$ and substituting the data of the problem, the asked speed becomes:

$$v_1 = \sqrt{Rg\left(1 - \frac{h}{2R}\right) - gh} = \sqrt{Rg\left(1 - \frac{3h}{2R}\right)} = 4.43\,\frac{\text{m}}{\text{s}}.$$

Remark. The fact that the circular paths join 'without break' does not mean that the object passes 'smoothly', because at the connection the normal reaction abruptly increases from zero to a very high value, allowing an elastic ball to be 'ejected' at the inflection point. Here the path cannot be considered as straight, unlike, for example, a sinus curve at its inflection. Let the mass of the sliding object be 1 kg: the normal reaction exerted on it at the inflection point of the curve increases from zero to a certain value of N for which $N - mg\cos\alpha = mv^2/R$, from which

$$N = m(g\cos\alpha + v^2/R) = 1\,\text{kg} \cdot \left(9.81\,\text{m/s}^2 \cdot \frac{4}{5} + \frac{4.43^2}{5}\,\text{m/s}^2\right) = 11.77\,\text{N}.$$

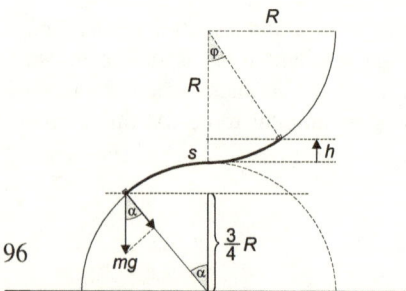

Solution of Problem 21. At the moment when the object detaches from the slope, the reaction force of the slope becomes zero, so Newton's second law in radial direction is:

$$mg\cos\alpha = m\frac{v^2}{R}.$$

According to the work–energy theorem:

$$mg[R(1-\cos\alpha)+h] = \frac{1}{2}mv^2,$$

from which the square of the speed is

$$v^2 = 2g[R(1-\cos\alpha)+h],$$

and, according to the given data, the cosine of α is

$$\cos\alpha = \frac{\frac{3}{4}R}{R} = \frac{3}{4}.$$

Plugging in all these formulas into Newton's second law (yet in parametric form), we get:

$$g\cos\alpha = \frac{2gR(1-\cos\alpha)+2hg}{R}.$$

From this the altitude h measured from the common horizontal tangent of the arcs is:

$$h = \left(\frac{3}{2}\cos\alpha - 1\right)R,$$

and substituting the value of $\cos\alpha$, we get that

$$h = \left(\frac{3}{2}\cdot\frac{3}{4}-1\right)\cdot R = \left(\frac{9}{8}-\frac{8}{8}\right)\cdot R = \frac{1}{8}R.$$

The whole distance covered by the small object on the slope is the sum of the distances covered on the concave and convex parts:

$$s = s_1 + s_2.$$

The first part of the distance can be determined from h and R:

$$s_1 = R\varphi = R\cdot\arccos\frac{R-h}{R} = R\cdot\arccos\left(1-\frac{h}{R}\right) = R\cdot\arccos\left(1-\frac{1}{8}\right) =$$
$$= R\cdot\arccos\frac{7}{8} = 0.5\text{ m}\cdot 0.505 \approx 0.253\text{ m}.$$

The second distance, according to the data given in the problem, is:

$$s_2 = R\alpha = R\cdot\arccos\frac{3}{4} = 0.5\text{ m}\cdot 0.7227 = 0.361\text{ m}.$$

Thus the small object covered a total distance of

$$s = s_1 + s_2 = 0.253\text{ m}+0.361\text{ m}=0.614\text{ m}=61.4\text{ cm},$$

on the slope, which has the parametric form

$$s = R\varphi + R\alpha = R\cdot(\varphi+\alpha) = R\cdot\left(\arccos\frac{3}{4}+\arccos\frac{7}{8}\right).$$

Solution of Problem 22. Let us solve this problem in general for an arbitrary initial angle $0 < \alpha_0 < 90°$.

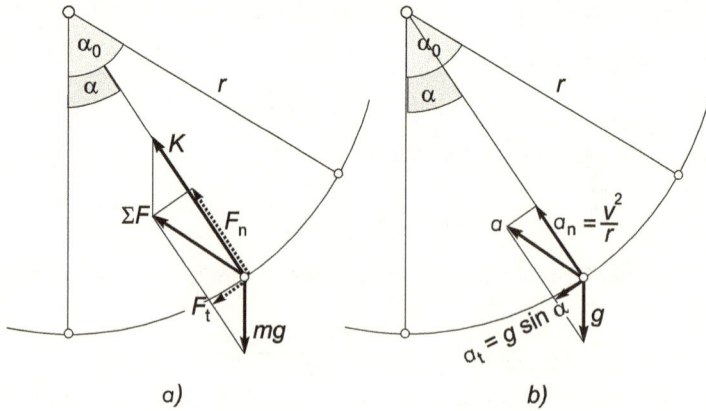

a)   b)

Figure a) shows the forces acting on the bob. The resultant force of gravitational force $m\vec{g}$ and tension $\vec{K}$ points towards the inside of the circle, its tangential component being equal to that of the gravitational force. Figure b) shows the accelerations of the bob, which can be derived from figure a) by dividing each force by the mass m of the bob. The magnitude of the net acceleration can be written into the form of:

$$a = \sqrt{a_n^2 + a_t^2} = \sqrt{\left(\frac{v^2}{r}\right)^2 + (g\sin\alpha)^2}. \tag{1}$$

The velocity of the bob can be calculated using the conservation of energy formula.

While the angle which the cord makes with the vertical decreases from α_0 to α, the bob's height decreases by:

$$|\Delta h| = r(\cos\alpha_0 - \cos\alpha).$$

Applying the conservation of energy formula and inputting the initial velocity as zero, we obtain:

$$mg|\Delta h| = mgr(\cos\alpha_0 - \cos\alpha) = \frac{1}{2}mv^2,$$

hence

$$v^2 = 2gr(\cos\alpha_0 - \cos\alpha).$$

Inserting this into equation (1), we get:

$$a = g\sqrt{[2(\cos\alpha - \cos\alpha_0)]^2 + \sin^2\alpha} = g\sqrt{\sin^2\alpha + 4[\cos^2\alpha - 2\cos\alpha\cos\alpha_0 + \cos^2\alpha_0]} =$$
$$= \sqrt{3\cos^2\alpha - 8\cos\alpha_0\cos\alpha + 4\cos^2\alpha_0 + 1}. \tag{2}$$

The bob will reach its minimum acceleration when the expression under the square root takes its minimum value. This expression is the second degree function of $\cos\alpha$:

$$3\cos^2\alpha - 8\cos\alpha_0\cos\alpha + (1 + 4\cos^2\alpha_0). \tag{3}$$

The general form of a quadratic function of x is:

$$ax^2 + bx + c.$$

By calculating the zeros of this function, you will find the x-intercepts of a parabola, with an axis parallel to the y-axis. These intercepts are symmetrical to the axis (and to the vertex) of the parabola, therefore the x-coordinate of the minimum point of the parabola is the arithmetic mean of the two zeros:

$$x_{\min} = (x_1 + x_2)/2,$$

where

$$x_1 = \frac{-b + \sqrt{b^2 - 4ac}}{2a}, \quad \text{and} \quad x_2 = \frac{-b - \sqrt{b^2 - 4ac}}{2a}.$$

Calculating their arithmetic mean gives:

$$x_{\min} = -\frac{b}{2a}.$$

Let us apply this to the second degree expression of $\cos\alpha$. The angle at which the bob reaches its minimum acceleration is given by:

$$\cos\alpha_{\min} = \frac{8\cos\alpha_0}{6} = \frac{4}{3}\cos\alpha_0. \tag{5}$$

Using this calculation in our case the initial angle is $\alpha_0 = 45°$ and the minimum acceleration is reached when:

$$\cos\alpha_{\min} = \frac{4}{3} \cdot \frac{\sqrt{2}}{2} = \frac{2\sqrt{2}}{3} = 0.9428$$

from which the angle formed by the cord and the vertical is:

$$\alpha_{\min} = 19.47°.$$

The question set in the problem is therefore answered.

Let us calculate some additional data regarding the minimum acceleration. Substituting equation (5) for equation (2), we arrive at a minimum acceleration of:

$$a_{\min} = g \cdot \sqrt{1 + 3 \cdot \frac{16\cos^2\alpha_0}{9} - 8 \cdot \frac{4\cos^2\alpha_0}{3} + 4\cos^2\alpha_0} =$$

$$= \frac{g}{9} \cdot \sqrt{(48 - 96 + 36)\cos_0^2 + 9} = \frac{g}{9} \cdot \sqrt{9 - 12\cos^2\alpha}. \tag{6}$$

In our case $\alpha_0 = 45°$, so $\cos\alpha_0 = \dfrac{\sqrt{2}}{2}$. Inserting this into equation (6), for the minimum value of the acceleration we get:

$$a_{\min} = \frac{g}{3}\sqrt{9 - 12\cdot\left(\frac{\sqrt{2}}{2}\right)^2} = \frac{\sqrt{3}}{3}\cdot g = 0.577g \approx 5.8\,\frac{\text{m}}{\text{s}^2}.$$

Angle φ formed by the minimum acceleration and the tangent of the path is:

$$\cos\varphi = \frac{g\sin\alpha}{g\frac{\sqrt{3}}{3}} = \frac{\sin 19.47°}{\sqrt{3}/3} = 0.5773,$$

thus $\varphi = 54.73°$, while the angle formed by the minimum acceleration and the horizontal is:

$$\varepsilon = \varphi - \alpha = 54.73° - 19.47° = 35.26°.$$

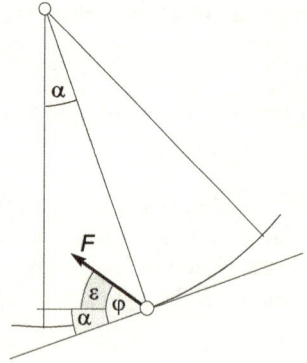

Solution of Problem 23. a) When the blocks move with the same acceleration, their acceleration equals the acceleration of their centre of mass, which can be determined easily. The sum of the external forces acting on the system equals the mass of the system times the acceleration of the centre of mass:

$$\sum F_{\text{ext}} = ma_{\text{centre}}.$$

Aplying this to the system of blocks, we obtain:

$$m_1 g\sin\alpha + m_2 g\sin\alpha - \mu_1 m_1 g\cos\alpha - \mu_2 m_2 g\cos\alpha = (m_1 + m_2)\cdot a_{\text{centre}}.$$

Using $m_1 = m_2 = m$ simplifies our equation to:

$$2mg\sin\alpha - (\mu_1 + \mu_2)mg\cos\alpha = 2ma_{\text{centre}},$$

from which we find:

$$a = g\left(\sin\alpha - \frac{\mu_1 + \mu_2}{2}\cos\alpha\right) = 10\,\frac{\text{m}}{\text{s}^2}\left(\sin 15° - \frac{0.4}{2}\cos 15°\right) = 0.656\,\frac{\text{m}}{\text{s}^2}.$$

Note that the upper block (if it was not connected to the lower block) would not start to move on the inclined plane by itself or would stop after being pushed downwards because the friction acting on it is greater than $mg\sin\alpha$. But as the friction acting on the lower block is small, the lower block moves down pulling the upper block with it.

b) The extension of the spring could be determined by applying Newton's second law to either block and substituting the value of acceleration calculated above. Let us now, however, calculate the extension directly, using only the given data and not the acceleration.

Newton's second law applied to the lower block gives:

$$mg\sin\alpha - \mu_2 mg\cos\alpha - D\Delta l = ma,$$

while applying Newton's second law to the upper block, we obtain:

$$mg\sin\alpha + D\Delta l - \mu_1 mg\cos\alpha = ma.$$

Subtracting the first equation from the second, the acceleration and $mg\sin\alpha$ cancel out:

$$2D\Delta l - \mu_1 mg\cos\alpha + \mu_2 mg\cos\alpha = 0,$$

from which we get:

$$\Delta l = \frac{m}{D}g\frac{\mu_1 - \mu_2}{2}\cdot\cos\alpha,$$

inserting the given data, we find:

$$\Delta l = \frac{3\,\mathrm{kg}}{200\,\mathrm{N/m}}\cdot 10\,\frac{\mathrm{m}}{\mathrm{s}^2}\cdot\frac{0.2}{2}\cdot\cos 15° = 0.01448 \approx 1.45\,\mathrm{cm}.$$

Solution of Problem 24. Consider the motion of the system. According to Newton's second law, with the notations of the figure,

$$F_2 - F_1 = (m+M)a_s, \tag{1}$$

where F_1 is the force of static friction, F_2 is the force of kinetic friction, and a_s is the acceleration of system.

Note that there are two friction forces of opposing directions, acting on the system at the same time. The first is opposing the motion, while the second, acting in the direction of the motion, advances translation and retards rotation.

The friction force F_1 is obtained by considering the torques acting on the cylinder:

$$F_1 R = \Theta\beta = \frac{1}{2}MR^2\frac{a_s}{R}.$$

Hence

$$F_1 = \frac{1}{2}Ma_s,$$

and

$$F_2 = \mu(mg - K\sin\alpha).$$

With the friction forces substituted in (1):

$$\mu(mg - K\sin\alpha) - \frac{1}{2}Ma_s = (m+M)a_s. \tag{2}$$

The tension force K acting on the string can be determined using Newton's second law applied to the cylinder:

$$K\cos\alpha - F_1 = Ma_s.$$

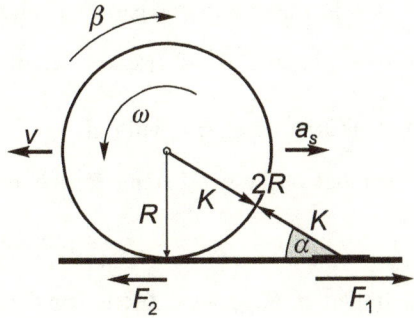

With the expression for F_1 substituted, K can be expressed:

$$K = \frac{3Ma_s}{2\cos\alpha}.$$

If this result is written in (2), the only unknown that remains is the acceleration:

$$\mu mg - \mu\frac{3Ma_s}{2\cos\alpha}\cdot\sin\alpha = \frac{1}{2}Ma_s + (m+M)a_s.$$

Hence the acceleration of the centre of mass of the cylinder (and the acceleration of the plate) is

$$a_s = \frac{2\mu m}{3M(1+\mu\tan\alpha)+2m}g.$$

According to the given information, $m = 2M$ and $\tan\alpha = \sqrt{3}/3$, thus:

$$a_s = \frac{4\mu}{3(1+\mu\tan\alpha)+4} = \frac{1.6}{3+0.4\cdot\sqrt{3}+4}\cdot10\,\frac{\text{m}}{\text{s}^2} = 2.08\,\frac{\text{m}}{\text{s}^2}.$$

Hence the distance covered and the time taken are

$$s = \frac{v_0^2}{2a_s}\cdot g = \frac{4\,\text{m}^2/\text{s}^2}{2\cdot2.08\ \text{m}/\text{s}^2} = 0.98\,\text{m} \quad\text{and}\quad t = \frac{2s}{v_0} = \frac{2\cdot0.98\,\text{m}}{2\ \text{m/s}} = 0.98\,\text{s}.$$

Solution of Problem 25. a) The hoop will get higher if there is friction, since in that case a part of its rotational energy (or possibly all of it) is also converted to gravitational potential energy. This statement can also be proved true by considering the forces acting on the hoop: as the hoop ascends, the speed of its centre of mass decreases. To decrease its angular velocity, there is an uphill friction force acting on the hoop, which represents a lifting force on the hoop.

It is instructive to compare the heights quantitatively: if the hoop rolls up the slope without slipping, it will rise to a height of $\Delta h_1 = \dfrac{\Delta E_{\text{kin}}}{mg} = \dfrac{\frac{1}{2}mv_0^2 + \frac{1}{2}\Theta\omega^2}{mg} = \dfrac{v_0^2}{g}$, while without friction its rise will only be $\Delta h_2 = \dfrac{E_{\text{transl}}}{mg} = \dfrac{\frac{1}{2}mv_0^2}{mg} = \dfrac{v_0^2}{2g}$.

The ratios of the two heights for a hoop and for a sphere are, respectively,

$$\frac{\Delta h_1}{\Delta h_2} = 2, \quad\text{and}\quad \frac{\Delta h_1}{\Delta h_2} = \frac{7}{5} = 1.4.$$

If there is only a weak friction on the slope and the hoop rolls with or without slipping, it will rise to a height Δh, such that

$$\Delta h_2 < \Delta h < \Delta h_1,$$

and part of the energy is dissipated.

b) If $r < R$, the hoop reaching the slope will roll on up the slope without a collision. On arrival, the speed of its centre of mass is v_0 and its angular speed is $\omega_0 = v_0/r$.

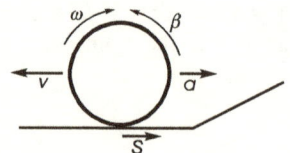

In the absence of friction (since there is no external torque acting on the hoop), the angular momentum of the hoop, and thus the angular speed too, will remain constant all the way. The hoop will slide up to a height of

$$h = v_0^2/2g,$$

where its speed is reduced to zero, and where it will then slide back to the base of the slope. It arrives at the base of the slope at a velocity of v_0 again, but in the opposite direction. Its sense of rotation does not change. Therefore, the hoop arriving back to the horizontal plane keeps sliding, and will continue to slide until the torque of the friction forces adjust the angular velocity to a value of $\omega = v/r$ 'in tune' with the instantaneous velocity and in the appropriate direction. In principle, this may occur in three different ways. Friction may reverse the sense of rotation, it may reverse the direction of velocity, or, in a special case it may reduce both to zero at the same time. The result will depend on the magnitude of rotational inertia. To solve the problem, this question needs to be investigated.

The diagrams below represent the three cases graphically. ($t = 0$ at the instant when the hoop arrives back down to the base of the slope.)

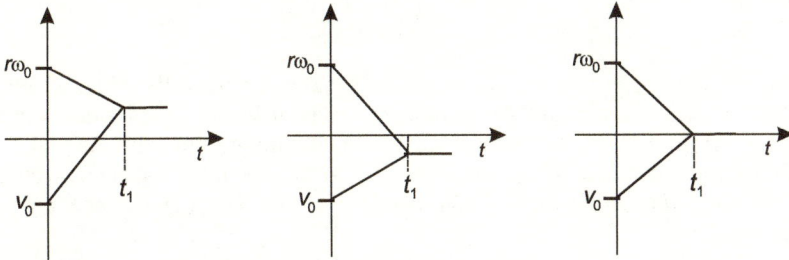

Calculations:
The acceleration of the centre of mass of the hoop after it has slid back down on the horizontal plane:

$$a = \mu g = \text{const.}$$

The angular acceleration of the hoop:

$$\beta = -\frac{\mu mgr}{mr^2} = -\frac{\mu g}{r} = \text{const.}$$

The speed and angular speed of the centre of the hoop expressed in terms of time:

$$v = -v_0 + at = -v_0 + \mu gt, \quad \text{and} \quad \omega = \omega_0 + \beta t = \omega_0 - \frac{\mu g}{r}t.$$

Sliding stops in a time t_1, such that

$$-v_0 + \mu gt_1 = \omega_0 r - \mu gt_1,$$

hence,

$$2\mu gt_1 = 2v_0, \quad \text{and} \quad t_1 = \frac{v_0}{\mu g} = \frac{3.5 \, \text{m/s}}{0.2 \cdot 10 \, \text{m/s}^2} = 1.75 \, \text{s}.$$

The speed of the centre of the hoop at the same time instant is

$$v = -v_0 + \mu g \frac{v_0}{\mu_0 g} = 0,$$

that is, we are dealing with the special case in which the hoop stops exactly when its angular speed *also* decreases to zero. Therefore it will not reverse either its velocity or angular velocity after its return.

Thus the hoop will stop in 1.75 s, which means that at 2.4 s, the time instant in question, it will be in the same position at the point of the horizontal plane where its coordinate is

$$s = x = -v_0 t_1 + \frac{1}{2}\mu g t_1^2 = -3.5\frac{\text{m}}{\text{s}} \cdot 1.75\,\text{s} + \frac{1}{2} \cdot 0.2 \cdot 10\,\frac{\text{m}}{\text{s}^2} \cdot 1.75^2\,\text{s}^2 = \approx -3.06\,\text{m},$$

with the origin at the base of the slope and the positive values of x under the inclined plane.

Remark. The case of a solid sphere is more complicated because the sphere will, after a while, continue to roll without slipping while its angular velocity is reversed. In this case, the given time interval is then made up of a decelerating part and a part of uniform motion. $\omega = 0$ at

$$t_1 = \frac{2}{5}\frac{v_0}{\mu g} = 0.7\,\text{s},$$

when the velocity is $v = v_0 - \mu g t_1 = 2.1$ m/s. The sphere rolls while slipping for this much time and then continues on unifomly. The distance rolled while slipping is $s_1 = v_0 t_1 - \mu g t_1 = 1.96$ m, and then it rolls without slipping until the interval of 2.4 s is over, covering a distance of $s_2 = v(t-t_1) = 3.57$ m. The total distance covered from the base of the slope during the 2.4 s is therefore $s = 5.53$ m. (The x axis now points the other way.)

A case of an object with cylindrical symmetry rolling back towards the slope may only occur if its rotational inertia is even greater than that of the hoop. (For example, a reel rolling with its narrow part on a track).

Solution of Problem 26. The motion of the block is retarded by the kinetic friction force and the force that is exerted by the dropped object parallel to their surface of contact. The force of kinetic friction is

$$S = \mu K,$$

where K is the normal force exerted by the ground on the block. This force has a small value before the collision and will therefore not change the speed of the block significantly during the 'infinitesimally short' duration of the collision. When the small mass falls onto the object, however, the normal force increases considerably, and thus friction can reduce the speed of the block by a finite value even 'in an instant'. Quantitatively:

The vertical component of the change in momentum of the small object equals the total impulse of the vertical forces acting on it:

$$\sum F_y \cdot \Delta t = \Delta m v_{1_y}.$$

In detail, since the small object loses its vertical velocity,

$$(mg - N)\Delta t = -mv_1,$$

where N is the mean magnitude of the normal component of the force exerted by the block on the small object (equal to the magnitude of the normal force acting *on the block*). Hence

$$N = mg + \frac{mv_1}{\Delta t}.$$

The resultant vertical force acting on the block is therefore $Mg + N - K = 0$, since the block does not accelerate vertically.

Thus the magnitude of the friction force acting on the block is

$$S = \mu K = \mu(N + Mg).$$

Consider the system comprising the block and the object dropped onto it. The change in momentum in the x direction is made up of the change in momentum $M\Delta u$ of the block and $m\Delta v_{1x} = mu$ of the small object, where u is the velocity of the block after the collision. From the law of impulse and momentum applied to the x components, with the coordinate axis pointing in the direction of the velocity v_2 of the block:

$$-\mu(N + Mg)\Delta t = M\Delta u + mu.$$

With the value of N substituted:

$$-\mu\left(mg + Mg + \frac{mv_1}{\Delta t}\right)\Delta t = M\Delta u + mu.$$

Multiplied by Δt:

$$-\mu(mg\Delta t + Mg\Delta t + mv_1) = M\Delta u + mu.$$

Since the collision is momentary, $\Delta t \to 0$, the only term of the expression in brackets not vanishing is mv_1. (Considering that $u = v_2 + \Delta u$), the change in velocity of the block is

$$\Delta u = -\frac{m(\mu v_1 + v_2)}{m + M} = -\frac{1\,\text{kg} \cdot (0.4 \cdot 10\,\text{m/s} + 2\,\text{m/s})}{1\,\text{kg} + 5\,\text{kg}} = -1\,\text{m/s}.$$

Thus the velocity of the block after the collision is

$$u = v_2 + \Delta u = \frac{Mv_2 - \mu mv_1}{m + M} = 1\,\frac{\text{m}}{\text{s}}.$$

Solution of Problem 27. According to Newton's second law applied to the radial components of the forces acting *on the ball*,

$$K - mg\cos\alpha = m\frac{v^2}{l},$$

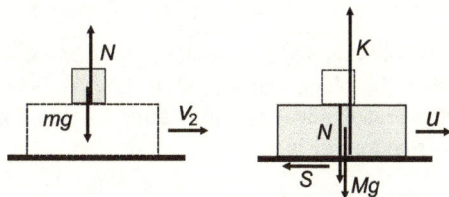

where K is the tension force acting on the string. According to the work-energy theorem,

$$mgl\cos\alpha = \frac{1}{2}mv^2.$$

From the two equations, the tension force is

$$K = 3mg\cos\alpha. \tag{1}$$

At the angle of the string to the vertical for which the static friction force is a maximum,

$$S = \mu_s(Mg + K\cos\alpha).$$

Newton's second law applied to *the block* at the time instant when the block starts to slide (that is, when it has not yet accelerated but when the static friction force has reached its maximum) is

$$\mu_s(Mg + K\cos\alpha) - K\sin\alpha = 0. \tag{2}$$

With the expression (1) of K written in (2), and rearranged:

$$\mu_s Mg + 3\mu_s mg\cos^2\alpha = 3mg\cos\alpha\sin\alpha.$$

Divided by g and with cosines expressed in terms of sines:

$$\mu_s M + 3\mu_s m - 3\mu_s m\sin^2\alpha = 3m\sin\alpha\sqrt{1 - \sin^2\alpha}.$$

Rearrangement leads to an equation that is quadratic in $\sin^2\alpha$. With the notation $x = \sin^2\alpha$ introduced:

$$9\left(1 + \mu_s^2\right)x^2 - \left[6\mu_s^2\left(\frac{M}{m} + 3\right) + 9\right]x + \mu_s^2\left(\frac{M^2}{m^2} + 6\frac{M}{m} + 9\right) = 0.$$

With the substitution of the given numerical data, the equation becomes simpler:

$$9.36x^2 - 10.2x + 1 = 0,$$

hence

$$x = \sin^2\alpha = \frac{10.2 \pm \sqrt{10.2^2 - 4\cdot9.36}}{2\cdot9.36},$$

that is,

$$x_1 = \sin^2\alpha_1 = 0.9808 \quad \text{and} \quad x_2 = \sin^2\alpha_2 = 0.1089.$$

The values obtained for the sine of the angle are

$$\sin\alpha_1 = \sqrt{0.9808} = 099036, \quad \text{and} \quad \sin\alpha_2 = \sqrt{0.1089} = 0.33004.$$

The block will start to slide when the string encloses an angle of

$$\alpha_1 = \arcsin 0.99036 = 82.038° \approx 82°$$

with the vertical.

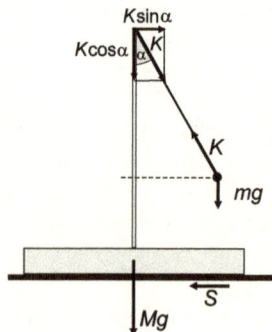

(Any angle α in the interval

$$\alpha_2 = \arcsin 0.33004 = 19.27° < \alpha < 82.038° = \alpha_1,$$

would satisfy the condition of sliding, provided that the block is held fixed until the string reaches that angle. However, under the present conditions the block will start to slide at $82.038°$, so any other angle is irrelevant for answering the question.)

Remark. The line of action of the tension force in the string does not pass through the centre of mass of the block, thus it also represents a torque about the centre of mass. As a result, the 'front' of the block is pressed harder against the ground than its rear end, and the value of the static friction force may become uncertain. However, since the solution is independent of the length of the pendulum and the only variable that the torque depends on in addition to the angle and the magnitude of the force is the height h of the rod, it can be made negligibly small. If the block is long enough relative to the rod, the effect of the torque becomes very small. (Note that the size of the ball imposes a limitation on shortening the string: the diameter of the ball must remain negligible relative to the length of the string, otherwise rotational kinetic energy should be considered in the work-energy theorem, too.)

Solution of Problem 28. The batten does not accelerate in the vertical direction, so Newton's second law for this direction is:

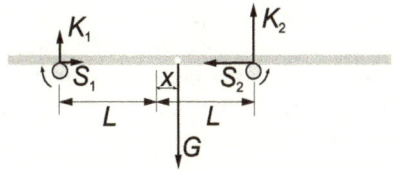

$$G - K_1 - K_2 = 0,$$

where G is the gravitational force exerted on the batten, K_1 and K_2 are the absolute values of the normal reactions exerted by the cylinders.

The batten does not rotate, thus the equation for the torques calculated for an axis through the centre of mass is:

$$K_1(L+x) - K_2(L-x) = 0.$$

Based on the above equations, the magnitudes of the normal reactions are:

$$K_1 = \frac{G(L-x)}{2L}, \quad\text{and}\quad K_2 = \frac{G(L+x)}{2L}.$$

Because, according to the problem, the cylinders rotate quickly, the relative speed of the batten and the surface of the cylinders is not zero, causing dynamic friction to be exerted between them and giving them each magnitudes of:

$$S_1 = \mu K_1, \quad\text{and}\quad S_2 = \mu K_2,$$

and although they are opposite, both are exerted towards the centre of the batten. Newton's second law for the horizontal forces is:

$$\mu K_2 - \mu K_1 = ma.$$

Substituting the values of the normal reactions:

$$\mu(K_2 - K_1) = -\mu G \frac{x}{L} = ma.$$

The force is proportional to the displacement and oppositely directed so the batten will undergo simple harmonic motion. Therefore, the net force exerted on the batten of mass m is:

$$\sum F = -\frac{\mu m g}{L} \cdot x,$$

and considering the force law of SHM which is: $\sum F = -m\omega^2 x$ we can find the angular frequency and the period of the motion, which are:

$$\omega = \sqrt{\mu g / L}, \quad \text{and} \quad T = 2\pi \sqrt{L / \mu g}.$$

Our result holds true unless the maximum speed of the batten does not reach the speed of any point on the surface of the rotating cylinder.

Solution of Problem 29. It is known that if the direction of the force exerted on an object placed onto a surface is such that its line of action is inside the so called 'frictional cone', then the object is not able to move regardless of the magnitude of the force. This is because the static frictional force, which is exerted in the plane of the surfaces in contact, is always greater than that component of the external force which is parallel to the surfaces in contact. (Of course the gravitational force is also meant to be part of this external force.)

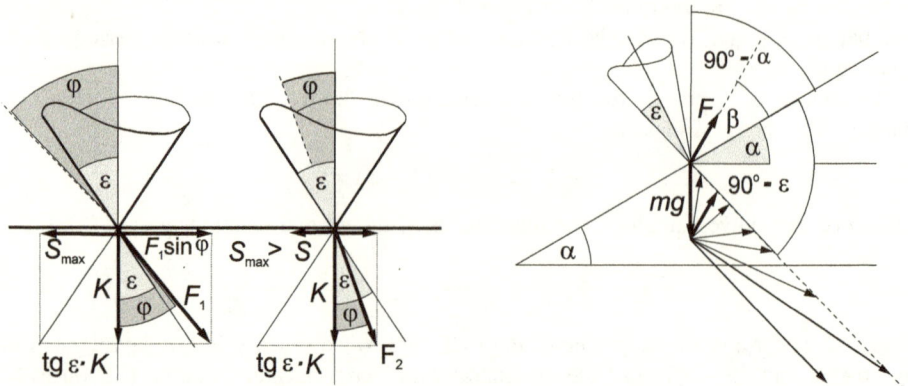

The figure on the left shows the forces exerted on a small object of negligible weight placed onto a horizontal plane. Let us apply Newton's second law to the boundary case when the object is in equilibrium. The equations for the components of the forces which are parallel and perpendicular to the surfaces are the following:

$$F \sin\varepsilon - \mu K = 0, \tag{1}$$

$$F \cos\varepsilon - K = 0. \tag{2}$$

Eliminating K

$$F \sin \varepsilon = \mu F \cos \varepsilon,$$

so

$$\mu = \tan \varepsilon,$$

where ε is the so called frictional angle, and the above mentioned frictional cone is the cone which is drawn around the normal to the plane, with the frictional angle being half of the vertex angle of the cone.

From the first equation it can be seen that if the line of action of the force is *outside the cone* (F_1), the object must move because the parallel component of F_1 is greater than the frictional force $(a \neq 0)$. If the line of action is inside the cone (F_2), the frictional force is always equal in magnitude and oppositely directed as the parallel component of the force, thus the object remains at rest. If the line of action is along the generator of the cone than the boundary case of the equilibrium is gained.

The figure in the left shows the forces exerted on the object and the frictional cone. The object can be pulled up along the plane if the line of action of the *resultant* of the gravitational force mg and the pulling force, which makes an angle of β with the plane, is outside the frictional cone. From the figure it can be seen that that if the object is pulled up uniformly the line of action of the resultant force must coincide with the generator of the cone. Because the angle between the normal of the plane and the generator of the cone is ε, the angle between the pulling force and the plane in the positive direction can only be

$$0 \leq \beta < (90° - \alpha)$$

(if $\beta = 90° - \alpha$, then the needed pulling force is mg)
and in the negative direction it can only be

$$0 \leq \beta < (90° - \varepsilon) \quad \text{thus} \quad 0 \leq \beta < (90° - \arctan\mu)$$

These angles are independent of the mass of the object. Naturally if $\beta \rightarrow 90° - \varepsilon$, then $F \rightarrow \infty$. If the absolute value of the angle is greater than this there is no force with which the object can be pulled (or pushed) up along the plane. The endpoints of the applicable pulling forces, $\vec{F}$, are along the line which makes an angle of $90° + \varepsilon$ with the inclined plane.

Solution of Problem 30. Newton's second law applied to the coin states that $S = = ma$, where S is the force of static friction. The coin starts to slip on the turntable when its acceleration reaches a value at which the force of static friction reaches its maximum: $S_{max} = \mu mg$ and can not increase any more.

After time t the acceleration of the coin has two components: the constant tangential acceleration and the increasing centripetal acceleration. Knowing that these components are perpendicular, we can use Pythagoras' theorem to find the magnitude of the net acceleration, which is:

$$a = \sqrt{(r\beta)^2 + (r\omega^2)^2},$$

where ω is the angular velocity of the turntable after time t. Writing the angular velocity as $\omega = \beta t$, we find that the acceleration of the coin is:

$$a = \sqrt{(r\beta)^2 + (r\beta^2 t^2)^2} = r\beta\sqrt{\beta^2 t^4 + 1}.$$

Inserting this into the law of motion of the coin, we get:

$$\mu mg = mr\beta\sqrt{\beta^2 t^4 + 1},$$

from which the time elapsed can be calculated as:

$$t = \frac{1}{\sqrt{\beta}} \cdot \sqrt[4]{\frac{\mu^2 g^2}{r^2 \beta^2} - 1} = 1.07 \, \text{s}.$$

Solution of Problem 31. Let us consider the thin-walled cylinders first. The friction force F_{f_1} due to the rod obviously points in the direction of the motion of the rod. Let us take the friction force F_{f_2} acting at the ground in the same direction. (After the solution of the equation system the sign of F_{f_2} will tell us the real direction.)

The law of the motion of the centre of mass for the cylinder with the components of the forces (as they happen to be collinear vectors) is:

$$F_{f_1} + F_{f_2} = ma_{cm}, \tag{1}$$

where a_{cm} is the acceleration of the centre of mass of the cylinder. The law for the moments of forces is

$$(F_{f_1} - F_{f_2})r = \Theta_{cm}\beta. \tag{2}$$

The kinematic constraint for no skidding is

$$a_{cm} = r\beta. \tag{3}$$

substituting the expression for a_{cm} from (3) into (1) the following relationship is acquired:

$$F_{f_1} + F_{f_2} = mr\beta \tag{4},$$

then by multiplying (4) by Θ_{cm}/m the following relationship is acquired:

$$(F_{f_1} + F_{f_2})\frac{\Theta_{cm}}{m} = \Theta_{cm} r\beta \tag{5},$$

finally by multiplying (2) by r the following equation is acquired:

$$(F_{f_1} - F_{f_2})r^2 = \Theta_{cm} r\beta \tag{6}.$$

The right sides of (5) and (6) are equal, so the left sides are also equal:

$$(F_{f_1} + F_{f_2})\frac{\Theta_{cm}}{m} = (F_{f_1} - F_{f_2})r^2.$$

From here the magnitude of the friction force exerted by the ground is

$$F_{f_2} = \frac{mr^2 - \Theta_{cm}}{\Theta_{cm} + mr^2}F_{f_1}.$$

Let us make use of the fact that the rotational inertia of a thin-walled cylinder for its axis is $\Theta_{\mathrm{cm}} = mr^2$:

$$F_{f_2} = \frac{mr^2 - mr^2}{mr^2 + mr^2} F_{f_1} = 0,$$

meaning there is no friction force between the table and the cylinders, and the minimum coefficient of friction required is $\mu = 0$. So in our case the cylinders roll without skidding even on a completely smooth surface.

Let us turn to the relationship between the cylinders and the rod now. The rod also moves on the cylinders without skidding, meaning the velocity and the acceleration of the topmost points of the cylinders are the same as those of the rod. But if there is no friction on the ground, the friction forces acting on the points that are touching the rod should be the same for both cylinders, considering this is the only way their accelerations can be the same. This is true despite the fact that as a result of the motion of the rod the normal forces N_1 and N_2 acting between the rod and the cylinders change continuously. The magnitude of N_1 starts from $Mg/4$ and its maximum value is $3Mg/4$ at the end of the process while for N_2 the opposite holds: it decreases from $3Mg/4$ to $Mg/4$, while $N_1 + N_2 = Mg$ is always true. Obviously, this can only be true if the coefficient of static friction between the cylinders and the rod is big enough to provide the relevant friction force F_{f_1} even in the case of the minimum normal force.

The equation of the motion of the rod is

$$F - 2F_{f_1} = Ma. \tag{7}$$

The law of the motion of the centre of mass for either cylinder is

$$a_{\mathrm{cm}} = \frac{F_{f_1}}{m}.$$

The rolling on both surfaces without skidding requires that $a_{\mathrm{cm}} = a/2$ holds. So

$$\frac{a}{2} = \frac{F_{f_1}}{m},$$

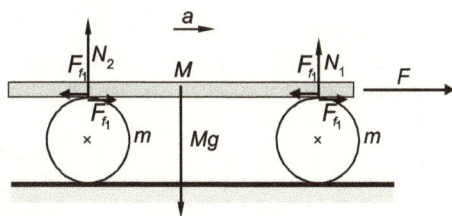

that is, $2F_{f_1} = ma$. Substituting this into (7) gives

$$F - ma = Ma,$$

that is,

$$a = \frac{F}{m + M} \quad \left(= 3\,\frac{\mathrm{m}}{\mathrm{s}^2} \right), \qquad \text{and} \qquad S = \frac{m}{2(m + M)} F.$$

With the given numerical values

$$F_{f_1} = \frac{12\,\mathrm{N} \cdot 1\,\mathrm{kg}}{2(1\,\mathrm{kg} + 3\,\mathrm{kg})} = 1.5\,\mathrm{N}.$$

So for the minimum coefficient of friction between the rod and the cylinders

$$\mu_{\min} = \frac{F_{f_1}}{N_{\min}} = \frac{F_{f_1}}{Mg/4} = \frac{4F_{f_1}}{Mg} = \frac{2m}{m+M} \cdot \frac{F}{Mg} = \frac{6}{30} = 0.2,$$

if $g \approx 10 \dfrac{\text{m}}{\text{s}^2}$ is used.

Based on relationship $v = \sqrt{2as}$, the final speed of the rod is

$$v = \sqrt{2\frac{F}{m+M} \cdot 2\frac{L}{3}} = \sqrt{2 \cdot 3\frac{\text{m}}{\text{s}^2} \cdot 2 \cdot \frac{3\,\text{m}}{3}} = 3.46\frac{\text{m}}{\text{s}}.$$

Solution of Problem 32. Since the brick slips on the cart, the net force acting on it is the kinetic friction: $S = \mu mg$. Therefore the brick has an acceleration of $a_1 = \mu g$ whose direction is the same as that of the acceleration of the cart. The next step is to determine the acceleration of the cart. Let us apply Newton's second law to the object that pulls the cart and to the cart itself. Let the masses of the object and cart be m_2 and m_3 respectively.

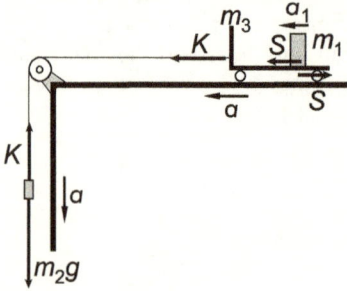

$$m_2 g - K = m_2 a,$$

$$K - \mu m_1 g = m_3 a.$$

If we add the two equations, K (which is the tension in the cord) cancels out, thus the acceleration of the cart (and of the object) turns out to be:

$$a = \frac{m_2 - \mu m_1}{m_2 + m_3} \cdot g.$$

Quite interestingly, the brick is assumed to be pointlike in the problem, therefore the difference in the distances covered by the cart and brick is the length of the cart ($l = 0.4\,\text{m}$):

$$\frac{1}{2}at^2 - \frac{1}{2}a_1 t^2 = l,$$

thus

$$\frac{1}{2} \cdot \frac{m_2 - \mu m_1}{m_2 + m_3} \cdot gt^2 - \frac{1}{2}\mu gt^2 = l.$$

Hence the coefficient of the kinetic friction between the brick and cart is:

$$\mu = \frac{m_2 gt^2 - 2l(m_2 + m_3)}{(m_1 + m_2 + m_3)gt^2} = \frac{5 \cdot 10 \cdot 0.64 - 2 \cdot 0.4 \cdot (5+3)}{(2+5+3) \cdot 10 \cdot 0.64} = 0.4.$$

Solution of Problem 33. Newton's second law applied to the small sphere gives:

$$mg - K = ma, \qquad (1)$$

where K is the magnitude of the normal forces exerted by the spheres on each other. Using the notion that the accelerations of the spheres are the same, and applying Newton's second law to the hollow sphere, we obtain:

$$Mg + K - kv^2 = Ma. \qquad (2)$$

Let us add equations (1) and (2) to determine the acceleration of the objects:

$$(m+M)g - kv^2 = (m+M)a,$$

hence

$$a = g - \frac{kv^2}{m+M}. \qquad (3)$$

Inserting this into equation (1) and solving for the required normal force, we get:

$$K = m(g-a) = m\left(g - g + \frac{kv^2}{m+M}\right) = \frac{m}{m+M}kv^2 =$$

$$= \frac{m}{m+m}kv^2 = \frac{1}{2}kv^2 = \frac{1}{2}\cdot 0.1\,\frac{\text{N}}{\text{m}^2\text{s}^2}\cdot v^2.$$

The function of force versus velocity is therefore a parabola. At the moment when the spheres are dropped, the velocity and air-drag are zero, meaning that the spheres are in free-fall (which is a state of weightlessness), and that the normal force K is also zero. During their fall the spheres accelerate causing their velocity and air-drag (which is opposite from their velocity) to accelerate as well. This, in turn, causes their acceleration to decrease. After a while they reach the terminal velocity (assuming constant air density and constant gravitational force) at which the resultant force is zero. Since the gravitational force acting on the system is equal to the air-drag:

$$(m+M)g = kv_{\text{max}}^2,$$

thus

$$v_{\text{max}} = \sqrt{\frac{m+M}{k}}\,g = \sqrt{\frac{m+m}{k}}\,g = \sqrt{\frac{8\,\text{kg} + 8\,\text{kg}}{0.1\,\frac{\text{N}}{\text{m}^2\,\text{s}^{-2}}}\cdot 10\,\frac{\text{m}}{\text{s}^2}} = 40\,\frac{\text{m}}{\text{s}}.$$

At that velocity the magnitude of the normal force is:

$$K_{\text{max}} = mg = 80\,\text{N}.$$

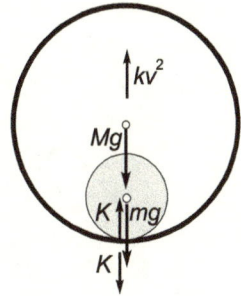

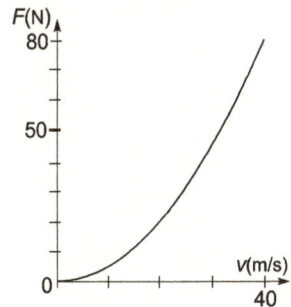

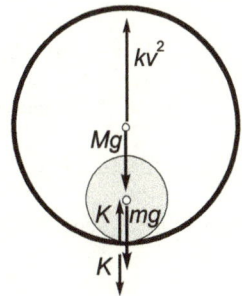

113

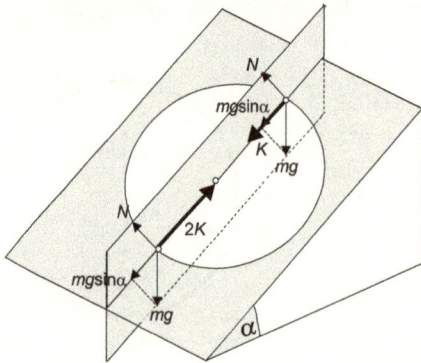

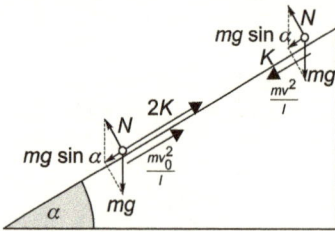

Solution of Problem 34. a) The equation of the motion of the small body in the bottom and top positions, considering the relationship between the tensions and the resultant of the normal force N exerted by the surface and the gravitational force mg (and replacing l by R), is:

$$2K - mg \cdot \sin\alpha = m\frac{v_0^2}{R},$$

and

$$mg \cdot \sin\alpha + K = m\frac{v^2}{R},$$

from which, by eliminating the tensions in the bottom and top positions, the following equation is acquired:

$$mg \cdot \sin\alpha + \frac{mv_0^2}{R} = 2 \cdot \left(\frac{mv^2}{R} - mg \cdot \sin\alpha\right).$$

Reorganizing:

$$3mg \cdot \sin\alpha - 2\frac{mv^2}{R} = -\frac{mv_0^2}{R},$$

from which

$$v_0 = \sqrt{2v^2 - 3gR \cdot \sin\alpha} = \sqrt{2 \cdot 9\frac{\text{m}^2}{\text{s}^2} - 3 \cdot 9.81\frac{\text{m}}{\text{s}^2} \cdot 0.2\,\text{m} \cdot 0.5} = 3.88\frac{\text{m}}{\text{s}}.$$

b) The work–kinetic energy theorem for the original and final states is

$$W_{\text{grav}} + W_{\text{f}} = \Delta E_{\text{kin}}, \quad \text{that is,} \quad -mg\,2R \cdot \sin\alpha - \mu mgR\pi \cdot \cos\alpha = \frac{1}{2}mv^2 - \frac{1}{2}mv_0^2.$$

From this the coefficient of friction is

$$\mu = \frac{v_0^2 - v^2}{2gR \cdot \pi\cos\alpha} - \frac{2}{\pi}\tan\alpha,$$

with numerical values

$$\mu = \frac{3.88^2 - 3^2}{2 \cdot 0.2 \cdot \pi \cdot 9.81 \cdot \cos 30°} - \frac{2}{\pi}\tan 30° = 0.1995 \approx 0.2.$$

c) After releasing the string, the body moves upwards on the slope along a straight line and covers distance x. Applying the work–kinetic energy theorem again for the initial and final states:

$$-mg(R+x)\sin\alpha - \mu\,mg \cdot \left(\frac{5}{2}R\pi + x\right)\cos\alpha = 0 - \frac{1}{2}mv_0^2.$$

From this

$$x = \frac{v_0^2 - (5\pi\mu\cos\alpha + 2\sin\alpha)Rg}{2(\sin\alpha + \mu\cos\alpha)g} =$$

$$= \frac{3.88^2 - (5\pi\cdot 0.2\cdot\cos 30° + 2\cdot\sin 30°)\cdot 0.2\cdot 9.81}{2\,(\sin 30° + 0.2\cos 30°)\cdot 9.81}\,\mathrm{m} \approx 0.59\,\mathrm{m}.$$

(Those who calculated with $g = 10\,\mathrm{m/s^2}$, acquired $v_0 = 3.87\,\mathrm{m/s}$ for the initial velocity, $\mu = 0.18$ for the coefficient of friction and $x = 0.62$ metres for the distance covered.)

Solution of Problem 35. Assume the ball is a pointmass as suggested by the figure. According to the work-energy theorem, the kinetic energy of the ball in point A equals the sum of the work done by the gravitational force and the spring:

$$mgs + \frac{1}{2}D(\Delta l)^2 = \frac{1}{2}mv^2,$$

where $\Delta l = x - L$, x and L are the extended and relaxed lengths of the spring. We used the notion that in its vertical position the spring will reach its relaxed length. Length x is provided by the Pythagorean theorem:

$$x = \sqrt{\overline{OC}^2 - \overline{OB}^2} = \sqrt{0.8\,\mathrm{m}^2 - 0.48\,\mathrm{m}^2} = \sqrt{0.4096\,\mathrm{m}^2} = 0.64\,\mathrm{m}.$$

The vertical displacement of the ball is $s = OA - OB = 0.8\,\mathrm{m} - 0.48\,\mathrm{m} = 0.32\,\mathrm{m}$. Using this, the speed turns out to be:

$$v = \sqrt{2gs + \frac{D}{m}(x - L)^2},$$

substituting known values, we find:

$$v = \sqrt{2\cdot 10\,\frac{\mathrm{m}}{\mathrm{s}^2}\cdot 0.32\,\mathrm{m} + \frac{75\,\mathrm{N/m}}{3.2\,\mathrm{kg}}(0.64\,\mathrm{m} - 0.32\,\mathrm{m})^2} = 2.97\,\frac{\mathrm{m}}{\mathrm{s}}.$$

Let us now determine the force exerted on the shell by the ball. At point A the only forces acting on the ball are the gravitational and normal forces, since the spring is in its relaxed state at that moment. Applying Newton's second law to the ball at that point, we obtain:

$$\vec{K} + \vec{G} = m\vec{a},$$

With the positive direction pointing upwards, we have:

$$K - mg = m\frac{v^2}{r},$$

from which the normal force (K) is:

$$K = mg + m\frac{v^2}{r} = 3.2\,\mathrm{kg}\cdot 10\,\frac{\mathrm{m}}{\mathrm{s}^2} + 3.2\,\mathrm{kg}\cdot\frac{2.97^2\,\mathrm{m}^2/\mathrm{s}^2}{0.8\,\mathrm{m}} = 67.3\,\mathrm{N}.$$

This is the same as the magnitude of the force exerted by the ball on the shell, since it and the normal force are both action-reaction forces.

Solution of Problem 36.

The equation of motion of the toy car in the direction of the relevant radius is

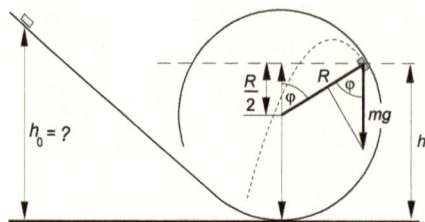

$$mg\cos\varphi + N = m\frac{v^2}{R}.$$

At the moment of detaching $N = 0$, and according to the data given in the problem, for the cosine of angle φ

$$\cos\varphi = \frac{R/2}{R} = 0.5,$$

that is, $\varphi = 60°$.

At the moment when the normal force N ceases, the equation of motion of the toy car in the radial direction is

$$mg\cos\varphi = m\frac{v^2}{R}. \tag{1}$$

From this, the remaining speed of the toy car at the moment of detaching is:

$$v^2 = Rg\cos\varphi. \tag{2}$$

From this position an oblique projection with this initial velocity and an initial angle of $\alpha = \varphi = 60°$ starts.

a) The height of the place the car starts from can be acquired from the work–kinetic energy theorem:

$$mg(h_0 - h) = \frac{1}{2}mv^2. \tag{3}$$

Substituting (2) into (3) gives $mg(h_0 - h) = \frac{1}{2}mgR\cos\varphi$.

From this

$$h_0 = h + \frac{1}{2}R\cos\varphi = \frac{3}{2}R + \frac{1}{2}R\cos\varphi = \frac{R}{2}(3 + \cos\varphi) = 1.75R = 56 \text{ cm}.$$

b) The maximum height is acquired if the maximum height y_{max} of the oblique projection is added to height h where the car detaches from the track:

$$h_{max} = h + y_{max} = h + \frac{v^2\sin^2\varphi}{2g} = \frac{3}{2}R + \frac{Rg\cos\varphi\cdot\sin^2\varphi}{2g} =$$

$$= \frac{R}{2}\left(3 + \frac{\sin\varphi\cdot\sin 2\varphi}{2}\right) = \frac{32}{2}\left(3 + \frac{1}{2}\cdot\frac{\sqrt{3}}{2}\cdot\frac{\sqrt{3}}{2}\right) \text{ cm} = 54 \text{ cm}.$$

In short: the toy car starts from height $h_0 = 56$ cm, detaches from the track at height $h = 48$ cm and reaches a maximum height $h_{\max} = 54$ cm. (The total height of the track is 64 cm.)

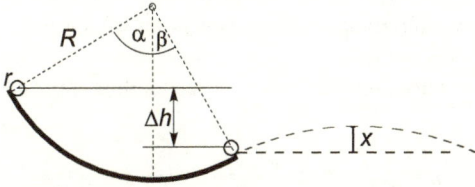

Solution of Problem 37. The centre of mass of the wheel undergoes projectile motion after leaving the ramp. Although it isn't stated clearly in the problem, x is the maximum height reached by the wheel measured from the right end of the ramp.

The direction of the wheel's velocity at the right end of the ramp forms an angle β with the horizontal. The maximum height reached by a projectile is given by the formula:

$$x = \frac{v_0^2 \sin^2 \beta}{2g},$$

where v_0 is the speed of the wheel's centre of mass at the right end of the ramp. Let us determine this speed. According to the work-kinetic energy theorem:

$$mg[(R-r)(1-\cos\alpha) - (R-r)(1-\cos\beta)] = \frac{1}{2}mv_0^2 + \frac{1}{2}mr^2\omega^2 = mv_0^2,$$

where r is the radius of the wheel, ω is the angular velocity of the wheel when leaving the ramp, which is $\omega = v_0/r$. Thus

$$\Delta h = (R-r)[(1-\cos\alpha) - (1-\cos\beta)] = \frac{v_0^2}{g},$$

and

$$\frac{v_0^2}{g} = (R-r)[1-\cos\alpha - 1 + \cos\beta] = (R-r)(\cos\beta - \cos\alpha).$$

Substituting this into the formula for x, we have:

$$x = \frac{1}{2}\sin^2\beta(\cos\beta - \cos\alpha)(R-r).$$

It can be seen that the answer depends on the radius of the wheel, which is not given. Let us therefore assume that the radius of the small wheel is small enough relative to R to be neglected, i.e. $r \ll R$. In that case our formula for x simplifies to:

$$x = \frac{1}{2}\sin^2\beta(\cos\beta - \cos\alpha)R,$$

inserting given data, we obtain

$$x = \frac{1}{2} \cdot \sin^2 30°(\cos 30° - \cos 60°) \cdot 1\,\text{m} =$$
$$= 0.5 \cdot 0.25 \cdot (0.866 - 0.5) \cdot 1\,\text{m} = 0.04575\,\text{m} \approx 4.58\,\text{cm}.$$

Solution of Problem 38. a) The equation of the motion of the car is

$$mg - N = m\frac{v^2}{\varrho},$$

where N is the normal force (its magnitude is equal to the unknown force exerted on the bridge) and ϱ is the radius of curvature belonging to the given point of the path. The essence of the problem is determining this value.

The relationship between the radius of curvature and the corresponding normal acceleration is:

$$a_n = \frac{v^2}{\varrho}.$$

In our case neither normal acceleration nor the radius of curvature is known. Luckily, in a simple case we can determine these values through elementary considerations. The parabola of oblique projectile motion comes in handy, it can be used to model the arc of the bridge and therefore its curvature as well. All we need to do, is find the angle and the initial velocity with which a thrown stone follows the longitudinal sectional line of the bridge. In the case of a thrown stone normal acceleration can be determined easily, and therefore if the stone is launched suitably, the radius of the curvature of our bridge will be in our grip. Let us determine the radius this way:
the range of the projectile motion is the same as the span of the bridge (d):

$$d = \frac{v_0^2 \sin 2\alpha}{g} = \frac{2v_0^2 \sin\alpha\cos\alpha}{g},$$

and the height of the projectile motion is the same as the height of the highest point of the bridge relative to the level of the banks:

$$h = \frac{v_0^2 \sin^2\alpha}{2g}.$$

The ratio of the two is

$$\frac{4\cos\alpha}{\sin\alpha} = \frac{d}{h},$$

from which

$$\tan\alpha = \frac{4h}{d} = 0.2 \quad \rightarrow \quad \alpha = \arctan 0.2 = 11.31°.$$

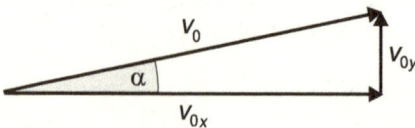

The vertical component of the initial velocity of the stone is

$$v_{0_y} = \sqrt{2gh} = 10\ \frac{m}{s},$$

and the horizontal component of the velocity is

$$v_{0_x} = \frac{v_{0_y}}{\tan\alpha} = \frac{10}{0.2}\frac{m}{s} = 50\ \frac{m}{s}.$$

Because at the highest point of the path the velocity of the stone is horizontal, its normal acceleration is the same as acceleration itself (which is g throughout the motion), therefore

$$a_n = g = \frac{v_x^2}{\varrho} \quad \rightarrow \quad \varrho = \frac{v_x^2}{g} = 250\,\text{m}.$$

With this the unknown normal force is

$$N = m\left(g - \frac{v_{\text{car}}^2}{\varrho}\right) = 1000\,\text{kg}\left(10 - \frac{400}{250}\right)\frac{\text{m}}{\text{s}^2} = 8400\,\text{N}.$$

b) The radius of curvature at the parabola point that belongs to 3/4 of the horizontal distance can be determined from the fact that the horizontal velocity component of the thrown stone is constant, therefore 3/4 of the time of the projectile flight belongs to 3/4 of the horizontal distance:

$$t_1 = \frac{3}{4}t_{\text{proj}} = \frac{3}{4}\cdot\frac{2v_0\sin\alpha}{g} = \frac{3}{2}\frac{v_0\sin\alpha}{g}.$$

The normal acceleration of the stone at this point of the path is

$$a_n = g\cos\varphi = \frac{v_1^2}{\varrho_1},$$

and according to the figure, the radius of curvature belonging to this point is

$$\varrho_1 = \frac{v_1^2}{g\cos\varphi} = \frac{v_1^2}{g\cdot\frac{v_x}{v_1}} = \frac{v_1^3}{gv_x},$$

where v_1 is the instantaneous velocity of the stone at the point in concern at time instant t_1. The time in concern is

$$t_1 = \frac{x_1}{v_x} = \frac{3}{4}\frac{d}{v_x} = \frac{300\,\text{m}}{4\cdot 50\,\text{m/s}} = \frac{3}{2}\,\text{s}.$$

With this, the square of the velocity of the stone at the point in concern is

$$v_1^2 = v_x^2 + v_y^2 = v_0^2\cos^2\alpha + (v_0\sin\alpha - gt_1)^2 =$$

$$= [50^2 + (10-15)^2]\frac{\text{m}^2}{\text{s}^2} = 2525\,\frac{\text{m}^2}{\text{s}^2},$$

and its instantaneous velocity is

$$v_1 = \sqrt{2525}\,\text{m/s} \approx 50.25\,\text{m/s}.$$

Therefore, the unknown radius of curvature is

$$\varrho_1 = \frac{v_1^3}{gv_x} = \frac{50.25^3}{10\cdot 50}\,\text{m} = 253.77\,\text{m} \approx 254\,\text{m}.$$

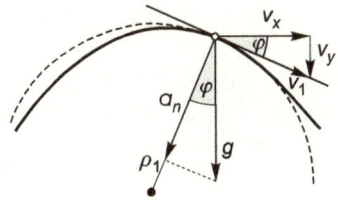

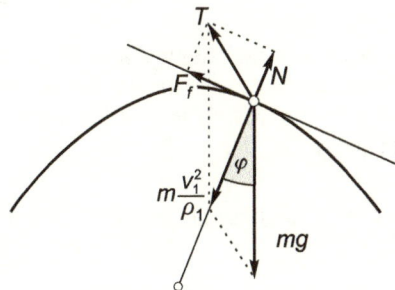

With these, the equation of the motion of the car can already be determined. Let us take into consideration that the car moves at uniform velocity throughout its motion, therefore it has only normal acceleration. The relationship between gravitational force mg, the so-called supporting force T, the normal force N and the static frictional force F_f is shown in the figure. From this, force T (which is the reaction to the force exerted on the bridge by the car) can be determined immediately using the cosine rule:

$$T = \sqrt{(mg)^2 + \left(m\frac{v_1^2}{\varrho}\right) - 2mg \cdot m\frac{v_1^2}{\varrho}\cos\varphi} = m\sqrt{g^2 + \frac{v_1^4}{\varrho^2} - 2\frac{v_1^2}{\varrho}g\cos\varphi} =$$

$$= 1000 \text{ kg}\sqrt{100 + \frac{160000}{254^2} - 2\cdot\frac{400}{254}\cdot10\cdot0.995} = 8434.47 \text{ N}.$$

If only the normal force exerted by the car is to be found, then the absolute value of N should be determined. This is acquired from the equation of the motion of the car in the normal direction:

$$mg\cos\varphi - N = m\frac{v_{car}^2}{\varrho_1},$$

where $\cos\varphi = v_x/v_1 = 50/50.25 = 0.9950$. From this

$$N = m\left(g\cos\varphi - \frac{v_{car}^2}{\varrho_1}\right) = 1000\left(10\cdot0.995 - \frac{400}{254}\right) \text{ N} = 8375.2 \text{ N}.$$

The resultant force of the static frictional forces that act on the tyres is acquired from the equation of the motion in the tangential direction. Taking into consideration that the car moves uniformly: $S - mg\sin\varphi = 0$, so

$$S = mg\sin\varphi = mg\sqrt{1 - \cos^2\varphi}.$$

Therefore the magnitude of the frictional force is

$$F_f = 1000 \text{ kg}\cdot10\frac{\text{m}}{\text{s}^2}\cdot\sqrt{1 - 0.995^2} = 998.75 \text{ N},$$

and obviously

$$T = \sqrt{8375.2^2 + 998.75^2} = 8434.5 \text{ N}.$$

First solution of Problem 39. a) Let K be the force exerted by the rod and let F be the tension in the thread. At the vertical position of the thread the velocity of the ball A is maximal, thus its acceleration is zero, $ma_A = 0$, so the equation of motion at that instant is:

$$K - mg - F = 0. \tag{1}$$

At the same time the equation of motion of the ball B is:

$$F - mg = ma_B, \tag{2}$$

and the energy conservation law gives the equation:

$$mgL = 2\cdot\frac{1}{2}mv_B^2 = mv_B^2. \tag{3}$$

(Here we have used the fact that $v_A = -v_B$ since the centre of mass moves along a vertical line, and the velocity of ball B is horizontal at the moment investigated.)

From this equation the velocities of the balls can be determined. From equation (3) the velocities of the balls are:

$$v_A = \sqrt{gL} = 4 \,\frac{\mathrm{m}}{\mathrm{s}}, \quad \text{and} \quad v_B = -v_A = -4 \,\frac{\mathrm{m}}{\mathrm{s}}.$$

Since $ma_A = 0$ the x component of the acceleration of the ball B is zero, while its total acceleration is the centripetal acceleration

$$a_B = \frac{v_B^2}{\varrho}, \tag{4}$$

where ϱ is the radius of curvature of the ball's trajectory at the lowest point. But this acceleration can be determined in a different way as well.

At this instant, the acceleration of the ball A is zero, and the masses of the balls are equal. Thus, the acceleration of the centre of mass is the average of the acceleration of the balls:

$$a_C = \frac{m \cdot 0 + m a_B}{m + m} = \frac{a_B}{2} \;\rightarrow\; a_B = 2a_C. \tag{5}$$

On the other hand, at this instant, the velocity of the centre of mass is $v_S = 0$ since the two balls of equal masses move at opposite velocities. This means that the centre of mass C is the instantaneous centre of rotation and that the angular speed of the thread is:

$$\omega = \frac{v_B}{\frac{L}{2}} = \frac{2v_B}{L}. \tag{6}$$

Since the centre of mass S accelerates upwards, the acceleration of the ball B is the sum of its acceleration relative to S and the acceleration of S. Using (5), we get:

$$a_B = a_C + a_{\mathrm{rel}} = a_C + \frac{L}{2}\omega^2 = \frac{a_B}{2} + \frac{L}{2}\omega^2.$$

Thus the acceleration of the ball B, calculated in the second way, is:

$$a_B = L\omega^2 = \frac{4v_A^2}{L}. \tag{7}$$

The accelerations (4) and (7), determined in the two different ways, are equal:

$$\frac{v_B^2}{\varrho} = \frac{4v_B^2}{L},$$

which gives the value of the radius of curvature:

$$\varrho = \frac{L}{4} = 0.4 \text{ m}.$$

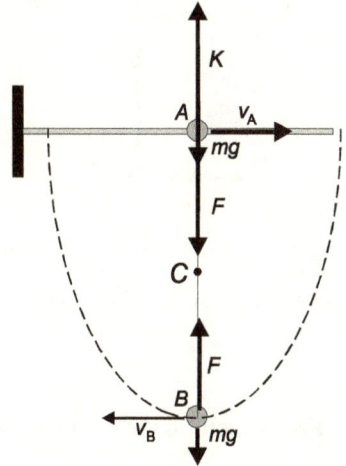

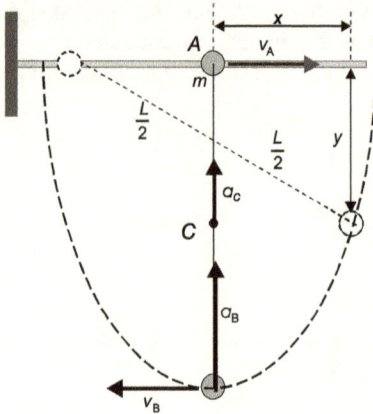

Summarizing, the accelerations of the two balls are:

$$a_A = 0,$$

and

$$a_B = \frac{v_B^2}{\varrho} = \frac{16 \text{ ms}^{-2}}{0.4 \text{ m}} = 40 \ \frac{\text{m}}{\text{s}^2},$$

(or in parametric form:

$$a_B = \frac{v_B^2}{\varrho} = \frac{gL}{\frac{L}{4}} = 4g.)$$

b) From equation (2) the tension in the thread is:

$$F = m(g + a_B) = 2 \text{ kg} \left(10 \ \frac{\text{m}}{\text{s}^2} + 40 \ \frac{\text{m}}{\text{s}^2} \right) = 100 \text{ N},$$

and from equation (1) the force exerted by the rod is:

$$K = mg + F = 20 \text{ N} + 100 \text{ N} = 120 \text{ N}.$$

Second solution of Problem 39. One may know that the trajectory of the ball B is an elliptic arc, and the radius of curvature at the endpoint of its major axis is $\varrho = \dfrac{b^2}{a}$, where a is the semimajor axis, and b is the semiminor axis, which are in our present case $a = L$ and $b = L/2$. Using these equations the radius of curvature can be determined immediately:

$$\varrho = \frac{\frac{L^2}{4}}{L} = \frac{L}{4}.$$

With this knowledge, the acceleration can be calculated directly from equation (4), while the other results can be obtained using the same way as before.

Third solution of Problem 39. Part a) of the problem can be solved in a shorter way as well. When the thread is vertical, the ball A has zero acceleration, thus the reference frame fixed to the ball is an inertial one. The acceleration of ball B is the same in all inertial reference frames, so we immediately know that:

$$a_B = \frac{v_{\text{rel}}^2}{r} = \frac{(2v_B)^2}{L} = \frac{4v_B^2}{L} = \frac{4 \cdot 4^2 \ \frac{\text{m}^2}{\text{s}^2}}{1.6 \text{ m}} = 40 \ \frac{\text{m}}{\text{s}^2},$$

where v_{rel} is the speed of ball B relative to ball A. In the first solution we saw that at the vertical position of the thread of the velocities of the balls have equal magnitude and opposite directions, due to the equal masses of the balls. It means that v_{rel} is just two times as much as the speed of any of the balls with respect to the ground.

Although it was not required in the problem, we deduced the equation of the orbit of the ball B. Because of the similarity of the two right triangles in the figure:

$$\frac{x}{\frac{L}{2}} = \frac{\sqrt{L^2 - y^2}}{L}$$

from which:

$$4x^2 + y^2 = L^2,$$

follows, which can also be written in the form

$$\frac{4x^2}{L^2} + \frac{y^2}{L^2} = 1, \quad \text{or} \quad \frac{x^2}{(L/2)^2} + \frac{y^2}{L^2} = 1.$$

This means that the orbit is an ellipse with semimajor axis $a = L/2$ and semiminor axis $b = L$:

$$\frac{4x^2}{L^2} + \frac{y^2}{L^2} = 1, \quad \text{or} \quad \frac{x^2}{(0.8 \text{ m})^2} + \frac{y^2}{(1.6 \text{ m})^2} = 1.$$

Solution of Problem 40. First, let us examine whether or not the marble can roll along the path at all (assuming that it rolls without sliding). In order for it to do this, it is necessary that the speed of its centre of mass at the top of the circular path exceeds the critical speed v_{crit} for which:

$$mg + K = ma_n = m\frac{v^2}{R - r},$$

where the normal reaction K becomes zero, making the value of the critical speed:

$$v_{\text{crit}} = \sqrt{(R - r)g}$$

In order to answer this, we have to apply the work-energy theorem:

$$mg[3R - (2R - r)] = \frac{1}{2}mv^2 + \frac{1}{2} \cdot \frac{2}{5}mr^2\omega^2,$$

from this we can express the speed, using the work-energy theorem, because the marble rolls without sliding $r\omega = v$, thus:

$$v^2 = \frac{10}{7}g(R + r) > (R - r)g = v_{\text{crit}}^2,$$

which is definitely greater than the critical speed, meaning that even at the topmost point the normal reaction is not zero.

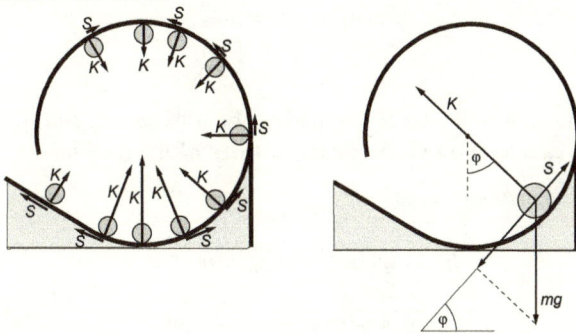

From now on, let us neglect r with respect to R since their ratio is $r/R = 0.005$. There are three forces exerted on the marble: the gravitational force, the frictional force and the normal reaction. The first one is constant. The second one is opposite to the direction of the motion until the marble reaches the bottom of the path. The third one is constant on the slope and along the circular part it decreases, until it reaches zero at the lowest point. Then, when the marble moves up, it increases for a while and its direction becomes the same as the direction of the motion, however, it then decreases again until it becomes zero at the top of the path. Then, once again, its direction changes. The normal reaction is always perpendicular to the path, along the slope it is constant, its maximum is at the bottom of the circular path and then it monotonic decreases until the top of the path. The frictional coefficient in question ensures that the rolling marble does not slide, and depends on the latter two forces. In depends on these two forces because the frictional force, which causes the appropriate angular acceleration β and which depends on the position of the marble, can be calculated as the product of the normal reaction and the minimum of the frictional coefficient. As a result, we have to determine the normal reaction K as a function of the position of the marble, the frictional force S and the maximum of their ratio.

$$\mu_{min} = \left[\frac{S}{K} \right]_{max},$$

because the coefficient of friction can be greater than this, but not smaller. This means that the maximum of the ratio S/K is the lower limit of the frictional coefficient.

It is worth examining the motion which occurs until the top of the path since it is there that the translational motion is the reverse of the upward translational motion of the marble (although the rotational motion is not). As a result, the asked frictional coefficients are the same at the same height.

Let us describe the motion of the marble in terms of the angle φ enclosed by the vertical and the radius connecting the centre of the circle and the marble. By applying Newton's second law, the frictional force can be calculated from the radial components, while the normal reaction can be calculated from the tangential components. This can also be done by using the equation written for the rotational motion and the work-energy theorem.

For the tangential components:

$$mg\sin\varphi - S = ma_t, \tag{1}$$

and

$$Sr = \Theta\beta = \Theta\frac{a_t}{r}, \tag{2}$$

where Θ is the moment of inertia of the marble about its centre, and a_t is the tangential component of the acceleration of the centre of mass of the marble.

For the radial components:

$$K - mg\cos\varphi = ma_n = m\frac{v^2}{R}, \tag{3}$$

and

$$mg\Delta h = \frac{1}{2}mv^2 + \frac{1}{2}\Theta\omega^2. \tag{4}$$

Here Δh is the height difference which equals $h - R + R\cos\varphi$, and ω^2 is equal to v^2/r^2. Using these

$$2mg(h - R + R\cos\varphi) = \frac{mr^2 + \Theta}{r^2}v^2. \tag{4'}$$

From equation (2)

$$a_t = \frac{Sr^2}{\Theta},$$

which can be written into equation (1) and we gain $mg\sin\varphi - S = m\dfrac{Sr^2}{\Theta}$ from which the frictional force is:

$$S = mg\sin\varphi \cdot \frac{\Theta}{\Theta + mr^2}.$$

From equation $(4')$

$$v^2 = 2g(h - R + R\cos\varphi) \cdot \frac{mr^2}{\Theta + mr^2},$$

which can be written into equation (3) and the normal reaction is:

$$K = mg\left[2\left(\frac{h}{R} - 1\right) \cdot \frac{mr^2}{\Theta + mr^2} + \frac{\Theta + 3mr^2}{\Theta + mr^2} \cdot \cos\varphi\right]$$

the necessary frictional coefficient is:

$$\mu = \frac{S}{K} = \frac{mg\sin\varphi\frac{\Theta}{\Theta + mr^2}}{mg\left[2\left(\frac{h}{R} - 1\right)\frac{mr^2}{\Theta + mr^2} + \frac{\Theta + 3mr^2}{\Theta + mr^2}\cos\varphi\right]} =$$

$$= \frac{\sin\varphi}{2\left(\frac{h}{R} - 1\right)\frac{mr^2}{\Theta} + \left(1 + \frac{3mr^2}{\Theta}\right)\cos\varphi}.$$

The maximum of the above function has to be determined. The approximate value of the maximum can be gained by plotting the graph, or from the derivative of the function a more punctual value can be calculated quite easily. Denoting the constants by A and B the function can be written in this form:

$$\mu = \frac{\sin\varphi}{A + B\cos\varphi}.$$

Let the numerator of the function be u and the denominator be v and apply the quotient rule. Thus the derivative is:

$$\left(\frac{u}{v}\right)' = \frac{u'v - uv'}{v^2} = \frac{\cos\varphi(A + B\cos\varphi) - \sin\varphi(-B\sin\varphi)}{(A + B\cos\varphi)^2}.$$

The function may have a maximum (or minimum) where the derivative is zero, thus the following equation must be solved:

$$A\cos\varphi + B\cos^2\varphi + B\sin^2\varphi = 0$$

Because
$$\sin^2 \varphi + \cos^2 \varphi = 1,$$
our equation can be simplified to the following form:
$$A \cos \varphi + B = 0$$
Its solution is:
$$\cos \varphi = -\frac{B}{A} = -\frac{3 + \frac{\Theta}{mr^2}}{2\left(\frac{h}{R} - 1\right)}.$$

(The second derivative shows that this is a maximum. The second derivative here is negative, which means that the first derivative changes from a positive to a negative, meaning the function first increases, and then decreases.)

The value of the asked frictional coefficient, with parameters and substituting $\cos \varphi$, can be expressed as:
$$\mu_{\min} = \frac{\Theta}{\sqrt{4(mr^2)^2 \left(\frac{h}{R} - 1\right)^2 - (\Theta + 3mr^2)^2}}.$$

Using that $\dfrac{h}{R} = 3$, and $\Theta = \dfrac{2}{5}mr^2$,
$$\mu = \frac{\frac{2}{5}mr^2}{\sqrt{4(mr^2)^2(2)^2 - \left(\frac{2}{5}mr^2 + 3mr^2\right)^2}} = \frac{2}{\sqrt{111}} = 0.1898 \approx 0.19.$$

Or, determining the value of $\cos \varphi$: $\cos \varphi = -\dfrac{3 + \frac{2mr^2/5}{mr^2}}{2(3-1)} = -0.85$, from which $\varphi = 148.2°$.

the frictional coefficient from the expression which contains the angle is:
$$\mu = \frac{\sin \varphi}{10 + 8.5 \cos \varphi} = \frac{0.527}{10 + 8.5 \cdot (-0.85)} = 0.1899 \approx 0.19.$$

It was expected to gain quite a large angle φ, greater than 90 degrees, at which point the frictional force has to take its maximum value. The gravitational force is away from the path and the normal reaction points towards the centre of the circular path causing the normal force to decrease quickly. On the other hand, because of the tangential acceleration (deceleration) of the marble, the angular acceleration demands quite a large frictional force which can be created only if there is a high frictional coefficient and if the normal reaction is small. The gained frictional coefficient is large enough to keep the marble rolling without slipping on the straight part of the path, since there the minimum frictional coefficient is $\mu_{\min} = 2\tan\alpha = 0.165$ which is smaller than the minimum frictional coefficient that we gained for the circular part of the path.

Solution of Problem 41. a) The speed of the ball is changed by the force components of the forces acting on it that are parallel with the track, so the speed can be maximum only where their sum is zero. Only gravitational force and spring force may have components parallel with the track (as the ball slides without friction, the force exerted by the track is perpendicular to the track), so at the place where speed has a maximum, the absolute values of the parallel components of gravitational force and spring force are equal:

$$F_{\text{spring}} \cos \delta = mg \cos \beta.$$

From this equation the mass of the ball can be determined if spring force and angle δ are known. The former can be determined from the elongation of the spring, the latter from the geometrical data of the arrangement. At the place where velocity is maximum, the length of the spring can be determined using the Pythagorean theorem:

$$l_2 = \sqrt{(R - R\sin\beta)^2 + (2R - R\cos\beta)^2} = R\sqrt{(1 - \sin\beta)^2 + (2 - \cos\beta)^2} =$$

$$= R\sqrt{6 - 2\sin\beta - 4\cos\beta} = 0.2\,\text{m}\sqrt{6 - 2\sin 34° - 4\cos 34°} = 25.02\,\text{cm}.$$

The elongation of the spring is

$$\Delta l_2 = l_2 - l_0 = 25.02\,\text{cm} - 20\,\text{cm} = 5.02\,\text{cm},$$

with it, the magnitude of spring force is

$$F_{\text{spring}} = R\Delta l = 100\frac{\text{N}}{\text{m}} \cdot 5.02\,\text{cm} = 5.02\,\text{N}.$$

Angle δ can be determined from angle γ shown in the figure:

$$\cos\gamma = \frac{R(1 - \sin\beta)}{l_2} = \frac{0.2\,\text{m} \cdot (1 - \sin 34°)}{0.25\,\text{m}} =$$

$$= 0.3523.$$

From this, $\gamma = 69.4°$, so

$$\delta = 180° - (\beta + \gamma) = 180° - (34° + 69.4°) = 76.6°.$$

With these the mass of the ball is

$$m = \frac{F_{\text{spring}} \cos\delta}{g \cos\beta} = \frac{5\,\text{N} \cdot \cos 76.6°}{9.81\frac{\text{N}}{\text{kg}} \cdot \cos 34°} = 143\,\text{g}.$$

b) The maximum speed of the ball can be determined from the work-kinetic energy theorem. The work done by the force exerted by the track is zero (because it is perpendicular to the track and therefore to velocity at any time), the kinetic energy of the ball is given by the work of the gravitational force and of the spring force:

$$mg(h_1 - h_2) + \frac{1}{2}k \cdot \left[(\Delta l_2)^2 - (\Delta l_1)^2 \right] = \frac{1}{2}mv^2.$$

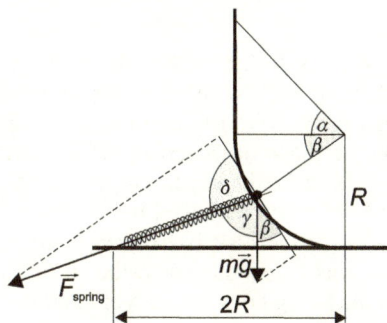

The still unknown data can be determined by using the geometrical data of the arrangement:

$$h_1 = 2R = 40 \, \text{cm}.$$

$$h_2 = R(1 - \sin\beta) = 8.82 \, \text{cm}.$$

$$l_1 = \sqrt{R^2 + (2R)^2} = R\sqrt{5} = 0.2 \, \text{m} \cdot 2.236 = 44.7 \, \text{cm}.$$

From here

$$\Delta l_1 = l_1 - l_0 = 44.7 \, \text{cm} - 20 \, \text{cm} = 24.7 \, \text{cm}.$$
$$\Delta l_2 = l_2 - l_0 = 25.02 \, \text{cm} - 20 \, \text{cm} = 5.02 \, \text{cm}.$$

With these

$$v = \sqrt{2g(h_2 - h_1) + \frac{k}{m}\left[(\Delta l_2)^2 - (\Delta l_1)^2\right]} =$$

$$= \sqrt{2 \cdot 9.81 \frac{\text{N}}{\text{kg}} \cdot (0.4 \, \text{m} - 0.0882 \, \text{m}) + \frac{100 \, \text{N/m}}{0.143 \, \text{kg}}[(0.247 \, \text{m})^2 - (0.0502 \, \text{m})^2]} = 6.86\frac{\text{m}}{\text{s}}.$$

First solution of Problem 42. (Using basic mathematics.) Let us assume that the object is very small to make sure that its rotational inertia is zero. Let us also assume that the action of hitting the disk is determined only by the length of the string and not by the shape of the object. However, the size of the object cannot be zero because that would make the tension in the string increase to infinity, and would subsequently cause the string to break well before the moment of impact.

While the disk is fixed and the string is not stretchable, the velocity of the object remains perpendicular to the string throughout the motion. This means that the tension in the string does not do work and that the speed of the object is constant: $|v| = 0.4 \, \text{m/s}$. All we have to do is simply calculate the distance covered by the object until it hits the disk and then use the formula $t = s/v$ to find the time elapsed until the impact.

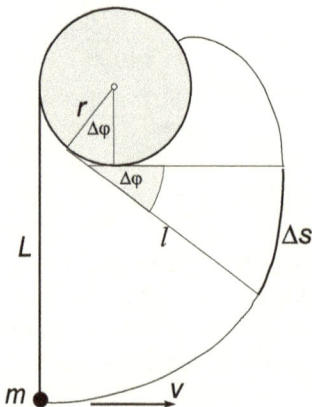

a) Let us consider a small time interval in which the string moves so that the angle enclosed by its initial and final positions is $\Delta\varphi$. The radii drawn to the points where the string touches the disk in its initial and final positions also from angle $\Delta\varphi$ as shown. In the considered time interval part of the string, whose length is $r\Delta\varphi$, gets wrapped around the disk, therefore the length of the unwrapped string decreases by

$$|\Delta l| = r \cdot \Delta\varphi.$$

In this time interval the length of the path of the object is:

$$\Delta s = l \cdot \Delta\varphi.$$

Isolating $\Delta\varphi$ from the first equation and inserting it into the second, we obtain:

$$\Delta s = \frac{l}{r} \cdot \Delta l.$$

The total distance covered by the object is the sum of the length of these path elements:

$$s = \sum_{i=1}^{n} \Delta s_i = \sum_{i=1}^{n} \frac{l}{r} \Delta l = \frac{1}{r} \sum_{i=1}^{n} l \cdot \Delta l = \frac{1}{2r} L^2.$$

This result can be found using that $\Delta l_i = L/n$ and $l = i \cdot L/n$. Thus, the expression inside the sum equals:

$$\sum_{i=1}^{n} i \cdot \frac{L}{n} \cdot \frac{L}{n} = \frac{L^2}{n^2} \sum_{i=1}^{n} i = \frac{L^2}{n^2} \cdot \frac{1+n}{2} \cdot n = L^2 \left(\frac{1}{2n^2} + \frac{1}{2} \right).$$

If n tends to infinity, the expression in the bracket tends to 1/2, therefore the total length of the path tends to:

$$s = \frac{L^2}{2r} = \frac{0.8^2 \, \text{m}^2}{2 \cdot 0.2 \, \text{m}} = 1.6 \, \text{m}.$$

Therefore, the time elapsed until the object hits the disk is:

$$T = \frac{L^2}{2rv} = 4 \, \text{s}.$$

b) The tension in the string provides the centripetal acceleration of the object, thus $F = \frac{mv^2}{l}$, where l is the instantaneous value of the radius of curvature of the object's path. Therefore, we need to find the length of the unwrapped string as a function of time. To do this, let us calculate the sum written in the previous part not for the whole path, but for an arbitrary $l < L$. In that case the distance covered by the object until that point is:

$$s = \frac{1}{r} \cdot \sum_{i=k}^{n} l \cdot \Delta l = \frac{1}{r} \sum_{i=k}^{n} i \cdot \frac{L}{n} \cdot \frac{L}{n} = \frac{L^2}{rn^2} \cdot \sum_{i=k}^{n} i =$$

$$= \frac{L^2}{rn^2} \cdot \left[\frac{(n+k)(n-k+1)}{2} \right] =$$

$$= \frac{L^2}{rn^2} \left[\frac{n^2 + nk - nk - k^2 + k + n}{2} \right] = \frac{L^2}{2r} \left[1 - \frac{k^2}{n^2} + \frac{k}{n^2} + \frac{1}{n} \right].$$

If $n \to \infty$ and $k \to \infty$, then the last two terms in the bracket tend to zero. Note that the second term multiplied by L^2 gives

$$\left(\frac{kL}{n} \right)^2,$$

where $\frac{kL}{n}$ is the unwrapped length of the string, so for the length of the path, we have:

$$s = \frac{1}{2r} (L^2 - l^2).$$

As the end of the string moves at constant speed, we obtain:

$$s = \frac{1}{2r}(L^2 - l^2) = vt,$$

from which the length of the unwrapped string (or the instantaneous radius of curvature) is:

$$l = \sqrt{L^2 - 2rvt}.$$

Therefore the tension in the string as a function of time can be expressed as:

$$F = \frac{mv^2}{l} = \frac{mv^2}{\sqrt{L^2 - 2rvt}} = \frac{0.6\,\text{kg} \cdot 0.4^2\,\frac{\text{m}^2}{\text{s}^2}}{\sqrt{0.8^2\,\text{m}^2 - 2 \cdot 0.2\,\text{m} \cdot 0.4\frac{\text{m}}{\text{s}} \cdot t}} = \frac{0.24\,\text{N}}{\sqrt{4 - 1\,\text{s}^{-1} \cdot t}}.$$

Second solution of Problem 42. (Using higher mathematics.)

Let the infinitesimal angle rotated be $d\varphi$. While rotating through this angle, the length of the string decreases by $r \cdot d\varphi$, so the change in the length of the unwrapped string is negative: $dl = -r \cdot d\varphi$. The length of the infinitesimal part of the path is $ds = l \cdot d\varphi$. Exterminating $d\varphi$ gives:

$$ds = -\frac{l}{r} \cdot dl.$$

The total length of the path is:

$$s = -\int_L^0 \frac{l}{r}\,dl = \frac{L^2}{2r} = 1.6\,\text{m}.$$

Therefore for the time elapsed until the impact, we obtain:

$$T = \frac{L^2}{2rv} = 4\,\text{s}.$$

The instantaneous radius of curvature is l, therefore the tension that provides the centripetal acceleration has magnitude mv^2/l. Let us express l as a function of time. To do this, let the upper limit of integration be l instead of 0 and let the distance covered be $s = vt$:

$$s = -\int_L^l \frac{l}{r}\,dl = \frac{1}{2r}(L^2 - l^2) = vt.$$

From which:

$$l = \sqrt{L^2 - 2rvt}.$$

The force as a function of time is therefore:

$$F = \frac{mv^2}{\sqrt{L^2 - 2rvt}}.$$

Solution of Problem 43. The string remains perpendicular to the instantaneous velocity of the object attached to its end, that is, to the tangent of its trajectory: it is always in the line of the normal to the trajectory. The normal force is provided by the combined action of the string and the force of gravity. At the position of the object where the normal component of the gravitational force alone is able to supply the centripetal force required, the string will become slack. While the free part of the string winding on the semi-cylinder is taut, it remains tangential to the cylindrical surface. Notice that when the string becomes slack, the part that has already wound up on the cylinder is longer than a quarter circle, that is, the object attached to the end has risen higher than the lowermost point of the semi-cylinder. It is only during the rising part of the motion that the force of gravity has a component that can pull the object along the direction of the string (that is, towards the point of suspension).

The position of the small object at the end of the string can be described in terms of the angle α enclosed by the free (straight) part of the string and the horizontal. The same angle is enclosed between the vertical and the radius drawn to the point where the line of the string touches the cylindrical surface. If the x axis of the coordinate frame is attached to the flat horizontal face of the semi-cylinder (in a direction perpendicular to the axis of the cylinder) and the y axis is set vertical, then the y coordinate of the point at the end of the string is

$$y = r \cdot \cos\alpha - s \cdot \sin\alpha. \tag{1}$$

The work-energy theorem can be used to express the instantaneous speed of the object in terms of y:

$$mgy = \frac{1}{2}mv^2.$$

Division by m and the substitution of y from (1) gives the following expression for the square of the speed:

$$v^2 = 2g(r \cdot \cos\alpha - s \cdot \sin\alpha). \tag{2}$$

At the time instant when the string becomes slack, the tension force in the string is zero, and the centripetal force required for moving in an orbit of instantaneous radius of curvature s is provided by the component of the gravitational force in the direction of the string:

$$mg \cdot \sin\alpha = m\frac{v^2}{s}.$$

Hence

$$s \cdot \sin\alpha = v^2/g,$$

and with the use of (2):

$$s \cdot \sin\alpha = 2(r\cos\alpha - s\sin\alpha).$$

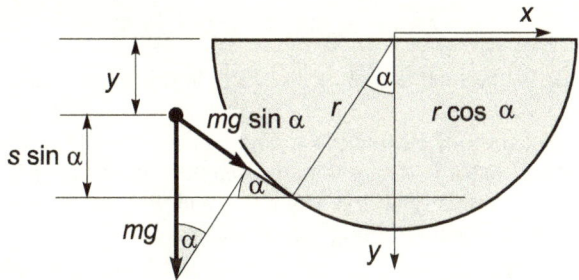

Division by $\cos\alpha$ gives

$$s\tan\alpha = 2r - 2s\tan\alpha.$$

The tangent of the angle corresponding to the position in question is obtained with $s = 0.96r$:

$$\tan\alpha = \frac{2r}{3s} = \frac{2r}{3 \cdot 0.96r} = 0.694,$$

and the angle is

$$\alpha = \arctan 0.694 = 34.8° = 0.607 \text{ radians.}$$

The total length of the string is therefore

$$L = s + \left(\alpha + \frac{\pi}{2}\right)r = 0.48\,\text{m} + \left(0.607 + \frac{\pi}{2}\right) \cdot 0.5\,\text{m} = 3.14r = 1.57\,\text{m},$$

that is, the total length of the string in this case is equal to the length of the semicircle.

Solution of Problem 44. The fact that the string connecting the two blocks is long means that it is longer than the height of the table (h), therefore the block of mass m_2 moves vertically all the way down and will not be pulled in the horizontal direction by block m_1 before hitting the ground.

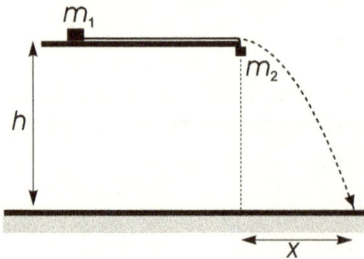

In the first phase of the motion the objects move with constant acceleration, which can be determined by using the laws of motion of the two objects:

$$m_2 g - K = m_2 a,$$
$$K = m_1 a,$$

where K is the tension in the string, a is the magnitude of the acceleration of both objects. (They move with the same acceleration because the string is not stretchable.) Adding the above equations, we get that the magnitude of the acceleration of the two objects is:

$$a = \frac{m_2}{m_1 + m_2} \cdot g.$$

The time taken by block m_2 to hit the ground is:

$$t = \sqrt{\frac{2h}{a}} = \sqrt{2gh \cdot \frac{m_2}{m_1 + m_2}}.$$

The velocity gained by the first block in that time is: $v = \sqrt{2ah} = \sqrt{2gh \cdot \dfrac{m_2}{m_1 + m_2}}$.

In the second phase of the motion the second block is at rest on the ground, while the first block moves towards the edge of the table at constant velocity. After leaving the table, the first block undergoes horizontal projection. Knowing that the distance covered in the vertical direction is h, we can calculate the time of fall as: $t_1 = \sqrt{2h/g}$.

The distance covered in the horizontal direction in that time is:

$$x = vt_1 = \sqrt{2gh \cdot \frac{m_2}{m_1 + m_2}} \cdot \sqrt{\frac{2h}{g}} = 2h\sqrt{\frac{m_2}{m_1 + m_2}}.$$

Note that our result is independent of g. Substituting given data, we find $x = 2\sqrt{5}/5 \, \text{m} \approx 0.896 \, \text{m}$.

Investigating the parametric formula gained for distance x, we can see that as the ratio of masses (m_1/m_2) increases from 0 to ∞, distance x decreases from $2h$ to 0.

Solution of Problem 45. Let us assume that the masses of the pendulums are negligible (or are included in the masses of the carts). The pendulums should be held in their previously calculated positions and should be released together with the carts, otherwise they would swing, which would have an unwanted effect on the movements of the carts. The positions in question could also be defined as the positions about which the pendulums would oscillate. (After these oscillations were damped, the pendulums would remain in these positions, but that would require a cord and track far too long.)

The first task is to determine the acceleration of the carts. Applying Newton's second law to each of the two carts (let K be the tension in the cord), we obtain:

$$K = m_1 a,$$

$$m_2 g \sin\alpha - K = m_2 a.$$

Adding the two equations, we get that the acceleration is:

$$a = \frac{m_2}{m_1 + m_2} g \sin\alpha.$$

A pendulum remains stationary relative to a cart if the acceleration of its bob equals the acceleration of the cart. The acceleration of the bob is caused by the net force of the gravitation and tension.

According to the figure, the angle enclosed by the vertical and the pendulum in cart m_1 that moves horizontally can be written as:

$$\tan\varphi_1 = \frac{a}{g} = \frac{m_2}{m_1 + m_2} \sin\alpha.$$

In case of cart m_2 that moves down the inclined plane, let us apply Newton's second law to the bob of the pendulum in directions that are parallel and perpendicular to the inclined plane. If the mass of the bob is m, we obtain:

$$mg\sin\alpha - K\sin\varepsilon = mg\frac{m_2\sin\alpha}{m_1 + m_2}, \qquad (1)$$

$$mg\cos\alpha - K\cos\varepsilon = 0, \qquad (2)$$

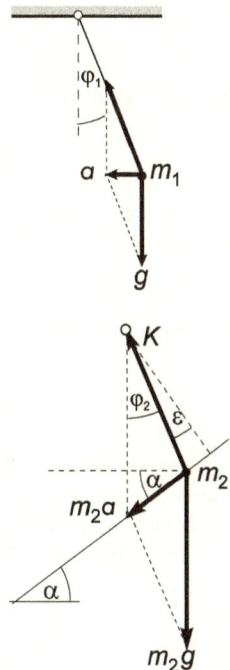

where ε is the angle formed by the pendulum and the normal to the inclined plane. Isolating the tension from the second equation, we have:

$$K = mg \frac{\cos \alpha}{\cos \varepsilon},$$

substituting this into the first equation, we find:

$$mg \sin \alpha - mg \tan \varepsilon \cos \alpha = mg \frac{m_2 \sin \alpha}{m_1 + m_2}.$$

Dividing the equation by $mg \cos \alpha$, we get:

$$\tan \varepsilon = \tan \alpha - \frac{m_2}{m_1 + m_2} \tan \alpha = \frac{m_1}{m_1 + m_2} \tan \alpha$$

The tangent of the angle enclosed by the vertical and the pendulum in cart m_2 ($\varphi_2 = \alpha - \varepsilon$) can be determined using the compound-angle formula:

$$\tan \varphi_2 = \tan(\alpha - \varepsilon) = \frac{\tan \alpha - \tan \varepsilon}{1 + \tan \alpha \cdot \tan \varepsilon}.$$

Substituting the expression for $\tan \varepsilon$, we find:

$$\tan \varphi_2 = \frac{m_2 \sin \alpha \cos \alpha}{m_1 + m_2 \cos^2 \alpha}.$$

Substituting known values, we get that the acceleration of the carts is:

$$a = \frac{51}{125} g = 4 \, \frac{\text{m}}{\text{s}^2},$$

the angle enclosed by the vertical and the pendulum in the cart moving horizontally is:

$$\tan \varphi_1 = \frac{51}{125} = 0.408, \qquad \rightarrow \qquad \varphi_1 = 22.2°$$

the angle enclosed by the vertical and the pendulum in the cart moving down the plane is:

$$\tan \varphi_2 = \frac{51}{118} = 0.4322, \qquad \rightarrow \qquad \varphi_2 = 23.37°$$

the angle formed by this pendulum and the normal to the inclined plane is:

$$\tan \varepsilon = \frac{6}{25} = 0.24, \qquad \rightarrow \qquad \varepsilon = 13.5.°$$

First solution of Problem 46. If the string is pulled with constant acceleration, it exerts a torque on the cube that tends to tilt the cube. Thus the base edge of the cube on the front is lifted off the plane, and the cube slides on its rear base edge. The torques of the string, the normal force of the ground and the force of gravity are in equilibrium.

Let F denote the force of the string, its vertical component being F_y, and let K be the normal force of the table. Based on the figure, Newton's second law can be used to set up equations for forces in the horizontal and vertical directions and for torques about the centre of the cube. With the notations of the figure,

$$K - F_y - G = 0, \tag{1}$$
$$F_y \cot \alpha = 3G, \tag{2}$$
$$Kx \cos \alpha + F_y(l - x)\cos \alpha = 3Gx \cos \alpha. \tag{3}$$

Furthermore,

$$\frac{l}{2} - x = \frac{l}{2}\tan \alpha. \tag{4}$$

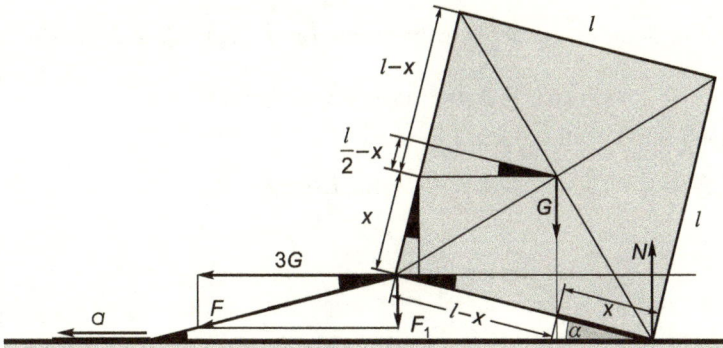

From (2) and (4),

$$F_y = 3G\left(1 - \frac{2x}{l}\right). \tag{5}$$

From (1) and (3),

$$(F_y + G)x + f_y(l - x) - 3Gx = 0. \tag{6}$$

Then the magnitude of the vertical component of the string force can be obtained from (5) and (6):

$$F_y = \frac{3}{4}G.$$

The force pressing on the ground is equal in magnitude to K:

$$K = F_y + G = \frac{7}{4}mg = 140\,\text{N}.$$

Thus the force exerted by the string is

$$F = \sqrt{F_y^2 + (3G)^2} = \sqrt{\frac{9}{16}G^2 + 9G^2} = \frac{3}{4}\sqrt{17}G = \frac{3}{4}\sqrt{17}\cdot 80\,\text{N} = 247.4\,\text{N}.$$

The base of the cube is lifted through an angle of

$$\alpha = \arctan\frac{F_y}{3G} = \arctan\frac{1}{4} = 14°$$

Second solution of Problem 46. From the figure:

$$F_x = 3G,$$

$$F_y = 3G\tan\alpha,$$

$$F = \frac{F_x}{\cos\alpha} = \frac{3G}{\cos\alpha},$$

$$K = G + F_y = G(1 + 3\tan\alpha).$$

The torques about the centre of mass:

$$Fl\frac{\sqrt{2}}{2}\sin(45° - 2\alpha) - Kl\frac{\sqrt{2}}{2}\sin(45° - \alpha) = 0.$$

With the substitution of the above expressions for F and K, and transformations to simplify,

$$3\sin(45° - 2\alpha) = (\cos\alpha + 3\sin\alpha)\sin(45° - \alpha).$$

With the application of the addition formula:

$$2\cos^2\alpha = 8\sin\alpha\cos\alpha.$$

Hence

$$\tan\alpha = \frac{1}{4}, \quad \text{and} \quad \alpha = 14°.$$

Thus

$$K = G(1 + 3\tan\alpha) = G\left(1 + 3\frac{1}{4}\right) = \frac{7}{4}G = 1.75G = 140\,\text{N},$$

and

$$F = \frac{3G}{\cos\alpha} = 247.3\,\text{N}.$$

Solution of Problem 47. a) In equilibrium (uniform motion in a straight line), the net torque of all forces must be 0. This occurs when there is no friction, which is only possible if the string is straight and if its extension passes through the centre of mass of the disc, (i.e. the string must be horizontal until the disc reaches its uniform speed). From that point onwards, the cart may even reduce its speed, and the slackened string may take any shape, while the disc will continue to travel uniformly. (Such an ideal case, however, will never occur in reality, the only realistic case is b).)

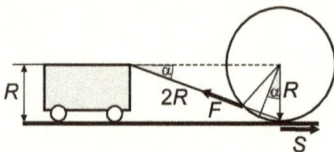

b) If there is friction, its torque needs to be counteracted by the torque of the string. (The force of gravity and the normal force have no torques about the centre of mass.) Consider the torques of the forces around the point where the disc touches the ground, a point moving along with uniform velocity in the inertial frame. Since neither the friction force S nor the normal force of the ground have torques around that point, the torque of the string must also be zero. This is only possible if the extension of the string passes through the point where the disc touches the ground.

The figure shows that the angle of inclination in question satisfies the equation

$$\sin\alpha = \frac{R}{2R+2R\sin\alpha}.$$

A quadratic equation is obtained for $\sin\alpha$:

$$2\sin^2\alpha+2\sin\alpha-1=0, \quad \text{and hence,} \quad \sin\alpha = \frac{-2\pm\sqrt{4+8}}{4}=\frac{\sqrt{3}}{2}-\frac{1}{2},$$

and the angle is $\alpha = 21.47°$, independently of the coefficient of friction. (This is surprising since it means that if a disc is pulled in this way on a plane with sudden changes of roughness, the string should not 'stir' at all, it should maintain its angle of $21.47°$ to the horizontal. However, if such an experiment is actually carried out, the disc will start to vibrate due to the finite speed of the effect transmitted in the string, and through non-equilibrium states it will amplify its non-harmonic oscillations.)

Solution of Problem 48. a) According to the problem, the system undergoes uniformly accelerated motion. Since the external forces are constant, this can only occur if the accelerations of the two bodies are equal and the same as the acceleration of the centre of mass. According to Newton's second law the magnitude of this is:

$$a = \frac{F_1+F_2}{m_1+m_2}.$$

The force exerted by the spring scale can be calculated by applying Newton's second law for any of the two objects. For example, if K is the force exerted on the object on the left handside, which has a mass of m_1, then:

$$F_1+K=m_1a,$$

From which

$$K=m_1a-F_1=m_1\frac{F_1+F_2}{m_1+m_2}-F_1=\frac{F_2m_1-F_1m_2}{m_1+m_2}=$$

$$=\frac{-10\,\text{N}\cdot10\,\text{kg}-20\,\text{N}\cdot2\,\text{kg}}{10\,\text{kg}+2\,\text{kg}}=-\frac{140}{12}\,\text{N}=-11.67\,\text{N}.$$

This is the force exerted by the spring on the object of mass m_1. The object of mass m_1 exerts a force of $11.67\,\text{N}$ on the spring.

b) The fact that F_1 and F_2 are swapped means that now F_1 is exerted on m_2 and F_2 is exerted on m_1 (in their original direction). So now the string between the objects and the spring must be substituted by a rod, otherwise we can only pull the spring balance. The system moves into the same direction with the same acceleration. In this case the force exerted by the spring scale on the object of mass m_1 is:

$$K=\frac{F_1m_1-F_2m_2}{m_1+m_2}=\frac{20\,\text{N}\cdot10\,\text{kg}-(-10\,\text{N}\cdot2\,\text{kg})}{10\,\text{kg}+2\,\text{kg}}=18.33\,\text{N}.$$

Thus, the force exerted on the spring by the object of mass m_1 is: $-18.33\,\text{N}$. (The negative spring force means that the spring is compressed.) c) If the mass of the two objects are equal, namely 6 kg, then the results in case of a) and b) are:

$$K = \frac{F_2 m - F_1 m}{m + m} = \frac{F_2 - F_1}{2} = \frac{-10\,\text{N} - 20\,\text{N}}{2} = -15\,\text{N},$$

and

$$K = \frac{F_1 - F_2}{2} = +15\,\text{N},$$

respectively. So the force exerted on the spring by the object of mass m_1 in case a) is $+15\,\text{N}$, in case b) it is $-15\,\text{N}$.

If the mass of any of the objects is zero than the spring balance reads the force exerted on that side which is $10\,\text{N}$, or $20\,\text{N}$.

Solution of Problem 49. a) Applying the work-kinetic energy theorem to the block's initial and final states, we get:

$$mg\Delta l_{\max} \cdot \sin\alpha - \frac{1}{2}D(\Delta l_{\max})^2 = 0,$$

hence

$$\Delta l_{\max} = \frac{2mg\sin\alpha}{D} = \frac{2 \cdot 30\,\text{N} \cdot 0.5}{80\,\text{N/m}} = \frac{3}{8}\,\text{m} = 0.375\,\text{m}.$$

The vertical displacement is therefore:

$$\Delta y = \Delta l \cdot \sin\alpha = \frac{2mg\sin^2\alpha}{D} = \frac{0.375}{2} = 0.1875\,\text{m} \approx 0.19\,\text{m} = 19\,\text{cm}.$$

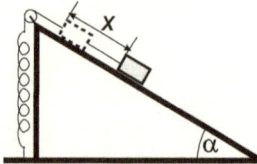

b) If friction can be neglected, the equilibrium position is defined by the equation:

$$D\Delta l_1 = mg\sin\alpha,$$

thus

$$\Delta l_1 = x = \frac{mg\sin\alpha}{D} = \frac{\Delta l_{\max}}{2} = 0.1875\,\text{m} \approx 19\,\text{cm}.$$

However, if friction is very small but can not be neglected, the equilibrium position of the block is not a point, but a small interval. In this case Newton's second law applied to the block being in equilibrium takes the form of:

$$mg\sin\alpha - D\Delta l \pm \mu mg\cos\alpha = 0.$$

Let $\Delta l = x$ be the distance between the block's original and equilibrium positions. The interval for x is defined by the inequalities:

$$mg\sin\alpha - \mu mg\cos\alpha \leq Dx \leq mg\sin\alpha + \mu mg\cos\alpha.$$

from which we have:

$$\frac{mg}{D}(\sin\alpha - \mu\cos\alpha) \leq x \leq \frac{mg}{D}(\sin\alpha + \mu\cos\alpha),$$

substituting known values, we find:

$$0.19 - 0.323\mu \le x \le 0.19 + 0.323\mu.$$

If the block is not simply placed onto the inclined plane in an equilibrium position, but reaches its final position from a state of motion as it does in our case, the exact place where it stops inside the above interval can also be determined, but that is a more difficult task to do.

Solution of Problem 50. The vertical displacement of the body that slides down the slope is the same in both cases, but in the case of a moving slope it requires twice as much time.

According to the quadratic distance relationship, the vertical acceleration component of the body is four times as much in the case of the stationary slope as in the case of the moving slope because for the distances travelled vertically in the two cases:

$$s_y = \frac{1}{2}a_{1y}t_1^2 = \frac{1}{2}a_{2y}(2t_1)^2,$$

from which

$$a_{1y} = 4a_{2y}.$$

Let us state the equation of the motion of the bodies, the constraining condition and the equation that expresses the special condition of the problem. Let us handle the horizontal and vertical components of the motion of the sliding body separately. As from here on the acceleration of the small body is used in the case of the moving slope, we will omit the indices 2. Using the notations of the figure, for the x component of the motion of the small body

$$N\sin\alpha - \mu N\cos\alpha = ma_x \qquad (1),$$

for the y component of the motion

$$mg - N\cos\alpha - \mu N\sin\alpha = ma_y \qquad (2),$$

for the wedge:

$$F - N\sin\alpha + \mu N\cos\alpha = MA \qquad (3)$$

the constraint condition:

$$a_y = (a_x - A)\tan\alpha \qquad (4)$$

the condition of the problem:

$$4a_y = g(\sin\alpha - \mu\cos\alpha)\sin\alpha \qquad (5).$$

Constraint condition (4) and condition (5) can be understood from the following figures:

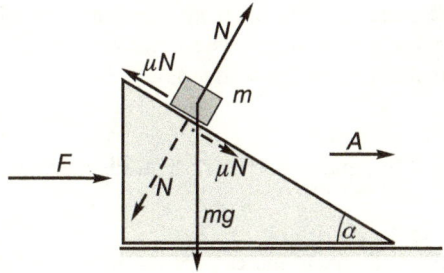

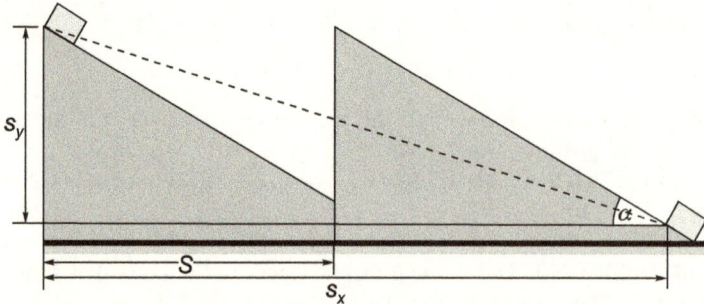

The vertical and horizontal distances travelled by the small body are s_y and s_x, respectively, the horizontal distance travelled by the wedge in the meantime is S. The height of the wedge is s_y and its base is $s_x - S$. With these the tangent of the angle of inclination of the wedge is

$$\tan \alpha = \frac{s_y}{s_x - S},$$

and the magnitude of vertical displacement is

$$s_y = (s_x - S)\tan \alpha.$$

From these, in the case of the moving slope the use of the quadratic distance law gives the following for the vertical acceleration of the body:

$$\frac{1}{2}a_y t^2 = \left(\frac{1}{2}a_x t^2 - \frac{1}{2}At^2\right)\tan \alpha,$$

after simplifying by $t^2/2$ (4) is acquired.

The right side of equation (5) is the vertical component of the acceleration $g(\sin \alpha - \mu \cos \alpha)$ of the body sliding down on a stationary slope: $a \cdot \sin \alpha$.

We have 5 independent equations for the 5 unknowns. From (5) a_y is expressed and substituted into (2) and (4), in (2) N is factored out:

$$mg - N(\cos \alpha + \mu \sin \alpha) = m\frac{g}{4}(\sin \alpha - \mu \cos \alpha)\sin \alpha, \qquad (2')$$

$$\frac{g}{4}(\sin \alpha - \mu \cos \alpha)\sin \alpha = (a_x - A)\tan \alpha, \qquad (4')$$

from $(2')$ the value of N is expressed, $(4')$ is divided by $\tan \alpha$:

$$N = mg\frac{1 - \frac{1}{4}(\sin \alpha - \mu \cos \alpha)\sin \alpha}{\cos \alpha + \mu \sin \alpha},$$

$$\frac{g}{4}(\sin \alpha - \mu \cos \alpha)\cos \alpha = a_x - A,$$

from which the acceleration of the wedge is $A = a_x - \frac{g}{4}(\sin \alpha - \mu \cos \alpha)\cos \alpha.$

Substituting the value of N into (1) and simplifying by m gives the following for a_x:

$$g\frac{\sin\alpha - \mu\cos\alpha}{\cos\alpha + \mu\sin\alpha}\left(1 - \frac{\sin\alpha - \mu\cos\alpha}{4}\sin\alpha\right) = a_x,$$

From (1) a_x is substituted into (3):

$$F = MA + ma_x,$$

(which could have been acquired from the theorem for the motion of the centre of mass directly) finally by substituting the value of A as function of a_x first and then by substituting the value of a_x from the parameters of the problem the requested force is acquired:

$$F = M\left[a_x - \frac{g}{4}(\sin\alpha - \mu\cos\alpha)\cos\alpha\right] + ma_x = (M+m)a_x - M\frac{g}{4}(\sin\alpha - \mu\cos\alpha)\cos\alpha =$$

$$= (M+m)g\frac{\sin\alpha - \mu\cos\alpha}{\cos\alpha + \mu\sin\alpha}\left(1 - \frac{\sin\alpha - \mu\cos\alpha}{4}\cdot\sin\alpha\right) - M\frac{g}{4}(\sin\alpha - \mu\cos\alpha)\cos\alpha,$$

reorganizing:

$$F = g(\sin\alpha - \mu\cos\alpha)\left[(M+m)\frac{4 - (\sin\alpha - \mu\cos\alpha)\sin\alpha}{4(\cos\alpha + \mu\sin\alpha)} - \frac{M}{4}\cos\alpha\right].$$

With numerical values:

$$F = 9.81\frac{\mathrm{m}}{\mathrm{s}^2}(0.5 - 0.2\cdot 0.866)\left[2\,\mathrm{kg}\frac{4 - (0.5 - 0.2\cdot 0.866)0.5}{4(0.866 + 0.2\cdot 0.5)} - \frac{1\,\mathrm{kg}}{4}0.866\right] = 5.67\,\mathrm{N}.$$

First solution of Problem 51. First we will solve this problem using Newton's second law. Let us apply it to the three objects in two perpendicular directions. Since the inclined plane also moves, these directions should be the horizontal (x) and vertical (y) directions. Let N be the normal force exerted by the inclined plane on block m_1, K be the tension in the cord, A be the acceleration of the inclined plane, a_{1x} and a_{1y} be the horizontal and vertical components of the acceleration of block m_1 respectively, a_{2x} and a_{2y} be the horizontal and vertical components of the acceleration of block m_2 respectively. Obviously a_{2x} and A are equal, therefore we have six unknowns. The seventh unknown, that we are to determine, is time t but this can be calculated using kinematical equations.

To solve the problem, we need to understand that the two blocks will be nearest to each other when the length of the cord on each side of the pulley is $h/2$. The distance between the two blocks — that takes its maximum (h) at the beginning of the motion and at the moment when the second block reaches the pulley — decreases in the first part of the motion and then increases. The distance will take its minimum value when the positions of the blocks are symmetrical about the bisector of the top angle of the inclined plane. In that position the two parts of the cord form an isosceles triangle, therefore to solve the problem, we simply need to determine the time taken by the hanging block to move a distance of $s_{2y} = h/2$ with acceleration a_{2y}, which is:

$$t = \sqrt{\frac{2 \cdot h/2}{a_{2y}}} = \sqrt{\frac{h}{a_{2y}}}. \tag{1}$$

Therefore, we have to find a_{2y} after setting up the following system of equations.

Equation (2) is Newton's second law applied to the inclined plane and block m_2 in the horizontal direction (assuming that their horizontal accelerations are equal), equations (3) and (4) are Newton's second law applied to block m_1 in the horizontal and vertical direction respectively, equation (5) is Newton's second law applied to block m_2 in the vertical direction, equation (6) is the kinematical restraining condition between block m_1 and the inclined plane, while equation (7) comes from the fact that the length of the cord is constant:

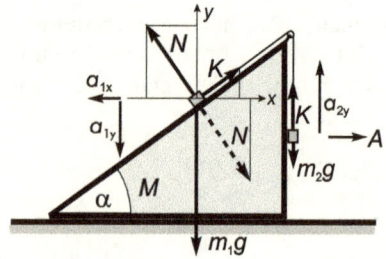

$$N \sin\alpha - K \cos\alpha = (M + m_2)A \tag{2}$$

$$N \sin\alpha - K \cos\alpha = m_1 a_{1x} \tag{3}$$

$$m_1 g - N \cos\alpha - K \sin\alpha = m_1 a_{1y} \tag{4}$$

$$K - m_2 g = m_2 a_{2y} \tag{5}$$

$$a_{1y} = (a_{1x} + A)\tan\alpha \tag{6}$$

$$a_{2y} = \frac{a_{1y}}{\sin\alpha}. \tag{7}$$

Equations (2)–(5) can be derived directly from the figure above, but equations (6) and (7) need to be explained.

There is a kinematical restraining condition between block m_1 and the inclined plane because the block has to remain on the inclined plane. The figure below shows the initial and final (after time t) positions of the system. While block m_1 moves s_{1y} down vertically, it covers a distance of s_{1x} in the horizontal direction. In this time the inclined plane moves a distance of S. It can be seen from the figure that the tangent of the angle of inclination is the ratio of lengths s_{1y} and $S + s_{1x}$, so:

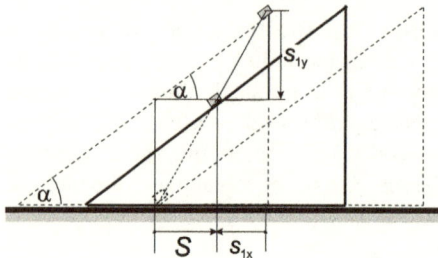

$$\tan\alpha = \frac{s_{1y}}{S + s_{1x}}.$$

Assuming that the initial velocities of each object are zero and that the accelerations are constants, we find that the ratio of distances are equal to the ratio of the corresponding accelerations:

$$\tan\alpha = \frac{\frac{1}{2}a_{1y}t^2}{\frac{1}{2}At^2 + \frac{1}{2}a_{1x}t^2} = \frac{a_{1y}}{A + a_{1x}},$$

hence
$$a_{1y} = (a_{1x} + A)\tan\alpha,$$
as was stated in equation (6).

As the length of the cord remains constant, the displacements of the two blocks relative to the inclined plane must be equal: $s_{1\text{rel}} = s_{2\text{rel}}$. Using that $s_{1\text{rel}} = s_{1y}/\sin\alpha$, we have
$$s_{2y} = \frac{s_{1y}}{\sin\alpha}.$$
Assuming again that the initial velocities are zero and the accelerations are constant, we find that:
$$a_{2y} = \frac{a_{1y}}{\sin\alpha},$$
as was stated in equation (7).

Let us now solve the system of equations. Multiplying equation (3) by $\cos\alpha$ and equation (4) by $\sin\alpha$, we obtain:
$$N\sin\alpha\cos\alpha - K\cos^2\alpha = m_1 a_{1x}\cos\alpha,$$
$$m_1 g\sin\alpha - N\cos\alpha\sin\alpha - K\sin^2\alpha = m_1 a_{1y}\sin\alpha.$$
After adding these two equations, we find that $N\sin\alpha\cos\alpha$ cancels out, and by factoring out K, its coefficient will be $\sin^2\alpha + \cos^2\alpha = 1$:
$$m_1 g\sin\alpha - K = m_1 a_{1x}\cos\alpha + m_1 a_{1y}\sin\alpha.$$
Let us solve equation (5) for K and substitute it into the above equation:
$$m_1 g\sin\alpha - m_2 a_{2y} - m_2 g = m_1 a_{1x}\cos\alpha + m_1 a_{1y}\sin\alpha. \qquad (8)$$
The right hand sides of equations (2) and (3) are equal:
$$(M + m)A = m_1 a_{1x},$$
thus
$$A = \frac{m_1}{M + m_2} a_{1x},$$
inserting this into equation (6), we have:
$$a_{1y} = \left(a_{1x} + \frac{m_1}{M + m_2} a_{1x}\right)\tan\alpha = \frac{M + m_1 + m_2}{M + m_2}\tan\alpha \cdot a_{1x},$$
which yields
$$a_{1x} = \frac{M + m_2}{M + m_1 + m_2} \cdot \frac{a_{1y}}{\tan\alpha} = \frac{M + m_2}{M + m_1 + m_2} \frac{\cos\alpha}{\sin\alpha} \cdot a_{1y}.$$
Let us now insert a_{1x} as expressed above and $a_{1y} = a_{2y}\sin\alpha$ from equation (7) into equation (8). The only unknown in this equation will be a_{2y}:
$$m_1 g\sin\alpha - m_2 a_{2y} - m_2 g = m_1 a_{2y}\sin\alpha \cdot \frac{M + m_2}{M + m_1 + m_2} \cdot \frac{\cos^2\alpha}{\sin\alpha} + m_1 a_{2y}\sin^2\alpha.$$

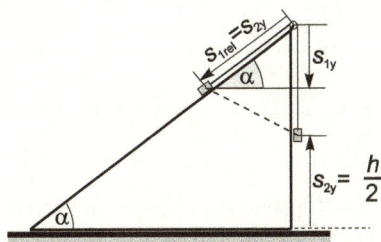

After some algebra, we find:

$$(m_1 \sin\alpha - m_2)g = \left[m_1 \left(\frac{M + m_2}{M + m_1 + m_2} \cos^2\alpha + \sin^2\alpha \right) + m_2 \right] \cdot a_{2y}.$$

After writing the coefficient of a_{2y} as one fraction, we have:

$$(m_1 \sin\alpha - m_2)g =$$
$$= \frac{m_1(M + m_2)\cos^2\alpha + m_1(M + m_1 + m_2)\sin^2\alpha + m_2(M + m_1 + m_2)}{M + m_1 + m_2} \cdot a_{2y}.$$

Let us write the second term of the numerator as:

$$m_1(M + m_1 + m_2)\sin^2\alpha = m_1(M + m_2)\sin^2\alpha + m_1\sin^2\alpha.$$

Factoring out $m_1(M + m_2)$ from the first term of the numerator and the first term of the expression above, we obtain

$$m_1(M + m_2)(\sin^2\alpha + \cos^2\alpha) = m_1(M + m_2),$$

which simplifies our equation to:

$$(m_1 \sin\alpha - m_2)g = \frac{m_1(M + m_2) + m_1^2\sin^2\alpha + m_2(M + m_1 + m_2)}{M + m_1 + m_2} \cdot a_{2y}.$$

Solving for a_{2y} gives:

$$a_{2y} = \frac{(m_1 \sin\alpha - m_2)(M + m_1 + m_2)}{m_1(M + m_2) + m_1^2\sin^2\alpha + m_2(M + m_1 + m_2)} \cdot g.$$

Substituting this into equation (1), the time in question takes the form of:

$$t = \sqrt{\frac{2s_{2y}}{a_{2y}}} = \sqrt{\frac{h[m_1(M + m_2) + m_1^2\sin^2\alpha + m_2(M + m_1 + m_2)]}{(m_1 \sin\alpha - m_2)(M + m_1 + m_2) \cdot g}}.$$

Substituting the given data, we find:

$$t = \sqrt{\frac{1\,\text{m}[7\,\text{kg}(2\,\text{kg} + 1\,\text{kg}) + 49\,\text{kg}^2 \cdot 0.36 + 1\,\text{kg}(2\,\text{kg} + 7\,\text{kg} + 1\,\text{kg})]}{(7\,\text{kg} \cdot 0.6 - 1\,\text{kg})(2\,\text{kg} + 7\,\text{kg} + 1\,\text{kg}) \cdot 10\,\frac{\text{m}}{\text{s}^2}}} =$$
$$= 0.389\,\text{s} \approx 0.39\,\text{s}.$$

Second solution of Problem 51. Let us solve the problem using conservation laws. The mechanical energy of the system is conserved:

$$m_1gh = m_1g\left(h - \frac{h}{2}\sin\alpha\right) + m_2g\frac{h}{2} + \frac{1}{2}m_1(v_{x1}^2 + v_{1y}^2) + \frac{1}{2}m_2v_{2y}^2 + \frac{1}{2}(M + m_2)V^2,$$

which yields:

$$m_1 g \frac{h}{2} \sin\alpha - m_2 g \frac{h}{2} = \frac{1}{2}(v_{1x}^2 + v_{1y}^2) + \frac{1}{2}m_2 v_{2y}^2 + \frac{1}{2}(M + m_2)V^2, \qquad (1)$$

where V is the horizontal velocity of the inclined plane (and of block m_2). The linear momentum of the system is conserved:

$$m_1 v_{1x} = (m_2 + M)V. \qquad (2)$$

Since the length of the cord is constant (see first solution):

$$v_{2y} = \frac{v_{1y}}{\sin\alpha}. \qquad (3)$$

As block m_1 remains on the inclined plane (see first solution):

$$v_{1y} = (v_{1x} + V)\tan\alpha. \qquad (4)$$

Let us now insert given data:

$$70\,\text{J}\cdot 0.6 - 10\,\text{J} = 7\,\text{kg}(v_{1x}^2 + v_{1y}^2) + 1\,\text{kg}\cdot v_{2y}^2 + 3\,\text{kg}\cdot V^2, \qquad (1')$$

$$7v_{1x} = 3V, \qquad (2')$$

$$v_{1y} = 0.6v_{2y}, \qquad (3')$$

$$v_{1y} = (v_{1x} + V)0.75. \qquad (4')$$

From equation $(2')$, we have

$$v_{1x} = \frac{3}{7}V, \qquad (2'')$$

which is then substituted into equation $(4')$ to get:

$$v_{1y} = \left(\frac{3}{7} + \frac{7}{7}\right)V \cdot \frac{3}{4} = \frac{10}{7} \cdot \frac{3}{4}V, \qquad (4'')$$

inserting this into equation $(3')$ gives:

$$\frac{10}{7} \cdot \frac{3}{4}V = 0.6v_{2y},$$

thus

$$V = \frac{4}{3} \cdot \frac{7}{10} \cdot 0.6v_{2y}, \qquad (5)$$

substituting this into equation $(2'')$, we find:

$$v_{1x} = \frac{3}{7} \cdot \frac{4}{3} \cdot \frac{7}{10} \cdot 0.6v_{2y} = \frac{4}{10} \cdot 0.6v_{2y}. \qquad (6)$$

Substituting equations (6), $(3')$ and (5) into equation $(1')$, we obtain an equation for v_{2y}:

$$32 = 7 \cdot \frac{16}{100} \cdot 0.36v_{2y}^2 + 7 \cdot 0.36v_{2y}^2 + v_{2y}^2 + 3 \cdot \frac{16}{9} \cdot \frac{49}{100} \cdot 0.36v_{2y}^2.$$

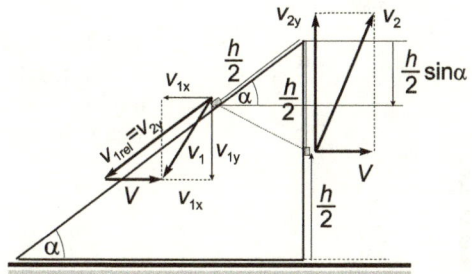

After some algebra, we find:

$$v_{2y}^2 = \frac{3200}{486.4} \frac{\text{m}^2}{\text{s}^2},$$

therefore the vertical velocity of block m_2 is:

$$v_{2y} = \sqrt{\frac{3200}{486.4}} = 2.5649 \frac{\text{m}}{\text{s}}$$

Using this, the time in question turns out to be:

$$t = \frac{2s_{2y}}{v_{2y}} = \frac{h}{v_{2y}} = \frac{1\,\text{m}}{2.5649 \frac{\text{m}}{\text{s}}} = 0.38978\,\text{s} \approx 0.39\,\text{s}.$$

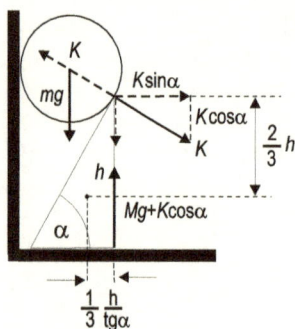

Fig. a)

Solution of Problem 52. a) First let us write down the equations of motion for the sphere as well as for the wedge, and the relation between their accelerations. The data referring to the sphere is denoted by lowercase letters, while the data ones corresponding to the wedge is denoted by uppercase letters. According to the figures a) and b), we get:

$$mg - K\cos\alpha = ma \tag{1}$$
$$K\sin\alpha = MA \tag{2}$$
$$a = A\tan\alpha \tag{3}$$

The last equation comes from the restriction that the sphere touches the top surface of the wedge during their motion. The distances covered by the sphere and by the wedge in time t are:

$$\Delta s = \frac{1}{2}at^2$$

$$\Delta S = \frac{1}{2}At^2,$$

since all the forces, and consequently the accelerations, are constant. According to figure b),

$$\Delta s = \Delta S \cdot \tan\alpha,$$

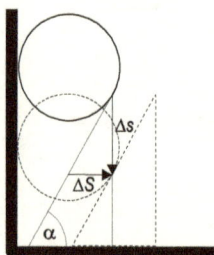

Fig. b)

thus

$$\frac{1}{2}at^2 = \frac{1}{2}At^2 \cdot \tan\alpha,$$

from which, by dividing with $\frac{1}{2}t^2$, equation (3) is obtained.

The mass ratio M/m is obtained by eliminating the quantities A and K from the system of equations. From equation (3):

$$A = \frac{a}{\tan\alpha}.$$

Plugging this into equation (2), K can be expressed:

$$K = M \frac{a}{\tan\alpha \cdot \sin\alpha}. \tag{4}$$

Inserting this into the equation (1), we get:

$$mg - M \frac{a}{\tan\alpha \cdot \sin\alpha} \cdot \cos\alpha = ma.$$

Rearranging this, and using the identity $\cos\alpha / \sin\alpha = 1/\tan\alpha$, we obtain:

$$mg = \left(\frac{M}{\tan^2\alpha} + m \right) \cdot a,$$

from which the acceleration of the sphere is:

$$a = \frac{mg}{\frac{M}{\tan^2\alpha} + m} = \frac{g\tan^2\alpha}{\frac{M}{m} + \tan^2\alpha}. \tag{5}$$

According to the figure a), the condition assuring that the wedge does not tilt, expressed in terms of torques relative to the centre of mass, reads as follows:

$$\frac{2}{3}Kh\sin\alpha + \frac{1}{3}K\cos\alpha \frac{h}{\tan\alpha} \le (Mg + K\cos\alpha) \frac{h}{3\tan\alpha}.$$

Here, we have used the fact that in the marginal case the line of action of the force exerted by the ground on the wedge is shifted to the right edge of the wedge.

After simplifying this equation by $h/3$ and multiplying by $\tan\alpha$, we get:

$$2K\sin\alpha \cdot \tan\alpha + K\cos\alpha \le Mg + K\cos\alpha.$$

Omitting the same terms on both sides, and inserting the expression of K from equation (4), we get:

$$2M \frac{a}{\tan\alpha \cdot \sin\alpha} \sin\alpha \cdot \tan\alpha \le Mg,$$

so the maximal acceleration of the sphere is:

$$a \le \frac{g}{2}.$$

Putting this into (5) we obtain the desired mass ratio M/m:

$$a = \frac{g\tan^2\alpha}{\frac{M}{m} + \tan^2\alpha} \le \frac{g}{2}, \quad \text{from which} \quad 2\tan^2\alpha \le \frac{M}{m} + \tan^2\alpha,$$

and finally the relation

$$\frac{M}{m} \ge \tan^2\alpha$$

is obtained. Thus the ratio M/m and the angle α should satisfy the inequality above.

b) If $\alpha = 60°$, then $\dfrac{M}{m} \geq \tan^2 60° = 3$ is the condition. Thus in the case of $\dfrac{M}{m} = 12$ the wedge does not tilt. According to the conservation of mechanical energy:

$$mgl\sin\alpha = \frac{1}{2}mv^2 + \frac{1}{2}MV^2.$$

The relation of the speeds is similar to that of the accelerations:

$$v = V\tan\alpha \quad \rightarrow \quad V = \frac{v}{\tan\alpha},$$

and using this in the previous equation we get:

$$2mgl\sin\alpha = mv^2 + M\frac{v^2}{\tan^2\alpha} = \left(m + \frac{M}{\tan^2\alpha}\right)\cdot v^2.$$

From this the speed of the sphere after covering a distance l along the wedge is:

$$v = \sqrt{\frac{2gl\sin\alpha}{1 + \frac{M}{m\tan^2\alpha}}} = \sqrt{\frac{2\cdot 9.81\ \text{ms}^{-2}\cdot 0.2\ \text{m}\cdot\sin 60°}{1 + \frac{12}{\tan^2 60°}}} \approx 0.82\ \frac{\text{m}}{\text{s}}.$$

Solution of Problem 53. One possible method would be to suspend a small ball onto a long cord that hangs from the top of the box. Let us wait until the oscillation of the pendulum stops and measure angle x, which is the angle enclosed by the cord and the line that is perpendicular to the top of the box. The bob of the pendulum is at rest with respect to the box, if its acceleration equals the acceleration of the box relative to the ground. The acceleration of the box is given by the expression:

$$a = g(\sin\alpha - \mu\cos\alpha)$$

The acceleration of the bob is caused by the net force of the gravitational force acting vertically and the tension exerted by the cord.

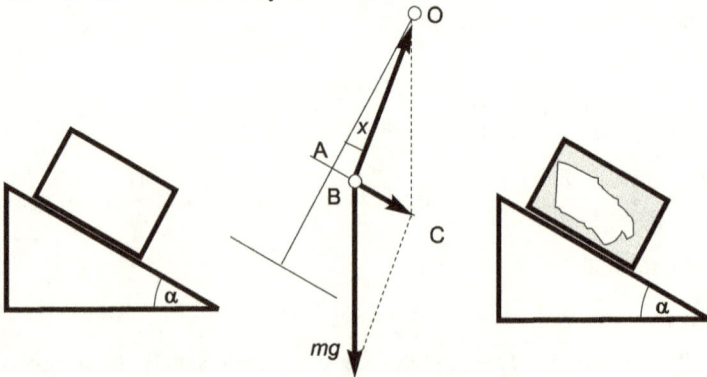

Let us use the figure above to apply Newton's second law to the bob in the directions that are parallel and perpendicular to the inclined plane.

In the perpendicular direction we have:

$$mg\sin\alpha - F\cos x = 0,$$

while in the parallel direction we obtain:

$$mg\sin\alpha - F\sin x = mg(\sin\alpha - \mu\cos\alpha),$$

hence

$$mg\cos\alpha - F\cos x = 0.$$

From which we find:

$$F\sin x = \mu mg\cos\alpha$$

$$F\cos x = mg\cos\alpha.$$

Dividing the first equation by the second, we get: $\tan x = \mu$. This way the coefficient of kinetic friction is determined. There are several methods that could be used to determine the angle of the inclined plane. Since we have three unknowns (μ, α, F) in the above equations, one more measurement is needs to be taken. The first possible method would be to measure the period of the pendulum that swings through a small angle. The pendulum inside the box accelerating down the inclined plane behaves as if it was placed into a uniform gravitational field in which the gravitational acceleration was $\vec{g'} = \vec{g} - \vec{a}$, where $\vec{a}$ is the acceleration of the box. The connection between this apparent gravitational acceleration and the tension is given by the equation:

$$F^2 = (mg\cos\alpha)^2 + (\mu mg\cos\alpha)^2 = m^2 g'^2,$$

where g' is the magnitude of the apparent gravitational acceleration, for which we get:

$$g' = g\cos\alpha\sqrt{1+\mu^2},$$

and therefore the period of the pendulum is:

$$T = 2\pi\sqrt{\frac{l}{g\cos\alpha\sqrt{1+\mu^2}}},$$

from which the angle of the inclined plane can be calculated as:

$$\alpha = \arccos\frac{l}{g\sqrt{1+\mu^2}} \cdot \frac{4\pi^2}{T^2}.$$

For example, if the mass of the bob is $m = 1\,\text{kg}$, angle x is measured to be 11.3^0, the length of the cord is $l = 1\,\text{m}$ and the period is found to be $T = 2.5\,\text{s}$, the coefficient of kinetic friction would be:

$$\mu = \tan 11.3° = 0.2,$$

while the angle of the inclined plane would be:

$$\alpha = \arccos\frac{1}{9.81\sqrt{1.04}} \cdot \frac{4\pi^2}{6.25} = 50.85°,$$

the acceleration of the box would be:

$$a = 9.81 \frac{m}{s^2}(\sin 50.85° - 0.2\cos 50.85°) = 6.37 \frac{m}{s^2},$$

and finally the tension in the cord (in the pendulum's stationary state) would be:

$$F = (mg\cos\alpha)\sqrt{1+\mu^2} = 9.81\,\text{N}\cos 50.85°\sqrt{1+0.04} = 6.32\,\text{N}.$$

A second possible method is to measure the tension. In this case the mass of the bob of the pendulum should be measured before getting into the box. Using the figure above, we obtain:

$$AB = AC - BC = mg\sin\alpha - mg(\sin\alpha - \mu\cos\alpha) = \mu\cos\alpha.$$

Thus

$$F^2 = (mg\cos\alpha)^2 + (\mu mg\cos\alpha)^2 = (mg)^2\cos^2\alpha \cdot (1+\mu^2),$$

which yields

$$\cos^2\alpha = \frac{F^2}{(mg)^2(1+\mu^2)},$$

hence

$$\cos\alpha = \frac{F}{mg\sqrt{1+\mu^2}} = \frac{F}{mg\sqrt{1+\tan^2 x}} = \frac{F\cos x}{mg},$$

therefore

$$\alpha = \arccos\frac{F\cos x}{mg}.$$

Substituting the values given in the example, we find:

$$\alpha = \arccos\frac{6.32 \cdot \cos 11.3°}{9.81} = 50.52°,$$

which equals approximately the previous result.

Note that these methods can only be used if the value of g is known and we are sure about the fact that the bottom and top of the box are parallel to the inclined plane. In any other case the quantities in question can not be determined.

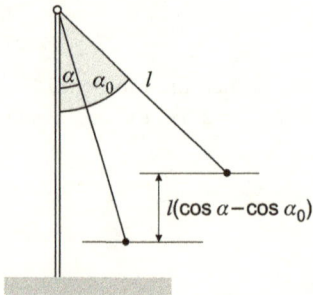

Solution of Problem 54. Newton's second law applied to the force components parallel to the string is

$$K - mg\cos\alpha = m\frac{v^2}{l}, \tag{1}$$

where K is the tension acting in the string. According to the work-energy theorem (applied to a general case of an initial angular displacement of α_0),

$$mgl(\cos\alpha - \cos\alpha_0) = \frac{1}{2}mv^2. \tag{2}$$

From (1) and (2):

$$K - mg\cos\alpha = 2mg(\cos\alpha - \cos\alpha_0),$$

and hence the tension K is

$$K = mg(3\cos\alpha - 2\cos\alpha_0).$$

The torque of the string is the only torque that the grip at the lower end needs to counteract: it must be able to exert an equal torque in the opposite direction. The figure shows that the torque of the tension force with respect to the lower end is

$$\tau = Kh\sin\alpha = mg((3\cos\alpha - 2\cos\alpha_0)\cdot h\cdot\sin\alpha.$$

Since the pendulum started from an initial position of $\alpha_0 = 90°$, $\cos\alpha_0 = 0$ and the torque in question is

$$\tau = 3mgh\cdot\sin\alpha\cos\alpha = 3mgh\frac{\sin 2\alpha}{2}.$$

This torque is a maximum if $\sin 2\alpha$ is a maximum, that is, at $2\alpha = 90°$, which means $\alpha = 45°$. Thus

$$\tau_{max} = 3mgh\sin 45°\cos 45° = \frac{3}{2}mgh = 9 \text{ Nm}.$$

It is worth noting that the tension force and the torque are both independent of the length of the string.

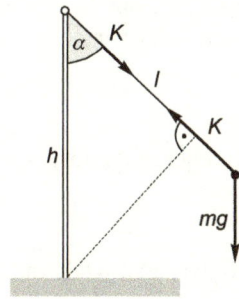

Solution of Problem 55. a) Since the external forces acting on the system are all vertical, the centre of mass of the system will not move horizontally. When the ball has left the hemisphere, it must move vertically upwards: since the ball slides all the way along the hemisphere, it cannot have a horizontal velocity component at separation. Otherwise, its horizontal velocity would be equal to that of the cart, which would mean a displacement of the centre of mass of the system to the left or to the right. After separation, the motion of the ball is vertical projection, and the cart is brought to rest again. Thus, all the energy is concentrated on the ball again, and the ball will rise back to its initial height.

Let X denote the displacement of the cart and let x denote the horizontal component of the displacement of the ball. As shown in the figure, the distance of the centre of mass of

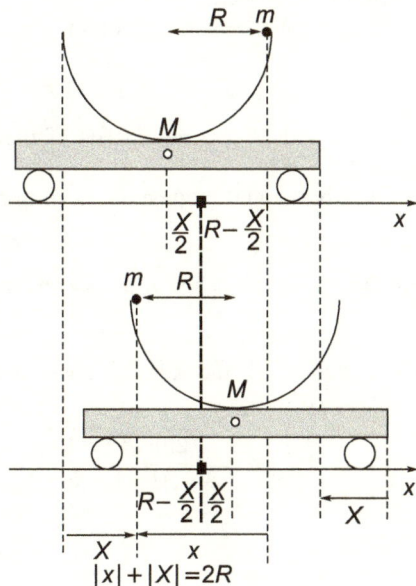

the cart from the common centre of mass is $X/2$, and the distance of the ball from there is $R - X/2$ metres. By definition of the centre of mass,

$$M\frac{X}{2} = m\left(R - \frac{X}{2}\right),$$

and hence the displaxement of the cart is

$$X = \frac{2m}{M+m}R$$

to the right, while the horizontal displacement of the ball is

$$x = \frac{2M}{M+m}R$$

to the left. With numerical data:

$$x = \frac{2 \cdot 2\,\text{kg}}{2\,\text{kg} + 0.5\,\text{kg}} \cdot 0.5\,\text{m} = 0.8\,\text{m}.$$

b) The normal force acting at the lowermost point of the path of the ball is obtained by applying Newton's second law:

$$N - mg = m\frac{v_{\text{rel}}^2}{R}, \tag{1}$$

where N is the normal force and v_{rel} is the speed of the ball relative to the cart. At that time instant the cart represents an inertial reference frame, therefore Newton's law is valid in it as well.

From the work-energy theorem,

$$mg(h+R) = \frac{1}{2}mv^2 + \frac{1}{2}MV^2, \tag{2}$$

where v and V are the speeds of the ball and the cart, respectively, relative to the ground.

Since horizontal momentum is conserved,

$$mv = MV. \tag{3}$$

Finally, the relationship of the speeds measured in the two reference frames is

$$v_{\text{rel}} = v + V.$$

The solution of the simultaneous equations for the magnitudes of the quantities involved is

$$V = \sqrt{\frac{2m^2g(h+R)}{M^2 + mM}} \quad \text{and} \quad v = \frac{M}{m}V = \sqrt{\frac{2Mg(h+R)}{M+m}},$$

$$N_{\text{max}} = \left(2\frac{Mm+m^2}{M} \cdot \frac{h+R}{R} + m\right)g =$$

$$= \left(2 \cdot \frac{2\,\text{kg} \cdot 0.5\,\text{kg} + 0.25\,\text{kg}^2}{2\,\text{kg}} \cdot \frac{0.5\,\text{m} + 0.5\,\text{m}}{0.5\,\text{m}} + 0.5\,\text{kg}\right) \cdot 10\,\frac{\text{m}}{\text{s}^2} = 30\,\text{N}.$$

Solution of Problem 56. a) When point A hits the ground, the rods form a straight line. As rods have constant length, the two ends of the system must have zero velocity at that moment, so the block of mass m_2 stops. Since only conservative forces act in this situation, the initial gravitational potential energy of the rods will be transformed into the rotational kinetic energy of the rods, which is independent of the mass of the block.

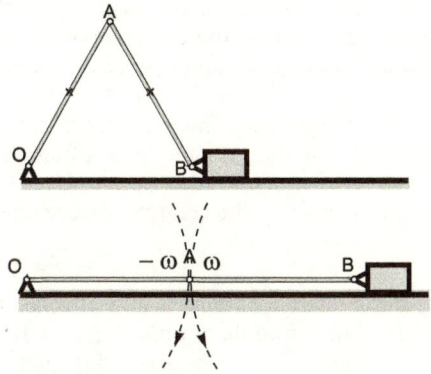

At the moment when point A hits the ground, the rotational kinetic energies of the two rods are equal. Assuming that the rotational inertia of a rod about its end is $\Theta = m_1 L^2/3$, the rotational kinetic energy of one rod is:

$$E_1 = \frac{1}{2}\Theta\omega^2 = \frac{1}{2}\cdot\frac{1}{3}m_1 L^2\omega^2.$$

The law of conservation of energy will take the form of:

$$2m_1 g\frac{L}{2}\sin\alpha = 2\cdot\frac{1}{2}\cdot\frac{1}{3}m_1 L^2\omega^2,$$

where $L/2\cdot\sin\alpha$ is the distance of the centre of mass of each rod from the ground in their initial position. As $\alpha = 60°$, we know that $\sin\alpha = \sqrt{3}/2$. Substituting this into the equation and isolating the angular velocity, we find:

$$\omega = \sqrt{\frac{3g\sqrt{3}}{2L}}.$$

We then use this to express the velocity of point A when hitting the ground:

$$v_A = L\omega = \sqrt{\frac{3gL\sqrt{3}}{2}} = \sqrt{\frac{3\cdot 9.81\text{ ms}^{-2}\cdot 0.5\,\text{m}\cdot\sqrt{3}}{2}} = 3.57\,\frac{\text{m}}{\text{s}}.$$

Note that the result does not depend on the masses of either the rods or the block.

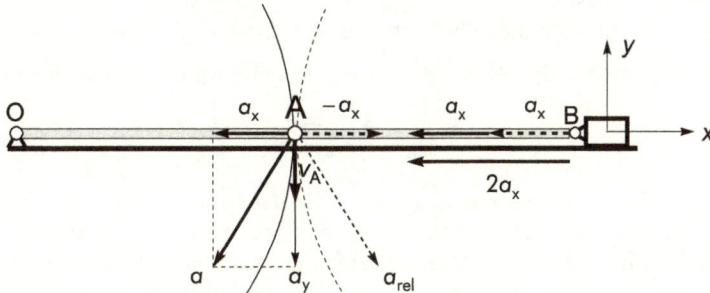

b) The acceleration of mass m_2 at the moment when point A hits the ground is made up of two different components: the first one is the horizontal component of the acceleration of point A (a_x), the second one is the horizontal component of the acceleration of point B relative to point A.

Let the reference frame be attached to point B, whose velocity becomes zero, when point A hits the ground. In this frame rod AB (and therefore point A) rotates in an accelerated motion around point B. The horizontal component of the acceleration of point A must be the centripetal acceleration, so

$$a_x = a_n = v_A^2/L$$

If the reference frame is now attached to point A, the horizontal acceleration of point B (and therefore that of mass m_2) will have the same magnitude as the one calculated above but will be in opposite directions. As the horizontal acceleration of point A in this situation has magnitude $a_x = a_n = v_A^2/L$ and points towards point O, therefore the total acceleration of point B and mass m_2 at the moment when $v_B = 0$ is:

$$a_B = 2a_x = 2v^2/L$$

Substituting known values gives:

$$a_B = 2a_x = 2 \cdot \frac{3g\sqrt{3L}}{2L} = 3\sqrt{3}g = 50.97 \, \frac{\text{m}}{\text{s}^2}$$

Note that this result is independent of the masses and of the lengths of the rods. (The force acting in hinge B is $F = m_2 a_B = 2\,\text{kg} \cdot 50.97 \, \frac{\text{m}}{\text{s}^2} = 101.94\,\text{N}$.)

Solution of Problem 57. a) During the tumbling of the triangle, the initial positional energy transfers into rotational kinetic energy. The side b lies on the ground, so only the edges a and c have non zero positional energy. This energy (relative to the ground, as zero level) can be expressed with the help of the height of the centre of mass of the rods. Notice that this height is $h_C = a/2$ for both rods. So, applying the conservation of energy for the initial state and the final state of the triangle (just before the triangle hits ground), we get:

$$(m_a + m_c)gh_C = \frac{1}{2}(\Theta_a + \Theta_c)\omega^2,$$

where Θ_a and Θ_c are the moments of inertia of the rods a and c with respect to the edge b, as rotation axis.

It is well known that the moment of inertia of a thin rod about an axis perpendicular to the rod at one of its endpoints is $\Theta = \frac{1}{3}ml^2$. In our case this applies for the side a:

$$\Theta_a = \frac{1}{3}m_a a^2.$$

The moment of inertia of the rod c is still to be determined. It can be obtained in a tricky way. First let us place the rod of length c and of mass m_c perpendicularly to the axis. Then let us 'compress' the rod, keeping its mass unchanged, to a size which is equal to the distance of the endpoint B of the oblique rod from the axis:

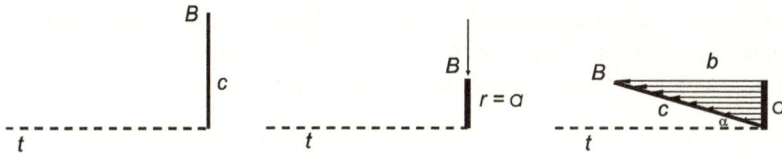

The moment of inertia of the compressed rod is $\Theta_c = \frac{1}{3} m_c r^2$, where $r = c \cdot \sin\alpha = a$ is the distance of point B from the axis. Finally, let us shear the rod in such a way that its length becomes again the original length, and every point of the rod moves parallel to the axis. This transformation does not change the moment of inertia, thus:

$$\Theta_c = \frac{1}{3} m_c c^2 \sin^2\alpha = \frac{1}{3} m_c a^2.$$

This result could have been obtained also by the definition of the moment of inertia:

$$\Theta_c = \sum m_i (l_i \sin\alpha)^2 = \sin^2\alpha \sum m_i l_i^2 = \sin^2\alpha \cdot \frac{1}{3} m_c c^2 = \frac{1}{3} m_c a^2.$$

Putting these results into the equation of energy conservation, and expressing the mass of each rod by the mass of rod c, we get that:

$$\left(\frac{3}{5} m_c + m_c\right) g \frac{1}{2} a = \frac{1}{2}\left(\frac{1}{3} \cdot \frac{3}{5} m_c + \frac{1}{3} m_c\right) a^2 \omega^2,$$

so

$$\frac{8}{5} m_c g a = \frac{8}{15} m_c a^2 \omega^2 \quad \rightarrow \quad 3g = a\omega^2$$

We have used the fact that $a = \frac{3}{5} c$, thus $m_a = \frac{3}{5} m_c$. Concluding, the value of the final velocity $v = a\omega$ of the vertex B is:

$$v = a\omega = \sqrt{3ga} \sqrt{3 \cdot 10 \text{ ms}^{-1} \cdot 0.3 \text{ m}} = 3 \,\frac{\text{m}}{\text{s}}$$

and it is directed vertically downwards.

b) In this case the centre of mass of the triangle may move only in vertical direction, since all the external forces are vertical. The vertical forces cannot give rise to rotation in horizontal plane (i.e. about vertical axis) either, thus the rod b lying on the ground just translates parallelly. At the moment when the triangle hits the ground none of its points have horizontal velocity due to the conservation of horizontal momentum. Thus, according to the law of energy conservation, the angular velocity just before hitting the ground, as well as the velocity of point B at this instant coincide with the result obtained in case a).

The place where B hits the ground is now by $a/3 =$ = 0.1 m closer to the initial position of side b then in case a). To obtain this the position of the centre of mass has to be determined.

According to Pythagoras' theorem, side b of the triangle has a length 0.4 m. Let us use a coordinate

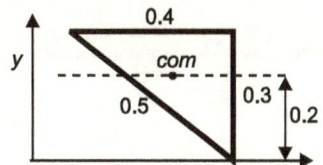

system whose x axis passes through the vertex B and parallel to the edge b, as it is shown in the figure. Then the y coordinate of the centre of mass of the triangle is simply the weighted average of the y coordinates of the centres of the three rods, so:

$$y = \frac{4 \cdot 0.3 + 3 \cdot 0.15 + 5 \cdot 0.15}{4 + 3 + 5} \text{ m} = 0.2 \text{ m}.$$

Here the numbers 3, 4 and 5 are the 'weights' proportional to the masses of the rods, and 0.3 m, 0.15 m are the y coordinates of the centres of the rods.

While in case a) the vertex B hits the ground $d_1 = a = 0.3$ m far from the initial vertical plane of the triangle, now the centre of mass remains in this plane, so the vertex B hits the ground only $d_2 = 0.2$ m far from the plane. (The distance between the places where B hits the ground in the two cases is $d' = 0.1$ m.)

Solution of Problem 58. Since no horizontal external force acts and the parts of the system are originally at rest, the centre of mass of the structure can move only vertically.

Let S_1, S_2 and S stand for the centres of mass of the two rods and the whole system, respectively. Then based on the Pythagorean theorem

$$\overline{S_1 S_2} = \sqrt{\left(\frac{l_2}{2}\right)^2 - \left(\frac{l_1}{2}\right)^2} = \sqrt{0.25 \text{ m}^2 - 0.09 \text{ m}^2} = \sqrt{0.16 \text{ m}^2} = 0.4 \text{ m}.$$

From the ratio of the masses of the rods (as $m_1 : m_2 = l_1 : l_2$):

$$\overline{S_1 S} = \overline{S_1 S_2} \cdot \frac{l_2}{l_1 + l_2} = 0.4 \text{ m} \cdot \frac{1 \text{ m}}{1.6 \text{ m}} = 0.25 \text{ m}.$$

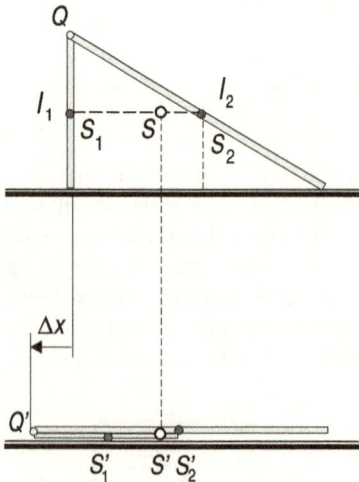

In the horizontal position of the rods, based on the figure:

$$\overline{S_1' S_2'} = \frac{l_2}{2} - \frac{l_1}{2} = 0.5 \text{ m} - 0.3 \text{ m} = 0.2 \text{ m},$$

according to the coordinate of the centre of mass (with S_1 in the origin):

$$\overline{S_1' S'} = \frac{0 + l_2 \cdot \overline{S_1' S_2'}}{l_1 + l_2} = \frac{0.2 \text{ m}}{1.6} = 0.125 \text{ m},$$

the distance between the joint and the centre of mass of the system is

$$\overline{Q' S'} = \overline{Q S_1'} + \overline{S_1' S'} = 0.3 \text{ m} + 0.125 \text{ m} = 0.425 \text{ m}.$$

Based on the figure, the requested displacement of the joint is

$$\Delta x = \overline{Q' S'} - \overline{S_1 S} = 0.425 \text{ m} - 0.25 \text{ m} = 0.175 \text{ m},$$

that is, the horizontal displacement of the common point of the rods is 17.5 cm in the direction of the tumbling, so point Q reaches the ground 17.5 cm to the left of the foot of rod l_1.

Determining the speed:

If in the horizontal position of the rods the speed of the common point (joint) is v, then the rods can only rotate around their free ends because v is perpendicular to the rods and in the horizontal direction the speed of the free endpoints of the rods is zero. The angular speeds of the two rods are therefore

$$\omega_1 = \frac{v}{l_1}, \quad \text{and} \quad \omega_2 = \frac{v}{l_2}.$$

The law of conservation of mechanical energy:

$$m_1 g \frac{l_1}{2} + m_2 g \frac{l_1}{2} = \frac{1}{2} \Theta_1 \omega_1^2 + \frac{1}{2} \Theta_2 \omega_2^2,$$

where the rotational inertias of the rods are calculated for their endpoints. If ϱ stands for the linear density of the rods ('the mass of a unit length'), then

$$m_1 = \varrho l_1 \quad \text{and} \quad m_2 = \varrho l_2.$$

With these, our equation can be written in the following form:

$$l_1 \varrho g \cdot \frac{l_1}{2} + l_2 \varrho g \cdot \frac{l_1}{2} = \frac{1}{2} \cdot \frac{1}{3} l_1 \varrho \cdot l_1^2 \frac{v^2}{l_1^2} + \frac{1}{2} \cdot \frac{1}{3} l_2 \varrho \cdot l_2^2 \frac{v^2}{l_2^2},$$

by dividing by ϱ, multiplying by 2, after combining the like terms the following equation is acquired:

$$l_1^2 g + l_1 l_2 g = \frac{1}{3} (l_1 + l_2) \cdot v^2,$$

after factoring out

$$3 l_1 (l_1 + l_2) \cdot g = (l_1 + l_2) \cdot v^2,$$

and from this the requested speed of impact is

$$v = \sqrt{3 l_1 g} = \sqrt{3 \cdot 0.6 \text{ m} \cdot 9.81 \text{ m/s}^2} = 4.2 \; \frac{\text{m}}{\text{s}}.$$

Solution of Problem 59. The figure shows that the vertical plane containing the rod is perpendicular to the axis of the cylinder, so the rod will move in that plane.

The change in gravitational potential energy can be determined by comparing the initial and final states. Since the system is conservative, the opposite of that change equals the total kinetic energy gained.

When point B reaches the cylinder, the rod and the radius drawn to it are perpendicular to each other. As seen in the figure, they enclose a triangle with sides

$$\overline{OB} = R, \quad \overline{BA} = 2R,$$
$$\overline{OA} = \sqrt{R^2 + 4R^2} = R\sqrt{5}.$$

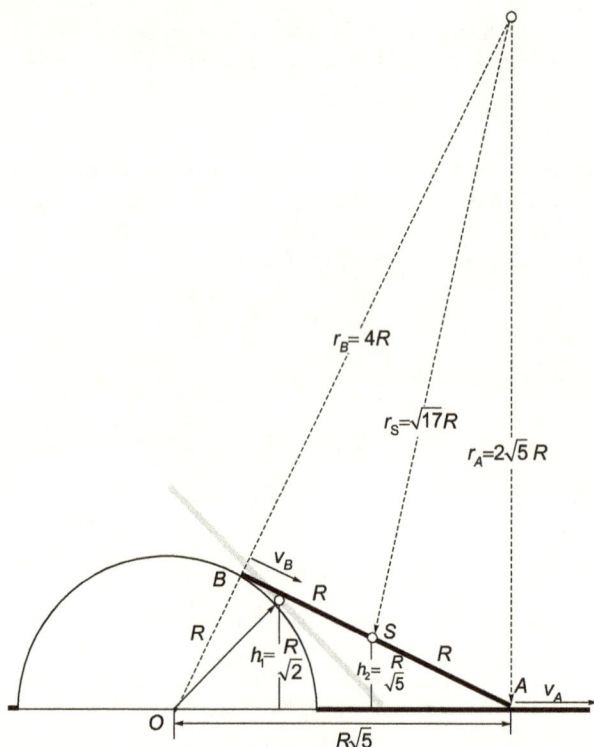

The distances of the centre of mass S of the rod from the horizontal plane in the initial and final positions are

$$h_1 = R\frac{\sqrt{2}}{2} \quad \text{and} \quad h_2 = R\frac{\sqrt{5}}{5},$$

since $h_2 : R = R : R\sqrt{5}$.

Energy is conserved:

$$mg(h_1 - h_2) = \frac{1}{2}mv_s^2 + \frac{1}{2}\Theta_s\omega^2.$$

The instantaneous speed v_s of the centre of mass (S) is determined by the instantaneous angular speed and the distance $r_B = \overline{CB}$ of the instantaneous axis of rotation C of the rod from the point S. Since the velocity of point A is horizontal and that of point B — at that time instant — is tangential to the cylinder, the instantaneous axis of rotation is the intersection of the perpendiculars drawn to these velocities.

From geometry, the instantaneous radius $r_A = \overline{CA}$ drawn to point A satisfies

$$r_A : R\sqrt{5} = 2R : R,$$

thus

$$r_A = 2R\sqrt{5}.$$

158

The instantaneous radius of rotation of point B is obtained from the Pythagorean theorem:

$$r_B = \sqrt{r_A^2 - 4R^2} = \sqrt{20R^2 - 4R^2} = 4R.$$

Finally, the instantaneous radius $r_S = \overline{CS}$ at the centre of mass is

$$r_S = \sqrt{\overline{CB}^2 + \overline{CS}^2} = \sqrt{16R^2 + R^2} = \sqrt{17}R.$$

Since the speed to be found is $v_B = r_B\omega$, the angular speed remains to be determined. The energy equation in terms of the unknown angular speed and the radius r_S obtained above is

$$mgR\left(\frac{\sqrt{2}}{2} - \frac{\sqrt{5}}{5}\right) = \frac{1}{2}m17R^2\omega^2 + \frac{1}{2}\cdot\frac{1}{12}m4R^2\omega^2 = \frac{26}{3}mR^2\omega^2.$$

The solution of the equation for ω is

$$\omega = \sqrt{\frac{3}{26}\left(\frac{\sqrt{2}}{2} - \frac{\sqrt{5}}{5}\right)\frac{g}{R}} = 0.5467\,\text{s}^{-1}.$$

Thus the speed of the point B of the rod at the time instant in question is

$$v_B = 4R\omega = 2.19\,\frac{\text{m}}{\text{s}}.$$

Solution of Problem 60. Let us assume that the rod is thin and homogeneous and moves in a vertical plane perpendicular to the edge of the table. The peg makes the rod rotate about its bottom end without translation until it leaves the table. During this time, the centre of mass of the rod gains a horizontal velocity because of the force exerted by the peg, and maintains this velocity after leaving the table, since during that time there is no force acting horizontally. The rod loses contact with the peg (and due to its being slim also with the edge of the table) when the direction of the acceleration of its centre of mass becomes vertical. From that moment the horizontal component of the velocity of the centre of mass remains constant. The rod itself undergoes both translation and rotation. Its centre of mass moves on the path of a horizontal projection, while the rod itself rotates about its centre of mass with a constant angular velocity.

Let us find the angle rotated until the rod reaches the position of leaving the table and the velocity of the centre of mass at that position.

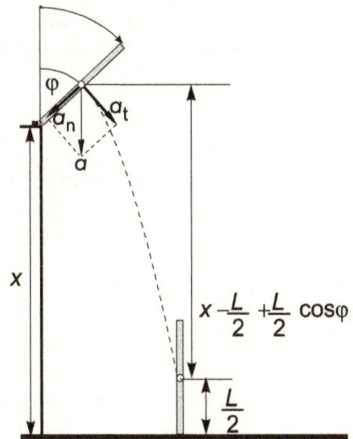

Let φ be the angle rotated until leaving the table and a_t and a_n be the tangential and normal components of the acceleration of the centre of mass respectively. In the position of leaving the table (shown in the figure) the following equations can be set up:

$$\tan\varphi = \frac{a_t}{a_n},$$

where

$$a_t = r\beta = \frac{L}{2}\beta$$

and

$$a_n = \frac{v_s^2}{r} = \frac{2v_s^2}{L},$$

where L is the length of the rod, $r = L/2$ is the radius of rotation of the centre of mass while being on the table, β is the angular acceleration of the rod in the position of leaving the table and v_s is the velocity of the centre of mass at the same instant. Substituting these into the expression for the tangent of the angle, we obtain:

$$\tan\varphi = \frac{r^2\beta}{v_s^2} = \frac{L^2\beta}{4v_s^2}. \tag{1}$$

Let us determine the velocity of the centre of mass and the angular acceleration. The first can be found using the work-kinetic energy theorem:

$$mg\Delta h_s = mg\frac{L}{2}(1-\cos\varphi) = \frac{1}{2}\Theta\omega^2 = \frac{1}{2}\cdot\frac{1}{3}mL^2\frac{4v_s^2}{L^2}.$$

where Δh_s is the vertical component of the displacement of the centre of mass. Using this to express the velocity, we find:

$$v_s^2 = \frac{3}{4}gL(1-\cos\varphi). \tag{2}$$

The angular acceleration can be expressed with the help of the torques about the stationary bottom end of the rod (using Newton's second law in angular form):

$$\beta = \frac{M}{\Theta} = \frac{mg\frac{L}{2}\sin\varphi}{\frac{1}{3}mL^2} = \frac{3}{2}\frac{g}{L}\sin\varphi. \tag{3}$$

Let us now substitute equations (2) and (3) into equation (1):

$$\tan\varphi = \frac{\sin\varphi}{\cos\varphi} = \frac{L^2\frac{3g}{2L}\sin\varphi}{4\cdot\frac{3}{4}gL(1-\cos\varphi)} = \frac{\sin\varphi}{2(1-\cos\varphi)},$$

from which:

$$\cos\varphi = \frac{2}{3}.$$

So the rod leaves the table after rotating through an angle φ, whose cosine is $\cos\varphi = = 2/3$, which gives $\varphi = 48.19° = 0.8411$ rad. Let us calculate other trigonometric functions of this angle: $\sin\varphi = \frac{\sqrt{5}}{3} = 0.7454$, $\tan\varphi = \frac{\sqrt{5}}{2} = 1.118$.

To investigate the movement of the rod after leaving the table, we need to find the rod's velocity along with its horizontal and vertical components. Using equation (2), these are:

$$v_s = \sqrt{\frac{3}{4}gL(1-\cos\varphi)} = \sqrt{\frac{3}{4}gL\left(1-\frac{2}{3}\right)} = \frac{1}{2}\sqrt{Lg},$$

$$v_{s_x} = v_s\cos\varphi = \frac{2}{3}v_s = \frac{2}{3}\cdot\frac{1}{2}\sqrt{Lg} = \frac{1}{3}\sqrt{Lg},$$

$$v_{s_y} = v_s\sin\varphi = \frac{\sqrt{5}}{3}v_s = \frac{\sqrt{5}}{3}\cdot\frac{1}{2}\sqrt{Lg} = \frac{\sqrt{5}}{6}\sqrt{Lg}.$$

The constant angular velocity of the rotation after leaving the table is:

$$\omega = \frac{v_s}{L/2} = \frac{2v_s}{L} = \frac{2\frac{1}{2}\sqrt{Lg}}{L} = \sqrt{\frac{g}{L}}.$$

After making these calculations, we can begin to answer the original question. The angle through which the rod should rotate while falling (if its bottom end is to initially reach the ground in the rod's vertical position) is $\alpha = \pi - \varphi = 180° - 48.19° = 131.81° = 2.3005\,\text{rad}$. The time needed for this is:

$$t = \frac{\pi - \varphi}{\omega} = \frac{\pi - \arccos\frac{2}{3}}{\sqrt{g/L}} = 2.3005 \cdot \sqrt{\frac{L}{g}}$$

The centre of mass moves on the path of a horizontal projection. It is to cover a vertical distance of:

$$x - \frac{L}{2} + \frac{L}{2}\cos\varphi = x - \frac{L}{2} + \frac{L}{2}\cdot\frac{2}{3} = x - \frac{L}{6}$$

where x is the height of the table. Using the equation for the distance covered in a vertical projection, we find:

$$x - \frac{L}{6} = v_{s_y}t + \frac{1}{2}gt^2 = \frac{\sqrt{5gL}}{6}\cdot 2.3005\sqrt{\frac{L}{g}} + \frac{1}{2}g\cdot 2.3005^2\cdot\frac{L}{g}.$$

Hence the height of the table is:

$$x = \left[\frac{1}{6} + \frac{2.3005\sqrt{5}}{6} + \frac{2.3005^2}{2}\right]L = 3.67L.$$

We still need to check that the normal force exerted by the table onto the bottom end of the rod still applies until the rod rotates through angle $\varphi = 48.19°$ because if not, the rod's bottom end will 'jump up' from the table, causing our calculation for the angular acceleration to be incorrect.

The bottom end of the rod would lift off, if the force K_y that is keeping the rod's end on the table was a negative normal force. Since the table cannot pull, there is no possibility for a negative normal force — meaning that the rod's end would lift before leaving the table. Let us calculate the angle at which the normal force gets to zero. It happens when the vertical component of the acceleration of the centre of mass equals the free-fall acceleration g. Let φ_1 be the angle the rod forms with the vertical in that position.

The vertical component of the acceleration can be written as the sum of the vertical components of the tangential and normal accelerations:

$$a_t \sin\varphi_1 + a_n \cos\varphi_1 = g.$$

Writing $a_t = \dfrac{L}{2}\beta$ and $a_n = \dfrac{2v^2}{L}$ and substituting the values of angular acceleration and velocity of the centre as given in equations (2) and (3), we find:

$$\frac{3}{4}g\sin^2\varphi_1 + \frac{3}{2}g(1-\cos\varphi_1)\cos\varphi_1 = g.$$

Let us divide by g, multiply by 4, and substitute $\sin^2\varphi_1 = 1-\cos^2\varphi_1$:

$$3(1-\cos^2\varphi_1) + 6\cos\varphi_1 - 6\cos^2\varphi_1 = 4.$$

Rearranging the equation, we get:

$$9\cos^2\varphi_1 - 6\cos\varphi_1 + 1 = 0.$$

The solution is:

$$\cos\varphi_1 = \frac{6 \pm \sqrt{36-36}}{18} = \frac{1}{3} \quad \rightarrow \quad \varphi_1 = 70.53°,$$

So the normal force K_y would get to zero at an angle $\varphi = 70.53°$, but as the rod leaves the table well before that, our previous calculations prove to be correct.

It is interesting to examine how the quantities describing the motion of the rod change as a function of time from the moment the rod leaves the table. Let us make calculations for a rod of length $1\,\mathrm{m}$. In that case:

$$\omega = \sqrt{\frac{g}{L}} = 3.162\ \mathrm{s}^{-1},$$

$$v_{sx} = \frac{1}{3}\sqrt{Lg} = 1.052\ \frac{\mathrm{m}}{\mathrm{s}},$$

$$v_{sy} = \frac{\sqrt{5}}{6}\sqrt{Lg} = 1.178\ \frac{\mathrm{m}}{\mathrm{s}},$$

The horizontal and vertical displacements of the centre of mass as a function of time are:

$$x_s = \frac{1}{3}\sqrt{Lg}\cdot t = 1.054\ \frac{\mathrm{m}}{\mathrm{s}}\cdot t,$$

$$y_s = \frac{\sqrt{5}}{6}\sqrt{Lg}\cdot t + \frac{1}{2}gt^2 = 1.178\ \frac{\mathrm{m}}{\mathrm{s}}\cdot t + 5\ \frac{\mathrm{m}}{\mathrm{s}^2}\cdot t^2,$$

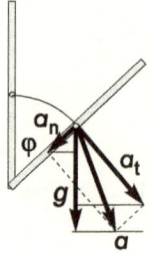

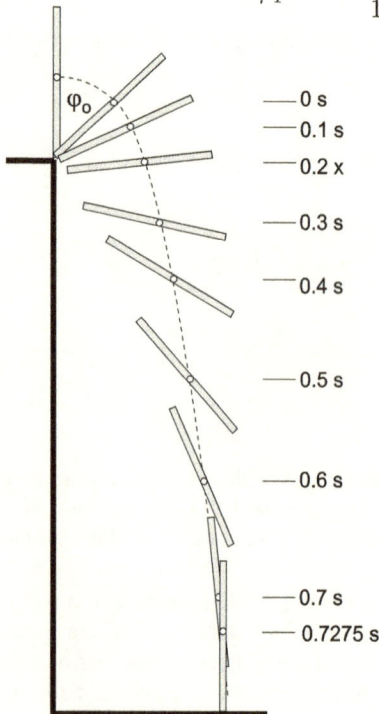

— 0 s
— 0.1 s
— 0.2 x
— 0.3 s
— 0.4 s
— 0.5 s
— 0.6 s
— 0.7 s
— 0.7275 s

The angle the rod forms with the vertical as a function of time is:

$$\varphi = \varphi_0 + \Delta\varphi = \varphi_0 + \omega t = 48.19° + 3.162 \cdot \frac{180°}{\pi} \cdot t,$$

where $\varphi_0 = 48.19°$ is the angle at which the rod leaves the table.

Let us set up a table of values for the above quantities (which are measured in metre, second and degree.)

t	0.1	0.2	0.3	0.4	0.5	0.6	0.7	0.7275
x_s	0.1052	0.2104	0.3156	0.4208	0.526	0.6312	0.7364	0.766785
y_s	0.1678	0.4356	0.8034	1.1712	1.839	2.5068	3.2746	3.503
$\Delta\varphi$	18.1°	36.2°	54.35°	72.46°	90.58°	108.7°	126.8°	131.8°
φ	66.29°	84.39°	102.54°	120.65°	138.77°	156.89°	174.99°	180°

Solution of Problem 61. a) According to Newton's second law with impulse and momentum

$$F_1 t_1 + F_2 t_2 + F_3 t_3 = mv,$$

and

$$\bar{F}(t_1 + t_2 + t_3) = mv.$$

From these, the average force is the arithmetic mean of the magnitudes of the forces acting in the different phases weighted by their durations:

$$\bar{F} = \frac{F_1 t_1 + F_2 t_2 + F_3 t_3}{t_1 + t_2 + t_3},$$

Its numerical value is

$$\bar{F} = \frac{10 \text{ N} \cdot 4 \text{ s} + 4 \text{ N} \cdot 14 \text{ s} - 15 \text{ N} \cdot 2 \text{ s}}{4 \text{ s} + 14 \text{ s} + 2 \text{ s}} = 3.3 \text{ N}.$$

b) According to the work-kinetic energy theorem:

$$F_1 s_1 + F_2 s_2 + F_3 s_3 = \frac{1}{2} mv^2,$$

and

$$\bar{F}(s_1 + s_2 + s_3) = \frac{1}{2} mv^2.$$

From these

$$\bar{F} = \frac{F_1 s_1 + F_2 s_2 + F_3 s_3}{s_1 + s_2 + s_3}.$$

The durations of the motion are given, but the distances belonging to the forces need to be determined. Calculating the distances:

$$s_1 = \frac{1}{2} a_1 t_1^2 = \frac{F_1}{2m} t_1^2 = \frac{10 \text{ N}}{2m} \cdot 4^2 \text{ s}^2 = \frac{80 \text{ kg} \cdot \text{m}}{m},$$

$$s_2 = v_1 t_2 + \frac{1}{2} a_2 t_2^2 = a_1 t_1 t_2 + \frac{1}{2} a_2 t_2^2 = \frac{F_1}{m} t_1 t_2 + \frac{F_2}{2m} t_2^2 =$$

$$= \frac{10 \text{ N} \cdot 4 \text{ s} \cdot 14 \text{ s}}{m} + \frac{4 \text{ N} \cdot 14^2 \text{ s}^2}{2m} = \frac{952 \text{ kg} \cdot \text{m}}{m},$$

$$s_3 = v_2 t_3 + \frac{1}{2} a_3 t_3^2 = (v_1 + a_2 t_2) \cdot t_3 + \frac{1}{2} a_3 t_3^2 = \left(\frac{F_1}{m} t_1 + \frac{F_2}{m} t_2 \right) \cdot t_3 + \frac{F_3}{2m} t_3^2 =$$

$$= \left(\frac{10 \text{ N} \cdot 4 \text{ s}}{m} + \frac{4 \text{ N} \cdot 14 \text{ s}}{m} \right) \cdot 2 - \frac{15 \text{ N} \cdot 2^2 \text{ s}^2}{2m} = \frac{162 \text{ kg} \cdot \text{m}}{m}$$

After substituting these, the average force is

$$\bar{F} = \frac{10 \text{ N} \cdot \frac{80}{m} + 4 \text{ N} \cdot \frac{952}{m} - 15 \text{ N} \cdot \frac{162}{m}}{\frac{80}{m} + \frac{952}{m} + \frac{162}{m}} = \frac{800 \text{ N} + 3808 \text{ N} - 2430 \text{ N}}{80 + 952 + 162} = 1.82 \text{ N}.$$

The same with parametric solution:

$$\bar{F} = \frac{F_1 \frac{F_1}{2m} t_1^2 + F_2 \left(\frac{F_1}{m} t_1 t_2 + \frac{F_2}{2m} t_2^2 \right) + F_3 \left[\left(\frac{F_1}{m} t_1 + \frac{F_2}{m} t_2 \right) \cdot t_3 + \frac{F_3}{2m} t_3^2 \right]}{\frac{F_1}{2m} t_1^2 + \left(\frac{F_1}{m} t_1 t_2 + \frac{F_2}{2m} t_2^2 \right) + \left(\frac{F_1}{m} t_1 + \frac{F_2}{m} t_2 \right) \cdot t_3 + \frac{F_3}{2m} t_3^2}$$

Simplifying by the mass of the body:

$$\bar{F} = \frac{\frac{1}{2} F_1^2 t_1^2 + F_1 F_2 t_1 t_2 + \frac{1}{2} F_2^2 t_2^2 + F_1 F_3 t_1 t_3 + F_2 F_3 t_2 t_3 + \frac{1}{2} F_3^2 t_3^2}{\frac{1}{2} F_1 t_1^2 + F_1 t_1 t_2 + \frac{1}{2} F_2 t_2^2 + F_1 t_1 t_3 + F_2 t_2 t_3 + \frac{1}{2} F_3 t_3^2} =$$

$$= \frac{(F_1 t_1 + F_2 t_2)^2 + [2(F_1 t_1 + F_2 t_2) + F_3 t_3] F_3 t_3}{F_1 t_1 (t_1 + 2t_2 + 2t_3) + F_2 t_2 (t_2 + 2t_3) + F_3 t_3^2},$$

with numerical values

$$\bar{F} = \frac{(10 \text{ N} \cdot 4 \text{ s} + 4 \text{ N} \cdot 14 \text{ s})^2 + [2 \cdot (10 \text{ N} \cdot 4 \text{ s} + 4 \text{ N} \cdot 14 \text{ s}) - 15 \text{ N} \cdot 2 \text{ s}] \cdot (-15 \text{ N} \cdot 2 \text{ s})}{10 \text{ N} \cdot 4 \text{ s} \cdot (4 \text{ s} + 2 \cdot 14 \text{ s} + 2 \cdot 2 \text{ s}) + 4 \text{ N} \cdot 14 \text{ s} \cdot (14 \text{ s} + 2 \cdot 2 \text{ s}) - 15 \text{ N} \cdot 4 \text{ s}^2} =$$

$$= 1.824 \text{ N}$$

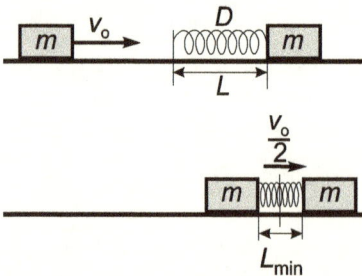

Solution of Problem 62. a) The collision is elastic. The spring connecting the two blocks will reach its maximum compression (shortest length) when the velocities of the two blocks become equal. At that moment, the blocks move with the velocity of the centre of mass of the system:

$$u = \frac{m_1 v_1 + m_2 v_2}{m_1 + m_2} = \frac{m}{2m} v_0 = \frac{v_0}{2}.$$

As there are only conservative forces present, the mechanical energy of the system is constant, so the initial kinetic energy of the second block is equal to the sum of the elastic potential energy of the spring and the kinetic energies of the two blocks at the moment when they move together:

$$\frac{1}{2} m_1 v_0^2 = \frac{1}{2} (m_1 + m_2) \frac{v_0^2}{4} + \frac{1}{2} D_0 x^2.$$

From this, as $m_1 = m_2 = m$, the compression of the spring is:

$$x = \sqrt{\frac{m v_0^2}{2 D_0}} = v_0 \sqrt{\frac{m}{2 D_0}} = 0.8 \frac{\text{m}}{\text{s}} \sqrt{\frac{1 \text{ kg}}{2 \cdot 250 \text{ N/m}}} = 3.58 \text{ cm}.$$

Therefore, the shortest length of the spring is: $L_{min} = L - x = 20 \text{ cm} - 3.58 \text{ cm} = 16.42 \text{ cm}.$ (The spring is assumed to remain straight during its compression.)

b) If the second block sticks to the spring, the motion of the blocks will be a simple harmonic oscillation in a reference frame attached to the centre of mass of the system. In this reference frame the centre of the spring is stationary, so the situation is the same as if an object of mass m would be connected to a spring of length $L/2$, whose other end is fastened to a wall. The spring constant doubles if the length of a spring is halved, so: $D = 2D_0$, therefore the period of oscillation for each block is:

$$T = 2\pi\sqrt{\frac{m}{2D_0}} = 2\pi\sqrt{\frac{1\,\text{kg}}{2\cdot 250\ \text{N/m}}} = 0.282\,\text{s}.$$

Solution of Problem 63. Let us always choose the reference frame moving at the velocity of the trolley before launching a ball (centre-of-mass reference frame) as a reference frame. The velocity changes which occur after the first launching are the same as the velocities themselves in the frame fixed to the ground (the process starts from rest). Let the number of launching be in the lower index of the velocity, V stand for the velocity of trolley, v stand for the velocity of the ball.

Due to the conservation of mechanical energy

$$E = \frac{1}{2}(M - m)V_1^2 + \frac{1}{2}mv_1^2. \tag{1}$$

Due to the conservation of momentum

$$(M - m)V_1 - mv_1 = 0. \tag{2}$$

From (2), the velocity of the ball is $v_1 = \dfrac{M - m}{m}V_1$, which is substituted into (1)

$$(M - m)V_1^2 + m\frac{(M - m)^2}{m^2}V_1^2 = 2E.$$

After rearrangement, the velocity of the trolley after the first launching is

$$V_1 = \Delta V_1 = \sqrt{\frac{2mE}{M(M - m)}}. \tag{3}$$

After the second launching, the change in the velocity of the trolley can be calculated using the same formula (3), the only difference being that M is now replaced by $M' = M - m$:

$$\Delta V_2 = \sqrt{\frac{2mE}{(M - m)(M - m - m)}} = \sqrt{\frac{2mE}{(M - m)(M - 2m)}},$$

after the third launching M is replaced by $M'' = M - 2m$:

$$\Delta V_3 = \sqrt{\frac{2mE}{(M - 2m)(M - 2m - m)}} = \sqrt{\frac{2mE}{(M - 2m)(M - 3m)}}.$$

The total change in the velocity of the trolley is equal to its velocity relative to the ground:

$$V_3 = \Delta V_1 + \Delta V_2 + \Delta V_3 =$$

$$= \sqrt{\frac{2mE}{M(M-m)}} + \sqrt{\frac{2mE}{(M-m)(M-2m)}} + \sqrt{\frac{2mE}{(M-2m)(M-3m)}} = 1.03 \ \frac{m}{s}.$$

Solution of Problem 64. The partially elastic collision means that the two bodies will not stick together after the collision but move with different velocities, and the total kinetic energy calculated with the speeds after the collision is less than the total kinetic energy before the collision. Thus, some part of the kinetic energy increases the internal energy of the objects, while the conservation of linear momentum holds true under any circumstance and the centre of mass of the two objects undergoes uniform straight line motion. As a general case, let us assume that the two objects move along the same straight line into the same direction, and the second one catches up to the first one. The first part of the collision lasts from the moment they touch each other and until they move, for an instant, at the same speed. Thus, the faster one slows down, the slower one speeds up to the speed at which the centre of mass of the bodies moves, which is:

$$c = \frac{m_1 v_1 + m_2 v_2}{m_1 + m_2}$$

During this process, the absolute values of the change in the linear momentum of the balls are the same, but their direction is opposite:

$$\Delta I_1 = m_1(c - v_1), \quad \text{and} \quad \Delta I_2 = m_2(c - v_2) = -\Delta I_1.$$

In the second part of the collision (until the balls are separated) more change on the linear momenta of the balls occur (the direction of the linear momentum might change as well), the linear momentum of the ball of mass m_2 further decreases and the linear momentum of the ball of mass m_1 further increases:

$$\Delta I_1' = m_1(u_1 - c), \quad \text{and} \quad \Delta I_2' = m_2(u_2 - c) = -\Delta I_1'.$$

If the collision is totally elastic, then for any object the change in its linear momentum in the first part is the same as the change in its linear momentum in the second part (both the direction and the magnitude). The $v_{rel_1} = v_1 - c$, and $v_{rel_1}' = u_1 - c$ are the velocities of the ball of mass m_1 and the $v_{rel_2} = v_2 - c$, and $v_{rel_2}' = u_2 - c$ are the velocities of the ball of mass m_2 with respect to the centre of mass of the balls before and after the collision respectively.

With respect to the centre of mass, it can be considered as if the two bodies (coming from two sides and arriving at the same time) collide with a wall of infinite mass (infinite because the centre of mass stays at rest). In case of a totally elastic collision the kinetic energy does not change, thus (in both cases) the speeds before and after the collision are equal. Thus,

$$v_1 - c = -(u_1 - c), \quad \text{and} \quad v_2 - c = -(u_2 - c).$$

If the collision is not totally elastic, then the speeds after the collision are smaller than before the collision, the ratio of these speeds is $0 \le k \le 1$ thus for example for the ball of mass m_1:

$$k = \frac{c - u_1}{v_1 - c}.$$

(Of course the ratio $k = \frac{c - u_2}{v_2 - c}$ is the same for the two balls, because if the change in the linear momentum of one body decreases by a factor of k, then that of the other must decrease by the same factor according to the conservation of linear momentum.) Thus, the speeds of the balls after collision are:

$$u_1 = (k+1)c - kv_1,$$
$$u_2 = (k+1)c - kv_2.$$

Therefore, the number k (the so called collision number or coefficient) is suitable to characterize the collision from the aspect of elasticity. If we would like to describe how inelastic the colision is, we may use the number $\alpha = 1 - k$. In case of the totally elastic collisions $k = 1$, and $\alpha = 0$; in case of the totally inelastic collisions $k = 0$, and $\alpha = 1$.

The change in the kinetic energy of the system is:

$$\Delta E = \frac{1}{2}m_1 u_1^2 + \frac{1}{2}m_2 u_2^2 - \frac{1}{2}m_1 v_1^2 - \frac{1}{2}m_2 v_2^2,$$

Which, after substituting the velocities after the collision, can be written as:

$$\Delta E = \frac{m_1 m_2}{2(m_1 + m_2)}(v_1 - v_2)^2 (k^2 - 1).$$

(Of course the lost energy is equal to $-\Delta E$.) In our case the ball of mass $m_1 = M$ was stationary thus using the notations $m_2 = m$ and $v_2 = v$ The result is:

$$\Delta E = \frac{mM}{2(m + M)}v^2 (k^2 - 2).$$

Solution of Problem 65. Each object has a speed of $v_0 = \sqrt{2gh}$ when arriving at the rigid, horizontal ground. The lower ball of mass m_1, arriving first, rebounds with an upward velocity of the same magnitude v_0 since the collision is elastic. It then collides with the ball of mass m_2 still travelling downwards at a speed of v_0. The velocities of the objects after they collide with each other are given by the equation

$$u_i = (k+1)c - kv_i,$$

where the value of the coefficient of restitution k is $k = 1$ for a totally elastic collision, v_1 and v_2 are the velocities of the objects before the collision, and $c = \dfrac{m_1 v_1 + m_2 v_2}{m_1 + m_2}$

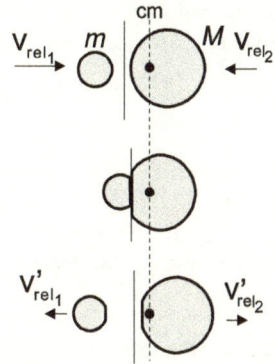

is the velocity of the common centre of mass of the two objects. Hence the velocities of the two objects after the collision are (with upward speeds taken as positive)

$$u_1 = 2 \cdot \frac{m_1 v_0 - m_2 v_0}{m_1 + m_2} - v_0 = v_0 \cdot \frac{m_1 - 3m_2}{m_1 + m_2}. \tag{1}$$

$$u_2 = 2 \cdot \frac{m_1 v_0 - m_2 v_0}{m_1 + m_2} + v_0 = v_0 \cdot \frac{3m_1 - m_2}{m_1 + m_2}. \tag{2}$$

a) To make the mass m_1 stay at rest after the second collision (the collision with the upper object), we need $u_1 = 0$. Therefore it follows from (1) that

$$m_1 - 3m_2 = 0,$$

that is, the ratio of the masses in question is

$$\frac{m_1}{m_2} = 3.$$

b) Then the speed of the rebounding ball obtained from (2) is

$$u_2 = v_0 \frac{9m_2 - m_2}{3m_2 + m_2} = 2v_0,$$

and the maximum height reached can be calculated from the law $h = v^2/2g$:

$$h_1 = \frac{4v_0^2}{2g} = 4 \cdot \frac{v_0^2}{2g} = 4h.$$

Solution of Problem 66. Due to friction, the blocks will decelerate with $a = \mu g = $ $= 1 \text{ m/s}^2$ before and after the collision. Let v_1 and v_2 be the velocities of the blocks just before, u_1 and u_2 be the velocities of the blocks right after the collision. Since the collision is elastic, we know that:

$$u_1 = \frac{(m_1 - m_2)v_1 + 2m_2 v_2}{m_1 + m_2}, \qquad u_2 = \frac{2m_1 v_1 + (m_2 - m_1)v_2}{m_1 + m_2}.$$

In our case the velocity of block m_2 is $v_2 = 0$ before the collision, therefore

$$u_1 = v_1/4, \qquad \text{and} \qquad u_2 = 5 \cdot v_1/4.$$

a) Since m_2 stops at the edge of the table, its velocity after the collision must be $u_2 = \sqrt{2as_2} = \sqrt{2\mu g s_2}$, which means that the velocity of m_1 before the collision should be $v_1 = 4u_2/5 = 4\sqrt{2\mu g s_2}/5$. Therefore, m_1 should be given an initial velocity of

$$v_{1_0} = \sqrt{v_1^2 + 2\mu g s_1} = \sqrt{\frac{16}{25} \cdot 2\mu g s_2 + 2\mu g s_1}$$

Since in our case $s_1 = s_2$, we find:

$$v_{1_0} = \sqrt{\left(\frac{16}{25} + 1\right) 2\mu g s_1} = \sqrt{\frac{41}{25}} = 1.28 \frac{\text{m}}{\text{s}}.$$

b) If now m_1 is to stop at the edge of the table, it must have a velocity of

$$u_1 = \sqrt{2\mu g s_2}$$

after the collision. This means that its velocity should be

$$v_1 = 4u_1 = 4\sqrt{2\mu g s_2}$$

before the collision. Therefore it should be given an initial velocity of

$$v'_{1_0} = \sqrt{v_1^2 + 2\mu g s_1} = \sqrt{16 \cdot 2\mu g s_2 + 2\mu g s_1} = \sqrt{(16+1)2\mu g s_1} = \sqrt{17} = 4.12\,\frac{\text{m}}{\text{s}}.$$

Solution of Problem 67. In order to be able to solve the problem uniquely, the two objects must be considered as point-like ones. Both will reach the bottom of the sphere of radius R at a speed of $v = \sqrt{2gR}$ at the same moment. Here they collide totally elastically, and both the energy and the linear momentum are conserved. For the elastic collision the following holds true:

$$u_1 = 2\frac{m_1 v_1 + m_2 v_2}{m_1 + m_2} - v_1$$

(where the velocities of the objects before collision are $v_1 = \sqrt{2gR}$ and $v_2 = -\sqrt{2gR}$) the velocities of the objects of masses m_1 and m_2 after the collision are:

$$u_1 = 2\frac{(m_1 - m_2)\sqrt{2gR}}{m_1 + m_2} - \sqrt{2gR} = \frac{m_1 - 3m_2}{m_1 + m_2}\sqrt{2gR} = -0.6\sqrt{2gR},$$

calculating similarly

$$u_2 = 2\frac{(m_1 - m_2)\sqrt{2gR}}{m_1 + m_2} + \sqrt{2gR} = \frac{3m_1 - m_2}{m_1 + m_2}\sqrt{2gR} = 1.4\sqrt{2gR}.$$

With this speed the object of mass m_1 rises to a height of $h_1 = u_1^2/2g = 0.36R = = 0.72\,\text{m}$, and the object of mass m_2 ascends to a height of $h_2 = u_2^2/2g = 1.96R = = 3.92\,\text{m}$ So it goes $1.92\,\text{m}$ above the rim of the hemisphere.

Solution of Problem 68. If the collision is assumed to be momentary, it is enough to consider the forces acting between the colliding bodies, gravitational forces can be neglected. It is practical to apply the equality of impulse to the change in momentum to the directions x parallel to the inclined plane and y perpendicular to it:

$$\sum F_x \cdot \Delta t = \sum \Delta p_x$$

and

$$\sum F_y \cdot \Delta t = \sum \Delta p_y.$$

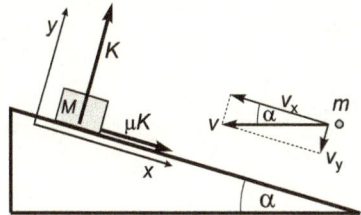

In detail, if axes are directed as shown in the figure:

$$\mu K \Delta t = (m+M)v_x - mv\cos\alpha, \tag{1}$$

$$K \Delta t = -mv\sin\alpha - 0, \tag{2}$$

where K is the mean value of the normal force exerted by the inclined plane on the block. (Before the collision, only the object of mass m has a velocity in the y direction, and neither object has any after the collision.)

More precisely,

$$\mu \int K(t)dt = (m+M)v_x - mv\cos\alpha,$$

$$\int K(t)dt = -mv\sin\alpha.$$

The term containing time is eliminated by substituting K from (2) into (1):

$$-\mu mv\sin\alpha = (m+M)v_x - mv\cos\alpha.$$

Hence the common speed of the objects moving together up the incline after the collision is

$$v_x = \frac{mv(\cos\alpha - \mu\sin\alpha)}{m+M}. \tag{3}$$

$$\left[v_x = \frac{0.4\,\text{kg} \cdot 12\,\text{m/s} \cdot (0.9600 - 0.2 \cdot 0.2798)}{0.4\,\text{kg} + 1.6\,\text{kg}} = 2.17\,\text{m/s} \right]$$

The acceleration of the object moving up the incline is

$$a = g(\sin\alpha + \mu\cos\alpha), \tag{4}$$

directed opposite to the velocity, and thus the stopping distance is

$$s = \frac{v_x^2}{2a}.$$

Hence with the use of the expressions (3) and (4):

$$s = \frac{\left(\frac{m}{m+M}\right)^2 v^2 (\cos\alpha - \mu\sin\alpha)^2}{2g(\sin\alpha + \mu\cos\alpha)}.$$

Numerically,

$$s = \frac{\left(\frac{0.4}{0.4+1.6}\right)^2 \cdot 144\,\frac{\text{m}^2}{\text{s}^2} \cdot (0.9600 - 0.2 \cdot 0.2798)^2}{2 \cdot 10\,\frac{\text{m}}{\text{s}^2} \cdot (0.2798 + 0.2 \cdot 0.9600)} = 0.499\,\text{m} \approx 0.5\ \text{m}.$$

Solution of Problem 69. With respect to the motion of the block, it does not matter whether the coefficients of static and kinetic friction are equal or not. In order for the block to slides back, it is necessary for the coefficient of static friction to be smaller then the tangent of the angle of inclination (so the angle of inclination must be greater then the 'critical angle' at which the block is just about to move). The turning of the block at the top of its path is momentary, thus this does not effect the time of the motion of the block. According to the problem, the interaction between the block and the bullet is momentary ('during the penetration the displacement of the block is negligible'), so during the interaction the system can be considered closed. (With respect to the internal forces the external ones are negligible.) Thus the total linear momentum of the system is conserved during the totally inelastic collision. The common initial speed is:

$$c = \frac{mv}{m+M}.$$

The block and the bullet embedded in it undergo uniformly decelerated motion, the acceleration of which has a magnitude of:

$$a_1 = g(\sin\alpha + \mu\cos\alpha)$$

The time of the upward motion until the block stops is

$$t_1 = \frac{c}{a_1} = \frac{mv}{2(m+M)g(\sin\alpha + \mu\cos\alpha)}.$$

The distance covered by the block during the upward motion is:

$$s = \frac{c^2}{2a_1} = \frac{m^2v^2}{2(m+M)^2g(\sin\alpha + \mu\cos\alpha)}.$$

After reaching the top, the block undergoes uniformly accelerated downward motion, covering the same distance as it covered when it moved up. The acceleration of this downward motion is:

$$a_2 = g(\sin\alpha - \mu\cos\alpha).$$

The time while it moves down is:

$$t_2 = \sqrt{\frac{2s}{a_2}} = \sqrt{\frac{m^2v^2}{(m+M)^2g(\sin\alpha + \mu\cos\alpha)g(\sin\alpha - \mu\cos\alpha)}} =$$

$$= \frac{mv}{(m+M)g} \cdot \frac{1}{\sqrt{\sin^2\alpha - \mu\cos^2\alpha}}.$$

The total time elapsed until the block reaches the buffer again is:

$$t_1 + t_2 = \frac{mv}{(m+M)g}\left(\frac{1}{\sin\alpha + \mu\cos\alpha} + \frac{1}{\sqrt{\sin^2\alpha - \mu^2\cos^2\alpha}}\right).$$

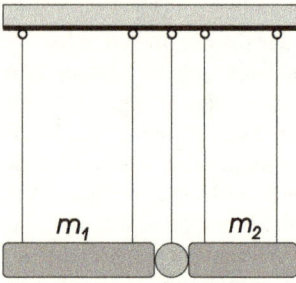

m_1 m_2

Solution of Problem 70. The bifilar hanging of the rods ensures that the rods undergo only translational motion. If their centres of mass are raised by a height of h, after releasing them, before the collision their speed will be $v = \sqrt{2gh}$. The linear momentum of the system is conserved during the inelastic (momentary) collision, but some part of the kinetic energy is distributed between the lots of degrees of freedom of the particles of the object which is deformed inelastically, which is the so called internal energy of the object. The decrease in the kinetic energy is equal to the work done in order to deform the object, thus the greater the change in the kinetic energy, the more efficient the hammering.

Because the mass of the ball, made of inelastic material, is negligible, the collision can be considered as the collision of two bodies. In case of an inelastic head-on collision of two objects the common speed of the objects can be calculated, and is equal to the speed of the centre of mass:

$$u = \frac{m_1 v_1 + m_2 v_2}{m_1 + m_2}.$$

Using the above speed the change in the kinetic energy is:

$$\Delta E_{\text{mech}} = \frac{1}{2}(m_1 + m_2) \cdot \frac{(m_1 v_1 + m_2 v_2)^2}{(m_1 + m_2)^2} - \frac{1}{2}m_1 v_1^2 - \frac{1}{2}m_2 v_2^2 =$$

$$= -\frac{1}{2} \cdot \frac{m_1 m_2}{m_1 + m_2} \cdot (v_2 - v_1)^2.$$

Considering the speeds of the colliding objects, the expression is symmetrical, so, from the point of view of the inelastic deformation, it is all the same whether or not the smaller or the greater object collides with the other, standing one of the same speed. From the point of view of the efficiency of the deformation, it is definitely better to move the smaller object, because less work is done while the smaller object is accelerated. This is why anvils are heavy, and in most of the cases they are fixed to the ground to increase their 'effective' mass. (During the hammering waves are generated in the Earth, thus some energy is lost, this is why it is not correct to add the mass of the Earth and the mass of the anvil).

The efficiency of the hammering is the quotient of the energy used to deform the ball and the total work done, thus if m_2 is the mass of the moving rod and considering that $v_1 = 0$:

$$\eta = \frac{\Delta E}{W_{\text{total}}} = \frac{\frac{1}{2} \cdot \frac{m_1 m_2}{m_1 + m_2} \cdot v_2^2}{\frac{1}{2}m_2 v_2^2} = \frac{m_1}{m_1 + m_2} = \frac{1}{1 + \frac{m_2}{m_1}}.$$

From the result, it can be seen that the efficiency is greater if the mass of the hammer m_2 is smaller with respect to the mass of the anvil. Of course, if the mass of the hammer is too small, we have to the anvil a lot of times in order to achieve the same result. This means that when the mass of the hammer is decreased, another factor decreases the efficiency, namely that whenever the hammer is raised, we have to raise the mass of our hand as well.

Solution of Problem 71. At the instant of the explosion the projectile was at rest. Because the explosion is momentary, the external (gravitational) force can be neglected compared to the internal forces. Thus the total linear momentum of the projectile during the explosion did not change. Therefore the two parts move in opposite directions after the explosion. Let us denote these velocities with v_1 and v_2, and the angle which is between the horizontal and the line which coincides with the velocity vectors with α and the time which elapses between the explosion and the moment of landing with t_1 and t_2. According to the conservation of linear momentum:

$$\frac{m_1}{m_2} = \frac{v_2}{v_1}.$$

From the datum which states that the covered horizontal distances are equal:

$$v_1 \cos\alpha \cdot t_1 = v_2 \cos\alpha \cdot t_2.$$

From these:

$$\frac{t_1}{t_2} = \frac{v_2}{v_1} = \frac{m_1}{m_2}.$$

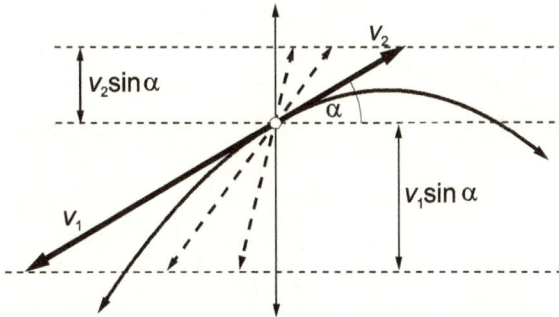

Since $m_2 > m_1$, it is true for the elapsed times as well that $t_2 > t_1$, so $t_2 = t_1 + T$ can only be true if the smaller part of the projectile is above the other, larger part, because the part that starts to move upward lands later.

Expressing the height of the explosion from the kinematic equations written for both parts:

$$h = v_1 \sin\alpha \cdot t_1 + \frac{1}{2}gt_1^2, \tag{1}$$

and

$$h = -v_2 \sin\alpha \cdot t_2 + \frac{1}{2}g(t_1 + T)^2. \tag{2}$$

173

Let us express v_2 and t_2 in terms of v_1 and t_1 and substitute them into the second equation:

$$h = -v_1 \frac{m_1}{m_2} \sin\alpha \cdot \frac{m_2}{m_1} t_1 + \frac{1}{2}g\left(\frac{m_2}{m_1}t_1\right)^2,$$

so

$$h = -v_1 \sin\alpha \cdot t_1 + \frac{1}{2}g\left(\frac{m_2}{m_1}t_1\right)^2. \tag{2'}$$

Adding the equations (1) and (2') :

$$2h = \frac{1}{2}g\left[t_1^2 + \left(\frac{m_2}{m_1}t_1\right)^2\right].$$

using $t_1 = t_2 - T = \dfrac{m_2}{m_1}t_1 - T$, can be written into t_1 :

$$t_1 = \frac{m_1}{m_2 - m_1}T,$$

Thus the height of the explosion is:

$$4h = g\left[\frac{m_1^2}{(m_2 - m_1)^2}T^2 + \frac{m_2^2}{m_1^2}\cdot\frac{m_1^2}{(m_2 - m_1)^2}T^2\right],$$

from which

$$h = \frac{1}{4}g\frac{m_1^2 + m_2^2}{(m_2 - m_1)^2}T^2 = \frac{1}{4}\cdot 9.8\,\frac{\mathrm{m}}{\mathrm{s}^2}\cdot\frac{9 + 36}{9}\cdot 16\ \mathrm{s}^2 = 194\,\mathrm{m}.$$

It worth to it introduce k for the ratio $\dfrac{m_2}{m_1}$ because it makes the calculation simpler:

$$k = \frac{m_2}{m_1} = \frac{v_1}{v_2} = \frac{t_2}{t_1}.$$

Because $t_2 - t_1 = T$

$$t_1 = t_2 - T = kt_1 - T,$$

from which

$$t_1 = \frac{T}{k - 1}, \tag{a}$$

and similarly

$$t_2 = \frac{kT}{k - 1}. \tag{b}$$

The height of the explosion is:

$$h = kv_2\sin\alpha \cdot t_1 + \frac{g}{2}t_1^2, \qquad \text{and} \qquad h = -v_2\sin\alpha \cdot t_2 + \frac{g}{2}t_2^2.$$

These two equations are an equation system with variables h and $v_2\sin\alpha$. Using the values expressed in (a) and (b) the solutions are:

$$h = \frac{g}{4}\cdot\frac{k^2 + 1}{(k - 1)^2}\cdot T^2 \quad \text{and} \quad v_2\sin\alpha = \frac{g(k + 1)}{4k}\cdot T.$$

From the data of the problem v_1 and v_2 cannot be calculated, just $v_1 \sin\alpha$ and $v_2 \sin\alpha$. The endpoints of the possible v_1 and v_2 velocity vectors are on parallel horizontal lines.

Using the data of our problem: $k = 2$, $t_1 = 4\,\text{s}$, $t_2 = 8\,\text{s}$, $h = 196\,\text{m}$, $v_1 \sin\alpha = 29.4\,\text{m/s}$, $v_2 \sin\alpha = 14.7\,\text{m/s}$.

Interesting results are gained if we calculate the speeds which belong to the different velocity-directions. For example there is no finite solution for v_1 if the angle is 0^0.

$10°$	$20°$	$30°$	$45°$	$60°$	$70°$	$80°$	$90°$	
169.3	85.95	58.8	36	33.95	31.28	29.85	29.4	(m/s)

Remark: If we would like to solve the problem for the special case when the velocities after the explosion are vertical, the result would not be unique. In this case the datum that the travelled horizontal distances are equal does not give any condition for the times of fall since the equation $v_1 \cos\alpha \cdot t_1 = v_2 \cos\alpha \cdot t_2$ is an identity because $\cos\alpha = \cos 90^0 = 0$. Thus the conditions of the problem can be satisfied for any height.

First solution of Problem 72. The simplest way to solve the problem is to apply the centre of mass theorem: the centre of mass of a system moves as if the total mass of the system was concentrated at the centre of the mass, and all the external forces acted upon it. In our case the centre of mass of the two pieces moves as if the projectile did not explode: it continues moving along the initial parabolic orbit of the projectile. (The explosion was caused by internal forces, and we neglect air resistance, as it is usual in these types of problems.) Let us follow the motion of both pieces and the centre of mass.

The position of the centre of mass is described by its coordinates. At the instant when the piece of mass $m_1 = m$ hits the ground, i.e. at time $t_2 = t_1 + \Delta t$ the coordinates of the centre of mass are:

$$x_{\text{cm}} = v_0 \cos\alpha \cdot t_2 = 150\,\frac{\text{m}}{\text{s}} \cdot \cos 60° \cdot 20\,\text{s} = 1500\,\text{m},$$

$$y_{\text{cm}} = v_0 \sin\alpha \cdot t_2 - \frac{1}{2}gt_2^2 = 150\,\frac{\text{m}}{\text{s}} \cdot \sin 60° \cdot 20\,\text{s} - \frac{10}{2}\,\frac{\text{m}}{\text{s}^2} \cdot 400\,\text{s}^2 = 598\,\text{m}.$$

The centre of mass divides the section between the two pieces into two parts with lengths

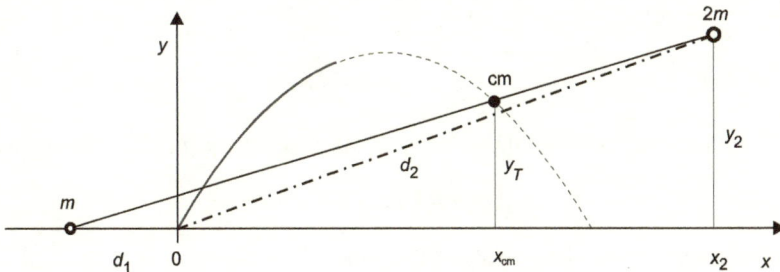

inversely proportional to the masses m and $2m$ at the ends. This means that from the centre of mass the distance of the piece m hitting the ground is twice as much as that of the other piece of mass $2m$. So, using the notations of the figure, the x coordinate of the piece of mass $2m$ satisfies the equation:

$$\frac{d_1 + x_2}{d_1 + x_{cm}} = \frac{500 \text{ m} + x_2}{500 \text{ m} + 1500 \text{ m}} = \frac{3}{2},$$

so

$$x_2 = \frac{6000 \text{ m}}{2} - 500 \text{ m} = 2500 \text{ m},$$

and for the y coordinate

$$\frac{y_2}{y_{cm}} = \frac{3}{2},$$

so

$$y_2 = \frac{3}{2} y_{cm} = \frac{3}{2} \cdot 598 \text{ m} = 897 \text{ m}.$$

Finally, the distance in question can be obtained with the help of Pythagoras' theorem:

$$d_2 = \sqrt{x_2^2 + y_2^2} = \sqrt{2500^2 \text{ m}^2 + 897^2 \text{ m}^2} = 2656 \text{ m}.$$

Second solution of Problem 72. A more complicated way of finding the solution is the following.

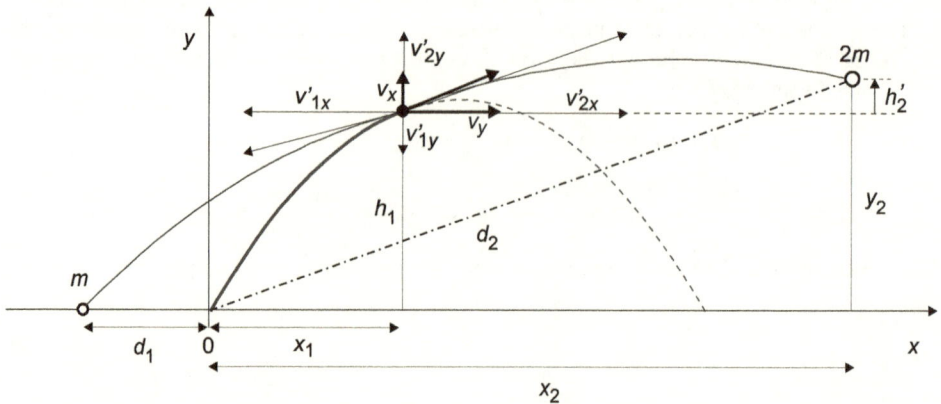

The horizontal component of the velocity of the projectile just before the explosion is:

$$v_x = v_0 \cos\alpha = 150 \frac{\text{m}}{\text{s}} \cdot 0.5 = 75 \frac{\text{m}}{\text{s}}.$$

The vertical component of the velocity of the projectile at the moment of the explosion is:

$$v_y = v_0 \sin\alpha - gt = 150 \frac{\text{m}}{\text{s}} \cdot 0.866 - 10 \frac{\text{m}}{\text{s}^2} \cdot 10 \text{ s} = 30 \frac{\text{m}}{\text{s}}.$$

The horizontal and vertical component of the momentum of the projectile at the moment of the explosion are:

$$I_x = 3m \cdot v_x = 3m \cdot 75 \; \frac{\text{m}}{\text{s}} = 225 \; \frac{\text{m}}{\text{s}} \cdot m$$

$$I_y = 3m \cdot v_y = 3m \cdot 30 \; \frac{\text{m}}{\text{s}} = 90 \; \frac{\text{m}}{\text{s}} \cdot m.$$

The altitude and the horizontal displacement of the projectile at the moment of the explosion are:

$$h_1 = v_0 \sin \alpha \cdot t_1 - \frac{1}{2} g t_1^2 = 150 \; \frac{\text{m}}{\text{s}} \cdot 0.866 \cdot 10 \; \text{s} - 5 \; \frac{\text{m}}{\text{s}^2} \cdot 100 \; \text{s}^2 = 800 \; \text{m},$$

$$x_1 = v_0 \cos \alpha \cdot t_1 = 150 \; \frac{\text{m}}{\text{s}} \cdot 0.5 \cdot 10 \; \text{s} = 750 \; \text{m}.$$

Calculated from the data given in the problem, the horizontal velocity component of the piece of mass $m_1 = m$ after the explosion is:

$$v'_{1x} = -\frac{x_1 + d_1}{\Delta t} = -\frac{750 \; \text{m} + 500 \; \text{m}}{10 \; \text{s}} = -125 \; \frac{\text{m}}{\text{s}}.$$

Since this piece falls from the altitude $h_1 = 800$ m to the ground in $\Delta t = 10$ s,

$$h_1 + v'_{1y} \Delta t - \frac{1}{2} g (\Delta t)^2 = 0,$$

so the vertical velocity component of this piece just after the explosion is:

$$v'_{1y} = \frac{1}{2} g \Delta t - \frac{h_1}{\Delta t} = 50 \; \frac{\text{m}}{\text{s}} - 80 \; \frac{\text{m}}{\text{s}} = -30 \; \frac{\text{m}}{\text{s}}.$$

Applying the law of conservation of momentum in the horizontal direction,

$$3m v_x = m v'_{1x} + 2m v'_{2x},$$

from which the horizontal velocity component of the piece of mass $2m$ is:

$$v'_{2x} = \frac{3 v_x - v'_{1x}}{2} = \frac{3 \cdot 75 - (-125)}{2} \; \frac{\text{m}}{\text{s}} = 175 \; \frac{\text{m}}{\text{s}}.$$

The momentum conservation law in the vertical direction is:

$$3m v_y = m v'_{1y} + 2m v'_{2y},$$

which means that the initial vertical velocity of the piece of mass $2m$ just after the explosion is:

$$v'_{2y} = \frac{3 v_y - v'_{1y}}{2} = \frac{3 \cdot 30 - (-30)}{2} \; \frac{\text{m}}{\text{s}} = 60 \; \frac{\text{m}}{\text{s}}.$$

After the explosion, this piece performs a projectile motion for a time Δt. The initial horizontal position (measured from the cannon) is x_1, the initial altitude is h_1, while the horizontal and vertical components of the initial velocity are v'_{2x} and v'_{2y}, respectively. During the time Δt, the altitude change of this piece of the projectile is

$$h'_2 = v'_{2y} \Delta t - \frac{1}{2} g (\Delta t)^2 = 60 \; \frac{\text{m}}{\text{s}} \cdot 10 \; \text{s} - 5 \; \frac{\text{m}}{\text{s}^2} \cdot 100 \; \text{s}^2 = 100 \; \text{m}$$

which means that the piece gets

$$h_2 = y_2 = h_1 + h_2' = 800 \text{ m} + 100\text{m} = 900\text{m}$$

high above the ground.

On the other hand, in a horizontal direction the fragment gets

$$x_2' = v_{2x}' \Delta t = 175 \, \frac{\text{m}}{\text{s}} \cdot 10 \text{ s} = 1750 \text{ m}$$

far from the place of explosion, so at a horizontal distance

$$x_2 = x_1 + x_2' = 750 \text{ m} + 1750 \text{ m} = 2500 \text{ m}$$

from the cannon.

It means that at the moment when the piece of mass $m_1 = m$ hits the ground, the distance of the other fragment of mass $m_2 = 2m$ from the cannon is:

$$d_2 = \sqrt{x_2^2 + y_2^2} = \sqrt{2500^2 \text{ m}^2 + 900^2 \text{ m}^2} = 2657 \text{ m}.$$

Solution of Problem 73. The initial momentum of the system consisting of the trolley and the object is $(M+m) \cdot V$. At the moment of the launch, an impulse is exerted on the trolley in a backward direction. Let U denote the new speed of the trolley. After the launch the speed of the object relative to the ground is $U+v$.

By the momentum conservation law,

$$MU + m(U+v) = (M+m)V.$$

The final speed U of the trolley can be expressed,

$$U = \frac{(M+m)V - mv}{M+m} = V - \frac{m}{M+m}v$$

so the speed of the object relative to the ground is:

$$v_{\text{ground}} = U + v = V - \frac{m}{M+m}v + v = V + \frac{M}{M+m}v = \frac{M(V+v)+mV}{M+m}.$$

Numerically:

$$v_{\text{ground}} = \frac{20 \text{ kg} \cdot \left(10 \, \frac{\text{m}}{\text{s}} + 2 \, \frac{\text{m}}{\text{s}}\right) + 2 \text{ kg} \cdot 10 \, \frac{\text{m}}{\text{s}}}{20 \text{ kg} + 2 \text{ kg}} \approx 11.82 \, \frac{\text{m}}{\text{s}}.$$

The kinetic energy of the object relative to the ground is:

$$E = \frac{1}{2}mv_{\text{ground}}^2 = \frac{1}{2} \cdot 2 \text{ kg} \cdot \left(11.82 \, \frac{\text{m}}{\text{s}}\right)^2 = 139.71 \text{ J}.$$

Solution of Problem 74. a) The speed of the body of mass m_1 at the moment of the collision is

$$u_1 = \sqrt{2gH}.$$

The speed of the centre of mass of the two balls at this moment is

$$v_{\mathrm{cm}} = \frac{m_1 u_1}{m_1 + m_2}.$$

The speed of the body with mass m_2 after the collision is

$$v_2 = 2v_{\mathrm{cm}} - u_2 = \frac{2m_1 u_1}{m_1 + m_2} = \frac{2m_1 \sqrt{2gH}}{m_1 + m_2},$$

because $u_2 = 0$, and for the body with mass m_1

$$v_1 = 2v_{\mathrm{cm}} - u_1 = \frac{2m_1 u_1}{m_1 + m_2} - u_1 = \frac{m_1 - m_2}{m_1 + m_2} \sqrt{2gH}.$$

The heights to which the bodies rise

$$h_1 = \frac{v_1^2}{2g} = \left(\frac{m_1 - m_2}{m_1 + m_2} \sqrt{2gH} \right)^2 \cdot \frac{1}{2g} = \left(\frac{m_1 - m_2}{m_1 + m_2} \right)^2 \cdot H,$$

and

$$h_2 = \frac{v_2^2}{2g} = \left(\frac{2m_1 \sqrt{2gH}}{m_1 + m_2} \right)^2 \cdot \frac{1}{2g} = \frac{4m_1^2}{(m_1 + m_2)^2} \cdot H.$$

Making use of the condition $h_1 = h_2$, from the previous two equations the $(m_1 - m_2)^2 = 4m_1^2$ quadratic equation is acquired. After rearrangement

$$m_2^2 - 2m_1 m_2 - 3m_1^2 = 0,$$

whose solution is:

$$m_2 = \frac{2m_1 \pm \sqrt{4m_1^2 + 12m_1^2}}{2} = \frac{2m_1 \pm 4m_1}{2}$$

and the physically realistic value of the unknown mass is $m_2 = 3m_1 = 0.6\,\mathrm{kg}$.

b) If the relationship $m_2 = 3m_1$ is substituted into any of the equations for the height to which the bodies rise, for the given ratio

$$h_1 = h_2 = \frac{4m_1^2}{(4m_1)^2} \cdot H = \frac{H}{4}$$

is acquired.

Solution of Problem 75. Since the friction is negligible, the forces between the two disks are radial, their tangential components are zero, so the disks do not start rotating after the collision.

From geometric considerations the angle α of the force acting on the disk, which is initially at rest, satisfies the following equation:

$$\sin \alpha = \frac{R}{2R} = 0.5 \rightarrow \alpha = \arcsin 0.5 = 30°.$$

Since this disk is initially at rest, both its acceleration and its velocity $\vec{u}_1$ makes this angle $\alpha = 30°$ with the initial velocity $\vec{v}_0$ of the other disk.

The velocity of the other disk and the speed of the first disk after the collision can be determined from the conservation law of energy and momentum.

According to the conservation of momentum:

$$m\vec{v}_0 = m\vec{u}_1 + m\vec{u}_2,$$

thus

$$\vec{v}_0 = \vec{u}_1 + \vec{u}_2. \tag{1}$$

According to the law of mechanical energy conservation:

$$\frac{1}{2}mv_0^2 = \frac{1}{2}mu_1^2 + \frac{1}{2}mu_2^2,$$

so

$$v_0^2 = u_1^2 + u_2^2. \tag{2}$$

By equation (1) the initial velocity and the final velocities form a triangle, and by (2) the sides of this triangle satisfy Pythagoras' theorem, so it is a right triangle, where u_1 and u_2 are the two legs of the triangle, and v_0 is the hypotenuse. With the notations of the figure: $\beta = 90°$, $\gamma = 60°$, so $\vec{u}_2$ makes an angle of $60°$ with $\vec{v}_0$.

From the triangle formed by the three vectors $\vec{u}_1$, $\vec{u}_2$ and $\vec{v}_0$ we get that:

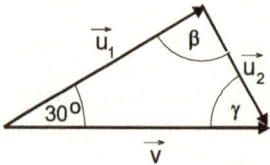

$$u_1 = v_0\cos 30° = v_0\frac{\sqrt{3}}{2} \approx 0.866\ \frac{\text{m}}{\text{s}},$$

$$u_2 = v_0\sin 30° = v_0\frac{1}{2} = 0.5\ \frac{\text{m}}{\text{s}}.$$

Solution of Problem 76. It is important to analyse the process in detail.

1. There are two elastic collisions in the process. The first one is between the disks A and B. Since their masses are equal, $m_A = m_B$, the two disks exchange velocities: A stops, and B starts moving at the speed v in the direction of the original velocity of A. (It seems as if the disk B had been given a velocity v instantaneously.)

2. After the instantaneous velocity-exchange, the second elastic collision takes place at the moment when the thread is suddenly stretched. It gives a pull to the two disks at its ends, by exerting an impulse of opposite direction and equal magnitude on the disks B and C. So the changes of momentum of the disks B and C have the same magnitude in opposite direction. (We could attribute the first collision as 'pushing', the second one as a 'pulling' collision.)

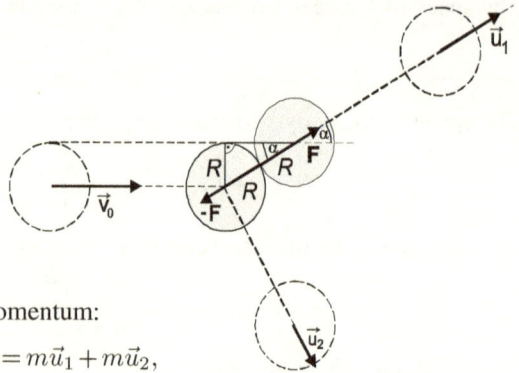

3. Although the centre of mass of the system consisting of the three disks moves at a speed $v/3$ in the direction of v, after the first collision the mass m_A can be omitted, and the whole process can be investigated as if the mass m_B had been suddenly given an initial velocity v.

4. Since initially the disk C is at rest, and there are no external forces, the centre of mass of the system consisting of the two remaining masses m_B and m_C performs a uniform motion at the speed $v/2$ in the direction of the initial trajectory of disk A.

5. The second collision can be the best understood by splitting the velocities in directions parallel and perpendicular to the thread. The impulse exerted by the thread has no perpendicular component, so in this direction the velocity components are unaltered. In the direction parallel to the thread, however, an elastic collision takes place between the two disks of equal masses, so in this direction the velocity components are exchanged. Using the fact that the angle $\alpha = 45°$, a simple geometric consideration states that in the direction parallel to the initial velocity $\vec{v}$ of A the velocity components of both B and C become $v/2$ after the collision. (This is, at the same time, the velocity of the centre of mass of the two disks, in accordance with the previous point).

6. Let the axis y be parallel to the trajectory of the disk A. The impulse exerted by the thread on the disk C has the same direction as the thread, thus C starts moving at a speed u_C in a direction making an angle $45°$ with the axis y.

7. Since the y component of this velocity is $u_{Cy} = v/2$, and because of the $45°$ angle, the x component of the velocity is also $u_{Cx} = v/2$.

8. Since in the x direction the centre of mass does not move, the x component of the velocity of B after the second collision has the same magnitude $u_{Bx} = v/2$ as u_{Cx} (but opposite direction). Thus the velocity u_B also makes also an angle of $45°$ with the y axis.

9. So after the second collision both disks have the speed

$$u_B = u_C = \sqrt{u_x^2 + u_y^2} = \sqrt{\frac{v^2}{4} + \frac{v^2}{4}} = v\frac{\sqrt{2}}{2}.$$

(It is the length of the diagonal of a square of side $v/2$).

10. The disk B moves perpendicularly to the initial direction of the thread, while disk C moves parallel to the thread. It means that the thread becomes loose immediately after the collision, and both disks perform a uniform motion.

11. The line passing through the midpoints of the disks becomes parallel to the initial velocity (trajectory) of disk A, when both disks cover the distance $\dfrac{l}{2} \cdot \dfrac{\sqrt{2}}{2}$ in the x direction at the speed $u_{Bx} = v/2$. The time needed for it, after the collisions, is:

$$t = \frac{\frac{l}{2} \cdot \frac{\sqrt{2}}{2}}{\frac{v}{2}} = \frac{l}{v} \cdot \frac{\sqrt{2}}{2} = \frac{1 \text{ m}}{2 \frac{\text{m}}{\text{s}}} \cdot \frac{\sqrt{2}}{2} = \frac{\sqrt{2}}{4} \approx 0.35(4) \text{ s}.$$

12. At this moment the distance of A from both of the other two disks is $l/2$, and the distance between B and C is:

$$l\frac{\sqrt{2}}{2} \approx 0.71 \text{ m}.$$

The details of the successive collisions are illustrated in a series of figures. The first and second figure show the velocities just after the first and second collision respectively. The third figure indicates the moment when the line of B and C is parallel to the trajectory of A.

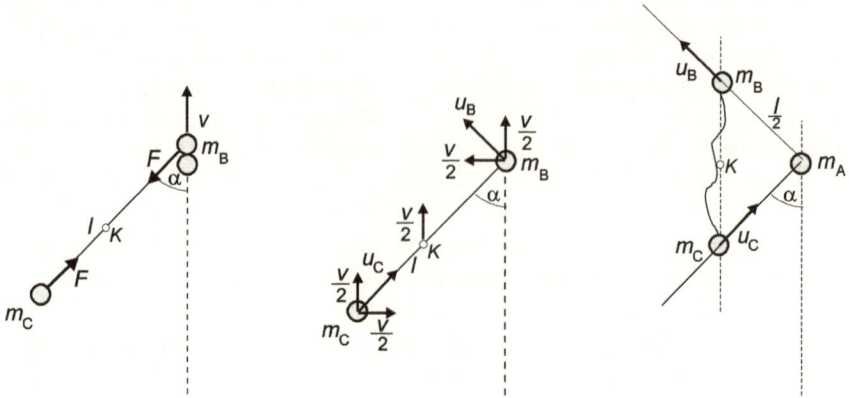

To complete the solution of the problem, we check the validity of the basic conservation laws for the process.

Check.

Statement:

I. The momentum is conserved.

II. The angular momentum is conserved.

III. The mechanical energy is conserved.

Proof:

I. We write separately the components of the momentum. In the y direction:

$$mv = mu_{By} + mu_{Cy} = m\frac{v}{2} + m\frac{v}{2} = mv.$$

In the x direction:

$$0 = mu_{Bx} + mu_{Cx} = m\frac{v}{2} + \left(-m\frac{v}{2}\right) = 0.$$

II. We calculate the angular momentum with respect to the initial position of the midpoint of the thread.

Initially the disks B and C are at rest, and the total angular momentum is carried by the (orbital) angular momentum of A. In the first collision this angular momentum is transferred to the disk B. In the second collision the impulse exerted by the thread is collinear with the thread, so it has no torque with respect to the midpoint of the thread and does not change the angular momenta of the disks. Formally:

$$mv\frac{l}{2}\cdot\frac{\sqrt{2}}{2} = mu_B\frac{l}{2} = m\frac{v}{2}\sqrt{2}\frac{l}{2} = mv\frac{l}{2}\cdot\frac{\sqrt{2}}{2}.$$

III. The total mechanical energy of the system is the sum of translational kinetic energies of its parts. The values of this sum before the first collision, and after the second collision are equal:

$$\frac{1}{2}m_Av_A^2 = \frac{1}{2}m_Bu_B^2 + \frac{1}{2}m_Cu_C^2 = \frac{1}{2}m_B\left(u_{Bx}^2 + u_{By}^2\right) + \frac{1}{2}m_C\left(u_{Cx}^2 + u_{Cy}^2\right) =$$
$$= \frac{1}{2}m\left(\frac{v^2}{4} + \frac{v^2}{4}\right) + \frac{1}{2}m\left(\frac{v^2}{4} + \frac{v^2}{4}\right) = \frac{1}{2}mv^2 = \frac{1}{2}m_Av_A^2,$$

since $m_A = m_B = m_C = m$.

Solution of Problem 77. In vertical direction the equation of motion of the released ball at the lowest point is:

$$K - mg = m\frac{v^2}{l}.$$

The speed v of the ball at this point is obtained from the energy conservation law:

$$mg\Delta h = \frac{1}{2}mv^2,$$

where Δh is the altitude loss of the ball, i.e., $l - l\cos\varphi_0 = l(1 - \cos\varphi_0)$. So the speed of the ball at its lowest position is:

$$v = \sqrt{2gl(1 - \cos\varphi_0)}.$$

The threshold force in the thread is:

$$K_1 = mg + m\frac{2gl(1 - \cos\varphi_0)}{l} = mg(3 - 2\cdot\cos\varphi_0) = mg(3 - 2\cdot\cos 60°) = 2mg.$$

Since the masses are equal, the two balls exchange their velocities in the totally elastic collision. The formula of the force in the second (shorter) thread is similar to that of the longer thread. The speed of the second ball is equal to the speed of the first ball, but in the centripetal acceleration $l/2$ has to be used for the radius. So

$$K_2 = mg + m\frac{2gl(1 - \cos\varphi)}{\frac{l}{2}} = mg\left(1 + \frac{4gl(1 - \cos\varphi)}{l}\right) = mg(5 - 4\cos\varphi),$$

where φ is the maximal initial angle of the longer pendulum, at which the threads do not break. This angle should be less than $60°$, since otherwise the first thread would break before the collision. We have to investigate the threshold condition for the second thread as well.

Since the two threads are made of the same material, the threshold force for the second thread is also $2mg$. From the equation $K_2 = 2mg$ we get the following condition for the angle φ:

$$2mg = (5 - 4\cos\varphi)mg,$$

from which the cosine of the maximal angle is

$$4\cos\varphi = 3.$$

It means that the threads do not break, if

$$\varphi < \arccos\frac{3}{4} = 41.4°.$$

Solution of Problem 78. Due to the elastic collision, the pendulum that was displaced initially stops and the second starts its oscillating motion at speed

$$v_0 = \sqrt{2gl(1 - \cos\alpha)}.$$

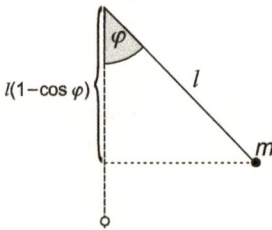

From this moment onwards, the system is closed (in the horizontal direction). In the extreme position of the pendulum $v = V$, where V stands for the instantaneous velocity of the trolley. The momentum balance is:

$$mv_0 = mv + MV = (m + M)V,$$

from this, the velocity of the trolley at the instant of maximum displacement is

$$V = \frac{m}{m + M}v_0.$$

The energy balance is:

$$\frac{1}{2}mv_0^2 = \frac{1}{2}(m + M)V^2 + mgl(1 - \cos\varphi),$$

where φ is the angle of the maximum displacement of the thread.

Substituting expressions $\left(\dfrac{m}{m+M}\right)^2 2gl(1 - \cos\alpha)$ for V^2 and $2gl(1 - \cos\alpha)$ for v_0^2, after simplifying and transformations the following expressions are acquired for the cosine of the unknown angle and the angle of the maximum displacement:

$$\cos\varphi = \frac{m + M\cos\alpha}{m + M}$$

$$\varphi = \arccos\frac{m + M\cos\alpha}{m + M} = 45.6°.$$

Solution of Problem 79. Assume that the rod is thin, and consider the time instant right before the collision. Let v_0 denote the speed of the centre of mass (the middle) of the rod relative to the ground, and let v_c denote the speed of the cart. Let $v_{e_{rel}}$ be the impact speed of the end of the rod that is wanted.

Since the external forces acting on the system have no horizontal components, horizontal momentum is conserved (the centre of mass of the system will not move in the horizontal direction):

$$mv_0 + 2mv_c = 0,$$

and hence the speed of the cart right before the collision is

$$v_c = -\frac{v_0}{2}. \qquad (1)$$

The speed of the middle of the rod relative to the cart is then

$$v_{0_{rel}} = v_0 - v_c = v_0 - \left(-\frac{v_0}{2}\right) = \frac{3}{2}v_0,$$

and the speed of the end of the rod relative to the cart is

$$v_{e_{rel}} = 2v_{0_{rel}} = 3v_0. \qquad (2)$$

To determine the speed of the centre of the rod before the collision, the work-energy theorem can be used:

$$mg \cdot \frac{L}{2} = \frac{1}{2}mv_0^2 + \frac{1}{2}\Theta_0\omega^2 + \frac{1}{2}(2m)v_c^2, \qquad (3)$$

where

$$\Theta_0 = \frac{1}{12}mL^2$$

is the moment of inertia of the rod about its centre of mass. With the use of (2), the angular velocity of the rod and the relative speed of its endpoint are related as follows:

$$\omega = \frac{v_{e_{rel}}}{L} = \frac{3v_0}{L}.$$

Substitution into the equation (3) multiplied by two gives

$$mgL = mv_0^2 + \frac{1}{12}mL^2 \cdot \frac{9v_0^2}{L^2} + 2m\frac{v_0^2}{4},$$

which simplifies to

$$gL = v_0^2 + \frac{3}{4}v_0^2 + \frac{v_0^2}{2} = \frac{9}{4}v_0^2.$$

Hence the speed of the centre of the rod relative to the ground right before the collision is

$$v_0 = \frac{2}{3}\sqrt{gL}, \qquad (4)$$

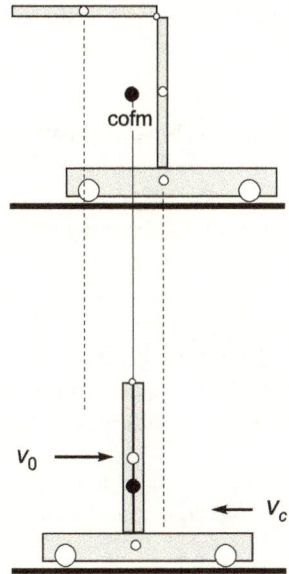

185

and thus the speed of the end of the rod relative to the cart is obtained from (2) and (4):

$$v_{e_{rel}} = 3v_0 = 2\sqrt{gL} = 8.94 \, \frac{m}{s}.$$

Solution of Problem 80. The speed of the weight at the 'collision' is:

$$v = \sqrt{2gh}.$$

Since the collision is instantaneous (very short), the effect of the gravitational force during the collision is negligible, thus the angular momentum of the system with respect to the axis of rotation is conserved:

$$mvR = muR + \frac{1}{2}MR^2\omega.$$

Since the thread is inelastic, it gives the constraint:

$$u = R\omega,$$

which can be put in the previous equation to obtain:

$$mv = mu + \frac{1}{2}Mu,$$

from which we get that

$$u = \frac{2m}{2m+M}v.$$

Substituting the numerical data:

$$u = \frac{2m}{2m+M}\sqrt{2gh} = \frac{2 \cdot 3 \text{ kg}}{2 \cdot 3 \text{ kg} + 2 \text{ kg}}\sqrt{2 \cdot 9.81 \, \frac{m}{s^2} \cdot 1.2 \text{ m}} = 3.64 \, \frac{m}{s}.$$

From this point on, the weight performs uniformly accelerated motion with initial speed u. The acceleration has to be determined.

The equation of motion of the weight is:

$$mg - K = ma,$$

and the equation of motion describing the rotation of the cylinder is:

$$KR = \frac{1}{2}MR^2\beta,$$

where $\beta = a/R$.

So the tension in the thread is:

$$K = \frac{1}{2}Ma.$$

Inserting it into the equation of motion, we get

$$mg - \frac{1}{2}Ma = ma,$$

which means that the acceleration of the weight is:

$$a = \frac{2m}{2m+M}g.$$

With numerical values:

$$a = \frac{2m}{2m+M}g = \frac{2 \cdot 3 \text{ kg}}{2 \cdot 3 \text{ kg} + 2 \text{ kg}} \cdot 9.81 \, \frac{\text{m}}{\text{s}^2} = 7.36 \, \frac{\text{m}}{\text{s}^2}.$$

The time needed for the first stage of the motion (until the collision) is:

$$t_1 = \sqrt{\frac{2h}{g}} = \sqrt{\frac{2.4 \text{ m}}{9.81 \, \frac{\text{m}}{\text{s}^2}}} = 0.495 \text{ s}.$$

The time of the second stage of the motion can be determined from the following kinematic equation:

$$h = ut + \frac{1}{2}at^2,$$

which has the more convenient form: $at^2 + 2ut - 2h = 0$.
The solution of this equation is:

$$t_2 = \frac{-u \mp \sqrt{u^2 + 2ah}}{a}.$$

The numerical value of the physically reasonable root is:

$$t_2 = \frac{-3.64 \, \frac{\text{m}}{\text{s}} + \sqrt{13.25 \, \frac{\text{m}^2}{\text{s}^2} + 2 \cdot 7.36 \, \frac{\text{m}}{\text{s}^2} \cdot 1.2 \text{ m}}}{7.36 \, \frac{\text{m}}{\text{s}^2}} = 0.261 \text{ s}.$$

Thus the weight covers the distance $2h$ in

$$t = t_1 + t_2 = 0.495 \text{ s} + 0.261 \text{ s} = 0.756 \text{ s}.$$

Solution of Problem 81. As the inclined plane is frictionless, the force exerted on the object that collides elastically with it can only be perpendicular to the plane. Let us assume that the object is a small ball, because this way the collision can only be central. (Otherwise the normal force exerted by the plane might not go through the centre of mass of the object, which will result in the rotation of the object. In that case the conservation of kinetic energy for the translational motions will not hold.)

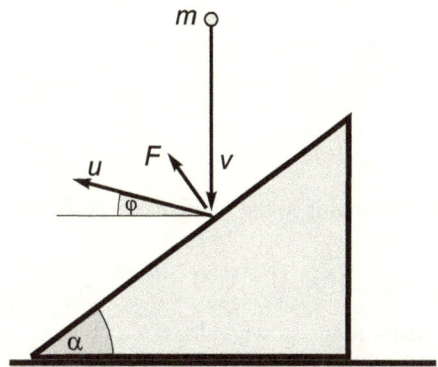

Let us also assume that the collision takes place in an instant, since then the gravitational force is negligible compared to the normal force, which makes our equations much simpler. The angle of the inclined plane simplifies our calculations, since: $\sin\alpha = \sin 36.78° \approx 0.6 = 3/5$; $\cos 36.78° \approx 0.8 = 4/5$; $\tan 36.78° \approx 0.75 = 3/4$; $\cot 36.78° \approx 1.3333 \approx 4/3$.

Let F be the average force exerted by the inclined plane and Δt be the duration of collision. Let us apply Newton's second law (expressed in terms of momentum) to the vertical and horizontal components and then use the conservation of linear momentum and energy for this situation:

$$F\Delta t\cos\alpha = mu_y - (-mv) = mu_y + mv \tag{1}$$

$$F\Delta t\sin\alpha = mu_x \tag{2}$$

$$mu_x = Mc \tag{3}$$

$$\frac{1}{2}mv^2 = \frac{1}{2}m(u_x^2 + u_y^2) + \frac{1}{2}Mc^2, \tag{4}$$

since $u^2 = u_x^2 + u_y^2$. We can eliminate the average force and the time interval by dividing equation (1) by equation (2):

$$\cot\alpha = \frac{u_y}{u_x} + \frac{v}{u_x},$$

thus

$$u_y = \cot\alpha \cdot u_x - v. \tag{5}$$

Let us solve equation (3) for the speed of the inclined plane:

$$c = \frac{m}{M}u_x. \tag{6}$$

After substituting the expressions for u_y and c into equation (4) and multiplying the equation by 2, we get an equation for u_x:

$$mv^2 = m(u_x^2 + \cot^2\alpha \cdot u_x^2 - 2\cdot\cot\alpha \cdot u_x v + v^2) + M\frac{m^2}{M^2}u_x^2.$$

Let us divide by m and rearrange the equation, to get:

$$0 = \left(1 + \cot^2\alpha + \frac{m}{M}\right)u_x^2 - 2\cdot\cot\alpha \cdot u_x v.$$

As $u_x \neq 0$, the equation can be divided by it. Solving for u_x leads us to:

$$u_x = \frac{2\cdot\cot\alpha}{1 + \cot^2\alpha + \frac{m}{M}} \cdot v.$$

Let us multiply the numerator and the denominator by $M\cdot\tan\alpha$:

$$u_x = \frac{2M}{(m+M)\tan\alpha + M\cot\alpha} \cdot v, \tag{7}$$

Substituting known values, we obtain:

$$u_x = \frac{2\cdot 18\,\text{kg}}{(6\,\text{kg} + 18\,\text{kg})\frac{3}{4} + 18\,\text{kg}\cdot\frac{4}{3}} \cdot 14\,\frac{\text{m}}{\text{s}} = 12\,\frac{\text{m}}{\text{s}}.$$

Inserting this result into equation (6), the speed of the inclined plane turns out to be:

$$c = \frac{m}{M} u_x = \frac{6}{18} \cdot 12 \, \frac{m}{s} = 4 \, \frac{m}{s}.$$

The general formula for the speed of the plane is:

$$c = \frac{m}{M} u_x = \frac{2m}{(m+M)\tan\alpha + M\cot\alpha} \cdot v,$$

multiplying the numerator and the denominator by $\tan\alpha$ gives:

$$c = \frac{2m \cdot \tan\alpha}{(m+M)\tan^2\alpha + M} \cdot v = \frac{2 \cdot 6\,\text{kg} \cdot \frac{3}{4}}{(6\,\text{kg} + 18\,\text{kg})\frac{9}{16} + 18\,\text{kg}} \cdot 14 \, \frac{m}{s} = 4 \, \frac{m}{s}.$$

The angle formed by the final velocity (u) of the ball and the horizontal can easily be determined by dividing equation (7) by equation (5):

$$\tan\varphi = \frac{u_y}{u_x} = \cot\alpha - \frac{v}{u_x} = \cot\alpha - v \cdot \frac{(m+M)\tan\alpha + M\cot\alpha}{2Mv}.$$

Multiplying the numerator and the denominator of the fraction by $\tan\alpha$, we have:

$$\tan\varphi = \cot\alpha - \frac{(m+M)\tan^2\alpha + M}{2M\tan\alpha} = \cot\alpha - \frac{1}{2}\left(\frac{m+M}{M}\tan\alpha + \cot\alpha\right) =$$

$$= \frac{1}{2}\left(\cot\alpha - \frac{m+M}{M}\tan\alpha\right).$$

Substituting known values, we find:

$$\tan\varphi = \frac{1}{2}\left(\frac{4}{3} - \frac{6\,\text{kg} + 18\,\text{kg}}{18\,\text{kg}} \cdot \frac{3}{4}\right) = \frac{1}{6},$$

from which the angle is $\varphi = \arctan\frac{1}{6} = 9.46°$. The velocity of the ball after the collision can now be calculated as:

$$u = \frac{u_x}{\cos\varphi} = \frac{12\,\text{m/s}}{\cos 9.46°} = 12.172 \, \frac{m}{s}.$$

First solution of Problem 82. The distance covered by the chest after the collision (independently of the mass) is $s = \frac{v_2^2}{2\mu g}$, where v_2 is the speed of the chest just after the collision. So this new speed has to be determined. The initial speed (just before the collision) changes abruptly because of two reasons:

1) during the collision the force pushing the ground, and consequently the friction force are both increased.

2) the momentum of the chest is increased by the horizontal momentum of the bag.

In this solution, let us assume that the inner surface of the chest is slippery, i.e. the friction between the bag and the chest is negligible. The slide of the bag is stopped by the side of the chest.

First, let us determine the vertical force between the bag and the chest during the collision.

The change of momentum of the falling bag is:

$$|\Delta(mv_y)| = m\sqrt{2gh},$$

where m is the mass of the bag. According to the impulse-momentum theorem, the average force acting on the bag during the collision is:

$$mg - K = \frac{\Delta(mv_y)}{\Delta t} = -\frac{m\sqrt{2gh}}{\Delta t} \quad \rightarrow \quad K = mg + \frac{m\sqrt{2gh}}{\Delta t}.$$

During the collision, the normal force between the ground and the chest increases by this value, too.

The change of the momentum of the chest and thus its new speed after the collision can be determined by the impulse-momentum theorem, using the impulse of the friction force:

$$\mu(Mg + K)\Delta t = \Delta(Mu),$$

where Δu is the change of speed of the chest. Inserting here the value of K above, we get:

$$\mu\left(Mg + mg + \frac{m\sqrt{2gh}}{\Delta t}\right) \cdot \Delta t = \Delta(Mu).$$

Since the collision is instantaneous (which means that $\Delta t \to 0$), after performing the multiplication with Δt, the first two terms in the bracket become negligible, the third term Δt cancels out, and we obtain that:

$$\mu m\sqrt{2gh} = \Delta(Mu) = M\Delta u.$$

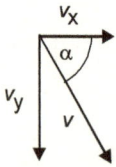

From here, the change of the speed of the chest is

$$\Delta u = \mu\frac{m}{M}\sqrt{2gh},$$

and it is opposite to the original velocity of the chest.

Now let us consider the horizontal interaction between the chest and the bag. According to the figure, the horizontal component of the velocity of the falling bag is

$$v_x = \frac{v_y}{\tan\alpha} = \cot\alpha\sqrt{2gh}.$$

In a horizontal direction an inelastic collision occurs between the chest and the bag, in which process the horizontal momentum is conserved:

$$m\cot\alpha\sqrt{2gh} + (v_1 - \Delta u)M = (M + m)v_2,$$

where v_2 is the common speed of the chest and the bag. Since the interaction is instantaneous, the displacement of the chest is negligible during the collision, and

190

after the collision the chest continues its decelerating motion from the place where the collision occurred. Writing into the previous equation the expression for Δu, we get:

$$m \cot \alpha \sqrt{2gh} + M \left(v_1 - \mu \frac{m\sqrt{2gh}}{M} \right) = (M+m)v_2.$$

Expressing the speed after the collision:

$$v_2 = \frac{m \cot \alpha \sqrt{2gh} + Mv_1 - \mu m \sqrt{2gh}}{m+M}.$$

Since in the problem $m = M$, the masses cancel out:

$$v_2 = \frac{\cot \alpha \sqrt{2gh} + v_1 - \mu \sqrt{2gh}}{2} = \frac{(\cot \alpha - \mu)\sqrt{2gh} + v_1}{2}.$$

The stopping distance does not depend on the mass, and its expression is:

$$s = \frac{v_2^2}{2\mu g} = \frac{v_1^2 + 2v_1(\cot \alpha - \mu)\sqrt{2gh} + (\cot \alpha - \mu)^2 2gh}{8\mu g}.$$

Numerically:

$$s = \frac{25 + 2 \cdot 5 \cdot (\cot 60° - 0.4) \cdot \sqrt{2 \cdot 9.81 \cdot 3} + (\cot 60° - 0.4)^2 2 \cdot 9.81 \cdot 3}{8 \cdot 0.4 \cdot 9.81} \; \text{m} = 1.29 \text{ m}.$$

If the sand bag had not fallen into the chest, then from the place of the instantaneous speed 5 m/s the stopping distance would have been

$$s' = \frac{v_1^2}{2\mu g} = \frac{25}{2 \cdot 0.4 \cdot 9.81} \approx 3.18 \text{ m},$$

so in this case the path covered by the chest would have been by $s' - s = 3.18$ m $- 1.29$ m $= 1.89$ m more.

Second solution of Problem 82. In the previous solution we divided the whole collision into two successive processes, in a somewhat arbitrary way. First, only the vertical interaction was considered, the intermediate speed of the chest was determined, and then the horizontal interaction was regarded as a separate collision, which determined the final, common speed of the chest and the bag. Now, with the help of the centre-of-mass theorem, we describe the whole collision process as a single event. Let us apply the centre-of-mass theorem in horizontal direction. The horizontal component of the net external force acting on the system, consisting of the chest and the bag, is the friction force. Let V_1 denote the speed of the centre of mass of the system before the collision, and let V_2 be the speed after collision.

We use the result obtained in the previous solution for the 'increase' of the normal force of the ground:

$$K = mg + \frac{m\sqrt{2gh}}{\Delta t}.$$

The change of horizontal momentum of the system is equal to the impulse of the friction force, thus:

$$S\Delta t = \Delta\left((M+m)V_x\right).$$

Inserting here the friction force S, we get that:

$$\mu(Mg+K)\Delta t = (M+m)\Delta V_x.$$

Writing here the expression above for the normal force of the ground:

$$\mu\left(Mg+mg+\frac{m\sqrt{2gh}}{\Delta t}\right)\Delta t = (M+m)\Delta V_x.$$

Performing the multiplication by Δt, and taking the limit $\Delta t \to 0$:

$$\mu m\sqrt{2gh} = (M+m)\Delta V_x.$$

From here, the change of the speed of the centre of mass is:

$$\Delta V_x = \mu\frac{m}{M+m}\sqrt{2gh}.$$

Initially, (before the collision) the horizontal speed of the centre of mass of the system is

$$V_{x1} = \frac{Mv_1+m\cot\alpha\sqrt{2gh}}{M+m},$$

so the final, common speed of the chest and the bag is:

$$V_{x2} = V_{x1} - \Delta V_x = \frac{Mv_1+m\cot\alpha\sqrt{2gh}}{M+m} - \mu\frac{m}{M+m}\sqrt{2gh}.$$

After the addition of the fractions,

$$V_{x2} = \frac{Mv_1+m\cot\alpha\sqrt{2gh}-\mu m\sqrt{2gh}}{M+m},$$

and using that $M=m$, we get that:

$$V_{x2} = \frac{v_1+\cot\alpha\sqrt{2gh}-\mu\sqrt{2gh}}{2} = \frac{v_1+(\cot\alpha-\mu)\sqrt{2gh}}{2}.$$

After the short time of the interaction, the chest and the bag will move with this common speed, so their stopping distance can be calculated from this speed:

$$s = \frac{V_{x2}^2}{2\mu g} = \frac{v_1^2+2v_1(\cot\alpha-\mu)\sqrt{2gh}+(\cot\alpha-\mu)^2 2gh}{8\mu g} = 1.29 \text{ m}.$$

Solution of Problem 83. The body slides up on the slope while the trolley accelerates until the body reaches the top of the slope. At this moment, the horizontal velocity component of the trolley and the body are the same and when the body leaves the slope, the constraining force ceases. The trolley moves uniformly at velocity V, the body completes vertical projection relative to the car and falls back tangentially on the upper end of the slope. (Relative to the ground the motion of the body is an oblique projectile motion with a horizontal velocity component $v_x = V$ and an initial vertical velocity component v_y that should be determined later.)

As the small body slides back on the slope, it accelerates the trolley further and then slides off it in the opposite direction. The interaction corresponds to an elongated perfectly elastic collision (in the case of equal masses the small body would stop on the horizontal ground).

Calculations: The horizontal component of momentum is conserved. For the velocities attained at the top of the slope:

$$mv = mv_x + MV,$$

mechanical energy is conserved:

$$\frac{1}{2}mv^2 = \frac{1}{2}mv_x^2 + \frac{1}{2}mv_y^2 + \frac{1}{2}MV^2 + mgR.$$

From the constraint condition it follows that $v_x = V$.

a) From the first equation

$$V = \frac{m}{m+M}v,$$

from which

$$V = v_x = 6\,\text{m/s}.$$

b) The flight time should be determined. For this, the initial vertical velocity component of the projectile motion is required, which can be determined from the second equation, the energy equation. Substituting V in place of v_x:

$$v_y = \sqrt{v^2 - \frac{m+M}{m}V^2 - 2gR},$$

substituting the value of V expressed with the initial velocity v of the body and combining the like terms gives for v_y:

$$v_y = \sqrt{\frac{M}{m+M}v^2 - 2gR} = 11.18\,\frac{\text{m}}{\text{s}}.$$

(The height of the projection from the upper end of the slope is

$$h' = \frac{v_y^2}{2g} = 6.25\,\text{m})$$

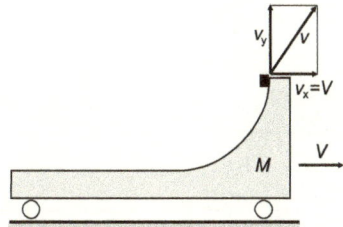

The time elapsed until return is

$$t = 2\frac{v_y}{g} = 2.24\,\text{s},$$

in this time the trolley moves through a distance of

$$s = Vt = 13.4\,\text{m}$$

(This corresponds to the 'horizontal range' of the obliquely projected body).
    Parametrically:

$$s = \frac{2m}{m+M}\frac{v^2}{g}\sqrt{\frac{M}{m+M} - \frac{2gR}{v^2}}.$$

c) The velocities of the two bodies at the moment of parting again can be determined either from the formulas of perfectly elastic collision or from the balance equations for energy and momentum.

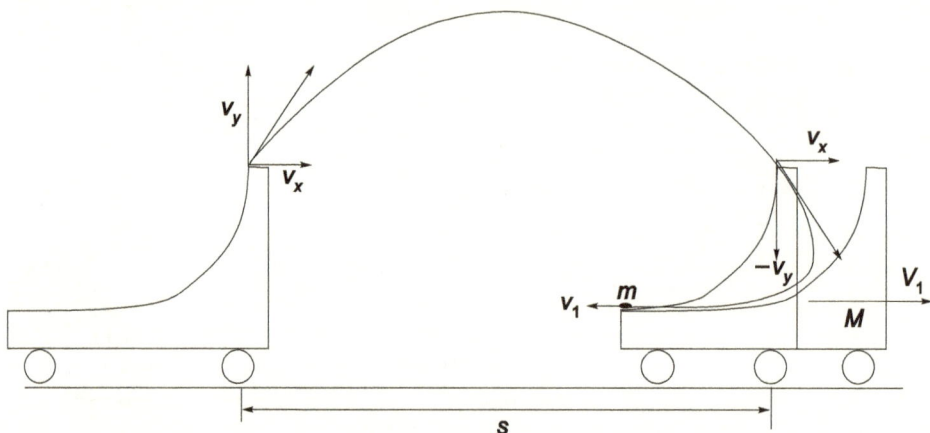

The energy balance is

$$\frac{1}{2}mv^2 = \frac{1}{2}mv_1^2 + \frac{1}{2}MV_1^2,$$

the momentum balance is

$$mv = mv_1 + MV_1.$$

The solution of the equation system is

$$v_1 = \frac{m-M}{m+M}v = -3\,\frac{\text{m}}{\text{s}} \quad \text{and} \quad V_1 = \frac{2M}{m+M}v = 12\,\frac{\text{m}}{\text{s}}.$$

Solution of Problem 84. a) Let A be the topmost point of the semi-cylinder. The length of the cart is a minimum if it accelerates to the minimum possible speed V during its contact with the small object, and thus covers the shortest possible distance during the time of the fall.

While the two objects are in contact, the cart keeps on accelerating, with the single exception of the time instant when the small object reaches the height of $2R$ on the semicircle.

The force exerted by the small object on the cart is the smallest if it slides onto the cart at the minimum possible speed. Since the condition for reaching the top is that the normal force N exerted by the track should remain $N \geq 0$ all the way, the cart will gain the smallest possible final speed if the normal force N decreases to 0 exactly at the topmost point. Let us go through the conditions required.

Condition 1:
$$N_A = 0. \tag{1}$$

When the object has reached point A, the cart moves on with uniform motion in a straight line, thus it becomes an inertial reference frame. In the reference frame of the cart, the small object moves along a circular path of radius R until it reaches A-ig, and then continues on a parabolic path as a projectile with a horizontal initial velocity. (In the reference frame attached to the ground, it reaches the cart with free fall along a vertical line, with zero initial velocity.) The next condition is provided by the circular motion in the reference frame of the cart:

Condition 2:
$$mg + N_A = m\frac{v_{rel}^2}{R},$$

and thus with (1),
$$g = \frac{v_{rel}^2}{R}. \tag{2}$$

Since there is no friction, all forces are conservative, the total mechanical energy of the system is conserved. Let v_0 denote the speed of the small object when it hits the cart (same as its initial speed of sliding onto the cart).

Condition 3:
$$\frac{1}{2}mv_0^2 = \frac{1}{2}mv_1^2 + \frac{1}{2}MV^2 + mgh,$$

where V is the speed of the cart and v_1 is the speed of the small object acquired by the time the small object rises to a height h above the surface of the cart. The small object needs to reach the point A at a height of $h = 2R$, and it needs to lose its speed there ($v_1 = 0$ is needed). Multiplied by two, the equation takes the form

$$mv_0^2 = MV^2 + 4mgR. \tag{3}$$

Since the small object is to stop at the topmost point of its path, its velocity relative to the cart at that point is the opposite of the velocity of the cart. In absolute value,
$$v_{rel} = V. \tag{4}$$

Since the external forces are all vertical, the sum of horizontal momenta is constant, that is,

Condition 4:

$$mv_0 = MV. \tag{5}$$

From (2) and (4):

$$V = \sqrt{gR}. \tag{6}$$

(6) is needed for answering question a) since the distance covered by the cart can be determined with (6) from the time of the fall from a height of $2R$. The distance covered in free fall is

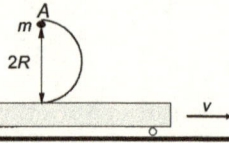

$$2R = \frac{1}{2}gt^2,$$

and hence the time of fall is

$$t = \sqrt{\frac{4R}{g}}.$$

In that time interval, the cart covers a distance of

$$s = Vt = \sqrt{gR} \cdot \sqrt{\frac{4R}{g}} = \sqrt{4R^2} = 2R.$$

Therefore the minimum cart length required is $L_{min} = 2s$, that is,

$$L_{min} = 4R = 4 \cdot 0.36\,\text{m} = 1.44\,\text{m}.$$

b) The equations for momentum (5) and energy (3) both have to be satisfied. The mass ratio of the small mass to the cart is not arbitrary. From (5) and (6),

$$v_0 = \frac{M}{m}V = \frac{M}{m}\sqrt{gR}. \tag{7}$$

Substituted into (3):

$$m\frac{M^2}{m^2}gR = MgR + 4mgR.$$

With both sides divided by m:

$$\frac{M^2}{m^2}gR = \frac{M}{m}gR + 4gR,$$

and hence, the quadratic equation

$$\frac{M^2}{m^2} - \frac{M}{m} - 4 = 0$$

is obtained for the mass ratio. With the notation $M/m = k$: $k^2 - k - 4 = 0$. Hence

$$k = \frac{1 \pm \sqrt{1+16}}{2} = 2.56(15),$$

that is, $M = 2.56 \cdot m$, and since $m = 1\,\text{kg}$, the mass of the cart is

$$M = 2.56\,\text{kg},$$

independently of R.

c) Since there is no friction, the small object was released at the height of

$$h = \frac{v_0^2}{2g},$$

which can be calculated with the use of (7):

$$h = \frac{1}{2}\left(\frac{M}{m}\right)^2 R = \frac{1}{2} \cdot 2.56^2 \cdot 0.36\,\text{m} = 1.18(1)\,\text{m}.$$

The small object slides onto the cart with a speed of

$$v_0 = \frac{M}{m}\sqrt{gR} = 2.56 \cdot \sqrt{9.8\,\frac{\text{m}}{\text{s}^2} \cdot 0.36} = 4.85(7)\,\frac{\text{m}}{\text{s}},$$

and the final speed of the cart is

$$V = \sqrt{gR} = \sqrt{9.8\,\frac{\text{m}}{\text{s}^2} \cdot 0.36\,\text{m}} = 1.89(6)\,\frac{\text{m}}{\text{s}}.$$

Solution of Problem 85. Although the setting of the problem doesn't state it exactly, let us assume that the disk is homogeneous and rotates around a vertical axis that goes through its centre. It is also important to state that the disk is much greater than the man, therefore the latter can be handled as a pointmass, which means that the man's rotational inertia when standing in the centre will be taken as zero.

Since there is no external torque acting on the system (friction and air resistance are neglected), the total angular momentum of the system remains unchanged. The total angular momentum of the system is the sum of the angular momentum of the disk ($\Theta_{\text{disk}} \cdot \omega$) and the moment of momentum of the man ($m_{\text{man}}vR$). Applying the conservation of angular momentum:

$$\Theta_{\text{disk}}\omega_1 + m_{\text{man}}R^2\omega_1 = \Theta_{\text{disk}}\omega_2 + 0,$$

since (as it was stated above) the man's rotational inertia is zero at the centre. Isolating the final angular velocity, we find:

$$\omega_2 = \frac{\Theta_{\text{disk}} + m_{\text{man}}R^2}{\Theta_{\text{disk}}} \cdot \omega_1.$$

The change in the total energy of the system is:

$$E_2 - E1 = \frac{1}{2}\Theta_{\text{disk}}\omega_2^2 - \left(\frac{1}{2}\Theta_{\text{disk}}\omega_1^2 + \frac{1}{2}m_{\text{man}}R^2\omega_1^2\right).$$

After substituting the expression for ω_2 and rearranging the equation, we have:

$$\Delta E = \frac{\Theta_{\text{disk}} + m_{\text{man}}R^2}{2\Theta_{\text{disk}}} m_{\text{man}}R^2\omega_1^2 = \frac{\Theta_{\text{disk}} + m_{\text{man}}R^2}{2\Theta_{\text{disk}}} m_{\text{man}}R^2 4\pi^2 n^2.$$

Using that the rotational inertia of a homogeneous disk about its axis of rotational symmetry is $\Theta_{disk} = \dfrac{1}{2}m_{disk}R^2$, the change in the energy can be written as:

$$\Delta E = \frac{m_{disk} + 2m_{man}}{2m_{disk}} \cdot m_{man}R^2 4\pi^2 n^2,$$

Substituting values gives: $\Delta E = \dfrac{300 + 160}{600} \cdot 80\,\text{kg} \cdot 25\,\text{m}^2 \cdot 4\pi^2 \cdot 0.01\ \text{s}^{-2} = 605.3\ \text{J}.$

The change in the kinetic energy of the system is $605.3\,\text{J}$, which means that the total energy of the system does not remain constant. This of course doesn't mean that the law of conservation of energy is violated, because the increase in the energy of the system is caused by the work done by the man's muscles, so biological (chemical) energy is transferred to kinetic energy in this case.

Solution of Problem 86. a) Conservation of angular momentum can be applied to the mass m, and the conservation of mechanical energy can be applied to the whole system:

$$mv_0 R = mvr. \tag{1}$$

$$Mg(R-r) + \frac{1}{2}mv_0^2 = \frac{1}{2}mv^2, \tag{2}$$

where v_0 is the smallest speed and v is the largest speed. With $v_0 = v\dfrac{r}{R}$, expressed from (1) and substituted into (2):

$$Mg(R-r) + \frac{1}{2}m\left(v\frac{r}{R}\right)^2 = \frac{1}{2}mv^2.$$

Rearranged:

$$2Mg(R-r) = mv^2\left(1 - \frac{r^2}{R^2}\right) = mv^2\frac{R^2 - r^2}{R^2} = mv^2\frac{(R+r)(R-r)}{R^2}.$$

The speeds are obtained by division through the whole equation by $(R-r)$ and rearrangement:

$$v = R\sqrt{2\frac{M}{m} \cdot \frac{g}{R+r}} = 0.4\,\text{m}\sqrt{2 \cdot \frac{2\,\text{kg}}{1\,\text{kg}} \cdot \frac{10\,\text{m/s}^2}{0.4\,\text{m}+0.1\,\text{m}}} = 3.58\,\frac{\text{m}}{\text{s}},$$

and

$$v_0 = v\frac{r}{R} = 3.58\,\frac{\text{m}}{\text{s}} \cdot \frac{0.1\,\text{m}}{0.4\,\text{m}} = 0.895\,\frac{\text{m}}{\text{s}} \approx 0.9\,\frac{\text{m}}{\text{s}}.$$

b) The conservation laws of angular momentum and mechanical energy can be used again, but this time the mass m has a velocity component v_1 normal to the string and a component v_2 parallel to the string. With these notations,

$$mv_0 R = mv_1 \frac{R}{2}, \qquad (3)$$

$$Mg\frac{R}{2} + \frac{1}{2}mv_0^2 = \frac{1}{2}m(v_1^2 + v_2^2) + \frac{1}{2}Mv_2^2. \qquad (4)$$

The solution of the simultaneous equations is

$$v_2 = \sqrt{\frac{MgR - 3mv_0^2}{m+M}} = \sqrt{\frac{2\,\mathrm{kg}\cdot 10\,\mathrm{m/s^2}\cdot 0.4\,\mathrm{m} - 3\cdot 1\,\mathrm{kg}\cdot 0.89^2\,\mathrm{m^2/s^2}}{1\,\mathrm{kg} + 2\,\mathrm{kg}}} = 1.368\frac{\mathrm{m}}{\mathrm{s}},$$

and from (3),

$$v_1 = 2v_0 = 1.78\,\mathrm{m/s}.$$

Therefore the mass m is moving at a speed of

$$v_{\frac{R}{2}} = \sqrt{v_1^2 + v_2^2} = 2.246\,\mathrm{m/s} \approx 2.25\,\mathrm{m/s},$$

and the speed of the mass M is

$$v_M = v_2 = 1.369\,\mathrm{m/s} \approx 1.37\,\mathrm{m/s}.$$

c) The accelerations can be determined by either of the two methods below: one using an inertial reference frame and the other using a rotating frame.

I. The acceleration of the mass m equals that of the end of the string. It has a centripetal component $a_n = r\omega^2 = v^2/r$ owing to the rotation of the horizontal segment of the string, and another component (a) owing to the decreasing length of the horizontal string segment. (At the time instants investigated, the instantaneous speed of the point of the string at the hole is 0.) Since the rotation of the string does not influence the motion of the mass M hanging from the string, the acceleration of the hanging object equals the acceleration component resulting from the change in length. Thus Newton's second law applied to the objects at the lowermost point gives the equations

$$Mg - F = Ma, \qquad (5)$$

$$F = m\left(a + \frac{v^2}{r}\right). \qquad (6)$$

The sum of (5) and (6) is $Mg = Ma + m\left(a + \frac{v^2}{r}\right)$,

and hence the acceleration a is

$$a = \frac{Mg - m\frac{v^2}{r}}{m+M}.$$

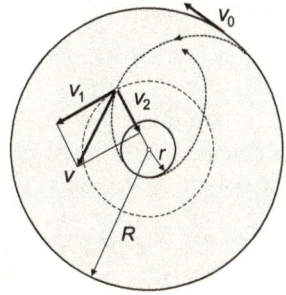

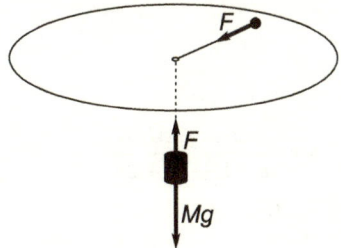

199

At the uppermost point:

$$a_0 = \frac{Mg - m\frac{v_0^2}{R}}{m + M}.$$

II. In a rotating reference frame, the angular acceleration is zero in the two extreme positions, and the mass m is momentarily at rest (thus there is no Coriolis-force either), the only inertial force acting on it is the centrifugal force:

$$F_{cf} = mr\omega^2 = m\frac{v^2}{r}. \qquad (7)$$

The equations are now

$$Mg - F = Ma,$$
$$F - F_{cf} = ma.$$

The sum of the two equations, with the expression of F_{cf} substituted from (7): $Mg - m\frac{v^2}{r} = (m + M)a$.

The expressions obtained for the accelerations are the same as those obtained in the inertial reference frame. In the two extreme positions,

$$a_0 = \frac{Mg - m\frac{v_0^2}{R}}{m + M} = \frac{2\,\text{kg} \cdot 10\,\frac{\text{m}}{\text{s}^2} - 1\,\text{kg} \cdot \frac{0.89^2\,\text{m}^2/\text{s}^2}{0.4\,\text{m}}}{1\,\text{kg} + 2\,\text{kg}} = 6\,\frac{\text{m}}{\text{s}^2},$$

and

$$a = \frac{Mg - m\frac{v^2}{r}}{m + M} = \frac{2\,\text{kg} \cdot 10\,\frac{\text{m}}{\text{s}^2} - 1\,\text{kg} \cdot \frac{3.58^2\,\text{m}^2/\text{s}^2}{0.1\,\text{m}}}{1\,\text{kg} + 2\,\text{kg}} = -36\,\frac{\text{m}}{\text{s}^2}.$$

Remark. It is instructive to determine the radii of curvature of the path of the mass m in the two extreme positions. They can be obtained from the equations

$$F_0 = m\frac{v_0^2}{\varrho_0} = m\left(a_0 + \frac{v_0^2}{R}\right) \qquad \text{and} \qquad F = m\frac{v^2}{\varrho} = m\left(a + \frac{v^2}{r}\right),$$

and the expressions of the speeds:

$$\varrho_0 = \frac{2(m + M)Rr}{mR(R + r) + 2Mr^2} \cdot r = \frac{2(1\,\text{kg} + 2\,\text{kg}) \cdot 0.4 \cdot 0.1\,\text{m}}{1\,\text{kg} \cdot 0.4\,\text{m}(0.4\,\text{m} + 0.1\,\text{m}) + 2 \cdot 2\,\text{kg} \cdot 0.01\,\text{m}^2} \cdot 0.1\,\text{m}$$
$$= 0.1\,\text{m},$$

and

$$\varrho = \frac{2(m + M)Rr}{mr(R + r) + 2MR^2} \cdot R = \frac{2(1\,\text{kg} + 2\,\text{kg}) \cdot 0.4 \cdot 0.1\,\text{m}}{1\,\text{kg} \cdot 0.1\,\text{m}(0.4\,\text{m} + 0.1\,\text{m}) + 2 \cdot 2\,\text{kg} \cdot 0.16\,\text{m}^2} \cdot 0.4\,\text{m}$$
$$= 0.14\,\text{m},$$

that is, $\varrho_0 = 0.25R = r$ and $\varrho = 0.35R = 1.4r$. Thus initially, the radius of curvature is smaller than the radius R, and finally it is greater than the radius r.

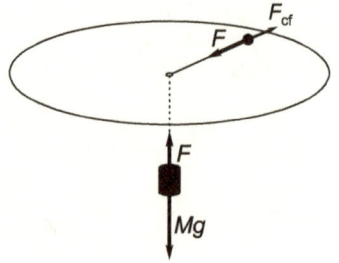

Solution of Problem 87. Let v_h and v_v, respectively, denote the magnitudes of the horizontal and vertical velocity components of the sliding object. Let m stand for the mass of the object, M for the mass of the cylinder, and let ω and Θ denote the angular velocity and moment of inertia of the cylinder about its axis.

a) Mechanical energy is conserved:

$$mgh = \frac{1}{2}m(v_v^2 + v_h^2) + \frac{1}{2}\Theta\omega^2. \tag{1}$$

Angular momentum is conserved. With respect to the axis of the cylinder, the sum of the angular momenta of the moving object and the cylinder is zero:

$$mv_h R - \Theta\omega = 0. \tag{2}$$

In order to determine the three unknowns (v_h, v_v, ω), a third equation is needed. It will be provided by the condition that the object remains on the track. Note that while the object descends through a height of h, the endpoint of the horizontal radius drawn to its position turns through a distance of $R\varphi_1$ in a horizontal direction, while the circumference of the cylinder rotates through $R\varphi_2$ in the opposite direction. The slope of the track ($\tan\alpha = h/2R\pi$) can be expressed in terms of these quantities:

$$\tan\alpha = \frac{h}{R(\varphi_1 + \varphi_2)} = \frac{\frac{1}{2}v_v t}{\frac{1}{2}R\omega_1 t + \frac{1}{2}R\omega t} = \frac{v_v}{v_h + R\omega} = \frac{h}{2R\pi}, \tag{3}$$

since the initial speed was zero and acceleration is constant.

The system of equations (1)–(2)–(3) becomes simpler with the use of the relationship $M = 5m$ of the masses and the formula $\Theta = \frac{1}{2}MR^2$ for the rotational inertia of the cylinder:

$$2mgh = m(v_h^2 + v_v^2) + 2.5mR^2\omega^2 \tag{1'}$$

$$mv_h R = 2.5mR^2\omega \tag{2'}$$

$$v_v = (v_h + R\omega)\frac{h}{2R\pi}. \tag{3'}$$

With (1') and (2') divided through by m, and (2') also divided by R,

$$2gh = v_h^2 + v_v^2 + 2.5R^2\omega^2 \tag{1''}$$

$$v_h = 2.5R\omega \tag{2''}$$

$$v_v = (v_h + R\omega)\frac{h}{2R\pi}. \tag{3'}$$

$R\omega$ can be expressed from (2'') and substituted into (1'') and (3'):

$$2gh = v_h^2 + v_v^2 + 2.5 \cdot \frac{v_h^2}{2.5^2} = \frac{3.5v_h^2 + 2.5v_v^2}{2.5},$$

that is,

$$5gh = 3.5v_h^2 + 2.5v_v^2, \tag{4}$$

and

$$v_v = \left(v_h + \frac{v_h}{2.5}\right) \cdot \frac{h}{2R\pi} = 3.5v_h \cdot \frac{h}{5R\pi}. \tag{5}$$

v_v is substituted from (5) into (4):

$$5gh = 3.5v_h^2 + 2.5 \cdot \left(\frac{3.5}{5}\right)^2 \cdot \frac{h^2}{R^2\pi^2}v_h^2 = \left(3.5 + 1.225\frac{h^2}{R^2\pi^2}\right)v_h^2,$$

and hence the horizontal component of the velocity of the small object is

$$v_h = \sqrt{\frac{5gh}{3.5 + 1.225 \cdot \frac{h^2}{R^2\pi^2}}} = R\pi\sqrt{\frac{5gh}{3.5R^2\pi^2 + 1.225h^2}}. \tag{6}$$

The angular speed of the revolution of the small object about the axis is

$$\omega_1 = \frac{v_h}{R} = \pi\sqrt{\frac{5gh}{3.5R^2\pi^2 + 1.225h^2}}. \tag{7}$$

The vertical component of the velocity of the small object is obtained from (5) and (6):

$$v_v = \frac{0.7h}{R\pi} \cdot v_h = 0.7h\sqrt{\frac{5gh}{3.5R^2\pi^2 + 1.225h^2}}. \tag{8}$$

The speed of the small object after completing one revolution is

$$v = \sqrt{v_h^2 + v_v^2} = \sqrt{(R^2\pi^2 + 0.49h^2) \cdot \frac{5gh}{3.5R^2\pi^2 + 1.225h^2}}.$$

Considering the special case represented by the given numerical data, namely that $h = R = L = 0.2$ m:

$$v = \sqrt{(\pi^2 + 0.49)\frac{5gL}{3.5\pi^2 + 1.225}} = 1.7\frac{\text{m}}{\text{s}^2}.$$

b) The time taken is calculated from the radius of the cylinder and the relative angular speed of the small object with respect to the cylinder:

$$\omega_{\text{rel}} = \omega_1 + \omega.$$

Since the acceleration is uniform, the mean angular velocity is

$$\overline{\omega} = \frac{\omega_{\text{rel}}}{2},$$

that is,

$$t = \frac{2\pi}{\overline{\omega}_{\text{rel}}} = \frac{4\pi}{\omega_1 + \omega}.$$

It follows from (2) that the angular velocities are related by the equation

$$m\omega_1 R^2 = 2.5mR^2\omega,$$

and thus

$$\omega_1 = 2.5\omega.$$

and

$$t = \frac{4\pi}{\omega_1 + 0.4\omega_1} = \frac{4\pi}{1.4\omega_1},$$

which can be combined with (7):

$$t = 4 \cdot \frac{1}{1.4} \sqrt{\frac{3.5R^2\pi^2 + 1.225h^2}{5gh}} = 4 \cdot \frac{1}{1.4} \sqrt{\frac{(3.5\pi^2 + 1.225)L}{5g}} = 1.08\,\text{s}.$$

Remark. The time taken by the object to cover a certain segment of its descent can also be determined by using the vertical velocity component: Note that $h = v_v t/2$, and hence with the use of (8):

$$t = \frac{2h}{v_v} = \frac{2h}{0.7h\sqrt{\frac{5gh}{3.5R^2\pi^2 + 1.225h^2}}} = \frac{2}{0.7}\sqrt{\frac{(3.5\pi^2 + 1225) \cdot L}{5g}} = 1.08\,\text{s}.$$

Solution of Problem 88. In the interaction between the ball and the disc angular momentum and mechanical energy are conserved. These result in two equations for the speed of the ball upon leaving and the angular speed of the disc.

The angular momentum of the ball after bowling is zero for the axis and the angular momentum of the originally stationary disc is also zero. Therefore, at the moment of detaching, the sum of the orbital angular momentum of the ball and the angular momentum of the disc are both zero:

$$mv_1 R - \frac{1}{2}MR^2\omega = 0, \tag{1}$$

because the ball leaves the rim in the direction of the tangent. The total energy at this moment is:

$$\frac{1}{2}mv^2 = \frac{1}{2}mv_1^2 + \frac{1}{2} \cdot \frac{1}{2}MR^2\omega^2. \tag{2}$$

from (1) the angular speed of the disc is

$$\omega = \frac{2mv_1 R}{MR^2} = 2\frac{m}{M} \cdot \frac{v_1}{R}.$$

If this is substituted into (2):

$$\frac{1}{2}mv^2 = \frac{1}{2}mv_1^2 + \frac{1}{2} \cdot \frac{1}{2}MR^2 \cdot 4\frac{m^2}{M^2} \cdot \frac{v_1^2}{R^2} = \left(\frac{m}{2} + \frac{m^2}{M}\right) \cdot v_1^2. \tag{3}$$

From (3) the speed of the ball upon leaving the the disc is

$$v_1 = v\sqrt{\frac{M}{M+2m}} = 3\frac{\text{m}}{\text{s}}\sqrt{\frac{2\,\text{kg}}{2\,\text{kg}+2\cdot1\,\text{kg}}} = 2.12\frac{\text{m}}{\text{s}}.$$

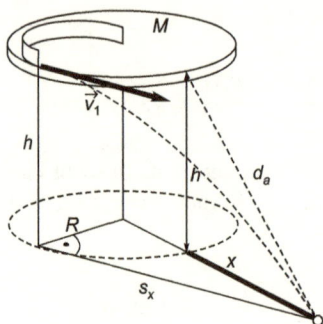

The time of falling is

$$\Delta t = \sqrt{\frac{2h}{g}} = \sqrt{\frac{2\cdot1\,\text{m}}{9.81\frac{\text{m}}{\text{s}^2}}} = 0.452\,\text{s}.$$

In the meantime the horizontal projection of the displacement of the ball is

$$s_x = v_1\Delta t = v_1\sqrt{\frac{2h}{g}} = 2.12\frac{\text{m}}{\text{s}}\cdot0.452\,\text{s} = 0.957\,\text{m}.$$

Let x stand for the distance between the projection of the rim of the disc on the ground and the place where the ball reaches the ground. Based on the figure

$$x = \sqrt{R^2 + v_1^2\Delta t^2} - R = \sqrt{R^2 + v^2\frac{M}{M+2m}\cdot\frac{2h}{g}} - R.$$

With numerical values:

$$x = \sqrt{(0.5\,\text{m})^2 + (3\,\text{m/s})^2\cdot\frac{2\,\text{kg}}{2\,\text{kg}+2\cdot1\,\text{kg}}\cdot\frac{2\cdot1\,\text{m}}{9.81\,\text{m/s}^2}} - 0.5\,\text{m} = 0.58\,\text{m}. \qquad (4)$$

a) The distance of the point where the ball reaches the ground from the rim of the disc is

$$d_\text{a} = \sqrt{h^2 + x^2} = \sqrt{1\,\text{m}^2 + (0.58\,\text{m})^2} = 1.156\,\text{m} \approx 1.16\,\text{m}.$$

b) Based on (2), during the time of falling the disc is rotating at an angular velocity

$$\omega = 2\frac{m}{M}\cdot\frac{v}{R}\sqrt{\frac{M}{M+2m}} = 2\cdot\frac{1\,\text{kg}}{2\,\text{kg}}\cdot\frac{3\frac{\text{m}}{\text{s}}}{0.5\,\text{m}}\sqrt{\frac{2\,\text{kg}}{2\,\text{kg}+2\cdot1\,\text{kg}}} = 4.24\,\text{s}^{-1}.$$

The total angular displacement until the ball reaches the ground is

$$\varphi = \omega\cdot t = 2\frac{m}{M}\cdot\frac{v}{R}\sqrt{\frac{2h}{g}\cdot\frac{M}{M+2m}} =$$

$$= 2\cdot\frac{1\,\text{kg}}{2\,\text{kg}}\cdot\frac{3\frac{\text{m}}{\text{s}}}{0.5\,\text{m}}\sqrt{\frac{2\,\text{m}}{9.81\,\text{m/s}^2}\cdot\frac{2\,\text{kg}}{2\,\text{kg}+2\cdot1\,\text{kg}}} = 1.92\,\text{rad} \approx 110°.$$

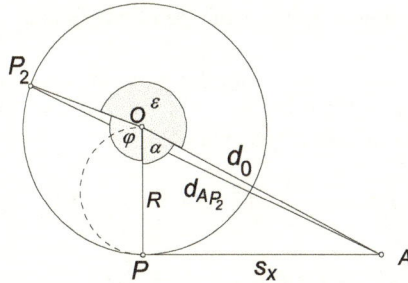

By analysing the figure the following statements can be made: Based on (4), the distance of the place where the ball reaches the ground from the place of the disc is

$$d_0 = \sqrt{R^2 + s_x^2} = \sqrt{R^2 + v_1^2 \frac{2h}{g}} = \sqrt{R^2 + v_1^2 \frac{M}{M+2m} \cdot \frac{2h}{g}} =$$

$$= \sqrt{(0.5\,\mathrm{m})^2 + (3\,\mathrm{m/s})^2 \cdot \frac{2\,\mathrm{kg}}{2\,\mathrm{kg} + 2 \cdot 1\,\mathrm{kg}} \cdot \frac{2 \cdot 1\,\mathrm{m}}{9.81\,\mathrm{m/s}^2}} = 1.08\,\mathrm{m}.$$

Let P_1 stand for the point of leaving on the projection of the rim of the disc on the ground and P_2 for the position of this projection when the ball reaches the ground. Let O stand for the foot of the axis and A stand for the point of impact on the ground. Let α stand for angle AOP_1 and ε for angle AOP_2. From the figure it can be seen that

$$\alpha = \arccos\frac{R}{d_0} = \arccos\frac{0.5}{1.08} = 1.09\ \mathrm{rad} = 62.4°,$$

and

$$\varepsilon = 2\pi - \varphi - \alpha = 6.28\ \mathrm{rad} - 1.92\ \mathrm{rad} - 1.09\ \mathrm{rad} = 3.27\ \mathrm{rad} = 187.5°.$$

According to the cosine rule, the distance between the point of impact and the projection of the rim, $(d_{AP_2} = \overline{AP_2})$ is:

$$d_{AP_2} = \sqrt{d_0^2 + R^2 - 2d_0 R \cos\varepsilon} =$$

$$= \sqrt{(1.08\,\mathrm{m})^2 + (0.5\,\mathrm{m})^2 - 2 \cdot 1.08\,\mathrm{m} \cdot 0.5\,\mathrm{m} \cdot \cos 187.5°} = 1.58\,\mathrm{m}.$$

Finally, according to the Pythagorean theorem, the distance between the point of impact and the point of leaving on the disc is

$$d_b = \sqrt{h^2 + d_{AP_2}^2} = \sqrt{h^2 + d_0^2 + R^2 - 2d_0 R \cos\varepsilon} = \sqrt{(1\,\mathrm{m})^2 + (1.58\,\mathrm{m})^2} = 1.87\,\mathrm{m}.$$

Solution of Problem 89. The pointmass is in a three-dimensional spherical motion, which is similar to the motion of a mass hanging on a string of length R. The direction of the maximum and minimum velocities (v_1 and v_2) must be horizontal since they occur at the deepest and highest point of the pointmass's path where the tangent to the path is horizontal.

We need to set up two equations to find the maximum and minimum velocities: one is the conservation of energy, the other is the conservation of angular momentum.

The conservation of energy can be written as:

$$mgh_1 + \frac{1}{2}mv_1^2 = mgh_2 + \frac{1}{2}mv_2^2,$$

hence

$$2g(h_1 - h_2) = v_2^2 - v_1^2. \tag{1}$$

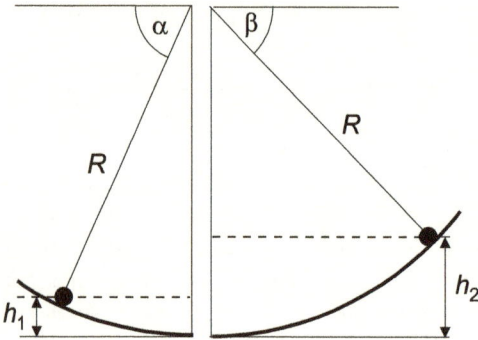

The conservation of angular momentum applies to the horizontal components, since the normal force always points towards the centre of the sphere, its horizontal component points towards the vertical axis of the sphere, while the horizontal component of the gravitational force is zero. This means that the line drawn from the vertical axis to the pointmass sweeps out equal areas in equal times. Let us apply this to the two extreme positions assuming that the velocities are equal to their horizontal components at those moments:

$$v_1 r_1 = v_2 r_2,$$

r_1 and r_2 can be expressed using the radius of the sphere R and heights h_1 and h_2:

$$r_1 = R\cos\alpha,$$
$$r_2 = R\cos\beta,$$

so the conservation of angular momentum will take the form of:

$$v_1 R\cos\alpha = v_2 R\cos\beta, \tag{2}$$

where α and β are the angles, which are formed by the radius that connects the pointmass to the centre of the sphere and the horizontal. Let us use the figure above to determine the cosines of these angles:

$$\cos\alpha = \frac{\sqrt{R^2 - (R - h_1)^2}}{R} = \frac{\sqrt{2Rh_1 - h_1^2}}{R},$$

$$\cos\beta = \frac{\sqrt{R^2 - (R - h_2)^2}}{R} = \frac{\sqrt{2Rh_2 - h_2^2}}{R}.$$

Writing these into equation (2), we have:

$$v_1\sqrt{2Rh_1 - h_1^2} = v_2\sqrt{2Rh_2 - h_2^2}. \tag{3}$$

Equations (1) and (3) form a set of equations with two unknowns. Let us take the square of equation (3), isolate v_2^2 and substitute it into equation (1) to find:

$$v_2^2 = v_1^2\frac{2Rh_1 - h_1^2}{2Rh_2 - h_2^2}$$

$$2g(h_2 - h_1) = v_1^2 - v_1^2\frac{2Rh_1 - h_1^2}{2Rh_2 - h_2^2} = \frac{2Rh_2 - 2Rh_1 - h_2^2 + h_1^2}{2Rh_2 - h_2^2}v_1^2,$$

from which

$$v_1 = \sqrt{\frac{2g(h_2 - h_1)(2Rh_2 - h_2^2)}{2Rh_2 - h_2^2 - 2Rh_1 + h_1^2}} = \sqrt{\frac{2g(h_2 - h_1)(2R - h_2)h_2}{2R(h_2 - h_1) + (h_1 - h_2)(h_1 + h_2)}}$$

Simplifying the fraction under the square root by $(h_2 - h_1)$, we obtain:

$$v_1 = \sqrt{2gh_2\frac{2R - h_2}{2R - (h_1 + h_2)}} = 2.5\,\frac{\text{m}}{\text{s}}$$

similarly (using the symmetry of the situation to exchange indices), we get:

$$v_2 = \sqrt{2gh_1\frac{2R - h_1}{2R - (h_1 + h_2)}} = 1.5\,\frac{\text{m}}{\text{s}}.$$

Solution of Problem 90. Assume the 3 kg object to be a point so that its rotational inertia can be neglected. Since friction and the rod's mass are negligible, the only force acting on the object is gravitational force, therefore the object undergoes free-fall. Its path being vertical, the object moves a distance of:

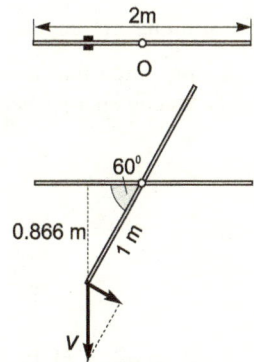

$$h = \sqrt{\left(\frac{L}{2}\right)^2 - \left(\frac{L}{4}\right)^2} = 0.866\,\text{m}$$

until it drops off from the rod. Its velocity at that moment is $v = \sqrt{2gh} = 4.16\,\text{m/s}$. The object's velocity can be resolved into components that are parallel and perpendicular to the rod. The latter equals the velocity of the rod's end at the moment when the object leaves the rod. After this moment the rod's end maintains its velocity, so its speed in the rod's vertical position is still:

$$v_P = v\cos\alpha,$$

where $\cos\alpha = \dfrac{L/4}{L/2} = 0.5$. Thus

$$v_P = 4.16\,\frac{\text{m}}{\text{s}} \cdot 0.5 = 2.08\,\frac{\text{m}}{\text{s}}.$$

Solution of Problem 91. The collision of the bullet and board is inelastic, therefore the conservation of energy can not be used in this situation. Since the board is initially vertical, the torques of the external forces acting on the board-bullet system are all zero at the point of suspension (hinge), therefore the conservation of moment of momentum can be applied to the collision of the bullet and board. Thus we have:

$$mvL = mL^2\omega + \frac{1}{3}ML^2\omega,$$

where mvL is the momentum of the bullet at the point of suspension before collision, ω is the angular velocity of the board and bullet moving together after the collision and $ML^2/3$ is the rotational inertia of the board about the axis that is perpendicular to the board and goes through its end. Isolating the angular velocity of the system after the collision, we get:

$$\omega = \frac{v}{L} \cdot \frac{1}{1 + M/3m}. \tag{1}$$

After the collision, there are only conservative forces acting on the system (neglecting air drag), whose works can be calculated easily. Before applying the work-kinetic energy theorem, let us determine the change in the kinetic energy of the system, which is:

$$E_{\text{kin}} = \frac{1}{2}m(\omega L)^2 + \frac{1}{2} \cdot \frac{1}{3}ML^2\omega^2 = \frac{1}{2}(m + M/3)\omega^2 L^2.$$

Substituting the angular velocity from equation (1), we find: $E_{\text{kin}} = \dfrac{1}{2} \cdot \dfrac{mv^2}{1 + M/3m}$.

The only force that does work on the system is the gravitational force, therefore the work-kinetic energy theorem takes the form of:

$$-mgL - Mg\frac{L}{2} = 0 - \frac{1}{2} \cdot \frac{mv^2}{1 + M/3m}.$$

Solving this for the initial velocity of the bullet, we find:

$$v = \sqrt{2gL(1 + M/2m)(1 + M/3m)} = 160\,\frac{\text{m}}{\text{s}}.$$

First solution of Problem 92. (Using the conservation of angular momentum). a) The speed of the body is $u = \sqrt{2gR}$ at the bottom (only conservative forces act). From the law of conservation of mechanical energy

$$mgR = \frac{1}{2}\left(\frac{1}{3}MR^2\right)\omega^2 + \frac{1}{2}mv^2. \tag{1}$$

From the law of conservation of angular momentum

$$muR = \frac{1}{3}MR^2\omega + mvR, \tag{2}$$

where muR and mvR are the angular momentums of the body and $\frac{1}{3}MR^2\omega$ is the angular momentum of the rod for its axis of rotation. According to the condition $v=0$, (1) and (2) may be written in the following form:

$$mgR = \frac{1}{6}MR^2\omega^2, \tag{1'}$$

$$muR = \frac{1}{3}MR^2\omega. \tag{2'}$$

Simplifying by R:

$$mg = \frac{1}{6}MR\omega^2, \tag{1''}$$

$$mu = \frac{1}{3}MR\omega. \tag{2''}$$

Dividing equation $(1'')$ by equation $(2'')$:

$$\frac{g}{u} = \frac{1}{2}\omega,$$

from which the angular speed is

$$\omega = \frac{2g}{u}.$$

If this is substituted into $(2'')$:

$$mu = \frac{1}{3}MR\frac{2g}{u},$$

from which the requested ratio is

$$\frac{M}{m} = \frac{3u^2}{2gR} = \frac{3 \cdot 2gR}{2gR} = 3.$$

b) Taking into consideration that the initial angular speed of the rod is

$$\omega = \frac{2g}{u} = \frac{2g}{\sqrt{2gR}} = \sqrt{\frac{2g}{R}},$$

based on the work–energy theorem

$$Mg\frac{R}{2}(1 - \cos\alpha) = \frac{1}{2} \cdot \frac{1}{3}MR^2\omega^2 = \frac{1}{3}MRg.$$

Simplifying by MgR:

$$1 - \cos\alpha = \frac{2}{3},$$

and from here

$$\cos\alpha = \frac{1}{3}, \quad \text{and} \quad \alpha = \arccos\frac{1}{3} = 70.53°.$$

Second solution of Problem 92. (Using impulse.) Let overline ($\overline{F}$) stand for the average force during the collision. $\overline{F_1}$ stands for the interaction between the rod and the small body (the two forces are equal but opposite, $\overline{F_1}$ stands for their absolute value) and $\overline{F_2}$ stands for the action of the axis of rotation on the rod (see the figure on the next page). With these the momentum theorem for the small body becomes

$$\overline{F_1}\Delta t = \Delta(mv) = m\sqrt{2gR}, \tag{1}$$

for the rod

$$\overline{F_1}\Delta t + \overline{F_2}\Delta t = \frac{1}{2}MR\omega, \tag{2}$$

the equation of motion for rotation becomes

$$\overline{F_1}\Delta t\frac{R}{2} - \overline{F_2}\Delta t\frac{R}{2} = \frac{1}{12}MR^2\omega. \tag{3}$$

Due to the absolutely elastic collision and the condition given in the problem

$$mgR = \frac{1}{2}\cdot\frac{1}{3}MR^2\omega^2. \tag{4}$$

From this the initial angular speed of the rod is

$$\omega = \sqrt{6\frac{m}{M}\frac{g}{R}}. \tag{4'}$$

Dividing (2) by (3) gives

$$\frac{\overline{F_1}+\overline{F_2}}{\overline{F_1}-\overline{F_2}} = \frac{6MR\omega}{2MR\omega} = 3.$$

From this we get

$$\overline{F_2} = \frac{1}{2}\overline{F_1}.$$

(We can see that $\overline{F_1}$ and $\overline{F_2}$ acting on the rod point in the same direction.)
Substituting this and (1) and (4') into (2) gives

$$m\sqrt{2gR}+\frac{1}{2}m\sqrt{2gR}=\frac{1}{2}MR\sqrt{6\frac{m}{M}\frac{g}{R}}.$$

Combining the like terms gives

$$m\frac{3}{2}\sqrt{2gR}=\frac{1}{2}MR\sqrt{6\frac{m}{M}\frac{g}{R}}.$$

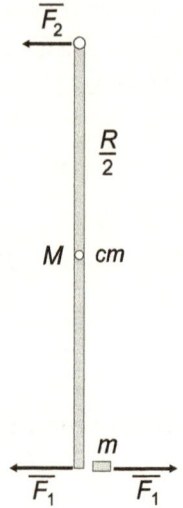

After squaring:

$$m^2 \cdot 9 \cdot 2gR = M^2 R^2 \cdot 6 \cdot \frac{m}{M}\frac{g}{R},$$

from which the requested ratio is

$$\frac{M}{m} = 3,$$

just as we acquired it from the first solution.

Solution of Problem 93. When the stick detaches from the hook, its centre of mass undergoes oblique projection. In the meantime, the stick rotates uniformly at the already acquired angular speed (the homogeneous gravitational force has no moment on the centre of mass). We determine the magnitude and the direction of the instantaneous velocity of the centre of mass (S) upon detachment and the angular speed of the stick, the rising time of the projection and from it the angular displacement of the stick and finally the angle enclosed by it and the horizontal.

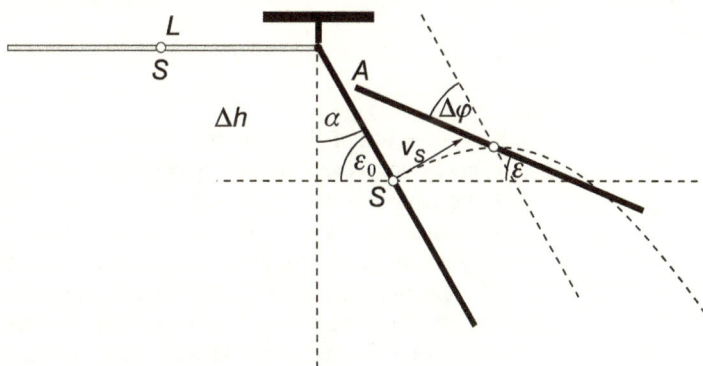

From the work–energy theorem:

$$mg\Delta h = \frac{1}{2}\Theta_A \omega^2.$$

In detail:

$$mg\frac{L}{2}\cos\alpha = \frac{1}{2} \cdot \frac{1}{3}mL^2\omega^2,$$

from which the angular speed is

$$\omega = \sqrt{\frac{3g}{L}\cos\alpha}\ .$$

From this the magnitude of the velocity of the centre of mass is

$$v_{\mathrm{s}} = \frac{L}{2}\omega.$$

The angle of projection is also α. With it the vertical component of the velocity of the projection is

$$v_{\mathrm{s_y}} = v_{\mathrm{s}} \cdot \sin\alpha.$$

The rising time (the moment of reaching the maximum height from the beginning of the projection) is

$$t_r = \frac{v_{s_y}}{g} = \frac{\frac{L}{2}\omega\sin\alpha}{g} = \frac{1}{2}\sqrt{\frac{3L}{g\cos\alpha}}\cdot\sin\alpha \quad (=0.1287\,\text{s}).$$

The angular displacement of the stick in the meantime is

$$\Delta\varphi = \omega\cdot\Delta t_r = \sqrt{3gL\cos\alpha}\cdot\frac{1}{2}\sqrt{\frac{3L}{g}}\cos\alpha\cdot\sin\alpha = \frac{3}{2}\cos\alpha\sin\alpha = \frac{3}{4}\sin 2\alpha \quad (=37.21°).$$

The angle enclosed by the stick and the horizontal in the beginning of the oblique projection is

$$\varepsilon = \frac{\pi}{2} - \alpha \; (= \frac{\pi}{2} - \frac{\pi}{6} = \frac{\pi}{3} = 60°),$$

and in the requested moment

$$\varepsilon = \varepsilon_0 - \Delta\varphi = \frac{\pi}{3} - \frac{3}{4}\sin 2\alpha = \frac{\pi}{3} - \frac{3}{4}\sin 60° = 0.3978\,\text{rad} = 22.78°.$$

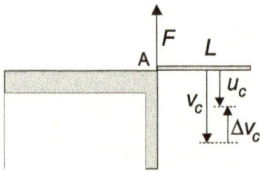

First solution of Problem 94. (Using angular momentum and energy conservation.) At the beginning of the interaction with the table the forces are vertical, and since the collision is instantaneous, by the time the rod falls down the forces already cease, thus there are no horizontal force components.

Let our reference point (A) be the end of the rod colliding with the table. Since the collision is instantaneous, the force F exerted by the table during the collision is much greater than the weight of the rod ($F \gg mg$), thus the latter can be disregarded during the collision. This means that the angular momentum with respect to point A is conserved. Indeed, the torque of the only external force F is zero with respect to A. Two conservation laws are applicable for the collision.

The law of angular momentum conservation is:

$$m\frac{L}{2}v_c = m\frac{L}{2}u_c + \Theta_c\omega, \tag{1}$$

where the left hand side is the angular momentum of the rod (not yet in rotation) before the collision, and the two terms on the right hand side are the orbital and spin angular momenta after the collision. (The rod performs planar motion, so the orbital and spin angular momenta are parallel vectors perpendicular to the plane of the motion, thus their magnitudes simply adds up). In the equation the speeds and the momentum of inertia refer to the centre of mass of the rod.

The law of energy conservation is:

$$\frac{1}{2}mv_c^2 = \frac{1}{2}mu_c^2 + \frac{1}{2}\Theta_c\omega^2. \tag{2}$$

In order to answer the problem's questions, the angular speed and the speed of the centre have to be determined after the collision. For these two unknowns we have two equations.

After simplifying (1) and (2) we get:

$$v_c = u_c + \frac{2\Theta_c}{mL}\omega,$$

$$v_c^2 = u_c^2 + \frac{\Theta_c}{m}\omega^2.$$

Taking the speeds to the left hand side of the equations:

$$v_c - u_c = \frac{2\Theta_c}{mL}\omega, \tag{1'}$$

$$v_c^2 - u_c^2 = \frac{\Theta_c}{m}\omega^2. \tag{2'}$$

Factorising the left hand side of $(2')$:

$$(v_c - u_c)(v_c + u_c) = \frac{\Theta_c}{m}\omega^2.$$

We divide $(2')$ by $(1')$:

$$v_c + u_c = \frac{L\omega}{2}. \tag{3}$$

By adding $(1')$ and (3) the speed u_c can be eliminated:

$$2v_c = \frac{2\Theta_c}{mL}\omega + \frac{L\omega}{2} = \frac{4\Theta_c + mL^2}{2mL}\omega,$$

and the unknown angular speed is:

$$\omega = \frac{4mL}{4\Theta_c + mL^2}v_c.$$

Putting in the moment of inertia of the rod, around the axis through the centre, perpendicular to the rod, we get:

$$\omega = \frac{4mL}{4\frac{1}{12}mL^2 + mL^2}\cdot v_c = \frac{4}{\frac{1}{3} + 1}\cdot\frac{v_c}{L} = 3\frac{v_c}{L}. \tag{4}$$

From equation $(1')$ the speed of the centre of mass after the collision is:

$$u_c = \frac{L\omega}{2} - v_c = \frac{L}{2}\cdot 3\frac{v_c}{L} - v_c = \frac{v_c}{2}.$$

The time needed for a whole revolution is:

$$T = \frac{2\pi}{\omega} = \frac{2\pi}{3v_c}L = \frac{2\pi}{3\sqrt{2gH}}L = \frac{2\pi}{3\sqrt{2\cdot10\,\frac{m}{s^2}0.8\,m}}\cdot0.4\text{ m} = 0.21\text{ s}.$$

During the revolution the centre of mass lowers by a distance of:

$$s = u_c T + \frac{1}{2}gT^2 = \frac{v_c}{2} \cdot \frac{2\pi}{3v_c}L + \frac{g}{2} \cdot \frac{4\pi^2 L^2}{9 \cdot 2gH} = \frac{\pi}{3}L\left(1 + \frac{\pi}{3}\frac{L}{H}\right).$$

Numerically:

$$s = \frac{\pi}{3}0.4 \text{ m} \cdot \left(1 + \frac{\pi}{3}\frac{0.4 \text{ m}}{0.8 \text{ m}}\right) = 0.64 \text{ m}.$$

Second solution of Problem 94. (Using energy conservation, impulse–momentum theorem and angular impulse–angular momentum theorem.) Let us direct the vertical axis of the coordinate frame downwards. All the velocities and forces are vertical, thus, considering only their vertical components, they can be treated as signed scalar quantities. Let the reference point be the centre of mass of the rod. The angular momentum of the rod is not conserved, because of the non-zero torque of the external force F. In the following equations the letters refer to the magnitude of the vectors. The impulse-momentum theorem for the collision is:

$$-F\Delta t = \Delta(mv_c) = m(u_c - v_c). \tag{1}$$

The angular impulse-angular momentum theorem is:

$$F \cdot r \cdot \Delta t = \Delta N.$$

Here $r = L/2$. In the centre-of-mass reference frame the orbital angular momentum is zero, and the initial angular speed is zero as well, so:

$$F\frac{L}{2}\Delta t = \Theta_c \Delta \omega = \Theta_c \omega. \tag{2}$$

The energy conservation law is:

$$\frac{1}{2}mv_c^2 = \frac{1}{2}mu_c^2 + \frac{1}{2}\Theta_c \omega^2. \tag{3}$$

Multiplying (1) by (-1), we get:

$$F\Delta t = m(v_c - u_c). \tag{1'}$$

After writing the moment of inertia into (2) and simplifying by $L/2$, we obtain:

$$F\Delta t = \frac{2}{L} \cdot \frac{1}{12}mL^2 = \frac{mL}{6}\omega. \tag{2'}$$

By comparing (1') and (2'):

$$v_c - u_c = \frac{L}{6}\omega, \tag{4}$$

and the form of (3) becomes simpler as well:

$$v_c^2 = u_c^2 + \frac{1}{12}L^2\omega^2. \tag{3'}$$

Rearranging this equation we get:

$$v_c^2 - u_c^2 = \frac{1}{12}L^2\omega^2.$$

After factorising, and dividing the equation by (4), from here the solution is the same as solution I.

Third solution of Problem 94. (Using angular impulse–angular momentum theorem, with reference point at the edge of the table.) Since the line of action of the force F passes through the end of the rod at the edge of the table, its torque is zero with respect to this point. The weight force can be disregarded because the collision is instantaneous. Thus, the total change of the angular momentum of the rod (with respect to point A) is zero:

$$F \cdot r \cdot \Delta t = \Delta N = 0,$$

so

$$0 = mu_c\frac{L}{2} - mv_c\frac{L}{2} + \Theta_c\omega.$$

Due to the conservation of energy:

$$\frac{1}{2}mv_c^2 = \frac{1}{2}mu_c^2 + \frac{1}{2}\Theta_c\omega^2.$$

These equations are identical to the ones written down in solution I, and the rest of the solution is the same as there.

Fourth solution of Problem 94. (Using general collision theory.) At the moment of collision, the rod can be considered as a weightlessly floating object since during the instantaneous interaction the role of the gravitational force is negligible. The collision process can be regarded equivalently as if the rod, floating at rest in the space, was hit by an upward moving 'table of infinite mass' at one of its ends. This interaction determines the angular speed of the rod after the collision, and thus the period of its rotational motion.

This process is equivalent to the collision of a rod, initially lying at rest on a very smooth (e.g. air cushion) table, and a pointlike particle of 'infinite mass', sliding towards the rod. First, let us solve this problem in a general, parametric way. Let m be the mass of the rod, and let M denote the mass of the pointlike particle sliding towards the rod at a speed V.

Furthermore, let u_c be the speed of the centre of mass of the rod, and let U be the speed of the masspoint M after collision.

With these notations the momentum conservation law is:

$$MV = MU + mu_C. \qquad (1)$$

Let the reference point of the angular momentum be the geometric point (at rest), where the collision takes place.

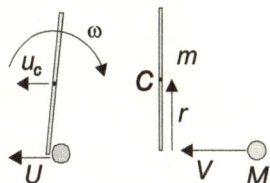

215

With respect to this point, both colliding objects have zero initial (spin and orbital) angular momentum, thus the conservation law of angular momentum has the following form:

$$0 = mu_c \frac{L}{2} - \frac{1}{12} mL^2 \omega, \tag{2}$$

where the first term is the orbital angular momentum and the second term is the spin angular momentum of the rod after collision. (The minus sign is due to the opposite direction of these angular momenta. See the figure.)

The energy conservation law is:

$$\frac{1}{2} MV^2 = \frac{1}{2} MU^2 + \frac{1}{2} mu_c^2 + \frac{1}{2} \cdot \frac{1}{12} mL^2 \omega^2. \tag{3}$$

From equation (2) the angular speed of the rod is:

$$\omega = \frac{6u_c}{L}. \tag{4}$$

Inserting it into (3), we get:

$$MV^2 = MU^2 + mu_c^2 + \frac{1}{12} mL^2 \frac{36u_c^2}{L^2} = MU^2 + 4mu_c^2. \tag{3'}$$

Equations (1) and $(3')$, written in a different form are:

$$M(V - U) = mu_c, \tag{1'}$$
$$M(V^2 - U^2) = 4mu_c^2. \tag{3''}$$

Factorising $(3'')$, we get:

$$M(V - U)(V + U) = 4mu_c^2, \tag{3'''}$$

and dividing it by equation $(1')$, we obtain:

$$(V + U) = 4u_c \;\longrightarrow\; u_c = \frac{(V + U)}{4}. \tag{4}$$

Inserting it into (1):

$$MV = MU + m \frac{(V + U)}{4} \;\longrightarrow\; 4MV = 4MU + mV + mU.$$

From here the speed of the masspoint M after collision can be expressed:

$$U = \frac{4M - m}{4M + m} V.$$

Writing it into (4), we obtain the speed of the centre of mass of the rod just after the collision is:

$$u_c = \frac{V + U}{4} = \frac{V + \frac{4M-m}{4M+m} V}{4} = \frac{4MV + mV + 4MV - mV}{16M + 4m} = \frac{8MV}{16M + 4m} = \frac{2MV}{4M + m}.$$

Now if $M \to \infty$, then $u_c \to \dfrac{V}{2}$, and from equation (4) the (constant) angular speed after the collision is:

$$\omega = \frac{6u_c}{L} = \frac{6\frac{V}{2}}{L} = 3\frac{V}{L} = \frac{3\sqrt{2gH}}{L}.$$

From here on the rest of the solution is the same as in solution I. The final results are the same as well.

First solution of Problem 95. This solution is based on the information that the mass of the small objects is negligible next to that of the rod, and meaning they will not influence the motion of the rod. (Their mass is certainly not negligible when their own motion is investigated.) Consider the motion of the rod first.

According to the work-energy theorem applied to the rod,

$$Mg\frac{L}{2}\sin\alpha = \frac{1}{2}\cdot\frac{1}{2}ML^2\omega^2.$$

Hence the angular speed expressed in terms of the angular displacement is

$$\omega = \sqrt{\frac{3g\sin\alpha}{L}}. \tag{1}$$

The law of torques applied about the axis of rotation states

$$Mg\frac{L}{2}\cos\alpha = \frac{1}{3}ML^2\beta,$$

and hence the angular acceleration β in terms of the angular displacement is

$$\beta = \frac{3}{2}g\cos\alpha \cdot \frac{1}{L}. \tag{2}$$

This result immediately shows that in the initial position ($\cos\alpha = 1$) the endpoint of the rod has an initial acceleration of $a_0 = 3g/2 > g$, thus the upper small object immediately lifts off the rod and falls freely along a vertical line. At the same time, the lower one is pressed downwards and made to accelerate. The force of static friction makes it move along a circular path for a while. At the angle α where the friction force is not able to provide the normal acceleration of the small object any more, it will also separate from the rod and continue to move along a parabolic projectile path. (Since the pointlike object is initially at the end of the rod, it will leave the rod immediately as it starts to slide, meaning there is no motion with kinetic friction along the bottom of the rod to be considered).

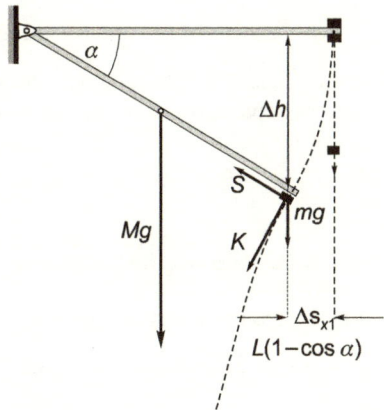

Newton's second law applied to the normal and tangential components of the motion of the small object at the time instant just before separation states:

$$S - mg\sin\alpha = mL^2\omega^2, \tag{3}$$

$$K + mg\cos\alpha = mL\beta, \tag{4}$$

where K is the normal force exerted by the rod and S is the maximum value of the static friction force:

$$S = \mu K. \tag{5}$$

With the value of K substituted from (4) into (5), and then the value of S substituted in (3):

$$\mu mL\beta - \mu mg\cos\alpha - mg\sin\alpha = mL\omega^2,$$

which is independent of m (note that $M \gg m$).

From (1) and (2),

$$\frac{3}{2}\mu\cos\alpha - \mu\cos\alpha - \sin\alpha = 3\sin\alpha.$$

Hence

$$\frac{1}{2}\mu\cos\alpha = 4\sin\alpha,$$

and the tangent of the angle where the separation occurs is

$$\frac{\sin\alpha}{\cos\alpha} = \tan\alpha = \frac{\mu}{8},$$

and

$$\alpha = \arctan\frac{\mu}{8} = \arctan 0.105 = 6°.$$

The small object has descended

$$\Delta h = L\sin\alpha = 1\,\text{m}\cdot\sin 6° = 0.1\,\text{m}$$

so far, moving together with the rod. Its horizontal displacement also equals that of the end of the rod:

$$\Delta s_{x1} = L(1-\cos\alpha) = 1\,\text{m}(1-0.9945) = 5.48\cdot 10^3\,\text{m} = 5.48\,\text{mm}.$$

The magnitudes of the velocity components of the projectile motion starting at the time instant of separation are obtained from (1):

$$v_{0x} = L\omega\sin\alpha = \sqrt{3gL\sin^3\alpha} = \sqrt{3\cdot 9.81\,\frac{\text{m}}{\text{s}^2}\cdot 1\,\text{m}\cdot\sin^3 6°} = 0.183\,\frac{\text{m}}{\text{s}},$$

$$v_{0y} = L\omega\cos\alpha = \sqrt{3gL\sin\alpha\cos^2\alpha} = \sqrt{3\cdot 1\,\text{m}\cdot 9.81\,\frac{\text{m}}{\text{s}^2}\cdot\sin 6°\cos^2 6°} = 1.744\,\frac{\text{m}}{\text{s}}.$$

Projectile motion starts at a height of

$$s_y = 2L - \Delta h = 2L - L\sin\alpha = L(2-\sin\alpha) = 1\,\text{m}(2-\sin 6°) = 1.9\,\text{m},$$

and the time of fall obtained from the relationship $t = \Delta v_y / g$ is

$$t = \frac{\sqrt{v_{0y}^2 + 2gs_y} - v_{0y}}{g} = 0.4685\,\text{s} \approx 0.47\,\text{s}.$$

The total horizontal displacement of the lower one of the two small objects is

$$\Delta x = \Delta s_{x1} + \Delta s_{x2} = L(1 - \cos\alpha) + v_{0x}t =$$

$$= 5.48 \cdot 10^{-3}\,\text{m} + 0.183\,\frac{\text{m}}{\text{s}} \cdot 0.47\,\text{s} = 9.15 \cdot 10^{-2}\,\text{m} = 9.15\,\text{cm}.$$

This is equal to the distance between the impact points of the two objects.

Second solution of Problem 95. This is a general solution for the case when the masses of the small objects are not negligible. The equations are set up for the small object and for the rod separately, and finally for the whole system:

$$S - mg\sin\alpha = mL\omega^2 \qquad (= ma_n \text{ for the normal direction}) \quad (1)$$

$$K + mg\cos\alpha = mL\beta \qquad (= ma_t \text{ for the tangential direction}) \quad (2)$$

$$S = \mu K \qquad (\text{for the time instant of separation}) \quad (3)$$

$$Mg\frac{L}{2}\cos\alpha - KL = \frac{1}{3}ML^2\beta \qquad (\text{for the rod}) \quad (4)$$

$$Mg\frac{l}{2}\sin\alpha + mgL\sin\alpha = \frac{1}{2}\cdot\frac{1}{3}ML^2\omega^2 + \frac{1}{2}m(L\omega)^2 \qquad (\text{for the system}) \quad (5)$$

The solution is

$$\omega = \sqrt{\frac{3g(M+2m)\sin\alpha}{L(M+3m)}}, \qquad L\beta = \frac{3M+6m}{2M+6m}\cdot g\cos\alpha,$$

and hence the tangent of the angle at which separation occurs is

$$\tan\alpha = \frac{M(M+3m)}{8M^2 + 42Mm + 54m^2}\cdot\mu = \frac{M}{8M+18m}\cdot\mu.$$

If $m = 0$, then $\tan\alpha = \frac{\mu}{8}$ and $\alpha = 6°$. The solution can be finished in the same way as solution 1.

Solution of Problem 96. The constraining force exerted by the half-rod (that really acts at the point of contact of the two halves) can be determined by using Newton's law of motion for the centre of mass of the lower half-rod. It is worth setting up the equation of motion for two components, the tangential one and the radial one.

Remarks on the figure:

1. Force K actually acts on the lower half-rod at the point of contact of the two half-rods. However, according to the law of motion of the centre of mass, the centre of mass moves as if the total mass of the body were concentrated there and all external

forces acted in the centre of mass. This is the reason why the drawing shows the force in the middle of the lower half-rod.

2. The direction of force K may also be a problem. It can be seen that force K should point 'forward', because the tangential acceleration of the centre of mass of the half-rod is greater than the acceleration that would arise from the tangential component of gravitational force. Let us use Newton's second law for angular motion ($M = \Theta\beta$) for the whole rod:

$$mg\frac{L}{2}\cos\varphi = \frac{1}{3}mL^2\beta.$$

From here, the angular acceleration is

$$\beta = \frac{3}{2}\frac{g}{L}\cos\varphi.$$

With this, the tangential acceleration of the lower half-rod, which moves on radius $3L/4$, is

$$a_t = \frac{3}{4}L \cdot \frac{3}{2}\frac{g}{L}\cos\varphi = \frac{9}{8}g\cos\varphi.$$

The tangential force required for this is

$$F_t = \frac{9}{8} \cdot \frac{m}{2}g\cos\varphi > \frac{m}{2}g\cos\varphi.$$

The missing force can be provided only by the other half-rod through the tangential component K_t of force K.

3. Some may ask why the angular acceleration of the lower half-rod is the same as the angular acceleration of the whole rod if gravitational force has no moment on the centre of mass; in addition, the moment of force K exerted by the upper half-rod on the half-rod acts in the opposite direction to the actual angular momentum. The total moment comes from the moment of this force and the moment of the elastic shearing stress due to the bending of the rod, this latter overcompensates the 'backward' moment of force K. (If the rod was not 'rigid', its outer half would lag behind the inner half in angular displacement, that is, the rod would fold during the rotation. This is prevented by the moment arising from the small bending).

The equation of the motion of the rod in tangential direction is

$$K_t + \frac{m}{2}g\cos\varphi = \frac{m}{2} \cdot a_t \quad , \tag{1}$$

in the radial direction

$$K_n - \frac{m}{2}g\sin\varphi = \frac{m}{2} \cdot a_n. \tag{2}$$

In order to determine the constraining force $K = \sqrt{K_t^2 + K_n^2}$, the normal and tangential accelerations should be determined from the dynamics of the process. For this, the

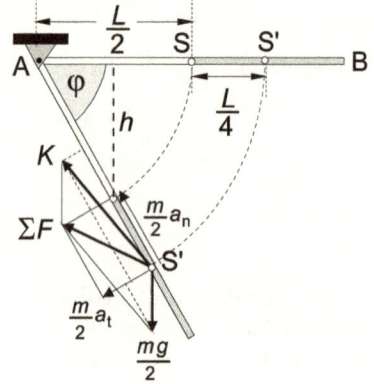

instantaneous angular velocity and angular acceleration are required. The first can be found from the work–energy theorem, the second from Newton's second law for angular motion. As the angular data of the half-rod are the same as the data of the whole rod, the following equations are true:

the work – energy theorem:

$$mhg = \frac{1}{2}\Theta \cdot \omega^2,$$

where

$$\Theta = \frac{1}{3}mL^2 \quad \text{and} \quad h = \frac{L}{2}\sin\varphi.$$

With this

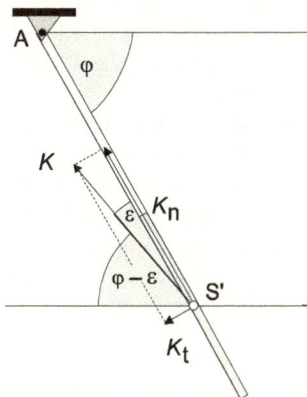

$$mg\frac{L}{2}\sin\varphi = \frac{1}{2}\frac{1}{3}mL^2\omega^2,$$

from here

$$L\omega^2 = 3g\sin\varphi. \tag{3}$$

Newton's second law for angular motion:

$$mg\frac{L}{2}\cos\varphi = \frac{1}{3}mL^2\beta,$$

from which

$$L\beta = \frac{3}{2}g\cos\varphi. \tag{4}$$

$a_t = \frac{3}{4}L\beta$ and by substituting $a_n = \frac{3}{4}L\omega^2$ and using (1), (2), (3) and (4):

$$K_t + \frac{m}{2}g\cos\varphi = \frac{m}{2}\frac{3}{4}L\beta = \frac{m}{2}\frac{3}{4}\frac{3}{2}g\cos\varphi = \frac{9}{16}mg\cos\varphi,$$

$$K_n - \frac{m}{2}g\sin\varphi = \frac{m}{2}\frac{3}{4}L\omega^2 = \frac{m}{2}\frac{3}{4}3g\sin\varphi = \frac{9}{8}mg\sin\varphi.$$

From here, the magnitudes of the two (perpendicular) components of the requested force are

$$K_t = \frac{9}{16}mg\cos\varphi - \frac{1}{2}mg\cos\varphi = mg\cos\varphi\left(\frac{9}{16} - \frac{8}{16}\right) = \frac{1}{16}mg\cos\varphi,$$

$$K_n = \frac{9}{8}mg\sin\varphi + \frac{1}{2}mg\sin\varphi = mg\sin\varphi\left(\frac{9}{8} + \frac{4}{8}\right) = \frac{26}{16}mg\sin\varphi.$$

With these the magnitude of the requested force is

$$K = \frac{mg}{16}\sqrt{\cos^2\varphi + 26^2\sin^2\varphi} = \frac{mg}{16}\sqrt{\frac{1}{4} + 26^2\frac{3}{4}} \approx$$

$$\approx 1.4076 \cdot mg.$$

For the direction of force K relative to the rod:

$$\tan\varepsilon = \frac{K_t}{K_n} = \frac{mg\cos\varphi}{16} \cdot \frac{16}{26\cdot mg\sin\varphi} = \frac{1}{26\cdot\tan\varphi} =$$

$$= \frac{1}{26\cdot\sqrt{3}},$$

from which $\varepsilon = \arctan\dfrac{\sqrt{3}}{78} = 1.272^0$, and the angle enclosed with the horizontal is $\alpha = \varphi - \varepsilon = 60° - 1.272^0 = 58.73°$.

First solution of Problem 97. Let us solve the problem by first using a reference frame which rotates with the disk. Let the centre of the disk be the origin, and one of the three axes of the frame be the axis of rotation. In this frame the rod is in static equilibrium.

Of course Newton's laws cannot be applied in non-inertial reference frames, but they can still be used if we introduce a fictitious, so-called inertial force. The law of motion in a non-inertial frame will take the same form as Newton's second law if a fictitious force is added to the real forces acting on the object. This inertial force can be calculated as the product of the opposite of the object's acceleration and its mass. The inertial force acting on a stationary object in a frame that rotates at constant angular velocity is the so-called centrifugal force.

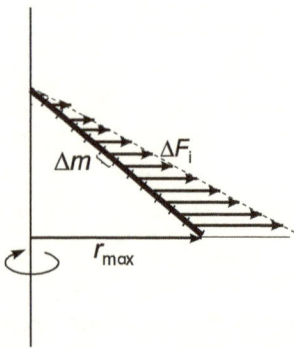

Centrifugal force depends on the position of the object, because the acceleration in a rotating frame changes with the distance from the centre. At the same time, centrifugal force is a volume force since it is proportional to the mass and in case of a homogeneous object (for which $\Delta m = \varrho\Delta V$) to the volume as well. (In this respect, it is similar to the gravitational force with the distinction that while gravitational force decreases, centrifugal force increases as we move away from the centre). In our case — as one end of the rod is on the rotation axis —the magnitude and point of action of the centrifugal force acting on the rod can be calculated in the following way.

Let us divide the rod into n equal parts. The magnitudes of centrifugal forces acting on these parts can be written as:

$$\Delta F_i = \Delta m r_i \omega^2$$

so the forces change from zero to $\Delta m r\omega^2$ as we move away from the centre. These forces are all perpendicular to the axis of rotation (therefore parallel to each other) and their magnitudes are in direct proportion to the distance from the centre, so their average is the arithmetic mean of the two extreme values $\Delta F_0 = 0$ and $\Delta F_n = \Delta m r_{\text{max}}\omega^2$:

$$\Delta\overline{F} = \frac{0 + \Delta m r_{\text{max}}\omega^2}{2},$$

hence the magnitude of centrifugal force acting on the whole rod can be calculated as:

$$F_{cf} = \sum \Delta \overline{F}_i = \frac{r_{\max}\omega^2}{2} \sum \Delta m_i = \frac{1}{2} m r_{\max} \omega^2.$$

More precisely the centrifugal force is the sum of an arithmetic sequence:

$$F = \sum_{i=1}^{n} \Delta F_i = \sum_{i=1}^{n} \frac{m}{n} \cdot i \cdot \frac{r_{\max}}{n} \cdot \omega^2 = \frac{m}{n^2} r_{\max} \omega^2 \sum_{i=1}^{n} i = \frac{m r_{\max} \omega^2}{n^2} \cdot \frac{1+n}{2} \cdot n$$

$$= m r_{\max} \omega^2 \left(\frac{1}{2n} + \frac{1}{2} \right).$$

If $n \to \infty$ then $1/(2n) \to 0$ and the magnitude of centrifugal force is: $F_{cf} = $
$= \frac{1}{2} m r_{\max} \omega^2.$

The second step is to determine the point of action of the centrifugal force, which is the resultant of parallel forces F_i. To do this, let us set up a model.

A vertical triangle in a uniform gravitational field provides the same distribution of forces if set as shown. Side AB is divided into n equal segments and vertical lines drawn from each point of division cut the triangle into n parts, whose weights (ΔG_i) show the same pattern as the centrifugal forces acting on the parts of the rod. We know that the point of action of the gravitational force acting on this triangle is at its centroid, which is at the 2/3 of its median. Therefore the line of action of the gravitational force divides side AB in the ratio $1:2$. Similarly the point of action of the centrifugal force divides the rod in the ratio $1:2$, so it is at a distance of $2L/3$ from the end that is above the axis or $L/3$ from the end that touches the disk.

Equations that express the conditions for translational and rotational equilibrium can now be set up. The condition for translational equilibrium in the vertical direction is:

$$mg - K = 0, \qquad (1)$$

while in the horizontal direction we have:

$$F_{cf} - S = 0, \qquad (2)$$

where K and S are the normal and frictional forces exerted by the disk respectively, and F_{cf} is the centrifugal force calculated above. As $K = mg$ from equation (1) and

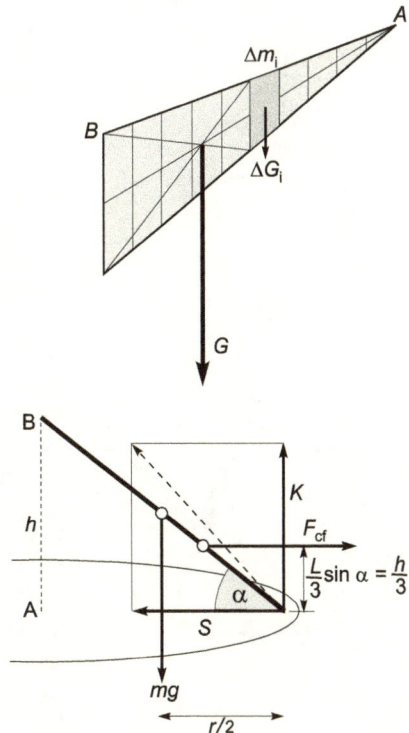

$F_{cf} = S$ from equation (2), we have two force couples, whose torques are $M_1 = mgr/2$ and $M_2 = F_{cf}L\sin\alpha/3$. respectively. (We use $r_{max} = r$ from now on.) The condition for rotational equilibrium is: $M_1 - M_2 = 0$, so

$$mg\frac{r}{2} = F_{cf}\frac{l}{3} \cdot \sin\alpha = \frac{1}{2}mr\omega^2 \cdot \frac{h}{3},$$

where $h = \overline{AB} = \sqrt{L^2 - r^2} = \sqrt{1\,\text{m}^2 - 0.64\,\text{m}^2} = 0.6$ m. Thus the required angular velocity is:

$$\omega = \sqrt{\frac{3g}{h}} = \sqrt{\frac{30\,\text{m/s}^2}{0.6\,\text{m}}} = \sqrt{50\,\text{s}^{-2}} = 7.07\,\text{s}^{-1}.$$

Second solution of Problem 97. Solving the problem in an inertial reference frame is much more complicated. In this case the rod is not in equilibrium, since every point of it (except for the top one) moves in a circle at constant angular velocity. According to Newton's second law, the vector sum of vertical forces mg and K should be zero (since the vertical acceleration of the centre of mass is zero), so they have to be equal in magnitude. In the horizontal direction the only force acting, which is the static friction S, should keep the centre of mass in a circular path, therefore:

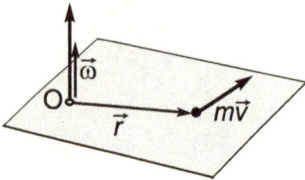

$$S = m\frac{r}{2}\omega^2 \qquad (1)$$

as the radius of the circular path of the centre of mass is $r/2$.

Let us now write Newton's second law in angular form:

$$\sum \vec{M} = \frac{\Delta\vec{N}}{\Delta t}, \qquad (2)$$

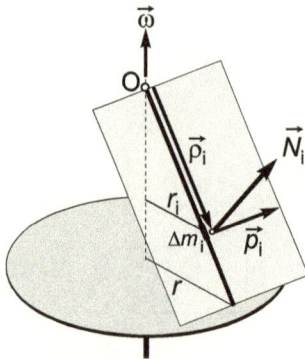

where the left-hand side is the resultant torque while the right-hand side is the time rate of change of the angular momentum. Note that both quantities should be defined with respect to the same point.

Let this point be the top of the rod (O), which remains stationary. Let us calculate the total angular momentum of the rod and then find its rate of change.

The total angular momentum is the sum of the angular momenta of its mass elements. The angular momentum of one mass element is defined as:

$$\vec{N} = \vec{\varrho} \times \vec{p} = \vec{\varrho} \times m\vec{v} = m[(\vec{\varrho} \times (\vec{\omega} \times \vec{r})],$$

where $\vec{\varrho}$ is the vector pointing from point O to the mass element, $\vec{p} = m\vec{v}$ is the linear momentum of the mass element, $\vec{r}$ is the vector pointing to the mass element from the centre of its circular path and $\vec{\omega}$ is the vector of angular velocity (given by the right-hand rule). In our case the vectors in the vector products are perpendicular to each other, therefore the sine of their enclosed angle is 1.

The velocity of the mass elements increases in proportion to their distance from the rotation axis, therefore their angular momenta are all different in magnitude and same in direction. The total angular momentum of the rod is the sum of the angular momenta of its mass elements. Let us divide the rod into n equal parts. As the mass of the rod is m, the mass of each mass element will be $\Delta m_i = m/n$. The magnitude of the vector pointing from O to each mass element is $\varrho_i = i \cdot L/n$, and the radius of the circular path of each mass element is given by $r_i = i \cdot r/n$. Since the angular momentum vectors of the mass elements are all parallel to each other (each being perpendicular to the plane defined by vectors $\vec{\varrho_i}$ and $\vec{v_i}$), their vector sum can be calculated simply as the sum of their magnitudes:

$$N = \sum_{i=1}^{n} \varrho_i \cdot \Delta m_i v_i = \sum_{i=1}^{n} \varrho_i \cdot \Delta m_i \cdot \omega \cdot r_i = \sum_{i=1}^{n} i \frac{L}{n} \cdot \frac{m}{n} \cdot \omega \cdot i \frac{r}{n}.$$

Removing the constants from the sum, we get:

$$\frac{mLr\omega}{n^3} \cdot \sum_{i=1}^{n} i^2,$$

thus we have to calculate the sum of squares of the first n integers, which can be written in the form of:

$$N = \frac{mLr\omega}{n^3} \cdot \frac{n(n+1)(2n+1)}{6} = \frac{mLr\omega}{6}\left(2 + \frac{3}{n} + \frac{1}{n^2}\right).$$

If $n \to \infty$, then the last two terms in the bracket tend to zero, so the total angular momentum of the rod tends to:

$$N = \frac{mLr\omega}{3}. \tag{3}$$

This is the magnitude of the total angular momentum of the rod, while its direction is perpendicular to the rod in the plane defined by the rod and the rotation axis as shown. As the rod rotates, so does its angular momentum, whose direction therefore changes throughout the motion. (This situation is similar to the uniform circular motion, in which the speed of the object is constant, but the direction of its velocity changes, therefore the object has a centripetal acceleration). Let us now determine the change in the angular momentum of the rod in time interval Δt, then divide the result by Δt to get the time rate of change of the angular momentum.

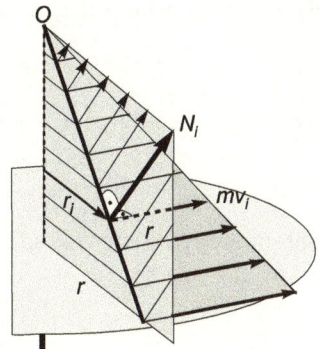

Let us first calculate the change in an arbitrary vector $\vec{a}$, which is perpendicular to the axis of rotation and has constant magnitude, while it is rotated through angle $\Delta\varphi$.

As shown in the figure, if the angle rotated is small, the length of the cord and the length of the arc are approximately equal, thus:

$$|\Delta \vec{a}| = a\Delta \varphi,$$

where $a = |\vec{a}|$. However, if $\vec{a}$ is no longer perpendicular to the rotation axis, but forms an angle α with it, the change in it will be given by the difference between its perpendicular components, hence

$$|\Delta \vec{a}| = a\Delta \varphi \cdot \sin \alpha.$$

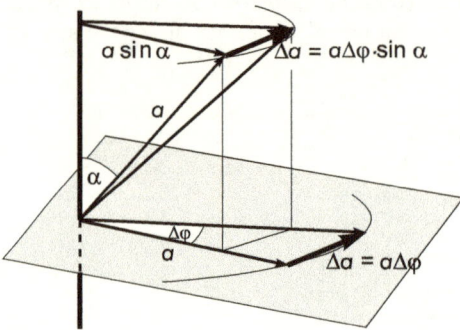

Applying this result to the angular momentum of the rod, we obtain:

$$\Delta N = N\Delta \varphi \cdot \sin \alpha,$$

using that for a uniform rotation $\Delta \varphi = = \omega \cdot \Delta t$, we get:

$$\Delta N = N\omega \Delta t \cdot \sin \alpha,$$

therefore the time rate of change of the angular momentum is:

$$\frac{\Delta N}{\Delta t} = N\omega \cdot \sin \alpha.$$

Newton's second law in angular form can now be written as:

$$\sum M = \frac{\Delta N}{\Delta t} = N\omega \sin \alpha. \qquad (4)$$

As the forces acting on the rod are all in one plane, their torques are all parallel, so the resultant torque can be calculated as the scalar sum of the magnitudes of these torques.

The torque of force S has the same direction as the angular momentum vector, while its magnitude with respect to point O is:

$$M_1 = SL\sin \alpha = m\frac{r}{2}\omega^2 L \cdot \sin \alpha, \qquad (5)$$

the torque exerted by force couple $[mg, K]$ is opposite in direction and has magnitude:

$$M_2 = mg\frac{r}{2} = mg\frac{L}{2}\cos \alpha. \qquad (6)$$

Substituting equations (5) and (6) into equation (4), we have:

$$SL\sin \alpha - mg\frac{L}{2}\cos \alpha = N\omega \sin \alpha,$$

Dividing by $\cos \alpha$ and using equations (1) and (3), we get:

$$m\frac{r}{2}\omega^2 L \cdot \tan \alpha - mg\frac{L}{2} = \frac{mLr\omega}{3} \cdot \omega \cdot \tan \alpha.$$

After rearrangement, we have:

$$\omega^2 \left(\frac{r}{2} - \frac{r}{3}\right) \cdot \tan\alpha = \frac{g}{2}.$$

From which the required angular velocity of the disk is:

$$\omega = \sqrt{\frac{3g}{r \cdot \tan\alpha}} = \sqrt{\frac{3g}{h}} = 7.07\,\mathrm{s}^{-1}.$$

The normal force exerted by the disk on the rod is $K = mg$, while for the horizontal static friction that points towards the axis of rotation, we get:

$$S = mr\omega^2/2 = mr\frac{3g}{h} = \frac{3}{2}\frac{r}{h}mg = \frac{3}{2}\cdot\frac{0.8}{0.6}mg = 2mg$$

The angle formed by the net force exerted by the disk and the horizontal can be calculated as:

$$\tan\varepsilon = \frac{mg}{m\frac{r}{2}\omega^2} = \frac{2g}{r\omega^2} = \frac{2g}{r\cdot\frac{3g}{(r\cdot\tan\alpha)}} = \frac{2\cdot\tan\alpha}{3} = \frac{2h}{3r} = \frac{2\cdot0.6}{3\cdot0.8} = 0.5,$$

thus

$$\varepsilon = \mathrm{arc}\ \tan 0.5 = 26.57°,$$

while the magnitude of the net force exerted by the disk is:

$$T = \frac{mg}{\sin\alpha} = \frac{mg}{0.4472} = 2.236\ mg,$$

or:

$$T = \sqrt{S^2 + K^2} = \sqrt{4m^2g^2 + m^2g^2} = \sqrt{5}\cdot mg = 2.236\ mg,$$

The angle formed by the rod and the horizontal is:

$$\alpha = \mathrm{arc}\ \tan\frac{h}{r} = \mathrm{arc}\ \tan\frac{0.6}{0.8} = 36.87°$$

Note that the line of action of the resultant force exerted by the disk does not pass through the centre of mass of the rod (although in case of an equilibrium or simple translation it would), therefore the resultant torque with respect to the centre of mass is not zero, which causes the angular momentum of the rod to change throughout the motion.

Solution of Problem 98. a) First we find the relation between the acceleration and the angular acceleration. Let a be the acceleration of the centre of the rod, a_1 the acceleration of its endpoint to which the cord is attached, and let β denote the angular acceleration of the rod. Since the geometric centre of the rod coincides with its centre of mass, $a_1 = a + l\beta/2$.

The equation of motion of the weight is:

$$m_1 g - K = m_1 a_1. \tag{1}$$

(Here we have used the fact that the cord is inelastic). Newton's second law for the centre of mass of the rod is:

$$K = ma, \tag{2}$$

and the equation of motion for the rotation is:

$$K \cdot \frac{l}{2} = \frac{1}{12} ml^2 \beta. \tag{3}$$

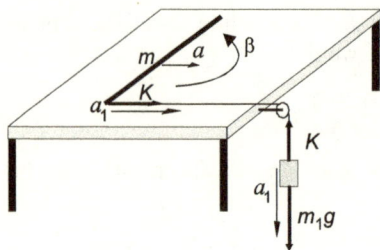

The kinematic relation between the accelerations and the angular acceleration is:

$$a_1 = a + \frac{l}{2} \beta. \tag{4}$$

From equation (4) the angular acceleration is:

$$\beta = \frac{2(a_1 - a)}{l}, \tag{5}$$

and inserting this and equation (2) into (3), we obtain that:

$$ma\frac{l}{2} = \frac{1}{12} ml^2 \cdot \frac{2(a_1 - a)}{l}.$$

After cancellation the following connection is obtained between the accelerations:

$$a = \frac{1}{3}(a_1 - a),$$

or

$$a_1 = 4a. \tag{6}$$

Writing equation (5) and (2) into (1), we get that

$$m_1 g - ma + m_1 4a,$$

so the acceleration of the centre of mass of the rod is:

$$a = \frac{m_1}{m + 4m_1} g. \tag{7}$$

Using equations (5) and (6), the angular acceleration of the rod is:

$$\beta = \frac{2(a_1 - a)}{l} = \frac{2(4a - a)}{l} = \frac{6a}{l}. \tag{8}$$

Now we can answer the questions of the problem.

The point of the rod, which has zero initial acceleration, is further from the end of the rod which is pulled by the cord, and closer to the other end. Let x denote the distance of this point from the centre of the rod. The acceleration of this point is zero if the magnitude of its relative acceleration a_{rel} with respect to the centre is equal to the acceleration of the centre, and points in the opposite direction:

$$x \cdot \beta = a.$$

Inserting here the angular acceleration from equation (8), we get:

$$x \cdot \frac{6a}{l} = a,$$

so the distance of the instantaneous rotation centre from the geometric centre of the rod is:

$$x = \frac{l}{6}.$$

b) The mass ratio in question can be determined from the expression of the acceleration of the centre of the rod:

$$a = \frac{m_1 g}{m + 4m_1} = \frac{g}{\frac{m}{m_1} + 4}.$$

It is clear that as $m_1 \to \infty$, the ratio $\frac{m}{m_1} \to 0$, and this minimises the denominator.

Thus to achieve the maximal acceleration, the mass of the weight should be large, $m \ll m_1$.

The possible maximal acceleration of the centre of the rod is:

$$a = \frac{g}{4}.$$

Solution of Problem 99. After the impulse, the rod slides freely, its centre of mass moving uniformly in a straight line. At the same time, it rotates about its centre of mass because of the torque of the impulse. If the impulse lasts for a time Δt, the centre of mass will gain a velocity of v_{cofm} and the angular velocity will be ω. Impulse equals change in momentum, and angular impulse equals change in angular momentum. With our notations:

$$F \Delta t = \Delta p = m v_{\text{cofm}} \quad \text{and} \quad F \frac{l}{2} \Delta t = \Delta L = \Theta \omega.$$

Speed and angular speed can be expressed from these equations:

$$\omega = \frac{F l \Delta t}{2 \Theta} \tag{1}$$

and

$$v_{\text{cofm}} = \frac{F \Delta t}{m}. \tag{2}$$

Let t denote the time of two revolutions of the rod. The corresponding angular displacement is

$$\omega t = 4\pi,$$

and hence

$$t = \frac{4\pi}{\omega}.$$

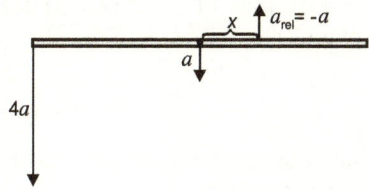

With the use of (1) and (2), the displacement of the centre of mass (as well as of every point of the rod) is

$$\Delta r = v_{\text{cofm}}t = \frac{F\Delta t}{m}\cdot\frac{4\pi}{\omega} = \frac{F\Delta t}{m}\cdot\frac{4\pi\cdot2\Theta}{Fl\Delta t} = \frac{8\pi\Theta}{ml}.$$

Since the rotational inertia about the centre of the rod is $\Theta = ml^2/12$, the magnitude of the displacement is

$$\Delta r = \frac{8\pi ml^2}{12ml} = \frac{2}{3}\pi l.$$

Solution of Problem 100. a) The discs will undergo rigid rotation with angular velocity ω_1 around the point of contact that is stationary in the inertial reference frame. According to the law of conservation of angular momentum (applying Steiner's parallel-axis theorem as well):

$$2\left(mvR - \frac{1}{2}mR^2\omega\right) = 2\left(\frac{1}{2}mR^2 + mR^2\right)\omega_1.$$

From this, the unknown angular velocity is $\omega_1 = 1\,\dfrac{1}{\text{s}}$. The rotation is in the direction opposite to the original.

b) According to the law of conservation of linear momentum, the discs can only move at velocities v_1 equal in magnitude but pointing in the opposite direction after the collision. From the symmetry it can be derived that the discs will assume angular velocities ω_1 equal in magnitude and in the same direction. The law of conservation of angular momentum holds:

$$2\left(mvR - \frac{1}{2}mR^2\omega\right) = 2\left(mv_1R + \frac{1}{2}mR^2\omega_1\right).$$

The law of conservation also holds for mechanical energies:

$$2\left(\frac{1}{2}mv^2 + \frac{1}{4}mR^2\omega^2\right) = 2\left(\frac{1}{2}mv_1^2 + \frac{1}{2}mR^2\omega_1^2\right).$$

After substitution:

$$6 = v_1 + 2\omega_1$$
$$132 = v_1^2 + 8\omega_1^2$$

The only physically realistic solution of the system of equations is

$$v_1 = -2\,\text{cm/s}, \quad \text{and} \quad \omega_1 = 4\,\text{s}^{-1}.$$

Both velocity and angular velocity change to the opposite of the original direction.

Solution of Problem 101. Case a). The mechanical energy of the compressed spring is transferred to the rotational kinetic energy of the two disks. Since the sum of the external torques is zero, the angular momentum is conserved. In this case, the two disks rotate in opposite direction at the same angular speed while the rod stays at rest.

$$E_{\text{spring}} = E_{\text{rot}},$$

$$N = 0.$$

In details:

$$\frac{1}{2}D(\Delta l)^2 = 2 \cdot \frac{1}{2} \cdot \Theta \omega_a^2,$$

and inserting the moment of inertia $\Theta = \frac{1}{2}mR^2$ of the disks, and simplifying by 2 we get that:

$$D(\Delta l)^2 = mR^2 \omega_a^2.$$

Finally, the angular speed of the disks is:

$$\omega_a = \frac{\Delta l}{R}\sqrt{\frac{D}{m}} = \frac{0.05}{0.1}\sqrt{\frac{1800 \text{ N/m}}{4 \text{ kg}}} = 10.607 \text{ 1/s}.$$

Case b). In this case, the two disks rotate in the same direction, but because the sum of the external torques is zero, as in the previous case, the total angular momentum of the system must remain zero. This is possible only if the rod (of negligible mass), along with the two disks, begins rotating in the opposite direction. Thus, the sum of the two (equal) spin angular momenta of the disks and the orbital angular momentum of the whole system have the same size but opposite direction. (We remark that if the rod were fixed, then this constrain would exert an external torque and the Earth would take over the angular momentum.)

The mechanical energy is conserved:

$$\frac{1}{2}D(\Delta l)^2 = 2 \cdot \frac{1}{2} \cdot \Theta \omega_b^2 + 2 \cdot \frac{1}{2}mv_c^2, \tag{1}$$

and the angular momentum is conserved as well:

$$2 \cdot \Theta \omega_b - 2 \cdot mv_c\frac{d}{2} = 0, \tag{2}$$

where v_c is the speed of the centre of the disks:

$$v_c = \frac{d}{2} \cdot \Omega, \tag{3}$$

and Ω is the angular speed of the rotating rod. Inserting (3) into equation (2):

$$2 \cdot \frac{1}{2}mR^2 \omega_b = 2 \cdot m\frac{d}{2} \cdot \Omega \cdot \frac{d}{2},$$

from which the angular speed of the rod is:

$$\Omega = 2\frac{R^2}{d^2}\omega_b, \quad \text{thus} \quad v_c = \frac{d}{2} \cdot \Omega = \frac{R^2}{d}\omega_b.$$

Putting this into equation (1) and multiplying by 2, we get:

$$D(\Delta l)^2 = mR^2\omega_b^2 + 2m\frac{R^4}{d^2}\omega_b^2 = mR^2\left(1 + \frac{2R^2}{d^2}\right)\cdot\omega_b^2.$$

The angular speed of the disks is:

$$\omega_b = \Delta l\frac{d}{R}\sqrt{\frac{D}{m(d^2+2R^2)}} = \frac{\Delta l}{R}\cdot\frac{d}{\sqrt{d^2+2R^2}}\sqrt{\frac{D}{m}} = \frac{d}{\sqrt{d^2+2R^2}}\cdot\omega_a.$$

Numerically:

$$\omega_b = \frac{\Delta l}{R}\cdot\frac{d}{\sqrt{d^2+2R^2}}\sqrt{\frac{D}{m}} = \frac{0.05}{0.1}\cdot\frac{0.25}{\sqrt{0.0625+2\cdot0.01}}\cdot\sqrt{\frac{1800\text{ N/m}}{4\text{ kg}}} = 9.23\,\frac{1}{\text{s}},$$

and in terms of the angular speed obtained in the first case:

$$\omega_b = 0.87\omega_a = 9.23\,\frac{1}{\text{s}}.$$

Solution of Problem 102. The motion can be divided into three stages: 1. from the start of the fall to reaching the table, 2. the collision with the table (which occurs in a negligible time interval, but is very important for finding the change of angular speed), 3. the slowing down of the rotation of the ring that has already stopped falling. Angular displacements can be considered to occur in the first and third stages only: φ_1 and φ_2. Since the collision itself is momentary, the angular displacement during the collision is negligible.

1. The time of fall of the ring is

$$t_0 = \sqrt{2h/g},$$

while the angular displacement is

$$\varphi_1 = \omega_0 t_0 = \omega_0\sqrt{2h/g}.$$

2. During the collision, there is a sudden and very large friction force slowing down the rotation. That force needs to be determined so that the time interval of the third stage can be determined from the angular speed after the collision. Since the total impulse equals the change in momentum,

$$(N - mg)\Delta t = \Delta mv,$$

where N is the mean normal force exerted by the table. Hence

$$N = \frac{\Delta mv}{\Delta t} + mg.$$

Thus the mean value of the friction force during the short time of the collision with the table is

$$F = \mu N = \mu \left(\frac{\Delta mv}{\Delta t} + mg \right). \tag{1}$$

During this short time interval, the angular impulse (the product of torque and time) equals the change in angular momentum:

$$\tau \Delta t = \Delta L,$$

where $\Delta L = \Theta \Delta \omega$ is the change in angular momentum of the ring. Now

$$Fr\Delta t = \Delta L, \tag{2}$$

since the friction force remains tangential to the ring and the ring is thin. Thus the moment arm of the friction force is the same everywhere, and the total torque of the friction force is obtained as a scalar sum of torques acting on small elementary arcs around the ring. By substituting (1) in (2), the equation

$$\mu \left(\frac{\Delta mv}{\Delta t} + mg \right) r\Delta t = \Delta L$$

is obtained. With the multiplication by $\mu r \Delta t$ carried out:

$$\mu \Delta mvr + \mu mgr\Delta t = \Delta L.$$

Since the collision is momentary, $\Delta t \to 0$, so $\mu mg\Delta t$ also tends to zero, that is, the second term is negligible. That leaves the following equation for the change in angular speed:

$$\mu \Delta mvr = \Delta L = \Theta \Delta \omega.$$

Since the ring is dropped from rest, $\Delta v = v$, as used in all the equations below. Note that the torque acts against the angular velocity, so the change in angular velocity is negative.

$$\Delta \omega = -\frac{\mu mvr}{\Theta} = -\frac{\mu mvr}{mr^2} = -\frac{\mu v}{r}. \tag{3}$$

The calculation of the change in angular velocity during the collision with the tabletop is thus completed.

3. From that point onwards, the rotation continues with a uniform angular deceleration until it finally stops. The initial angular velocity of the third stage is

$$\omega_1 = \omega_0 + \Delta \omega,$$

and the angular acceleration of the third stage equals

$$\beta_1 = \frac{\tau}{\Theta} = \frac{\mu mgr}{\Theta} = \frac{\mu g}{r}. \tag{4}$$

The time taken to stop is

$$t_1 = \frac{\omega_1}{\beta_1} = \frac{\omega_0 + \Delta \omega}{\frac{\mu g}{r}} = \frac{\omega_0 + \Delta \omega}{\mu g} \cdot r. \tag{5}$$

(4) and (5) are used to determine the angular displacement during the third stage:

$$\varphi_2 = \frac{1}{2}\beta_1 t_1^2 = \frac{1}{2}\cdot\frac{\mu g}{r}\cdot\left(\frac{\omega_0+\Delta\omega}{\mu g/r}\right)^2 = \frac{(\omega_0+\Delta\omega)^2}{2\mu g}\cdot r.$$

With the expression (3) of $\Delta\omega$ substituted:

$$\varphi_2 = \frac{(\omega_0-\frac{\mu v}{r})^2}{2\mu g}r = \frac{\left(\omega_0-\frac{\mu\sqrt{2gh}}{r}\right)^2}{2\mu g}\cdot r.$$

The total angular displacement is

$$\varphi = \varphi_1+\varphi_2 = \omega_0\sqrt{\frac{2h}{g}}+\frac{\left(\omega_0-\frac{\mu\sqrt{2gh}}{r}\right)^2}{2\mu r}\cdot r,$$

and the number of revolutions made is

$$z = \frac{\varphi}{2\pi} = \frac{1}{2\pi}\left(\omega_0\sqrt{\frac{2h}{g}}+\frac{\left(\omega_0-\frac{\mu\sqrt{2gh}}{r}\right)^2}{2\mu g}r\right) =$$

$$= \frac{1}{2\pi}\left(21\frac{1}{\text{s}}\sqrt{\frac{2\cdot0.2\,\text{m}}{10\,\text{m/s}^2}}+\frac{\left(21\frac{1}{\text{s}}-\frac{0.3\sqrt{2\cdot10\,\text{m/s}^2\cdot0.2\,\text{m}}}{0.1\,\text{m}}\right)^2}{2\cdot0.3\cdot10\,\text{m/s}^2}\cdot0.1\,\text{m}\right) =$$

$$= \frac{1}{2\pi}(4.2+3.75) = 1.265.$$

(The angular displacements are $\varphi_1 = 4.2$ rad $= 240.64°$ in the first stage, 0 in the second stage and $\varphi_2 = 3.75$ rad $= 214.86°$ in the third stage, which add up to a total of $\varphi = 455.5°$.)

Solution of Problem 103. a) The sphere reaches the cart with a speed of $v_1 = \sqrt{2gh} = 5\,\text{m/s}$. The magnitude of the y component of the change in its momentum owing to the collision is

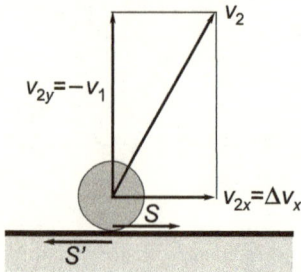

$$\Delta p_y = 2mv_y = 2m\sqrt{2gh} = 800\ \text{Ns},$$

and the magnitude of the horizontal component is

$$\Delta p_x = S\Delta t,$$

where S is the mean friction force. The mean normal force acting during the collision is

$$K = \frac{\Delta p_y}{\Delta t} = \frac{2m\sqrt{2gh}}{\Delta t}.$$

Thus the sphere gains a horizontal momentum of

$$p_x = \Delta p_x = S\Delta t = \mu K\Delta t = \mu\frac{2m\sqrt{2gh}}{\Delta t}\Delta t = 2\mu m\sqrt{2gh} = 80 \text{ Ns.}$$

The external forces are all vertical, so the total change in horizontal momentum of the system is 0, that is,

$$MV = mv_{2x},$$

after the collision, where the horizontal speed of the sphere is

$$v_{2x} = \frac{\Delta p_x}{m} = 2\mu v_1 = 2\mu\sqrt{2gh} = 1\,\frac{\text{m}}{\text{s}},$$

and the speed of the cart is

$$V = \frac{m}{M}v_{2x} = 2\frac{m}{M}\mu v_1 = 2\mu\frac{m}{M}\sqrt{2gh} = 0.4\,\frac{\text{m}}{\text{s}}.$$

Since the deformation is perfectly elastic, the sphere rebounds and rises to the initial height again. Thus the vertical component of the velocity of rebound is equal in magnitude to the speed v_1 of the sphere reaching the cart. After the collision, the sphere follows a parabolic projectile path and the time interval between the two collisions, i.e. the time of the projectile motion is

$$t = \frac{2v_1}{g} = \sqrt{\frac{8h}{g}} = 1\,\text{s.}$$

During this time, the sphere travels a horizontal distance of

$$\Delta x = v_{2x}t = 2\mu\sqrt{16h^2} = 8\mu gh = 1\,\text{m}$$

to the right relative to the ground, while the cart travels

$$\Delta X = Vt = \frac{m}{M}\Delta x = \frac{80}{200}\cdot 1\,\text{m} = 0.4\,\text{m}$$

to the left. The distance between the two impact points is

$$d = \Delta X + \Delta x = 1.4\,\text{m.}$$

Therefore the length of the cart needs to be at least

$$L = 2d = 16\mu h\frac{m+M}{M} = 2.8\,\text{m.}$$

b) In the case when the rotation decelerates until the touching point on the cart stops relative to the cart (that is the point where rolling would start), the tangential speed of the great circle of the sphere sliding on the cart is

$$v_{\text{rel}} = V + v_{2x}.$$

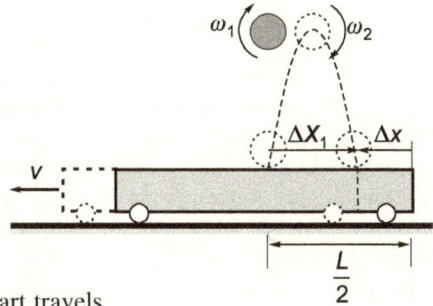

Thus the minimum possible value of the angular speed after rebounding is

$$\omega_2 = \frac{v_{\text{rel}}}{R} = \frac{V + v_{2x}}{R} = 2\mu\frac{m+M}{RM}\sqrt{2gh} = 0.2\frac{280\,\text{kg}}{0.2\,\text{m}\cdot 200\,\text{kg}}\sqrt{2\cdot 10\,\frac{\text{m}}{\text{s}^2}\cdot 1.25\,\text{m}} = 7\,\text{s}^{-1},$$

where v_{rel} is the speed of the lowermost point of the circumference of the ball relative to the cart.

The mean value of the decelerating torque of the kinetic friction force is $|\vec{\tau}| = SR$, where

$$S = \mu K = \mu\frac{2m\sqrt{2gh}}{\Delta t},$$

and hence

$$|\vec{\tau}| = \mu\frac{2m\sqrt{2gh}}{\Delta t}R = \left|\frac{\Theta\Delta\omega}{\Delta t}\right|.$$

Δt cancels out, therefore

$$|\Delta\omega| = \omega_1 - \omega_2 = \mu\frac{2m\sqrt{2gh}}{\frac{2}{5}mR^2}R = \frac{5\mu\sqrt{2gh}}{R} = \frac{0.5\sqrt{2\cdot 10\,\text{m/s}^2\cdot 1.25\,\text{m}}}{0.2\,\text{m}} = 12.5\,\text{s}^{-1},$$

and thus the minimum possible value of the initial angular speed is

$$\omega_{1\min} = \omega_2 + |\Delta\omega| = 7\,\text{s}^{-1} + 12.5\,\text{s}^{-1} = 19.5\,\text{s}^{-1}.$$

c) In the case of the angular speed calculated in b), the sphere is not sliding during the second collision, and thus mechanical energy is only dissipated during the first collision. Since the deformation of the cart is perfectly elastic, the kinetic energy of the motion in the y direction is not changed by the collision. As a result of the the friction force, the translational kinetic energies of the motion (of both the ball and the cart) in the x direction increase, while rotational kinetic energy decreases. The amount of mechanical energy dissipated is equal to the total work done by friction.

According to the work-energy theorem,

$$\Delta E_{\text{kin}} = \sum W = W_{m\to M} + W_{M\to m} = \frac{1}{2}MV^2 + \frac{1}{2}mv_x^2 + \frac{1}{2}\Theta(\omega_2^2 - \omega_1^2),$$

where the first and second terms are the translational kinetic energies gained by the cart and the ball, respectively, and the third term is the loss of rotational kinetic energy of the ball.

With the calculated numerical data:

$$\Delta E_{\text{kin}} = \frac{1}{2}\cdot 200\,\text{kg}\cdot 0.4^2\,\frac{\text{m}^2}{\text{s}^2} + \frac{1}{2}\cdot 80\,\text{kg}\cdot 1\,\frac{\text{m}^2}{\text{s}^2} + \frac{1}{2}\cdot\frac{2}{5}\cdot 80\,\text{kg}\cdot 0.2^2\,\text{m}^2(7^2 - 19.5^2)\frac{1}{\text{s}^2} =$$
$$= -156\,\text{J}.$$

[With the results substituted parametrically and the operations carried out:

$$\Delta E_{\text{mech}} = -\frac{m(4m + 14M)}{M}\mu^2 gh.]$$

d) The total work of the friction force was calculated in c). The work done by the sphere on the cart is

$$W_{m \to M} = \frac{1}{2}MV^2 = 4\frac{m^2}{M}\mu^2 gh = 4 \cdot \frac{80^2 \, \text{kg}^2}{200 \, \text{kg}} \cdot 0.01 \cdot 10 \, \frac{\text{m}}{\text{s}^2} \cdot 1.25 \, \text{m} = +16 \, \text{J},$$

and the work done by the cart on the sphere is

$$W_{M \to m} = \sum W - W_{m \to M} = -2\frac{(4m + 7M)m}{M}\mu^2 gh = -167 \, \text{J} - 16 \, \text{J} = -172 \, \text{J}.$$

(Since the translational kinetic energy of the sphere increases, it is its rotational kinetic energy that must decrease.)

e) The cart gains a kinetic energy of

$$\Delta E_M = W_{m \to M} = +16 \, \text{J},$$

and the translational kinetic energy of the sphere increases by

$$\Delta E_{m_{\text{trans}}} = \frac{1}{2}mv_{2x}^2 = \frac{1}{2}m(2\mu\sqrt{2gh})^2 = 4\mu^2 mgh = 4 \cdot 0.01 \cdot 80 \, \text{kg} \cdot 10 \, \frac{\text{m}}{\text{s}^2} \cdot 1.25 \, \text{m} = +40 \, \text{J}$$

during the first collision. Finally, the change in the rotational energy of the sphere is

$$\Delta E_{m_{\text{rot}}} = \Delta E_{\text{mech}} - \frac{1}{2}MV^2 - \frac{1}{2}mv_x^2 = -156 \, \text{J} - 16 \, \text{J} - 40 \, \text{J} = -212 \, \text{J}.$$

Parametrically:

$$\Delta E_{m_{\text{rot}}} = \frac{1}{2}\Theta(\omega_2^2 - \omega_1^2) = -2mgh\frac{4m + 9M}{M}\mu^2.$$

Since the change is negative, it decreases, as expected.

A summary of the energy changes:

The total mechanical energy is initially

$$E_{\text{mech}_1} = mgh + \frac{1}{2}\Theta\omega_1^2 = 1000 \, \text{J} + 243.36 \, \text{J} = \mathbf{1243.36} \, \text{J}.$$

The mechanical energy after the collision is

$$E_{\text{mech}_2} = \frac{1}{2}MV^2 + \frac{1}{2}m(v_2^2 + v_1^2) + \frac{1}{2}\Theta\omega_2^2 = 16 \, \text{J} + 1040 \, \text{J} + +31.36 \, \text{J} = \mathbf{1087.36} \, \text{J}.$$

The difference of the two values (the mechanical energy dissipated) is $\Delta E_{\text{mech}} = -156 \, \text{J}$.

The decrease in the rotational kinetic energy is $\Delta E_{\text{rot}} = \frac{1}{2}\Theta(\omega_2^2 - \omega_1^2) = \mathbf{-212} \, \text{J}$.

The total work done by friction, that is the change in the total mechanical energy of the system is

$$\sum W_{\text{fr}} = \Delta E_{\text{mech}} = -156 \, \text{J},$$

which is made up of two components: $\sum W_{\text{fr}} = \Delta E_{\text{rot}} + \Delta E_{\text{trans}}$, that is,

$-156\,\text{J} \Big\langle$

$-212\,\text{J}$ (change in rotational energy)

$+56\,\text{J}$ (change in translational energy)

Solution of Problem 104. The problem becomes solvable only if the ball of mass M is assumed to be pointlike as it is suggested by the figure.

Let us apply the work-kinetic energy theorem. The normal force and static friction do not do any work, therefore the work of the gravitational force equals the change in the kinetic energy of the system:

$$W_{\text{grav}} = \Delta E_{\text{kin}}.$$

The height of the centre of the mass of the cylinder does not change, therefore the gravitational force does work only on the ball of mass M. This work is given by the formula $W_{\text{grav}} = Mg(R+r)$, thus the work-kinetic energy takes the form of:

$$Mg(R+r) = \frac{1}{2}mv_0^2 + \frac{1}{2}\Theta\omega^2 + \frac{1}{2}MV^2.$$

Let us find the connection between the velocities and the angular velocity. Since the cylinder rolls without slipping, the velocity of its centre of mass must be:

$$v_0 = r\omega. \tag{1}$$

The velocity (V) of the ball must be perpendicular to the ground because point P is the instantaneous axis of rotation, thus the instantaneous radius of rotation of the ball lies on the ground.

Velocity V is the resultant of the translational velocity of point O (which is the centre of mass of the cylinder) and the velocity with which the ball rotates about point O. Using that v_0 and V are perpendicular, we get:

$$V^2 = (R\omega)^2 - v_0^2 = \omega^2(R^2 - r^2). \tag{2}$$

Substituting equations (1) and (2) into the work-kinetic energy theorem, we obtain:

$$Mg(R+r) = \frac{1}{2}m(\omega r)^2 + \frac{1}{2}\cdot\frac{1}{2}mr^2\omega^2 + \frac{1}{2}M(R^2 - r^2)\omega^2,$$

where $\Theta = \frac{1}{2}mr^2$ is the rotational inertia of the cylinder. Solving the equation for ω, we find:

$$\omega = \sqrt{\frac{2g(R+r)}{R^2 + r^2(3m/2M - 1)}} = 3.25\ \text{s}^{-1},$$

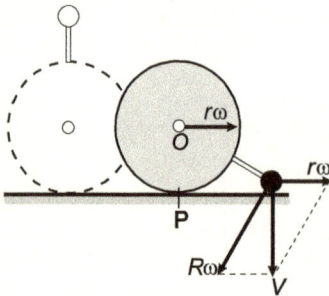

thus the ball hits the ground with a velocity of:

$$V = \omega\sqrt{R^2 - r^2} = (R+r)\sqrt{\frac{2g(R-r)}{R^2 + r^2(3m/2M - 1)}} = 1.3 \,\frac{\text{m}}{\text{s}}.$$

First solution of Problem 105. Assuming that the hoop stays vertical, we are dealing with motion in a plane. Since the system starts from rest, in the absence of horizontal forces the common centre of mass S of hoop and weight will descend (with a non-uniform acceleration) along a vertical line. During the fall, if the centre of the hoop is displaced to the left of the vertical line drawn through the centre of mass, the weight will be displaced to the right. Since the hoop and the weight have equal masses, the centre of mass S is at the midpoint of the radius connecting the centre of the hoop to the weight, that is, at a distance of $r/2$ from each. Thus their horizontal motions (displacement, instantaneous velocity, the x component of acceleration) are symmetrical. The centre of the hoop does not accelerate vertically. Its horizontal acceleration vector first points to the left and then to the right.

a) In the position investigated by the problem, the centre of the hoop is at rest, its acceleration $\vec{a}_0$ is equal and opposite to the component $\vec{a}_{1x}$ of the acceleration of the weight. Therefore it is enough to determine the horizontal component of the acceleration of the weight.

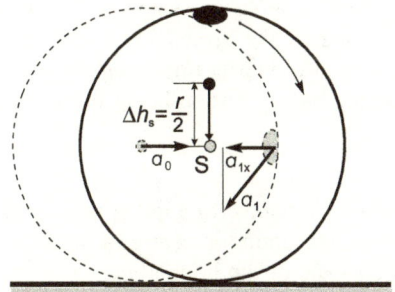

Since the centre of the hoop is at rest (instantaneous axis of rotation), the speed of the centre of mass S is

$$v_S = \frac{r}{2}\omega,$$

and the speed of the weight is

$$v_1 = r\omega = 2v_S, \tag{1}$$

both in the vertical direction. ω denotes the instantaneous angular velocity of the hoop. At the same time instant, the horizontal component of the acceleration of the weight is equal to the centripetal acceleration of its rotation about the centre of mass (since the horizontal acceleration of point S stays 0 throughout), that is,

$$a_{1x} = \frac{v_{\text{rel}}^2}{\frac{r}{2}} = \frac{2v_{\text{rel}}^2}{r}, \tag{2}$$

where, as obtained from (1), the speed of the weight relative to the centre of mass is

$$v_{\text{rel}} = v_1 - v_S = v_1 - \frac{v_1}{2} = \frac{v_1}{2}. \tag{3}$$

The speed v_1 of the weight needs to be determined. The work-energy theorem can be used:

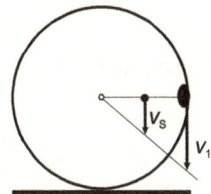

$$mg\Delta h = \frac{1}{2}mv_1^2 + \frac{1}{2}\Theta_0\omega^2,$$

239

where $\Delta h = r$ is the fall of the weight, and $\Theta_0 = mr^2$ is the moment of inertia of the hoop about its own centre of mass (O). Since the motion of the hoop at this time instant is pure rotation, its translational kinetic energy is 0, and for the same reason the speed of the weight is $v_1 = r\omega$. With these results, the work-energy theorem takes the form

$$mgr = \frac{1}{2}mv_1^2 + \frac{1}{2}mr^2\omega^2 = mv_1^2.$$

Hence the speed of the weight after a fall of r is

$$v_1 = \sqrt{rg}. \qquad (4)$$

From (2), (3) and (4), therefore, the x component of the acceleration of the weight and also the acceleration of the centre of the hoop has a magnitude of

$$|a_0| = |a_{1x}| = \frac{2v_{\mathrm{rel}}^2}{r} = \frac{2(v_1/r)^2}{r} = \frac{2\frac{rg}{4}}{r} = \frac{rg}{2} = \frac{1\,\mathrm{m}\cdot 10\,\frac{\mathrm{m}}{\mathrm{s}^2}}{2} = 5\,\frac{\mathrm{m}}{\mathrm{s}^2}$$

and a horizontal direction, both pointing towards the centre of mass S.

b) The force pressing on the ground is equal and opposite to the normal force K exerted by the ground. Consider the net torque about the centre of mass S. It equals moment of inertia times angular acceleration. The torque of the gravitational force $2mg$ acting on the system being 0, the equation will only contain the normal force K:

$$K\frac{r}{2} = \Theta_S\beta, \qquad (5)$$

where β stands for angular acceleration, and Θ_S is the moment of inertia of the system about the common centre of mass. It is the sum of the moments of inertia of the weight (Θ_1) and of the hoop (Θ_h).

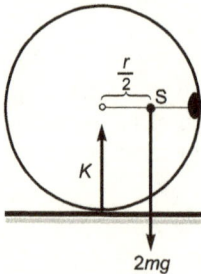

The moment of inertia of the weight is

$$\Theta_1 = m\left(\frac{r}{2}\right)^2 = m\frac{r^2}{4},$$

and that of the hoop, with the parallel-axis theorem:

$$\Theta_h = \Theta_0 + md^2 = mr^2 + m\left(\frac{r}{2}\right)^2 = mr^2 + m\frac{r^2}{4}.$$

The sum of them is

$$\Theta_S = mr^2 + \frac{mr^2}{4} + \frac{mr^2}{4} = \frac{3}{2}mr^2.$$

Substituted in (5):

$$K\frac{r}{2} = \frac{3}{2}mr^2\beta,$$

that is,

$$K = 3mr\beta. \qquad (6)$$

The angular acceleration β and the acceleration a_S of the centre of mass S are related by the equation

$$a_s = \frac{r}{2}\beta,$$

since the centre of mass only accelerates vertically and the centre of the hoop only accelerates horizontally. The acceleration of the centre of mass is obtained by applying Newton's second law to the system:

$$a_S = \frac{\sum F}{\sum m} = \frac{2mg - K}{2m} = g - \frac{K}{2m}.$$

Thus the angular acceleration is

$$\beta = \frac{2a_S}{r} = \frac{2g}{r} - \frac{K}{mr}.$$

Substituted in (6):

$$K = 3mr\left(\frac{2g}{r} - \frac{K}{mr}\right) = 6mg - 3K, \quad \text{and hence} \quad 4K = 6mg.$$

Thus the magnitude of the normal force acting between the hoop and the ground is

$$K = \frac{3}{2}mg = \frac{3}{2} \cdot 50\,\text{N} = 75\,\text{N}.$$

Second solution of Problem 105. We will give a general solution to the problem in terms of the angle α enclosed by the vertical and the radius drawn to the weight.

With the notations of the previous solution, the speeds of the centre of mass and the centre of the hoop are expressed in terms of α as follows:

$$v_S = \frac{r}{2} \cdot \omega \cdot \sin\alpha, \tag{1'}$$

$$v_0 = \frac{r}{2} \cdot \omega \cdot \cos\alpha. \tag{2'}$$

It follows from the work-energy theorem that

$$2mg \cdot \frac{r}{2}(1 - \cos\alpha) = \frac{1}{2}(2m)v_S^2 + \frac{1}{2}\Theta_S\omega^2, \tag{3'}$$

where $\Theta_S = 1.5mr^2$. Angular speed is expressed from (1'):

$$\omega = \frac{2v_S}{r\sin\alpha},$$

and substituted in (3'):

$$2mg \cdot \frac{r}{2}(1 - \cos\alpha) = \frac{2mv_S^2}{2} + \frac{1}{2} \cdot \frac{3}{2}mr^2 \cdot \frac{4v_S^2}{r^2\sin^2\alpha}.$$

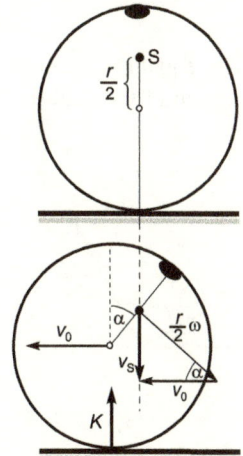

The equation can be divided through by m, a factors of 2 cancelled in the first term and 4 and r^2 cancelled in the second term:

$$rg(1 - \cos\alpha) = v_S^2 + \frac{3v_S^2}{\sin^2\alpha} = v_S^2 \cdot \frac{\sin^2\alpha + 3}{\sin^2\alpha}.$$

With the substitution of $\sin^2\alpha = 1 - \cos^2\alpha$ in the numerator:

$$rg(1 - \cos\alpha) = v_S^2 \cdot \frac{4 - \cos^2\alpha}{\sin^2\alpha}.$$

Hence the speed of the centre of mass in terms of α is

$$v_S = \sin\alpha\sqrt{\frac{gr(1 - \cos\alpha)}{4 - \cos^2\alpha}}. \tag{4'}$$

The speed of the centre of the hoop can be expressed in a similar way from $(2')$:

$$v_0 = \cos\alpha\sqrt{\frac{gr(1 - \cos\alpha)}{4 - \cos^2\alpha}}. \tag{5'}$$

The angular velocity expressed from $(1')$ is $\omega = 2v_S/r\sin\alpha$:

$$\omega = \sqrt{\frac{4g(1 - \cos\alpha)}{r(4 - \cos^2\alpha)}}. \tag{6'}$$

The angular acceleration is obtained from the net torque: $K \cdot \dfrac{r}{2}\sin\alpha = \beta\Theta$, hence

$$\beta = K \cdot \frac{r}{2\Theta} \cdot \sin\alpha = \frac{K\frac{r}{2}\sin\alpha}{\frac{3}{2}mr^2} = \frac{K\sin\alpha}{3mr}. \tag{7'}$$

The equation obtained by applying Newton's second law to the system describes the motion of the centre of mass:

$$2ma_S = 2mg - K. \tag{8'}$$

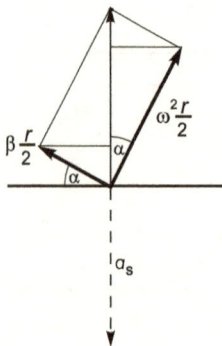

The acceleration of the centre of mass will be determined with the help of the acceleration of the centre of the hoop relative to a reference frame attached to the centre of mass and moving with a translational motion: The vertical component of this acceleration is the negative of the acceleration of the centre of mass.

The normal and tangential accelerations of the centre of the hoop are $a_n = \omega^2 \cdot r/2$ and $a_t = \beta \cdot r/2$. The sum of their vertical components is the negative of the acceleration of point S, thus the magnitude of the acceleration, as shown in the figure, is

$$a_S = \frac{r}{2} \cdot \omega^2 \cdot \cos\alpha + \frac{r}{2} \cdot \beta \cdot \sin\alpha. \tag{9'}$$

The solution of the simultaneous equations provides the acceleration a_0 and the force K in question. The acceleration in $(9')$ is substituted in $(8')$:

$$K = 2mg - 2m \cdot \frac{r}{2} \cdot \omega^2 \cdot \cos\alpha - 2m \cdot \frac{r}{2} \beta \cdot \sin\alpha.$$

The angular velocity ω is taken from $(6')$ and the angular acceleration β is taken from $(7')$:

$$K = 2mg - 2m \cdot \frac{r}{2} \cdot \frac{4g(1-\cos\alpha)}{r(4-\cos^2\alpha)} \cdot \cos\alpha - 2m \cdot \frac{r}{2} \cdot \frac{K\sin\alpha}{3mr} \cdot \sin\alpha.$$

r is cancelled in the second term, and $2mr$ is cancelled in the last term of the right-hand side. The terms containing K are transferred to the left-hand side and the common factors are pulled out on each side:

$$K\left(1 + \frac{\sin^2\alpha}{3}\right) = 2mg\left(1 - \frac{2(1-\cos\alpha)\cdot\cos\alpha}{4-\cos^2\alpha}\right).$$

$\sin^2\alpha$ is replaced with $1 - \cos^2\alpha$, and common denominators are applied:

$$K \cdot \frac{4 - \cos^2\alpha}{3} = 2mg \cdot \frac{4 - \cos^2\alpha - 2(1-\cos\alpha)\cos\alpha}{4 - \cos^2\alpha}.$$

Hence the normal force in question is

$$K = 2mg\frac{3(4 + \cos^2\alpha - 2\cos\alpha)}{(4 - \cos^2\alpha)^2}. \tag{10'}$$

The acceleration of the centre of the hoop is given by the horizontal component of its acceleration relative to the centre of mass, since the centre is not accelerating vertically:

$$a_0 = \frac{r}{2} \cdot \beta \cdot \sin\alpha - \frac{r}{2} \cdot \omega^2 \cdot \sin\alpha = \frac{K\sin\alpha}{3mr} \cdot \frac{r}{2} \cdot \cos\alpha - \frac{4g(1-\cos\alpha)}{r(4-\cos^2\alpha)} \cdot \frac{r}{2} \cdot \sin\alpha.$$

With the substitution of the value of K from $(10')$, rearrangement and the use of a common denominator:

$$a_0 = \frac{[(4+\cos^2\alpha - 2\cos\alpha)\cos\alpha - 2(1-\cos\alpha)(4-\cos^2\alpha)]\sin\alpha}{(4-\cos^2\alpha)^2} \cdot g.$$

The answers to the problem's questions are obtained by substituting 90^0 for α:

$$a_0 = -\frac{8}{16}g = -\frac{g}{2}, \quad \text{and} \quad K = \frac{24}{16}mg = \frac{3}{2}mg = 1.5 \cdot 50\,\text{N} = 75\,\text{N}.$$

Third solution of Problem 105. The first question of the problem can be answered in an unusual way. The acceleration of the centre of the hoop at the time instant when the angular displacement of the weight is $90°$ is obtained directly as the normal acceleration calculated at the point where the tangent to its trajectory is vertical: $a_{1x} = v_1^2/\varrho$. The magnitude of the acceleration is determined as in Solution 1, and the centre of curvature ϱ of the trajectory is easily obtained by noticing that the motion of the common centre

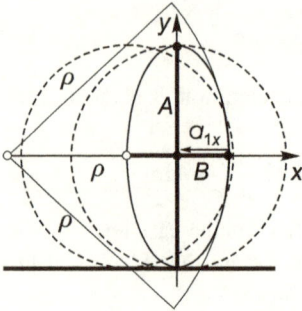

of mass (S) is vertical and the motion of the centre of the hoop is horizontal. Therefore the weight is moving along an arc of an ellipse with a semimajor axis of $A = r$ and semiminor axis $B = r/2$. (The semi-axes are now denoted by capital letters to distinguish the semimajor axis from the symbol of acceleration.) The radius of curvature of the ellipse at the endpoint of its minor axis is

$$\varrho = \frac{A^2}{B}, \qquad \text{which now means} \qquad \varrho = \frac{r^2}{\frac{r}{2}} = 2r.$$

Since the speed of the weight (as obtained in the first solution) is

$$v_1 = \sqrt{rg},$$

the acceleration of the weight (and thus of the centre of the hoop as well) has a magnitude of

$$a_{1x} = a_0 = \frac{v_1^2}{\varrho} = \frac{rg}{2r} = \frac{g}{2} = 5\,\frac{\text{m}}{\text{s}^2}.$$

Proof of the elliptical shape of the trajectory:

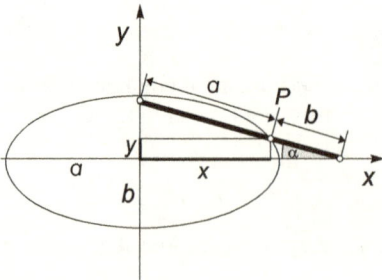

If two given points of a straight line are moving along a pair of lines intersecting at right angles, then the path of all other points on the moving line will form an ellipse. As shown in the figure, let the point P divide the line segment cut out of the line by the axes into segments of a and b. The coordinates of P are

$$x = a\cos\alpha,$$
$$y = b\sin\alpha.$$

The square of the second equation is

$$y^2 = b^2 \sin^2\alpha = b^2(1 - \cos^2\alpha),$$

where $\cos\alpha$ is x/a from the first equation. Thus α can be eliminated:

$$y^2 = b^2\left(1 - \frac{x^2}{a^2}\right),$$

Division by b^2 and rearrangement gives

$$\frac{x^2}{a^2} + \frac{y^2}{b^2} = 1,$$

which is known as the central equation of an ellipse.

(It can be shown in a similar way that the trajectories of points on the line that lie outside the line segment between the axes are also ellipses.)

Proof of the formula for the radius of curvature at the endpoint of the minor axis:

Consider the motion of a point moving in an elliptical path as a composition of two perpendicular simple harmonic motions of the same angular frequency. The resulting Lissajous figure becomes an ellipse if there is a phase shift of $90°$ between the two oscillations. Then the point only has a normal acceleration at the endpoints of the axes, which is equal to the maximum acceleration of the oscillation along the relevant axis. Thus the acceleration at the endpoints of the major axis is

$$a_A = A\omega^2,$$

where A is the amplitude of that oscillation. The speed of the point at the same time instant is the maximum speed of the oscillation along the minor axis:

$$v_{B_{\max}} = B\omega,$$

where B is the amplitude of this acceleration. Therefore

$$\omega^2 = \frac{v_{B_{\max}}^2}{B^2}.$$

The normal accelerations, the speed and the radius of curvature are related by

$$a = \frac{v^2}{\varrho}, \quad \text{so} \quad \varrho = \frac{v^2}{a}.$$

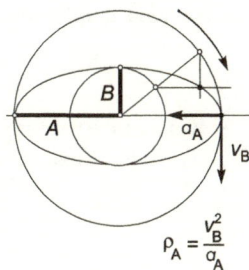

In this problem,

$$\varrho_A = \frac{B^2\omega^2}{A\omega^2} = \frac{B^2}{A},$$

as stated above. Note that the radius of curvature at the endpoints of the minor axis, obtained in a similar way, is

$$\varrho_B = \frac{A^2}{B}.$$

Solution of Problem 106. The particles will be handled as pointmasses. Let l_1 and l_2 be the extended lengths of the springs. The outer spring provides the necessary centripetal force for the outer particle, so:

$$D(l_2 - L) = m3L \cdot \omega^2.$$

The inner particle is kept on a circular path by the net force of tensions in the two springs:

$$D(l_1 - L) - D(l_2 - L) = ml_1\omega^2.$$

Let us exterminate l_2 by adding the two equations:

$$D(l_1 - L) = 3mL\omega^2 + ml_1\omega^2,$$

from which the extended length of the inner spring is:

$$l_1 = L \cdot \frac{D + 3m\omega^2}{D - m\omega^2}.$$

Since the sum of the extended lengths of the springs should be $l_1 + l_2 = 3L$, the extended length of the outer spring can be written as:

$$l_2 = 3L - l_1 = 3L - L \cdot \frac{D + 3m\omega^2}{D - m\omega^2} = L \cdot \frac{2D - 6m\omega^2}{D - m\omega^2}.$$

Let us substitute the expression for l_2 into the first equation. After some algebra, we get:

$$3m^2\omega^4 - 8Dm\omega^2 + D^2 = 0.$$

The solution of this equation can be written into the form of:

$$\omega = \sqrt{\frac{D}{3m}(4 \pm \sqrt{13})},$$

hence $\omega_1 = 5.04$ s^{-1}, $\omega_2 = 1.15$ s^{-1}.

Note that the results are independent of the relaxed lengths of the springs (L). Root ω_1 has no physical meaning, because in that case $D < m\omega^2$, which means that the result for l_1 would be negative. Therefore the solution of the problem is: $\omega_2 = 1.15$ s^{-1}. Thus the extended lengths of the springs are:

$$l_1 = (-2 + \sqrt{13})L = 1.61L, \qquad l_2 = (5 - \sqrt{13})L = 1.39L.$$

Solution of Problem 107. The role of the beetle is negligible in the motion of the ring. The equations for the acceleration a and angular acceleration β of the ring are

$$m_0 g \sin\alpha - F_f = m_0 a$$

$$F_f R = m_0 R^2 \beta$$

$$a = R\beta,$$

where a is the acceleration of the centre of the ring. From the equation system it comes that

$$a = \frac{g \sin\alpha}{2}. \tag{1}$$

After $5/4$ turns, that is, after travelling a distance of $s = = 5R\pi/2$, the square of the speed of the centre of mass is

$$v^2 = 2as = \frac{5}{2} R\pi g \sin\alpha. \tag{2}$$

At the moment in question, the radial component of the acceleration of the beetle is collinear with the acceleration of the centre of the disc and the centripetal acceleration of the point of the ring occupied by the beetle (measured in

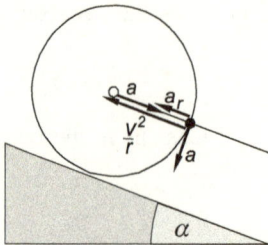

a coordinate system that moves with the ring but does not rotate). The direction of the latter is opposite to the acceleration of the centre in the direction of the slope, so at this moment the acceleration of the beetle in the direction of the centre (that is, along the slope) is

$$a_\mathrm{r} = \frac{v^2}{R} - a,$$

and the acceleration in the direction of the tangent of the ring (that is, perpendicular to the slope) is a in the inertial reference frame. Let us take our coordinate system fixed to the slope with axis x being parallel with it and axis y being perpendicular to it. The acceleration of the beetle is caused by the gravitational force and the clinging force C, whose components have magnitudes C_x and C_y.

The equations of the motion of the beetle in the x and y directions are:

$$C_x - mg\sin\alpha = m\left(\frac{v^2}{R} - a\right), \qquad (3)$$

$$mg\cos\alpha - C_y = ma. \qquad (4)$$

Substituting (1) and (2) into (3) gives

$$C_x = mg\sin\alpha + m\frac{5}{2}\pi g\sin\alpha - m\frac{g\sin\alpha}{2} = \frac{1}{2}mg(1+5\pi)\sin\alpha,$$

with numerical values

$$C_x = 0.5\cdot 10^{-3}\,\mathrm{kg}\cdot 9.81\,\frac{\mathrm{m}}{\mathrm{s}^2}\cdot(1+5\pi)\sin 20° = 0.028\,\mathrm{N},$$

and (4) gives

$$C_y = mg\left(\cos\alpha - \frac{\sin\alpha}{2}\right) = 10^{-3}\,\mathrm{kg}\cdot 9.81\,\frac{\mathrm{m}}{\mathrm{s}^2}\cdot(\cos 20° - 0.5\cdot\sin 20°) = 0.00754\,\mathrm{N}.$$

The magnitude of the resultant clinging force is

$$C = \sqrt{C_x^2 + C_y^2} = \sqrt{(28\cdot 10^{-3})^2\,\mathrm{N}^2 + (7.54\cdot 10^{-3})^2\,\mathrm{N}^2} =$$
$$= 28.997\cdot 10^{-3}\,\mathrm{N} \approx 29\cdot 10^{-3}\,\mathrm{N}.$$

(It can be seen that at this speed the radial acceleration is already dominant.)
The direction of the resultant force relative to the surface of the slope is

$$\tan\gamma = \frac{C_y}{C_x} = \frac{7.54}{28} = 0.2693 \quad \rightarrow \quad \gamma = \arctan 0.2693 = 15°,$$

and relative to the ground, in a direction upwards along the slope it is $\gamma' = 20° + 15° = 35°$.

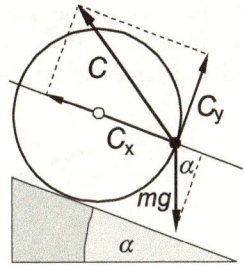

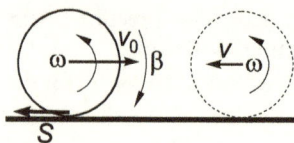

Solution of Problem 108. Let us direct the horizontal axis of the coordinate system from left to right. The dynamic frictional force exerted on the backward rotating wheel is independent of the speed of the hoop, thus the acceleration of the centre of mass of the hoop is $a = -\mu g$, and its angular velocity decreases with an angular acceleration of $\beta = M/\Theta = \mu M r / M r^2 = \mu g / r$. In order for the hoop to move backward, it must start at a greater angular speed than the angular speed at which it is to be thrown — in the case where the angular speed and the speed of the wheel decreases to zero at the same time. The first graph shows the velocity of the centre of mass v as a function of time and the speed of a particular point of the hoop $r\omega$ with respect to the centre of mass (so in a moving coordinate system) as a function of time. To answer the first part of the question, let us examine the boundary case where the rotation of the wheel stops at the same time as the speed of the centre of mass decreases to zero. The initial angular speed can be calculated from the kinematic equations:

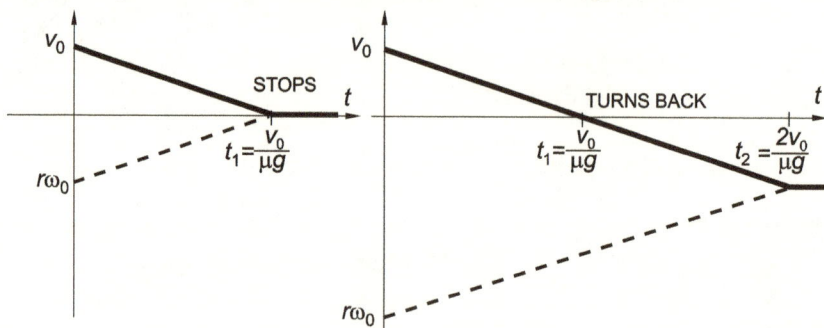

Translational motion of centre of mass:

$$v = v_0 - \mu g t,$$

rotation about the centre of mass:

$$\omega = -\omega_0 + \beta t = -\omega_0 + \frac{\mu g}{r} t.$$

The time of deceleration from the first equation:

$$0 = v_0 - \mu g t_1 \quad \rightarrow \quad t_1 = \frac{v_0}{\mu g}.$$

If this is written into the equation for the angular speed, and satisfying the condition that $\omega = 0$ we gain:

$$0 = -\omega_0 + \frac{\mu g}{r} t_1 = -\omega_0 + \frac{\mu g}{r} \frac{v_0}{\mu g} = -\omega_0 + \frac{v_0}{r}.$$

From this the condition for the initial angular speed is

$$|\omega_0| > \left| \frac{v_0}{r} \right|.$$

For the second part of the question we can answer similarly, using the second graph:

$$-v_0 = v_0 - \mu g t_2 \qquad \rightarrow \qquad t_2 = \frac{2v_0}{\mu g},$$

because the hoop must reach its initial speed as it moves backwards, and after this it is to roll without skidding thus the following relationship must be satisfied: $v = r\omega = $ $= \text{constant}$. Thus the equation for the rotation in the second case is:

$$\omega = -\omega_0 + \frac{\mu g}{r} t_2,$$

in which $\omega = -\frac{v_0}{r}$, thus:

$$-\frac{v_0}{r} = -\omega_0 + \frac{\mu g}{r} \frac{2v_0}{\mu g},$$

from which the asked angular speed is:

$$\omega_0 = \frac{3v_0}{r}$$

which is independent of the coefficient of dynamic friction.

Solution of Problem 109. The ball gained a horizontal velocity of v_x and an angular velocity of ω after being hit back, but when it bounces back from the table, it loses both, therefore the loss in its kinetic energy is:

$$-\Delta E = \frac{1}{2} m v_x^2 + \frac{1}{2} \Theta \omega^2.$$

Note that this is also the total loss in the ball's mechanical energy since the collision is elastic, which means that the ball bounces back to its initial height, so the energy stored in the elastic deformation of the ball will all be transformed into kinetic energy in the vertical direction.

To be able to solve the problem, we need to know the rotational inertia of the ping-pong ball. We know that the rotational inertia of a spherical shell about an axis going through its centre is given by the formula:

$$\Theta = \frac{2}{5} m \frac{R^5 - r^5}{R^3 - r^3},$$

where m is the mass of the shell, while R and r are the outer and inner radii of the shell respectively. As the wall of a ping-pong ball is very thin, we have to find out where the above formula tends to if r tends to R. Since both the numerator and denominator of the fraction tends to zero, we need to use a little algebra to find its exact value.

Let us use the general formula:

$$a^n - b^n = (a - b)(a^{n-1} + a^{n-2}b + \cdots + ab^{n-2} + b^{n-1}).$$

Applying this to both the numerator and denominator of the fraction, we find:

$$\frac{R^5 - r^5}{R^3 - r^3} = \frac{(R-r)(R^4 + R^3 r + R^2 r^2 + R r^3 + r^4)}{(R-r)(R^2 + Rr + r^2)}.$$

Dividing by $(R-r)$ and using that r equals R, we get:

$$\frac{R^5 - r^5}{R^3 - r^3} = \frac{R^4 + R^4 + R^4 + R^4 + R^4}{R^2 + R^2 + R^2} = \frac{5}{3}R^2.$$

Substituting this into the formula for the rotational inertia, we get that the rotational inertia of the ping-pong ball is:

$$\Theta = \frac{2}{5}m \cdot \frac{5}{3}R^2 = \frac{2}{3}mR^2.$$

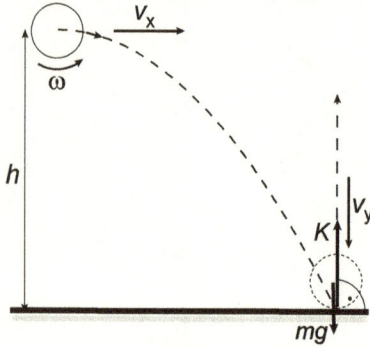

Let v_y be the vertical component of the velocity of the ball at the moment of hitting the table. This velocity can be calculated from the initial height of the ball using the formula:

$$v_y = \sqrt{2gh}.$$

Although we need the initial horizontal velocity (v_x) and angular velocity (ω) of the ball to calculate the lost mechanical energy, these quantities are not given. Let us assume that both of the above quantites should turn to zero in the same time interval. Let this time interval be $\Delta\tau$. If Δt is the time of the vertical compression of the ball, then the average vertical force acting on the ball, which is given by the rate of change of its linear momentum, must be:

$$\sum F = K - mg = \frac{\Delta p}{\Delta t} = \frac{2mv_y}{\Delta t},$$

where K is the normal force exerted by the table on the ball and mg is the gravitational force. Isolating the normal force, we get:

$$K = mg + \frac{2mv_y}{\Delta t}. \tag{1}$$

Therefore friction acting on the surface of the spinning ball is:

$$S = \mu K = \mu\left(mg + \frac{2mv_y}{\Delta t}\right). \tag{2}$$

If the deceleration of the horizontal translation (and rotation) of the ball takes time $\Delta\tau$, then the change in the horizontal linear momentum of the ball can be written as:

$$mv_x = S\Delta t = \mu\left(mg + \frac{2mv_y}{\Delta t}\right)\cdot\Delta\tau.$$

If the time of deceleration equals the time of deformation, i.e. $\Delta t = \Delta\tau$, then our equation is simplified to:

$$mv_x = \mu\left(mg + \frac{2mv_y}{\Delta t}\right)\cdot\Delta t.$$

Multiplying the expression in the bracket by Δt, we obtain:

$$mv_x = \mu(mg\Delta t + 2mv_y).$$

Since the collision occurs in a very short time ($\Delta t \rightarrow 0$), the first term in the bracket can be neglected. Thus the horizontal velocity (v_x) of the ball is found to be:

$$v_x = 2\mu v_y. \tag{3}$$

The time needed to decelerate the rotation of the ball equals the time of the deceleration of the horizontal translation, therefore the average angular deceleration is:

$$\beta = \frac{\omega}{\Delta\tau}.$$

This means that the net torque acting on the ball should be:

$$M = \Theta\beta,$$

substituting the average quantities, we obtain:

$$Sr = \Theta\frac{\omega}{\Delta\tau},$$

which yields:

$$\omega = \frac{Sr}{\Theta} \cdot \Delta\tau.$$

Substituting the friction from equation (2), we get:

$$\omega = \frac{\mu\left(mg + \frac{2mv_y}{\Delta t}\right) R}{\Theta} \cdot \Delta\tau.$$

If $\Delta t = \Delta\tau$ and $\Delta t \rightarrow 0$, the initial angular velocity of the ball is:

$$\omega = \frac{2\mu mv_y R}{\Theta}. \tag{4}$$

Using equations (3) and (4), we can now calculate the loss in the mechanical energy of the ball:

$$-\Delta E = \frac{mv_x^2}{2} + \frac{\Theta\omega^2}{2} = 2m\mu^2 v_y^2 + \frac{2m^2\mu^2 v_y^2 R^2}{\Theta}.$$

Substituting the expressions for the vertical component of velocity ($\sqrt{2gh}$) and the rotational inertia ($2mR^2/3$), we get that the maximum heat produced by the collision is:

$$Q = -\Delta E = 4\mu^2 mgh + 6\mu^2 mgh = 10\mu^2 mgh.$$

Inserting given data, the quantities used in the solution are: $v_y = 2$ m/s, $v_x = 1$ m/s, $\omega = 150$ s^{-1}, while the loss of mechanical energy or the maximum heat produced is:

$$Q_{max} = 10 \cdot 0.25^2 \cdot 0.003\,\text{kg} \cdot 10\,\frac{\text{m}}{\text{s}^2} \cdot 0.2\,\text{m} = 3.75 \cdot 10^{-3}\,\text{J}.$$

Note that our result gives the upper limit of the heat produced in the collision. It is possible that the time of deceleration of the horizontal translation and rotation is less than the time of deformation, i.e. $\Delta\tau < \Delta t$. In that case the values of v_x and ω will be less than the ones given in equations (3) and (4), thus the loss of mechanical energy will also be less than the one given in our final result. The maximum heat is produced when $\Delta\tau = \Delta t$.

Solution of Problem 110. According to the condition given in the problem, the centres of mass of the two objects move with the same acceleration (a).

Since both objects roll without slipping, angular velocities of the rim and cylinder are:

$$\omega_1 = \frac{v}{r_1} \quad \text{and} \quad \omega_2 = \frac{v}{r_2}$$

respectively, where v is the component of the velocity of the centres of mass parallel to the inclined plane.

The angular accelerations of the rim and cylinder are:

$$\beta_1 = \frac{a}{r_1} \quad \text{and} \quad \beta_2 = \frac{a}{r_2}.$$

The rotational inertia of the rim and cylinder are:

$$\Theta_1 = m_1 r_1^2 \quad \text{and} \quad \Theta_2 = \frac{1}{2} m_2 r_2^2.$$

The net torque acting on the cylinder must be:

$$M_2 = \Theta_2 \beta_2 = \frac{m_2 r_2^2}{2} \cdot \frac{a}{r_2} = \frac{m_2 r_2}{2} \cdot a. \tag{1}$$

The acceleration of the centres of mass can be determined using the work-kinetic energy theorem. While the objects move through a distance s, their displacement in the vertical direction is $s\sin\varphi$, so the work of the gravitational force on them is:

$$W_{\text{grav}} = (m_1 + m_2) g \cdot s \cdot \sin\varphi.$$

(Since the forces move in opposite direction and do their work through the same distances and since the objects do not slip, the work done on the objects by the external forces add up to zero.)

The change in the kinetic energy of the system is:

$$\Delta E_{\text{kin}} = \frac{m_1 v^2}{2} + \frac{m_2 v^2}{2} + \frac{\Theta_1 \omega_1^2}{2} + \frac{\Theta_2 \omega_2^2}{2} =$$

$$= \frac{v^2}{2} \cdot \left[m_1 + m_2 + \frac{m_1 r_1^2}{r_1^2} + \frac{m_2 r_2^2}{2 r_2^2} \right] = \frac{v^2}{2} \cdot (2m_1 + 1.5 m_2).$$

Using that in case of a constant acceleration and zero initial velocity $v^2 = 2as$, the change in the kinetic energy can be written as:

$$\Delta E_{\text{kin}} = as(2m_1 + 1.5 m_2),$$

According to the work-kinetic energy theorem $\sum W = \Delta E_{\text{kin}}$, hence we obtain:

$$(m_1 + m_2)g \cdot s \cdot \sin\varphi = as(2m_1 + 1.5m_2).$$

Isolating the acceleration of the centres of mass, we obtain:

$$a = g \cdot \frac{(m_1 + m_2)\sin\varphi}{2m_1 + 1.5m_2}. \tag{2}$$

In this equation we have two unknowns (m_2 and a). A new equation can be obtained by determining the torque acting on the cylinder and substituting it into equation (1). There are two forces acting on the cylinder: the gravitational force ($m_2 g$) and the resultant of the static friction and normal force exerted by the rim, which is called the force of support (T) that acts in point Q, where the rim and cylinder touch. The net force and net torque of these two forces cause the acceleration (a) and the angular acceleration (β) of the cylinder respectively.

To determine the torque of force T, let us resolve it into radial (T_r) and tangential components (T_t). Since the torques of both $m_2 g$ and T_r are zero about the centre of mass of the cylinder, the net torque equals the torque of force T_t, whose moment arm is r_2.

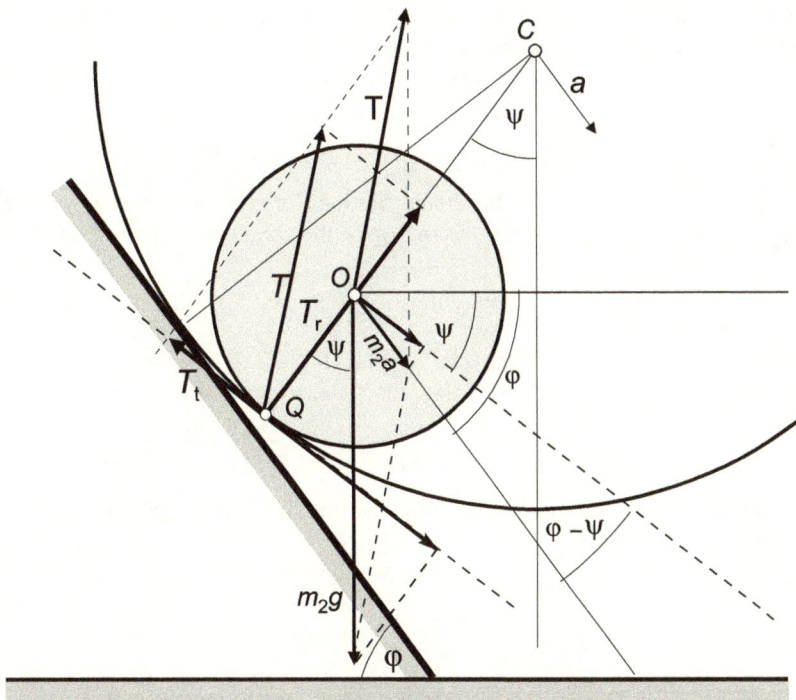

The magnitude of force T_t according to the figure is:

$$|T_t| = m_2 g \cdot \sin\psi - m_2 a \cdot \cos(\varphi - \psi),$$

inserting this into equation (1), we get:

$$[m_2 g \cdot \sin\psi - m_2 a \cdot \cos(\varphi - \psi)]r_2 = \frac{1}{2} m_2 r_2^2 \cdot \frac{a}{r_2}.$$

Isolating the acceleration, we find:

$$a = \frac{2g\sin\psi}{1 + 2\cos(\varphi - \psi)}. \tag{3}$$

Assuming that the right hand sides of equations (2) and (3) are equal, we get that the ratio of masses (m_2/m_1) of the two objects is:

$$\frac{m_2}{m_1} = \frac{\sin\psi}{\sin\varphi - 3\sin\psi + 2\sin\varphi\cos(\varphi - \psi)} - 1.$$

Substituting the given data, we find: $\varphi = 53^0 08'$, $\psi = 36^0 52'$, $\sin\varphi = \cos\psi = 0.8$, $\cos\varphi = \sin\psi = 0.6$. $m_2/m_1 = 8/67$, hence $m_2 = 8 \cdot 670\,\text{g}/67 = 80\,\text{g}$, and the magnitude of the acceleration is $a = 30g/73 = 0.411\ g \approx 4.03\,\text{m/s}^2$.

Solution of Problem 111. a) In order to have the centre of mass of the ball stay at rest, the sum of all forces acting on it should be zero. The forces acting on the ball are gravitational force, normal force and static friction force.

For these $\vec{K} + \vec{G} + \vec{F}_f = 0$.

For tangential direction:

$$mg\sin\alpha - F_f = 0.$$

The static friction force should be $F_f = mg\sin\alpha$, where according to the condition $\sin\alpha = d/R$ and

$$d = \sqrt{R^2 - \frac{9}{16}R^2} = \frac{R}{4}\sqrt{7}, \quad \text{that is,} \quad \sin\alpha = \frac{\sqrt{7}}{4}.$$

From this, $\alpha = 41.41°$.

With this, the static friction force is

$$F_f = mg\sin\alpha = 20\frac{\sqrt{7}}{4} = 13.23 \text{ N}.$$

The tangential acceleration of the point of the ball in contact is equal to the acceleration of the cylinder:

$$a_t = r\beta_{\text{ball}},$$

where

$$\beta_{\text{ball}} = \frac{F_f r}{\frac{2}{5}mr^2} = \frac{5g\sin\alpha}{2r}.$$

With this, we have determined the tangential acceleration of the ball and the nappe of the wheel of fortune:

$$a_t = \frac{5}{2}g\sin\alpha.$$

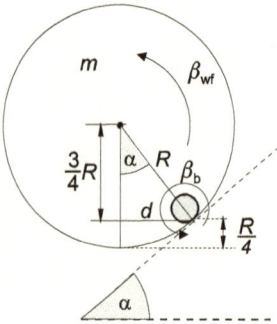

The angular acceleration of the wheel of fortune is

$$\beta_{\text{wf}} = \frac{5g}{2R}\sin\alpha.$$

This is caused by the signed sum of the torques acting on it:

$$M - M_{\text{sf}} = \Theta_{\text{wf}}\beta_{\text{wf}},$$

where $M_{\text{sf}} = F_f R$. For the torque produced

$$M = F_f R + \Theta_{\text{wf}} \cdot \frac{a_t}{R} = mg\sin\alpha \cdot R + \Theta_{\text{wf}} \cdot \frac{5}{2}\frac{g}{R}\sin\alpha.$$

Finally, the rotational inertia of the wheel of fortune should be determined.
Let us determine the mass of a unit surface area. The total surface area of the wheel of fortune is the sum of the area of the nappe, which is $\frac{R}{2} \cdot 2R\pi$, and the area of the two bases, which is $2 \cdot R^2\pi$. With this the mass of a unit surface area is

$$\varrho = \frac{m}{A} = \frac{m}{2R^2\pi + \frac{R}{2}2R\pi} = \frac{m}{3R^2\pi}.$$

The rotational inertia is additive:

$$\Theta_{\text{nappe}} = m_n R^2 = \varrho A_n R^2 = \frac{m}{3R^2\pi} \cdot 2R\pi\frac{R}{2} \cdot R^2 = \frac{m}{3}R^2,$$

$$\Theta_{\text{base}} = \frac{1}{2}m_b R^2 = \frac{1}{2}2\varrho \cdot A_b R^2 = \cdot \varrho R^2\pi \cdot R^2 = \frac{m}{3R^2\pi} \cdot R^2\pi R^2 = \frac{m}{3}R^2.$$

(The two are accidentally equal.)
With these the rotational inertia of the wheel of fortune is

$$\Theta_{\text{wf}} = \frac{2}{3}mR^2.$$

The torque that should be produced by us is

$$M = mg\sin\alpha R + \frac{2}{3}mR^2 \cdot \frac{5}{2}\frac{g}{R}\sin\alpha = mgR\sin\alpha\left(1 + \frac{5}{3}\right) = \frac{8}{3}mgR\sin\alpha =$$

$$= \frac{8}{3}20 \cdot 0.54 \cdot \frac{\sqrt{7}}{4} \text{ Nm} \approx 19.1 \text{ Nm}.$$

b) The work done by us is

$$W = \Delta E_{\text{wf}} + \Delta E_{\text{ball}} = \frac{1}{2}\Theta_{\text{wf}}\omega_{\text{szk}}^2 + \frac{1}{2}\Theta_{\text{ball}}\omega_{\text{ball}}^2 = \frac{1}{2} \cdot \frac{2}{3}mR^2\omega_{\text{wf}}^2 + \frac{1}{2} \cdot \frac{2}{5}mr^2\omega_{\text{ball}}^2.$$

Because of the constraining condition $R^2\omega_{\text{wf}}^2 = r^2\omega_{\text{ball}}^2$, that is,

$$W = \frac{1}{3}mR^2\omega_{\text{wf}}^2 + \frac{1}{5}mR^2\omega_{\text{wf}}^2 = mR^2\omega_{\text{wf}}^2\left(\frac{1}{3} + \frac{1}{5}\right) = \frac{8}{15}mR^2 \cdot \omega_{\text{wf}}^2.$$

Here the angular speed of the wheel of fortune after $t = 2$ s is

$$\omega_{\text{wf}} = \beta_{\text{wf}}' t = \frac{5}{2} \frac{g}{R} \sin\alpha \cdot t.$$

With this the work done by us in 2 seconds is

$$W = \frac{8}{15} \cdot mR^2 \frac{25}{4} \frac{g^2}{R^2} \sin^2\alpha \cdot t^2 = \frac{10}{3} \cdot mg^2 \sin^2\alpha \cdot t^2 = \frac{10}{3} \cdot 2 \text{ kg} \cdot 100 \frac{m^2}{s^4} \cdot 4 \text{ s}^2 \cdot \frac{7}{16} =$$
$$= 1166.67 \text{ J}.$$

c) The requested two angular accelerations are

For the wheel of fortune:

$$\beta_{\text{wf}} = \frac{a_t}{R} = \frac{5}{2} \frac{g}{R} \sin\alpha = 2.5 \cdot \frac{10 \frac{m}{s^2}}{0.54 \text{ m}} \frac{\sqrt{7}}{4} = 30.62 \frac{1}{s^2}.$$

For the ball:

$$\beta_{\text{ball}} = 6 \cdot \beta_{\text{wf}} = 183.73 \frac{1}{s^2}.$$

Solution of Problem 112. Let a_1 and a_2 be the accelerations of the centres of mass of the cylinder and the board respectively, both relative to the ground. Friction S acts on the cylinder and points backwards, while friction S' (of the same magnitude) makes the board move forward. First, we should decide whether the cylinder slips on the board or rolls without slipping. Let us therefore determine the minimum value of coefficient of friction that is needed for the cylinder to roll without slipping. If the coefficient given in the problem is greater than this minimum, the cylinder will not slip on the board, otherwise it will, in which case we would need to alter some of our equations. (The equation expressing the relation between the accelerations and the angular acceleration of the cylinder would be lost, but a new one, that gives the value of the kinetic friction, would be gained.)

Let us apply Newton's second law to the cylinder and the board and then Newton's second law in angular form to the cylinder. Using that $S' = S$, our equations take the form of:

$$F - S = m_1 a_1,$$
$$S = m_2 a_2,$$
$$Sr = \Theta\beta.$$

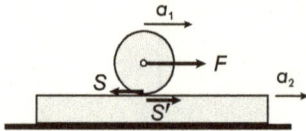

If we assume that the cylinder rolls without slipping, we obtain:

$$\beta = \frac{a_1 - a_2}{r},$$

and because the cylinder is solid, we get $\Theta = \frac{1}{2}mr^2$.

Let us rewrite our equations as:

$$F - S = m_1 a_1 \qquad \rightarrow \qquad a_1 = \frac{F - S}{m_1} \tag{1}$$

$$S = m_2 a_2 \qquad \rightarrow \qquad a_2 = \frac{S}{m_2} \tag{2}$$

$$Sr = \frac{1}{2} m_1 r^2 \frac{a_1 - a_2}{r}. \tag{3}$$

Substituting the acceleration as given in equations (1) and (2) into equation (3), we get:

$$S = \frac{m_2}{3m_2 + m_1} F = 12.6 \, \text{N},$$

and thus the minimum coefficient of friction needed for the cylinder to roll without slipping is:

$$\mu = \frac{S}{m_1 g} = \frac{12.6}{30 \cdot 9.8} = 0.042 < 0.1,$$

which means that the cylinder does not slip on the board. Therefore we can use our original equations to solve the problem. Substituting the expression for friction into equations (1) and (2), we obtain:

$$a_1 = \frac{F}{m_1} \cdot \frac{2m_2 + m_1}{3m_2 + m_1} = 1.05 \, \frac{\text{m}}{\text{s}^2},$$

$$a_2 = \frac{F}{3m_2 + m_1} = 0.21 \, \frac{\text{m}}{\text{s}^2}.$$

Force F causes the cylinder to move a distance of $s = a_1 t^2 / 2 = 1.05 \, \text{m/s}^2 \cdot 4\text{s}^2 / 2 = 2.1 \, \text{m}$, therefore the work done by it is:

$$W = Fs = \frac{1}{2} \frac{F^2}{m_1} \cdot \frac{2m_2 + m_1}{3m_2 + m_1} t^2 = 92.82 \, \text{J}.$$

Solution of Problem 113. Let m be the mass of the spheres, R is their radius, and let r denote the radius of the hole. (As we shall see later, the final results do not depend on m and R, so for simplicity we can assume that these data are the same for both spheres.) According to Newton's second law, written for the linear motion of the centre of mass, and for the angular motion, we get (for both spheres) that:

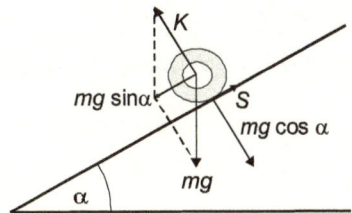

$$mg\sin\alpha - S = ma$$

$$SR = \Theta \frac{a}{R},$$

Where a is the acceleration of the centre of mass of the spheres, S is the static friction force, and Θ is the moment of inertia with respect to the centre of mass. Since the spheres roll without sliding, the angular acceleration β of the spheres are

$$\frac{a}{R} = \beta.$$

From the second equation, the static friction force is:

$$S = \Theta \frac{a}{R^2},$$

and inserting it into the first equation, we get that:

$$mg\sin\alpha - \Theta \frac{a}{R^2} = ma,$$

so the acceleration of the centre of mass is:

$$a = \frac{mg\sin\alpha}{m + \frac{\Theta}{R^2}}. \tag{I.}$$

Putting it back into the first equation,

$$S = \frac{\Theta}{R^2} \frac{mg\sin\alpha}{m + \frac{\Theta}{R^2}},$$

which can be written in a simpler form, if both the numerator and the denominator are divided by Q/R^2:

$$S = \frac{mg\sin\alpha}{\frac{mR^2}{\Theta} + 1}. \tag{II.}$$

No sliding occurs, if the static friction force satisfies the inequality

$$S \leq \mu_0 mg\cos\alpha,$$

so if the coefficient of static friction is large enough:

$$\mu_0 \geq \frac{S}{mg\cos\alpha}.$$

Writing here S from (II.), we get that:

$$\mu_0 \geq \frac{mg\sin\alpha}{\frac{mR^2}{\Theta} + 1} \cdot \frac{1}{mg\cos\alpha}, \tag{III.}$$

so

$$\mu_0 \geq \frac{\tan\alpha}{\frac{mR^2}{\Theta} + 1}.$$

Since $\Theta \propto mR^2$, both the acceleration (I.) and the threshold for the coefficient of static friction are independent of m and R, we can assume that these data are the same for the spheres.

a) The rolling times are equal, if the accelerations are the same. From equation (I.) we can see that the accelerations depend only on the moments of inertia, so these latter quantities have to be calculated.

The moment of inertia of the solid sphere is:

$$\Theta_S = \frac{2}{5}mR^2,$$

while that of the hollow sphere (or spherical shell) is (from data table):

$$\Theta_H = \frac{2}{5}m\frac{R^5 - r^5}{R^3 - r^3},$$

where R is the outer, r is the inner radius. In our case $r = R/2$, which means that:

$$\Theta_H = \frac{2}{5}m\frac{R^5 - \left(\frac{R}{2}\right)^5}{R^3 - \left(\frac{R}{2}\right)^3} = \frac{2}{5}mR^2\frac{\frac{32-1}{32}}{\frac{8-1}{8}} = \frac{2}{5}mR^2\frac{31\cdot 8}{32\cdot 7} = \frac{2}{5}mR^2\frac{31}{28} = \frac{31}{28}\Theta_S.$$

Expressing Θ_H with the mass and the radius,

$$\Theta_H = \frac{31}{28}\Theta_T = \frac{31}{28}\cdot\frac{2}{5}mR^2 = \frac{31}{70}mR^2.$$

Now substituting the values Θ_S and Θ_H into equation (I.), a relationship can be derived between the slopes α_T and α_H of the incline in the two cases:

$$a_S = \frac{mg\sin\alpha_S}{m + \frac{\Theta_S}{R^2}} = \frac{mg\sin\alpha_H}{m + \frac{\Theta_S}{R^2}} = a_H.$$

Inserting here the moments of inertia:

$$\frac{mg\sin\alpha_S}{m + \frac{\frac{2}{5}mR^2}{R^2}} = \frac{mg\sin\alpha_H}{m + \frac{\frac{31}{70}mR^2}{R^2}}.$$

After cancellation, we get that:

$$\frac{\sin\alpha_S}{1 + \frac{2}{5}} = \frac{\sin\alpha_H}{1 + \frac{31}{70}} \quad\rightarrow\quad \frac{5\sin\alpha_S}{7} = \frac{70\sin\alpha_H}{101},$$

which means that the slope of the incline in the second experiment is:

$$\sin\alpha_H = \frac{505}{490}\sin\alpha_S = \frac{505}{490}\sin 30° = 0.5153,$$

so

$$\alpha_H = \arcsin 0.5153 = 31.8°.$$

b) The threshold values for the coefficients of static friction are obtained by writing the moments of inertia into the equation (III.). We obtain that the solid sphere is rolling without sliding if:

$$\mu_{S0} \geq \frac{\tan\alpha_S}{\frac{mR^2}{\Theta_S} + 1} = \frac{\tan\alpha_S}{\frac{mR^2}{\frac{2}{5}mR^2} + 1} = \frac{2\tan\alpha_S}{7} = \frac{2\tan 30°}{7} = 0.165.$$

Similarly, the condition for the slidefree rolling of the hollow sphere is:

$$\mu_{HO} \geq \frac{\tan\alpha_H}{\frac{mR^2}{\Theta_H}+1} = \frac{\tan\alpha_H}{\frac{mR^2}{\frac{31}{70}mR^2}+1} = \frac{31\tan\alpha_H}{101} = \frac{31\tan 31°}{101} = 0.184.$$

It can be seen that for slidefree rolling, the threshold value of the coefficient of static friction is greater in the second case, since the hollow sphere has a greater moment of inertia, so a greater torque is needed for its angular acceleration.

Solution of Problem 114. In the first part of the motion the work done by the weight force is converted to translational and rotational kinetic energy of the sphere, while the static friction force and the normal force of the semi-cylinder do no work. But on the other side of the semi-cylinder only the translational kinetic energy is transformed back to potential energy, because of the lack of friction there is no torque acting on the sphere causing its angular velocity to remain constant. Thus on the other side, the sphere reaches a height smaller than it had initially. We have to determine the rotational kinetic energy at the bottom of the semi-cylinder. According to the work-energy theorem:

$$mg\Delta h_1 = \frac{1}{2}mv_c^2 + \frac{1}{2}\cdot\frac{2}{5}mr^2\omega^2 = \frac{7}{10}mv_c^2 \text{ m},\tag{1}$$

where we have used that $r\omega = v_c$. (This last relation holds also for curved surfaces; if not, the circular ramp would continue horizontally at the bottom and a sudden jump in the angular velocity would occur, something that is impossible.)

From equation (1),

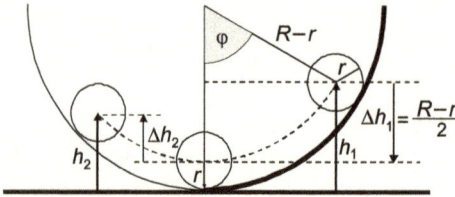

$$mv_C^2 = \frac{10}{7}mg\Delta h_1,\tag{2}$$

where Δh_1 is the vertical displacement of the centre of the sphere, until it reaches the bottom of the semi-cylinder. As the figure shows, it is:

$$\Delta h_1 = \frac{R-r}{2}.\tag{3}$$

Indeed, the radius to the initial position makes an angle of 60° with the vertical radius to the final position, and thus they form an equilateral triangle, whose horizontal altitude intersects the opposite side at the midpoint.

As it is well known, the rotational kinetic energy is:

$$E_{\text{rot}} = \frac{1}{2}\Theta\omega^2 = \frac{1}{2}\cdot\frac{2}{5}mr^2\omega^2 = \frac{1}{5}mv_C^2.$$

The maximal height reached by the sphere on the other side is determined by the energy conservation law:

$$mg\Delta h_1 = mg\Delta h_2 + E_{\text{rot}} = mg\Delta h_2 + \frac{1}{5}mv_C^2.$$

Inserting here the expressions (2) and (3), we have:

$$mg\frac{R-r}{2} = mg\Delta h_2 + \frac{1}{5}\frac{10}{7}mg\Delta h_1 = mg\Delta h_2 + \frac{2}{7}mg\frac{R-r}{2} = mg\Delta h_2 + \frac{1}{7}mg(R-r).$$

Dividing the equation by mg, and then expressing Δh_2, we get that:

$$\frac{R-r}{2} = \Delta h_2 + \frac{1}{7}(R-r),$$

and

$$\Delta h_2 = \frac{R-r}{2} - \frac{R-r}{7} = \frac{7(R-r)-2(R-r)}{14} = \frac{5}{14}(R-r) =$$
$$= \frac{5}{14}\cdot(1-0.2) \text{ m} = \frac{5}{14}\cdot 0.8 \text{ m} = 0.286 \text{ m}.$$

So at the highest position the vertical distance between the centre of the sphere and the bottom of the semi-cylinder is:

$$h_2 = r + \Delta h_2 = 0.2 \text{ m} + 0.286 \text{ m} = 0.486 \text{ m} = 48.6 \text{ cm}.$$

We remark that at the initial position this height was

$$h_1 = r + \Delta h_1 = 0.2 \text{ m} + 0.4 \text{ m} = 0.6 \text{ m}.$$

Solution of Problem 115. Our first task is to investigate whether or not the disk slips on the cart, because this will affect the set-up of our equations. Let us therefore determine the minimum coefficient of friction needed for the disk to roll without slipping. If the coefficient given in the problem is greater than or equal to that, the disk rolls without slipping, otherwise it will slip on the surface of the cart. Before determining the minimum coefficient, let us answer one more question: does the friction acting on the disk point in the direction of its acceleration (i.e. forward) or in the opposite direction?

In order to find the answer, let us imagine what would happen if the surface of the cart was frictionless. In that case, due to the horizontal force F exerted at the top of the disk, its centre of mass would move with an acceleration of:

$$a = F/m,$$

while the points on its perimeter would have an acceleration of

$$a_t = r\beta = r\frac{Fr}{\Theta} = \frac{Fr^2}{mr^2/2} = \frac{2F}{m} = 2a$$

with respect to the centre of mass.
Thus point P, where the disk touches the cart, would move to the left with an acceleration of $\vec{a}_P = \vec{a} + \vec{a}_t = -\vec{a}$ with respect to the ground, meaning it would slip

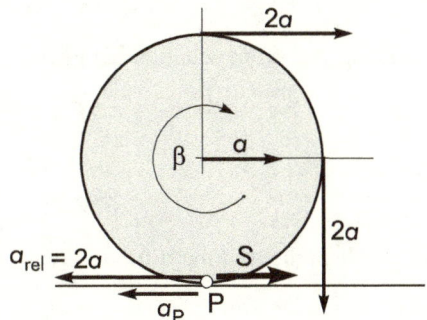

backward. Therefore if the surface of the cart is not frictionless, the friction acting on the disk points forward, while the one acting on the cart points backward.

Now we can start determining the minimum coefficient of friction needed for the disk to roll without slipping. Let the acceleration of the centre of mass of the disk be a, while that of the cart be A. In the present situation, all important vectors are horizontal, we can set up our equations using only their magnitudes. Our equations will be the following: Newton's second law applied to the centre of mass of the disk (1); Newton's second law in angular form applied to the disk (2); the restraining condition that prevents the disk from slipping (3); Newton's second law applied to the cart (4).

$$F + S = ma, \tag{1}$$
$$Fr - Sr = \Theta\beta, \tag{2}$$
$$\beta = \frac{a + A}{r}, \tag{3}$$
$$S = MA. \tag{4}$$

Let us solve this system of equations for friction S. Substituting $\Theta = \frac{1}{2}mr^2$ and equation (3) into equation (2) and then dividing it by r, we obtain:

$$F + S = ma, \, . \tag{1}$$
$$F - S = \frac{1}{2}mr^2\frac{a + A}{r^2} = \frac{1}{2}m(a + A), \tag{2'}$$
$$S = MA. \tag{4}$$

Let us now substitute the acceleration of the cart from equation (4) into equation (2') and then simplify by r^2 and multiply by 2 to get:

$$2F - 2S = ma + \frac{S}{M}m.$$

Inserting ma from equation (2) gives:

$$2F - 2S = F + S + \frac{m}{M}S,$$

hence

$$F = 3S + \frac{m}{M}S = \frac{3M + m}{M}S,$$

from which the minimum friction required is:

$$S = \frac{M}{3M + m}F.$$

Using that the maximum of friction can be written as $S = \mu mg$,

$$\mu mg = \frac{M}{3M + m} \cdot F,$$

from which we get that the minimum coefficient of friction needed for the disk to roll without slipping is:

$$\mu = \frac{M}{3M+m} \cdot \frac{F}{mg} = \frac{5\,\text{kg}}{25\,\text{kg}} \cdot \frac{100\,\text{N}}{100\,\text{N}} = \frac{1}{5} = 0.2 > 0.1.$$

This means that in our case the disk slips on the cart. After having ascertained this, let us investigate the motion of the system.

a) As the disk slips, one equation (the restraining condition) is 'lost', but at the same time a new one is gained, since the kinetic friction can be written in the form of $S = \mu mg$. Therefore, our equations will be:

$$F + \mu mg = ma \tag{5}$$

$$\mu mg = MA \tag{6}$$

$$Fr - \mu mgr = \frac{1}{2}mr^2\beta. \tag{7}$$

Our three unknowns (a, A and β) can easily be calculated from the above equations one by one:

$$a = \frac{F}{m} + \mu g = \frac{100\,\text{N}}{10\,\text{kg}} + 0.1 \cdot 10\,\frac{\text{m}}{\text{s}^2} = 11\,\frac{\text{m}}{\text{s}^2} \text{ to the right} \tag{8}$$

$$A = \mu\frac{m}{M}g = 0.1 \cdot \frac{10\,\text{kg}}{5\,\text{kg}} \cdot 10\,\frac{\text{m}}{\text{s}^2} = 2\,\frac{\text{m}}{\text{s}^2} \text{ to the left} \tag{9}$$

$$\beta = \frac{2F}{mr} - \mu\frac{2g}{r} = \frac{200\,\text{N}}{10\,\text{kg}\cdot 0.2\,\text{m}} - 0.1 \cdot \frac{20\,\text{m/s}^2}{0.2\,\text{m}} = 90\,\frac{1}{\text{s}^2}. \tag{10}$$

b) The kinetic energy of the system is the sum of the kinetic energies of the two objects. The energy of the disk is the sum of its translational and rotational energy:

$$E_{\text{disk}} = \frac{1}{2}mv^2 + \frac{1}{2}\Theta\omega^2, \tag{11}$$

while the energy of the cart is:

$$E_{\text{cart}} = \frac{1}{2}MV^2. \tag{12}$$

Let us therefore calculate the speed of the cart and the angular velocity of the disk at the moment when the length of the unwound string becomes $L = 2\,\text{m}$.

Let t be the time needed for the string to reach an unwound length of L. During this time the disk rotates through an angle of:

$$\varphi = \frac{1}{2}\beta t^2,$$

where $\varphi = L/r$, which yields

$$t = \sqrt{\frac{2\varphi}{\beta}} = \sqrt{\frac{2L}{r\beta}}.$$

Substituting β from equation (10), we find:

$$t = \sqrt{\frac{2L}{r \cdot \frac{2F-2\mu mg}{mr}}} = \sqrt{\frac{mL}{F-\mu mg}}, \tag{13}$$

Substituting known values gives:

$$t = \sqrt{\frac{10\,\text{kg}\cdot 2\,\text{m}}{100\,\text{N} - 0.1\cdot 10\,\text{kg}\cdot 10\,\text{m/s}^2}} = \sqrt{\frac{2}{9}\,\text{s}^2} = \sqrt{0.2222}\,\text{s} = 0.471\,\text{s}.$$

In that time the disk gains an angular velocity of:

$$\omega = \beta t = 90\,\text{s}^{-2}\cdot 0.471\,\text{s} = 42.4\,\text{s}^{-1}$$

while its centre of mass gains a speed of

$$v = at = 11\,\frac{\text{m}}{\text{s}^2}\cdot 0.471\,\text{s} = 5.18\,\frac{\text{m}}{\text{s}}.$$

Inserting these into equation (11) and assuming that the rotational inertia of the disk is $\Theta = mr^2/2$, we obtain:

$$E_{\text{disk}} = \frac{1}{2}ma^2t^2 + \frac{1}{2}\cdot\frac{1}{2}mr^2\cdot\beta^2 t^2.$$

Substituting the acceleration from equation (8), the angular acceleration from equation (10) and the time taken from equation (13), we find that the total kinetic energy of the disk is:

$$E_{\text{disk}} = \frac{m}{2}\left[\left(\frac{F+\mu mg}{m}\right)^2\frac{mL}{F-\mu mg} + \frac{1}{2}r^2 4\left(\frac{F-\mu mg}{mr}\right)^2\frac{mL}{F-\mu mg}\right].$$

After some algebra, this can be written into the form of:

$$E_{\text{disk}} = \frac{1}{2}L\frac{(F+\mu mg)^2 + 2(F-\mu mg)^2}{F-\mu mg} =$$

$$= \frac{1}{2}L\frac{F^2 + 2\mu mgF + \mu^2 m^2 g^2 + 2F^2 - 4F\mu mg + 2\mu^2 m^2 g^2}{F-\mu mg},$$

hence

$$E_{\text{disk}} = \frac{L}{2}\cdot\frac{3(F^2+\mu^2 m^2 g^2) - 2F\mu mg}{F-\mu mg}. \tag{14}$$

Inserting the given data, we find:

$$E_{\text{disk}} = \frac{3\cdot(10000\,\text{N}^2 + 100\,\text{N}^2) - 2\cdot 100\,\text{N}\cdot 10\,\text{N}}{100\,\text{N} - 10\,\text{N}}\cdot\frac{2\,\text{m}}{2} = 314.44\,\text{J}.$$

One part of this energy is caused by the translational motion of the disk:

$$E_{\text{transl}} = \frac{1}{2}mv^2 = \frac{1}{2}\cdot 10\,\text{kg}\cdot 5.18^2\,\frac{\text{m}^2}{\text{s}^2} = 134.44\,\text{J},$$

the other part is caused by the rotation of the disk:

$$E_{\rm rot} = \frac{1}{2} \cdot \frac{1}{2} mr^2 \omega^2 = \frac{1}{4} \cdot 10\,{\rm kg} \cdot 0.04\,{\rm m}^2 \cdot 42.4^2\,{\rm s}^{-2} = 180\,{\rm J}$$

The kinetic energy of the cart (neglecting the rotational energies of its wheels) can be determined according to equation (12) using equations (9) and (13):

$$E_{\rm cart} = \frac{1}{2} M A^2 t^2 = \frac{1}{2} M \frac{\mu^2 m^2 g^2}{M^2} \cdot \frac{mL}{L - \mu mg} = \frac{(\mu mg)^2 L}{2\frac{M}{m}(F - \mu mg)}.$$

Substituting known data, we find:

$$E_{\rm cart} = \frac{1}{2} \cdot 5\,{\rm kg} \cdot 4 \left(\frac{\rm m}{{\rm s}^2}\right)^2 \cdot 0.22222\,{\rm s}^2 = 2.22\,{\rm J}.$$

(The velocity of the cart is $V = At = 2\,{\rm m/s}^2 \cdot 0.471\,{\rm s} = 0.942\,{\rm m/s}$.)

Therefore, the total kinetic energy of the system is:

$$E_{\rm kin} = E_{\rm transl} + E_{\rm rot} + E_{\rm cart} = 134.2\,{\rm J} + 180\,{\rm J} + 2.22\,{\rm J} = 316.66\,{\rm J}.$$

[In general, the total kinetic energy of the system can be written as:

$$E_{\rm total} = \frac{L}{2} \cdot \frac{3F^2 + \left(3 + \frac{m}{M}\right)(\mu mg)^2 - 2F\mu mg}{F - \mu mg}.]$$

c) In order to determine the work done by force F, we need to find the displacement s of the end of the string, because in case of a constant force, the work done can be calculated as $W = Fs$.

$$s = s_0 + r\varphi = s_0 + L = \frac{1}{2} at^2 + L.$$

substituting the expressions for a and t, we get:

$$s = \frac{1}{2} \cdot \frac{F + \mu mg}{m} \cdot \frac{mL}{F - \mu mg} + L = \frac{1}{2} \cdot \frac{F + \mu mg}{F - \mu mg} L + L = \frac{3F - \mu mg}{2(F - \mu mg)} \cdot L.$$

Thus the work done by force F can be written as:

$$W = Fs = \frac{3F^2 - \mu mgF}{2(F - \mu mg)} \cdot L,$$

Inserting given data, we find:

$$W = \frac{3 \cdot 10000\,{\rm N}^2 - 100\,{\rm N} \cdot 10\,{\rm N}}{2 \cdot (100\,{\rm N} - 10\,{\rm N})} \cdot 2\,{\rm m} = 322.22\,{\rm J}.$$

This is the end of the solution.

Remarks: The kinetic energy of the system is less than the work done by force F. This is due to the fact that the disk slips on the cart, therefore part of the energy of the system is dissipated through the work of frictional force. Let us check this statement via calculations.

The total energy given to the system equals the work done by force F: $W = 322.22$ J. The total kinetic energy of the system is: $E_{\text{kin}} = 316.66$ J, so the dissipated energy (or in other words the lost mechanical energy) must be: $-\Delta E_{\text{mech}} = -(316.66 \text{ J} - 322.22 \text{ J}) = 5.56$ J. Therefore, $k = \Delta E / W = 1.73\%$.

Although it can be seen that the conservation of mechanical energy does not hold for this case, the work-energy theorem is still true: The sum of the works done by the external and internal forces acting on the system equals the change in the system's kinetic energy.

Let us calculate these works one by one. The work of force F (which is the external force) is already known, therefore the only forces, whose works should be determined, are the friction exerted by the cart on the disk and the friction exerted by the disk on the cart. Let us calculate the latter first.

The work of the friction acting on the cart can be calculated according to equation (12) using equations (9) and (13):

$$W_{\text{disk} \to \text{cart}} = S \cdot s_{\text{cart}} = S \cdot \frac{1}{2} A t^2 = \mu m g \cdot \frac{1}{2} \frac{\mu m g}{M} \cdot \frac{Lm}{F - \mu m g} = \frac{(\mu m g)^2 L}{2 \frac{M}{m} (F - \mu m g)}.$$

Inserting given data, we find:

$$W_{\text{disk} \to \text{cart}} = \frac{100 \, \text{N}^2 \cdot 2 \, \text{m}}{2 \cdot 0.5 (100 \, \text{N} - 10 \, \text{N})} = \frac{20}{9} \, \text{J} = 2.2222 \, \text{J}.$$

Calculating the work done by the friction acting on the disk proves more difficult as the distance covered by the perimeter of the disk should be determined with respect to the cart. The work done by this force will be negative since the displacement is opposite the direction of the force. $W_{\text{cart} \to \text{disk}} = -S \cdot s'$. Where $s' = r\varphi - s$, and s is the displacement of the centre of the disk.

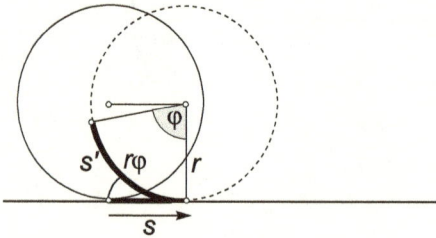

The calculation of the distance covered by the perimeter of the disk can be explained the following way. If a disk rotates around a fixed axis, the distance covered by a point on its perimeter is $r\varphi$, while if the disk slips without rotation, its perimeter moves through a distance of s. In our case, however, since both movements are present and are done in opposite directions, the distance covered will be the difference of the distances above: $r\varphi - s$.

The work done by the friction acting on the disk can also be calculated by assuming that the instantaneous power is the product of the force and the instantaneous velocity: $P = F \cdot v$. The bottom of the disk has a velocity

$$v = v_0 - r\omega$$

relative to the cart, where v_0 is the velocity of the centre of the disk and $r\omega$ is the angular velocity of the disk. We can write the work in terms of power as: $W = \overline{P} \cdot t$, where $\overline{P}$ is the average power and t is the elapsed time. In case of a constant force and zero initial velocity:

$$\overline{P} = \frac{P_{\max}}{2} = F \cdot \frac{v_{\max}}{2}.$$

So the work done by the friction on the disk is:

$$W_{\text{cart} \to \text{disk}} = \overline{P} \cdot t = \mu m g \frac{v_{\max}}{2} \cdot t = \mu m g \cdot \frac{(v_0 - r\omega)}{2} \cdot t = \mu m g \cdot (s - r\varphi) =$$
$$= \mu m g \cdot \left(\frac{1}{2} a t^2 - r\varphi \right) = \mu m g \cdot \left(\frac{1}{2} a t^2 - L \right).$$

Substituting the acceleration from equation (8) and the time from equation (13), we obtain:

$$W_{\text{cart} \to \text{disk}} = \mu m g \left(\frac{1}{2} \frac{F + \mu m g}{m} \cdot \frac{mL}{F - \mu m g} - L \right) =$$
$$= \mu m g \left(\frac{F + \mu m g}{2(F - \mu m g - 1)} \right) L = \mu m g \frac{3\mu m g - F}{2(F - \mu m g)} \cdot L.$$

Inserting given data, we find:

$$W_{\text{cart} \to \text{disk}} = 10\,\text{N} \cdot \frac{3 \cdot 10\,\text{N} - 100\,\text{N}}{2(100\,\text{N} - 10\,\text{N})} \cdot 2\,\text{m} = \frac{-70}{9}\,\text{J} = -7.778\,\text{J}.$$

So the total work done by the internal forces is:

$$\sum W_{\text{fric}} = 2.222\,\text{J} - 7.778\,\text{J} = -5.56\,\text{J},$$

which equals the dissipated energy. Therefore, the work-kinetic energy theorem can be written as:

$$W_{\text{ext}} + W_{\text{int}} = 322.22\,\text{J} - 5.56\,\text{J} = 316.66\,\text{J} = \Delta E_{\text{kin}},$$

which proves our statement.

Solution of Problem 116. Let us write Newton's second law for both objects and the constraint of the problem in order to gain the accelerations of the objects. Using the notations shown in the figure, Newton's second law for the block is (where S is the static frictional force and A is the acceleration of the block):

$$F - S = MA, \tag{1}$$

Newton's second law for the translational motion of the centre of mass of the ball is (a is the acceleration of the centre of mass of the ball)

$$S = ma, \tag{2}$$

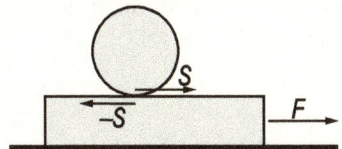

Newton's second law for the rotational motion of the ball (R is the radius of the ball, β is the angular acceleration of the ball):

$$SR = \frac{2}{5}mR^2\beta, \tag{3}$$

The constraints for rolling without sliding are:

$$A = a + R\beta, \quad \text{and} \quad \beta = \frac{A-a}{R}. \tag{4}$$

substituting (4) into (3), cancelling R, and then adding (1) and (2) and expressing S from (2) and substituting it into (3), the acceleration of the ball and the block will be:

$$a = \frac{2F}{2m + 7M}$$

$$A = \frac{7}{2}a = \frac{7F}{2m + 7M}.$$

The displacements of the ball and the block are shown in the figure. The area of the shaded region of the velocity–time graph is proportional to the distance covered by the ball on the block, which is half of the length of the block l.

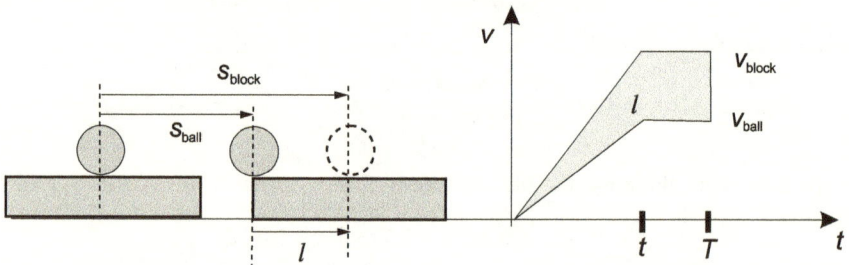

The speeds of the block and the ball with respect to the ground at the end of the accelerating period are:

$$V = At, \quad \text{and} \quad v = at.$$

the distances covered by the block and the ball during the time T are:

$$s_{\text{block}} = \frac{1}{2}At^2 + At(T - t),$$

$$s_{\text{ball}} = \frac{1}{2}at^2 + at(T - t),$$

where t is the time during which the force is exerted on the block, $T - t$ is the time of uniform motion until the ball falls off. The ball falls off if $l = s_{block} - s_{ball}$, so the equation for the asked time T is:

$$l = \frac{1}{2}(A - a)t^2 + (A - a)t(T - t),$$

from which

$$T = \frac{l}{(A-a)t} + \frac{t}{2}.$$

the maximum of time t can be gained if the distance along which the ball is accelerated is equal to half of the length of the block:

$$l = \frac{1}{2}(A-a)t^2,$$

from which the longest time while the force is exerted and the ball is on the block is:

$$t = \sqrt{\frac{2l}{A-a}}.$$

Note: In the solution we assumed that the ball has uniform density. Otherwise even the accelerations of the objects would not be constant. If the centre of mass of the ball is the geometric centre of the ball, but the ball is not solid, its moment of inertia Θ, calculated for the centre of mass, must be given. Assuming this, the relative acceleration of the two objects would be:

$$A - a = \frac{F \cdot \frac{mR^2}{\Theta}}{m\left(1 + \frac{m}{M} + \frac{mR^2}{\Theta}\right)}.$$

Let us illustrate the above statements with an example: $m = 0.1\,\text{kg}$, $R = 2\,\text{cm}$, $M = 0.4\,\text{kg}$, $F = 0.03\,\text{N}$, $l = 0.4\,\text{m}$ and the time while the force is exerted is $t = 2\,\text{s}$. Using these data the accelerations of the two objects are:

$$A = \frac{7 \cdot 0.03\,\text{N}}{2 \cdot 0.1\,\text{kg} + 7 \cdot 0.4\,\text{kg}} = 0.07\,\frac{\text{m}}{\text{s}^2},$$

$$a = \frac{2}{7}A = 0.02\,\frac{\text{m}}{\text{s}^2},$$

The relative acceleration is :

$$A - a = 0.05\,\frac{\text{m}}{\text{s}^2},$$

the maximum time of the acceleration is

$$t = \sqrt{\frac{0.8\,\text{m}}{0.05\,\frac{\text{m}}{\text{s}^2}}} = 4\,\text{s}$$

thus during the 2 seconds while the force is exerted the ball does not reach the end of the block. Thus the total time until the ball falls off in this case is

$$T = \frac{0.4}{0.05\,\frac{\text{m}}{\text{s}^2} \cdot 2\,\text{s}} + \frac{2\,\text{s}}{2} = 5\,\text{s}.$$

Solution of Problem 117. Let a be the acceleration of mass m. According to Newton's second law, the tension in the string is:

$$K = m(g - a).$$

Forces acting on the cylinder are the tension in the string, the gravitational force, kinetic frictions S_1 and S_2 and finally the normal forces N_1 and N_2 exerted by the wall and the ground respectively. Let us apply Newton's second law and its angular form to the cylinder (the former is written separately for the horizontal and vertical directions):

$$K + S_2 - N_1 = 0, \tag{1}$$

$$Mg - N_2 - S_1 = 0, \tag{2}$$

$$KR - S_1 R - S_2 R = \Theta \beta. \tag{3}$$

Since the string does not slip on the cylinder and cannot be stretched, the relationship between the acceleration of the object and the angular acceleration of the cylinder is given by:

$$\beta = \frac{a}{R}. \tag{4}$$

Kinetic frictions can be written as:

$$S_1 = \mu N_1, \tag{5}$$

$$S_2 = \mu N_2. \tag{6}$$

Isolating normal forces from equation (1) and (2) and inserting them into equation (5) and (6) give:

$$S_1 = \mu(K + S_2), \tag{5'}$$

$$S_2 = \mu(Mg - S_1). \tag{6'}$$

Substituting S_2 from equation $(6')$ into equation $(5')$, we have that:

$$S_1 = \mu[K + \mu(Mg - S_1)] = \mu K + \mu^2 Mg - \mu^2 S_1.$$

Solving for S_1 and writing the tension in terms of the acceleration leads us to:

$$S_1 = \frac{\mu(K + \mu Mg)}{1 + \mu^2} = \frac{\mu(mg - ma + \mu Mg)}{1 + \mu^2}.$$

Let us now substitute S_1 from equation $(5')$ into equation $(6')$ to determine the kinetic friction exerted by the ground:

$$S_2 = \mu\left(Mg - \frac{\mu(K + \mu Mg)}{1 + \mu^2}\right) = \frac{\mu(Mg - \mu K)}{1 + \mu^2},$$

writing K in terms of the acceleration gives:

$$S_2 = \frac{\mu(Mg - \mu mg + \mu ma)}{1 + \mu^2}.$$

By substituting the expressions for the forces into equation (3), we will have a linear equation for the acceleration. Let us divide equation (3) by the radius first:

$$K - S_1 - S_2 = \Theta \frac{a}{R^2}.$$

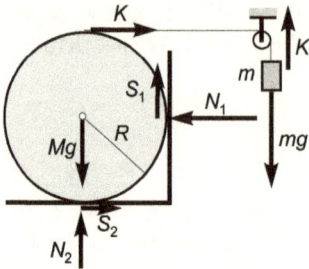

Substituting the expressions for K, S_1 and S_2, we find:

$$mg - ma - \frac{\mu mg - \mu ma + \mu^2 Mg}{1 + \mu^2} - \frac{\mu Mg - \mu^2 mg + \mu^2 ma}{1 + \mu^2} = \frac{\Theta}{R^2} a.$$

Let us solve the above equation for a:

$$a = \frac{m + 2\mu^2 m - \mu m - \mu^2 M - \mu M}{\frac{\Theta}{R^2} + \mu^2 \frac{\Theta}{R^2} + m + 2\mu^2 m - \mu m} \cdot g.$$

Dividing the numerator and the denominator of the fraction by M, we obtain:

$$a = \frac{\frac{m}{M}(1 - \mu + 2\mu^2) - \mu(1 + \mu)}{\frac{m}{M}(1 - \mu + 2\mu^2) + \frac{\Theta}{MR^2}(1 + \mu^2)} \cdot g.$$

Using that the rotational inertia of a solid cylinder about its axis of symmetry is $\Theta = \frac{1}{2}MR^2$, we find:

$$a = \frac{\frac{m}{M}(1 - \mu + 2\mu^2) - \mu(1 + \mu)}{\frac{m}{M}(1 - \mu + 2\mu^2) + \frac{1}{2}(1 + \mu^2)} \cdot g.$$

Substituting known values, we get:

$$a = \frac{\frac{11\,\text{kg}}{8\,\text{kg}}(1 - 0.5 + 2 \cdot 0.5^2) - 0.5(1 + 0.5)}{\frac{11\,\text{kg}}{8\,\text{kg}}(1 - 0.5 + 2 \cdot 0.5^2) + \frac{1}{2}(1 + 0.5^2)} \cdot 10\,\frac{\text{m}}{\text{s}^2} = 3.125\,\frac{\text{m}}{\text{s}^2}.$$

Note that this result is independent of the radius of the cylinder. If the acceleration is now taken to be zero, the condition for the cylinder to start rotating is:

$$\frac{m}{M} \geq \frac{\mu(1 + \mu)}{1 - \mu + 2\mu^2}.$$

If m/M is less than that, the cylinder and the object attached to the string remains at rest.

Solution of Problem 118. The cylinder can move without rotation if the torque of S_1 — which is the kinetic friction acting on the point where the cylinder touches the ground — is compensated by the torque of S_1', which is the static friction acting on the point where the cylinder touches the cube. Therefore, S_1' should be equal to S_1 and should point downwards, increasing the weight of the cylinder.

Let us apply Newton's second law to the vertical direction:

$$mg - K_1 + S_1 = 0,$$

from which the normal force exerted by the ground is:

$$K_1 = mg + S_1$$

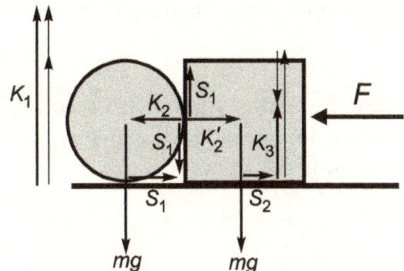

and so the kinetic friction acting on the ground can be written as:

$$S_1 = \mu K_1 = \mu(mg + S_1).$$

hence

$$S_1 = \frac{\mu}{1 - \mu} mg. \tag{1}$$

Newton's second law applied to the horizontal components takes the form of:

$$K_2 - S_1 = ma,$$

where K_2 is the normal force exerted by the cube. Isolating K_2, we find:

$$K_2 = ma + S_1.$$

In the extreme case that marks off pure translation from rolling, the magnitude of static friction acting at the point where the cylinder touches the cube can be written as:

$$S_1' = \mu_0 K_2 = \mu_0(ma + S_1). \tag{2}$$

Using that $S_1 = S_1'$ and substituting S_1 from equation (1) into equation (2), we obtain:

$$\frac{\mu}{1 - \mu} mg = \mu_0 ma + \mu_0 \frac{\mu}{1 - \mu} mg.$$

Isolating the acceleration of cylinder, we get:

$$a = \frac{\mu}{\mu_0} \cdot \frac{1 - \mu_0}{1 - \mu} \cdot g. \tag{3}$$

Let us now examine the motion of the cube. The kinetic friction acting at its bottom can be determined by using the formula $S_2 = \mu K_3$, where K_3 is the normal force exerted by the ground on the cube. To find K_3 let us apply Newton's second law to the vertical direction:

$$mg - S_1 - K_3 = 0,$$

hence

$$K_3 = mg - S_1 = mg - \frac{\mu}{1 - \mu} mg = \frac{1 - 2\mu}{1 - \mu} mg,$$

so the magnitude of kinetic friction S_2 is:

$$S_2 = \frac{\mu(1 - 2\mu)}{1 - \mu} mg. \tag{4}$$

Newton's second law applied to the cube in the horizontal direction takes the form of:

$$F - S_2 - K_2' = ma,$$

where K_2' and K_2 are action-reaction forces, therefore they are equal in magnitude and opposite in direction. Using that $K_2 = ma + S_1$, the minimum value of the pushing force turns out to be:

$$F = ma + S_2 + K_2 = ma + S_2 + ma + S_1 = 2ma + S_1 + S_2.$$

Substituting equations (1), (3) and (4) into the above equation, we find:

$$F = 2m \frac{\mu}{\mu_0} \cdot \frac{1-\mu_0}{1-\mu} g + \frac{\mu}{1-\mu} mg + \mu \frac{1-2\mu}{1-\mu} mg.$$

After rearranging the expression, we get:

$$F = \frac{2\mu(1-\mu_0\mu)}{\mu_0(1-\mu)} mg = \frac{2 \cdot 0.2(1-0.6 \cdot 0.2)}{0.6(1-0.2)} \cdot 12 \, \text{kg} \cdot 10 \, \frac{\text{m}}{\text{s}^2} = 88 \, \text{N}.$$

So the motion of the cylinder will be purely translational if the pushing force is greater than $88 \, \text{N}$. Note that the system requires a minimum of $F_0 = 2mg\mu_0 = 144 \, \text{N}$ to start moving, therefore if the cube and cylinder begin moving, the pushing force can be decreased to $88 \, \text{N}$ to keep the cylinder's motion purely rotational. If the magnitude of the pushing force is decreased further, the cylinder will start rolling, rubbing the side of the cube. If the force becomes less than $F = 2mg\mu = 48 \, \text{N}$, the system stops. The magnitudes of other quantities when the force is $F = 88 \, \text{N}$ are: $a = \frac{1}{6}g = 1.67 \, \frac{\text{m}}{\text{s}^2}$, $S_1 = 30 \, \text{N}$, $S_2 = 18 \, \text{N}$, $K_1 = 150 \, \text{N}$, $K_2 = 50 \, \text{N}$, $K_3 = 90 \, \text{N}$, $\sum F = ma = 20 \, \text{N}$.

Solution of Problem 119. Let us find out what happens. Each of the three objects will remain at rest if both $m_3g < \mu_2 m_2 g$ and $m_3g < \mu_1(m_1+m_2)g$ are true. Since in our case none of the above inequalities hold, this is not the solution of the problem. The board will start to move if

$$\mu_2 m_2 g > \mu_1(m_1+m_2)g.$$

Since the data given satisfies this inequality, we can state that the board starts to move. The next step is to decide whether the brick slips on the board or moves together with it.

Let us assume that the brick slips on the board. In this case both frictions take their maximum values, thus applying Newton's second law to each of the three objects and eliminating the tension, we get that the accelerations of the board and brick are:

$$a_1 = \frac{\mu_2 m_2 g - \mu_1(m_1+m_2)g}{m_2} = 0.15g,$$

$$a_2 = \frac{m_3g - \mu_2 m_2 g}{m_2+m_3} = 0.1g.$$

This means that the acceleration of the board would be greater than that of the brick, which is impossible. Therefore, the only solution of the problem is that the board and brick move together with the same acceleration. In this case the magnitude of friction between the board and brick can be anything between zero and its maximum value. From the laws of motion of the two objects, we get that their acceleration is:

$$a = \frac{m_3 - \mu_1(m_1+m_2)}{m_1+m_2+m_3} \cdot g = 0.12g = 1.18 \, \frac{\text{m}}{\text{s}^2}.$$

The magnitude of static friction between the board and brick is:

$$S = \frac{m_1 m_3 + \mu_1(m_1+m_2)(m_2+m_3)}{m_1+m_2+m_3} = 6.28 \, \text{N},$$

while for the tension, we get:

$$K = \frac{(m_1 + m_2)(1 + \mu_1)}{m_1 + m_2 + m_3} m_3 g = 8.63 \, \text{N},$$

and finally the magnitude of kinetic friction between the board and table is:

$$S_k = \mu_1 (m_1 + m_2) g = 3.92 \, \text{N}.$$

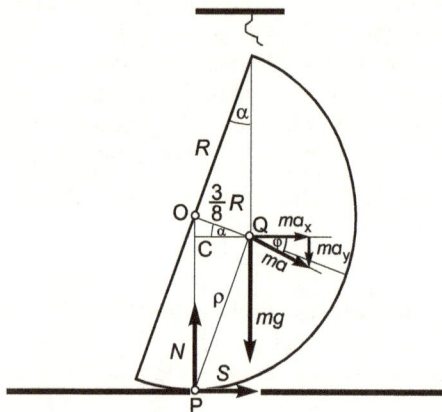

Solution of Problem 120. The hemisphere starts to push the surface after burning the string and as its centre of gravity is not above its point of support, it will undergo an accelerating rolling motion. The horizontal component of the acceleration of the centre of mass is caused by the static friction S, while the vertical component is due to the gravitational force mg and the normal force N. The angular acceleration of rotation β is caused by the torques acting around the rotational axis.

Let us apply Newton's second law separately to the horizontal and vertical components and the angular form for the rotation. Note that $\sum M = \Theta \beta$ holds only if the torques are taken about a point that has no acceleration or about the centre of mass. Therefore in this case torques will be taken about point Q, which is the centre of mass of the hemisphere.

Let α be the angle that the plane of the great circle bounding the hemisphere forms with the vertical, and φ be the angle that the initial acceleration of the centre of mass forms with the horizontal. Newton's second law for the horizontal and vertical components are:

$$S = ma \cdot \cos\varphi, \tag{1}$$

$$mg - N = ma \cdot \sin\varphi, \tag{2}$$

Newton's second law in angular form is:

$$Nk_1 - Sk_2 = \Theta_s \beta, \tag{3}$$

where $k_1 = \frac{3}{8} R \cos\alpha$, $k_2 = R(1 - \frac{3}{8}\sin\alpha)$, Θ_s is the rotational inertia of the hemisphere about the axis that goes through the centre of mass parallel to the bounding great circle and β is the initial angular acceleration of the hemisphere.

The minimum value of the coefficient of static friction that should be calculated is:

$$\mu = \frac{S}{N}.$$

To be able to solve the system of equations above, we need to calculate the rotational inertia Θ_s of the hemisphere first and then to determine the relationship between the acceleration of the centre of mass and the angular acceleration.

Let us start from the fact that the rotational inertia of a sphere about its centre is:
$$\Theta = \frac{2}{5}MR^2.$$

As the rotational inertia is additive, the rotational inertia of a sphere can be taken as the sum of the rotational inertias of two symmetrical hemispheres:
$$\Theta_{\text{sphere}} = 2 \cdot \Theta_{\text{hemisphere}}.$$

If the mass of the hemisphere is m, the equation will take the form of:
$$\frac{2}{5}(2m)R^2 = 2 \cdot \frac{2}{5}mR^2,$$

which shows that the rotational inertia of a hemisphere with mass m and radius R about any diameter of its bounding great circle is:
$$\Theta_O = \frac{2}{5}mR^2.$$

We can also arrive to the above result by imagining that with the help of a half-plane whose bounding line is a diameter of the sphere and which is rotated 180^0 from its original position, the mass of the sphere is 'swept' into the volume of a hemisphere. Although the density of the hemisphere will be twice that of the sphere, because all pointmasses of the sphere move along a half-circle and thus their distances from the centre remain unchanged, there will be no change in the sum: $\Theta = \sum_{i=1}^{n} m_i r_i^2$, which allows us to draw the conclusion that the rotational inertias of a sphere and hemisphere of the same mass and about the same diameter are equal. The next step is to determine the rotational inertia of a hemisphere about its centre of mass. Applying Steiner's law:
$$\Theta_O = \Theta_s + md^2,$$

where d is the distance between the two axes, Θ_s in our case is therefore:
$$\Theta_s = \Theta_O - md^2 = \frac{2}{5}mR^2 - m\left(\frac{3}{8}R\right)^2 = \frac{83}{320}mR^2. \tag{4}$$

The trigonometric functions of the angle describing the initial position of the hemisphere are:
$$\cos\alpha = \frac{R}{BQ} = \frac{8}{\sqrt{73}} = 0.9363,$$

since $BQ = \sqrt{R^2 + (3R/8)^2} = R \cdot \frac{\sqrt{73}}{8} = 1.068R.$
$$\sin\alpha = \frac{3R/8}{\sqrt{73}R/8} = \frac{3}{\sqrt{73}} = 0.3511,$$

$$\tan\alpha = \frac{3}{8} = 0.375 \quad \rightarrow \quad \alpha = 20.5560°.$$

The trigonometric functions of the angle of the acceleration vector are:

$$\tan\varphi = \frac{CQ}{CP} = \frac{3R\cos\alpha/8}{R - 3R\sin\alpha/8} = \frac{3\cos\alpha}{8 - 3\sin\alpha} = \frac{24}{8\sqrt{73} - 9} = 0.4044,$$

hence $\varphi = 22.017°$.

$$\sin\varphi = 0.3749, \quad \text{and} \quad \cos\varphi = 0.9271.$$

And finally the relationship between the acceleration of the centre of mass and the angular acceleration is:

$$a = \varrho \cdot \beta, \tag{5}$$

where ϱ is the instantaneous radius of rotation, i.e. the distance of the centre of mass from the instantaneous centre of rotation (P). (Note that it is important that when the hemisphere starts to move, point P is not only at rest but also has an increasing but initially zero acceleration. This is due to the fact that point P is the point of a cycloid, where the rolling circle touches the ground. In general, this point is at rest, but has an acceleration v^2/R towards the centre of the circle. In this case, however, the initial velocity of the centre of the circle is zero, therefore the initial acceleration of point P reduces to zero as well, which makes it possible to write the acceleration of the centre of mass in a reference frame fixed to point P as $a = \varrho \cdot \beta$.)

The instantaneous radius of rotation can be determined using triangle PQC:

$$\varrho = \frac{CQ}{\sin\varphi} = \frac{3R\cos\alpha}{8\sin\varphi} = 0.9368R.$$

Let us now return to equations (1), (2) and (3). Using equation (1) to isolate a, substituting it into equation (3) then dividing it by R and using equation (5) lead us to:

$$\frac{3}{8}\cos\alpha \cdot N - \left(1 - \frac{3}{8}\sin\alpha\right) \cdot S = \frac{\Theta_s}{R\varrho} \cdot \frac{S}{m\cos\varphi}.$$

dividing by N and using that $\mu = S/N$, we obtain:

$$\frac{3}{8}\cos\alpha - \left(1 - \frac{3}{8}\sin\alpha\right)\mu = \mu\frac{\Theta_s}{R\varrho m\cos\varphi}.$$

isolating the coefficient of static friction from the equation, we get:

$$\mu = \frac{\frac{3}{8}\cos\alpha}{\left(1 - \frac{3}{8}\sin\alpha\right) + \frac{\Theta_s}{R\varrho m\cos\varphi}}.$$

Multiplying both the numerator and the denominator of the fraction by $\cos\varphi$ and multiplying both the numerator and the denominator of the second term of the denominator by R, we have:

$$\mu = \frac{3\cos\alpha\cos\varphi}{8\cos\varphi - 3\sin\alpha\cos\varphi + 8\frac{\Theta_s}{mR^2} \cdot \frac{R}{\varrho}}.$$

Substituting known values gives:

$$\mu = \frac{3 \cdot 0.9363 \cdot 0.9271}{8 \cdot 0.9271 - 3 \cdot 0.3511 \cdot 0.9271 + 8 \cdot \frac{83}{320} \cdot \frac{1}{0.9368}} = 0.3009.$$

(If the hemisphere does not slip at the start of its motion, it will not slip afterwards either. Since the line of action of N will get closer to the centre of mass, its torque will decrease and so will the angular acceleration. This makes the horizontal component of the acceleration decrease as well, which means that less static friction will be needed.)

Let us carry out some extra calculations for additional information.

Use equation (1) and (2) to determine the initial magnitude of the static friction and normal force:

$$S = \mu N$$

Substituting into equation (1) and dividing equation (2) by equation (1), we get:

$$\frac{mg - N}{\mu N} = \tan \varphi,$$

from which the magnitudes of the forces are:

$$N = \frac{1}{1 + \mu \tan \varphi} \cdot mg = 0.8915 mg, \qquad S = \mu N = 0.2628 mg,$$

while the magnitudes of the acceleration vector and its components are:

$$a = \frac{S}{m \cos \varphi} = 0.2894g = 2.84 \, \frac{\mathrm{m}}{\mathrm{s}^2},$$

$$a_x = a \cos \varphi = 0.268g = 2.632 \, \frac{\mathrm{m}}{\mathrm{s}^2}, \qquad a_y = a \sin \varphi = 0.1085g = 1.064 \, \frac{\mathrm{m}}{\mathrm{s}^2}.$$

First solution of Problem 121. Let us solve the problem investigating the energies of the system. The work done by the gravitational force on the object moving down equals the change in the kinetic energy of the system. (The sum of the works of the internal forces is zero in this situation.) Using this, we can determine the instantaneous velocity of the object after an infinitesimal displacement (Δh). Since the cylinders are far from each other, the change in the angle of the cord between them can be neglected during an infinitesimal displacement, therefore all forces and accelerations may be considered to be constant. Thus, assuming that the initial velocity of the object is zero and therefore $v = \sqrt{2as}$, we can determine the acceleration of the object by simply substituting the expression previously gained for the velocity. Applying the work-kinetic energy theorem, we obtain:

$$mg\Delta h = \frac{1}{2}mv^2 + \frac{1}{4}mr^2\omega_1^2 + \frac{1}{2}mv_0^2 + \frac{1}{4}mr^2\omega_2^2,$$

where on the right-hand side the first term is the translational energy of the object moving down, the second is the rotational energy of the pulley, while the third and fourth are the translational and rotational energies of the cylinder on the ground.

From now on let v_c denote the instantaneous velocity of the object, since this equals the velocity of the segment of the cord coming down from the pulley. The velocity of the centre of the mass of the cylinder is denoted by v_0. Dividing the above equation by m, we find:

$$g\Delta h = \frac{1}{2}v_c^2 + \frac{1}{4}v_c^2 + \frac{1}{2}v_0^2 + \frac{1}{4}v_0^2. \qquad (1)$$

Let us determine the connection between the two velocities in order to be able to express the velocity of the object in terms of the displacement from the above equation.

Point C (shown in the figure) is the instantaneous centre of rotation of the cylinder (since its instantaneous velocity is 0). Let point A be the point of tangency on the line of the cord. The instantaneous radius of point A is $CA = \varrho$. The velocity of the centre of mass of the cylinder is $v_0 = r\omega_2$.

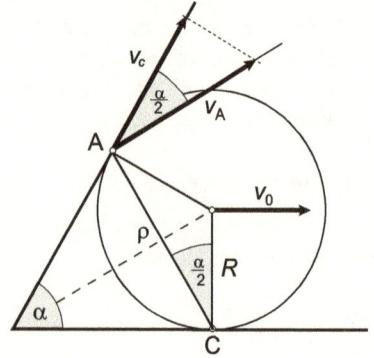

Using these notations, the instantaneous velocity of point A of the cylinder is:

$$v_A = \varrho\omega_2 = 2r\cos\frac{\alpha}{2}\omega_2 = v_0 2\cos\frac{\alpha}{2}.$$

This is also the velocity of the point of the cord that is in point A. The component of this velocity that is perpendicular to the cord does not play any part in moving the cord. The parallel component, however, gives the velocity, whose magnitude equals the speed of the object moving down. Therefore the velocity of the object is:

$$v_c = v_A \cos\frac{\alpha}{2} = v_0 2\cos^2\frac{\alpha}{2}. \qquad (2)$$

Since $a = \Delta v/\Delta t$, the same relation exists between the accelerations of the object and of the centre of mass of the cylinder:

$$a_c = a_0 2\cos^2\frac{\alpha}{2},$$

which can also be written in the form of:

$$a_c = a_0(1 + \cos\alpha). \qquad (3)$$

Isolating v_0 from equation (2) and substituting it into equation (1), we get an equation for the velocity of the object:

$$g\Delta h = \frac{1}{2}v_c^2 + \frac{1}{4}v_c^2 + \frac{1}{2}\cdot\frac{v_c^2}{4\cos^4\frac{\alpha}{2}} + \frac{1}{4}\cdot\frac{v_c^2}{4\cos^4\frac{\alpha}{2}},$$

which yields:

$$v_c = \sqrt{2\cdot\frac{8\cos^4\frac{\alpha}{2}g}{12\cos^4\frac{\alpha}{2}+3}\cdot\Delta h}$$

thus the acceleration of the object moving down is:

$$a_c = \frac{8\cos^4\frac{\alpha}{2}}{12\cos^4\frac{\alpha}{2}+3} \cdot g,$$

after some algebra, this can be written into the form of:

$$a_c = \frac{2}{3} \cdot \frac{(1+\cos\alpha)^2}{(1+\cos\alpha)^2+1} \cdot g,$$

substituting known values, we find:

$$a_c = \frac{2}{3} \cdot \frac{(1+0.5)^2}{(1+0.5)^2+1} \cdot g = 0.461g = 4.53 \,\frac{\text{m}}{\text{s}}.$$

Second solution of Problem 121. The problem can also be solved using the laws of motion. Let K_1, K_2 and K_3 be the tensions acting in the vertical, inclined and horizontal parts of the cord respectively.

Applying Newton's second law to the object, we obtain:

$$mg - K_1 = ma_c, \tag{1}$$

Applying Newton's second law in angular form to the pulley, we get:

$$K_1 r - K_2 r = \Theta\frac{a_c}{r}, \tag{2}$$

The law of motion of the centre of mass of the cylinder is:

$$K_2\cos\alpha + K_3 = ma_0, \tag{3}$$

Applying Newton's second law in angular form to the rolling cylinder, we have:

$$K_2 r - K_3 r = \Theta \cdot \frac{a_0}{r}. \tag{4}$$

Dividing equation (2) by r and adding it to equation (1), we get:

$$mg - K_2 = \left(m + \frac{\Theta}{r^2}\right) a_c. \tag{I.}$$

Let us divide equation (4) by r and then add it to equation (3). Using equation (3) of the first solution, that gives the relation between a_c and a_0, we find:

$$K_2(1+\cos\alpha) = \left(m + \frac{\Theta}{r^2}\right)\frac{a_c}{1+\cos\alpha},$$

isolating K_2, we have:

$$K_2 = \left(m + \frac{\Theta}{r^2}\right)\frac{a_c}{(1+\cos\alpha)^2} \tag{II.}$$

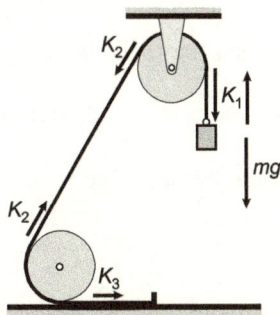

Substituting the above expression for K_2 into equation (I) and isolating a_c, we get:

$$a_c = \frac{m(1+\cos\alpha)^2}{\left(m+\frac{Q}{r^2}\right)[1+(1+\cos\alpha)^2]} \cdot g,$$

dividing by m yields:

$$a_c = \frac{(1+\cos\alpha)^2}{(1+\Theta/mr^2)[1+(1+\cos\alpha)^2]} \cdot g.$$

It can be useful to determine the other quantities describing the motion of the system as well. After some algebra (not detailed here), we would get that the tension in the vertical cord is:

$$K_1 = m(g-a_c) = \frac{1+\frac{\Theta}{mr^2}[1+(1+\cos\alpha)^2]}{(1+\Theta/mr^2)[1+(1+\cos\alpha)^2]} \cdot mg,$$

the tension in the inclined cord can be calculated from equation (II):

$$K_2 = \frac{(m+\Theta/2r^2)a_c}{(1+\cos\alpha)^2} = \frac{1}{1+(1+\cos\alpha)^2}mg,$$

the tension in the horizontal cord can be determined using equation (4):

$$K_3 = K_2 - \frac{\Theta}{r^2}a_0 = \frac{1-\Theta\cos\alpha/mr^2}{(1+\Theta/mr^2)[1+(1+\cos\alpha)^2]}mg,$$

while the acceleration of the centre of mass of the cylinder is:

$$a_0 = \frac{a_c}{1+\cos\alpha} = \frac{(1+\cos\alpha)}{(1+\Theta/mr^2)[1+(1+\cos\alpha)^2]}.$$

Substituting given data and using that for a solid cylinder $\Theta/mr^2 = 0.5$, we find:

$$a_c = \frac{6}{13} \cdot g = 0.462g = 4.528\,\frac{\text{m}}{\text{s}^2},$$

$$a_0 = \frac{4}{13} \cdot g = 0.308g = 3.02\,\frac{\text{m}}{\text{s}^2},$$

$$K_1 = \frac{7}{13} \cdot mg = 0.538mg = 42.26\,\text{N},$$

$$K_2 = \frac{4}{13} \cdot mg = 0.308mg = 14.15\,\text{N},$$

$$K_3 = \frac{2}{13} \cdot mg = 0.154mg = 12.08\,\text{N}.$$

Solution of Problem 122. The pulley-system rotates with a constant angular acceleration. Let R and $2R$ be the radii of the smaller and greater pulleys respectively. The ratio of the masses of the pulleys are given by the ratio of their volumes which is the same as the ratio of their radii squared, thus $m_1 : m_2 = 1 : 4$. Asssuming that their total mass is $5\,\text{kg}$, we get $m_1 = 1\,\text{kg}$ and $m_2 = 4\,\text{kg}$. The rotational inertia of the pulley-system around the rotational axis is:

$$\Theta = \frac{1}{2}m_1 R^2 + \frac{1}{2}4m_1(2R)^2 = \frac{17}{2}m_1 R^2.$$

Substituting known values, we find:

$$\Theta = \frac{17}{2}\cdot 1\,\text{kg}\cdot 0.1^2\,\text{m}^2 = 0.085\,\text{kg}\cdot\text{m}^2.$$

Applying Newton's second law to the two hanging blocks (using the notation shown in the figure) gives:

$$mg - K_1 = ma_1 \quad \text{and} \quad mg - K_2 = ma_2.$$

From Newton's second law in angular form applied to the pulley-system, we obtain:

$$K_1 \cdot R + K_2 \cdot 2R = \Theta\beta.$$

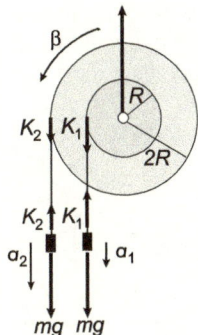

Assuming that the pulleys rotate together and that the strings are unstretchable, we gain:

$$a_1 = R\beta, \quad \text{and} \quad a_2 = 2R\beta = 2a_1.$$

Using the above system of equations to isolate K_2, we find:

$$K_2 = mg - \frac{6R^2 m^2 g}{\Theta + 5mR^2} = \frac{17m_1 m - 12m^2}{17m_1 + 10m}\cdot g = -\,0.83\,\text{N}.$$

Having a negative value for tension means that the left string pushes the hanging block instead of pulling it, which is impossible. In reality the left strings remains slack, $K_2 = 0$, thus $a_2 = g$, which means that the block hanging from the greater pulley undergoes freefall and the left string doesn't play any part in rotating the pulley-system. Let us use this information to set up a new system of equations:

$$mg - K_1 = ma_1,$$

$$K_1 \cdot R = \Theta\beta,$$

$$a_1 = R\beta.$$

The solutions of the system of equations are:

$$\beta = 50.4\,\text{s}^{-2}; \quad a_1 = 0.51g = 5.04\,\frac{\text{m}}{\text{s}^2}; \quad a_2 = g = 9.8\,\frac{\text{m}}{\text{s}^2}.$$

The times needed for the hanging blocks to move down into a depth of $4.9\,\text{m}$ are:

$$t_1 = \sqrt{2s/a_1} = 1.39\,\text{s}, \quad \text{and} \quad t_2 = \sqrt{2s/g} = 1\,\text{s}.$$

Solution of Problem 123. As the axis of symmetry remains stationary, so does the centre of mass of the disk-system, therefore the resultant of the forces acting on it should be zero. Since there is no friction, the only horizontal forces acting on the disks are the ones exerted by the cords. The sum of these two forces can only be zero if their magnitudes are equal and the pulleys are positioned in such a way that the cords run parallel to each other.

Since the cords that exert forces of the same magnitude are wrapped around disks of different radii, the net torque will not be zero, and so the disk-system will rotate around its stationary axis of symmetry with constant angular acceleration. At the same time, m_1 and m_2 accelerate downwards and upwards respectively. Let us calculate the value of m_2 by determining the tensions in the cords.

Let β be the angular acceleration of the disk-system. The acceleration of m_1 can be written as:

$$a_1 = r_1\beta,$$

so Newton's second law takes the form of:

$$m_1g - F = m_1r_1\beta,$$

isolating F, which is the tension in the cord, we get:

$$F = m_1g - m_1r_1\beta. \tag{1}$$

Let us apply Newton's second law to m_2:

$$F - m_2g = m_2r_2\beta,$$

isolating F, we find:

$$F = m_2g + m_2r_2\beta. \tag{2}$$

The rotation of the disk-system is caused by the tensions in the two cords.

According to Newton's second law in angular form:

$$F(r_1 - r_2) = \Theta\beta. \tag{3}$$

Substituting the expression for the force given in equation (1), we obtain:

$$(m_1g - m_1r_1\beta)(r_1 - r_2) = \Theta\beta,$$

from which the angular acceleration can be isolated as:

$$\beta = \frac{m_1g(r_1 - r_2)}{\Theta + m_1r_1(r_1 - r_2)}. \tag{4}$$

Assuming that the right-hand sides of equations (1) and (2) are equal and substituting the expression for the angular acceleration, we get an equation for m_2:

$$m_2g + m_2r_2\frac{m_1g(r_1 - r_2)}{\Theta + m_1r_1(r_1 - r_2)} = m_1g - m_1r_1\frac{m_1g(r_1 - r_2)}{\Theta + m_1r_1(r_1 - r_2)}.$$

Let us write both sides as one fraction and divide them by g:

$$m_2\frac{\Theta + m_1r_1(r_1 - r_2) + m_1r_2(r_1 - r_2)}{\Theta + m_1r_1(r_1 - r_2)} = \frac{\Theta + m_1r_1(r_1 - r_2) - m_1r_1(r_1 - r_2)}{\Theta + m_1r_1(r_1 - r_2)}m_1$$

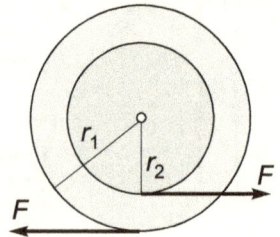

After multiplying by the denominator and expanding the numerator on the right-hand side, we obtain:

$$m_2 = m_1 \frac{\Theta}{\Theta + m_1(r_1 - r_2)(r_1 + r_2)} = m_1 \frac{\Theta}{\Theta + m_1(r_1^2 - r_2^2)}.$$

Substituting known values, we find:

$$m_2 = 5 \, \text{kg} \frac{0.25}{0.25 + 5(0.09 - 0.04)} = 2.5 \, \text{kg}.$$

(According to equation (4), the angular acceleration of the disks is: $\beta = 12.5 \ \text{s}^{-1}$. The tension in the cords can be calculated from equation (1): $F = 31.25 \, \text{N}$.)

Solution of Problem 124. The printed letters will be clear if the cylinder rolls on the wall without slipping. (In reality printing obviously also requires the cylinder to be pushed onto the wall, but in our case this is impossible as the cords are vertical. If there was a normal force acting to push the cylinder onto the wall, the problem would become inexplicit because of the presence of static friction, therefore the solution for the acceleration would be an interval instead of a single value.)

If the cords were wrapped around the cylindrical surface, the cylinder could be made to roll without slipping by simply keeping the ends of the cords in our stationary hands. In this case, however, the cords run down from disks of smaller radius than R, and therefore the tangential acceleration of an arbitrary point on the cylindrical surface in a reference frame attached to the axis of the cylinder is greater than the acceleration of the axis of the cylinder in a reference frame attached to the wall. Therefore if the ends of the cords were held stationary, the letters on the cylindrical surface would move upwards relative to the wall, which would make the text printed onto the wall smudgy. This means that the ends of the cords should be accelerated downwards to achieve clear printing (rolling without slipping).

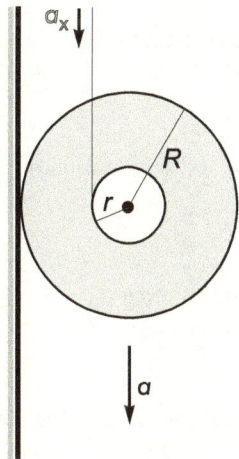

Let a be the acceleration of the axis (or centre of mass) of the cylinder, a_x be the acceleration of the ends of the cords and K be the tension in the cords. Applying Newton's second law to the cylinder, we have:

$$mg - K = ma. \tag{1}$$

The cylinder rotates with a constant angular acceleration. Writing Newton's second law in angular form (torques are taken about the centre of mass), we obtain:

$$Kr = \Theta\beta, \tag{2}$$

where β is the angular acceleration of the cylinder. If the cylinder rolls on the wall without slipping, the connection between its acceleration and angular acceleration is given by:

$$a = R\beta. \tag{3}$$

As the cords are unstretchable:

$$a = a_x + r\beta. \tag{4}$$

Let us solve equation (3) for the angular acceleration and substitute it into equation (4):

$$a = a_x + r\frac{a}{R},$$

so the connection between the two linear accelerations is determined by the geometry of the system:

$$a_x = a\frac{(R-r)}{R}. \tag{5}$$

The acceleration of the centre of mass can be calculated from equations (1) and (2). Isolating the tension in equation (2) and using equation (3), we get:

$$K = \frac{\Theta}{r} \cdot \frac{a}{R},$$

Let us now substitute this into equation (1):

$$mg - \frac{\Theta}{r} \cdot \frac{a}{R} = ma,$$

after rearranging this, we obtain:

$$mg = \left(\frac{\Theta}{rR} + m\right)a,$$

so the acceleration of the centre of mass can be expressed as:

$$a = \frac{mg}{\frac{\Theta}{rR} + m} = \frac{mgrR}{\Theta + mrR}.$$

Substituting this into equation (5), we can calculate the required acceleration of the ends of the cords:

$$a_x = \frac{mgrR}{\Theta + mrR} \cdot \frac{R-r}{R} = \frac{mgr}{\Theta + mrR}(R-r).$$

Knowing that the rotational inertia of a homogeneous solid cylinder around its axis of symmetry is $\Theta = mR^2/2$, we have:

$$a_x = \frac{mgr}{\frac{1}{2}mR^2 + mrR}(R-r) = \frac{2r(R-r)}{R^2 + 2rR}g.$$

Let us now use the connection between the two radii: $R = 3r$, which will simplify our formula. We obtain that the acceleration of the ends of the cords should be:

$$a_x = \frac{2r(3r-r)}{9r^2 + 2r \cdot 3r}g = \frac{4}{9+6}g = \frac{4}{15}g \approx 0.267g = 2.616\,\frac{m}{s^2}.$$

Additional data: the acceleration of the centre of mass is

$$a = \frac{a_x R}{(R-r)} = \frac{4}{15}g \cdot \frac{3r}{3r-r} = 0.4g,$$

the tension in the cords is $K = m(g-a) = m(1-0.4)g = 0.6mg$ and finally the angular acceleration of the cylinder is $\beta = 0.4g/R$.

Remark: The problem can also be solved if cords run down from the disks in such a way that they lie on the outer sides of the disks. In that case the ends of the cords should be accelerated with a_y pointing upwards. The system of equations and the method of solution are similar to the one shown above. The results in this second case are:

$$a_y = \frac{8}{3}g; \quad a = 2g; \quad K = 3mg; \quad \beta = \frac{2g}{R}.$$

Solution of Problem 125. a) Between the time the thread stretches for the first time and the time it becomes loose, an 'elastic collision' practically happens (not in the nature of a usual elastic 'push' but in the nature of an elastic 'pull'). As no external forces act, the law of conservation of momentum holds, and as no dissipative forces act either, the law of conservation of mechanical energy holds as well.

This collision consists of half of a harmonic oscillation. Let us change to a centre-of-mass coordinate system. From the moment of the stretching of the thread, the distance travelled in time t by the trolleys with mass m_1 and m_2 are Δx_1 and Δx_2 respectively. Based on the theorem about the motion of the centre of mass, for the magnitudes of these displacements

$$\frac{\Delta x_1}{\Delta x_2} = \frac{m_2}{m_1}. \tag{1}$$

holds. On the other hand, the magnitude of the force (exerted on both bodies) by the spring is

$$F = k(\Delta x_1 + \Delta x_2). \tag{2}$$

Expressing Δx_2 from (1) and substituting it into (2) gives

$$F = k\left(\Delta x_1 + \frac{m_1}{m_2}\Delta x_1\right) = k\frac{m_1+m_2}{m_2}\Delta x_1 = k_1^*\Delta x_1. \tag{3}$$

The motion of any trolley – until the thread is stretched – can be regarded as the motion of a point mass attached to a spring with spring constant k^*, which, as we know, is a harmonic oscillation. According to this, the half period of the oscillation of the trolley with mass m_1 (and similarly, symmetrically of the trolley with mass m_2) is:

$$t_1 = \frac{T}{2} = \pi\sqrt{\frac{m_1}{k_1^*}} = \sqrt{\frac{m_1 m_2}{k(m_1+m_2)}} = \sqrt{\frac{2m^2}{k\cdot 3m}} = \sqrt{\frac{2m}{3k}} = \sqrt{\frac{16\,\text{kg}}{3\cdot 23.3\,\text{N/m}}} = 1.5\,\text{s}.$$

(Remark: The same numerical value is acquired for the trolley with mass m_2, for which $k_2^* = 3k$, while the value of k_1^* was $\frac{3}{2}k$.)

285

The (relative) velocity of the two trollies relative to each other until the start of the half oscillation was

$$v_{\text{rel}} = v_0 = 2\,\text{m/s},$$

so at the end it is -1 times this value due to symmetry reasons, so the additional time elapsed until the collision of the rear trolley and the spring is

$$t_2 = \frac{l}{v_0} = \frac{1\,\text{m}}{2\,\frac{\text{m}}{\text{s}}} = 0.5\,\text{s}.$$

Thus the total time elapsed from the stretching of the thread to the collision with the spring is

$$t = t_1 + t_2 = 1.5\,\text{s} + 0.5\,\text{s} = 2\,\text{s}.$$

b) As the process is symmetrical (the other half of the period elapses between the compression and the stretching of the spring) and the relative velocity is -1 times the original value, the time elapsed from the collision of the trolley and the spring to the second stretching of the thread is

$$t_b = t_a = 2\,\text{s},$$

and from the first stretching of the string it is

$$t'_b = 2t_a = 4\,\text{s}.$$

Solution of Problem 126. Let us apply Newton's second law for the motion of the small body and for the rotational motion of the disc. Let K_2 be the tension exerted in the thread on the left-hand side, and K_1 be the tension in the thread in the right-hand side, Δl_1 is the total extension of the spring when the small body is displaced by Δh. This

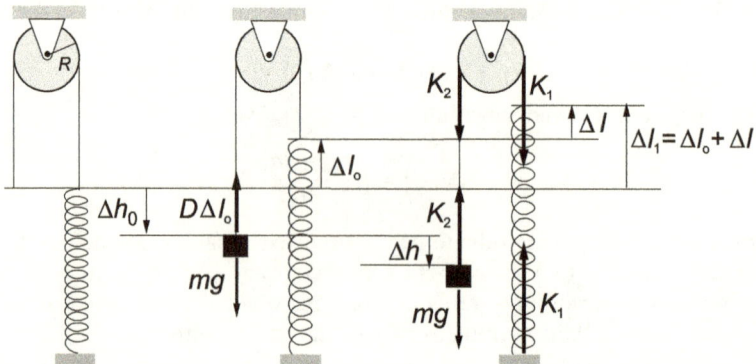

consists of the initial elongation of the spring which belongs to the equilibrium position, for which $\Delta l_0 = -\Delta h_0$, and the excess elongation caused by the displacement of the small body, which is $\Delta l = -\Delta h$, and thus: $\Delta l_1 = \Delta l_0 + \Delta l$. The disc does not effect the initial elongation Δl_0 which belongs to the equilibrium position. Its magnitude can be calculated from the equation: $mg - D\Delta l_0 = 0$, thus: $\Delta l_0 = mg/D$. (D denotes the spring constant.) Therefore our equations are:

$$K_2 - mg = ma \tag{1}$$

$$(K_1 - K_2)R = \Theta \cdot \beta \tag{2}$$

$$K_1 - D\Delta l_1 = 0 \tag{3}$$

$$\Delta l_0 - \frac{mg}{D} = 0. \tag{4}$$

The thread does not slide on the disc thus $\beta = a/R$, so equation (2) can be written in the form:

$$K_1 - K_2 = \frac{\Theta}{R^2} a. \tag{2'}$$

Adding equation (1) and (2) and substituting K_1 from equation (3) we gain:

$$D\Delta l_1 - mg = ma + \Theta \frac{a}{R^2} = \left(m + \frac{\Theta}{R^2}\right) a. \tag{5}$$

Expressing Δl_1 in terms of the extension with respect to the initial elongation equation (5) will be the following:

$$D\Delta l_0 + D\Delta l - mg = a \left(m + \frac{\Theta}{R^2}\right).$$

Considering equation (4):

$$mg + D\Delta l - mg = D\Delta l = a \left(m + \frac{\Theta}{R^2}\right).$$

In this equation a is the acceleration of the small body. This can be expressed with the displacement of the small body $\Delta h = -\Delta l$ and finding the common denominator the following is gained:

$$-D\Delta h = a \cdot \frac{mR^2 + \Theta}{R^2}$$

from this the acceleration of the small body is:

$$a = -\frac{DR^2}{mR^2 + \Theta} \cdot \Delta h,$$

so the acceleration of the small body is proportional to the displacement and oppositely directed, which means that the system undergoes simple harmonic motion, applying Newton's second law:

$$\sum F = ma = -\frac{mDR^2}{mR^2 + \Theta} \cdot \Delta h.$$

The spring constant which may characterize this motion is:

$$D^* = \frac{mDR^2}{mR^2 + \Theta}$$

thus the period of the linear oscillation of the small body and the rotational oscillation of the disc is:

$$T = 2\pi \sqrt{\frac{m}{D^*}} = 2\pi \sqrt{\frac{mR^2 + \Theta}{DR^2}} = 2\pi \sqrt{\frac{m + \Theta/R^2}{D}}.$$

The absolute value of the acceleration of the resulted oscillatory motion cannot exceed the acceleration due to gravity g, otherwise the thread will sometimes get loose and the small body at its end will start 'jumping'. The maximum value of the amplitude, according to the inequality $a \leq g$, is:

$$A = \Delta l_{max} \leq \frac{mR^2 + \Theta}{DR^2} \cdot g.$$

Solution of Problem 127. The motion of the disc is a planar motion since the springs and the threads are on both sides of the disc symmetrically, meaning there is no net torque exerted on the disc which would turn the disc out of its plane.

The motion of the disc until it reaches the lowest point can be split into two main characteristic parts: while the threads are tight, and after the threads get loose. The first part lasts until the disc reaches its greatest speed, as well as its greatest angular speed. After this the speed of the centre of mass decreases, whilst the angular speed of the rotation remains constant, thus the threads winds down from the axle at an increasing rate —supposing that they are long enough. (If the threads are completely flexible they are not able to exert a 'pushing force' on the disc.)

Let us examine the first part of the motion. Applying Newton's second law for the translational motion of the centre of mass (because the two springs pull)

$$mg - K - 2D\Delta l = ma,$$

where K is the tension exerted by the threads, Δl is the extension of the spring, as well as the displacement of the centre of mass of the disc, and a is the acceleration of the centre of mass of the disc.

According to Newton's second law for the rotational motion of the disc:

$$Kr = \Theta \cdot \beta = \Theta \cdot \frac{a}{r}.$$

(β is the angular acceleration of the disc.) Substituting K from this equation into the first one, the acceleration becomes:

$$a = \frac{mg - 2D\Delta l}{m + \Theta/r^2}.$$

The threads get loose when the speed is the greatest. This happens when the spring force and the gravitational force are equal.

$$2D\Delta l_0 = mg,$$

from this the displacement of the disc in the first part of the motion is: $\Delta l_0 = mg/(2D)$.

Let us write the value of the acceleration as a function of the displacement measured from the equilibrium position. The instantaneous extension of the spring is $\Delta l = \Delta l_0 + y$, where y is the displacement. Using this the force is:

$$ma = m\frac{mg - 2D(\Delta l_0 + y)}{m + \Theta/r^2} = m\frac{mg - 2D\frac{mg}{2D} - 2Dy}{m + \Theta/r^2} = -\frac{2Dm}{m + \Theta/r^2} \cdot y = -D^* y.$$

It can be seen that this part of the motion is the first quarter of a simple harmonic motion the equivalent spring constant of which is: $D^* = 2Dm/[m + \Theta/r^2]$. The time of this motion is:

$$t_1 = \frac{T_1}{4} = \frac{\pi}{2}\sqrt{\frac{m}{D^*}}$$

Substituting the value of D^* the time is:

$$t_1 = \frac{\pi}{2}\sqrt{\frac{m}{2Dm/[m + \Theta/r^2]}} = \frac{\pi}{2}\sqrt{\frac{m + \Theta/r^2}{2D}}.$$

The next part of the motion is again a simple harmonic motion, in which the springs, and not the threads, exert forces. From the equilibrium position to the lowest position again one-quarter of the period elapses, and now the equivalent spring constant can be calculated from the spring constant of the springs, which is $2D$. At the lowest position the centre of the mass of the disc is in equilibrium, as well as rotating at the maximum angular speed. The time at this part of the motion is:

$$t_2 = \frac{\pi}{2}\sqrt{\frac{m}{2D}}.$$

Thus, the total time until the disc reaches the lowest position is:

$$t = t_1 + t_2 = \frac{\pi}{2}\sqrt{\frac{m + \Theta/r^2}{2D}} + \frac{\pi}{2}\sqrt{\frac{m}{2D}}.$$

Using the data of the problem: $t = 4.71\,\text{s} + 1.28\,\text{s} = 5.99 \approx 6\,\text{s}$.

The depth of the equilibrium position is $\Delta l_0 = mg/2D = 6.67\,\text{m}$, and the length of the second part of the motion can be calculated from the maximum speed for which

$$v_{\text{max}} = A_1\frac{2\pi}{T_1} = A_2\frac{2\pi}{T_2},$$

where $A_1 = \Delta l_0$, and A_2 is the asked further descent. From this

$$A_2 = A_1\frac{T_2}{T_1} = \frac{mg}{2D}\frac{T_2}{T_1} = \frac{mg}{2D}\sqrt{\frac{mr^2}{mr^2 + \Theta}} = 1.81\,\text{m}.$$

Thus the greatest descent of the centre of mass of the disc is $6.67\,\text{m} + 1.81\,\text{m} = 8.48\,\text{m}$.

Solution of Problem 128. When the body of mass m is placed on the unstretched spring (Figure 1), it assumes a new equilibrium position (Figure 2). The initial compression Δl_0 can be found by using Newton's second law:

$$k\Delta l_0 - mg = 0,$$

from which the initial compression is

$$\Delta l_0 = \frac{mg}{k} = \frac{0.1 \text{ kg} \cdot 10 \frac{\text{m}}{\text{s}^2}}{20 \frac{\text{N}}{\text{m}}} = 0.05 \text{ m}.$$

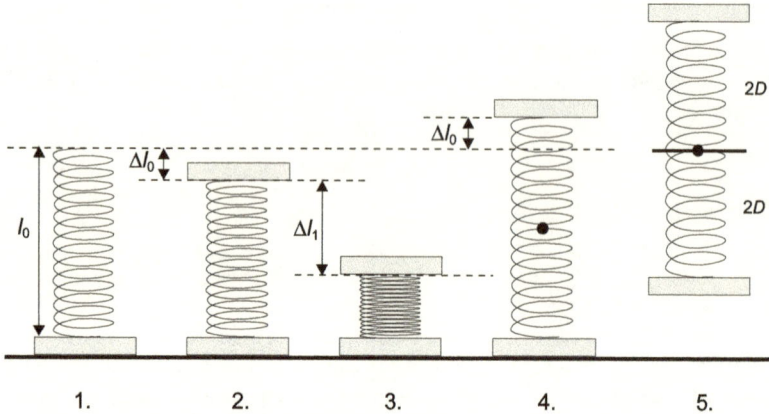

When the spring is compressed by an additional Δl_1 (Figure 3) and then released, the upper body starts to rise with a certain acceleration, passes through the equilibrium position and stretches the spring more. When the elongation of the spring reaches the absolute value of the initial compression Δl_0 (Figure 4), it exerts the same force as the weight of the body placed on it at both ends, so the resultant force acting on the lower body is exactly zero (the vector sum of spring force and gravitational force). The body lying on the ground starts to rise at this moment. (The lower body certainly leaves the ground because the maximum compression of the spring is greater than the compression until the equilibrium position.) At this moment, the length of the spring is $l_0 + \Delta l_0$.

From this moment on, the system moves freely. The centre of mass undergoes vertical projection, the bodies attached to the ends of the spring undergo simple harmonic motion relative to the centre of mass. These two oscillations that are opposite to each other correspond to the oscillating motion of a body of mass m connected to a spring of length $l_0/2$ and spring constant $2k$. (In the freely falling coordinate system the centre of mass of the system of bodies moves uniformly or remains at rest, that is, it can be 'substituted by a wall of infinite mass' to which the two half-springs are fixed. The spring constant of the half-spring is twice as much as the spring constant of the original spring.)

In order to determine the amplitude of the oscillation produced (which determines the maximum distance between the two bodies), we require the relative velocity of the oscillating bodies relative to the centre of mass. For this reason, first we determine the 'absolute velocity' of the upper body, that is, its velocity relative to the ground at the moment when the lower body leaves the ground.

In phase 4 shown in the figure, for the upper body the law of conservation of energy holds because only conservative forces act. (The gravitational potential energy cancels out in the calculation because the gravitational force only shifts the equilibrium position of the oscillation. So as long as the lower body is on the ground, the motion can be described as if an oscillation of amplitude $\Delta l_1 = 0.15$ m would happen on a horizontal spring of length $l_0 - \Delta l_0 = 0.25$ m and spring constant $k = 20$ N/m.)

The instantaneous displacement of the oscillation at the moment in concern is $y = 2\Delta l_0$, that is, $y = \dfrac{2mg}{k}$. The energy of the oscillation (the total energy of the oscillating system) is equal to the maximum elastic energy at every moment:

$$\frac{1}{2}ky^2 + \frac{1}{2}mv^2 = \frac{1}{2}kA^2,$$

that is,

$$k\frac{4m^2g^2}{k^2} + mv^2 = kA^2,$$

After simplifying and reorganising, the following value is acquired for velocity:

$$v = \sqrt{\frac{kA^2}{m} - \frac{4mg^2}{k}} = \sqrt{\frac{20\,\frac{\text{N}}{\text{m}} \cdot 0.15^2\,\text{m}^2}{0.1\,\text{kg}} - \frac{4 \cdot 0.1\,\text{kg} \cdot 100\,\frac{\text{m}^2}{\text{s}^2}}{20\,\frac{\text{N}}{\text{m}}}} = \sqrt{2.5}\,\frac{\text{m}}{\text{s}} = 1.58\,\frac{\text{m}}{\text{s}}.$$

If we make use of the already calculated partial data and set up the conservation of energy without dimensions, we acquire the following simple equation:

$$\frac{1}{2}20 \cdot (0.1)^2 + \frac{1}{2}0.1 \cdot v^2 = \frac{1}{2}20 \cdot (0.15)^2, \quad \rightarrow \quad v^2 = 2.5\,\frac{\text{m}^2}{\text{s}^2} \quad \rightarrow \quad v = 1.58\,\frac{\text{m}}{\text{s}}.$$

When the upper body reaches this velocity, the lower body leaves the ground at initial velocity $v_0 = 0$. The velocity of the centre of mass is half of the velocity of the upper body then: $v_{\text{cm}} = v/2 = 0.79$ m/s. The length of the spring is $l_0 + \Delta l_0 = 0.35$ m then. The bodies continue to move away from each other. From this time onward, the motion of the two bodies is determined by the vertical projection describing the motion of the centre of mass and the symmetric oscillation about the centre of mass. Amplitude A' of the new, free oscillation is determined from the law of conservation of energy again.

The displacement of the oscillating bodies in phase 4 is

$$y' = \frac{\Delta l_0}{2} = \frac{mg}{2k} = \frac{0.1\,\text{kg} \cdot 10\,\frac{\text{m}}{\text{s}^2}}{2 \cdot 20\,\frac{\text{N}}{\text{m}}} = 0.025\ \text{m}.$$

The magnitude of their original velocity relative to the centre of mass is

$$v_{\text{rel}} = v - v_{\text{cm}} = v - \frac{v}{2} = \frac{v}{2} = \frac{1.58}{2}\,\frac{\text{m}}{\text{s}} = 0.79\,\frac{\text{m}}{\text{s}}.$$

The conservation of energy for one of the bodies is

$$E_{\text{kin}} + E_{\text{el}} = E_{\text{total}} = \frac{1}{2}kA'^2,$$

in our case

$$\frac{1}{2}mv_{\text{rel}}^2 + \frac{1}{2}2ky'^2 = \frac{1}{2}2kA'^2.$$

Substituting the relative velocity:

$$m\left(\frac{v}{2}\right)^2 + 2k\left(\frac{mg}{2k}\right)^2 = 2kA'^2.$$

Parametrically, after dividing by $2D$:

$$\frac{m}{8k}\left[\frac{k}{m}(\Delta l_1)^2 - 4\frac{mg^2}{k}\right] + \frac{m^2g^2}{4k^2} = A'^2.$$

Rearranging:

$$A' = \sqrt{\frac{(\Delta l_1)^2}{8} - \frac{m^2g^2}{4k^2}} = \sqrt{\frac{0.15^2 \text{ m}^2}{8} - \frac{0.01 \text{ kg}^2 \cdot 100 \frac{\text{m}^2}{\text{s}^4}}{4 \cdot 400 \frac{\text{N}^2}{\text{m}^2}}} = 4.67 \text{ cm}.$$

[With the already calculated partial data our equation is

$$\frac{1}{2} \cdot 0.1 \cdot (0.79)^2 \text{ m}^2 + \frac{1}{2}40 \cdot (0.025)^2 = \frac{1}{2}40A'^2,$$

from which

$$A' = \sqrt{0.002185} = 0.0467 \text{ m} = 4.67 \text{ cm}.]$$

With this, the requested maximum distance is

$$l_{\max} = l_0 + 2A' = 30 \text{ cm} + 2 \cdot 4.67 \text{ cm} = 39.35 \text{ cm}.$$

We should check whether or not the lower body reaches the ground before the distance between the two bodies reaches the maximum.

When the distance between the two bodies is maximum, their instantaneous velocities relative to the ground are the same as the instantaneous velocity of the centre of mass. So if the time elapsed from leaving the ground to the maximum elongation of the spring is less than the rising time of the centre of mass, (that is, the centre of mass is still rising when the distance between the two bodies is maximum) the lower body does not reach the ground 'too soon'.

The rising time of the centre of mass is

$$t_{\text{cm}} = \frac{v_{\text{cm}}}{g} = \frac{0.79}{10} \text{ s} = 0.079 \text{ s}.$$

The oscillating bodies move for less than one quarter of the period between phases 4 and 5. The quarter of the period is

$$T = \frac{1}{4} \cdot 2\pi\sqrt{\frac{m}{2k}} = \frac{\pi}{2}\sqrt{\frac{0.1 \text{ kg}}{40 \text{ N/m}}} = 0.0785 \text{ s},$$

so the centre of mass of the system is still moving upward when the distance between the bodies reaches the maximum.

Remark: Those who wanted to determine the velocity of the upper body, by taking the gravitational potential energy into consideration, reached the correct solution in the following way: by setting up the work–kinetic energy theorem between the lowest (that is, stationary) position and position 4:

$$\Sigma W = \Delta E_{\text{kin}}.$$

The left side of the equation contains the sum of the works done by the spring and by the gravitational force. The work done by the spring is positive until it becomes loose and then it is negative, the work done by the gravitational force is negative throughout the process.

$$\frac{1}{2}k(\Delta l_0 + \Delta l_1)^2 - \frac{1}{2}k(\Delta l_0)^2 - mg(\Delta l_1 + 2\Delta l_0) = \frac{1}{2}mv^2 - 0.$$

After squaring and multiplying by 2:

$$k(\Delta l_0)^2 + 2k\Delta l_0 \Delta l_1 + k(\Delta l_1)^2 - k(\Delta l_0)^2 - 2mg\Delta l_1 - 4mg\Delta l_0 = mv^2.$$

After combining the like terms and substituting $\Delta l_0 = mg/k$:

$$2k\frac{mg}{k}\Delta l_1 + k(\Delta l_1)^2 - 2mg\Delta l_1 - 4mg\frac{mg}{k} = mv^2.$$

The sum of the first and third terms is 0, dividing by m and taking the square root, the requested velocity is

$$v = \sqrt{\frac{k}{m}(\Delta l_1)^2 - 4\frac{mg^2}{k}} = \sqrt{\frac{k}{m}[(\Delta l_1)^2 - 4(\Delta l_0)^2]} =$$

$$= \sqrt{\frac{20}{0.1} \cdot (0.15^2 - 4 \cdot 0.05^2)} \; \frac{\text{m}^2}{\text{s}^2} = \sqrt{2.5} \; \frac{\text{m}}{\text{s}} = 1.58 \; \frac{\text{m}}{\text{s}},$$

the same as the previous result.

Solution of Problem 129. As the hung body causes an elongation of Δl of the spring in equilibrium:

$$m \cdot g = D \cdot \Delta l. \tag{1}$$

While moving, the body undergoes forced oscillation. The frequency of the external shocks is equal to the natural frequency of the elastic system because of the 'high amplitude' (resonance). The shocks follow each other with a time interval

$$T_g = \frac{x}{v}$$

due to the small shocks received at the fittings, when the first wheels of the truck arrive at the fittings.

In the case of resonance the natural period of the system is equal to the period of the external shocks:

$$T_g = 2\pi\sqrt{\frac{m}{D}} = \frac{x}{v}, \tag{2}$$

Substituting the expression $m/D = \Delta l/g$ acquired from (1)

$$2\pi\sqrt{\frac{\Delta l}{g}} = \frac{x}{v},$$

from which the speed of the truck can be expressed:

$$v = \frac{x}{2\pi}\sqrt{\frac{g}{\Delta l}} = \frac{20 \text{ m}}{2\pi}\cdot\sqrt{\frac{9.81 \text{ m/s}^2}{0.1 \text{ m}}} = 31.53\,\frac{\text{m}}{\text{s}} = 113.5\,\frac{\text{km}}{\text{h}}.$$

Solution of Problem 130. The block needs to cover a distance of $x_1 = s - L = 0.92$ m for the spring attached to it to reach the wall. In doing so, its speed is reduced from v_0 to

$$v_1 = \sqrt{v_0^2 - \mu g(s-L)} = \sqrt{4\frac{\text{m}^2}{\text{s}^2} - 0.2\cdot10\frac{\text{m}}{\text{s}^2}\cdot0.92\text{ m}} = 0.566\,\frac{\text{m}}{\text{s}},$$

since the distance is covered with a uniform acceleration of $a = \mu g$ directed against its velocity. The time taken to cover this distance is

$$t_1 = \frac{s - L}{\bar{v}} = \frac{2(s-L)}{v_0 + v_1} = 0.717\,\text{s},$$

and the average speed during this time interval is $\bar{v} = (v_0 + v_1)/2 = (2 \text{ m/s} + 0.566 \text{ m/s})/2 = 1.283 \text{ m/s}$.

The next task is to determine the further distance x_2 covered by the block from the time instant of the spring touching the wall to the time instant of its stopping the first time (i.e. the maximum compression of the spring). The work-energy theorem can be applied: (owing to friction, mechanical energy is not conserved.)

$$-\mu mgx_2 - \frac{1}{2}Dx_2^2 = 0 - \frac{1}{2}mv_1^2,$$

which leads to a quadratic equation for x_2:

$$Dx_2^2 + 2\mu mgx_2 - mv_1^2 = 0.$$

The solution of the equation is

$$x_2 = \frac{-2\mu mg \pm \sqrt{4\mu^2m^2g^2 + 4mv_1^2 D}}{2D} = \frac{\mu mg}{D}\left(\sqrt{1 + \frac{Dv_1^2}{m\mu^2g^2}} - 1\right).$$

Numerically:

$$x_2 = \frac{0.2\cdot10 \text{ m s}^{-2}}{100 \text{ N/m}}\left(\sqrt{1 + \frac{100\cdot0.566^2}{1\cdot0.04\cdot100}} - 1\right) = 0.04\,\text{m}.$$

This distance was needed in order to calculate the time taken to cover it. The total time taken is made up of three parts: t_1 is the time until the spring reaches the wall, t_2 is the time taken by the block to stop the first time, and t_3 is the time interval from the start of the rebound to the second (final) stop of the block. t_2 and t_3 are a little more complicated to determine.

Consider each of these stages of the motion as part of an appropriate simple harmonic motion, a type of motion that is easy to discuss. That can be done — in each of the two stages separately — since the kinetic friction force represents a constant force acting on the block in addition to the harmonic force (in a direction collinear with it), and the resultant of two such forces is also a harmonic force.

The stage of the motion corresponding to the time interval t_2 could arise if the spring were attached to the wall and stretched to the position where the forces exerted by the spring and friction on the block are in equilibrium. Then the object would be (suddenly) given a speed, such that when approaching the wall to a distance of $s - L$ (that is, the distance where the spring reaches the wall during the actual motion), its speed should be exactly v_1. From that point onwards, the motion is identical to the one investigated by the problem. This stage of the motion is thus described as a part of simple harmonic oscillation. Thus the displacement x_2 belongs to a simple harmonic oscillation of angular frequency

$$\omega = \sqrt{\frac{D}{m}} = \sqrt{\frac{100\,\text{N/m}}{1\,\text{kg}}} = 10\,\text{s}^{-1},$$

and amplitude

$$A = x_0 + x_1,$$

where x_0 is the extension of the spring stretched to the position where friction and tension forces are in equilibrium. Therefore

$$x_0 = \frac{\mu m g}{D} = \frac{0.2 \cdot 1\,\text{kg} \cdot 10\,\text{m\,s}^{-2}}{100\,\text{N/m}} = 0.02\,\text{m}.$$

If the block was started from this equilibrium position, a quarter of the oscillation period would elapse until it stops, that is,

$$t^* = \frac{T}{4} = \frac{\pi}{2}\sqrt{\frac{m}{D}} = \frac{\pi}{2}\sqrt{\frac{1\,\text{kg}}{100\,\text{N/m}}} = \frac{\pi}{20} = 0.157\,\text{s}.$$

Therefore the task is to determine the time t it takes to attain the displacement x_0, and subtract it from $T/4$ to get the time t_2. The time t is obtained from the simple relationship

$$x_0 = A\sin\omega t.$$

Hence

$$t = \frac{1}{\omega}\arcsin\frac{x_0}{A} = \sqrt{\frac{m}{D}}\arcsin\frac{x_0}{x_0 + x_1} = \sqrt{\frac{1\,\text{kg}}{100\,\text{N\,m}^{-1}}}\arcsin\frac{0.02}{0.06} = 0.034\,\text{s},$$

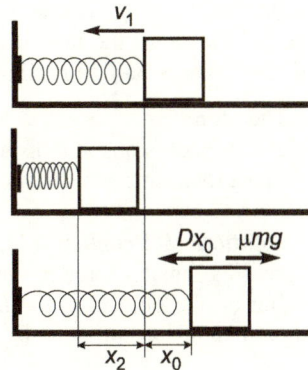

and thus the time taken to stop first is

$$t_2 = \frac{T}{4} - t = 0.157\,\text{s} - 0.034\,\text{s} = 0.123\,\text{s}$$

The distance covered by the object after rebounding can be determined from the work-energy theorem again. From the first stopping to the second (final) stopping,

$$\frac{1}{2}Dx_3^2 - \mu mg x_3 = 0.$$

Hence

$$x_3 = \frac{2\mu mg}{D} = \frac{2 \cdot 0.2 \cdot 10\,\text{N}}{100\,\text{N/m}} = 0.04\,\text{m},$$

that is, the speed of the object decreases to zero at the very same position where it started the second stage of its motion. At that point the spring was unstretched, thus it must be unstretched again. Therefore, the object will stop at a distance of $L = 0.08\,\text{m} = 8\,\text{cm}$ from the wall, that is, at a distance equal to the relaxed length of the spring.

The time of this last stage of the motion is easily obtained by considering that at the beginning of this time interval the force acting on the block was a maximum, and it is also a maximum just before the final stop, but directed oppositely. (The maximum force was exerted by kinetic friction acting in addition to the spring force decreasing to zero.) Thus the object covered exactly half an oscillation period. The time of half a period is

$$t_3 = \frac{T}{2} = \frac{1}{2} \cdot 2\pi\sqrt{\frac{m}{D}} = \frac{\pi}{10}\,\text{s} = 0.314\,\text{s}.$$

Remark: There is another way to see that the third stage of the motion is half an oscillation period. Note that the equilibrium position of the oscillation is now shifted to the left by x_0, that is, the amplitude of the new stage of the oscillation is $A_1 = x_1 - x_0 = 0.02\,\text{m}$. Since x_3 is exactly the double of this, that is, $x_3 = 0.04\,\text{m} = 2 \cdot 0.02\,\text{m} = 2A_1$, the third stage of the motion is, indeed, a simple harmonic motion covering a distance of $2A_1$, that is half an oscillation.

Therefore,
a) the block stops at a distance of $d = 0.08\,\text{m} = 8\,\text{cm}$ from the wall, and
b) the total time of its motion is $t_t = t_1 + t_2 + t_3 = 0.717\,\text{s} + 0.123\,\text{s} + 0.314\,\text{s} = 1.154\,\text{s}$.

Solution of Problem 131. The object will start to lift off the ground when the increasing tension force in the spring becomes equal to the constant gravitational force acting on the object: $mg = D\Delta L_1 = Dv_0 t_1$, where $v_0 = 0.5\,\text{m/s}$ is the speed of the upper end of the spring and t_1 is the time elapsed until the object starts to rise. Hence,

$$t_1 = \frac{mg}{Dv_0} = \frac{20\,\text{N}}{80\,\frac{\text{N}}{\text{m}} \cdot 0.5\,\frac{\text{m}}{\text{s}}} = 0.5\,\text{s}.$$

The extension of the spring at that time instant is

$$\Delta L_1 = \frac{mg}{D} = \frac{20\,\text{N}}{80\frac{\text{N}}{\text{m}}} = 0.25\,\text{m}.$$

The distance of the upper end of the spring above ground as a function of time is

$$h = L_0 + v_0 t = 0.6\,\text{m} + 0.5\,\frac{\text{m}}{\text{s}} \cdot t.$$

To be able to see what happens next, let us temporarily attach the reference frame to the uniformly moving upper end of the spring. From that point of view, the object is seen to recede at a uniform speed of $-v_0$ until equilibrium is reached and then to perform a simple harmonic oscillation with a maximum speed of $-v_0$. Therefore, the situation is analogous to that of an object hanging in equilibrium on a spring stretched by $\Delta L_1 = mg/D$ and suddenly given a downward speed of v_0 to make it oscillate harmonically.

Since the maximum speed and angular frequency of the oscillation are determined by the given information, the amplitude can be calculated. The angular frequency is

$$\omega = \sqrt{D/m} = \sqrt{80\,\text{N}\,\text{m}^{-1}/2\,\text{kg}} = \sqrt{40}\,\text{s}^{-1} \approx 6.32\,\text{s}^{-1}.$$

Given the maximum speed and the angular fequency, the amplitude is obtained from the equation

$$v_0 = v_{\text{max}} = A\omega = A\sqrt{D/m}$$

as follows:

$$A = v_0\sqrt{\frac{m}{D}} = 0.5\,\frac{\text{m}}{\text{s}}\sqrt{\frac{2\,\text{kg}}{80\,\text{N/m}}} = 7.91 \cdot 10^{-2}\,\text{m}.$$

The length of the spring at the time instant when the object starts to rise is

$$L_0 + \Delta L_1 = L_0 + \frac{mg}{D} = 0.6\,\text{m} + \frac{20}{80}\,\text{m} = 0.85\,\text{m}.$$

The period is

$$T = 2\pi\sqrt{\frac{m}{D}} = \frac{2\pi}{\omega} = \frac{2\pi}{\sqrt{40}}\,\text{s} \approx 1\,\text{s}.$$

After the time instant t_1 when the oscillation starts, the instantaneous height y of the object, the length L of the spring, the extension ΔL of the spring and the speed v of the object are given by the functions (1), (2), (3) and (4), respectively:

$$y = v_0(t - t_1) - v_0\sqrt{\frac{m}{D}} \cdot \sin\left[\sqrt{\frac{D}{m}}(t - t_1)\right].$$

With the factor v_0 taken out:

$$y = v_0\left\{t - t_1 - \sqrt{\frac{m}{D}} \cdot \sin\left[\sqrt{\frac{D}{m}}(t - t_1)\right]\right\}. \tag{1}$$

$$L = h - y = L_0 + v_0 t - v_0(t - t_1) + v_0\sqrt{\frac{m}{D}} \cdot \sin\left[\sqrt{\frac{D}{m}}(t - t_1)\right].$$

With the factor v_0 taken out:

$$L = L_0 + v_0 \left\{ t_1 + \sqrt{\tfrac{m}{D}} \cdot \sin \left[\sqrt{\tfrac{D}{m}} (t - t_1) \right] \right\}. \tag{2}$$

$$\Delta L = L - L_0 = v_0 t - v_0 (t - t_1) + v_0 \sqrt{\tfrac{m}{D}} \cdot \sin \left[\sqrt{\tfrac{D}{m}} (t - t_1) \right].$$

With the factor v_0 taken out:

$$\Delta L = v_0 \left\{ t_1 + \sqrt{\tfrac{m}{D}} \cdot \sin \left[\sqrt{\tfrac{D}{m}} (t - t_1) \right] \right\}. \tag{3}$$

$$v = v_0 - A\omega \cdot \cos[\omega(t - t_1)] = v_0 - v_0 \cdot \cos \left[\sqrt{\tfrac{D}{m}} (t - t_1) \right].$$

With the factor v_0 taken out:

$$v = v_0 \left\{ 1 - \cos \left[\sqrt{\tfrac{D}{m}} (t - t_1) \right] \right\}. \tag{4}$$

Numerically:

$$y = 0.625 \, \text{m} - 0.079 \, \text{m} \cdot \sin \left[6.32 \, \text{s}^{-1} (t - 0.5 \, \text{s}) \right], \tag{1'}$$

$$L = 0.85 \, \text{m} + 0.079 \, \text{m} \cdot \sin \left[6.32 \, \text{s}^{-1} (t - 0.5 \, \text{s}) \right], \tag{2'}$$

$$\Delta L = 0.25 \, \text{m} + 0.079 \, \text{m} \cdot \sin \left[6.32 \, \text{s}^{-1} (t - 0.5 \, \text{s}) \right], \tag{3'}$$

$$v = 0.5 \, \tfrac{\text{m}}{\text{s}} - 0.5 \, \tfrac{\text{m}}{\text{s}} \cdot \cos \left[6.32 \, \text{s}^{-1} (t - 0.5 \, \text{s}) \right]. \tag{4'}$$

a) The answer is obtained from the function y by substituting $t = 1.75 \, \text{s}$ in (1) or (1'). 1.75 s after the upper end of the spring starts to move, the height of the object will be

$$y = 0.625 \, \text{m} - 0.079 \, \text{m} \cdot \sin(6.32 \, \text{s}^{-1} \cdot 1.25 \, \text{s}) = 0.546 \, \text{m}.$$

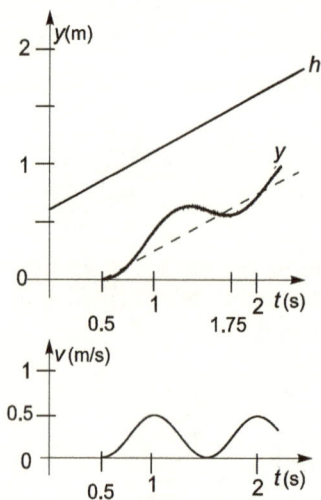

b) The work done by the lifting force is expressed from the work-energy theorem applied to the object lifted:

$$W + W_{\text{grav}} + W_{\text{spring}} = \Delta E_{\text{kin}},$$

that is,

$$W - mg \cdot y - \tfrac{1}{2} D (\Delta L)^2 = \tfrac{1}{2} mv^2.$$

Hence

$$W = \tfrac{1}{2} mv^2 + mg \cdot y + \tfrac{1}{2} D (\Delta L)^2,$$

where the speed of the object is calculated from (4'):

$$v = 0.5 \, \tfrac{\text{m}}{\text{s}} - 0.5 \, \tfrac{\text{m}}{\text{s}} \cdot \cos(6.32 \, \text{s}^{-1} 1.25 \, \text{s}) = 0.53 \, \text{m/s},$$

and the extension of the spring is obtained from (3'):

$$\Delta L = 0.25 \, \text{m} + 0.079 \, \text{m} \cdot \sin(6.32 \, \text{s}^{-1} \cdot 1.25 \, \text{s}) = 0.329 \, \text{m}.$$

With these data, the work done is

$$W = \tfrac{1}{2} \cdot 2 \, \text{kg} \cdot 0.53^2 \, \tfrac{\text{m}^2}{\text{s}^2} + 20 \, \text{N} \cdot 0.546 \, \text{m} + \tfrac{1}{2} \cdot 80 \, \tfrac{\text{N}}{\text{m}} \cdot 0.329^2 \, \text{m}^2 = 15.53 \, \text{J}.$$

c) The instantaneous power at the time instant investigated is $P = F_{\text{spring}}v_0$, where F_{spring} is the force exerted by the hand on the upper end of the spring (the equal and opposite reaction force to the instantaneous force exerted by the spring on the hand). The magnitude of that force is $F_{\text{spring}} = D\Delta L$, where $\Delta L_1 = v_0 t_1$ at the time instant in question. Thus

$$P = Dv_0^2 t_1 = 80\,\frac{\text{N}}{\text{m}} \cdot 0.25\,\frac{\text{m}^2}{\text{s}^2} \cdot 0.5\,\text{s} = 10\,\text{W}.$$

The power versus time function can be investigated on two separate intervals. During the interval t_1 while the object is at rest, $P = F_{\text{spring}}v_0 = D\Delta Lv_0$, where $\Delta L = v_0 t$. Hence

$$P = Dv_0^2 \cdot t = 20\,\text{W}\,\text{s}^{-1} \cdot t$$

in the time interval $0 \le t \le t_1 = 0.5\,\text{s}$.

After the time instant t_1, the power is $P = D\Delta L \cdot v_0$, where ΔL is obtained from (3). Parametrically:

$$P = Dv_0^2 \left\{ t_1 + \sqrt{\frac{m}{D}}\sin\left[\sqrt{\frac{D}{m}}(t - t_1)\right] \right\},$$

and numerically:

$$P = 80\,\frac{\text{N}}{\text{m}} \cdot 0.25\,\frac{\text{m}^2}{\text{s}^2}\left\{ 0.5\,\text{s} + \sqrt{\frac{2\,\text{kg}}{80\,\text{N/m}}} \cdot \sin\left[6.32\,\text{s}^{-1}(t - 0.5\,\text{s})\right] \right\} =$$

$$= 10\,\text{W} + \sqrt{10}\,\text{W} \cdot \sin\left[6.32\,\text{s}^{-1}(t - 0.5\,\text{s})\right].$$

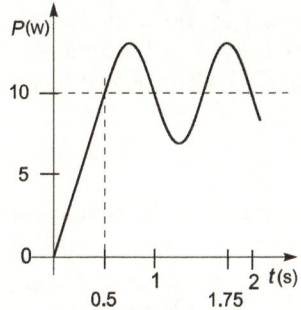

Solution of Problem 132. After releasing, the body on the spring performs simple harmonic motion, the amplitude of which is the difference between its initial and equilibrium position. In the equilibrium position the sum of the forces acting on the body is zero, so:

$$mg = D\Delta l.$$

It means that the amplitude of the oscillation is:

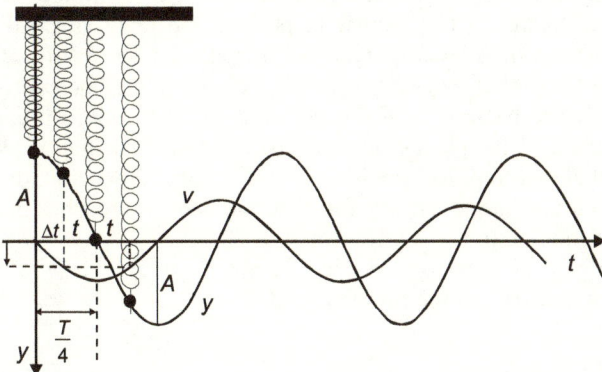

$$A = \Delta l = \frac{mg}{D}.$$

The period and the angular frequency of the harmonic motion are:

$$T = 2\pi \sqrt{\frac{m}{D}},$$

and

$$\omega = \sqrt{\frac{D}{m}}.$$

Let us direct the y axis vertically downwards. The velocity, as a function of time elapsed from the release of the body, is a sine function:

$$v = A\omega \cdot \sin\omega t = \frac{mg}{D} \cdot \sqrt{\frac{D}{m}} \cdot \sin\sqrt{\frac{D}{m}} \cdot t = g\sqrt{\frac{m}{D}} \sin\sqrt{\frac{D}{m}} \cdot t.$$

So the time needed to achieve the speed $v=0.5$ m/s is:

$$t = \frac{1}{\omega}\arcsin\frac{v}{A\omega} = \sqrt{\frac{m}{D}}\arcsin\left(\frac{v}{mg}D\sqrt{\frac{m}{D}}\right) = \sqrt{\frac{m}{D}}\arcsin\left(\frac{v}{g}\sqrt{\frac{D}{m}}\right).$$

Thus, from its release, the body reaches the speed $v = 0{,}5$ m/s after

$$t = \sqrt{\frac{m}{D}}\arcsin\left(\frac{v}{g}\sqrt{\frac{D}{m}}\right) = \sqrt{\frac{1.25 \text{ kg}}{250 \text{ Nm}^{-1}}} \cdot \arcsin\left(\frac{0.5 \text{ ms}^{-1}}{9.81 \text{ ms}^{-2}}\sqrt{\frac{250 \text{ Nm}^{-1}}{1.25 \text{ kg}}}\right) =$$

$$= 0.05692 \text{ s} \approx 57 \text{ ms}$$

for the first time.

Solution of Problem 133. a) Let us investigate the motion of the body in the reference frame attached to point B, in which the end B of the rubber thread is at rest, and the body starts moving at the speed $v_0 = 1$ m/s to the left (according to the convention of the figure). (It is similar to pushing the body attached to an initially unstretched spring.) Our reference frame is inertial, and the net force acting on the body (exerted by the rubber thread) is harmonic, therefore the body performs harmonic oscillation until it gets back to its initial position. (At that moment, the rubber thread becomes unstretched.) This process is a half period of the oscillation. When the body returns to its initial position, its speed is v_0 to the right. After this, the rubber thread becomes loose and does not exert any force, so the body approaches the point B with a linear, uniform motion.

a) At the extreme position of the oscillation the initial kinetic energy is wholly converted to elastic energy of the rubber thread:

$$\frac{1}{2}mv_0^2 = \frac{1}{2}DA^2,$$

so the amplitude of the oscillation is

$$A = \sqrt{\frac{mv_0^2}{D}} = \sqrt{\frac{1 \text{ kg} \cdot 1 \frac{m^2}{s^2}}{100 \frac{N}{m}}} = 0.1 \text{ m}.$$

It means that the longest distance between the points A and B is

$$L_0 + A = 0.5 \text{ m} + 0.1 \text{ m} = 0.6 \text{ m} = 60 \text{ cm}.$$

b) Until the body catches up to point B, it performs a half period of the oscillation, and then—when the rubber thread gets loose—it covers the distance L_0 to the point B at a constant speed v_0, so the unknown time is:

$$t = \frac{T}{2} + \frac{L_0}{v_0} = \pi \sqrt{\frac{m}{D}} + \frac{L_0}{v_0} = \pi \sqrt{\frac{1 \text{ kg}}{100 \frac{N}{m}}} + \frac{0.5 \text{ m}}{1 \frac{m}{s}} = 0.814 \text{ s}.$$

Solution of Problem 134. a) The length of the pipe determines the wavelength of the standing wave in it. Thus the wavelengths are the same in the two cases. From this point of view it is not important whether the pipe is open or closed at the end. The frequencies of the sounds differ because the speed of sound is not the same in air and in helium.

The speed of sound can be obtained from data tables. For example at $0°C$ it is:

$$c_{\text{air}} = 331.8 \text{ m/s}$$

$$c_{He} = 970 \text{ m/s}.$$

The relation between the sound speed and wavelength is $c = \nu\lambda$, which means that the ratio of the two frequencies is:

$$\frac{c_{He}}{c_{\text{air}}} = \frac{\nu_{He}\lambda}{\nu_{\text{air}}\lambda} = \frac{\nu_{He}}{\nu_{\text{air}}} = \frac{970}{331.8} = 2.923.$$

This ratio is approximately $3:1$, so the sound in helium is by a tritave, i.e., by an octave and a fifth higher than the normal a' tone. It is close to the e''' tone, do–do–sol. (More precisely, by half of a half tone, i.e., by $\sqrt[24]{2}$ lower than this: $\sqrt[24]{2} \cdot 2.923 \approx 3.00$. Only a few people would notice this difference.)

The frequency of the sound in helium is $\nu_{He} = 1286 \text{ Hz}$.

b) In the case of the open pipe half of the wavelength of the fundamental mode is equal to the length of the pipe, while in the case of the closed pipe the quarter of the wavelength gives the pipe length. So the length of the pipe depends only on whether or not it is open or closed, and not on the gas we blow into it.

Performing the calculations with air, the lengths of the different pipes are:

$$l_{\text{open}} = \frac{\lambda}{2} = \frac{c_{\text{air}}}{2\nu_{\text{air}}} = \frac{331.8 \text{ m/s}}{2 \cdot 440 \text{ 1/s}} = 0.377 \text{ m} = 37.7 \text{ cm}.$$

$$l_{\text{closed}} = \frac{\lambda}{4} = \frac{c_{\text{air}}}{4\nu_{\text{air}}} = \frac{l_{\text{open}}}{2} = 18.85 \text{ cm}.$$

Solution of Problem 135. The distance between points that are in the same phase is an integral multiple of the wavelength:

$$k\lambda = 5 \text{ m} \tag{4}$$

The distance between the points that are in the opposite phase is an odd multiple of the half-wavelength:

$$(2l+1)\frac{\lambda}{2} = 1.5 \text{ m}, \tag{2}$$

where the values of k and l are

$$k = 1, 2, 3, \ldots \qquad \text{and} \qquad l = 0, 1, 2, \ldots$$

Producing the ratio of the corresponding sides of (1) and (2):

$$\frac{k\lambda}{(2l+1)\frac{\lambda}{2}} = \frac{5}{1.5},$$

from which

$$k = \frac{5}{3}(2l+1). \tag{3}$$

As k is an integer, $2l+1$ should be divisible by 3. The values of l that satisfy this condition are

$$l_1 = 1, \quad l_2 = 4, \quad l_3 = 7, \quad \ldots$$

And the corresponding values of k are

$$k_1 = 5, \quad k_2 = 15, \quad k_3 = 25, \quad \ldots$$

respectively. With these the possible values of the wavelength (e.g. according to (1)) are

$$\lambda_1 = \frac{5}{5} \text{ m} = 1 \text{ m}, \qquad \lambda_2 = \frac{5}{15} \text{ m} = \frac{1}{3} \text{ m}, \qquad \lambda_3 = \frac{5}{25} \text{ m} = \frac{1}{5} \text{ m}, \qquad \ldots$$

so infinitely many wavelengths satisfy this condition.

Remark: The corresponding values of k can be produced in the following way:
In (3) $(2l+1)$ is divisible by 3 only if l is of the form $(3q+1)$, where $q = 0, 1, 2, \ldots$, because then

$$2l+1 = 2(3q+1)+1 = (6q+2)+1 = 6q+3 = 3(2q+1),$$

so based on (3)

$$k = \frac{5}{3}(2l+1) = \frac{5}{3} \cdot 3 \cdot (2q+1) = 5 \cdot (2q+1),$$

and with this the possible wavelengths are

$$\lambda = \frac{5 \text{ m}}{k} = \frac{1}{2q+1} \text{ m}. \tag{4}$$

q	0	1	2	3	...
k	5	15	25	35	...
$\lambda = \dfrac{5}{k}$	1	$\dfrac{1}{3}$	$\dfrac{1}{5}$	$\dfrac{1}{7}$	...

(It can be observed that according to (4), the denominator of λ gives the sequence of odd numbers.)

The snapshot of the waves of the first three wavelengths are

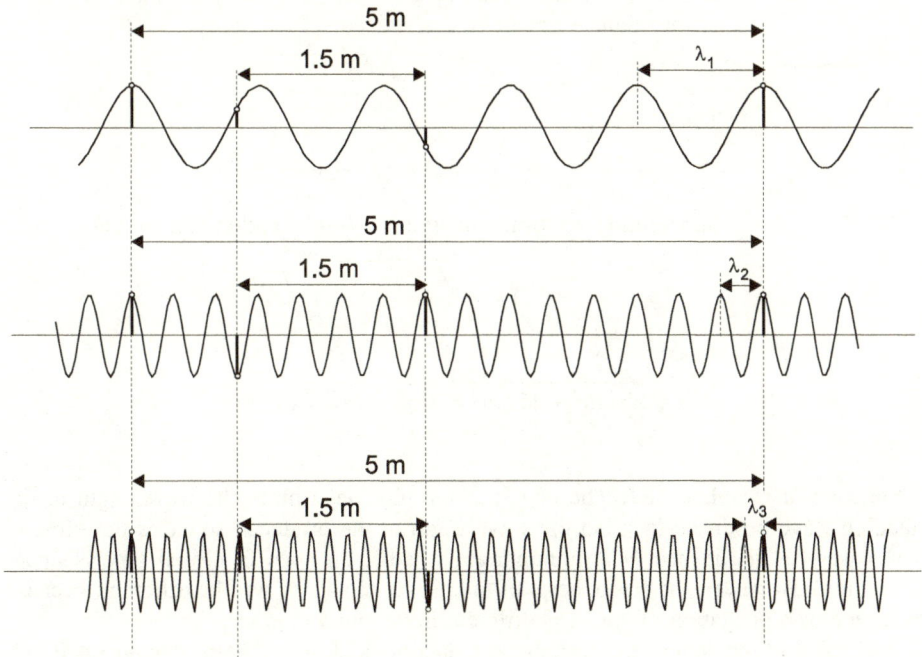

Solution of Problem 136. Let us handle the chandelier as a bob of simple pendulum on a 4 m long cord. The period of such a pendulum is given by:

$$T = 2\pi\sqrt{\frac{l}{g}} = 2\pi\sqrt{\frac{4\,\text{m}}{10\,\text{m/s}^2}} = 3.9738 \approx 4\,\text{s}.$$

Therefore the pendulum makes a quarter oscillation in $1\,\text{s}$, so at the time of the second earthquake shock the cord is vertical and the chandelier moves with a speed of:

$$v = A_1\omega, \tag{1}$$

where A_1 is the amplitude of the first oscillation, which equals the displacement of the ground in the first shock ($x = 5$ cm). The angular frequency of the first oscillation is:

$$\omega = \frac{2\pi}{T} = \sqrt{\frac{g}{l}}.$$

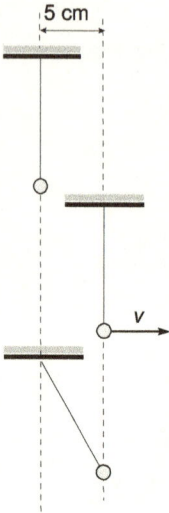

As in the second shock the point of suspension moves suddenly to the left by 5 cm, the final oscillation of the chandelier is defined by the situation in which the displacement of the pendulum is $x = 5$ cm and the chandelier has a speed of v. Using the formula between the displacement and speed of a simple pendulum, the final amplitude of the chandelier can be determined:

$$v = \omega\sqrt{A^2 - x^2}. \tag{2}$$

Thus

$$A = \sqrt{\frac{v^2}{\omega^2} + x^2}$$

Substituting v^2 from equation (1) into equation (2), we get:

$$A = \sqrt{\frac{A_1^2\omega^2}{\omega^2} + x^2} = \sqrt{A_1^2 + x^2},$$

hence:

$$A = \sqrt{25\,\text{cm}^2 + 25\,\text{cm}^2} = \sqrt{50\,\text{cm}^2} = 7.071\,\text{cm}.$$

Solution of Problem 137. The length of the pipe determines the wavelength of the standing wave produced in it, so the wavelength of the produced sound is the same in both cases (in this respect it is unimportant whether an open or closed pipe is under discussion). However, the frequencies of the produced sounds will be different, because the speed of propagation of sound is different in helium and in air.

According to the data of the formula and data booklet, it is $330\,\text{m/s}$ in air (at $0\,°\text{C}$) and $970\,\text{m/s}$ in helium.

(The same data are acquired from relationship

$$c = \sqrt{\frac{c_\text{p}}{c_\text{V}} \cdot \frac{R}{M} T},$$

after substituting the values taken from the formula and data booklet, where c_p and c_V are specific heats of the gas at constant pressure and constant volume, while M is the molar mass of the gas.)

According to relationship $\nu = c/\lambda$, the pipe produces higher frequency sound when the speed of propagation is higher in it. This takes place in the case of helium (i.e. the frequency is higher by the same factor as the speed of propagation in helium relative to air). Therefore the requested ratio and the frequency of the sound made by the pipe filled with helium are

$$\frac{\nu_{\text{helium}}}{\nu_{\text{air}}} = \frac{c_{\text{helium}}}{c_{\text{air}}} = \frac{970\,\text{m/s}}{330\,\text{m/s}} = 2.94,$$

$$\nu_{\text{helium}} = \frac{c_{\text{helium}}}{c_{\text{air}}} \cdot \nu_{\text{air}} = \frac{970\,\text{m/s}}{330\,\text{m/s}} \cdot 440\,\text{Hz} = 1290\,\text{Hz}.$$

Solution of Problem 138. Attaching the lead weight to the spoke of the wheel a physical pendulum is created, the period of which, for small displacements, can be calculated with the formula

$$T = 2\pi\sqrt{\frac{\Theta}{mgs}}$$

where Θ is the rotational inertia calculated for the axis of rotation, m is the total mass, g is the acceleration due to gravity and s is the distance between the centre of mass and the axis of rotation.

Because of the additive, the moment of inertia of the wheel with the lead weight on it is

$$\Theta = \Theta_0 + ml^2,$$

where Θ_0 is the moment of inertia of the wheel without the lead weight. In our case the total mass of the system is $M + m$. Using this, the measured period is:

$$T = 2\pi\sqrt{\frac{\Theta_0 + ml^2}{(M+m)gs}}.$$

Now we have to calculate the distance s, balancing the wheel, its centre of mass is at (the middle of) its axle, the centre of mass divides the distance between the lead weight and the centre of the wheel in the ratio of the masses, but it is closer to the heavier mass, so:

$$s : (l - s) = m : M,$$

From this:

$$s = \frac{m}{M+m} \cdot l.$$

substituting this into the formula of the period:

$$T = 2\pi\sqrt{\frac{\Theta_0 + ml^2}{(M+m)g\frac{ml}{M+m}}} = 2\pi\sqrt{\frac{\Theta_0 + ml^2}{mgl}}.$$

The mass of the wheel could be cancelled, thus its moment of inertia can be calculated. Its value is:

$$\Theta_0 = mgl\left(\frac{T}{2\pi}\right)^2 - ml^2 = 0.01577\,\text{kg}\cdot\text{m}^2.$$

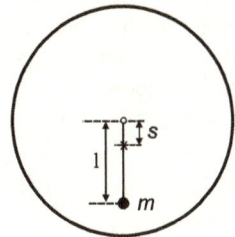

Solution of Problem 139. Sound propagates at speed c relative to the air in every direction, but not relative to the ship. Let $\mathbf{v}$ stand for the speed of the ship relative to the air and $\mathbf{c}$ for the speed of sound relative to the air. Then

$$\mathbf{c} = \mathbf{v} + \mathbf{c}_{\text{toship}},$$

where $\mathbf{c}_{\text{toship}}$ is the speed of the propagation of sound relative to the ship. From here $\mathbf{c}_{\text{toship}} = \mathbf{c} - \mathbf{v}$.

Moving from A to C vectors $\mathbf{v}$ and $\mathbf{c}$ point in the same direction, so the speed of sound relative to the ship is $c_{\text{toship}} = |\mathbf{c} - \mathbf{v}| = c - v$, moving from C to A the velocity of the ship and the velocity of sound point in opposite directions. Therefore $c_{\text{toship}} = |\mathbf{c} + \mathbf{v}| = c + v$. According to these, the sound travels along the course $A - C - A$ in time

$$\Delta t_1 = \frac{l}{c-v} + \frac{l}{c+v} = \frac{2lc}{c^2 - v^2} = \frac{2l}{c} \cdot \frac{l}{1 - \frac{v^2}{c^2}}.$$

Moving from A to B and from B to A $\mathbf{v}$ is perpendicular to $\mathbf{c}$, so in both cases

$$c_{\text{toship}} = |\mathbf{c} - \mathbf{v}| = \sqrt{c^2 - v^2}.$$

According to this, sound travels along the course $A - B - A$ in time

$$\Delta t_2 = \frac{2l}{c} \cdot \frac{1}{\sqrt{1 - \frac{v^2}{c^2}}}.$$

Introducing the notation $k = \dfrac{1}{\sqrt{1 - \frac{v^2}{c^2}}}$ and subtracting the two equations from each other a quadratic equation is acquired for k.

$$\Delta t = \frac{2l}{c}(k^2 - k) \quad \rightarrow \quad \frac{2l}{c}k^2 - \frac{2l}{c}k - \Delta t = 0, \quad (\text{where} \quad \Delta t = \Delta t_1 - \Delta t_2).$$

The roots of this equation are: $k_1 = 1.0004265$ and $k_2 = -0.0004265$, but only k_1 can be a solution, because in the case of $|k| < 1$ the expression for the speed of the ship would contain a negative number under the root, so it would not be valid on the set of real numbers.

Once k is known, the speed of the ship can be calculated:

$$v = c\sqrt{1 - \frac{1}{k^2}} = 320\frac{\text{m}}{\text{s}} \cdot \sqrt{1 - \frac{1}{1.0004265}} = 9.34\frac{\text{m}}{\text{s}} = 33.6\frac{\text{km}}{\text{h}}.$$

Solution of Problem 140. The solution of the problem is essentially based on geometric optics, since the propagation properties of seismic waves are analogous to that of light waves.

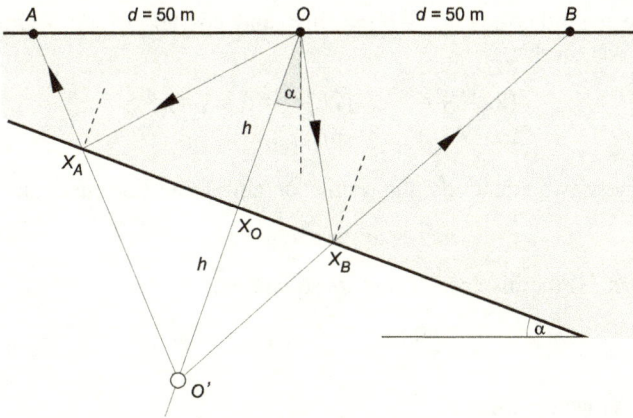

The place of explosion plays the role of light source, the topmost layer is optically less dense, and the inclined rock plate acts as a reflecting mirror, as it is shown in the figure.

Data: $d = 50$ m is the distance of the geophones at A and B from the place of explosion denoted by O

$$t_0 = 0.2 \text{ s}$$

$$t_A = 0.26 \text{ s}$$

$$t_B = 0.34 \text{ s}$$

Our task is to determine the propagation speed v of seismic waves in the topmost layer, the distance h of the inclined rock plate from the place of explosion and the angle of inclination α of the rock plate in east–west direction.

a) With the above introduced notations, using the law of reflection and the cosine formula for the side AO' of the triangle $AO'O$, we get that:

$$(2h)^2 + d^2 - 2 \cdot (2h)d\cos(90° - \alpha) = (vt_A)^2. \tag{1}$$

Here we have assumed that the length of $OX_A A$ equals the shortest distance between A and O', i.e., $OX_A + X_A A = O'A$, where O' is the mirror image of the the place of explosion. Furthermore, the angle $O'OA\angle$ equals $(90° - \alpha)$, since the two angles denoted by α in the figure have pairwise orthogonal rays. Thus the product of the speed of wave propagation and the time gives just the distance $O'A$.

By similar reasoning applied for the triangle $OO'B$ we get that:

$$(2h)^2 + d^2 - 2(2h)d\cos(90° + \alpha) = (vt_B)^2. \tag{2}$$

Finally for the distance OO' we obtain:

$$2h = vt_0 \tag{3}$$

The unknown quantities can be determined from these three equations. The propagation speed of seismic waves is obtained from the first two equations, using trigonometric identities.

Applying the identities $\cos(90° - \alpha) = \sin\alpha$ and $\cos(90° + \alpha) = -\sin\alpha$ in the first two equations, we get that:

$$(2h)^2 + d^2 - 2\cdot(2h)d\sin\alpha = (vt_A)^2, \tag{1'}$$

$$(2h)^2 + d^2 + 2\cdot(2h)d\sin\alpha = (vt_B)^2. \tag{2'}$$

Summarizing these two equations, the terms containing the sine functions cancel out:

$$8h^2 + 2d^2 = v^2(t_A^2 + t_B^2). \tag{4}$$

From equation (3) the distance h and its square are:

$$h = \frac{vt_0}{2} \qquad \rightarrow \qquad h^2 = \frac{v^2 t_0^2}{4}. \tag{5}$$

Putting it into (4) we obtain that:

$$2v^2 t_0^2 + 2d^2 = v^2(t_A^2 + t_B^2),$$

which means that the propagation speed of seismic waves is:

$$v = \frac{d\sqrt{2}}{\sqrt{t_A^2 + t_B^2 - 2\cdot t_0^2}} = \frac{50 \text{ m}\cdot\sqrt{2}}{\sqrt{0.26^2 \text{ s}^2 + 0.34^2 \text{ s}^2 - 2\cdot 0.2^2 \text{ s}^2}} = 220 \ \frac{\text{m}}{\text{s}}.$$

b) The (perpendicular) distance h of the place of explosion from the inclined rock plate is obtained from equation (5) and the propagation speed:

$$h = \frac{vt_0}{2} = \frac{220 \ \frac{\text{m}}{\text{s}}\cdot 0.2 \text{ s}}{2} = 22 \text{ m}.$$

c) The inclination angle of the rock plate can be obtained for example from equation (1'):

$$\sin\alpha = \frac{(2h)^2 + d^2 - (vt_A)^2}{2\cdot(2h)d} = \frac{(2\cdot 22 \text{ m})^2 + (50 \text{ m})^2 - \left(220 \ \frac{\text{m}}{\text{s}}\cdot 0.26 \text{ s}\right)^2}{2\cdot(2\cdot 22 \text{ m})\cdot 50 \text{ m}} = 0.2646,$$

which yields

$$\alpha = \arcsin 0.2646 = 15.34°.$$

Solution of Problem 141. The greatest possible speed (at which the vehicle does not fly away) is determined by the gravitational field of the planet which gives an upper bound for the centripetal acceleration of the vehicle moving on the surface of the planet — supposed to have a spherical shape — and thus it gives an upper bound for the speed of the vehicle. (Naturally, if the planet is hilly, the concave parts of the speed of the vehicle can be arbitrary and it will still touch the surface.) Thus in case of the greatest possible speed the centripetal acceleration of the vehicle is equal to the gravitational acceleration due to the planet, which is $\dfrac{v^2}{r} = g$. Thus the greatest speed is $v = \sqrt{rg}$

If the density of the Earth is ϱ, then the gravitational force is: $F = G \cdot \varrho \cdot \dfrac{4r^3\pi}{3} \cdot \dfrac{m}{r^2}$, therefore the acceleration of free fall is $g = G \cdot \dfrac{4\pi}{3} \varrho \cdot r$, where G is the gravitational constant. Substituting this into the expression of the greatest speed:

$$v = r\sqrt{\frac{4\pi}{3} \cdot G\varrho,}$$

if the data of the Earth are substituted into this formula ($r = 6370$ km, $\varrho_{\text{average}} = 5500$ kg/m^3) it gives the orbital velocity of $v_{\text{Earth}} = 7.89$ km/s. In case of a radius 500 times smaller the critical speed will also be 500 times smaller, so $v = 15.8$ m/s $= 56.88$ km/h.

Note: it is quite difficult to reach this maximum speed, with a land vehicle in case of a spherical planet, because the closer the speed of the vehicle to this maximum speed the smaller the normal force between the wheels and the ground, thus the increase of the tangential speed can be produced by smaller and smaller tangential acceleration.

Solution of Problem 142. a) The mass of the spaceship is negligible relative to the mass of the Earth, therefore the Earth can be assumed to be stationary, thus the law of motion of the spaceship in its original orbit is:

$$G \cdot \frac{Mm}{r_1^2} = m\frac{v^2}{r_1},$$

isolating the velocity of the spaceship (which is measured in a translating reference frame moving together with the Earth, which therefore can be assumed to be an inertial reference frame), we find:

$$v = \sqrt{G\frac{M}{r_1}},$$

hence the initial kinetic energy of the spaceship is:

$$E_{\text{kin}_1} = \frac{1}{2}mv^2 = G \cdot \frac{Mm}{2r_1}. \qquad (1)$$

The total mechanical energy of an orbiting spaceship is the sum of its kinetic and potential energies. If the spaceship moves in a circular orbit of radius $AF = r_1$, its kinetic energy is $GMm/2r_1$, while its potential energy (assuming that the potential energy is defined to be zero at infinity) is:

$$E_{\text{pot}_1} = -G \cdot \frac{Mm}{r_1}. \qquad (2)$$

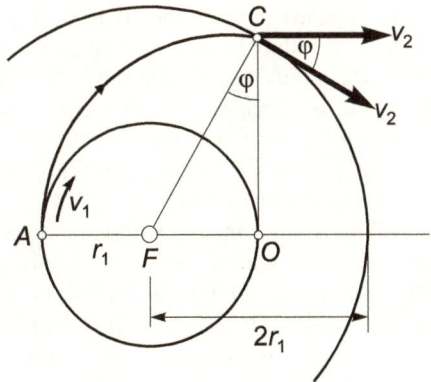

According to equation (1), the kinetic energy of the spaceship in a circular orbit of radius $2r_1$ is:

$$E_{\text{kin}_2} = G \cdot \frac{Mm}{4r_1},\qquad(3)$$

while its potential energy is:

$$E_{\text{pot}_2} = -G\frac{Mm}{2r_1}.\qquad(4)$$

The total energy in the circular orbit of radius $r_2 = 2r_1$ is $E_{total_2} = E_{total_1} + \Delta E_{\text{kin}}$, since in point A, where the magnitude of velocity changes instantaneously, the potential energy does not change yet, therefore:

$$E_{\text{kin}_2} + E_{\text{pot}_2} = E_{\text{kin}_1} + E_{\text{pot}_1} + \Delta E_{\text{kin}}.$$

Substituting equations (1), (2), (3) and (4), we obtain:

$$G\frac{Mm}{4r_1} - G\frac{Mm}{2r_1} = G\frac{Mm}{2r_1} - G\frac{Mm}{r_1} + \Delta E_{\text{kin}}.$$

Hence the increase in the kinetic energy of the spaceship in point A is:

$$\Delta E_{\text{kin}} = \frac{1}{4}G\frac{Mm}{r_1} = \frac{1}{2}\cdot G\frac{Mm}{2r_1} = \frac{1}{2}E_{\text{kin}_1},$$

which means that during the first course correction in point A the kinetic energy of the spaceship should be increased by 50%.

b) After the first course correction the spaceship moves in an elliptical orbit in which its total mechanical energy remains constant. The second task is to change the elliptical orbit into a circular orbit. Since during the second correction only the direction of the velocity is changed, the total mechanical energy of the spaceship is the same in its new circular orbit as it was in the transfer ellipse.

According to Kepler's laws, the total mechanical energy of a spaceship orbiting the Earth depends on only the semimajor axis of its orbit. Since the mechanical energies of the spaceship in the transfer ellipse (between points A and C) and in the outer circle (of radius r_2) are the same, the semimajor axes of the two orbits should also be equal. In the case of the outer circle the semimajor axis is $a_{\text{circ}} = 2r_1$, therefore the semimajor axis of the transfer ellipse is also $a_{\text{ell}} = 2r_1$. By measuring distance $2r_1$ starting from point A onto the line going through point F, we get the centre of the transfer ellipse, which is point O on the inner circle. Point C, which is the point where the elliptical orbit intersects the line perpendicular to AF and going through point O, is the end of the semiminor axis of the transfer ellipse. This is the point where the second course correction should be carried out. (The first appropriate moment mentioned in the problem is therefore the moment when the spaceship reaches point C.) Since $FC = 2r_1$ and $FO = r_1$, the angle enclosed by them is $\varphi = 30^0$. This is the angle by which the direction of the velocity should be changed. During the second course correction the total mechanical energy of the spaceship remains constant in a translating (approximately inertial) reference frame, therefore the work done by the engine increases the kinetic energy of the exhaust products.

c) The time taken by the spaceship to move from point A to C can be determined using Kepler's second law. If the period in the transfer ellipse is T_2, then the areal velocity can be written as:

$$f = \frac{\Delta A}{\Delta t} = \frac{\pi ab}{T_2},$$

where a and b are the semiaxes of the ellipse and $\pi ab = A_{\text{ell}}$ is the area of the ellipse. Kepler's second law states that the areal velocity (i.e. the ratio of the area swept out by the line joining the spaceship to the focal point to time) is $f = $ constant. In our case the area swept out by the line in time Δt is the area of the quarter of the ellipse minus the area of triangle OFC:

$$\Delta A = \frac{\pi ab}{4} - \frac{ab}{4} = \frac{ab(\pi - 1)}{4}.$$

The time taken is given by the ratio of the area to the areal velocity, which is:

$$\Delta t = \frac{\Delta A}{f} = \frac{ab(\pi - 1)}{4} : \frac{\pi ab}{T_2} = \frac{\pi - 1}{4\pi} \cdot T_2 \approx 0.17 T_2.$$

Applying Kepler's third law, the period in the outer circular orbit (and in the transfer ellipse) can be expressed in terms of the period in the inner circular orbit:

$$\frac{T_2^2}{T_1^2} = \frac{(2r_1)^3}{r_1^3} = 8,$$

hence

$$T_2 = T_1 \cdot \sqrt{8} = 2\sqrt{2} \cdot T_1,$$

thus the time spent on the transfer ellipse is:

$$\frac{(\pi - 1)\sqrt{2}}{2\pi} \cdot T_1 \approx 0.482 \cdot T_1.$$

Solution of Problem 143. The remark of the problem that the 'acceleration due to gravity at the surface of the Earth is known' implies that it is expected to use this datum instead of any other data, which might be found in a data booklet (i.e. gravitational constant, mass of the Earth etc.).

Applying Newton's second law to the motion of the satellite, the radius of the orbit of the satellite can be calculated:

$$G\frac{Mm}{r^2} = mr\omega^2,$$

where M is the mass of the Earth, m is the mass of the satellite G is the gravitational constant, r is the radius of the orbit and ω is the angular speed of the circular motion.

The latest one is $\omega = \dfrac{2\pi}{T}$ in terms of the period which is given. From the equation the radius of the orbit is:

$$r = \sqrt[3]{\frac{GM}{\omega^2}}.$$

Assuming that the gravitational acceleration at the surface of the Earth is

$$g_0 = \frac{GM}{R_F^2},$$

where R_F is the radius of the Earth, substituting $GM = g_0 R_F^2$, the radius of the orbit is:

$$r = \sqrt[3]{\frac{g_0 R_F^2}{\omega^2}} = \sqrt[3]{\frac{g_0 R_F^2 T^2}{4\pi^2}} =$$

$$= \sqrt[3]{\frac{9.81\,\mathrm{m/s^2} \cdot 6370000^2\,\mathrm{m^2} \cdot (90 \cdot 60)^2 \mathrm{s^2}}{4\pi^2}} = 6649544\,\mathrm{m} \approx 6650\,\mathrm{km}.$$

Thus the height at which the satellite orbits above the surface of the Earth is:

$$r - R_F = 6650\,\mathrm{km} - 6370\,\mathrm{km} = 280\,\mathrm{km}$$

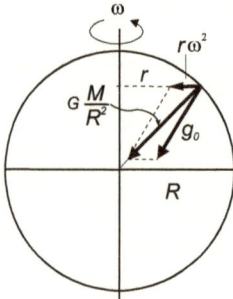

(Note: in the solution we used the approximation that the Earth was considered to be an inertial frame of reference when we assumed that the acceleration of a freely falling object at the surface of the Earth is the same as the acceleration due to the gravitational pull between the Earth and the satellite at the same place. In reality, the value of g_0 contains the rotation of the Earth, thus the acceleration of a freely falling object, measured here, slightly differs from the acceleration of an object, which is also released here, with respect to an inertial frame of reference: $g_0 < G\dfrac{M}{R_F^2}$. According to the figure, the appropriate relationship between the acceleration of a freely falling object and the acceleration due to the gravitational pull at the latitude of 45 degrees is:

$$g_0 = \sqrt{\left(G\frac{M}{R_F^2}\right)^2 + \left(R_F \sin 45° \cdot \frac{4\pi^2}{T^2}\right)^2 - 2G\frac{M}{R_F^2} R_F \sin 45° \cdot \frac{4\pi^2}{T^2} \cos 45°}.$$

The sum of the second and the third terms of the radicand is approximately $0.33\,\mathrm{m^2/s^4}$, which is negligibly small with respect to the first term because the sum is approximately three-thousandths of the first term.)

Solution of Problem 144. Two cases should be distinguished, depending on whether or not the satellite moves in the direction of the rotation of the Earth or opposite to it.

a) Let T_a be the orbital period of the satellite moving in the direction of the rotation of the Earth, and let T_E denote the period of the rotation of the Earth. In the given time $t = 6$ hours, the angular displacement of the satellite is equal to one whole turn plus the angular displacement of the Earth, since the satellite returns to the same point above the equator where it was initially. The angular displacements can be calculated by using the formula $\varphi = \omega t$, and the relation between the angular speed and period is $\omega = 2\pi/T$.

The exact value of the period of the rotation of the Earth with respect to the inertial reference frame determined by the distant fixed stars is 1 *sidereal day* = 86 163.4 s. However, we would not make a big error, if instead, we used the *solar day* as an approximation: 1 solarday = 24 hours = 86 400 s. The difference between the two days is due to the revolution of the Earth around the Sun. Indeed, in one solar day the Earth accomplishes one rotation with respect to the Sun, i.e., it shows the same point of the equator towards the Sun. But during this time, the Earth makes an angular displacement $2\pi/365$ along its orbit, so its total angular displacement with respect to the distant stars is by this angle larger than a whole turn. The time needed for this extra turn is one 365th of the 24 hours, so $86\,400/365.2422 = 236.555$. The sidereal day is obtained by substituting this time from the solar day: $(86\,400 - 236.555)$ s = 86 163.4 s.

According to the facts above, the equation is:

$$\frac{2\pi}{T_a}t = 2\pi + \frac{2\pi}{T_E}t.$$

From this equation the orbital period of the satellite can be determined. Dividing by 2π, we get:

$$\frac{t}{T_a} = 1 + \frac{t}{T_E}.$$

So the orbital period of the satellite is:

$$T_a = \frac{t}{1 + \frac{t}{T_E}} = \frac{t \cdot T_E}{t + T_E} = \frac{6\text{ h} \cdot 24\text{ h}}{6\text{ h} + 24\text{ h}} = \frac{144}{30}\text{ h} = 4.8\text{ h}.$$

b) Denoting by T_b the orbital period of the satellite, if it orbits opposite to the rotation of the Earth, we get:

$$\frac{2\pi}{T_b}t = 2\pi - \frac{2\pi}{T_E}t.$$

Dividing by 2π, we get:

$$\frac{t}{T_b} = 1 - \frac{t}{T_E}.$$

So the orbital period of the satellite is:

$$T_b = \frac{t}{1 - \frac{t}{T_E}} = \frac{t \cdot T_E}{T_E - t} = \frac{6\text{ h} \cdot 24\text{ h}}{24\text{ h} - 6\text{ h}} = 14418\text{ h} = 8\text{ h}.$$

Now that we know in both cases the orbital period of the satellite, the altitude of the orbit can be obtained by using Newton's law of gravitation:

$$G\frac{M_E m}{r_a^2} = m r_a \frac{4\pi^2}{T_a^2},$$

from where the radius of the satellite orbit is:

$$r_a = \sqrt[3]{\frac{GM_E T_a^2}{4\pi^2}}.$$

Instead of the universal gravitational constant G we can use the acceleration due to gravity g:

$$mg = G\frac{M_E m}{R_E^2}, \qquad \text{so} \qquad GM_E = gR_E^2.$$

Inserting it into the previous equation, we get:

$$r_a = \sqrt[3]{\frac{GM_E T_a^2}{4\pi^2}} = \sqrt[3]{\frac{R_E^2 g T_a^2}{4\pi^2}} =$$

$$= \sqrt[3]{\frac{(6370 \cdot 10^3)^2 \ \text{m}^2 \cdot 9.81 \ \frac{\text{m}}{\text{s}^2} \cdot (4.8 \cdot 3600)^2 \ \text{s}^2}{4\pi^2}} = 14439712 \ \text{m} \approx 14440 \ \text{km}.$$

Similarly, if the satellite orbits opposite to the rotation of the Earth, then the radius of the orbit is:

$$r_a = \sqrt[3]{\frac{R_E^2 g T_b^2}{4\pi^2}} = \sqrt[3]{\frac{(6370 \cdot 10^3)^2 \ \text{m}^2 \cdot 9.81 \ \frac{\text{m}}{\text{s}^2} \cdot (8 \cdot 3600)^2 \ \text{s}^2}{4\pi^2}} =$$

$$= 20298208 \ \text{m} \approx 20300 \ \text{km}.$$

Thus the altitudes of the orbits (above the surface of the Earth) are:

In case a): $h_a = r_a - R_E = 14440 \ \text{km} - 6370 \ \text{km} = 8070 \ \text{km}.$

In case b): $h_b = r_b - R_E = 20300 \ \text{km} - 6370 \ \text{km} = 13930 \ \text{km}.$

Solution of Problem 145. Because the spaceship is kept in a circular orbit by the gravitational force, which is a radial force, the plane of the circular orbit must contain the centre of the Earth. The spaceship can be considered pointlike and its mass is negligible with respect to the mass of the Earth, so it does not effect the motion of the Earth. The intersection of the plane of the orbit and the surface of the Earth, which is considered a sphere, is one of its great circles. If the spaceship must remain above the same point of the Earth, this point can only be on one of the great spheres of the Earth. During the rotation of the Earth, only those points of the surface move along a great circle which is along the equator of the Earth, meaning that the condition is satisfied for any point on the equator of the Earth.

The speed of the spaceship with respect to a reference frame which is moving with the Earth (but does not rotate with respect to the stars) is determined by the angular speed of the Earth and the radius of the orbit of the spaceship according to Newton's second law:

$$G \cdot \frac{Mm}{r^2} = mr\omega^2,$$

where $G = 6.672 \cdot 10^{-11} \, \dfrac{\text{N} \cdot \text{m}^2}{\text{kg}^2}$ is the gravitational constant, $M = 5.974 \cdot 10^{24} \, \text{kg}$ is the mass of the Earth, m is the mass of the spacehip, and r is the asked distance between the spaceship and the centre of the Earth. Using the above equation the value of this radius is:

$$r = \sqrt[3]{\frac{GM}{\omega^2}},$$

and thus the speed of the spaceship with respect to the reference frame which is moving with the Earth (but not rotating) is $v = r\omega$.

ω is equal to the angular speed of the Earth. Because $\omega = 2\pi/T$, where T is the period of the rotation of the Earth. If this is known, the speed of the spaceship can be calculated:

$$v = \omega \sqrt[3]{\frac{GM}{\omega^2}} = \sqrt[3]{GM\omega} = \sqrt[3]{\frac{G2\pi M}{T}}.$$

What is the value of T? It can be calculated easily if it is not found in a table. The time between two consecutive solar noons is known: it is 24 hours, which is 86400 seconds. This is called a solar day. This is longer than the amount of time it takes the Earth to complete one revolution about its axis, because while it revolves 360° with respect to the inertial frame of reference, its centre moves forward along its orbit about the Sun, thus the Earth has to rotate more than 360° in order that the Sun should be above the same point again. Let us determine the period of the rotation in the inertial frame of reference (sidereal day) in solar seconds.

Let α be the angle subtended by the arc along which the Earth moves during one solar day to the Sun. During this time, the Earth turns an angle of

$$\varphi = 2\pi + \alpha = \omega T_{So},$$

where ω is the angular speed of the rotation of the Earth in an inertial frame of reference, and T_{So} is a solar day.

The angle turned during one day α, counting 365.26 solar days in one year is

$$\alpha = \frac{2\pi}{365.26},$$

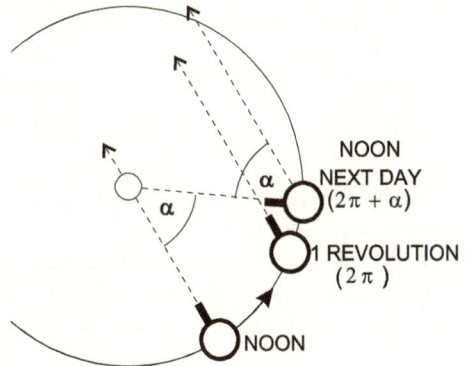

where 365.26 is the length of one year in solar days. Because one solar day is $T_{So} =$
$= \dfrac{2\pi + \alpha}{\omega}$, and one sidereal day is $T_{Si} = \dfrac{2\pi}{\omega}$ long, their ratio is:

$$\frac{T_{Si}}{T_{So}} = \frac{2\pi}{\omega} \cdot \frac{\omega}{2\pi + \alpha} = \frac{2\pi}{2\pi + \dfrac{2\pi}{365.26}} = \frac{365.26}{366.26},$$

Thus one sidereal day expressed in solar days is:

$$T_{Si} = \frac{365.26}{366.26} \cdot T_{So} = \frac{365.26}{366.26} \cdot 86400 \,\text{s} = 86164.102 \,\text{s}.$$

Now we can answer the question asked in the problem:

$$v = \sqrt[3]{\frac{6.672 \cdot 10^{-11} \,\text{Nm}^2/\text{kg}^2 \cdot 5.973 \cdot 10^{24} \,\text{kg} \cdot 2\pi}{86164.1 \,\text{s}}} = 3074.45 \,\frac{\text{m}}{\text{s}}.$$

Note that the distance between the spaceship and the centre of the Earth is $r =$
$= 42161.252$ km, and the distance between the spaceship and the surface of the Earth
is 35790.23 km.

Solution of Problem 146. The possible methods are based on either Newton's second
law ($\sum F = ma$) or the conservation of linear momentum ($\sum I = \text{constant}$). The
spaceship in free fall can be assumed to be an inertial system and its mass can be
considered to be infinitely greater than the mass to be measured.

In the first method, we can use a calibrated dynamometer to measure the force acting
on the object and measure its acceleration (using a stop watch and a meter bar) at the
same time. The mass of the object is the ratio of the force and acceleration.

In the second method, the object is attached to a dynamometer and is put into a
circular orbit moving at constant speed. The dynamometer measures the centripetal
force, meanwhile the radius of the circle and the number of revolutions are also
measured. The mass of the object is given by the formula:

$$m = \frac{F_{\text{dyn.}}}{R 4\pi^2 n^2}.$$

If the dynamometer is not calibrated, we need to know its spring constant (k) and
measure its extension.

In the third method, the object is fastened in between two springs of known spring
constant and the period of oscillation of the system is measured. If the masses of the
springs are negligible, the mass of the object is given by the formula:

$$m = k \frac{T^2}{4\pi^2}.$$

The conservation of linear momentum is used in the fourth method. Let us collide the
object to a second object of known mass initially at rest. If the collision is completely

inelastic, the mass of the object can be determined by measuring its initial velocity (v) and the final velocity of the system (u) using the formula:

$$m = m_0 \frac{u}{v - u},$$

where m_0 is the known mass of the second object.

The fifth method is also based on the conservation of linear momentum. Let us attach the object to be measured and a second object of known mass to two ends of a strong spring of unknown spring constant. The spring is then compressed and released. After a short period of accelerating motion, the objects leave the spring and move at constant speed. If the distances covered by the two objects in equal times are measured, the unknown mass can be determined using the formula:

$$m = m_0 \frac{s_0}{s}.$$

In the sixth method, the conservation of energy formula is used. Let us fasten one end of a spring of known spring constant to the wall of the spaceship. The object is attached to the other end of the spring, which is then compressed and released. After leaving the spring, the object moves at constant speed. Measuring the speed of the object and the compression of the spring, we get the mass of the object using the formula:

$$m = k \frac{(\Delta l)^2}{v^2}.$$

Solution of Problem 147. a) Let R_1 and R_2 stand for the radii of the circular orbits, v_1 and v_2 for the orbital speeds, u_1 and u_2 for the speeds of the satellite on the transitional ellipse at distances R_1 and R_2 from the planet.

According to the fundamental law of dynamics:

$$m \frac{v^2}{R} = G \cdot \frac{mM}{R^2} \quad \Rightarrow \quad v_1^2 = \frac{GM}{R_1} \quad \text{and} \quad v_2^2 = \frac{GM}{R_2} \tag{1}$$

$$mR \frac{4\pi^2}{T^2} = G \frac{mM}{R^2} \quad \Rightarrow \quad T_1^2 = \frac{4\pi^2}{GM} R_1^3 \quad \text{and} \quad T_2^2 = \frac{4\pi^2}{GM} R_2^3 \tag{2}$$

The semimajor axis of the transitional elliptical orbit is

$$a = \frac{R_1 + R_2}{2}. \tag{3}$$

Applying Kepler's third law to the satellite orbiting on the circular orbit with radius R_1 and to the transitional elliptical orbit:

$$\frac{T^2}{T_1^2} = \frac{a^3}{R_1^3},$$

or by making use of (3)

$$T^2 = T_1^2 \frac{(R_1 + R_2)^3}{8R_1^3}.$$

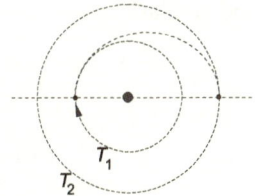

Introducing the periods instead of the radii based on (2):

$$T^2 = T_1^2 \frac{(T_1^{2/3} + T_2^{2/3})^3}{8T_1^2} = \frac{(T_1^{2/3} + T_2^{2/3})^3}{8},$$

from which

$$T = \frac{(T_1^{2/3} + T_2^{2/3})^{3/2}}{2^{3/2}} = \frac{(8^{2/3} + 27^{2/3})^{3/2}}{2^{3/2}} \text{ hours} = \frac{(\sqrt{4+9})^3}{2^{3/2}} \text{ hours} =$$

$$= \sqrt{\frac{13^3}{8}} \text{ hours} = 16.572 \text{ hours}.$$

As the suitable moment for changing over to the circular orbit with radius R_2 is when the satellite reaches the endpoint of the major axis of the transitional ellipse (then velocity is perpendicular to the line connecting the satellite and the planet), the course correction requires

$$T_{\text{correction}} = \frac{T}{2} = 8.286 \text{ hours}.$$

b) Let us apply the law of conservation of energy and of angular momentum to the satellite moving on the transitional ellipse.

$$\frac{1}{2}mu_1^2 - G\frac{mM}{R_1} = \frac{1}{2}mu_2^2 - G\frac{mM}{R_2},$$

$$u_1 R_1 = u_2 R_2.$$

From the equation system u_1 and u_2 can be expressed: by substituting $u_2 = u_1 \frac{R_1}{R_2}$, dividing by $m/2$

$$u_1^2 - 2G\frac{M}{R_1} = u_1^2 \frac{R_1^2}{R_2^2} - 2G\frac{M}{R_2} \quad \Rightarrow \quad u_1^2 \frac{R_2^2 - R_1^2}{R_2^2} = 2GM\frac{R_2 - R_1}{R_1 R_2}$$

from which

$$u_1^2 = \frac{GM}{R_1} \cdot \frac{2R_2}{R_1 + R_2},$$

and similarly

$$u_2^2 = \frac{GM}{R_2} \cdot \frac{2R_1}{R_1 + R_2},$$

by using (1):

$$u_1^2 = v_1^2 \frac{2R_2}{R_1 + R_2} \quad \text{and} \quad u_2^2 = v_2^2 \frac{2R_1}{R_1 + R_2},$$

and by using (2):

$$u_1^2 = v_1^2 \frac{2T_2^{2/3}}{T_1^{2/3} + T_2^{2/3}} \quad \text{and} \quad u_2^2 = v_2^2 \frac{2T_1^{2/3}}{T_1^{2/3} + T_2^{2/3}}.$$

The relative changes in velocity are:

$$\frac{u_1}{v_1} = \sqrt{\frac{2T_2^{2/3}}{T_1^{2/3} + T_2^{2/3}}} = \sqrt{\frac{2 \cdot 27^{2/3}}{8^{2/3} + 27^{2/3}}} = \sqrt{\frac{2 \cdot 9}{4 + 9}} = \sqrt{\frac{18}{13}} = 1.1767$$

this is a 17.67 % increase,

$$\frac{v_2}{u_2} = \sqrt{\frac{T_1^{2/3} + T_2^{2/3}}{2T_1^{2/3}}} = \sqrt{\frac{8^{2/3} + 27^{2/3}}{2 \cdot 8^{2/3}}} = \sqrt{\frac{4 + 9}{2 \cdot 4}} = \sqrt{\frac{13}{8}} = 1.2747,$$

this is a 27.47 % increase.

Solution of Problem 148. The number of photons arriving on the mirror is constant and the fluctuation can be neglected, meaning that the change in the momentum of the photons is uniform and that the force acting on the mirror is constant in time. Because of the 100% reflexivity of the mirror the change in the momentum of the photons is exactly twice as much as the momentum delivered by them, namely, as the mirror moves extremely slowly, there is practically no change in the colour of the reflected photons (their wavelength does not increase).

The force acting on the mirror is the reaction to the force exerted on the photons by the mirror, so their magnitudes are equal:

$$F = \frac{\Delta p}{\Delta t},$$

where Δp is the total change in momentum in time Δt. Its magnitude is $\Delta p = A\Delta p_1 = A\frac{2E_1 \cdot \Delta t}{c}$. Here p_1 is the momentum intensity and ΔE_1 is the energy flux intensity, that is, the energy arriving on a unit area in one second. With this, the requested force is:

$$F = \frac{\Delta p}{\Delta t} = \frac{A\Delta p_1}{\Delta t} = \frac{A2E_1\Delta t}{c\Delta t} = \frac{2AE_1}{c},$$

with numerical values:

$$F = \frac{2 \cdot 100 \cdot 10^{-4}\,\mathrm{m}^2 \cdot 1250\frac{\mathrm{J}}{\mathrm{m}^2 \cdot \mathrm{s}}}{3 \cdot 10^8\,\frac{\mathrm{m}}{\mathrm{s}}} = 8.33 \cdot 10^{-8}\,\mathrm{N}.$$

The moment of this force sets the system into rotation. The magnitude of this moment is:

$$M = F \cdot r,$$

because due to the constant force distribution (force intensity independent of the position) the changing 'intensity of the moment of force', which depends on position and changes linearly with radius can be calculated as the arithmetic mean of the minimum and maximum intensity of the moment of force, that is, the arm r that belongs to the centre of the mirror. Therefore:

$$M = 8.33 \cdot 10^{-8}\,\mathrm{N} \cdot 0.2\,\mathrm{m} = 1.67 \cdot 10^{-8}\,\mathrm{N\,m}.$$

The angular acceleration of the structure can be determined from the fundamental equation of dynamics for rotating motion ($\beta = M/\Theta$). So in order to determine the angular acceleration, the rotational inertia of the mirror should be calculated for the axis supported by the bearings. For the calculation Steiner's parallel-axis theorem is applied:

$$\Theta = \Theta_{cm} + md^2,$$

where Θ_{cm} is the rotational inertia of the body for the axis that passes through the centre of mass of the body, m is the total mass of the body, d (here r) is the distance between the axis that passes through the centre of mass and another axis that is parallel with it.

The rotational inertia of a thin square plate for an axis that passes through its centre of mass and is parallel with one of the sides of the square is $\Theta_{cm} = (1/12)m \cdot a^2$, where m is the mass of the square, a is the length of its side. (This result can also be obtained by assuming that the square consists of thin rods that are parallel with the side and have a rotational inertia $(1/12)\Delta m \cdot a^2$ each and then summing up each of these.)

So the rotational inertia of the mirror structure for the axis of rotation can be calculated from Steiner's parallel-axis theorem and then angular acceleration can be calculated with the rotational inertia:

$$\Theta = \Theta_{cm} + mr^2 = \frac{1}{12}ma^2 + mr^2 = \frac{1}{12} \cdot 0.02\,\text{kg} \cdot 0.1^2\,\text{m}^2 + 0.02\,\text{kg} \cdot 0.2^2\,\text{m}^2 =$$
$$= 8.17 \cdot 10^{-4}\,\text{kg m}^2.$$

$$\beta = \frac{M}{\Theta} = \frac{\frac{2AE_1}{c} \cdot r}{\frac{1}{12}ma^2 + mr^2} = \frac{8.33 \cdot 10^{-8}\,\text{N} \cdot 0.2\,\text{m}}{8.17 \cdot 10^{-4}\,\text{kg m}^2} = 2.04 \cdot 10^{-5}\,\text{s}^{-2}.$$

Finally, the angular displacement in 1 minute is:

$$\varphi = \frac{\beta}{2}t^2 = \frac{2.04 \cdot 10^{-5}\,\text{s}^{-2}}{2} \cdot 3600\,\text{s} = 0.0367\,\text{rad} \approx 2.1^\circ.$$

It is questionable whether a bearing support that allows this operation can be produced.

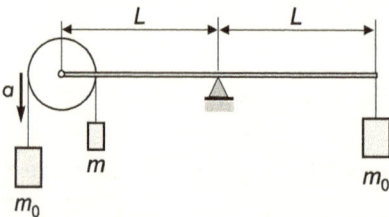

Solution of Problem 149. If the axis of the pulley remains at rest, Newton's second law applied to the two blocks hanging from the pulley will take the form of:

$$m_0 g - K = m_0 a$$

$$K - mg = ma$$

(We used that m is less than m_0. This can be derived from the fact that the sum of tensions in the string should be equal to $m_0 g$, but if m was greater than or equal to m_0, the sum of tensions would be greater than $m_0 g$. We also used that the magnitudes of the accelerations of each block are the same. For each block the positive direction was chosen to be in the direction of its acceleration.)

We add the two equations to get:

$$(m_0 - m)g = (m_0 + m)a,$$

from which the acceleration of the blocks is: $a = \dfrac{m_0 - m}{m_0 + m} \cdot g$.

Either of the first two equations can be used to determine the tensions in the string:

$$K = mg + ma = mg\left(1 + \frac{m_0 - m}{m_0 + m}\right) = \frac{2m_0 m}{m_0 + m}g.$$

Taking the double of this, we get the resultant of the two tensions, which is equal to the gravitational force $m_0 g$ acting on the other end of the lever, so:

$$\frac{4mm_0}{m_0 + m}g = m_0 g.$$

Thus $m = \dfrac{m_0}{3}$.

The acceleration of the two blocks is:

$$a = \frac{m_0 - m_0/3}{m_0 + m_0/3}g = \frac{2}{3}g.$$

Solution of Problem 150. The shape of the hole can be described by angle α, for which:

$$\tan\alpha = \frac{d}{h},$$

where d is the diameter and h is the depth of the hole. Let c and L be the lengths of the parts of the rod that are inside and outside the hole respectively, and G be the weight of the coat hanged onto the end of the rod. In the extreme case the maximum frictional forces act at both contact points. (Coefficients of kinetic and static friction are assumed to be the same.)

The forces exerted by the wall (as shown in the figure) are: F_1, μF_1, F_2, μF_2. The rod is in equilibrium if the resultant force and resultant torque on it are zero. Let us write the condition for translational equilibrium separately for the horizontal and vertical components of forces:

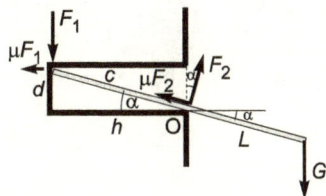

$$G + F_1 - F_2\cos\alpha - \mu F_2\sin\alpha = 0, \qquad (1)$$
$$F_2\sin\alpha - \mu F_2\cos\alpha - \mu F_1 = 0. \qquad (2)$$

The sum of torques about point O is:

$$GL\cos\alpha - F_1 c\,\cos\alpha - \mu F_1 c\,\sin\alpha = 0. \qquad (3)$$

Thus we have a system of equations with three unknowns that can easily be determined. Let us isolate F_2 from equation (2):

$$F_2 = \frac{\mu F_1}{\sin\alpha - \mu\cos\alpha}. \qquad (4)$$

Substitute it into equation (1):

$$G + F_1 - \frac{\mu F_1}{\sin\alpha - \mu\cos\alpha}(\cos\alpha + \mu\sin\alpha) = 0.$$

F_1 can be factored out from the second and third terms:

$$G + \frac{\sin\alpha - \mu\cos\alpha + \mu(\cos\alpha + \mu\sin\alpha)}{\sin\alpha - \mu\cos\alpha}F_1 = 0.$$

Isolating F_1, we find:

$$F_1 = \frac{\sin\alpha - \mu\cos\alpha}{2\mu\cos\alpha - \sin\alpha(1 - \mu^2)}G.$$

Dividing both the numerator and the denominator by $\cos\alpha$, we obtain:

$$F_1 = \frac{\tan\alpha - \mu}{2\mu - (1 - \mu^2)\tan\alpha}G, \tag{5}$$

Substituting $\tan\alpha = d/h$ and multiplying both the numerator and denominator by h lead us to:

$$F_1 = \frac{d - \mu h}{2\mu h - (1 - \mu^2)d}G = \frac{2 - 0.2\cdot 6}{2\cdot 0.2\cdot 6 - (1 - 0.04)\cdot 2}G = 1.667G.$$

Force F_2 can be calculated by substituting the value of F_1 into equation (4):

$$F_2 = \frac{\mu}{2\mu\cos\alpha - (1 - \mu^2)\sin\alpha}\cdot G,$$

where

$$\cos\alpha = \frac{h}{\sqrt{h^2 + d^2}}, \qquad \sin\alpha = \frac{d}{\sqrt{h^2 + d^2}}.$$

Substitute these trigonometric functions into the expression obtained for F_2:

$$F_2 = \frac{\mu\sqrt{h^2 + d^2}}{2\mu h - (1 - \mu^2)d}G = \frac{0.2\sqrt{40}}{2\cdot 0.2\cdot 6 - (1 - 0.04)\cdot 2}G = 2.635G.$$

Length L can be determined using equation (3):

$$L = \frac{F_1}{G}c\frac{\cos\alpha + \mu\sin\alpha}{\cos\alpha} = \frac{F_1}{G}c(1 + \mu\tan\alpha),$$

where

$$c = \sqrt{d^2 + h^2} = \sqrt{2^2 + 6^2}\text{ cm} = \sqrt{40}\text{ cm}.$$

Substituting the value of F_1 as given in equation (5), we find that the length of the part of the rod that should be outside the hole is independent of G:

$$L = \frac{(\tan\alpha - \mu)(1 + \mu\tan\alpha)}{2\mu - (1 - \mu^2)\tan\alpha}c.$$

Using that $\tan\alpha = d/h$ and $c = \sqrt{d^2 + h^2}$, we get:

$$L = \frac{(d - \mu h)(h + \mu d)}{2\mu h - (1 - \mu^2)d}\cdot\frac{\sqrt{d^2 + h^2}}{h} = \frac{(2 - 0.2\cdot 6)(6 + 0.2\cdot 2)}{2\cdot 0.2\cdot 6 - (1 - 0.04)2}\frac{\sqrt{40}}{6} = 11.24\text{ cm}.$$

Therefore the length of the rod which is to be used as a coat-hanger should be at least:

$$l = L + c = 11.24\text{ cm} + \sqrt{40}\text{ cm} = 11.24\text{ cm} + 6.33\text{ cm} = 17.56\text{ cm}.$$

6.3 Statics

Solution of Problem 151. Notations: $L = 1$ m, $m_{\text{rod}} = 1$ kg, $\alpha = 30°$, $l = 1.3$ m, $m = 0.2$ kg.

In the process on one hand, the centre of mass of the rod is lifted (by a quarter of a metre due to the simple numerical values), and on the other hand, the weight is raised by Δh. Essentially this latter quantity has to be determined.

The work done on the rod is:

$$W_{\text{rod}} = m_{\text{rod}} g \Delta h_{\text{rod}} = m_{\text{rod}} g \frac{L}{4} = 1 \text{ kg} \cdot 10 \frac{\text{m}}{\text{s}^2} \cdot 0.25 \text{ m} = 2.5 \text{ J}.$$

The rise of the weight can be determined according to the figures. Since the pulley is moving along the thread without friction, it is always in the lowest possible position. The tension in the thread balances the weight force, and the tension in the two sides of the thread are equal. Otherwise, they would have a net torque on the pulley. The weight force is vertical, so the sum of the forces exerted by the two sides of the thread has to be vertical, too. But since the forces in the two sides of the thread are of equal magnitude, and their sum is vertical, they make the same angle to the vertical (as well as to the horizontal). If one side of the thread is reflected in the vertical or horizontal line across the pulley, then the line of the image coincides with the other side of the thread. We use these geometric facts to determine the height of the weight.

According to Pythagoras' theorem, the position of the pulley below the horizontal rod is:

$$h_2 = \frac{1}{2}\sqrt{l^2 - L^2} = \frac{1}{2}\sqrt{1.3^2 \text{ m}^2 - 1^2 \text{ m}^2} = 0.415 \text{ m}.$$

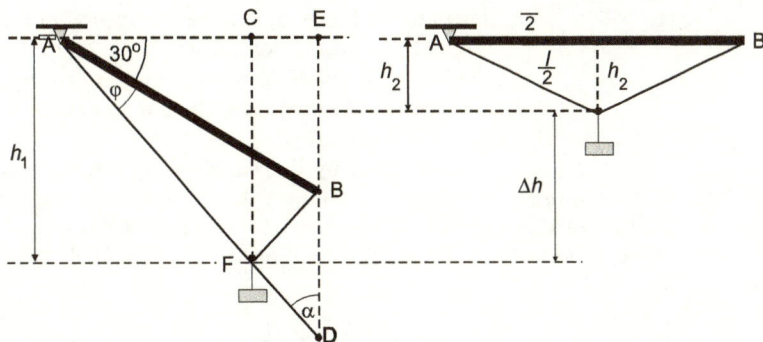

Initially, at the inclined position of the rod the pulley was at a distance $h_1 = CF$ below the horizontal line passing through the top end of the rod. The length of CF has to be determined. First, we calculate the angle of the thread with respect to the horizontal. According to the figure,

$$\cos(\varphi + 30°) = \frac{AE}{AD} = \frac{L \cdot \cos 30°}{l} = \frac{1 \text{ m} \cdot 0.866}{1.3} = 0.666 \rightarrow \varphi + 30° = 48.228°,$$

so the length of ED is:

$$ED = l \cdot \sin(\varphi + 30°) = 1.3 \text{ m} \cdot \sin 48.228° = 0.97 \text{ m}.$$

Since $EB = 0.5$ m, the length of BD is: $BD = ED - EB = 0.97 \text{ m} - 0.5 \text{ m} = 0.47 \text{ m}$.

The BFD triangle is an isosceles triangle, $BF = FD$. The horizontal line passing through F crosses halfway to the opposite side, so

$$h_1 = CF = EB + \frac{BD}{2} = 0.5 \text{ m} + \frac{0.47}{2} \text{ m} = 0.735 \text{ m}.$$

The vertical distance, by which the pulley and the weight rise, is

$$\Delta h = |h_2 - h_1| = 0.735 \text{ m} - 0.415 \text{ m} = 0.320 \text{ m}.$$

The work needed to lift the weight is:

$$W_{\text{weight}} = mg\Delta h = 0.2 \text{ kg} \cdot 10 \, \frac{\text{m}}{\text{s}^2} \cdot 0.320 \text{ m} = 0.640 \text{ J}.$$

Thus the total work needed to lift the rod is:

$$W_{\text{rod}} + W_{\text{weight}} = 2.5 \text{ J} + 0.640 \text{ J} = 3.14 \text{ J}.$$

First solution of Problem 152. The solution of this problem is an 'interval' of positions, which can be determined by examining the two extreme cases in which the beads just start to slip. In the first solution we will use Newton's second law.

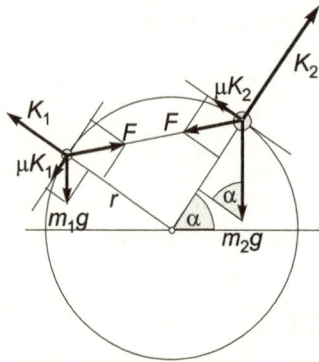

Let us describe the position of the system with the help of angle α, which is the angle formed by the horizontal and the radius drawn to the greater bead as shown. Since the beads are on the ends of a quarter-circle, the string forms an angle of $45°$ with the radii drawn to the beads. Let F be the tension in the string, K_1 and K_2 be the normal forces acting on the beads and let us use notation $m = m_1$ and $2m = m_2$ in order to simplify our equations. The unknowns are therefore α, F, K_1 and K_2.

Let us start by investigating the situation in which the greater bead is in its most right position. (If the greater bead was moved further to the right, it would slip down on the loop pulling the smaller bead with it.)

Let us apply Newton's second law to the two beads in tangential and normal directions:

$$m_2 g \sin\alpha + F\frac{\sqrt{2}}{2} - K_2 = 0, \tag{1}$$

$$\mu K_2 + F\frac{\sqrt{2}}{2} - m_2 g \cos\alpha = 0, \tag{2}$$

$$m_1 g \cos\alpha + F\frac{\sqrt{2}}{2} - K_1 = 0, \tag{3}$$

$$\mu K_1 + m_1 g \sin\alpha - F\frac{\sqrt{2}}{2} = 0. \tag{4}$$

Eliminating the normal forces by multiplying equations (1) and (3) by μ and adding them to equations (2) and (4) respectively, we find that the only unknowns remaining are α and F. After factoring out $F\dfrac{\sqrt{2}}{2}$, our equations take the form of:

$$\mu m_2 g \sin\alpha + F\frac{\sqrt{2}}{2}(\mu+1) - m_2 g \cos\alpha = 0, \tag{5}$$

$$\mu m_1 g \cos\alpha + m_1 g \sin\alpha + F\frac{\sqrt{2}}{2}(\mu-1) = 0. \tag{6}$$

Solving (6) for $F\dfrac{\sqrt{2}}{2}$ gives:

$$F\frac{\sqrt{2}}{2} = \frac{\mu m_1 g \cos\alpha + m_1 g \sin\alpha}{1-\mu},$$

which is then substituted into equation (5) to give:

$$\mu m_2 g \sin\alpha + (\mu m_1 g \cos\alpha + m_1 g \sin\alpha)\frac{\mu+1}{1-\mu} - m_2 g \cos\alpha = 0.$$

Let us divide by g and factor out $\sin\alpha$ and $\cos\alpha$:

$$\sin\alpha(\mu m_2 - \mu^2 m_2 + \mu m_1 + m_1) + \cos\alpha(\mu^2 m_1 + \mu m_1 - m_2 + \mu m_2) = 0,$$

which yields

$$\sin\alpha[\mu m_2(1-\mu) + m_1(1+\mu)] = \cos\alpha[(1-\mu)m_2 - \mu m_1(1+\mu)],$$

from which the tangent of the required angle is:

$$\tan\alpha = \frac{(1-\mu)m_2 - \mu m_1(1+\mu)}{\mu m_2(1-\mu) + m_1(1+\mu)}.$$

Substituting known values, we find:

$$1-\mu = 1-0.15 = 0.85,$$

$$1+\mu = 1+0.15 = 1.15,$$

$$\mu = 0.15,$$

hence

$$\tan\alpha = \frac{0.85(2m) - 0.15 \cdot m \cdot 1.15}{0.15(2m)0.85 + m \cdot 1.15} = \frac{1.7 - 0.172}{0.285 + 1.15} = \frac{1.5275}{1.405} = 1.0872,$$

thus

$$\alpha = \arctan 1.0872 = 47.39°.$$

Let us now investigate the other extreme position of the system. The equations will be the same as in the previous case, but with opposite indices. Therefore the solution can be obtained by exchanging the indices in the previous result.

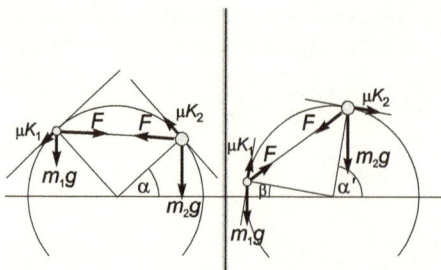

This is because the two extreme cases are symmetrical in their topology, i.e. the second case can be gained from the first one using a transformation, in which the corresponding vectors differ in direction and magnitude, but their role in the situation and the directions of their components remain the same relative to each other.

Note that if the indices are exchanged, the solution will now give angle β, which is the angle formed by the horizontal and the radius drawn to the smaller bead.

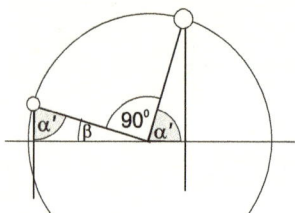

Since we want to find the angle formed by the horizontal and the radius drawn to the greater bead (let this be α'), we will use $\alpha' = 90° - \beta$ (as shown in the figure) to determine the required angle. Technically this means that after exchanging the indices in the formula for the tangent of angle, we also need to take its reciprocal.

The original solution was:

$$\tan\alpha = \frac{(1-\mu)m_2 - \mu m_1(1+\mu)}{\mu m_2(1-\mu) + m_1(1+\mu)}.$$

After exchanging the indices, we get:

$$\tan\beta = \frac{(1-\mu)m_1 - \mu m_2(1+\mu)}{\mu m_1(1-\mu) + m_2(1+\mu)}.$$

Taking its reciprocal gives:

$$\tan\alpha' = \frac{1}{\tan\beta} = \frac{\mu m_1(1-\mu) + m_2(1+\mu)}{(1-\mu)m_1 - \mu m_2(1+\mu)}.$$

Substituting known values, we obtain:

$$\tan\alpha' = \frac{0.15 \cdot m \cdot 0.85 + (2m) \cdot 1.15}{0.85 \cdot m - 0.15 \cdot (2m) \cdot 1.15} = 4.8069,$$

from which we find that the angle describing the other extreme position is:

$$\alpha' = \arctan 4.8069 = 78.25°.$$

Second solution of Problem 152. Let ε be the angle for which $\tan\varepsilon = \mu$. We will prove that if the resultant $\sum F$ of all forces, except for the normal force K and friction S, acting on a body, has a line of action whose angle formed with the normal is greater than ε the the body will slip no matter how small the magnitude of the resultant is.

However, if the line of action of the above force encloses an angle less than ε with the normal, the body will not slip, no matter how great the magnitude of the resultant is.

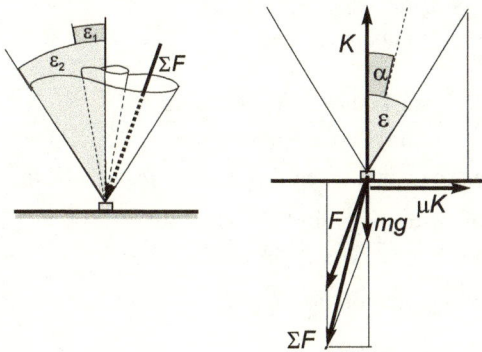

In other words, if the line of action of the above force is inside a cone, whose axis is the normal and whose cone angle is 2ε (see figure), the body will not slip. If it isn't the case, it will. So, the body will not slip if:

$$\mu K \geq S,$$

if $\sum F$ is the resultant of all forces except for the normal force and friction, then the above inequality takes the form of:

$$\mu \cdot \sum F \cos\alpha \geq \sum F \sin\alpha,$$

in the extreme case, using that $\alpha_{\max} = \varepsilon$, we find:

$$\mu \cos\varepsilon = \sin\varepsilon,$$

thus: $\tan\varepsilon = \mu$, as it was stated.

Let us now investigate the extreme cases of the beads finding triangles in which the angle formed by the horizontal and the radius drawn to the greater bead can be expressed with the help of angle ε.

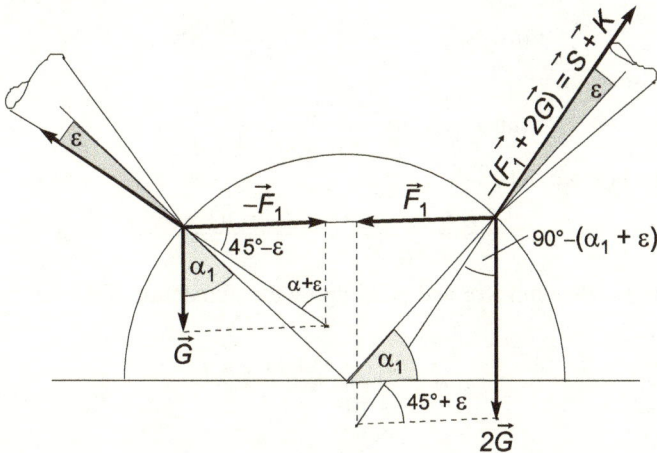

In the situation when the greater bead is in its right extreme position, let us apply the law of sines to the triangles formed by the forces shown:

$$\frac{2G}{F} = \frac{\sin(45° + \varepsilon)}{\cos(\alpha + \varepsilon)}, \quad \text{and} \quad \frac{G}{F} = \frac{\sin(45° - \varepsilon)}{\sin(\alpha + \varepsilon)},$$

where $G = mg$ is the weight of the smaller bead. Dividing the first equation by the second gives:

$$2 = \tan(\alpha + \varepsilon) \frac{\sin(45° + \varepsilon)}{\sin(45° - \varepsilon)}.$$

Thus

$$\tan(\alpha + \varepsilon) = 2 \cdot \frac{\sin(45° - \varepsilon)}{\sin(45° + \varepsilon)} = 2 \cdot \frac{\sin 45° \cos \varepsilon - \cos 45° \sin \varepsilon}{\sin 45° \cos \varepsilon + \cos 45° \sin \varepsilon}.$$

Dividing the numerator and denominator by $\cos \varepsilon$ and using that $\tan \varepsilon = \mu$, we obtain:

$$\tan(\alpha + \varepsilon) = 2 \cdot \frac{\sin 45° - \cos 45° \cdot \tan \varepsilon}{\sin 45° + \cos 45° \cdot \tan \varepsilon} = 2 \cdot \frac{\sin 45° - \mu \cos 45°}{\sin 45° + \mu \cos 45°}$$

Let us use that $\sin 45° = \cos 45°$ to simplify our equation:

$$\tan(\alpha + \varepsilon) = 2 \cdot \frac{1 - \mu}{1 + \mu} = 2 \cdot \frac{0.85}{1.15} = 1.4783,$$

hence $\alpha + \varepsilon = \arctan 1.4783 = 55.92°$, and since $\tan \varepsilon = \mu = 0.15$, we find that $\varepsilon = \arctan 0.15 = 8.53°$, so the angle in question is:

$$\alpha = 55.92° - 8.53° = 47.39°.$$

If the tangent of the angle in question is to be expressed parametrically, the solution continues as:

$$\tan(\alpha + \varepsilon) = \frac{\tan \alpha + \tan \varepsilon}{1 - \tan \alpha \cdot \tan \varepsilon} = \frac{\tan \alpha + \mu}{1 - \tan \alpha \cdot \mu} = 2 \cdot \frac{1 - \mu}{1 + \mu}.$$

Thus

$$\tan \alpha + \mu = 2 \cdot \frac{1 - \mu}{1 + \mu} - 2 \cdot \frac{1 - \mu}{1 + \mu} \cdot \mu \tan \alpha.$$

Factoring out $\tan \alpha$ gives:

$$\tan \alpha \left(1 + 2\mu \frac{1 - \mu}{1 + \mu} \right) = 2 \cdot \frac{1 - \mu}{1 + \mu} - \mu.$$

After some algebra, we obtain:

$$\tan \alpha \cdot \frac{1 + \mu + 2\mu(1 - \mu)}{1 + \mu} = \frac{2(1 - \mu) - (1 + \mu)\mu}{1 + \mu}.$$

Multiplying by the denominator and dividing by the numerator of the left hand side, we obtain:

$$\tan \alpha = \frac{2(1 - \mu) - (1 + \mu)\mu}{1 + \mu + 2\mu(1 - \mu)},$$

which yields:

$$\tan \alpha = \frac{2 - 3\mu - \mu^2}{1 + \mu + 2\mu - 2\mu^2} = \frac{2 - (3 + \mu)\mu}{1 + (3 - 2\mu)\mu} = \frac{2 - 3.15 \cdot 0.15}{1 + 2.7 \cdot 0.15} = 1.0872,$$

thus $\alpha = \arctan 1.0872 = 47.39°$.

The other extreme case can be investigated similarly. In that case the law of sines applied to the two triangles give:

$$\frac{2G}{F'} = \frac{\sin(45° - \varepsilon)}{\cos(\alpha' - \varepsilon)},$$

$$\frac{G}{F'} = \frac{\sin(45° + \varepsilon)}{\sin(\alpha' - \varepsilon)}.$$

After dividing the first equation by the second and substituting the value of ε, we find that:

$$\tan(\alpha' - \varepsilon) = 2.7057$$

from which we get that the angle of the second extreme case is $\alpha' = 78.25°$.

Solution of Problem 153. The weight of the mass standard differs due to the difference in the density of the air, and thus the buoyant force is different on them. Let M_s stand for the mass of the mass standard, ϱ for the density of air, ϱ_{Plexi}, in short ϱ_p for the density of Plexiglas, ϱ_{Cu} for the density of copper, m for the unknown mass of Plexiglas. For the equilibrium of the balance, which is assumed to be equal-armed:

$$M_s g - \frac{M_s}{\varrho_{Cu}} \varrho g = mg - \frac{m}{\varrho_p} \varrho g.$$

From this

$$M_s = m \frac{\varrho_{Cu}}{\varrho_p} \cdot \frac{\varrho_p - \varrho}{\varrho_{Cu} - \varrho}.$$

Applying this to the measurements in wet and in dry air, the following expression is acquired for the apparent difference of the two masses:

$$\Delta M_s = M_s' - M_s = m \frac{\varrho_{Cu}}{\varrho_p} \cdot \left[\frac{\varrho_p - \varrho_2}{\varrho_{Cu} - \varrho_2} - \frac{\varrho_p - \varrho_1}{\varrho_{Cu} - \varrho_1} \right].$$

After transformation and simplifying:

$$\Delta M_s = m \frac{\varrho_{Cu}}{\varrho_p} \frac{(\varrho_{Cu} - \varrho_p)(\varrho_1 - \varrho_2)}{(\varrho_{Cu} - \varrho_2)(\varrho_{Cu} - \varrho_1)} \approx m \frac{\varrho_{Cu}}{\varrho_p} \frac{(\varrho_{Cu} - \varrho_p)(\varrho_1 - \varrho_2)}{\varrho_{Cu}^2} =$$

$$= m \frac{(\varrho_{Cu} - \varrho_p)(\varrho_1 - \varrho_2)}{\varrho_p \varrho_{Cu}},$$

where ϱ_1 and ϱ_2 are the densities of wet and dry air respectively. Here, $\varrho_1 - \varrho_2$ is the difference of the densities of dry and wet air, which can be derived from the theorem of partial pressures, and is thus equal to the difference of the densities of dry air and water vapour at pressure $p = 2 \cdot 10^3$ Pa and temperature $T = 296$ K. As

$$pV = \frac{m}{M}RT, \qquad \varrho = \frac{pM}{RT},$$

$$\varrho_1 - \varrho_2 = \frac{p}{RT}[M_{\text{air}} - M_{\text{H}_2\text{O}}] = 8.94 \cdot 10^{-3} \text{kg/m}^3.$$

(We made use of the molar mass of air, $M_{\text{air}} = 29 \cdot 10^{-3}\text{kg/mol}$.) With this, the unknown mass of Plexiglas is

$$m = \Delta M_{\text{s}} \cdot \frac{\varrho_{\text{p}}\varrho_{\text{Cu}}}{(\varrho_{\text{Cu}} - \varrho_{\text{p}})(\varrho_1 - \varrho_2)} = 15.3 \text{ g},$$

where $\Delta M_{\text{s}} = 10^{-4} \text{ g}$.

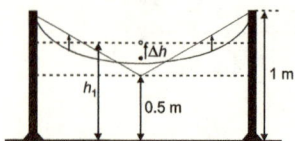

Solution of Problem 154. When the middle of the chain is pulled down, the centre of mass rises. If the chain is released, the centre of mass should fall due to the gravitational force. This is the only way that the system reaches its minimum potential energy only this way. When the middle link of the chain is pulled downwards, more mass elements move downwards than upwards. Let Δh stand for the rise of the centre of mass. Let us apply the work–energy theorem for the process:

$$W - mg\Delta h = 0.$$

From here, the change in the height of the centre of mass is

$$\Delta h = \frac{W}{mg} = \frac{0.5 \text{ J}}{2 \text{ kg} \cdot 9.81 \text{ N/kg}} = 2.55 \text{ cm}.$$

In the final state, the stretched chain segments are (approximately) straight, their centres of mass are in the mid-points of the segments, that is, they are at height $h_1 = 75$ cm from the ground, so their common centre of mass is also at this height. Originally, it was lower by Δh than this, that is,

$$h_0 = h_1 - \Delta h = 75 \text{ cm} - 2.55 \text{ cm} = 72.45 \text{ cm}$$

from the ground.

Solution of Problem 155. The easiest way to calculate the work is if we split it into three parts. Let W_1 be the work done until the top of the cube reaches the boundary, W_2 be the work done until the bottom of the cube reaches the boundary and W_3 be the work done while the cube is moved in the oil.

In the first part, the tension (thus the force exerted by us) K_1 is constant, in the second part the force decreases linearly until the bottom of the cube reaches the oil as well, then it is constant K_2. The total work done is the sum of these works:

$$W = W_1 + W_2 + W_3 = K_1 d + \frac{K_1 + K_2}{2}l + K_2 d,$$

where d is the distance between the boundary and the bases of the cube and l is the edge of the cube. In the middle part the average force can be calculated as the arithmetic mean of the initial and final values of the force.

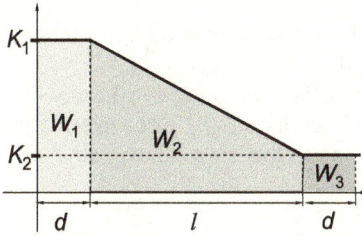

The cube must be pulled very slowly in order not to cause any whirls when the water displaces the cube, and the water-oil boundary remains horizontal. Newton's second law for the three part is:

$$K_1 + F_{1_\text{upth}} - G = 0,$$

Substituting the appropriate data:

$$K_1 = (\varrho - \varrho_w)l^3 g.$$

Similarly $K_2 + F_{2_\text{upth}} - G = 0$, from which $K_2 = (\varrho - \varrho_o)l^3 g$, and

$$\frac{K_1 + K_2}{2} = \frac{2\varrho - \varrho_w - \varrho_o}{2} \cdot l^3 g,$$

where ϱ is the density of the cube, ϱ_w is the density of water, and ϱ_o is the density of oil.

The work performed:

$$W = (\varrho - \varrho_o)l^3 gd + \frac{2\varrho - \varrho_w - \varrho_o}{2} \cdot l^3 gl + (\varrho - \varrho_o) \cdot l^3 gd,$$

so the work done is:

$$W = \frac{2\varrho - \varrho_w - \varrho_o}{2} \cdot l^3 g(2d + l).$$

Substituting the data:

$$W = \frac{(3.4 - 1 - 0.8) \cdot 10^{-3}\,\text{kg/m3}}{2} \cdot 0.008\ \text{m}^3 \cdot 9.8\,\text{m/s}^2(0.1 + 0.2)\,\text{m} = 18.82\ \text{J}.$$

Our solution is correct only if the tank is very big, otherwise the position of the boundary between the two liquids would change.

Solution of Problem 156. Investigating the second position of the wood, we can determine the exact place of its centre of mass and its weight. The conditions for translational and rotational equilibrium take the form of:

$$G + F - F_b = 0,$$

$$Gx - F\frac{l}{2} = 0,$$

where x is the distance of the centre of mass from the geometric centre. Multiplying the first equation by x and subtracting it from the second equation, we get:

$$x = \frac{F_b}{F_b - F} \cdot \frac{l}{2} = \frac{F}{\varrho_w A l g - F} \cdot \frac{l}{2} = \frac{80}{400 - 80} \cdot \frac{4\,\text{m}}{2} = 0.5\,\text{m}.$$

The weight of the wood can be calculated using the first equation:

$$G = \varrho_w A l g - F = 400\,\text{N} - 80\,\text{N} = 320\,\text{N}.$$

Therefore the mass of the wood is $m = 32\,\text{kg}$, while its density is $\varrho = 32\,\text{kg}/40\,\text{dm}^3 = 0.8\,\text{kg}/\text{dm}^3$.

The work done by us will be calculated in three steps. First we push down the wood in its vertical position until it submerges in water. While doing so, the force exerted by us increases from 0 to $F = 80\,\text{N}$, therefore the work done in this step can be calculated using the average force $\dfrac{F}{2} = 40\,\text{N}$.

Let y be the height of the wood above water level in its first position. This height can be determined assuming that the gravitational and buoyant forces are equal in magnitude:

$$l A \varrho = (l - y) A \varrho_w,$$

which yields:

$$y = l \frac{\varrho_w - \varrho}{\varrho_w} = 4\,\text{m} \cdot \frac{1 - 0.8}{1} = 0.8\,\text{m}.$$

Thus the work done in the first step is:

$$W_1 = \frac{F}{2} y = 40\,\text{N} \cdot 0.8\,\text{m} = 32\,\text{J}.$$

In the second step, the wood is slowly rotated about its centre of mass into a horizontal position. The work done by the gravitational force during the rotation is zero. The work done by the buoyant force acting on the geometric centre of the wood is:

$$W_b = -F_b \cdot x,$$

since the centre of mass of the displaced water is in the geometric centre of the wood. According to the work-kinetic energy theorem, the sum of the works done on the wood is equal to the change in its kinetic energy, which is zero. Therefore the work done by us, can be calculated using that:

$$W_2 - W_b = 0, \quad \text{hence} \quad W_2 = F_b \cdot x = 400\,\text{N} \cdot 0.5\,\text{m} = 200\,\text{J}.$$

In the third step, we let the wood move up to water level exerting a downward force of $F = 80\,\text{N}$. The distance moved by the wood is:

$$\Delta h = \frac{l}{2} + x - \frac{\sqrt{A}}{2}$$

Thus the work done by us, in the third step is:

$$W_3 = -F\left(\frac{l}{2} + x - \frac{\sqrt{A}}{2}\right) = -80\,\text{N}(2.5 - 0.05)\,\text{m} = -80 \cdot 2.45\,\text{J} = -196\,\text{J}.$$

Therefore the total work done by us while moving the wood from its initial position to its final position is:

$$W = W_1 + W_2 + W_3 = 32\,\text{J} + 200\,\text{J} - 196\,\text{J} = 36\,\text{J}.$$

Solution of Problem 157. The high-pressure air which was pumped into the rigid container does not push the originally half-submerged plank into the water any deeper. This is because the pressure exerted on the plank from above increases, since according to Pascal's law the air pushes the water as well. This pressure is conveyed in the fluid and the same excess pressure is exerted on the plank from below. Whilst from the point of view of the flotation the effect of air at atmospheric pressure is negligible, the high pressure air in the closed container has considerable density, and in this case the upthrust due to the air is comparable to the upthrust due to the water. So now the plank floats at the boundary of two media. We have to find the total upthrust exerted by the two media.

The width of the plank is d, and the width of that part which is submerged in water is x, the density of water is ϱ, the density of air at a pressure of 100 atmosphere is ϱ_1. This lattest one can be calculated from the gas laws. For the standard conditions:

$$p_0 V_0 = \frac{m}{M} RT \qquad \rightarrow \qquad p_0 = \frac{m}{V_0}\frac{RT}{M}$$

and for the high pressure state:

$$pV = \frac{m}{M} RT \qquad \rightarrow \qquad p = \frac{m}{V}\frac{RT}{M},$$

where $m/V_0 = \varrho_0$ and $m/V = \varrho_1$. After dividing the two equations the density of the high-pressure air can be expressed:

$$\varrho_1 = \frac{p}{p_0}\varrho_0 = 100 \cdot 0.0013\,\frac{\text{g}}{\text{cm}^3} = 0.13\,\frac{\text{g}}{\text{cm}^3}$$

Using this, we can apply Newton's second law:

$$Ad\varrho g - Ax\varrho g - A(d-x)\varrho_1 g = 0,$$

where A is the area of the base of the plank. From this, the height of the part of the plank which is submerged is:

$$x = d \cdot \frac{\varrho_0 - \varrho_1}{\varrho - \varrho_1} = 10\,\text{cm} \cdot \frac{0.5 - 0.13}{1 - 1.13} = 4.25\,\text{cm}.$$

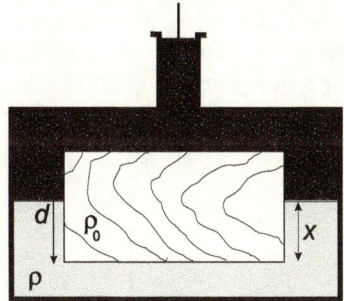

6.4 Fluids

Solution of Problem 158. Since the mass of the sphere is negligible, initially a negligibly small part of its whole volume submerges into the water. (If we assume that the sphere is a balloon, and it is filled with air, then the mass of the air can also be neglected, that is why the density of air is not given.) While the sphere is slowly pushed into the water, the kinetic energy of the system consisting of the water and the sphere does not change, so according to the work–energy theorem, the sum of the works done by all forces acting on the system is zero. There are two forces doing work, the external pushing force and the weight of the water. The air pressure does not do work because the volume of the system is constant. Since the mass of the sphere is negligible, the work done by the external pushing force is the opposite of the work done by the weight force on the water. (Indeed, their sum is zero.)

a) If the sphere is pushed down in a lake, then the rearrangement of the water during the process can be observed as the water displaced by the sphere at the bottom of the lake moves to the top of the lake in a very thin layer, while the rest of the water remains at its original position.

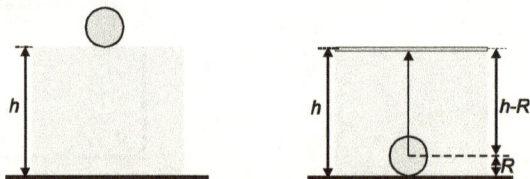

The centre of mass of the displaced water gets higher by $(h - R)$, therefore the work done by the weight force on the water is $W_{\text{weight}} = -m_{\text{water}}g(h - R)$. This means that the work of the external pushing force is:

$$W = m_{\text{water}}g(h - R) = \varrho V_{\text{sphere}}g(h - R) = \frac{4}{3}R^3\pi\varrho g(h - R),$$

and numerically:

$$W = \frac{4}{3} \cdot 0.008 \text{ m}^3 \cdot \pi \cdot 10^3 \, \frac{\text{kg}}{\text{m}^3} \cdot 9.81 \, \frac{\text{m}}{\text{s}^2} \cdot 0.8 \text{ m} = 263 \text{ J}.$$

b) If the sphere is pushed down into the tank of base area A, then it can be observed as the displaced water gets to the top of the tank and forms there a layer with a thickness of:

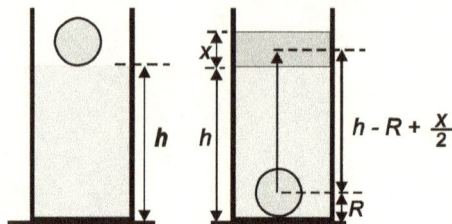

$$x = \frac{V_{\text{sphere}}}{A} = \frac{4R^3\pi}{3A},$$

while the position of the rest of the water does not change. The centre of mass of the displaced water rises by

$$\left(h - R + \frac{x}{2}\right),$$

so the work done by the external force is:

$$W = \frac{4}{3}R^3\pi\varrho g\left(h - R + \frac{x}{2}\right) = \frac{4}{3}R^3\pi\varrho g\left(h - R + \frac{4R^3\pi}{6A}\right).$$

Numerically:

$$W = \frac{4}{3}\cdot 0.2^3 \text{ m}^3\cdot\pi\cdot 10^3 \frac{\text{kg}}{\text{m}^3}\cdot 9.81 \frac{\text{m}}{\text{s}^2}\cdot\left(0.8 \text{ m} + \frac{4\cdot 0.2^3 \text{ m}^3\cdot\pi}{6\cdot 0.5 \text{ m}^2}\right) = 274 \text{ J}.$$

Solution of Problem 159. First of all, let us examine whether the container is floating or submerged. The mass of the container is 13 kg and the volume of the water in it is $6 \text{ dm} \cdot 2 \text{ dm} \cdot 1 \text{ dm} = 12 \text{ dm}^3$, which means there is an additional mass of 12 kg. Therefore the total mass, which is 25 kg, divided by the volume of the container, which is $V = 4 \text{ dm}^2\cdot 6 \text{ dm} = 24 \text{ dm}^2$, gives an average density of $\varrho_{\text{average}} = 25/24 \text{ kg/dm}^3 > 1 \text{ kg/dm}^3$, which is greater than the density of water, meaning that the container is at the bottom of the tank.

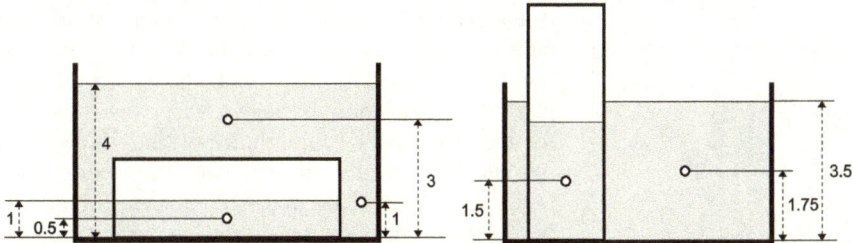

The total work done can be determined by calculating the change in the potential energy of the system. Assuming that moving the container is done slowly, the energy dissipation can be neglected.

Let us set the potential energy at the bottom of the tank to zero.

First, the initial potential energy of the system must be determined. Calculating the potential energy of the water outside the container is done in two steps. Let us handle the masses of water above the container and on the sides of it separately. At the initial state the water above the container has its centre of mass at a height of 3 dm and has a volume of $20 \text{ dm}^2\cdot 2 \text{ dm} = 40 \text{ dm}^3$, which is equivalent to a mass of 40 kg. The volume of the water on the sides of the container can be calculated as the total volume of the water in the tank, which is $20 \text{ dm}^2\cdot 4 \text{ dm} - 24 \text{ dm}^3 = 56 \text{ dm}^3$, minus the volume of the water above the container: $56 \text{ dm}^3 - 40 \text{ dm}^3 = 16 \text{ dm}^3$. This gives 16 kg for the mass of water whose centre of mass is at a height of 1 dm. The mass of water inside the container is 12 kg, and its centre of mass is at 0.5 dm from the bottom. Finally, the container itself has a mass of 13 kg and its centre of mass is at a height of 1 dm.

Thus the initial potential energy of the system (that consists of the water inside and outside the container and the container itself) is:

$$E_{p_1} = 400 \text{ N}\cdot 0.3 \text{ m} + 160 \text{ N}\cdot 0.1 \text{ m} + 120 \text{ N}\cdot 0.05 \text{ m} + 130 \text{ N}\cdot 0.1 \text{ m} = 155 \text{ J}.$$

Let us now calculate the potential energy of the system after setting the container in its upright position:

The part of the base of the tank that is not covered by the container is $20\,\mathrm{dm}^2 - 4\,\mathrm{dm}^2 = 16\,\mathrm{dm}^2$, which means that the $56\,\mathrm{dm}^3$ water outside the container fills the tank to a level of $56\,\mathrm{dm}^3/16\,\mathrm{dm}^2 = 3.5\,\mathrm{dm}$, therefore the centre of mass of the water in the tank is at a height of $1.75\,\mathrm{dm}$. The centre of mass of the water inside the container and that of the container itself are at a distance of $1.5\,\mathrm{dm}$ and $3\,\mathrm{dm}$ from the bottom. So the potential energy of the system in its final state is: $E_{p_2} = 560\,\mathrm{N}\cdot 0.175\,\mathrm{m} + 120\,\mathrm{N}\cdot 0.15\,\mathrm{m} + 130\,\mathrm{N}\cdot 0.3\,\mathrm{m} = 155\,\mathrm{J}$. Our results show that the potential energy of the system is the same in the initial and the final positions, therefore the total work done on the system is zero. This means that the work that is given to the system at a given stage will be given back to us at another stage.

Note that in spite of the fact that our work input is gained back at a given stage of the motion, this work cannot be used for anything.

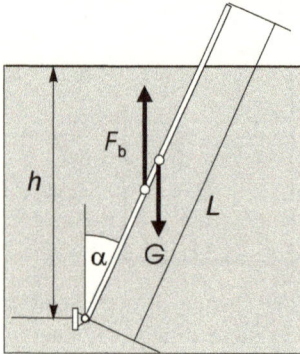

Solution of Problem 160. The rod is in equilibrium if the sum of the torques of gravitational force and buoyant force is zero. Since the density of the rod is less than the density of water both in case a), and b), part of the rod must be above water level — except for the two trivial equilibrium positions in which the rod stands vertically up or down. The reason for this is the following: if the rod is completely immersed in water, the point of action of both the gravitational and the buoyant force is at the geometrical centre of the rod, so the moment arms of the two forces are the same, but as the gravitational force $\varrho_{\text{water}} Alg$ is always greater than the buoyant force ϱAlg, the sum of their torques will never be zero.

The upper end of the rod will rise until it reaches a position in which the torque of the buoyant force (due to the change in the moment arm and in the amount of displaced water) that is acting on the part under water, will reach the same magnitude as the torque of the gravitational force that is acting at the centre of the rod.

Let the equilibrium position be given by angle α, which is the angle formed by the rod and the vertical. The sum of the torques of the gravitational and buoyant force can be written as:

$$\varrho ALg\frac{L}{2}\sin\alpha - \varrho_w A\frac{h}{\cos\alpha}g\frac{h}{2\cos\alpha}\sin\alpha = 0,$$

Where A is the cross-sectional area of the rod and ϱ_w is the density of water. This leads us to

$$\cos\alpha = \frac{h}{L}\sqrt{\frac{\varrho_w}{\varrho}}.$$

Substituting values in case a) gives:

$$\cos\alpha = \frac{0.8}{1}\sqrt{\frac{1}{0.5}} = 1.1313 > 1,$$

which is impossible, so in case a) there are only the two trivial equilibrium positions: at $\alpha_1 = 0°$ the equilibrium is stable and at $\alpha_2 = 180°$ the equilibrium is unstable. For every other angle $0 < \alpha < 180°$ the torque of the buoyant force is greater than that of the gravitational force.

In case b), we get three equilibrium positions:

$$\cos\alpha = \frac{0.8}{1}\sqrt{\frac{1}{0.853}} = 0.866,$$

so the two torques will cancel once they reach the angle $\alpha = 30°$. The equilibrium positions are therefore: $\alpha_1 = 0°$ and $\alpha_2 = 180°$ both being unstable and $\alpha_3 = 30°$, which is stable.

Solution of Problem 161. If the cart is released and left on its own, its motion will be rather complicated. When the cart suddenly starts to move, some water usually spills out, and the water that remains in the cart starts to oscillate. This means that instead of the cart and the hanging object having a constant acceleration, they will undergo a very complicated motion that cannot be described using basic mathematics. Let us therefore assume that the string is very long, the table is very high and the cart is not released suddenly, but keeping one hand on it, we increase its acceleration slowly to the final constant value. Our calculations below will all concern this final state of the system.

The volume of water in the cart is $V = ahl = 1\,\text{dm}\cdot 0.9\,\text{dm}\cdot 2\,\text{dm} = 1.8\,\text{dm}^3$ initially, therefore the initial mass of water is $m_1 = 1.8\,\text{kg}$. Thus the mass of the cart itself is $m_3 = M - m_1 = 0.2\,\text{kg}$.

When the cart moves with constant acceleration, the surface of the water is not horizontal, but forms an angle α with the horizontal. Angle α is determined by the equation:

$$\tan\alpha = \frac{a}{g}.$$

Since the level of water was quite high initially, it is almost guaranteed that some water will spill out. In order to check this, let us assume that no water spills out and see what follows from that. In this case, the acceleration of the cart and water can be determined by applying Newton's second law to the cart (adding the total mass of water to the cart's own mass) and the hanging object, from which we obtain:

$$a = \frac{m_2}{M + m_2}\cdot g,$$

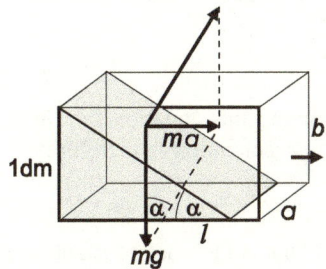

which yields:

$$\tan\alpha = \frac{a}{g} = \frac{m_2}{M+m_2} = \frac{1.2}{2+1.2} = 0.375 \quad \text{hence} \quad \alpha = 20.55°.$$

If a line that encloses this angle with the horizontal was drawn through the centre of the horizontal surface of water, it would pass well above the top of the back wall of the cart, which means that some water does indeed spill out. Let us now solve the problem using this statement.

Since part of the water — whose mass is still unknown — spills out, the total mass of the cart gets changed as well. The first task is to find out the mass of water that remains in the cart in case the water surface forms an angle α with the horizontal. The volume of water inside the cart can be determined by calculating the volume of a triangular prism, which (using the notations of the figure) can be written as:

$$\frac{1}{2} \cdot \frac{b}{\tan\alpha} \cdot a \cdot b = \frac{1}{2} \cdot \frac{1\,\text{dm}}{\tan\alpha} \cdot 1\,\text{dm} \cdot 1\,\text{dm} = \frac{1}{2\tan\alpha}\text{litre},$$

thus the mass of water in question is

$$m_1' = \frac{1}{2\tan\alpha}\,\text{kg}.$$

The laws of motion of this system are:

$$m_2 g - K = m_2 a,$$

$$K = (m_3 + m_1')a.$$

From which the acceleration of the cart and object is:

$$a = \frac{m_2}{m_3 + m_1' + m_2} \cdot g.$$

The tangent of the angle of inclination of the water surface therefore can be written as:

$$\tan\alpha = \frac{a}{g} = \frac{m_2}{m_3 + m_1' + m_2} = \frac{1.2}{0.2 + \frac{1}{2}\tan\alpha + 1.2}.$$

Solving this equation for $\tan\alpha$, we find $\tan\alpha = 0.5$, ($\alpha = 26.57°$). The magnitude of the acceleration is therefore:

$$a = g \cdot \tan\alpha = 0.5g \approx 4.9\,\frac{\text{m}}{\text{s}^2}.$$

This is the final constant acceleration of the cart. The water remaining in the cart has volume $V' = 1$ litre and mass $m_1' = 1$ kg, which means that 0.8 litre of water was spilled out. The water level at the back of the cart is at the top of the wall. (If we got a value for $\tan\alpha$ that was less than 0.5, the cross section of the water inside the cart would be a trapezoid and not a triangle, therefore the volume of a trapezoid based prism should be determined to find the volume of the water remaining in the cart.)

Solution of Problem 162. The material in the container moves with a constant normal acceleration whose value is different for each point of the container. This is ensured by the constraining force of the individual concentric layers. This is similar to the hydrostatic pressure in liquid supported by the gravitational field arising from the constraining force exerted by the individual layers on each other: due to the rotation radial pressure is created along the cylindrical surfaces coaxial, while the axis of rotation and pressure difference is created between the layers. Therefore, the body placed in the liquid experiences not only an Archimedean bouyant force but also a force that acts towards the axis.

The force is the same as the force exerted by the surroundings on a liquid element that is placed into the same position and has the same size. This liquid element is forced to accelerate radially by its surroundings, which 'takes no interest' in the material filling the boundary of the liquid element, be that a liquid of the same density or some other material.

Similarly to Archimedes' principle, we could state the following: On every body immersed into a rotating liquid (and rotating with it), besides the Archimedean bouyant force — caused by gravity — the liquid also exerts a centripetal force whose magnitude is the same as the force that would act on a liquid element displaced by the body at the same position. (This force depends on its position; it is directly proportional to the distance between the centre of mass of the body — in the case of a homogeneous body the geometrical centre — and the axis of rotation.)

Because of the above, bodies whose density is smaller than the density of water accelerate not only upwards but also 'inwards'. Water, whose density is higher, is forced to move further from the axis. The magnitude of the vertical and horizontal (radial) forces can be acquired from the suitable equations of motion. The line of action of these two forces is in the vertical plane that contains the axis of rotation. When the bead has taken its stationary position, gravity, the two Archimedean bouyant forces and the tension in the thread ensure the circular motion.

The equations of motion in the y and x directions in the inertial reference frame are

$$\varrho_w V g - \varrho_{\text{body}} V g - T_y = 0$$
$$\varrho_w V r \omega^2 - T_x = \varrho_{\text{body}} V r \omega^2.$$

From these, the magnitude of the two components of tension force is:

$$T_y = (\varrho_w - \varrho_{\text{body}}) \cdot V g$$

and

$$T_x = (\varrho_w - \varrho_{\text{body}}) \cdot V r \omega^2.$$

The ratio of the two is (independent of the densities)

$$\tan \varphi = \frac{T_x}{T_y} = \frac{r \omega^2}{g}.$$

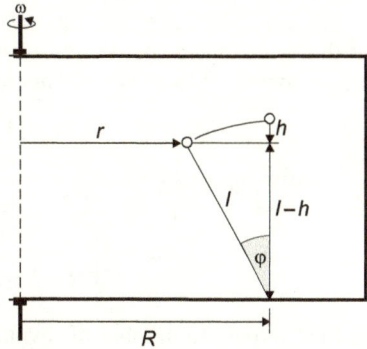

From geometry

$$\tan\varphi = \frac{R-r}{l-h}.$$

From the equality of the two

$$\frac{r\omega^2}{g} = \frac{R-r}{l-h}.$$

The distance r of the bead from the axis of rotation (the radius of its circular orbit) is unknown. This can be determined from the length of the thread and the given sinking of the bead. Since the density of the bead is smaller than the density of water, it will move inwards. Using the Pythagorean theorem

$$r = R - \sqrt{l^2 - (l-h)^2} = R - \sqrt{(2l-h)\cdot h}.$$

Substituting this into the previous equation and rearranging for ω gives

$$\omega = \sqrt{\frac{g\sqrt{(2l-h)\cdot h}}{(l-h)\cdot\left(R-\sqrt{(2l-h)\cdot h}\right)}} = 9.68 \text{ s}^{-1},$$

and the requested number of revolutions is

$$n = \frac{\omega}{2\pi} = 1.54 \text{ s}^{-1}.$$

Solution of Problem 163. a) The pressure at the bottom is obviously the same because the total mass of the water is the same, so the force on the bottom must also be the same. On the other hand, at height h_1 measured from the bottom the pressure increases. This is because of thermal expansion, which causes some material to move above the horizontal surface taken at h_1. The increase in pressure is proportional to the amount of material that moves above the level:

$$\Delta p_1 = \varrho' g \Delta h.$$

Here the new density of water is

$$\varrho' = \frac{\varrho}{1 + \beta\cdot\Delta t}$$

and

$$\Delta h_1 = \frac{\Delta V_1}{A} = \frac{V_1\beta\Delta t}{A} = \frac{h_1\cdot A\cdot\beta\Delta t}{A} = h_1\beta\Delta t.$$

With this the requested increase in pressure is

$$\Delta p_1 = \varrho g \Delta h_1 = \varrho\cdot g\cdot h_1\cdot\frac{\beta\Delta t}{1+\beta\Delta t} =$$

$$= 10^3 \frac{\text{kg}}{\text{m}^3}\cdot 9.81\frac{\text{m}}{\text{s}^2}\cdot 0.2\,\text{m}\cdot\frac{0.00013\ ^\circ\text{C}^{-1}\cdot 80\ ^\circ\text{C}}{1+0.00013\ ^\circ\text{C}^{-1}\cdot 80\ ^\circ\text{C}} = 20.2\,\text{Pa}.$$

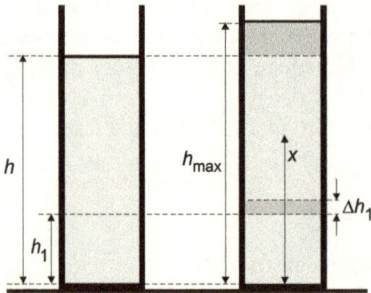

b) The pressure increase–height function consists of three parts. The first interval is $0 \leq x \leq h$ (where x stands for the distance measured from the bottom of the container), the second is $h \leq x \leq h_{\max}$, the third is $h_{\max} \leq x \leq \infty$. For this last interval Δp_{III} is obviously 0.

We have already determined the pressure increase function in the first interval. Its maximum is at $x = h$, its value is

$$\frac{h}{h_1} \cdot \Delta p_1 = 3\Delta p_1 = 60.6 \, \text{Pa}.$$

We have to determine the domain of the middle interval. This is

$$h \leq x \leq h_{\max}, \qquad \text{,that is} \qquad h \leq x \leq h(1 + \beta \Delta t).$$

the numerical value of $h_{\max}$ is

$$h_{\max} = 60 \, \text{cm} \cdot (1 + 0.00013 \, ^{\circ}\text{C}^{-1} \cdot 80 \, ^{\circ}\text{C}) = 60.62 \, \text{cm}.$$

The requested functions in the three intervals are

$$\Delta p_{\mathrm{I}} = \varrho g x \cdot \frac{\beta \Delta t}{1 + \beta \Delta t} = 100.97 \frac{\text{Pa}}{\text{m}} \cdot x,$$

$$\Delta p_{\mathrm{II}} = \frac{\varrho}{1 + \beta \, \Delta t} g(h_{\max} - x) = \frac{\varrho}{1 + \beta \, \Delta t} g[h \cdot (1 + \beta \Delta t) - x] =$$

$$\varrho g h - \frac{\varrho}{1 + \beta \, \Delta t} g \cdot x = \varrho g \left(h - \frac{x}{1 + \beta \Delta t} \right) = 5886 \, \text{Pa} - 9709 \frac{\text{Pa}}{\text{m}} \cdot x.$$

$$\Delta p_{\mathrm{III}} = 0,$$

respectively.

The acquired functions are shown by the following figures:

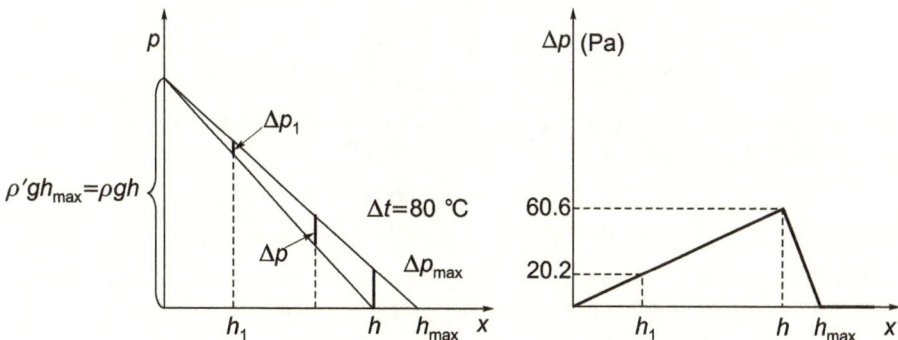

Chapter 7

Thermodynamics Solutions

7.1 Thermal expansion

Solution of Problem 164. Steel is also heated with the paraffin. The problem does not state whether the coefficients of thermal expansion are calculated at a temperature of 0 °C or 18 °C or 20 °C. Let us assume that all of these data are calculated at a temperature of 0 °C, though the difference between the coefficients at different temperatures is quite small.

The coefficient of volumetric expansion of steel is $\beta_s = 3 \cdot \alpha_s = 3.6 \cdot 10^{-5} 1/°C$. If the volume of the steel ball at a temperature of 0 °C is V_s, then at 20 °C its volume is $V_s(1 + 3.6 \cdot 10^{-5} \cdot 20)$, and at 100 °C its volume is $V_s(1 + 3.6 \cdot 10^{-5} \cdot 100)$.

If the density of the paraffin at 0 °C is ϱ_0, its volumetric thermal expansion coefficient is β_p, then the density of the paraffin at a temperature of $t_1 = 20$ °C-on, or at 100 °C is:

$$\varrho_{20} = \frac{m}{V_0(1 + \beta_p t_1)} = \frac{\varrho_0 V_0}{V_0(1 + \beta_p t_1)} = \frac{\varrho_0}{1 + \beta_p t_1}, \quad \text{or} \quad \varrho_{100} = \frac{\varrho_0}{1 + \beta_p t_2}.$$

The upthrust is the product of the volume of the immersed ball, the density of the liquid, and the acceleration due to gravity, so at temperatures 20 °C and 100 °C the values of the upthrust are:

$$F_{20} = \frac{V_s(1 + 3.6 \cdot 10^{-5} \cdot 20)\varrho_0 g}{1 + \beta_p \cdot 20 \, °C} = 0.2145 \, \text{N},$$

$$F_{100} = \frac{V_s(1 + 3.6 \cdot 10^{-5} \cdot 100)\varrho_0 g}{1 + \beta_p \cdot 100 \cdot 1/°C} = 0.200 \, \text{N}.$$

If the first equation is divided by the second, the volume of the steel ball and the density of the paraffin at a tempeature of 0 °C can be cancelled.

$$\frac{(1 + 3.6 \cdot 10^{-5} \cdot 20)(1 + \beta_p \cdot 100 \cdot 1/°C)}{(1 + 3.6 \cdot 10^{-5} \cdot 100)(1 + \beta_p \cdot 20 \cdot 1/°C)} = \frac{0.2145}{0.200}.$$

From this equation which is a linear equation for β_p the volumetric thermal expansion coefficient of paraffin at a temperature of 0 °C can be calculated:

$$\beta_p = 0.963 \cdot 10^{-3} \, 1/°C.$$

Solution of Problem 165. As the temperature of the brass sphere increases, its volume increases as well. The homogeneous, solid sphere expands uniformly in all directions. Its total mass remains constant, but every elementary part of the sphere gets a bit farther from the axis of rotation, thus the moment of inertia of the sphere increases. The scaling of the volume, due to the temperature increase, does not change the expression describing the moment of inertia of the sphere:

$$\Theta = \frac{2}{5}mR^2.$$

Let R' denote the increased radius of the sphere, and let α be the linear thermal expansion coefficient of brass. After the temperature increase Δt the new moment of inertia is

$$\Theta' = \frac{2}{5}mR'^2 = \frac{2}{5}mR^2(1+\alpha\Delta t)^2.$$

With a lack of torque the angular momentum of the freely rotating sphere remains constant, so the following equation holds:

$$\Theta \cdot \omega = \Theta' \cdot \omega'.$$

From here, the ratio of frequencies (which is the same as the ratio of angular velocities) is:

$$\frac{\omega}{\omega'} = \frac{2\pi f}{2\pi f'} = \frac{f}{f'} = \frac{\Theta'}{\Theta} = \frac{\frac{2}{5}mR^2(1+\alpha\Delta t)^2}{\frac{2}{5}mR^2} = (1+\alpha\Delta t)^2.$$

Taking the square root of the equation:

$$1+\alpha\Delta t = \sqrt{\frac{f}{f'}},$$

so the maximal temperature increase in question is:

$$\Delta t = \frac{\sqrt{\frac{f}{f'}}-1}{\alpha} = \frac{\sqrt{1.01}-1}{1.84\cdot10^{-5}\frac{1}{°C}} = 271 \ °C.$$

Solution of Problem 166. From the equilibrium of torques, the following equation is obtained for the angle of inclination of the rod to the horizontal at $4\,°C$:

$$\varrho_{0Al} L_0 (A_e - A_i)g\frac{L_0}{2}\cos\varphi_0 - \varrho_{0w}\frac{h_0}{\sin\varphi_0}A_e g\frac{h_0}{2\sin\varphi_0} = 0.$$

Hence

$$\sin\varphi_0 = \frac{h_0}{L_0}\sqrt{\frac{\varrho_{0w}A_e}{\varrho_{0Al}(A_e - A_i)}} = \frac{0.6}{1}\sqrt{\frac{1\cdot1.2}{2.7\cdot0.2}} = 0.8944,$$

and the initial angle is $\varphi_0 = \arcsin 0.8944 = 63.43°$.

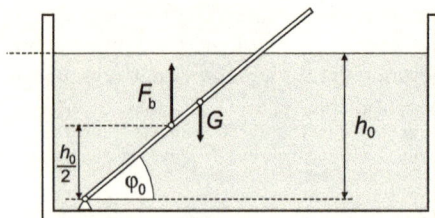

The tube, the water and the tank all expand when heated. The interior of the tank expands as if it were solid glass. The geometric dimensions and the densities all change:

$$\varrho_w = \frac{\varrho_{0w}}{1+\beta_w\Delta t} \quad (=961.9\,\text{kg/m}^3),$$

$$\varrho_{Al} = \frac{\varrho_{0Al}}{1+3\alpha_{Al}\Delta t} \quad (=2682.6\,\text{kg/m}^3).$$

The new length of the tube is

$$L = L_0(1+\alpha_{Al}\Delta t) \quad (=1.00216\,\text{m}),$$

and the new water height is

$$h = \frac{V}{A} = \frac{A_0 h_0(1+\beta_w\Delta t)}{A_0(1+2\alpha_{glass}\Delta t)} = h_0\frac{1+\beta_w\Delta t}{1+2\alpha_{glass}\Delta t} \quad (=0.6229\,\text{m}),$$

where A_0 is the original base area of the tank. The sine of the new angle of inclination is

$$\sin\varphi = \frac{h}{L}\sqrt{\frac{\varrho_w}{\varrho_{Al}}\cdot\frac{A_e}{A_e-A_i}} = \frac{h_0(1+\beta_w\Delta t)}{L_0(1+2\alpha_{glass}\Delta t)(1+\alpha_{Al}\Delta t)}\sqrt{\frac{\varrho_{0w}(1+3\alpha_{Al}\Delta t)A_e}{\varrho_{0Al}(1+\beta_w\Delta t)(A_e-A_i)}}.$$

(Since the ratio of the cross-sectional areas of the tube does not change). With the substitution of numerical data:

$$\sin\varphi = 0.91162, \quad \text{and hence} \quad \varphi = \arcsin 0.91162 = 65.73°.$$

Thus the change in the angle of inclination is

$$\Delta\varphi = 65.73° - 63.43° = 2.3°,$$

the tube will rise.

Solution of Problem 167. Since the temperature is not mentioned in the problem, we may assume that the process takes place very slowly, and that the temperature remains constant. In this case, Boyle's law holds true for the process.

Let us denote the volume of the porous material (material with a lot of holes in it) by x

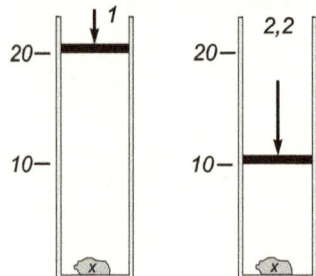

(which is the difference between the volume enclosed by the envelope-surface of the material and the total volume of the holes, which contain air). According to Boyle's law:

$$p_1 V_1 = p_2 V_2,$$

so the equation for the air confined in the syringe, whose initial volume is $V_1 = V_1' - x$ and whose final volume is $V_2 = V_2' - x$, is :

$$1\,\text{atm}\cdot(20\text{ cm}^3 - x) = 2.2\,\text{atm}\cdot(10\text{ cm}^3 - x).$$

Thus the volume of the porous material is:

$$x = 1.67\text{ cm}^3.$$

7.2 Ideal gas processes

Solution of Problem 168. Let us start from the properties of gases at standard reference conditions. The molar volume of both gases at standard reference conditions is $V_{0M} = 22.41$ dm^3. Thus in this state, 30 g mixture of gases, which contains 2 g of hydrogen and 28 g of nitrogen, is a 50 percent volume mixture. However, the temperature of the gases in the problem is 27 °C, so, applying Charles's law, the molar volume of the gases is:

$$V_M = V_{0M}\frac{T}{T_0} = 22.41 \text{ dm}^3 \cdot \frac{300 \text{ K}}{273 \text{ K}} = 24.63 \text{ dm}^3.$$

Since an amount of $m_{\text{mixture}} = 500$ g mixture is needed in every minute, from both gases a volume $\dfrac{m_{\text{mixture}}}{M_{\text{mixture}}} = \dfrac{500 \text{ g}}{30 \text{ g}} = 16.67$ times greater than the molar volume should be provided for the mixture. So the volume of the gases flowed in the tubes per minute is:

$$\Delta V = \frac{m_{\text{mixture}}}{M_{\text{mixture}}} \cdot V_{0M}\frac{T}{T_0} = 16.67 \cdot 24.63 \text{ dm}^3 = 410.58 \text{ dm}^3.$$

The volume of the gases passed through the tubes per second is:

$$\frac{\Delta V}{\Delta t} = \frac{410.58 \text{ dm}^3}{60 \text{ s}} = 6.84 \frac{\text{dm}^3}{\text{s}}.$$

This quantity is the volumetric flow rate I, which, according to the continuity equation, can be expressed as

$$I = Av,$$

where A is the cross section of the tubes, and v is the (average) speed of the flow. Thus the speed of both gases in the tubes is:

$$v = \frac{I}{A} = \frac{\Delta V}{A\Delta t} = \frac{6.84 \text{ dm}^3/\text{s}}{0.1 \text{ dm}^2} = 68.4 \frac{\text{dm}}{\text{s}} = 6.84 \frac{\text{m}}{\text{s}}.$$

Solution of Problem 169. Applying Newton's second law to the piston in its final position, we get:

$$p_r A - p_l A = m_p a, \qquad (1)$$

where p_r and p_l are the pressures in the right and left part respectively, A is the base area of the cylinder, and a is the acceleration of the piston of mass m_p. In the piston's final position, its acceleration will be the same as the acceleration of the cylinder. Initially the volume of the gas in the left part is $V_l = 0.8$ dm^3, so the piston is initially at a distance

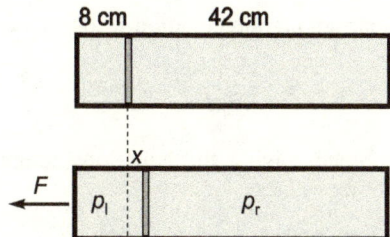

of $l_l = V_l/A = 0.8\,\mathrm{dm} = 8\,\mathrm{cm}$ from the left base of the cylinder. Similarly the piston's distance from the right base of the cylinder is: $l_r = V_r/A = 4.2\,\mathrm{dm} = 42\,\mathrm{cm}$.

The final position of the piston is determined by its distance from the cylinder's left base, which is $y = l_l + x$, where x is the distance between the piston's initial and final positions. When the piston comes to rest (relative to the cylinder) in its final position, all points in the system have the same acceleration, so according to Newton's second law:

$$F = a_{cm} \sum m,$$

from which the acceleration of the centre of mass (a_{cm}) is:

$$a_{cm} = \frac{F}{m_p + m_c} = \frac{2.5\,\mathrm{N}}{(0.2 + 0.8)\,\mathrm{kg}} = 2.5\,\frac{\mathrm{m}}{\mathrm{s}^2}.$$

Applying Newton's second law to the piston again, we get:

$$(p_r - p_l)A = m_p \frac{F}{m_p + m_c} = 0.2\,\mathrm{kg} \cdot 2.5\,\frac{\mathrm{m}}{\mathrm{s}^2} = 0.5\,\mathrm{N},$$

where p_r and p_l are the final pressures of the gases in the right and left part respectively. Applying Boyle's law to the gases in the two parts, we obtain:

$$V_l p = (l_l + x)A p_l,$$
$$V_r p = (l_r - x)A p_r,$$

where p is the initial pressure in both parts. This leads us to

$$p_r = \frac{V_r p}{(l_r - x)A},$$
$$p_l = \frac{V_l p}{(l_l + x)A},$$
$$p_r - p_l = \frac{m_p a}{A}.$$

Substituting the expressions for the final pressures into the equation above, we find:

$$\frac{V_r}{l_r - x}p - \frac{V_l}{l_l + x}p = m_p a = m_p \frac{F}{m_p + m_c}. \tag{2}$$

Rearranging the equation leads to a quadratic equation for x:

$$x^2 + \left[\frac{V_r + V_l}{m_p F}(m_p + m_c)p + l_l - l_r\right] \cdot x + \frac{V_r l_l - V_l l_r}{m_p F}(m_p + m_c)p - l_r l_l = 0.$$

Since solving the equation parametrically is far too complicated, let us substitute known values:

$$x^2 + \left(\frac{5000\,\mathrm{cm}^3}{0.2\,\mathrm{kg} \cdot 2.5\,\mathrm{N}} \cdot 1\,\mathrm{kg} \cdot 0.02\,\frac{\mathrm{N}}{\mathrm{cm}^2} + 8\,\mathrm{cm} - 42\,\mathrm{cm}\right)x -$$

$$- \frac{4200\,\mathrm{cm}^3 \cdot 8\,\mathrm{cm} - 800\,\mathrm{cm}^3 \cdot 42\,\mathrm{cm}}{0.2\,\mathrm{kg} \cdot 2.5\,\mathrm{N}} \cdot 1\,\mathrm{kg} \cdot 0.02\,\frac{\mathrm{N}}{\mathrm{cm}^2} - 8\,\mathrm{cm} \cdot 42\,\mathrm{cm} = 0$$

hence:

$$x^2 + 166\,\text{cm} \cdot x - 336\,\text{cm}^2 = 0$$

The solution is:

$$x = \frac{-166 \pm \sqrt{166^2 + 4 \cdot 336}}{2}\,\text{cm} = 2\,\text{cm},$$

So the final position of the piston will be at a distance of $y = l_l + x = 8\,\text{cm} + 2\,\text{cm} = 10\,\text{cm}$ from the left base of the cylinder.

Remark: The solution becomes a bit shorter if known values are substituted right into equation (2) without units, which gives:

$$\frac{4200}{42 - x} \cdot 0.02 - \frac{800}{8 + x} \cdot 0.02 = 02 \cdot 2.5$$

hence

$$\frac{84}{42 - x} - \frac{16}{8 + x} = 0.5.$$

rearranging the equation leads us to:

$$x^2 + 166x - 336 = 0$$

which is the same as the one obtained from the parametric equation in the solution.

For additional information, the final pressures on the two sides of the piston are:

$$p_l = \frac{800\ \text{cm}^3 \cdot 0.02\,\text{N/cm}^2}{10\,\text{cm} \cdot 100\,\text{cm}^2} = 0.016\ \frac{\text{N}}{\text{cm}^2},$$

$$p_r = \frac{4200\ \text{cm}^3 \cdot 0.02\,\text{N/cm}^2}{40\,\text{cm} \cdot 100\,\text{cm}^2} = 0.021\,\text{N/cm}^2.$$

Solution of Problem 170. Note that in this problem the change in the height of the mercury level cannot be neglected, since the base area of the container is small. When the volume of the air in the cylinder decreases, so does the mercury level, and assuming that the base areas of the container and cylinder are in the ratio $2:1$, we get that the decrease in the height of the mercury level is one half of the decrease in the height of the air-column in the cylinder.

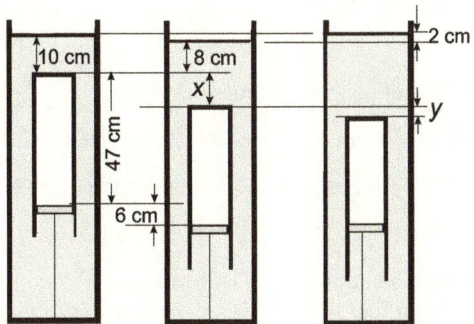

The cylinder will be in equilibrium if the mass of the cylinder and the thickness of its walls can be neglected, and if the external pressure acting on its top end equals its internal pressure (due to the enclosed air).

a) Let centimetres of Mercury (cmHg) be the unit of pressure. The atmospheric pressure can be assumed to be the normal 76 cmHg. Let x be the distance moved down by the top of the cylinder when the cord is shortened by Δl. In this case the mercury level decreases by

$$\Delta h = \frac{x - \Delta l}{2}$$

Applying Boyle's law to the air inside the cylinder, we obtain:

$$(p_0 + h_0) \cdot L = \left(p_0 + x + h_0 - \frac{x - \Delta l}{2} \right) \cdot (L + \Delta l - x),$$

where p_0 is the atmospheric pressure, h_0 is the height of mercury above the cylinder in the initial position and L is the initial height of the air column inside the cylinder. Substituting known values, we get:

$$(75 \,\text{cm} + 10 \,\text{cm}) \cdot 47 \,\text{cm} =$$

$$= \left(76 \,\text{cm} + x + 10 \,\text{cm} - \frac{x - 6 \,\text{cm}}{2} \right) \cdot (47 \,\text{cm} + 6 \,\text{cm} - x).$$

Rearranging this, we get a quadratic equation for x:

$$x^2 + 125 \,\text{cm} \cdot x - 1350 \,\text{cm}^2 = 0.$$

The solution of this equation is:

$$x = 10 \,\text{cm},$$

which is the distance moved down by the cylinder. Thus the mercury level in the container decreases by $\Delta h = \dfrac{10 \,\text{cm} - 6 \,\text{cm}}{2} = 2 \,\text{cm}.$

b) If the container is now filled with mercury up to the original level, the cylinder moves further down because of the increasing external pressure. Let this additional distance moved down be y. Applying Boyle's law again to the initial and final (third) state, we obtain:

$$(p_0 + h_0) \cdot L = (p_0 + h_0 + x + y) \cdot (L + \Delta l - x - y).$$

Substituting given values, we get:

$$(76 \,\text{cm} + 10 \,\text{cm}) \cdot 47 \,\text{cm} = (76 \,\text{cm} + 20 \,\text{cm} + y)(47 \,\text{cm} + 6 \,\text{cm} - 10 \,\text{cm} - y),$$

rearranging this, we get a quadratic equation for y:

$$y^2 + 53 \,\text{cm} \cdot y - 86 \,\text{cm}^2 = 0,$$

whose solution is $y = 1.58 \,\text{cm}$.

Therefore the volume of the mercury that should be poured into the container is:

$$\Delta V = A_{\text{container}} \Delta h + A_{\text{cylinder}} \cdot y.$$

Substituting known values, we find:

$$\Delta V = 20 \,\text{cm}^2 \cdot 2 \,\text{cm} + 10 \,\text{cm}^2 \cdot 1.58 \,\text{cm}^2 = 55.8 \,\text{cm}^3.$$

Solution of Problem 171. The initial separation between the pistons is

$$d = \frac{V_1}{A} = \frac{2000\,\text{cm}^3}{100\,\text{cm}^2} = 20\,\text{cm}.$$

After the compression, the air forms a cylinder of length x cm, and accordingly, the spring is also compressed by x cm. The piston on the left is held in equilibrium by the combined effect of the external air pressure, the pressure of the enclosed gas and the force of the spring, therefore the pressure of the enclosed gas needs to grow to a value of

$$p_2 = p_1 + \frac{Dx}{A} = 10^5\,\text{Pa} + \frac{1000\,\text{N/m}}{10^{-2}\,\text{m}^2} \cdot x,$$

where D is the spring constant. Then the volume of the enclosed gas is

$$V_2 = A \cdot x = 10^{-2}\,\text{m}^2 \cdot x.$$

Since temperature is constant, Boyle's law can be applied:

$$p_1 V_1 = p_2 V_2 = \left(p_1 + \frac{Dx}{A} \right) Ax.$$

Rearranged by the powers of x:

$$Dx^2 + p_1 Ax - p_1 V_1 = 0, \tag{1}$$

and the solution of the equation is

$$x = \frac{-p_1 A \pm \sqrt{p_1^2 A^2 + 4 D p_1 V_1}}{2D}.$$

Numerically, the equation (1) is

$$10^3 \frac{\text{N}}{\text{m}} \cdot x^2 + 10^3\,\text{N} \cdot x - 2 \cdot 10^2\,\text{N\,m} = 0,$$

which simplifies to $5x^2 + 5x - 1 = 0$, and the solution is

$$x = \frac{-5 \pm \sqrt{25 + 20}}{10} = 0.1708\,\text{m} \approx 0.171\,\text{m}.$$

Hence the volume of the air in the final position is

$$V_2 = A \cdot x = 10^{-2}\,\text{m}^2 \cdot 0.171\,\text{m} = 1.71 \cdot 10^{-3}\,\text{m}^3 = 1.71\,\text{dm}^3.$$

Solution of Problem 172. The equation of the line passing through the points 2 and 4 is

$$p = \frac{p_2 - p_1}{T_1 - T_4} \cdot T - p_1, \tag{1}$$

where T and p denote the abcissa and ordinate of any point of the line. Since the point 3 also lies on this line, its coordinates T_3 and p_3 satisfy the equation:

$$p_3 = \frac{p_2 - p_1}{T_1 - T_4} \cdot T_3 - p_1. \tag{2}$$

T_3 needs to be determined to calculate p_3. It can be obtained from the universal gas equation applied to the states 1 and 3, also considering that $3V_3 = V_1$:

$$T_3 = T_1 \cdot \frac{p_3 V_3}{p_1 V_1} = T_1 \frac{p_3 V_1}{p_1 3 V_1} = T_1 \frac{p_3}{3 p_1}. \tag{3}$$

With (3) substituted in (2):

$$p_3 = \frac{p_2 - p_1}{T_1 - T_4} \cdot T_1 \frac{p_3}{3 p_1} - p_1.$$

With algebraic transformations and the substitution of numerical data:

$$p_3 = \frac{3 p_1^2 (T_1 - T_4)}{(p_2 - p_1) T_1 - 3 p_1 (T_1 - T_4)} =$$

$$= \frac{3 \cdot 10^{10} \, \text{Pa}^2 (500 \, \text{K} - 200 \, \text{K})}{3 \cdot 10^5 \, \text{Pa} \cdot 500 \, \text{K} - 3 \cdot 10^5 \, \text{Pa} (500 \, \text{K} - 200 \, \text{K})} = 1.5 \cdot 10^5 \, \text{Pa}.$$

Solution of Problem 173. Let us draw in the graph the line corresponding to the isobaric process passing through point B. In this coordinate system it is a straight line going through the origin and point B, according to Charles's law. The points of this line represent states of the same pressure. Thus the following ratios are equal:

$$\frac{V}{V_B} = \frac{T}{T_B}.$$

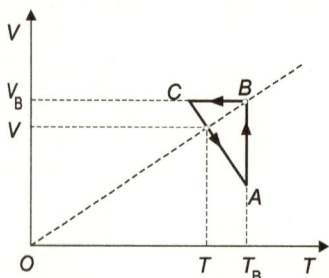

The solution of the problem is determined by the intersection of the isobaric line and the straight segment AC. From the previous equation, the temperature T can be expressed as a function of the volume V:

$$T = \frac{T_B}{V_B} V. \tag{1}$$

On the other hand, the equation of the straight line AC is:

$$V - V_C = \frac{V_A - V_B}{T_B - T_C} \cdot (T - T_C). \tag{2}$$

Substituting T from equation (1) into equation (2), we obtain an equation for the volume V corresponding to the state of the subprocess $C \to A$, which has the same pressure as state B has:

$$V - V_C = \frac{V_A - V_B}{T_B - T_C} \cdot \left(\frac{T_B}{V_B} \cdot V - T_C \right).$$

Expressing V from this equation we get the volume in question:

$$V = V_C \cdot \frac{V_A T_C - V_C T_A}{V_A T_A - 2 V_C T_A + V_C T_C} = 12 \, \text{dm}^3 \cdot \frac{5 \cdot 273 - 12 \cdot 373}{5 \cdot 373 - 2 \cdot 12 \cdot 373 + 12 \cdot 273} \approx 9.8 \, \text{dm}^3.$$

Thus during the subprocess $C \to A$, at the volume $V = 9.8$ dm^3 the gas has the same pressure as in state B.

Solution of Problem 174. a) If the mercury level sinks by x cm, then the rise in the other arm is also x cm. If we calculate in the Hgcm unit of pressure, then we get a very simple equation for the requested rise in the level.

The initial pressure of the enclosed air is $p_0 = 76$ Hgcm, the final pressure is $p_1 = (76 + 2x)$ Hgcm.

According to Boyle's law

$$p_0 h_0 A = (p_0 + 2x)(h_0 + \Delta h + x)A.$$

In our case $\Delta h = -10$ cm $= -h_0/2$. Substituting this and simplifying by A gives

$$p_0 h_0 = (p_0 + 2x)\left(\frac{h_0}{2} + x\right),$$

numerically

$$76 \text{ Hgcm} \cdot 20 \text{ cm} = (76 + 2x) \text{ Hgcm} \cdot (10 + x) \text{ cm}.$$

From here, (omitting the dimensions) equation

$$x^2 + 48x - 380 = 0$$

is acquired, whose positive solution is

$$x = \frac{-48 + \sqrt{48^2 + 4 \cdot 380}}{2} \text{ cm} = 6.9 \text{ cm}.$$

If the competitor calculates in the SI system, his or her equations gain the following forms:

$$p_0 h_0 A = (p_0 + 2\varrho g x)\left(\frac{h_0}{2} + x\right)A,$$

rearranged according to the decreasing powers of x:

$$2\varrho g x^2 + (p_0 + \varrho g h_0)x - \frac{p_0 h_0}{2} = 0.$$

From here on, it is worth calculating only numerically:

$$2 \cdot 13.6 \cdot 10^3 \, \frac{\text{kg}}{\text{m}^3} \cdot 9.8 \, \frac{\text{m}}{\text{s}^2} \cdot x^2 +$$

$$+ \left(10^5 \, \frac{\text{N}}{\text{m}^2} + 13.6 \cdot 10^3 \, \frac{\text{kg}}{\text{m}^3} \cdot 9.8 \, \frac{\text{m}}{\text{s}^2} \cdot 0.2 \text{ m}\right) \cdot x - \frac{10^5 \, \frac{\text{N}}{\text{m}} \cdot 0.2 \text{ m}}{2} = 0.$$

that is,

$$266832 \, \frac{1}{\text{m}^3} \cdot x^2 + 126683.2 \, \frac{1}{\text{m}^2} \cdot x - 10^4 \, \frac{1}{\text{m}} = 0,$$

dividing by the coefficient of x^2 gives

$$x^2 + 0.474768 \text{ m} \cdot x - 0.0374768 \text{ m}^2 = 0.$$

The positive solution of the equation is

$$x = \frac{-0.474768 + \sqrt{0.474768^2 + 4 \cdot 0.0374768}}{2} \text{ m} = 0.0689 \text{ m} \approx 6.9 \text{ cm}.$$

b) The energy of the gas does not change because its temperature is constant. The work done while pushing down the piston partly increases the potential energy of the mercury, partly covers the energy released during the cooling of the walls. The change in the energy of mercury appears only in the change in potential energy.

By comparing the initial and final states, it is clear that — although the mercury level sinks in the left arm by the same value as it rises by in the right one — its potential energy increases. This can be calculated as if the amount of mercury that fits into the volume corresponding to a sink of x in a tube of cross-sectional area A is lifted above the original common level and put into the other arm. The centre of mass of this part of mercury rises exactly by x. Therefore the change in the energy of mercury is

$$\Delta E = \Delta m g x,$$

where $\Delta m = \varrho A x$, that is,

$$\Delta E = \varrho A x g x = \varrho A g x^2 = 13.6 \cdot 10^3 \, \frac{\text{kg}}{\text{m}^3} \cdot 2 \cdot 10^{-4} \text{ m}^2 \cdot 9.8 \, \frac{\text{m}}{\text{s}^2} \cdot (6.9 \cdot 10^{-2})^2 \text{ m}^2 =$$

$$= 0.1269 \text{ J} \approx 0.13 \text{ J}.$$

Solution of Problem 175. In describing this phenomenon, it is practical to measure pressure by the height of the mercury column, i.e. in centimetres of mercury. ($1.013 \cdot 10^5$ Pa ≈ 76 cmHg.) Let x, y, z and v denote the heights of the mercury columns after the pressure increase. Let p denote the pressure of the air entrapped between the two mercury columns, let p_0 be the external atmospheric pressure, and let p_1 be the increased air pressure. Let h stand for the lengths of the vertical segments of the glass tube, and let d stand for the horizontal segments. There are 5 unknowns: x, y, z, v and p. 5 equations are needed.

The first equation will be Boyle's law applied to the enclosed air.

$$p_0 V_0 = p V.$$

According to the data not included in the wording of the problem, and only indicated in the figure, the vertical segments of the glass tube are initially filled with mercury to exactly half their height. Thus the total length of the enclosed gas column equals the combined length of one vertical tube segment and one horizontal connection. The initial volume is therefore

$$V_0 = (h + d)A.$$

The cross sectional area A cancels out of the Boyle's law equation. According to the figure,

$$(d+h) \cdot p_0 = (d+2h-y-z) \cdot p, \tag{1}$$

provided that temperature stays constant throughout.

The second and third equations express the equilibrium of the branches in each of the two U-shaped parts of the tube. On the left, the condition for equilibrium in the final state is

$$p_0 + (v-z) = p, \tag{2}$$

and on the right it is

$$p_1 - (y-x) = p. \tag{3}$$

The remaining two equations are provided by the volumes (lengths) of the mercury columns being constant:

$$v+z = h, \tag{4}$$

$$y+x = h. \tag{5}$$

The equations may be solved as follows. The difference of (3) and (5) gives

$$p+2y = p_1 + h. \tag{6}$$

$$[p+2y = 384.8 \text{ cmHg}]$$

And from the difference of (2) and (4),

$$p_0 - 2z = p - h. \tag{7}$$

$$[76 - 2z = p - 152 \text{ cmHg}]$$

The difference of (6) and (7) divided by 2 and rearranged:

$$y+z = \frac{p_0 + p_1}{2} + h - p. \tag{8}$$

$$[y+z = 306.4 \text{ cmHg} - p]$$

Substituting (8) into (1) we have

$$(d+h)p_0 = \left[d+2h - \left(\frac{p_0+p_1}{2} + h - p\right)\right]p = dp + hp - \frac{p_0+p_1}{2}p + p^2.$$

This is an equation in a single unknown for the pressure of the entrapped air. Rearranged, it will have the following form:

$$p^2 + \left(d+h - \frac{p_0+p_1}{2}\right)p - (d+h)p_0 = 0.$$

$$[p^2 + 13.6 \text{ cmHg} \cdot p - 12768 \text{ cmHg}^2 = 0]$$

Now it would be too complicated to continue the solution parametrically. The quadratic equation is solved by using the numerical coefficients:

$$p = \frac{-13.6 \text{ cmHg} + \sqrt{13.6^2 \text{ cmHg}^2 + 4 \cdot 12768 \text{ cmHg}^2}}{2} = 106.4 \text{ cmHg}.$$

If the result is substituted into (6), the following value is obtained for the height of the mercury column in the third tube:

$$y = \frac{p_1 + h - p}{2} = \frac{232.8 + 152 - 106.4}{2} \cdot \text{cmHg} = 139.2 \text{ cmHg},$$

that is, the height of the mercury column in the third tube is 139.2 cm. The values of p and y are now substituted into (3):

$$x = p + y - p_1 = 106.4 \text{ cmHg} + 139.2 \text{ cmHg} - 232.8 \text{ cmHg} = 12.8 \text{ cmHg},$$

that is, the height of the mercury column in the fourth tube is $x = 12.8$ cm.

The value of z is obtained from (7) by substituting the numerical value of p:

$$z = \frac{p_0 + h - p}{2} = \frac{76 + 152 - 106.4}{2} \cdot \text{cmHg} = 60.8 \text{ cmHg}.$$

Finally, the value of z is substituted in (4) to give v:

$$v = h - z = 152 \text{ Hgcm} - 60.8 \text{ cmHg} = 91.2 \text{ cmHg}.$$

The results are therefore as follows: $p = 106.4$ cmHg $= 1.4 \cdot 10^5$ Pa, $x = 12.8$ cm, $y = 139.2$ cm, $z = 60.8$ cm, $v = 91.2$ cm.

Solution of Problem 176. The boiling point of ether being 35 °C means that ether boils at that temperature at normal atmospheric pressure. Since there is a mercury column lying over the ether in the tube, the pressure at the surface of the ether is greater than normal atmospheric pressure, meaning that the ether is initially in the liquid state. (The pressure of 19 cm of mercury is equal to $1/4$ of the atmospheric pressure, thus the total pressure on the ether is $5/4$ of the atmospheric pressure, $\approx 1.25 \cdot 10^5$ Pa.) If the tube is inverted, the pressure p_e of the ether and the pressure of the mercury will balance the atmospheric pressure, that is,

$$p_e + 19 \text{ cmHg} = 76 \text{ cmHg},$$

and hence

$$p_e = 57 \text{ cmHg} = \frac{3}{4}p_0$$

At $3/4$ of the atmospheric pressure the ether at the boiling-point temperature will evaporate to form an unsaturated vapour.

In the liquid state, the volume of the enclosed ether is

$$V_e = Al_e = 0.2 \text{ cm}^2 \cdot 0.25 \text{ cm} = 0.05 \text{ cm}^3,$$

where A is the cross-sectional area of the tube and l_e is the length of the liquid ether column. The mass of the ether is

$$m = \varrho \cdot V_e = 0.7 \frac{\text{g}}{\text{cm}^3} \cdot 0.05 \text{ cm}^3 = 0.0035 \text{ g}.$$

The molar mass of ether is $M =$ (relative molecular mass) $\cdot$ g/mol, therefore the quantity of ether enclosed is

$$n = \frac{m}{M} = \frac{0.035\,\text{g}}{74\,\text{g/mol}} = 0.000473\,\text{mol}.$$

The volume of this quantity of ether at atmospheric pressure and a temperature of $0\,^\circ\text{C}$ is

$$V_{e0} = V_n \cdot n = 22.41 \cdot 10^3\,\frac{\text{cm}^3}{\text{mol}} \cdot 4.73 \cdot 10^{-4}\,\text{mol} = 10.6\,\text{cm}^3.$$

The universal gas equation can be used to determine the volume of this quantity of ether under the conditions present in the inverted tube:

$$\frac{p_0 V_{e0}}{T_0} = \frac{p_e V}{T}, \quad \text{that is,} \quad \frac{1 \cdot 10.6\,\text{cm}^3}{273\,\text{K}} = \frac{\frac{3}{4} \cdot V}{273\,\text{K} + 35\,\text{K}},$$

and hence the volume of the ether vapour in the inverted tube is

$$V = 15.95\,\text{cm}^3.$$

The length of the column of the ether vapour is

$$l = \frac{V}{A} = \frac{15.95\,\text{cm}^3}{0.2\,\text{cm}^2} = 79.75\,\text{cm},$$

that is, the upper end of the mercury column is $79.75\,\text{cm}$ below the closed end and its lower end is at $98.75\,\text{cm}$. Thus the experiment can only be carried out if the length of the glass tube is at least $99\,\text{cm}$.

Solution of Problem 177. As seen in the figure, the balance of pressures for the hydrogen means

$$p_0 + \varrho g h = p_{H_2}, \qquad (1)$$

and for the oxygen:

$$p_0 + \varrho g h = p_{O_2} + \varrho g(x - y). \qquad (2)$$

According to the universal gas equation,

$$p_{H_2} A x = N_{H_2} kT \qquad (3)$$

and

$$p_{O_2} A y = N_{O_2} kT. \qquad (4)$$

The height of the water column pressing on the hydrogen is

$$h = x + \Delta h. \qquad (5)$$

Since water is incompressible,

$$x + y = \Delta h. \qquad (6)$$

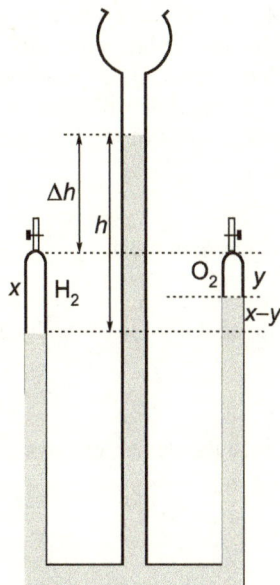

It follows from the composition of the water molecule that

$$N_{H_2} = 2N_{O_2}. \qquad (7)$$

This system of simultaneous equations leads to a quadratic equation in x: With (7) written in (3):

$$p_{H_2} Ax = 2N_{O_3} kT. \qquad (3')$$

(3') divided by (4):

$$\frac{p_{H_2} x}{p_{O_2} y} = 2 \qquad \rightarrow \qquad x = 2\frac{p_{O_2}}{p_{H_2}} y.$$

With p_{H_2} and p_{O_2} substituted from (1) and (2):

$$x = 2\frac{p_0 + \varrho g h - \varrho g(x-y)}{p_0 + \varrho g h} y.$$

With h from (5) and $y = \Delta h - x$ from (6):

$$x = 2\frac{p_0 + \varrho g(x + \Delta h) - \varrho g(x - \Delta h + x)}{p_0 + \varrho g(x + \Delta h)} (\Delta h - x).$$

The quadratic equation obtained by rearrangement is

$$\varrho g x^2 - (3p_0 + 7\varrho g \Delta h)x + 2\left[p_0 \Delta h + 2\varrho g (\Delta h)^2\right] = 0.$$

With the numerical data (with all quantities in SI units):

$$9.8x^2 - 368.6x + 239.2 = 0.$$

Hence the height of the hydrogen column is $x = 0.660(43)\,\text{m} = 660\,\text{mm}$, and the height of the oxygen column is $y = \Delta h - x = 0.339(54)\,\text{m} = 339\,\text{mm}$. (The height of the hydrogen column is a little smaller than the double of the height of the oxygen column since the external pressure on the hydrogen is larger than on the oxygen: $660\,\text{mm} <$ $< 2 \cdot 339\,\text{mm} = 678\,\text{mm}$.)

The mass of the hydrogen produced is obtained from the gas equation:

$$p_{H_2} V_{H_2} = \frac{m}{M} RT,$$

which now means

$$[p_0 + (x + \Delta h)\varrho g] Ax = \frac{m}{M} RT.$$

Hence the mass of the hydrogen is

$$m = \frac{M}{RT} [p_0 + (x + \Delta h)\varrho g] Ax = 24.712\,\text{mg}.$$

Since the device extracts $\Delta m = 0.6$ mg of hydrogen per minute, this quantity takes

$$t = \frac{\Delta m}{m} = 2471.2\,\text{s} = 41.187 \text{ minutes}$$

to produce. Thus the average speed of the rising water level in the middle tube is

$$v = \frac{\Delta h}{t} = \frac{1000 \text{ mm}}{2471.2 \text{ s}} = 0.4 \frac{\text{mm}}{\text{s}}.$$

(The motion is not strictly uniform, since as time passes, the growing water column imposes a growing pressure retarding the increase of the volumes of the gases developed.)

Solution of Problem 178. The initial volume of the enclosed air is $V_1 = V + A \frac{l}{2}$ ($= 1020 \text{ cm}^3$). After heating, the volume becomes $V_2 = V + Al$ ($= 1040 \text{ cm}^3$). According to the gas law

$$\frac{p_1 V_1}{T_1} = \frac{p_2 V_2}{T_2},$$

from which the unknown temperature is

$$T_2 = \frac{p_2 V_2}{p_1 V_1} \cdot T_1.$$

In this expression only pressure p_2 is unknown. This pressure comes from the external atmospheric pressure $p_1 = p_0$ and the hydrostatic pressure. Since the container is narrow, the external mercury level rises considerably, thus leading to an increase in pressure at the bottom of the tube. Our task is to determine this increase.

The increase in the volume of the expanding air is $\Delta V =$
$= A \frac{l}{2}$ ($= 20 \text{ cm}^3$). This air displaces the same volume of mercury, therefore the rise in the mercury level is

$$\Delta h = \frac{\Delta V}{a^2 - A} = \frac{A \frac{l}{2}}{a^2 - A} \ (= 2.5 \text{ cm}),$$

where $a^2 - A$ ($= 8 \text{ cm}^2$) is the cross-sectional area of the mercury column. (The cross-sectional area of the wall of the tube can be neglected according to the wording of the problem). With this, the hydrostatic pressure of the mercury at the bottom of the tube is

$$p_{\text{Hg}} = \varrho g \left(\frac{l}{2} + \Delta h \right) = 13600 \frac{\text{kg}}{\text{m}^3} \cdot 9.81 \frac{\text{m}}{\text{s}^2} \cdot 22.5 \cdot 10^{-2} \text{ m} =$$
$$= 30018.6 \text{ Pa},$$

and the total pressure is

$$p_2 = p_0 + p_{\text{Hg}} = 130018.6 \text{ Pa}.$$

With this, the unknown temperature is

$$T_2 = 283 \text{ K} \cdot \frac{130018.6 \text{ Pa} \cdot 1040 \text{ cm}^3}{10^5 \text{ Pa} \cdot 1020 \text{ cm}^3} = 375.1 \text{ K} = 102.1 \text{ °C}.$$

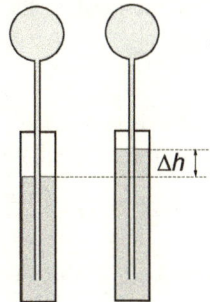

357

Solving parametrically:

$$T_2 = T_1 \frac{V + Al}{(V + A\frac{l}{2})p_0} \left[p_0 + \varrho g \left(\frac{l}{2} + \frac{\frac{Al}{2}}{a^2 - A} \right) \right],$$

after simplifying

$$T_2 = T_1 \frac{\left(2p_0 + \varrho g l \frac{a^2}{a^2 - A} \right)(V + Al)}{p_0(2V + Al)}.$$

Solution of Problem 179. a) Since the container and the piston are heat insulators, the energy released by the heater is equal to the heat absorbed by the gas. During the isobaric process, a part of this energy increases the internal energy of the gas, the other part of it covers the work done by the gas.

The ideal gas law provides us a relationship between the mass of the gas and the other thermodynamic quantities:

$$pV = \frac{M}{m} RT.$$

For the isobaric process we have

$$p\Delta V = \frac{m}{M} R\Delta T.$$

Using this formula, we have two equations for the two isobaric processes. In the first case the mass of the gas is m, in the second case $m - \Delta m$:

$$m = \frac{p_1 \Delta V_1 M}{R\Delta T_1}, \quad \text{and} \quad m - \Delta m = \frac{p_2 \Delta V_2 M}{R\Delta T_2}.$$

In these two equations the two unknowns are m and M. Expressing the molar mass from the first equation, and inserting it into the second one, we get that:

$$M = \frac{mR\Delta T_1}{p_1 \Delta V_1}, \quad \text{so} \quad m - \Delta m = \frac{p_2 \Delta V_2 m R\Delta T_1}{p_1 \Delta V_1 R\Delta T_2} = \frac{p_2 \Delta V_2 m \Delta T_1}{p_1 \Delta V_1 \Delta T_2}.$$

The mass of the gas can be determined from the last equation:

$$m - \frac{p_2 \Delta V_2 m \Delta T_1}{p_1 \Delta V_1 \Delta T_2} = \Delta m \quad \rightarrow \quad m \left(1 - \frac{p_2 \Delta V_2 \Delta T_1}{p_1 \Delta V_1 \Delta T_2} \right) = \Delta m \quad \rightarrow$$

$$\rightarrow \quad m = \frac{\Delta m}{\left(1 - \frac{p_2 \Delta V_2 \Delta T_1}{p_1 \Delta V_1 \Delta T_2} \right)} = \frac{\Delta m \cdot p_1 \Delta V_1 \Delta T_2}{p_1 \Delta V_1 \Delta T_2 - p_2 \Delta V_2 \Delta T_1}.$$

Using this result, the molar mass is:

$$M = \frac{mR\Delta T_1}{p_1 \Delta V_1} = \frac{\Delta m \cdot p_1 \Delta V_1 \Delta T_2 R\Delta T_1}{(p_1 \Delta V_1 \Delta T_2 - p_2 \Delta V_2 \Delta T_1)p_1 \Delta V_1} =$$

$$= \frac{\Delta m \cdot R}{(p_1 \Delta V_1 \Delta T_2 - p_2 \Delta V_2 \Delta T_1)} \Delta T_1 \Delta T_2.$$

Numerically, we get that:

$$m = \Delta m \cdot \frac{p_1 \Delta V_1 \Delta T_2}{p_1 \Delta V_1 \Delta T_2 - p_2 \Delta V_2 \Delta T_1} = 5 \text{ g} \frac{139.2 \cdot 5 \cdot 46.88}{139.2 \cdot 5 \cdot 46.88 - 130.5 \cdot 8 \cdot 29.3} = 80 \text{ g}.$$

(The units in the fraction after Δm cancel out, so they are omitted.)

b) The molar mass is:

$$M = \frac{mR\Delta T_1}{p_1 \Delta V_1} = \frac{80 \text{ g} \cdot 8.31 \frac{\text{J}}{\text{mol·K}} \cdot 29.3 \text{ K}}{139.2 \text{ kPa} \cdot 5 \cdot 10^{-3} \text{ m}^3} = 28 \frac{\text{g}}{\text{mol}}.$$

Since the gas in the container is diatomic, we can conclude that originally there was 80 g nitrogen gas in the container.

c) Knowing the type of the gas, its specific heat at constant pressure can be obtained from data tables. Using this, the energy released by the heater in the first process is:

$$Q_p = c_p m \Delta T_1 = 1038 \frac{\text{J}}{\text{kg·K}} \cdot 0.08 \text{ kg} \cdot 29.3 \text{ °C} = 2433.1 \text{ J}.$$

Solution of Problem 180. a) Initially the pressure of the air in the pipe is the same as the external air pressure p_0. After the pipe is pulled higher, the pressure p_1 of the air in it becomes

$$p_1 = p_0 - h\varrho_{\text{water}}g = p_0 - 0.5 \text{ m} \cdot 10^3 \frac{\text{kg}}{\text{m}^3} \cdot 9.81 \frac{\text{m}}{\text{s}^2} = p_0 - 4905 \text{ Pa}.$$

According to Boyle's law:

$$l_0 p_0 = l_1 p_1,$$

thus

$$0.6 \text{ m} \cdot p_0 = 0.63 \text{ m} \cdot (p_0 - 4905 \text{ Pa}).$$

From this

$$0.03 p_0 = 0.63 \cdot 4905 \text{ Pa} = 3090.15 \text{ Pa},$$

and the external pressure is:

$$p_0 = \frac{3090.15 \text{ Pa}}{0.03} = 103005 \text{ Pa}.$$

(For the sake of completeness, we note that the pressure of the air in the pipe has the value

$$p_1 = p_0 - 4905 \text{ Pa} = 103005 \text{ Pa} - 4905 \text{ Pa} = 98100 \text{ Pa},$$

by the first equation.)

b) If the water level in the pipe is decreased by 16 cm, then the length of the enclosed air column is increased by this value. In order to maintain the equilibrium, the pressure of the enclosed air has to increase as well by the pressure of the missing water column of height 16 cm. So the new air pressure inside the pipe is:

$$p_2 = p_1 + \varrho g \Delta h,$$

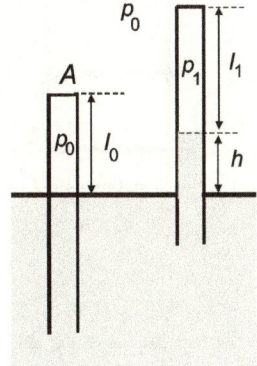

where $\Delta h = 16$ cm is the increase of the length of the air column. The new volume of the air is:

$$V_2 = (l_1 + \Delta h) \cdot A.$$

Comparing the initial and the final state by the ideal gas law, we get:

$$\frac{p_1 l_1 A}{T_1} = \frac{(p_1 + \varrho g \Delta h) \cdot (l_1 + \Delta h) \cdot A}{T_2},$$

which means that the new temperature is:

$$T_2 = \frac{(p_1 + \varrho g \Delta h) \cdot (l_1 + \Delta h)}{p_1 l_1} T_1.$$

Numerically:

$$T_2 = \frac{\left(98100 \text{ Pa} + 10^3 \text{ } \frac{\text{kg}}{\text{m}^3} \cdot 9.81 \text{ } \frac{\text{m}}{\text{s}^2} \cdot 0.16 \text{ m}\right) \cdot (0.63 \text{ m} + 0.16 \text{ m})}{98100 \text{ Pa} \cdot 0.63 \text{ m}} \cdot 278 \text{ K} =$$
$$= 354.2 \text{ K} = 81.2 \text{ }^\circ\text{C}.$$

Solution of Problem 181. The pressure and the volume of the gas below the lower piston are:

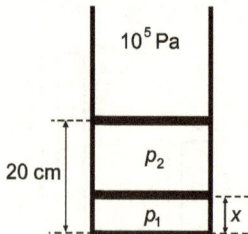

$$p_1 = p_2 + \frac{mg}{A} = p_0 + \frac{mg}{A} + \frac{mg}{A} = p_0 + \frac{2mg}{A} =$$
$$= 10^5 \text{ Pa} + \frac{2 \cdot 1 \text{ kg} \cdot 10 \text{ } \frac{\text{m}}{\text{s}^2}}{10^{-3} \text{ m}^2} = 120000 \text{ Pa}.$$

$$V_1 = x \cdot A.$$

After the pistons are lifted, the new pressure and volume here become:

$$p_1' = \left(y + \frac{mg}{A}\right) = y + 10000 \text{ Pa},$$
$$V_1' = (x + 0.04 \text{ m}) \cdot A$$

where $y = p_2'$ is the final pressure between the two pistons. In the initial state the pressure and the volume of the gas between the pistons are:

$$p_2 = p_0 + \frac{mg}{A} = 10^5 \text{ Pa} + \frac{1 \text{ kg} \cdot 10 \text{ } \frac{\text{m}}{\text{s}^2}}{10^{-3} \text{ m}^2} = 110000 \text{ Pa}.$$
$$V_2 = (0.2 \text{ m} - x) \cdot A,$$

and in the final state:

$$p_2' = y \quad \text{and} \quad V_2' = [(0.2 \text{ m} + 0.1 \text{ m}) - (x + 0.04 \text{ m})] \cdot A = (0.26 - x) \cdot A.$$

At constant temperature Boyle's law is valid for the two gases:

$$p_1 V_1 = p_1' V_1' \quad \text{and} \quad p_2 V_2 = p_2' V_2'.$$

Inserting the volumes and pressures, the cross section cancels out and we get:

$$120000 \text{ Pa} \cdot x = (y + 10000 \text{ Pa})(x + 0.04 \text{ m})$$

$$110000 \text{ Pa} \cdot (0.2 \text{ m} - x) = y(0.26 \text{ m} - x)$$

Expressing the pressure of the upper gas from the second equation, we get:

$$y = \frac{110000 \text{ Pa} \cdot (0.2 \text{ m} - x)}{(0.26 \text{ m} - x)}.$$

Writing it into the first equation, we obtain:

$$120000 \text{ Pa} \cdot x = \left[\frac{110000 \text{ Pa} \cdot (0.2m - x)}{(0.26 \text{ m} - x)} + 10000 \text{ Pa} \right] \cdot (x + 0.04 \text{ m})$$

and after dividing both sides by 10000, and multiplying by the denominator,

$$12 \text{ Pa} \cdot x \cdot (0.26 \text{ m} - x) = (11 \text{ Pa} \cdot 0.2 \text{ m} - 11 \text{ Pa} \cdot x + 1 \text{ Pa} \cdot 0.26 \text{ m} - 1 \text{ Pa} \cdot x)(x + 0.04 \text{ m}).$$

Now we carry out the operations in the equation:

$$3.12 \text{ Pa} \cdot \text{m} \cdot x - 12 \text{ Pa} \cdot x^2 = 2.46 \text{ Pa} \cdot x + 0.0984 \text{ Pa} \cdot \text{m}^2 - 12 \text{ Pa} \cdot x^2 - 0.48 \text{ Pa} \cdot \text{m} \cdot x$$

and write the equation in a simpler form:

$$1.14 \text{ Pa} \cdot \text{ m} \cdot x = 0.0984 \text{ Pa} \cdot \text{m}^2.$$

Dividing this equation by $1.14 \text{ Pa} \cdot \text{m}$, for the distance of the lower piston from the bottom of the cylinder in the final state, we get that:

$$x = \frac{0.0984 \text{ Pa} \cdot \text{m}^2}{1.14 \text{ Pa} \cdot \text{m}} = 0.0863 \text{ m} = 8.63 \text{ cm}.$$

With the help of this result, the problem's question can be easily answered. After removing the upper piston from the cylinder, the pressure of the gas below the other piston becomes the sum of the external pressure and the pressure due to the weight of the piston: 110000 Pa. The new volume is determined by Boyle's law:

$$p_1 \cdot A \cdot x = p_2'' \cdot A \cdot z.$$

The cross section cancels out. With the numerical data the equation reads:

$$120000 \text{ Pa} \cdot 0.0863 \text{ m} = 110000 \text{ Pa} \cdot z,$$

and the new height of the piston is:

$$z = \frac{12 \text{ Pa} \cdot 0.0863 \text{ m}}{11 \text{ Pa}} = 0.0941 \text{ m} = 9.41 \text{ cm}.$$

(Remark: the calculations would have been simpler if we had omitted the units in the equations. Furthermore, if we had not insisted on using SI units, but had instead measured the lengths in centimetres, then the numbers would have been more convenient as well.)

Solution of Problem 182. The mean specific heat of a gas mixture at constant volume can be determined from the formula $U = c_v mT$ and the additive property of energy $(U = U_1 + U_2 + U_3)$:

$$c_{v_{\text{mix}}} mT = c_{v_1} m_1 T + c_{v_2} m_2 T + c_{v_3} m_3 T = c_{v_1} \alpha_1 mT + c_{v_2} \alpha_2 mT + c_{v_3} \alpha_3 mT,$$

where α_i is the percentage of the ith component. Division by mT gives

$$c_{v\text{mix}} = \alpha_1 c_{v_1} + \alpha_2 c_{v_2} + \alpha_3 c_{v_3}.$$

(Note that the result is the arithmetic mean weighted with the percentages:

$$c_{v\text{mix}} = \frac{\alpha_1 c_{v_1} + \alpha_2 c_{v_2} + \alpha_3 c_{v_3}}{\alpha_1 + \alpha_2 + \alpha_3},$$

where $\alpha_1 + \alpha_2 + \alpha_3 = 1$.)

With the molecular expressions of the individual specific heats:

$$c_{v\text{mix}} = \alpha_1 \frac{f_1}{2} \frac{R}{M_1} + \alpha_2 \frac{f_2}{2} \frac{R}{M_2} + \alpha_3 \frac{f_3}{2} \frac{R}{M_3} =$$

$$= \left(0.755 \cdot \frac{5}{2} \cdot \frac{1}{28} + 0.323 \cdot \frac{5}{2} \cdot \frac{1}{32} + 0.013 \cdot \frac{3}{2} \cdot \frac{1}{40} \right) \cdot \frac{8.31}{10^{-3}} \frac{\text{J}}{\text{kg} \cdot \text{K}} = 714.85 \frac{\text{J}}{\text{kg} \cdot \text{K}}.$$

(The air investigated here contained no carbon-dioxide, that is why the result differs somewhat from the value $712 \, \text{J}/(\text{kg} \cdot \text{K})$ found in tables.)

Solution of Problem 183. Let M be the unknown mass of the ice block, and let m_1, m_2 and $m = 0.3$ kg denote the masses of the steams let into the system. The notation for the equilibrium temperatures at the different stages are $t_1 = 10 \, °\text{C}$, $t_2 = 15 \, °\text{C}$ and $t_3 = 23 \, °\text{C}$. The heat balance equation after the first stage, in parametric form, is:

$$L_c m_1 + c_w m_1 \Delta t_{1w} + L_m M + c_w M \Delta t_{1M} = 0.$$

Here L_c is the condensation heat of steam (the inverse of the boiling heat), L_m is the melting heat of ice, and the Δt's, with different subscripts, denote the appropriate temperature changes.

It is more advantageous to treat this equation, as well as the following three ones, numerically, plugging in the numerical values of the different thermal constants from a material table:

$$-2.256 \cdot 10^6 \frac{\text{J}}{\text{kg}} \cdot m_1 + 4200 \frac{\text{J}}{\text{kg} \, °\text{C}} \cdot m_1 \cdot (-90 \, °\text{C}) + 334960 \frac{\text{J}}{\text{kg}} \cdot M +$$

$$+ 4200 \frac{\text{J}}{\text{kg} \, °\text{C}} \cdot M \cdot 10 \, °\text{C} = 0,$$

which gives us the following relation between the mass of the ice and the steam:

$$m_1 = 0.143113 \cdot M.$$

The equation of heat balance of the second stage, in parametric form is:

$$L_c m_2 + c_w m_2 \Delta t_{2w} + c_w (m_1 + M) \Delta t_{2M} = 0.$$

and in numerical form:

$$-2.256 \cdot 10^6 \; \frac{J}{kg} \cdot m_2 + 4200 \; \frac{J}{kg \, °C} \cdot m_2 \cdot (-85 \; °C) + 4200 \; \frac{J}{kg \, °C} \cdot (M + m_1) \cdot 5 \; °C = 0,$$

which leads to the mass of the steam in the second stage:

$$m_2 = 0.0091869 \cdot M.$$

Finally, the heat balance equation of the third stage, in parametric form, is:

$$L_c m_3 + c_w m_3 \Delta t_{3w} + c_w (m_1 + m_2 + M) \Delta t_{3M} = 0,$$

and in numerical form:

$$-2.256 \cdot 10^6 \; \frac{J}{kg} \cdot 0.3 \; kg + 4200 \; \frac{J}{kg \, °C} \cdot 0.3 \; kg \cdot (-77 \; °C) +$$

$$+ 4200 \; \frac{J}{kg \, °C} \cdot (0.1523M + M) \cdot 8 \; °C = 0,$$

and solving the equation, we obtain that the mass of the ice block initially in the container is:

$$M = 19.986 \; kg \approx 20 \; kg.$$

First solution of Problem 184. In solid or liquid phases matter is in a bound state, which means that the sum of the kinetic energy of the particles (due to thermal motion) and the interaction energy is negative. In the solid phase the particles are more strongly bound than in the liquid phase, thus the absolute value of the (negative) energy of the solid phase is larger than that of the liquid phase. During the solidification (freezing) process matter gets into a state of lower energy and transmits the energy difference into its environment.

If water is cooled down in a very careful way, in the liquid phase, it can be cooled well beyond its freezing point without crystallization. This phenomenon is called supercooling. To initiate the freezing, small crystal seeds should be present, around which the crystallization process starts. (The supercooled state is unstable.)

When crystallization starts, the (negative) energy of the system decreases further, in such a way that the system transmits a part of its energy to the environment. The energy released during the freezing of the supercooled water heats up the system to freezing point, so while a part of the supercooled water becomes ice, the other part of it remains water at 0 degrees. If all this occurs in an insulated container, the total energy of the ice–water mixture remains constant.

Let m_i denote the mass of the solidified water (ice), let m be the mass of the total amount of (supercooled) water, and let L_0 be the solidification heat of water (melting heat of ice).

A part of the heat released during the crystallization of ice of mass m_i heats up the unfrozen water of mass $m - m_i$, the other part of it heats up the ice from temperature

$-9\,^{\circ}\mathrm{C}$ to $0\,^{\circ}\mathrm{C}$. Thus a new equilibrium state of ice and water is reached at $0\,^{\circ}\mathrm{C}$. Since energy does not leak from the isolated container, the heat balance equation is:

$$c_i m_i \Delta t + c_w (m - m_i) \Delta t - m_i L_0 = 0.$$

After rearranging the equation and expressing the mass of the ice, we get:

$$m_i [L_0 + (c_w - c_i) \Delta t] = c_w m \Delta t,$$

$$m_i = \frac{c_w m \Delta t}{L_0 + (c_w - c_i) \Delta t} = \frac{4187 \,\frac{\mathrm{J}}{\mathrm{kg \cdot K}} \cdot 18 \,\mathrm{kg} \cdot 9 \,\mathrm{K}}{334960 \,\frac{\mathrm{J}}{\mathrm{kg}} + (4187 - 2093.4) \,\frac{\mathrm{J}}{\mathrm{kg \cdot K}} \cdot 9 \,\mathrm{K}} = 1.9172 \,\mathrm{kg} \approx 2 \,\mathrm{kg}.$$

In the solution we neglected the facts that the heat of freezing (L_0) is given at the freezing point and that the specific heat may vary with the temperature.

Second solution of Problem 184. In this solution we neglect only the temperature dependence of the specific heat. The solution is based on the fact that if the system gets from an initial state in two different ways to the same final state, then the energy changes corresponding to the two ways are the same.

First let us carefully transfer enough heat from outside into the isolated container so that it will heat up the total amount of supercooled water to the freezing point, i.e., to $0\,^{\circ}\mathrm{C}$. In this way we get 18 kg water at temperature $0\,^{\circ}\mathrm{C}$. Then let us withdraw the same amount of heat from the system, so that the internal energy of the system will become the same as at the beginning. This will make a part of the water freeze so that the system reaches the same final state as we had obtained via another way, i.e., initiating the freezing by slightly shaking the container, or by throwing a small ice crystal into the supercooled water. Let us determine the amount of ice produced by the distraction of the heat transmitted in the first step.

The heat needed to increase the temperature of the supercooled water from $-9\,^{\circ}\mathrm{C}$ to $0\,^{\circ}\mathrm{C}$ is:

$$Q_{\mathrm{in}} = c_w m \Delta t = 4187 \,\frac{\mathrm{J}}{\mathrm{kg \cdot K}} \cdot 18 \,\mathrm{kg} \cdot 9 \,\mathrm{K} = 678294 \,\mathrm{J}.$$

So now we have 18 kg water at $0\,^{\circ}\mathrm{C}$. Next we take out the same amount of heat as we put in in the first step, due to which a part of the water freezes: $Q_{\mathrm{out}} = m_i L_0$. It means that the mass of the frozen ice is:

$$m_i = \frac{Q_{\mathrm{out}}}{L_0} = \frac{Q_{\mathrm{in}}}{L_0} = \frac{678294 \,\mathrm{J}}{334960 \,\mathrm{J/kg}} = 2.025 \,\mathrm{kg} \approx 2 \,\mathrm{kg}.$$

The small (approximately 5%) difference between the two solutions is due to the exclusions mentioned above. The value of L_0 is different in the two solutions.

Solution of Problem 185. a) When the piston is pushed downwards, the density of the saturated water vapour does not change. A part of it condenses, and as a result the water level rises gradually while the vapour space is compressed both from below and from above. Let x stand for the height of the water column in the final state, y for the

descent of the piston. Let the original masses of the water and vapour phase be m_w and m_v, and the final masses be m'_w and m'_v, respectively.
In the initial state:

$$m_w = Ah_1\varrho_w = Ah_1 n\varrho_v$$

$$m_v = Ah_2\varrho_v.$$

The total mass of the material in the cylinder is

$$m_w + m_v = Ah_1 n\varrho_v + Ah_2\varrho_v = A\varrho_v(nh_1 + h_2).$$

In the final state:

$$m'_w = A\varrho_w x = An\varrho_v x,$$

$$m'_v = A(h - y - x)\varrho_v.$$

The total mass in this state is

$$m'_w + m'_v = An\varrho_v x + A(h - y - x)\varrho_v = A\varrho_v(nx + h - y - x).$$

The total masses written in the two different ways are equal:

$$A\varrho_v(nh_1 + h_2) = A\varrho_v(nx + h - y - x),$$

that is,

$$nh_1 + h_2 = nx + h - y - x.$$

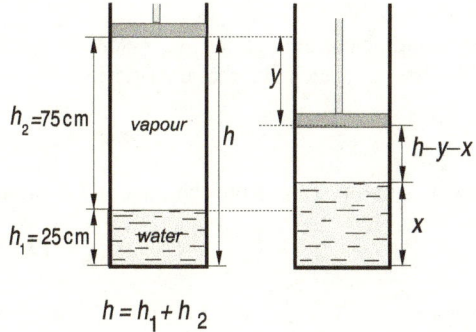

$h_2 = 75\,cm$ vapour

$h_1 = 25\,cm$ water

$h = h_1 + h_2$

Making use of the fact that the given final volume of the vapour is $V = A(h - y - x)$:

$$nh_1 + h_2 = nx + \frac{V}{A},$$

from which

$$x = h_1 + \frac{h_2}{n} + \frac{V}{nA} = 25\ \text{cm} + \frac{75\ \text{cm}}{2} - \frac{4500\ \text{cm}^3}{2 \cdot 100\ \text{cm}^2} = 40\ \text{cm} = 4\ \text{dm}.$$

Substituting this into expression $h - y - x = \dfrac{V}{A}$ for the volume gives

$$y = h - x - \frac{V}{A} = 100\ \text{cm} - 40\ \text{cm} - \frac{4500\ \text{cm}^3}{100\ \text{cm}^2} = 15\ \text{cm} = 1.5\ \text{dm}.$$

So the piston should be pushed down by 1.5 dm.

b) In the final state, there is only water under the piston, whose mass is equal to the total initial mass of the water and the vapour, that is, to value

$$m_w + m_v = A\varrho_v(nh_1 + h_2)$$

determined in part a). In the final state, the mass of the water is

$$m = Azn\varrho_v,$$

where z is the final height of the water column. With it

$$Azn\varrho_v = A\varrho_v(nh_1 + h_2),$$

from which $nz = nh_1 + h_2$, and with this

$$z = h_1 + \frac{h_2}{n} = 25 \text{ cm} + \frac{75 \text{ cm}}{2} = 62.5 \text{ cm} = 6.25 \text{ dm.}$$

So the piston should be pushed down by $h_1 + h_2 - z = 25 \text{ cm} + 75 \text{ cm} - 62.5 \text{ cm} = 37.5 \text{ cm}$ in order to have all saturated vapour condense.

Solution of Problem 186. The process is adiabatic. The massive wall accelerates until the pressure on both sides becomes the same. As the piston is thermally insulated, it does not gain energy from the gas through transfer of heat. The change in the kinetic energy of the piston is equal to the sum of the works done on it (work-kinetic energy theorem):

$$\frac{1}{2}mv^2 = W_1 + W_2.$$

In an adiabatic change the works done by the two gases are equal to minus one times the change in their internal energies, so

$$\frac{1}{2}mv^2 = -\Delta E_1 - \Delta E_2.$$

As it is known (e.g. from the data and formula booklet):

$$W_{\text{gas}} = \frac{p_1V_1 - p_2V_2}{\gamma - 1},$$

where

$$\gamma = \frac{c_p}{c_V},$$

the ratio of specific heats.

Using this in our case, the values belonging to the second state are indicated with commas ($'$) and the equation is reorganised:

$$\frac{1}{2}mv^2 = \frac{p_1V_1 + p_2V_2}{\gamma - 1} - \frac{p_1'V_1' + p_2'V_2'}{\gamma - 1}.$$

As the wall does not accelerate upon reaching the maximum speed, the pressures of the two gases are equal, that is, $p_1' = p_2'$ have the common value p_c for a moment, and the total volume does not change by moving the piston (wall) ($V_1' + V_2' = V_1 + V_2$), our equation gains the following form:

$$\frac{1}{2}mv^2 = \frac{p_1V_1 + p_2V_2}{\gamma - 1} - \frac{p_c(V_1 + V_2)}{\gamma - 1}.$$

All we have to do now is determine the common pressure p_c. In order to determine it, we can use the state equation for adiabatic change of state (Poisson's equation):

$$p_1 V_1^\gamma = p_k V'^\gamma_1,$$

$$p_2 V_2^\gamma = p_k V'^\gamma_2,$$

from which

$$V_1' = \left(\frac{p_1}{p_c}\right)^{\frac{1}{\gamma}} \cdot V_1, \quad \text{and} \quad V_2' = \left(\frac{p_2}{p_c}\right)^{\frac{1}{\gamma}} \cdot V_2.$$

By adding these and taking into consideration that the total volume is constant:

$$V_1 + V_2 = \left(\frac{p_1}{p_c}\right)^{\frac{1}{\gamma}} \cdot V_1 + \left(\frac{p_2}{p_c}\right)^{\frac{1}{\gamma}} \cdot V_2.$$

From this, the common pressure after raising the fractions to the given power and reorganising is

$$p_c^{\frac{1}{\gamma}} = \frac{p_1^{\frac{1}{\gamma}} V_1 + p_2^{\frac{1}{\gamma}} V_2}{V_1 + V_2},$$

from which the common pressure is

$$p_c = \frac{\left(p_1^{\frac{1}{\gamma}} V_1 + p_2^{\frac{1}{\gamma}} V_2\right)^\gamma}{(V_1 + V_2)^\gamma}.$$

If it is substituted into the formula for the kinetic energy of the wall, the requested speed can be expressed:

$$v = \sqrt{\frac{2}{(\gamma-1)m} \left[p_1 V_1 + p_2 V_2 - \frac{\left(p_1^{\frac{1}{\gamma}} V_1 + p_2^{\frac{1}{\gamma}} V_2\right)^\gamma}{(V_1+V_2)^{\gamma-1}}\right]} = 5.017 \, \frac{m}{s} \approx 5 \, \frac{m}{s},$$

In detail, with numerical values

$$\left(\frac{2}{\frac{2}{3} \cdot 2 \, \text{kg}} \left\{ 4 \cdot 10^5 \, \text{Pa} \cdot 3 \cdot 10^{-3} \, \text{m}^3 + 2.5 \cdot 10^5 \, \text{Pa} \cdot 2 \cdot 10^{-3} \, \text{m}^3 - \right.\right.$$

$$\left.\left. - \frac{[(4 \cdot 10^5 \, \text{Pa})^{0.6} \cdot 3 \cdot 10^{-3} \, \text{m}^3 + (2.5 \cdot 10^5)^{0.6} \cdot 2 \cdot 10^{-3} \, \text{m}^3]^{\frac{5}{3}}}{(3 \cdot 10^{-3} \, \text{m}^3 + 2 \cdot 10^{-3} \, \text{m}^3)^{\frac{2}{3}}} \right\} \right)^{-1/2} = 5.017 \, \frac{m}{s} \approx 5 \, \frac{m}{s}.$$

where $\gamma = 5/3$, $\gamma - 1 = 2/3$, $1/\gamma = 0.6$.

First solution of Problem 187. The pressure of the gas mixture can only be increased by decreasing the volume since, owing to the thermal insulation of the vessel, the process must be adiabatic. Concerning the temperature, volume and pressure of the gas mixture, it does not make a difference whether or not you assume that the two gases, initially, of different molar heats and degrees of freedom, are separated by a thin insulating and freely moving wall. Then — since the given data refer to $0\,°C$ and atmospheric pressure — the two gases fill volumes determined by their quantities. There is exactly 1 mole of helium, so $V_{0_{He}} = 22.41$ dm^3, and half a mole of oxygen, so $V_{0_{O_2}} = 11.205$ dm^3. When the piston is pressed to increase the pressure from $p_0 = 10^5$ Pa to $p_1 = 2 \cdot 10^5$ Pa, both gas compartments are compressed, while their temperatures increase to different extents. At this stage, the volumes of the individual gases can be expressed from the equation of adiabatic change. The ratios of the molar specific heats are $5/3 = \gamma_1$ for helium and $7/5 = \gamma_2$ for oxygen. Thus

$$p_0 V_{0_{He}}^{\gamma_1} = p_1 V_{1_{He}}^{\gamma_2}.$$

Hence the volumes of helium and oxygen after the compression are

$$V_{1_{He}} = V_{0_{He}} \left(\frac{p_0}{p_1}\right)^{\frac{1}{\gamma_1}} = 22.41 \text{ dm}^3 \frac{1}{2^{\frac{3}{5}}} = 14.785 \text{ dm}^3.$$

$$V_{1_{O_2}} = V_{0_{O_2}} \left(\frac{p_0}{p_1}\right)^{\frac{1}{\gamma_2}} = 11.205 \text{ dm}^3 \frac{1}{2^{\frac{5}{7}}} = 6.829 \text{ dm}^3.$$

The volume of the gas mixture at $p_1 = 2 \cdot 10^5$ Pa is now

$$V = V_{1_{He}} + V_{1_{O_2}} = 14.785 \text{ dm}^3 + 6.829 \text{ dm}^3 = 21.615 \text{ dm}^3.$$

This is not the final volume yet, since the temperatures of the two gases are different. The balancing of temperatures will involve a change in volumes (now at constant pressure). The different temperatures of the two gases are given by the universal gas equation:

$$T_{1_{He}} = T_0 \frac{p_1 V_{1_{He}}}{p_0 V_{0_{He}}} = 273 \text{ K} \cdot \frac{2 \cdot 10^5 \text{ Pa} \cdot 14.785 \text{ dm}^3}{1 \cdot 10^5 \text{ Pa} \cdot 22.41 \text{ dm}^3} = 360.22 \text{ K}.$$

$$T_{1_{O_2}} = T_0 \frac{p_1 V_{1_{O_2}}}{p_0 V_{0_{O_2}}} = 273 \text{ K} \cdot \frac{2 \cdot 10^5 \text{ Pa} \cdot 6.829 \text{ dm}^3}{1 \cdot 10^5 \text{ Pa} \cdot 11.205 \text{ dm}^3} = 332.765 \text{ K}.$$

Now the two gases have the same pressure but different temperatures. The divider of the two compartments is then removed 'in two steps'. First it is imagined to turn into a light and thermally conducting piston, and finally the piston is removed. In the first stage, the temperatures of the two gases are balanced, while the external piston is continually adjusted to maintain the constant pressure of $p_1 = 2 \cdot 10^5$ Pa. (This involves the displacement of the external piston, and thus the final total volume will change.) At the end of this process, temperature and pressure are both equal in the two compartments, that is, they are in complete equilibrium. If the (imaginary) piston is now removed, the two gases will mix until chemical concentrations are also balanced, and the whole process will stop.

The common temperature can be determined by using the equal absolute values of the energies absorbed and given off (since there is no energy entering or leaving the vessel any more). Now, with the thermally conducting piston still in, the gases transfer energy to each other until the mean kinetic energy per degree of freedom is balanced between the two compartments. Meanwhile they do work on each other since their volumes change. The work can be expressed in terms of the molar specific heats at constant pressure:

$$n_{He}C_{ph}(T_{1_{He}} - T) = n_{O_2}C_{po}(T - T_{1_{O_2}}),$$

and hence,

$$T = \frac{n_{He}C_{ph}T_{1_{He}} + n_{O_2}C_{po}T_{1_{O_2}}}{n_{He}C_{ph} + n_{O_2}C_{po}} =$$

$$= \frac{1\,\text{mol}\cdot 20.5\,\frac{\text{J}}{\text{mol}\cdot\text{K}}\cdot 360.22\,\text{K} + 0.5\,\text{mol}\cdot 28.7\,\frac{\text{J}}{\text{mol}\cdot\text{K}}\cdot 332.785\,\text{K}}{1\,\text{mol}\cdot 20.5\,\frac{\text{J}}{\text{mol}\cdot\text{K}} + 0.5\,\text{mol}\cdot 28.7\,\frac{\text{J}}{\text{mol}\cdot\text{K}}} = 348.92\,\text{K}.$$

The combined volume of the two compartments is obtained by adding the individual final volumes of the two gases, which can be calculated from the gas equations for constant pressure:

$$V'_{He} = V_{1_{He}}\frac{T}{T_{1_{He}}} = 14.785\,\text{dm}^3\cdot\frac{348.92\,\text{K}}{360.22\,\text{K}} = 14.321\,\text{dm}^3,$$

$$V'_{O_2} = V_{1_{O_2}}\frac{T}{T_{1_{O_2}}} = 6.829\,\text{dm}^3\cdot\frac{348.92\,\text{K}}{332.785\,\text{K}} = 7.160\,\text{dm}^3.$$

If the thermally conducting wall is now removed altogether, the two gases will mix, but neither the temperature nor the pressure will change anymore. Thus the final temperature of the gas mixture is

$$T = 348.92\,\text{K},$$

and its volume is

$$V = V'_{He} + V'_{O_2} = 14.321\,\text{dm}^3 + 7.160\,\text{dm}^3 = 21.481\,\text{dm}^3.$$

Second solution of Problem 187. The result is obtained faster by using the mean molar heat ratio of the gas mixture, which is obtained as follows: The internal energy of the gas mixture is an additive quantity, so at a temperature T, the total internal energy of a mixture of n_1 moles of one gas of molar specific heat C_{v1} and n_2 moles of another gas of molar specific heat C_{v2} is

$$n_1 C_{v_1}T + n_2 C_{v2}T = (n_1 + n_2)C_v T,$$

where the mean molar heat at constant volume is

$$C_v = \frac{n_1 C_{v1} + n_2 C_{v2}}{n_1 + n_2},$$

that is, the arithmetic mean weighted with the numbers of moles. The molar heat at constant pressure is

$$(n_1 C_{p1} + n_2 C_{p2})\Delta T = (n_1 + n_2)C_p\Delta T.$$

369

Hence the mean molar heat at constant pressure is

$$C_p = \frac{n_1 C_{p1} + n_2 C_{p2}}{n_1 + n_2}.$$

The ratio of the mean molar specific heats is

$$\gamma = \frac{c_p}{c_v} = \frac{C_p}{C_v} = \frac{n_1 C_{p1} + n_2 C_{p2}}{n_1 C_{v1} + n_2 C_{v2}}.$$

With the given information substituted, the value of the ratio for the gas mixture investigated is

$$\gamma = \frac{1 \text{ mol} \cdot 20.5 \ \frac{\text{J}}{\text{mol} \cdot \text{K}} + 0.5 \text{ mol} \cdot 28.7 \ \frac{\text{J}}{\text{mol} \cdot \text{K}}}{1 \text{ mol} \cdot 12.3 \ \frac{\text{J}}{\text{mol} \cdot \text{K}} + 0.5 \text{ mol} \cdot 20.5 \ \frac{\text{J}}{\text{mol} \cdot \text{K}}} = 1.5455.$$

This makes all calculations much simpler. The initial volume is obtained from the universal gas equation:

$$V_0 = \frac{(N_1 + N_2)kT}{p} =$$

$$= \frac{(6 \cdot 10^{23} + 3 \cdot 10^{23}) \cdot 1.38 \cdot 10^{-23} \ \frac{\text{J}}{\text{K}} \cdot 273 \text{ K}}{10^5 \text{ Pa}} = 33.91 \cdot 10^{-3} \text{ m}^3 = 33.91 \text{ dm}^3.$$

The equation of adiabatic change states $p_0 V_0^\gamma = p_1 V^\gamma$. Hence

$$V = V_0 \left(\frac{p_0}{p_1} \right)^{\frac{1}{\gamma}} = 33.91 \, \text{dm}^3 \cdot \frac{1}{2^{\frac{1}{\gamma}}} = 21.654 \, \text{dm}^3.$$

The difference from the value above is caused by the fact that the given molar heats are rounded values. (In calculating the mean molar heat ratio γ, these roundings influenced the result in a different way.)

The final temperature is simply obtained from the universal gas equation again:

$$T = T_0 \frac{pV}{p_0 V_0} = 273 \text{ K} \cdot \frac{2 \cdot 10^5 \text{ Pa} \cdot 21.654 \, \text{dm}^3}{1 \cdot 10^5 \text{ Pa} \cdot 33.91 \, \text{dm}^3} = 348.661 \text{ K},$$

in good agreement with the first solution above.

Solution of Problem 188. a) In equilibrium, both pressure and temperature are the same on both sides. The state equation for the two gases after the equilibrium is reached:

$$p_c(V_1 - \Delta V) = N_1 k T_c, \tag{1}$$

$$p_c(V_2 + \Delta V) = N_2 k T_c, \tag{2}$$

Dividing (1) by (2) gives $\dfrac{V_1 - \Delta V}{V_2 + \Delta V} = \dfrac{N_1}{N_2}$, multiplying by the denominators:

$$V_1 N_2 - \Delta V N_2 = V_2 N_1 + \Delta V N_1,$$

from which the volume swept by the piston is:

$$\Delta V = \frac{N_2 V_1 - N_1 V_2}{N_1 + N_2}. \tag{3}$$

The relationship between the numbers of particles and the initial data of the gases is given by the state equation:

$$p_1 V_1 = N_1 k T_1, \qquad p_2 V_2 = N_2 k T_2.$$

From these, the numbers of particles can be substituted into (3):

$$\Delta V = \frac{\frac{p_2 V_2}{k T_2} V_1 - \frac{p_1 V_1}{k T_1} V_2}{\frac{p_1 V_1}{k T_1} + \frac{p_2 V_2}{k T_2}}.$$

After simplifying and factoring out:

$$\Delta V = \frac{(p_2 T_1 - p_1 T_2) V_1 V_2}{V_1 p_1 T_2 + p_2 V_2 T_1} = \frac{(3 \cdot 10^5 \cdot 350 - 2 \cdot 10^5 \cdot 280) \cdot 4 \cdot 5}{2 \cdot 10^5 \cdot 4 \cdot 280 + 3 \cdot 10^5 \cdot 5 \cdot 350} \ \text{dm}^3 = 1.31 \ \text{dm}^3.$$

The displacement of the piston is

$$\Delta s = \frac{\Delta V}{A} = \frac{1.31 \ \text{m}^3}{1 \ \text{dm}^2} = 1.31 \ \text{dm}.$$

(Those who start with the gas law written for the changes in the state of the gases enclosed in the two parts, end up with the following:

$$\frac{p_1 V_1}{T_1} = \frac{p_c (V_1 - \Delta V)}{T_c}, \tag{1'}$$

$$\frac{p_2 V_2}{T_2} = \frac{p_c (V_2 + \Delta V)}{T_c}. \tag{2'}$$

(1') divided by (2') gives

$$\frac{p_1 V_1 T_2}{p_2 V_2 T_1} = \frac{V_1 - \Delta V}{V_2 + \Delta V}.$$

After rearrangement the change in volume is acquired immediately.)

Those who start with the conservation of the total energy of the gases enclosed in the cylinder can write up the following:

$$E = \frac{3}{2} p_1 V_1 + \frac{5}{2} p_2 V_2 = \frac{3}{2} \cdot 2 \cdot 10^5 \frac{\text{N}}{\text{m}^2} \cdot 4 \cdot 10^{-3} \ \text{m}^3 + \frac{5}{2} \cdot 3 \cdot 10^5 \frac{\text{N}}{\text{m}^2} \cdot 5 \cdot 10^{-3} \ \text{m}^3 =$$
$$= 1200 \text{J} + 3750 \text{J} = 4950 \text{J}.$$

The energy in the new equilibrium expressed with the common temperature is

$$\frac{3}{2} N_1 k T_c + \frac{5}{2} N_2 k T_c = \left(\frac{3}{2} \frac{p_1 V_1}{T_1} + \frac{5}{2} \frac{p_2 V_2}{T_2} \right) T_c.$$

From the equality of the total energy in the initial and in the final states:

$$T_c = \frac{\frac{3}{2}p_1 V_1 + \frac{5}{2}p_2 V_2}{\frac{3}{2}\frac{p_1 V_1}{T_1} + \frac{5}{2}\frac{p_2 V_2}{T_2}} = \frac{3p_1 V_1 + 5p_2 V_2}{3p_1 V_1 T_2 + 5p_2 V_2 T_1} \cdot T_1 T_2.$$

With numerical values, after simplifying by the powers of 10 and the suitable units:

$$T_c = \frac{3 \cdot 2 \cdot 4 + 5 \cdot 3 \cdot 5}{3 \cdot 2 \cdot 4 \cdot 280 \text{ K} + 5 \cdot 3 \cdot 5 \cdot 350 \text{ K}} \cdot 350 \text{ K} \cdot 280 \text{ K} = 294.3 \text{ K}.$$

The common pressure reached in equilibrium is

$$p_c = \frac{(N_1 + N_2)kT_k}{V_1 + V_2} = \frac{\left(\frac{p_1 V_1}{T_1} + \frac{p_2 V_2}{T_2}\right)T_c}{V_1 + V_2} = \frac{\frac{2 \cdot 10^5 \text{ Pa} \cdot 4}{350} + \frac{3 \cdot 10^5 \text{ Pa} \cdot 5}{280}}{4 + 5} \cdot 294.3 = 2.5 \cdot 10^5 \text{ Pa}.$$

The change in volume is acquired from the gas law written e.g. for helium:

$$\frac{p_1 V_1}{T_1} = \frac{p_c(V_2 - \Delta V)}{T_c},$$

from which

$$\Delta V = V_2 - T_c \cdot \frac{p_1 V_1}{p_c T_1} = 4 \cdot 10^{-3} \text{ m}^3 - 294.3 \text{ K} \cdot \frac{2 \cdot 10^5 \frac{\text{N}}{\text{m}^2} \cdot 4 \cdot 10^{-3} \text{ m}^3}{2.5 \cdot 10^5 \text{ Pa} \cdot 350 \text{ K}} = 1.31 \text{ dm}^3.$$

So the displacement of the piston is $\Delta s = \Delta V / A = 1.31$ dm.

b) If the piston is permeable, the pressure, the temperature and the density of both gas mixtures will be the same on both sides. The piston can be in equilibrium in any state. Its place is determined by the rate of the equalisation of the temperature and the diffusion speed of the different materials.

c) If the piston allows only helium to diffuse into the other part, the piston will move to the end position on the side that originally contained only helium, the sum of partial pressures will always be greater in the mixture. The helium concentration strives to equalise in the process. (Concentration is an intensive state variable like pressure and temperature.)

First solution of Problem 189. The fact that the containers are connected does not make it impossible to maintain a temperature difference between them, but ensures that the pressure is the same in each of the three containers. Therefore the masses of gases in the containers must change, gas should flow to the coolest container from the other two.

The quantities describing the initial and final state are shown. The initial temperature pressure, the initial mass of gas (which is the equivalent of 1 mole per container) and the final temperatures in each container are known. The volumes of the containers and the total mass of gas remains unchanged throughout the process. The final pressure and change in energy can be determined easily by using the conservation of matter principle and applying the equation of state to the different containers.

The total number of moles is constant (there is no leak in the system), so:

$$n_1 + n_2 + n_3 = 3n_0, \tag{1}$$

where $n_0 = 1$ mole. Applying the equation of state to any of the containers in its initial state, we have:

$$p_0 V = n_0 R T_0, \tag{2}$$

Applying the equation of state to each container in their final states, we get:

$$pV = n_1 R T_1, \tag{3}$$

$$pV = n_2 R T_2, \tag{4}$$

$$pV = n_3 R T_3, \tag{5}$$

where $T_2 = T_0$. Isolating the number of moles using equations (3), (4) and (5) and inserting them into equation (1), we obtain:

$$\frac{pV}{RT_1} + \frac{pV}{RT_2} + \frac{pV}{RT_3} = 3n_0. \tag{1'}$$

Let us isolate R/V from equation (2):

$$\frac{R}{V} = \frac{p_0}{n_0 T_0},$$

and multiply equation (1') by R/V:

$$p\left(\frac{1}{T_1} + \frac{1}{T_2} + \frac{1}{T_3}\right) = 3n_0 \frac{R}{V} = 3n_0 \frac{p_0}{n_0 T_0} = 3\frac{p_0}{T_0}.$$

From which the final pressure is:

$$p = 3\frac{p_0}{T_0} \cdot \frac{T_1 T_2 T_3}{T_1 T_2 + T_1 T_3 + T_2 T_3},$$

simplify this expression using $T_2 = T_0$:

$$p = 3p_0 \frac{T_1 T_3}{T_1 T_0 + T_1 T_3 + T_0 T_3},$$

substituting known values, we find:

$$p = 3 \cdot 10 \, \frac{\text{N}}{\text{cm}^2} \cdot \frac{373 \cdot 573}{373 \cdot 473 + 373 \cdot 573 + 473 \cdot 573} = 9.7 \, \frac{\text{N}}{\text{cm}^2}.$$

The total internal energy of the gas in its final state is:

$$U = U_1 + U_2 + U_3 = c_v m_1 T_1 + c_v m_2 T_2 + c_v m_3 T_3,$$

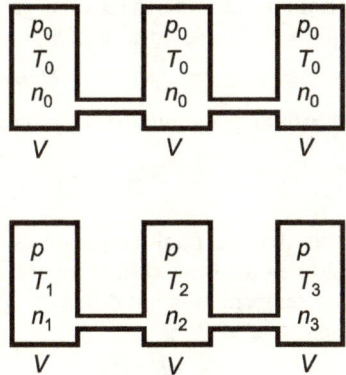

assuming that the mass of a gas can be written as the product of its molar mass and number of moles, we obtain:

$$U = c_v M (n_1 T_1 + n_2 T_2 + n_3 T_3).$$

Substituting the number of moles isolated from equations (3), (4) and (5), we get:

$$U = c_v M \left(n_0 \frac{T_0}{p_0} \frac{p}{T_1} T_1 + n_0 \frac{T_0}{p_0} \frac{p}{T_2} T_2 + n_0 \frac{T_0}{p_0} \frac{p}{T_3} T_3 \right).$$

Note that the final temperatures of gases cancel out, which means that the energies of gases in the three different containers are the same in spite of the fact that their masses and temperatures are different. Therefore the total internal energy of oxygen gas in its final state is:

$$U = 3 c_v M n_0 \frac{T_0}{p_0} p = 3 c_v M n_0 \cdot 3 \frac{T_1 T_0 T_3}{T_1 T_0 + T_1 T_3 + T_0 T_3}.$$

Substituting known values, we find:

$$U = 3 \cdot 670 \, \frac{J}{kg \, K} \cdot 32 \cdot 10^{-3} \frac{kg}{mol} \cdot 1 \, mol \cdot \frac{473 \, K}{10^5 \, \frac{N}{m^2}} \cdot 9.7 \cdot 10^4 \, \frac{N}{m^2} = 29510.6 \, J.$$

The initial internal energy is:

$$U_0 = 3 c_v M n_0 T_0 = 3 \cdot 670 \, \frac{J}{kg \, K} \cdot 32 \cdot 10^{-3} \frac{kg}{mol} \cdot 1 \, mol \cdot 473 \, K = 30423 \, J.$$

So the total energy of oxygen decreased — energy flew out of the system throughout the process. The change in the total internal energy of oxygen gas is:

$$\Delta U = U - U_0 = 29510.6 \, J - 30423 \, J = -912.4 \, J.$$

Second solution of Problem 189. The problem can also be solved by using the number of molecules and the degree of freedom. The total number of molecules is constant:

$$N_1 + N_2 + N_3 = 3 N_0. \tag{1'}$$

Using the equation of state, we get:

$$p_0 V = N_0 k T_0, \tag{2'}$$
$$p V = N_1 k T_1, \tag{3'}$$
$$p V = N_2 k T_2, \tag{4'}$$
$$p V = N_3 k T_3. \tag{5'}$$

Isolating the number of molecules and substituting them into equation (1'), we obtain:

$$\frac{pV}{kT_1} + \frac{pV}{kT_2} + \frac{pV}{kT_3} = 3 \frac{p_0 V}{kT_0},$$

Let us divide by V/k-val and then isolate the final pressure:

$$p = 3 p_0 \frac{T_1 T_3}{T_1 T_0 + T_1 T_3 + T_0 T_3} = 9.7 \, \frac{N}{cm^2},$$

as $T_2 = T_0$.

If the change in the energy is now calculated using the degree of freedom, there will be a slight difference in our answer compared to the previous solution. This is caused by the fact that although the specific heat of oxygen is given as 670 J/(kg K), in reality it is less than that [653 J/(kg K)]. Let us express the final total energy using the degree of freedom:

$$U = \frac{f}{2}k(N_1T_1 + N_2T_2 + N_3T_3),$$

Substitute the expressions for the number of moles and V isolated from equation (2'):

$$U = \frac{f}{2}k\left(\frac{pV}{k} + \frac{pV}{k} + \frac{pV}{k}\right) = \frac{f}{2}3pV = \frac{f}{2}3p\frac{N_0kT_0}{p_0}.$$

Substituting known values, we find:

$$U = \frac{5}{2} \cdot 3 \cdot 9.7\,\frac{\mathrm{N}}{\mathrm{cm}^2} \cdot \frac{6 \cdot 10^{23} \cdot 1.38 \cdot 10^{-23}\ \mathrm{J/K} \cdot 427\,\mathrm{K}}{10\,\mathrm{N/cm}^2} = 25721.2\,\mathrm{J},$$

The initial total energy is:

$$U_0 = \frac{f}{2} \cdot 3N_0kT_0 = \frac{5}{2} \cdot 3 \cdot 6 \cdot 10^{23} \cdot 1.38 \cdot 10^{-23} \cdot 427\,\mathrm{K} = 26612.8\,\mathrm{J},$$

so the change in the energy is:

$$\Delta U = U - U_0 = 25721.2\,\mathrm{J} - 26612.8\,\mathrm{J} = -891.6\,\mathrm{J}.$$

The difference between the two results for the change in energy means a relative error of: $\dfrac{912.4 - 891.6}{891.6} = 0.0234 = 2.34\%.$

First solution of Problem 190. Let us determine the missing data in states A and B first. According to the figure, the unknown pressure in state A is related to the given data as follows: $p_A/(V_0 - V_A) = p_0/V_0$, and so

$$p_A = \frac{V_0 - V_A}{V_0}p_0 = \frac{1}{3}p_0 \quad (=0.4 \cdot 10^5\,\mathrm{Pa}). \tag{1}$$

Similarly, the pressure in state B satisfies $p_B/(V_0 - V_B) = p_0/V_0$, and so

$$p_B = \frac{V_0 - V_B}{V_0}p_0 = \frac{7}{12}p_0 \quad (=0.7 \cdot 10^5\,\mathrm{Pa}). \tag{2}$$

The unknown temperature in state B is determined by using the universal gas equation:

$$T_B = \frac{p_B V_B}{p_A V_A}T_A = \frac{35}{32}T_A \quad (=328.1\,\mathrm{K}). \tag{3}$$

The product Nk will be needed below. It can be obtained from the relationship $p_A V_A = NkT_A$. With the use of equation (1) and the given information $V_A = 2V_0/3$:

$$Nk = \frac{p_A V_A}{T_A} = \frac{\frac{1}{3}p_0 \cdot \frac{2}{3}V_0}{T_A} = \frac{2}{9}\frac{p_0 V_0}{T_A} \quad \left(=1.067\,\frac{\mathrm{J}}{\mathrm{K}}\right). \tag{4}$$

The function $p(V)$ describing the process is provided by the equation of the line passing through the points $(0;p_0)$ and $(V_0;0)$:

$$p(V) = -\frac{p_0}{V_0}V + p_0 = p_0\left(1 - \frac{V}{V_0}\right). \tag{5}$$

The function $T(V)$ is obtained from (4) and (5):

$$T(V) = \frac{p(V)\cdot V}{Nk} = p_0\left(1 - \frac{V}{V_0}\right)\cdot\frac{V}{Nk} = p_0\cdot\frac{9T_A}{2p_0V_0}\cdot\left(1 - \frac{V}{V_0}\right)V =$$

$$= \frac{9}{2}T_A\left(1 - \frac{V}{V_0}\right)\frac{V}{V_0} = \frac{9}{2}T_A\left[\frac{V}{V_0} - \left(\frac{V}{V_0}\right)^2\right]. \tag{6}$$

Let $Q(V)$ denote the heat absorbed by the gas from the surroundings while its volume changes from V_A to V. Let us determine the function $Q(V)$.

According to the first law of thermodynamics,

$$\Delta U_{(V_A\to V)} = Q(V) + W_{(V_A\to V)}.$$

Hence

$$Q(V) = \Delta U_{(V_A\to V)} - W_{(V_A\to V)}. \tag{7}$$

Therefore, the task is to find the change in internal energy and the work done on the gas during a decrease of volume from V_A to any V. The energy change is obtained from the formula $\Delta U = \frac{f}{2}Nk\Delta T$ with the use of (4) and (6):

$$\Delta U = \frac{5}{2}Nk(T - T_A) = \frac{5}{2}\cdot\frac{2}{9}\frac{p_0V_0}{T_A}\left\{\frac{9}{2}T_A\left[\frac{V}{V_0} - \left(\frac{V}{V_0}\right)^2\right] - T_A\right\} =$$

$$= p_0v_0\left[\frac{5}{2}\left(\frac{V}{V_0}\right) - \frac{5}{2}\left(\frac{V}{V_0}\right)^2 - \frac{5}{9}\right]. \tag{8}$$

The work done on the gas is represented by 'the area under the graph' over the interval $V_A\to V$:

$$W = -\frac{p_A+p}{2}(V - V_A).$$

With the use of (1), (5) and $V_A = 2V_0/3$:

$$W = -\frac{1}{2}\left[\frac{1}{3}p_0 + p_0\left(1 - \frac{V}{V_0}\right)\right]\cdot\left(V - \frac{2}{3}V_0\right) = -\frac{1}{2}\left[\frac{4}{3}p_0 - p_0\frac{V}{V_0}\right]\left(V - \frac{2}{3}V_0\right).$$

With the indicated operations and rearrangement carried out, the expression obtained for the work is

$$W = -p_0V_0\left[\left(\frac{V}{V_0}\right) - \frac{1}{2}\left(\frac{V}{V_0}\right)^2 - \frac{4}{9}\right]. \tag{9}$$

Thus, with the substitution of (8) and (9) in (7), the function $Q(V)$ is

$$Q(V) = p_0 V_0 \left\{ \left[\frac{5}{2} \left(\frac{V}{V_0} \right) - \frac{5}{2} \left(\frac{V}{V_0} \right)^2 - \frac{5}{9} \right] + \left[\left(\frac{V}{V_0} \right) - \frac{1}{2} \left(\frac{V}{V_0} \right)^2 - \frac{4}{9} \right] \right\}.$$

Simplified and rearranged:

$$Q(V) = p_0 V_0 \left[\frac{7}{2} \left(\frac{V}{V_0} \right) - 3 \left(\frac{V}{V_0} \right)^2 - 1 \right]. \tag{10}$$

The analysis of the function $Q(V)$ provides the following information. The net heat absorbed increases until the gas is gradually compressed from the initial volume of V_A to $7V_0/12$. The net heat absorbed so far is

$$Q_{\text{absorbed}} = Q \left(\frac{7}{12} V_0 \right) = p_0 V_0 \left[\frac{7}{2} \cdot \frac{7V_0}{12V_0} - 3 \cdot \left(\frac{7V_0}{12V_0} \right)^2 - 1 \right] =$$

$$= p_0 V_0 \left(\frac{49}{24} - \frac{3 \cdot 49}{144} - 1 \right) = \frac{p_0 V_0}{48} = \frac{1.2 \cdot 10^5 \, \text{Pa} \cdot 12 \cdot 10^{-3} \, \text{m}^3}{48} = 30 \, \text{J}.$$

As the gas is compressed further from the volume $7V_0/12$, it gives off heat. That heat is obtained as the difference of the total heat transfer during the whole process and the heat transfer during the compression to $7V_0/12$, since

$$Q_{(V_A \to V_B)} = Q_{(V_A \to \frac{7}{12} V_0)} + Q_{(\frac{7}{12} V_0 \to V_B)},$$

where

$$Q_{(V_A \to \frac{7}{12} V_0)} = Q_{\text{absorbed}} = \frac{p_0 V_0}{48} = 30 \, \text{J}.$$

With the substitution of $V_B = 5V_0/12$ in the function $Q(V)$ (10), the total heat transfer during the whole process is

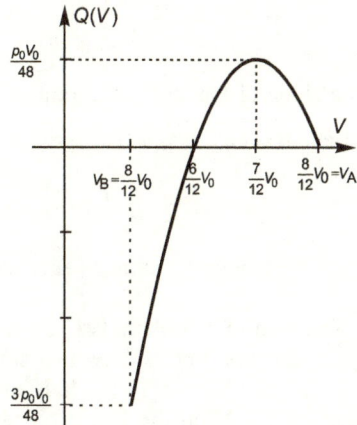

$$Q_{(V_A \to V_B)} = p_0 V_0 \left(-3 \cdot \frac{25}{144} + \frac{7}{2} \cdot \frac{5}{12} - 1 \right) = -p_0 V_0 \frac{9}{144} = -\frac{3 p_0 V_0}{48}.$$

Thus the heat absorbed by the gas is

$$Q_{(\frac{7}{12} V_0 \to V_B)} = Q_{(V_A \to V_B)} - Q_{(V_A \to \frac{7}{12} V_0)} = -\frac{3 p_0 V_0}{48} - \frac{p_0 V_0}{48} = -\frac{p_0 V_0}{12}.$$

With numerical data:

$$Q_{(\frac{7}{12} V_0 \to V_B)} = -\frac{1}{12} \cdot 1.2 \cdot 10^5 \, \text{Pa} \cdot 12 \cdot 10^{-3} \, \text{m}^3 = -120 \, \text{J},$$

therefore the heat given off during the process is $Q_{\text{off}} = 120 \, \text{J}$.

Second solution of Problem 190. There is another way to determine the volume V_x down to which heat is absorbed. The gas absorbs heat while its volume decreases to V_x, but gives off heat when it is compressed further. This implies that in a small neighbourhood of V_x there is no heat absorbed or given off. More accurately, the $p(V)$ diagram of the process touches the curve of the adiabatic process passing through the point $[V_x, p(V_x)]$. Consider the adiabatic curve passing through an arbitrary point $[V, p]$. The slope of the curve is expressed as follows:

$$p = c \cdot V^{-\gamma} \quad (c = \text{constant}),$$

$$\frac{dp}{dV} = -\gamma c V^{-\gamma-1} = -\gamma \frac{cV^{-\gamma}}{V},$$

therefore

$$\frac{dp}{dV} = -\gamma \frac{p}{V}. \tag{8}$$

Along the curve $p(V)$ of the process investigated, the slope of the adiabatic curve at volume V can be expressed with (8):

$$\left(\frac{dp}{dV}\right)_{\text{adiabat}} = \left(\frac{dp}{dV}\right)_{\text{process}} = -\gamma \frac{p_0}{v}\left(1 - \frac{V}{V_0}\right)$$

The slope of the $p(V)$ diagram of the gas is $-\dfrac{p_0}{V_0}$ for all volumes. The slopes can be set equal. Thus (given that $\gamma = 7/5$ for oxygen gas),

$$-\frac{7}{5}\frac{p_0}{V_x}\left(1 - \frac{V_x}{V_0}\right) = -\frac{p_0}{V_0}, \quad \text{andso} \quad V_x = \frac{7}{12}V_0.$$

Then the solution continues as above.

Solution of Problem 191. a) We work with exactly 1 mol of hydrogen gas in this cyclic process. Let us draw the isothermal curves of the hydrogen gas for temperatures $T_1 = 273\,\text{K}$, $T_2 = 2 \cdot T_1 = 546\,\text{K}$ and $T_3 = 819\,\text{K}$ on the p-V diagram. The cycle starts at point 1. When the hydrogen reaches point 2, its pressure doubles and so does its temperature, which is therefore $546\,\text{K}$. The heat absorbed by the gas in this process is:

$$Q_1 = c_v m \Delta T_1 = 10100 \frac{\text{J}}{\text{kg K}} \cdot 2 \cdot 10^{-3}\,\text{kg} \cdot 273\,\text{K} = 5514.6\,\text{J}.$$

When the gas is heated to $T_3 = 819\,\text{K}$, its temperature is increased to $T_3/T_2 = 1.5$ times its previous value, therefore its new volume becomes $1.5 V_1 = 1.5 \cdot 22.4 \cdot 10^{-3}\,\text{m}^3 = 33.6$ litre. The heat absorbed by the gas in this second process is:

$$Q_2 = c_p m \Delta T_2 = 14280 \frac{\text{J}}{\text{kg K}} \cdot 2 \cdot 10^{-3}\,\text{kg} \cdot 273\,\text{K} = 7797\,\text{J}.$$

The total heat absorbed by the gas is $Q_{\text{absorbed}} = Q_1 + Q_2 = 13311.6\,\text{J}$ so far. In the third process heat is rejected from the gas.

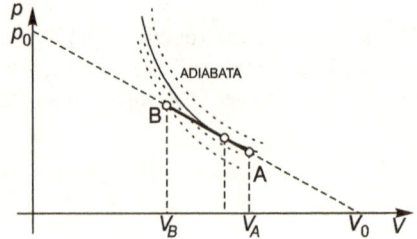

The efficiency of the cycle is the ratio of the work done by the gas to the heat absorbed by the gas. (The rejected heat in the third process does not have any effect on the efficiency.)

The work done by the gas is given by the enclosed area, which is:

$$W = \frac{1}{2}\Delta p \Delta V = \frac{1}{2} \cdot 10^5 \text{ Pa} \cdot 11.2 \cdot 10^{-3} \text{ m}^3 = 560 \text{ J}.$$

Hence the efficiency in question is:

$$\eta = \frac{W}{Q_1 + Q_2} = \frac{560}{13311.6} = 4.2\%.$$

b) The equation of the line that passes through points 1 and 3 is:

$$\frac{p - p_1}{V - V_1} = \frac{p_3 - p_1}{V_3 - V_1}.$$

Rearranging this, we get:

$$p = \frac{p_3 - p_1}{V_3 - V_1} \cdot V + \frac{p_1 V_3 - p_3 V_1}{V_3 - V_1}.$$

Using the equation of state, we can express the pressure in terms of temperature, which can then be substituted into the equation of the line. This way we can express the temperature in terms of volume during process 3–1. Since we have 1 mol of hydrogen gas, $p = RT/V$.

Thus the temperature can be expressed in terms of volume as:

$$T = \frac{1}{R} \cdot \frac{p_3 - p_1}{V_3 - V_1} \cdot V^2 + \frac{1}{R} \cdot \frac{p_1 V_3 - p_3 V_1}{V_3 - V_1} \cdot V.$$

Substituting the given data, we find:

$$T = 1074437 \frac{\text{K}}{\text{m}^6} \cdot V^2 - 12033.69 \frac{\text{K}}{\text{m}^3} \cdot V.$$

The temperature therefore changes as a second degree function of volume during process 3-1. Now, by isolating now the volume instead of the pressure from the equation of state, we obtain a similar connection between the temperature and pressure:

$$T = \frac{1}{R} \cdot \frac{V_3 - V_1}{p_3 - p_1} \cdot p^2 + \frac{1}{R} \cdot \frac{p_3 V_1 - p_1 V_3}{p_3 - p_1} \cdot p.$$

Substituting the given data, we find:

$$T = 1.35 \cdot 10^{-8} \frac{\text{Km}^4}{\text{N}^2} \cdot p^2 + 1.35 \cdot 10^{-3} \frac{\text{Km}}{\text{N}} \cdot p.$$

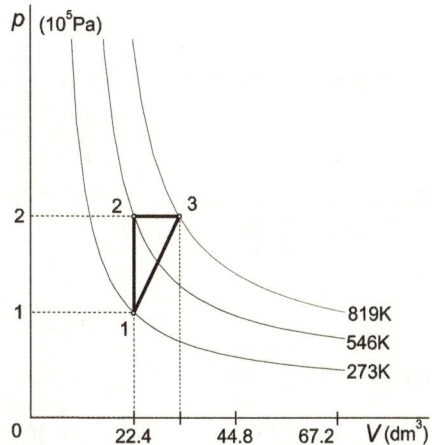

Obviously, during processes 1–2 and 2–3 the temperature changes as a linear function of pressure and volume respectively:

$$T = \frac{T_1}{V_1} \cdot V = 12187.5 \; \frac{\text{K}}{\text{m}^3} \cdot V, \quad \text{and} \quad T = \frac{T_1}{p_1} \cdot p = 2.73 \cdot 10^{-3} \; \frac{\text{Km}^2}{\text{N}} \cdot p.$$

Solution of Problem 192. For process $1 \to 2$ it is true that

$$V^2 = \frac{2 \cdot 10^{-3}}{600} \; \frac{\text{m}^6}{\text{K}} \cdot T.$$

From this

$$T = 3 \cdot 10^5 \; \frac{\text{K}}{\text{m}^6} \cdot V^2.$$

If this is substituted into the universal gas law $pV = nRT$:

$$p = 1 \text{ mol} \cdot 8.31 \; \frac{\text{J}}{\text{mol} \cdot \text{K}} \cdot 3 \cdot 10^5 \; \frac{\text{K}}{\text{m}^6} \cdot V \approx 25 \cdot 10^5 \; \frac{\text{Pa}}{\text{m}^3} \cdot V. \tag{1}$$

Similarly, for process $3 \to 4$

$$V^2 = \frac{2 \cdot 10^{-3}}{300} \; \frac{\text{m}^6}{\text{K}} \cdot T,$$

from which

$$T = 1.5 \cdot 10^5 \; \frac{\text{K}}{\text{m}^6} \cdot V^2.$$

If this is substituted into the universal gas law $pV = nRT$:

$$p = 1 \text{ mol} \cdot 8.31 \; \frac{\text{J}}{\text{mol} \cdot \text{K}} \cdot 1.5 \cdot 10^5 \; \frac{\text{K}}{\text{m}^6} \cdot V \approx 12.5 \cdot 10^5 \; \frac{\text{Pa}}{\text{m}^3} \cdot V. \tag{2}$$

From the equations the state variables can be calculated:
For state ①. From the figure:

$$V_1 = \sqrt{10^{-3} \text{ m}^6} = 3.16 \cdot 10^{-2} \text{ m}^3,$$

$$T_1 = 300 \text{ K},$$

and from (1)

$$p_1 = 25 \cdot 10^5 \; \frac{\text{Pa}}{\text{m}^3} \cdot V_1 = 25 \cdot 10^5 \; \frac{\text{Pa}}{\text{m}^3} \cdot 3.16 \cdot 10^{-2} \text{ m}^3 = 0.79 \cdot 10^5 \text{ Pa},$$

similarly, for state ② from the figure

$$V_2 = \sqrt{2 \cdot 10^{-3} \text{ m}^6} = 4.47 \cdot 10^{-2} \text{ m}^3,$$

$$T_2 = 600 \text{ K},$$

and from (1)

$$p_2 = 25 \cdot 10^5 \; \frac{\text{Pa}}{\text{m}^3} \cdot V_2 = 25 \cdot 10^5 \; \frac{\text{Pa}}{\text{m}^3} \cdot 4.47 \cdot 10^{-2} \text{ m}^3 = 1.118 \cdot 10^5 \text{ Pa}.$$

For state ③ from the figure

$$V_3 = V_2 = 4.47 \cdot 10^{-2} \text{ m}^3,$$

$$T_3 = T_1 = 300 \text{ K},$$

and from (2)

$$p_3 = 12.5 \cdot 10^5 \, \frac{\text{Pa}}{\text{m}^3} \cdot V_3 = 12.5 \cdot 10^5 \, \frac{\text{Pa}}{\text{m}^3} \cdot 4.47 \cdot 10^{-2} \text{ m}^3 = 0.56 \cdot 10^5 \text{ Pa}.$$

For state ④ from the figure

$$V_4 = V_3 = 3.16 \cdot 10^{-2} \text{ m}^3,$$

$$T_4 = \frac{T_1}{2} = 150 \text{ K},$$

and from (2)

$$p_4 = 12.5 \cdot 10^5 \, \frac{\text{Pa}}{\text{m}^3} \cdot V_4 = 12.5 \cdot 10^5 \, \frac{\text{Pa}}{\text{m}^3} \cdot 3.16 \cdot 10^{-2} \text{ m}^3 = 0.4 \cdot 10^5 \text{ Pa}.$$

Based on these data, the p–V diagram can be created:

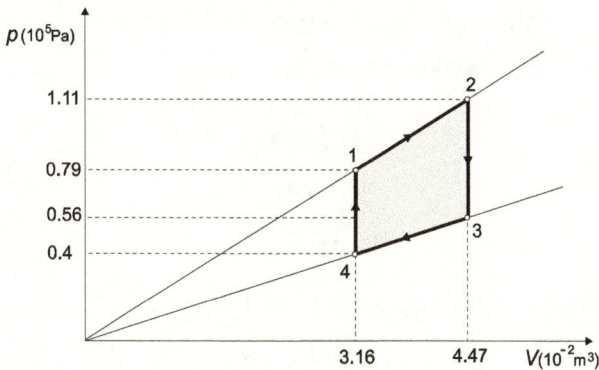

The useful work is

$$W = \frac{p_1 + p_2}{2}(V_2 - V_1) - \frac{p_3 + p_4}{2}(V_2 - V_1) = \frac{p_1 + p_2 - (p_3 + p_4)}{2}(V_2 - V_1),$$

with numerical values:

$$W = \frac{0.79 + 1.11 - 0.56 - 0.4}{2} \cdot 10^5 \, \frac{\text{N}}{\text{m}^2} \cdot (4.47 - 3.16) \cdot 10^{-2} \text{ m}^3 = 615.7 \text{ J}.$$

The heat absorbed is

$$Q_{\text{in}} = Q_{41} + Q_{12} = \Delta E_{41} + \Delta E_{12} - W_{12} =$$

$$= \frac{f}{2} nR(T_1 - T_4) + \frac{f}{2} nR(T_2 - T_1) + \frac{p_1 + p_2}{2}(V_2 - V_1),$$

in short:

$$Q_{\text{in}} = \frac{f}{2}nR(T_2 - T_4) + \frac{p_1 + p_2}{2}(V_2 - V_1) =$$

$$= \frac{5}{2} \cdot 1 \text{ mol} \cdot 8.31 \frac{\text{J}}{\text{mol} \cdot \text{K}} \cdot (600 - 150) \text{ K} + \frac{0.79 + 1.11}{2} \cdot 10^5 \text{ Pa} \cdot (4.47 - 3.16) \cdot 10^{-2} \text{ m}^3 =$$

$$= 10593.2 \text{ J}.$$

The efficiency is

$$\eta = \frac{W}{Q} = \frac{615.7 \text{ J}}{10593.2 \text{ J}} = 0.0581 = 5.81\%.$$

Solution of Problem 193. a) Applying the equation of state to the initial and final situation and assuming that $V_1 = V_2 = V$, we get:

$$p_1 V = N_1 k T_1, \tag{1}$$

$$p_2 V = N_2 k T_2,$$

where N_2 is the sum of the 80% of N_1 and the double of the 20% of N_1. Therefore in the final state:

$$V p_2 = (0.8 N_1 + 2 \cdot 0.2 N_1) k T_2 = 1.2 N_1 k T_2. \tag{2}$$

Dividing equation (2) by equation (1) gives:

$$\frac{p_2}{p_1} = 1.2 \frac{T_2}{T_1},$$

which yields:

$$p_2 = 1.2 \cdot p_1 \cdot \frac{T_2}{T_1}.$$

b) The initial internal energy of the gas is given by:

$$U_1 = \frac{f_1}{2} N_1 k T_1,$$

while the energy at temperature T_2 is:

$$U_2 = \frac{f_1}{2} \cdot 0.8 N_1 k T_2 + \frac{f_2}{2} \cdot 2 \cdot 0.2 N_1 k T_2,$$

where $f_1 = 5$ and $f_2 = 3$ are the degrees of freedom of a diatomic and monatomic gas respectively. Using this, we obtain:

$$U_2 = \left(\frac{5}{2} \cdot 0.8 + \frac{3}{2} \cdot 0.4 \right) N_1 k T_2 = 2.6 N_1 k T_2.$$

Therefore the ratio of energies is:

$$\frac{U_2}{U_1} = \frac{\frac{f_1}{2} \cdot 0.8 N_1 k T_2 + \frac{f_2}{2} \cdot 0.4 N_1 k T_2}{\frac{f_1}{2} \cdot N_1 k T_1} =$$

$$= \frac{0.8 f_1 + 0.4 f_2}{f_1} \cdot \frac{T_2}{T_1} = \frac{4 + 1.2}{5} \frac{T_2}{T_1} = \frac{2.6}{2.5} \cdot \frac{T_2}{T_1} = 1.04 \frac{T_2}{T_1}.$$

First solution of Problem 194. $\Delta p / \Delta V$ is positive, because if it was negative, then the maximum temperature of the gas would be $5\,°C$ during the process. Let T_0 and V_0 stand for the initial data and let $\left| \dfrac{\Delta p}{\Delta V} \right|$ be x.

Our task can be rephrased as follows: we are looking for the gradient of all straight lines passing through point (V_0, p_0) of the state plane that are between the vertical direction and the gradient of the tangent of the isothermal curve belonging to temperature $T_{\max}$ and belong to the compression of the gas. These fall into an interval closed from the left and open from the right. From the right the limiting value of the gradient $-\infty$. Knowing this, we only have to find the left boundary of the interval, that is, the gradient of the line with the highest gradient (its absolute value is the smallest) that has a common point with the isothermal curve belonging to temperature $T_{\max}$. From the property of the hyperbola it can be seen that every straight line passing through point $(V_0, p_{0)})$ has two points of intersection with it except for the 'vertical' line, the 'horizontal' line and the lines belonging to the points of tangency (in the case of the latter we can speak about two coinciding points of intersection). See the graph of Solution 2 as well.

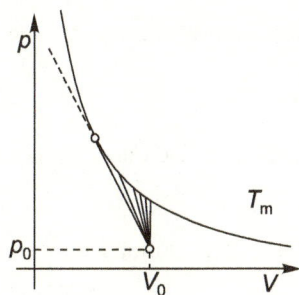

Let us use the universal gas law.
For the initial data of an ideal gas

$$p_0 V_0 = N k T_0,$$

the relationship between the relevant data is

$$p V = N k T.$$

According to the condition for compression

$$\frac{p - p_0}{V - V_0} = -x.$$

From here, the pressure at any time is

$$p = -x V + x V_0 + p_0.$$

Substituting this into the gas law rearranged for T gives

$$T = \frac{1}{Nk} p V = \frac{1}{Nk} \left[-x V^2 + (p_0 + x V_0) V \right] = -\frac{x}{Nk} V^2 + \frac{p_0 + x V_0}{Nk} V.$$

This function is quadratic in V (its graph is an inverted parabola that passes through the origin), so the volume belonging to the maximum temperature is halfway between the two zeros of the function, that is, the volume belonging to the maximum temperature is the arithmetic mean of the two solutions of equation

$$-\frac{x}{Nk}V^2 + \frac{p_0 + xV_0}{Nk}V = 0,$$

that is, of equation

$$V(-xV + p_0 + V_0) = 0.$$

So

$$V_{\text{max}} = \frac{p_0 + xV_0}{2x}.$$

If this is substituted into the gas law, then the maximum temperature is acquired:

$$T_{\text{max}} = \frac{(p_0 + xV_0)^2}{4Nkx}.$$

This gives the quadratic equation

$$V_0^2 x^2 - 2Nk(2T_{\text{max}} - T_0)x + p_0^2 = 0$$

for x. Its solutions are

$$x_{1,2} = \frac{2Nk(2T_{\text{max}} - T_0) \pm \sqrt{4N^2k^2(2T_{\text{max}} - T_0)^2 - 4p_0^2 V_0^2}}{2V_0^2}.$$

Taking into consideration that $p_0 V_0 = NkT_0$, substituting this and factoring out Nk/V_0^2 gives

$$x = \frac{Nk}{V_0^2}\left(2T_{\text{max}} - T_0 \pm 2\sqrt{T_{\text{max}}(T_{\text{max}} - T)}\right).$$

With numerical values

$$x = \frac{6 \cdot 10^{23}\,\frac{1}{\text{mol}} \cdot 1\,\text{mol} \cdot 1.38\,\frac{\text{J}}{\text{K}}}{3 \cdot 10^{-2}\,\text{m}^3} \cdot \left(2 \cdot 344\,\text{K} - 278\,\text{K} \pm 2\sqrt{344\,\text{K}(344\,\text{K} - 288\,\text{K})}\right) =$$

$$= \begin{cases} 6.54 \cdot 10^6\,\dfrac{\text{Pa}}{\text{m}^3} \\[2mm] 9.995 \cdot 10^5\,\dfrac{\text{Pa}}{\text{m}^3} \end{cases}$$

Only the steeper graph of the first result corresponds to a compression. So the solution of the problem is

$$-\infty < \frac{\Delta p}{\Delta V} \leq -6.54 \cdot 10^6\,\frac{\text{Pa}}{\text{m}^3}.$$

Second solution of Problem 194. (Using coordinate geometry). The general equation of straight lines passing through point (p_0, V_0) is

$$p - p_0 = a(V - V_0). \tag{1}$$

The equation of the hyperbola (isothermal curve) is

$$p = \frac{nRT_{\max}}{V} \tag{2}$$

Let us find the value of gradient a where the common points (points of intersection) of the straight line and the hyperbola coincide, that is, the gradient of the tangent of the hyperbola that passes through point (p_0, V_0). By substituting (2) into (1) the coordinates of the points of intersection are acquired:

$$\frac{nRT_{\max}}{V} - p_0 = a(V - V_0).$$

From here, a mixed quadratic equation is acquired for V:

$$aV^2 + (p_0 - aV_0)V - nRT_{\max} = 0.$$

In the case of tangency the D discriminant is zero, so

$$D = (p_0 - aV_0)^2 + 4anRT_{\max} = 0,$$

which gives another quadratic equation for the gradient a:

$$V_0^2 a^2 + (4nRT_{\max} - 2V_0 p_0)a + p_0^2 = 0.$$

Taking $p_0 V_0 = nRT_0$ into consideration, the following expression is acquired for the solution:

$$a_{1,2} = -nR \frac{2T_{\max} - T_0 \pm 2\sqrt{T_{\max}^2 - T_{\max}T_0}}{V_0^2}.$$

This is the same as in the first solution.

Third solution of Problem 194. (Using derivative). The pressure-volume function with maximum temperature is:

$$p = \frac{nRT_{\max}}{V}, \tag{1}$$

The gradient belonging to volume V is equal to the differential

$$a = \frac{\Delta p}{\Delta V} \rightarrow \frac{dp}{dV} = \frac{-nRT_{\max}}{V^2} \tag{2}.$$

The equation of the straight line passing through points (p_0, V_0) and (p, V) is

$$\frac{p - p_0}{V - V_0} = a, \tag{3}$$

where a is the gradient of the equation.

Making the two gradients [(2) and (3)] equal and making use of (1):

$$\frac{\frac{nRT_{\max}}{V} - p_0}{V - V_0} = -\frac{nRT_{\max}}{V^2}.$$

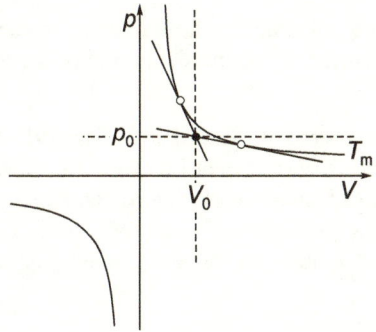

This gives a mixed quadratic equation for V:

$$p_0 V^2 - 2nRT_{\max}V + nRT_{\max}V_0 = 0,$$

whose solutions are

$$V_{1,2} = nR\frac{T_{\max} \pm \sqrt{T_{\max}(T_{\max} - T_0)}}{p_0}.$$

If the result is substituted into (2), then the requested gradient is acquired:

$$a = -\frac{nRT_{\max}}{V_{1,2}^2} = -\frac{T_{\max}p_0^2}{nR\left(T_{\max} \pm \sqrt{T_{\max}(T_{\max} - T_0)}\right)^2}.$$

By substituting the numerical values we acquire the previous solutions. (By removing the root from the denominator the above expressions are also acquired parametrically.)

First solution of Problem 195. If the temperature of the atmosphere rises, a part of the absorbed heat increases its internal energy, while the rest of the heat is converted to mechanical work due to the expansion of the gas. In our problem this work increases the gravitational potential energy of the atmosphere. (Indeed, the centre of mass of an air column in the atmosphere gets higher.)

$$Q = \Delta E_{\text{grav}} + \Delta U.$$

From here, the increase of the gravitational potential energy is:

$$\Delta E_{\text{grav}} = Q - \Delta U.$$

The change of the internal energy ΔU can be written as:

$$\Delta U = \frac{f}{2}Nk\Delta T.$$

How can the absorbed heat Q be determined?

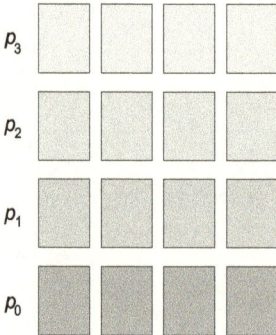

Let us imagine that the atmosphere was divided into small 'air parcels', and each parcel was wrapped into a weightless 'bag' which is infinitely stretchable. The pressure p_0 in the lowest bags arises from the weight of the air column above them, which is unchanged in the process, therefore the pressure in the lowest parcels remains the same during the temperature increase. According to the same logic, the pressure also remains constant in the air parcels at higher levels. Thus in each parcel the enclosed air undergoes an isobaric process at its own pressure, while the bags expand in vertical direction. (In lateral direction the neighbouring parcels prevent the expansion.)

p_3

p_2

p_1

p_0

During the isobaric expansion the air in the ith bag absorbs the heat

$$Q_i = \frac{f+2}{2} N_i k \Delta T.$$

Summarizing these expressions for all the bags, we get:

$$Q = \sum Q_i = \frac{f+2}{2} \left(\sum N_i \right) k \Delta T = \frac{f+2}{2} N k \Delta T.$$

So the change of the gravitational potential energy is:

$$\Delta E_{\text{grav}} = Q - \Delta U = \frac{f+2}{2} N k \Delta T - \frac{f}{2} N k \Delta T = N k \Delta T = \frac{m}{M} R \Delta T. \qquad (1)$$

The total mass m of the atmosphere can be determined from the air pressure at the surface of the Earth. (Indeed, the force pushing the area A of the surface of the Earth comes from the weight of the air above this area.)

$$p_0 A = \frac{m}{4 R_E^2 \pi} g A, \qquad (2)$$

where

$$\frac{m}{4 R_E^2 \pi} = m_A$$

is the mass of the air column above a unit area of the Earth, R_E is the radius of the Earth, and $m_A A$ is the mass of the air above the area A.

The height of the atmosphere is negligibly small with respect to the radius of the Earth. Consequently, the air column above the area A can be regarded as a straight prism, and the dependence of the gravitational acceleration g on the altitude is also negligible. The weight of the air in a straight prism of base A gives the force pushing the surface A:

$$F = m_A A g = p_0 A.$$

From equation (2) the total mass of the atmosphere is:

$$m = \frac{4 R_E^2 \pi p_0}{g} = \frac{4 \cdot (6370 \cdot 10^3 \text{ m})^2 \pi \cdot 10^5 \text{ Pa}}{10 \, \frac{\text{m}}{\text{s}^2}} = 5.1 \cdot 10^{18} \text{ kg}.$$

Writing this into equation (1), we obtain that the increase of the gravitational potential energy of the atmosphere is:

$$\Delta E_{\text{grav}} = \frac{4 R_E^2 \pi p_0}{M g} R \Delta T = \frac{m}{M} R \Delta T = \frac{5.1 \cdot 10^{18} \text{ kg}}{29 \cdot 10^{-3} \, \frac{\text{kg}}{\text{mol}}} \cdot 8.31 \, \frac{\text{J}}{\text{mol} \cdot \text{K}} \cdot 1 \text{ K} = 1.46 \cdot 10^{21} \text{ J}.$$

Second solution of Problem 195. Let us start with the barometric formula. According to it, the density of the air at the altitude h is:

$$\varrho = \varrho_0 e^{-\frac{m_0 g h}{k T}},$$

where ϱ_0 is the density of the air at sea level and m_0 is the mass of an air molecule.

At the altitude h the mass of an air layer of area A and height Δh is:

$$\Delta m = \Delta V \varrho = A \Delta h \varrho = A \Delta h \varrho_0 e^{-\frac{m_0 g h}{kT}},$$

and its gravitational potential energy is:

$$\Delta E_{\text{grav}_A} = \Delta m g h = A \Delta h \varrho_0 e^{-\frac{m_0 g h}{kT}} \cdot g h.$$

These energies have to be summarized along the whole height ($h \to \infty$) of the air column of base area A. As $\Delta h \to 0$, in doing so we get the following integral:

$$E_{\text{grav}_A} = g A \varrho_0 \int_0^\infty h e^{-\frac{m_0 g h}{kT}} \cdot dh.$$

We can find in the integral table, in the chapter of exponential functions, that the primitive function for this indefinite integral is:

$$\int x e^{ax} dx = \frac{e^{ax}}{a^2} (ax - 1).$$

Taking into consideration that in our case a is negative and denoting it by $-\alpha$, we get that:

$$\int x e^{-\alpha x} dx = \frac{e^{-\alpha x}}{\alpha^2} (-\alpha x - 1).$$

Applying the fundamental theorem of calculus, the definite integral is:

$$\int_0^\infty x e^{-\alpha x} dx = \left[\frac{e^{-\alpha x}}{(-\alpha)^2} (-\alpha x - 1) \right]_0^\infty = 0 - \frac{1}{\alpha^2} (0 - 1) = \frac{1}{\alpha^2}.$$

Comparing the abstract integral with the integral appearing in the formula for the gravitational potential energy, we can see that α takes the value

$$\alpha = \frac{m_0 g}{kT},$$

so the integral defining the gravitational potential energy is :

$$E_{\text{grav}_A} = g A \varrho_0 \cdot \frac{1}{\alpha^2} = g A \varrho_0 \left(\frac{kT}{m_0 g} \right)^2.$$

From the universal gas law, the relationship between the density and the pressure of the gas is:

$$p_0 V_0 = N_0 kT \ \to \ p_0 = \frac{N_0 kT}{V_0} = \frac{N_0 kT}{\frac{m}{\varrho_0}} = \frac{\varrho_0 kT}{\frac{m}{N_0}} = \frac{\varrho_0 kT}{m_0}.$$

This means that the density at sea level is:

$$\varrho_0 = \frac{p_0 m_0}{kT}.$$

In the problem, the pressure at sea level is given. Writing the density at sea level into the formula of the gravitational potential energy:

$$E_{\text{grav}_A} = gA\frac{p_0 m_0}{kT}\left(\frac{kT}{m_0 g}\right)^2 = p_0 A\frac{kT}{m_0 g}.$$

Instead of using the molar mass of one air molecule, the molar mass of the air has to be used. The relationship between the two masses is obtained by comparing the two forms of the universal gas law:

$$pV = NkT,$$

$$pV = \frac{m}{M}RT.$$

From here, kT equals

$$kT = \frac{m}{N}\frac{RT}{M} = m_0\frac{RT}{M},$$

and using it, the gravitational potential energy of an air column can be expressed with the data given in the problem:

$$E_{\text{grav}_A} = p_0 A\frac{kT}{m_0 g} = p_0 A\frac{RT}{Mg}.$$

Summing up this for the whole surface of the Earth, we obtain that:

$$E_{\text{grav}} = p_0 4R_E^2\pi\frac{R}{Mg}T.$$

Thus the change of the gravitational potential energy of the atmosphere is:

$$E_{\text{grav}} = p_0 4R_E^2\pi\frac{R}{Mg}\Delta T.$$

This result is equal to the result obtained in the first (elementary) solution.

Solution of Problem 196. a) The initial volume and pressures can be determined using the ideal gas law and the relationship between the pressures:

$$p_1 V_0 = n_1 RT_1$$

$$p_2 V_0 = n_2 RT_2$$

$$p_2 = p_1 + \frac{mg}{A}.$$

From these equations the pressures above and under the piston can be determined. Dividing the first equation by the second one:

$$\frac{p_1}{p_1 + \frac{mg}{A}} = \frac{n_1 T_1}{n_2 T_2}. \quad \text{After rearranging:} \quad p_1\left(1 - \frac{n_1 T_1}{n_2 T_2}\right) = \frac{mg}{A}\cdot\frac{n_1 T_1}{n_2 T_2}.$$

So the pressure above the piston is:

$$p_1 = \frac{mgn_1T_1}{\left(1 - \frac{n_1T_1}{n_2T_2}\right)An_2T_2} = \frac{mg}{A} \cdot \frac{n_1T_1}{(n_2T_2 - n_1T_1)} =$$

$$= \frac{0.5 \text{ kg} \cdot 9.81 \text{ m/s}^2}{0.01 \text{ m}^2} \cdot \frac{0.05 \cdot 183}{0.03 \cdot 319 - 0.05 \cdot 183} = 10685.9 \text{ Pa}.$$

And the pressure under the piston is:

$$p_2 = p_1 + \frac{mg}{A} = 10685.9 \text{ Pa} + \frac{0.5 \text{ kg} \cdot 9.81 \text{ m/s}^2}{0.01 \text{ m}^2} = 11176.4 \text{ Pa}.$$

From the first equation the common volume of the two gases is:

$$V_0 = \frac{n_1RT_1}{p_1} = \frac{A}{mg} \cdot R(n_2T_2 - n_1T_1).$$

Numerically:

$$V_0 = \frac{0.05 \text{ mol} \cdot 8.31 \frac{\text{J}}{\text{mol} \cdot \text{K}} \cdot 183 \text{ K}}{10685.9 \frac{\text{N}}{\text{m}^2}} = 0.00712 \text{ m}^3 = 7.12 \text{ dm}^3.$$

To determine the final temperature T of the system and the displacement Δx of the piston, we use the combined gas law and the law of energy conservation.

The combined gas law, written for the two gases separately between their initial and final states, gives the following two equations:

$$\frac{p_1V_1}{T_1} = \frac{p(V_0 + xA)}{T}, \tag{1}$$

$$\frac{p_2V_0}{T_2} = \frac{(p + \frac{mg}{A}) \cdot (V_0 - xA)}{T}. \tag{2}$$

The law of energy conservation for the whole process in the isolated cylinder has the form:

$$\Delta E_1 + \Delta E_2 + \Delta E_3 + \Delta E_4 = 0.$$

Detailing the terms, we get:

$$\frac{f_1}{2}n_1R(T - T_1) + \frac{f_2}{2}n_2R(T - T_2) + cm(T - T_0) + mg\Delta x = 0. \tag{3}$$

The three unknowns are T, p and x. The above three equations unambiguously determine their values. The solution of the problem can be considerably simplified by noticing that the pressure arising from the weight of the piston is much less than the pressure of the gases, and thus it is negligible. (The pressure in the upper part of the cylinder is 10685.9 Pa, in the lower part it is 11176.4 Pa, while the pressure due to the weight of the piston is

$$p_P = \frac{mg}{A} = \frac{0.5 \text{ kg} \cdot 9.81 \text{ m/s}^2}{0.01 \text{ m}^2} = 490.5 \text{ Pa},$$

which is less than 4.6%.)

With this, exclusions (1) and (2) have the form:

$$\frac{p_1 V_0}{T_1} = \frac{p \cdot (V_0 + xA)}{T}, \tag{1'}$$

$$\frac{p_2 V_0}{T_2} = \frac{p \cdot (V_0 - xA)}{T}. \tag{2'}$$

Dividing $(1')$ by $(2')$ the unknowns p and T cancel out. (This does not mean, however, that the result is independent of the temperature and pressure change, since in the exact equation there is the term mg/A as well.)

$$\frac{p_1 V_0}{T_1} \cdot \frac{T_2}{p_2 V_0} = \frac{V_0 + xA}{V_0 - xA},$$

Rearranging the equation:

$$p_1 T_2 V_0 - p_1 T_2 Ax = p_2 T_1 V_0 + p_2 T_1 Ax$$
$$(p_1 T_2 - p_2 T_1) \cdot V_0 = (p_2 T_1 + p_1 T_2) \cdot Ax,$$

from which the displacement of the piston is:

$$x = \frac{p_1 T_2 - p_2 T_1}{p_1 T_2 + p_2 T_1} \cdot \frac{V_0}{A} = \frac{10685.9 \cdot 319 - 11176.4 \cdot 183}{11176.4 \cdot 183 + 10685.9 \cdot 319} \cdot \frac{0.00712 \text{ m}^3}{0.01 \text{ m}^2} = 0.178 \text{ m} \approx 18 \text{ cm}.$$

From the energy balance equation (3), we get that the final temperature is:

$$T = \frac{(f_1 n_1 T_1 + f_2 n_2 T_2) R + (2cT_0 + 2g\Delta x) m}{(f_1 n_1 + f_2 n_2) R + 2cm}.$$

Since

$$2cT_0 = 2 \cdot 210 \cdot 373 \text{ J/kg} = 156660 \text{ J/kg}$$

and

$$2g\Delta x = 2 \cdot 9.81 \cdot 0.18 \text{ m}^2/\text{s}^2 = 3.5316 \text{ m}^2/\text{s}^2,$$

which is only 0.0022543% of the former quantity, the term $2g\Delta x$ can be neglected again. So the final temperature, in a simpler way, is:

$$T = \frac{(f_1 n_1 T_1 + f_2 n_2 T_2) R + 2cmT_0}{(f_1 n_1 + f_2 n_2) R + 2cm}.$$

Numerically:

$$T = \frac{(3 \cdot 0.05 \text{ mol} \cdot 183 \text{ K} + 5 \cdot 0.03 \text{ mol} \cdot 319 \text{ K}) \cdot 8.31 \frac{\text{J}}{\text{mol K}} + 2 \cdot 210 \frac{\text{J}}{\text{kg mol}} \cdot 0.5 \text{ kg} \cdot 373 \text{ K}}{(3 \cdot 0.05 \text{ mol} + 5 \cdot 0.03 \text{ mol}) \cdot 8.31 \frac{\text{J}}{\text{mol K}} + 2 \cdot 210 \frac{\text{J}}{\text{kg K}} \cdot 0.5 \text{ kg}} =$$
$$= 371.57 \text{ K}$$

If we start from the energy balance equation (where we made a relatively smaller exclusion) and put the temperature value obtained into the combined gas law, then in a slightly more complicated way a better result is obtained for the displacement of the piston. Expressing the pressure p from equation (1) and plugging it into (2), the following second order equation is obtained for x:

$$\frac{p_2 V_0}{T_2} = \left(\frac{p_1 V_0}{T_1} \cdot \frac{T}{V_0 + xA} + \frac{mg}{A} \right) \cdot (V_0 - xA).$$

After performing the multiplication on the right hand side:

$$\frac{p_2 V_0}{T_2} = \frac{p_1 V_0^2 T}{T_1} \cdot \frac{1}{V_0 + xA} - \frac{p_1 V_0 T}{T_1} \cdot \frac{xA}{V_0 + xA} + \frac{mg}{A} V_0 - \frac{mg}{A} xA = 0.$$

Multiplying the equation by $V_0 + xA$ we get:

$$\frac{p_2 V_0^2 T}{T_2} + \frac{p_2 V_0 T}{T_2} Ax = \frac{p_1 V_0^2 T}{T_1} - \frac{p_1 V_0 T}{T_1} Ax + \frac{mg}{A} V_0^2 + mg V_0 x - mg V_0 x - mg Ax^2 = 0.$$

Collecting the terms with the same power of x we get a quadratic equation:

$$mg Ax^2 + \left(\frac{p_2}{T_2} + \frac{p_1}{T_1} \right) \cdot V_0 T Ax + \left(\frac{p_2}{T_2} - \frac{p_1}{T_1} \right) \cdot V_0^2 T - \frac{mg}{A} V_0^2 = 0.$$

Putting in here the numerical data, first we calculate each coefficient separately, and then apply the quadratic formula:

$$0.04905 \cdot x^2 + 2.47168 \cdot x - 0.46482438 = 0.$$

$$x = \frac{-2.47168 \pm \sqrt{2.47168^2 + 4 \cdot 0.04905 \cdot 0.46482438}}{2 \cdot 0.04905} = 0.187 \, \text{m} = 18.7 \, \text{cm}.$$

Both ways of finding the solution are acceptable. Of course, a calculation with reasonably rounded values also gives the right result:

$$x = \frac{-2.47 \pm \sqrt{2.47^2 + 4 \cdot 0.05 \cdot 0.46}}{2 \cdot 0.05} \, \text{m} \approx 0.185537968 \, \text{m} = 0.186 \, \text{m} = 18.6 \, \text{cm}.$$

Solution of Problem 197. If Δp stands for the magnitude of the change in pressure and ΔN stands for the number of escaped particles, then based on the state equation:

$$\Delta N = \frac{\Delta p \cdot V}{kT} = \frac{0.01 \, \text{pV}}{kT} = \frac{0.01 \cdot 5 \cdot 10^4 \, \text{Pa} \cdot 80 \, \text{m}^3}{1.38 \cdot 10^{-23} \cdot 295 \, \text{K}} = 9.826 \cdot 10^{24}.$$

Let us determine the number of particles that escape through the hole in a unit time, that is, the magnitude of the particle flow. Based on secondary school knowledge, we can only answer it in the nature of an estimate. We shall show two such trains of thought.

I. Let v stand for the average speed of the translating motion of the particles. Then in time t $\frac{1}{6}$ of the particles present in a cylindrical space of volume $V_1 = vtA$ leave through the hole. (Factor $\frac{1}{6}$ takes the directional distribution of the speed of the molecules into consideration.) This number is

$$N_1 = \varrho V_1 = \frac{1}{6} \cdot \frac{N}{V} Avt,$$

where ϱ is the particle density, so the intensity of particle flow is

$$I = \frac{N_1}{t} = \frac{1}{6} A v \cdot \frac{N}{V}. \tag{1}$$

The mean velocity v can be calculated from the temperature:

$$\frac{1}{2} m_0 v^2 = \frac{3}{2} kT,$$

where m_0 is the mass of one molecule and from here

$$v = \sqrt{\frac{3kT}{m_0}} = \sqrt{\frac{3RT}{M}} = \sqrt{\frac{3 \cdot 8.31 \, \frac{J}{mol \cdot K} \cdot 295 \text{ K}}{32 \cdot 10^{-3} \, \frac{kg}{mol}}} = 479 \, \frac{m}{s}.$$

The number of particles N can be acquired from the state equation:

$$N = \frac{pV}{kT} = 100 \Delta N = 9.826 \cdot 10^{26}.$$

The initial value of the particle flow can be calculated by substituting N and v into (1):

$$I = \frac{1}{6} \cdot 10^{-7} \text{ m}^2 \cdot 479 \, \frac{m}{s} \cdot \frac{9.826 \cdot 10^{26}}{80 \text{ m}^3} = 9.8 \cdot 10^{19} \, \frac{1}{s}.$$

As in the process under investigation the number of particles hardly changes, we do not have to deal with its decrease. The requested time is

$$t = \frac{\Delta N}{I} = \frac{9.826 \cdot 10^{24}}{9.8 \cdot 10^{19} \text{ s}^{-1}} = 100\,265 \text{ s} = 27.8 \text{ hours.}$$

(So there is enough time to fix the flaw.)

II. Let v_x stand for the mean of the velocity components of the particles perpendicular to the hole. In time t half of the particles present in a space with volume $A v_x t$ escape through the hole. So the intensity of the particle flow is

$$I' = \frac{1}{2} A v_x \frac{N}{V} \tag{1'}$$

The value of v_x can be acquired from the temperature:

$$\frac{1}{2} m_0 v_x^2 = \frac{1}{2} kT,$$

from which the (root mean square) speed is:

$$v_x = \sqrt{\frac{kT}{m_0}} = \sqrt{\frac{RT}{M}} = 277 \, \frac{m}{s}.$$

After determining the number of particles, the intensity of particle flow can be determined:

$$I' = \frac{1}{2} 10^{-7} \text{ m}^2 \cdot 277 \, \frac{\text{m}}{\text{s}} \cdot \frac{9.826 \cdot 10^{26}}{80 \text{ m}^3} = 1.7 \cdot 10^{20} \, \frac{1}{\text{s}}.$$

The estimated time with this train of thought is

$$t' = \frac{\Delta N}{I'} = \frac{0.01 \cdot N}{I'} = \frac{9.826 \cdot 10^{24}}{1.7 \cdot 10^{20}} = 57800 \text{ s} = 16 \text{ hours}.$$

(The calculation that takes speed distribution into consideration gives a value of

$$I'' = \frac{1}{\sqrt{2\pi}} A \frac{N}{V} \sqrt{\frac{RT}{M}} = \sqrt{\frac{2}{\pi}} I' = 0.8 I' = 1.36 \cdot 10^{20} \, \frac{1}{\text{s}}$$

for the intensity of particle flow, with which the requested time is

$$t'' = \frac{\Delta N}{I''} = \frac{9.826 \cdot 10^{24}}{1.36 \cdot 10^{20} \text{ s}^{-1}} = 72250 \text{ s} = 20.1 \text{ hours}.$$

The elementary solutions given through both trains of thought are around the correct value, their order of magnitude is the same.)

Solution of Problem 198. Since the volume and temperature of the helium gas are given, we need to caluclate its pressure to find its mass. According to the equation of state:

$$pV = \frac{m_{\text{He}}}{M_{\text{He}}} RT,$$

solving for the mass of the helium, we get:

$$m_{\text{He}} = \frac{pV M_{\text{He}}}{RT}. \tag{1}$$

In order to determine the pressure of the helium gas, let us apply Newton's second law to the cylinder-piston system and then to the piston itself. Let the masses of piston and cylinder be m and M respectively, and let K be the tension in the string. (The mass of helium gas can be neglected.) If the system is considered, the internal forces cancel out:

$$(m+M)g - K = (m+M)a, \tag{2}$$

Forces acting on the cylinder are gravitational force (mg) and the force ($p_0 A$) due to the atmospheric pressure both pointing downwards and the tension and pA exerted by the helium both pointing upwards.

$$mg + p_0 A - K - pA = ma. \tag{3}$$

As we have three unknowns (K, a, p) one more equation is needed. This will be Newton's second law in angular form applied to the pulley. Using that $\beta = a/r$, we obtain:

$$Kr = \Theta \frac{a}{r}. \tag{4}$$

Isolating the tension gives:

$$K = \frac{\Theta a}{r^2}. \tag{5}$$

Inserting this into equations (2) and (3), we get:

$$(m+M)g - \frac{\Theta a}{r^2} = (m+M)a \tag{6}$$

$$mg + p_0 A - \frac{\Theta a}{r^2} - pA = ma. \tag{7}$$

Now we have two equations with two unknowns (a and p). In equation (6) the acceleration can be isolated as:

$$a = \frac{m+M}{\frac{\Theta}{r^2} + m + M} g. \tag{8}$$

Let us solve equation (7) for the pressure and substitute equation (8):

$$pA = mg + p_0 A - \left(\frac{\Theta}{r^2} + m \right) \cdot \frac{m+M}{\frac{\Theta}{r^2} + m + M} \cdot g,$$

after some algebra, we get:

$$p = \frac{mg}{A} + p_0 - \frac{(\Theta + mr^2)(m+M)}{A[\Theta + (m+M)r^2]} \cdot g.$$

Substituting this into equation (1), we obtain the expression for the mass of the helium gas:

$$m_{\text{He}} = \left(\frac{mg}{A} + p_0 - \frac{(\Theta + mr^2)(m+M)}{A[\Theta + (m+M)r^2]} \cdot g \right) \cdot \frac{AlM_{\text{He}}}{RT} =$$

$$= \left(mg + p_0 A - \frac{(\Theta + mr^2)(m+M)}{\Theta + (m+M)r^2} \cdot g \right) \frac{lM_{\text{He}}}{RT}.$$

Using that $m + M = 50\,\text{kg}$ and $mr^2 = 1\,\text{kg} \cdot \text{m}^2$ and substituting known values, we find:

$$m_{\text{He}} = \left[250\,\text{N} + 10^5 \frac{\text{N}}{\text{m}^2} 0.04\,\text{m}^2 - \frac{(3\,\text{kg}\,\text{m}^2 + 1\,\text{kg}\,\text{m}^2)(50\,\text{kg})}{3\,\text{kg}\,\text{m}^2 + 50\,\text{kg} \cdot 0.04\,\text{m}^2} 10 \frac{\text{m}}{\text{s}^2} \right] \cdot$$

$$\cdot \frac{0.896\,\text{m} \cdot 4 \cdot 10^{-3} \frac{\text{kg}}{\text{mol}\,\text{K}}}{8.31 \frac{\text{J}}{\text{mol}\,\text{K}} \cdot 273\,\text{K}} = 0.000395\,\text{kg},$$

so the mass of the helium gas inside the container is $m_{\text{He}} \approx 0.4\,\text{g}$.

Solution of Problem 199. If the piston with the weight on it moves down by x with respect to the initial position, then the net force acting on it is:

$$F_n = mg - (p - p_0)A, \tag{1}$$

where p is the increased pressure of the gas. Since the gas in the cylinder undergoes an adiabatic process, and its volume is proportional to the height of the piston, the equation

$$p_0 h^\gamma = p(h-x)^\gamma,$$

is satisfied, so

$$p = p_0 \left(\frac{h}{h-x} \right)^\gamma = p_0 \left(1 - \frac{x}{h} \right)^{-\gamma}.$$

Since the amplitude of the oscillation is small, $x \ll h$, the approximation $(1 \pm \alpha)^n \approx 1 \pm n\alpha$ can be applied:

$$p = p_0 \left(1 + \gamma \frac{x}{h} \right). \tag{2}$$

Writing the pressure from equation (2) into equation (1), the following is obtained for the net force acting on the piston:

$$F_n = mg - (p - p_0)A = mg - \left(p_0 + p_0 \gamma \frac{x}{h} - p_0 \right) A = mg - \frac{\gamma p_0 A}{h} x.$$

It can be seen that the net force is the sum of a constant force and a harmonic force (which is proportional to x and has opposite direction). We know —by the analogy of a mass suspended on a spring— that this kind of force results in a harmonic motion. The equilibrium position is determined by the equation $F_n(x_0) = 0$:

$$x_0 = \frac{mgh}{\gamma A p_0} = \frac{14 \text{ kg} \cdot 9.81 \frac{\text{m}}{\text{s}^2} \cdot 0.5 \text{ m}}{1.4 \cdot 0.01 \text{ m}^2 \cdot 10^5 \text{ Pa}} = 0.04905 \text{ m} \approx 5 \text{ cm}.$$

Since the oscillation started from its extreme position, the amplitude has the same value: $A = 5$ cm.

Using again the analogy with the spring, the frequency of the oscillation can be calculated. The spring constant is the multiplier of x in the formula of the net force:

$$D = \frac{\gamma p_0 A}{h} = \frac{1.4 \cdot 10^5 \text{ Pa} \cdot 0.01 \text{ m}^2}{0.5 \text{ m}} = 2800 \frac{\text{N}}{\text{m}}.$$

From here the frequency of the oscillation is:

$$\nu = \frac{1}{2\pi} \sqrt{\frac{D}{m}} = \frac{1}{2\pi} \sqrt{\frac{2800 \frac{\text{N}}{\text{m}}}{14 \text{ kg}}} = 2.25 \text{ Hz}.$$

The maximal speed of the piston (the velocity amplitude) is:

$$v_{\max} = A\omega = A 2\pi\nu = A\sqrt{\frac{D}{m}} = 0.05 \text{ m} \sqrt{\frac{2800 \frac{\text{N}}{\text{m}}}{14 \text{ kg}}} \approx 0.71 \frac{\text{m}}{\text{s}}.$$

Solution of Problem 200. According to the first law of thermodynamics, $\Delta E = Q + W$, from which the heat absorbed by the gas is $Q = \Delta E - W = \Delta E + W_{\text{gas}}$.

First, let us determine in percents what ratio of the absorbed heat increases the internal energy and what ratio is given off in the form of work.

$$\frac{\Delta E}{Q} = \frac{c_v m \Delta T}{c_p m \Delta T} = \frac{c_v}{c_p} = \frac{1}{\gamma} = \frac{1}{1.4} = 0.7143 = 71.43\%,$$

and consequently

$$\frac{W_{\text{gas}}}{Q} = 1 - 0.7143 = 28.57\%.$$

It means that the increase of the internal energy of the gas, and the work done by the gas are

$$\Delta E = 0.7143 Q = 0.7143 \cdot 3988 \text{ kJ} = 2848.6 \text{ kJ},$$

$$W = 3988 \text{ kJ} - 2848.6 \text{ kJ} = 1139.4 \text{ kJ}.$$

7.3 First law of thermodynamics

Solution of Problem 201. a) Let A be the cross-sectional area of the cylinder, m be the mass of the piston, h be the initial height of the air column, h_1 be the height of the empty part above the piston, p_0 be the atmospheric pressure, ϱ_{Hg} and ϱ_1 be the densities of mercury and air (in its initial state) and finally let c_v be the specific heat of air at constant volume.

Note that ϱ_1 need not have been given as it can be determined from the other data. (Assuming that the molar mass of air is known.)

The initial pressure of the enclosed air is $p_1 = p_0 + mg/A$, while its final (maximum) pressure is

$$p_2 = [p_0 + (m + m_{\text{Hg}})g/A] = p_0 + mg/A + \varrho_{\text{Hg}} g x.$$

According to Boyle's law:

$$V_2 = \frac{p_1}{p_2} V_1$$

substituting the expressions for p_1, p_2, V_1 and V_2, we get:

$$(h + h_1 - x)A = \frac{p_0 + \frac{mg}{A}}{p_0 + \frac{mg}{A} + \varrho_{\text{Hg}} g x} \cdot Ah.$$

Let us divide the equation by A and multiply by the denominator of the fraction:

$$\left(p_0 + \frac{mg}{A} + \varrho_{\text{Hg}} g x\right)(h + h_1 - x) = \left(p_0 + \frac{mg}{A}\right) h.$$

After rearranging this according to the powers of x, we get:

$$\varrho_{\text{Hg}} g x^2 - [\varrho_{\text{Hg}} g(h_1 + h) - (p_0 + mg/A)]x - (p_0 + mg/A)h_1 = 0.$$

This is a second degree equation of x. By calculating x, we can also determine the mass of the mercury, assuming that $m_{\text{Hg}} = \varrho_{\text{Hg}} \cdot xA$.

Let us substitute known data:

$$p_0 = 10\frac{N}{cm^2}; \qquad \frac{mg}{A} = \frac{72}{20}\frac{N}{cm^2} = 3.6\frac{N}{cm^2};$$

$$\varrho_{Hg}g = 13.6 \cdot 10^{-3}\frac{kg}{cm^3} \cdot 10\frac{m}{s^2} = 0.136\frac{N}{cm^3}.$$

Inserting these into the equation, we obtain:

$$0.136\frac{N}{cm^3} \cdot x^2 - \left(0.136\frac{N}{cm^3} \cdot 40\,cm - 13.6\frac{N}{cm^2}\right) \cdot x - 13.6\frac{N}{cm^2} \cdot 7\,cm = 0.$$

Dividing the equation by unit N/cm^2, we find:

$$0.136\frac{1}{cm} \cdot x^2 + 8.16 \cdot x - 95.2\,cm = 0.$$

The solution is:

$$x = \frac{-8.16 + \sqrt{8.16^2 + 4 \cdot 95.2 \cdot 0.136}}{2 \cdot 0.136}\,cm = 10\,cm.$$

So the volume of the mercury column is:

$$V_{Hg} = xA = 10\,cm \cdot 20\,cm^2 = 200\,cm^3,$$

from which the required mass is:

$$m_{Hg} = \varrho_{Hg} \cdot V_{Hg} = 13.6\frac{g}{cm^3} \cdot 200\,cm^3 = 2720\,g.$$

b) The heat transferred to the air can be determined using the first law of thermodynamics:

$$\Delta U = Q + W,$$

from which

$$Q = \Delta U - W = \Delta U + W_{gas}, \tag{1}$$

where W is the work done on the gas and W_{gas} is the work done by the gas.

The change in the internal energy of the air can be written as:

$$\Delta U = c_v m \Delta T, \tag{2}$$

while the work done by the gas can be calculated using the arithmetic mean of pressures p_2 and p_3 (since the mass of mercury that has run out is in direct proportion to the change in volume):

$$W_{gas} = \frac{p_2 + p_3}{2} \cdot \Delta V. \tag{3}$$

The pressure of air in its most compressed state is:

$$p_2 = p_0 + \frac{mg}{A} + \varrho_{Hg}gh = 10\frac{N}{cm^2} + 3.6\frac{N}{cm^2} + 1.36\frac{N}{cm^2} = 14.96\frac{N}{cm^2},$$

while in its final state it is:

$$p_3 = p_0 + \frac{mg}{A} = p_1 = 13.6 \frac{N}{cm^2}.$$

The mass of air can be determined using the initial values of its density and volume:

$$m_{air} = \varrho_1 A h = 1.8 \frac{g}{dm^3} \cdot 20 \, cm^2 \cdot 33 \, cm = 1.118 \, g.$$

Assuming that the pressure of the air is the same ($p_1 = p_3 = p_0 + mg/A$) in its first and third (final) state, the change in its temperature can easily be determined (the same way as in the case of an isobaric process):

$$\frac{V_1}{V_3} = \frac{T_1}{T_3},$$

Isolating for T_3 gives:

$$T_3 = T_1 \frac{V_3}{V_1}.$$

Let us substitute the expressions for the volumes:

$$T_3 = T_1 \frac{(h + h_1) A}{h A} = T_1 \frac{h + h_1}{h} = 273 \, K \cdot \frac{40 \, cm}{33 \, cm} = 330.91 \, K,$$

so the change in the temperature is:

$$\Delta T = T_3 - T_1 = 57.91 \, K \approx 58 \, K.$$

Using equations (1), (2) and (3) and substituting known values, we get that the heat transmitted to the air is:

$$Q = 0.7 \frac{J}{g \, K} \cdot 1.188 \, g \cdot 58 \, K + \frac{13.6 + 14.96}{2} \frac{N}{cm^2} \cdot 200 \, cm^3 \cdot 10^{-2} \frac{m}{cm} =$$

$$= 48.23 \, J + 28.65 \, J = 76.79 \, J.$$

In this process the internal energy of the gas is increased by $48.23 \, J$, while $28.65 \, J$ is the work done by the gas. The former energy remains in the system, while the latter increases the energy of the environment.

Solution of Problem 202. The cylinder is rising slowly, that is, it remains in equilibrium. Therefore, the pressure of the gas in the cylinder is constant, which means that we are dealing with an isobaric process.

The heat absorbed at constant pressure is

$$Q = C_p n \Delta T, \tag{1}$$

where C_p is the molar heat at constant pressure, n is the number of moles, and ΔT is the change in temperature.

The relationship between the two molar heats is

$$C_p - C_v = R,$$

and hence

$$C_p = R + C_v. \tag{2}$$

The pressure of the enclosed helium is obtained from the equilibrium of the forces acting on the cylinder:

$$mg + pA - p_0 A = 0.$$

Hence

$$p = p_0 - \frac{mg}{A}. \tag{3}$$

Assume that the cylinder has walls of negligible thickness, that is $A_{\text{inner}} \approx A_{\text{outer}}$. The number of moles can be expressed by substituting (3) into the universal gas equation applied to the initial state:

$$n = \frac{pV_1}{RT_1} = \frac{\left(p_0 - \frac{mg}{A}\right)Al_1}{RT_1} = \frac{(p_0 A - mg)l_1}{RT_1}. \tag{4}$$

Since the process is isobaric, the final temperature of the enclosed gas is

$$T_2 = T_1 \frac{V_2}{V_1} = T_1 \frac{l_2}{l_1}.$$

Hence the change in temperature is

$$\Delta T = T_2 - T_1 = T_1 \frac{l_2 - l_1}{l_1}. \tag{5}$$

The extracted heat in question is obtained by substituting the expressions (2), (4) and (5) in (1):

$$Q = (R + C_v) \cdot \frac{(p_0 A - mg)l_1}{RT_1} \cdot T_1 \frac{l_2 - l_1}{l_1} = (p_0 A - mg)(l_2 - l_1)\left(\frac{C_v}{R} + 1\right),$$

which is independent of the initial temperature. Numerically:

$$Q = (10^5 \frac{\text{N}}{\text{m}^2} \cdot 2 \cdot 10^{-3}\,\text{m}^2 - 80\,\text{N})(0.896\,\text{m} - 1.12\,\text{m})\left[\frac{12.3\frac{\text{J}}{\text{mol} \cdot \text{K}}}{8.31\frac{\text{J}}{\text{mol} \cdot \text{K}}} + 1\right] = -66.7\,\text{J}.$$

Thus the heat extracted from the helium is $66.7\,\text{J}$.

Remark: the problem can also be solved by using the first law of thermodynamics:

$$\Delta U = Q + W = Q - W_{\text{gas}},$$

hence

$$Q = \Delta U + W_{\text{gas}} = C_v n \Delta T + p \Delta V.$$

Substitution of the above data gives the same result.

Solution of Problem 203. a) Since the work done by the gas is positive, the gas expands. This means that heat must have been given to the gas, therefore the external temperature must be higher than the initial temperature of the gas. Applying the work-energy theorem to the piston (that is moving up), we get:

$$W_{\text{gas}} - mgx - \frac{1}{2}Dx^2 - p_0 Ax = 0,$$

rearranging this, we get:

$$Dx^2 + 2(p_0 + mg)x - 2W_{\text{gas}} = 0.$$

The displacement of the piston (or the extension of the spring) is given by the quadratic formula:

$$x = \frac{-2(p_0 A + mg) + \sqrt{4(p_0 A + mg)^2 + 8DW_{\text{gas}}}}{2D} =$$

$$= \sqrt{\left(\frac{p_0 A + mg}{D}\right)^2 + \frac{2W_{\text{gas}}}{D}} - \frac{p_0 A + mg}{D} =$$

$$= \frac{1}{D}\left[\sqrt{(p_0 A + mg)^2 + 2W_{\text{gas}}D} - (p_0 A + mg)\right].$$

Inserting given data, we find:

$$x = \frac{1}{2.67 \cdot 10^5 \, \frac{\text{N}}{\text{m}}} \cdot \left[\sqrt{(10^5 \, \text{Pa} \cdot 0.5 \, \text{m}^2 + 6000 \, \text{N})^2 + 2 \cdot 1800 \, \text{J} \cdot 2.67 \cdot 10^5 \, \frac{\text{N}}{\text{m}}} -\right.$$

$$\left. - \left(10^5 \, \text{Pa} \cdot 0.5 \, \text{m}^2 + 600 \, \text{kg} \cdot 10 \, \frac{\text{m}}{\text{s}^2}\right)\right] = 0.03 \, \text{m} = 3 \, \text{cm}.$$

To find the external temperature, let us apply the equation of state to the helium gas in its initial and final states:

$$T_2 = T_1 \cdot \frac{p_2 V_2}{p_1 V_1} = T_1 \cdot \frac{\left(p_0 + \frac{mg}{A} + \frac{Dx}{A}\right) A(h_0 + x)}{\left(p_0 + \frac{mg}{A}\right) A h_0} = T_1 \cdot \frac{(p_0 A + mg + Dx)(h_0 + x)}{(p_0 + mg)h_0},$$

where h_0 is the height of the initial position of the piston.
Substituting known data gives:

$$T_2 = 218 \, \text{K} \frac{\left(10^5 \, \text{Pa} \cdot 0.5 \, \text{m}^2 + 6000 \, \text{N} + 2.67 \cdot 10^5 \, \frac{\text{N}}{\text{m}} \cdot 0.03 \, \text{m}\right)(0.32 + 0.03) \, \text{m}}{(10^5 \, \text{Pa} \cdot 0.5 \, \text{m}^2 + 6000 \, \text{N}) \cdot 0.32 \, \text{m}} =$$

$$= 273.04 \, \text{K},$$

so the external temperature is $273 \, \text{K}$.

b) To be able to determine the heat added to the gas, we need to calculate the mass of the helium first. Using the equation of state, we get:

$$m = \frac{p_1 V_1 M}{RT_1} = \frac{\left(p_0 + \frac{mg}{A}\right) A h_0 M}{RT_1} = 40\,\text{g},$$

which is exactly 10 mol. The change in the temperature of the helium gas is:

$$\Delta T = T_2 - T_1 = 273\,\text{K} - 218.4\,\text{K} = 54.6\,\text{K},$$

therefore the change in its internal energy is:

$$\Delta U = C_v n \Delta T = 12.3\frac{\text{J}}{(\text{mol}\cdot\text{K})}\cdot 10\text{ mol}\cdot 54.6\,\text{K} = 6716\,\text{J}.$$

According to the fist law of thermodynamics:

$$\Delta U = Q + W = Q - W_{\text{gas}},$$

hence the heat given to the gas is:

$$Q = \Delta U + W_{\text{gas}} = 6716\,\text{J} + 1800\,\text{J} = 8516\,\text{J}.$$

The change in the internal energy of the gas can also be calculated using the degree of freedom:

$$\Delta U = \frac{f}{2}NK\Delta T, \tag{1}$$

and

$$p_1 V_1 = NkT_1. \tag{2}$$

Rearranging equation (2) gives:

$$Nk = \frac{p_1 V_1}{T_1},$$

which can be substituted into equation (1) to get:

$$\Delta U = \frac{f}{2}\cdot\frac{p_1 V_1}{T_1}\cdot\Delta T = \frac{3}{2}\frac{(p_0 A + mg)h_0}{T_1}\cdot\Delta T,$$

inserting given data, we find:

$$\frac{3}{2}\cdot\frac{(10^5\,\text{Pa}\cdot 0.5\,\text{m}^2 + 6000\,\text{N})\cdot 0.32\,\text{m}}{218.4\,\text{K}}\cdot 54.6\,\text{K} = 6720\,\text{J}.$$

The small difference in the results is due to the slight inaccuracy of the molar specific heat of the helium.

Solution of Problem 204. While the helium is kept inside the container by the piston, it expands adiabatically, which means that:

$$TV^{\gamma-1} = \text{constant.}$$

The ratio of molar specific heats for helium is:

$$\gamma = \frac{c_p}{c_v} = \frac{f+2}{f} = \frac{5}{3},$$

where f is the degree of freedom. This yields $\gamma - 1 = 2/3$. At the moment when the piston reaches the top of the cylinder, the temperature of helium is given by the equation:

$$546\,\text{K} \cdot 5.6^{2/3} = T \cdot 11.2^{2/3},$$

thus the temperature is

$$T = \frac{546}{\sqrt[3]{2^2}} = 344\,\text{K}.$$

Let us apply the work-kinetic energy theorem to the piston. The sum of the works done by the forces acting on the piston equals the change in the piston's kinetic energy. As the initial and final speeds of the piston are both zero, the change in its kinetic energy is also zero. Thus the work-kinetic energy theorem can be written as:

$$W_{\text{gas}} + W_{\text{grav}} + W_{\text{atm}} = 0,$$

where the first term is the work done by the helium undergoing adiabatic expansion, the second is the work done by the gravitational force, and the third is the work done by the atmosphere. These works can be expressed as:

$$W_{\text{gas}} = -\Delta U_{\text{gas}},$$

because in case of an adiabatic expansion, the loss of internal energy of the gas is converted into the work done by the gas. As the internal energy of a gas depends on its temperature only, the work done by the helium gas can be determined:

$$W_{\text{gas}} = -\Delta U_{\text{gas}} = -c_v m \Delta T = -n C_v (T_2 - T_1) =$$
$$1\ \text{mol} \cdot 12.6\ \text{J/(mol\,K)} \cdot (546 - 344)\ \text{K} \approx 2536\,\text{J}.$$

The work done by the gravitational force is negative:

$$W_{\text{grav}} = -mgx = -8\,\text{kg} \cdot 9.8\,\frac{\text{m}}{\text{s}^2} \cdot x = -78.4\,\text{N} \cdot x.$$

The atmosphere does work while the piston is inside the container, since this is when the air inside the container is lifted up. Once the piston leaves the cylinder, it will continuously exchange positions with the air, but will not lift it. (Air drag acting on the piston is neglected.) The work done by the atmosphere is also negative, because the force is opposite the displacement:

$$-p_0 \Delta V = -p_0 A \Delta h = -10.12\,\frac{\text{N}}{\text{cm}^2} \cdot 100\,\text{cm}^2 \cdot 0.56\,\text{m} = -567\,\text{J}.$$

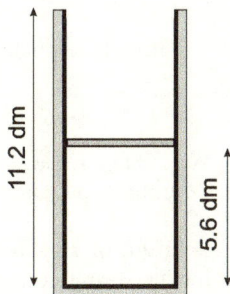

Therefore the distance moved by the piston can be written as:

$$x = \frac{W_{\text{gas}} + W_{\text{grav}}}{mg},$$

substituting given data, we find:

$$x = \frac{2536 \text{ J} - 567 \text{ J}}{78.4 \text{ N}} = 25 \text{ m}.$$

We assumed that the temperature changes at the same rate everywhere in the helium gas during its adiabatic expansion.

Solution of Problem 205. a) Let index 1 stand for the initial variables of the gas, k for the spring constant, A for the cross-sectional area of the cylinder and x for the displacement of the piston. At the end of the heating, the pressure of the gas is

$$p_2 = p_1 + \frac{kx}{A}, \tag{1}$$

its volume is

$$V_2 = V_1 + Ax. \tag{2}$$

By using (1) and (2), the universal gas law gives

$$\frac{p_1 V_1}{T_1} = \frac{(p_1 + \frac{kx}{A})(V_1 + Ax)}{T_2}.$$

From these a quadratic equation is acquired for x:

$$kx^2 + \left(p_1 A + \frac{kV_1}{A}\right)x + \left(p_1 V_1 - \frac{p_1 V_1 T_2}{T_1}\right) = 0. \tag{3}$$

It is advisable to substitute the numerical values into the variables now and work on with the numerical equation. The coefficient of the quadratic term is $a = 2000 \ \frac{\text{N}}{\text{m}}$, the coefficient of the linear term is

$$b = 10^5 \ \frac{\text{N}}{\text{m}} \cdot 0.03 \text{ m}^2 + \frac{2000 \ \frac{\text{N}}{\text{m}} \cdot 0.024 \text{ m}^3}{0.03 \text{ m}^2} = 4600 \text{ N},$$

and the constant term is

$$c = 10^5 \ \frac{\text{N}}{\text{m}} \cdot 0.024 \text{ m}^3 - \frac{10^5 \ \frac{\text{N}}{\text{m}^2} \cdot 0.024 \text{ m}^3 \cdot 360 \text{ K}}{300 \text{ K}} = -480 \text{ Nm}.$$

Substituting these numerical values into (3) gives

$$2000x^2 + 4600x - 480 = 0,$$

dividing by 40 gives $50x^2 + 115x - 12 = 0$.
Its solution is

$$x = \frac{-115 \pm \sqrt{115^2 + 4 \cdot 50 \cdot 12}}{100} \text{ m} = \frac{-115 \pm 125}{100} \text{ m} = 0.1 \text{ m}.$$

This is the displacement of the piston.

b) The heat absorbed by the gas can be determined from the first law of thermodynamics:

$$\Delta U = Q + W = Q - W_{\text{gas}},$$

where W is the work done on the gas, W_{gas} is the work done by the gas. From this the heat absorbed by the gas is

$$Q = \Delta U + W_{\text{gas}}. \tag{4}$$

According to the work-energy theorem ($\sum W = \Delta E_{\text{kin}}$) for the piston (as in our case the change in the kinetic energy of the piston is 0):

$$W_{\text{gas}} + W_{\text{atmosphere}} + W_{\text{spring}} = 0,$$

in detail

$$W_{\text{gas}} - p_e A x - \frac{1}{2} k x^2 = 0,$$

if the work done by the gas is substituted into (4), for the heat delivered by the heating filament this equation gives

$$Q = \Delta U + p_e A x + \frac{1}{2} k x^2. \tag{5}$$

Here the magnitude of the second term is

$$p_e A x = 10^5 \text{ Pa} \cdot 0.03 \text{ m}^2 \cdot 0.1 \text{ m} = 300 \text{ J},$$

and the magnitude of the third term is

$$\frac{1}{2} k x^2 = \frac{1}{2} \cdot 2000 \, \frac{\text{N}}{\text{m}} \cdot 0.01 \text{ m}^2 = 10 \text{ J}.$$

Our further task is to determine the internal energy of the gas. This can be done in several ways.

1. By determining the mass of the gas from the state equation, and the specific heat of the gas from the data and formula booklet:

$$\Delta U = c_v m \Delta T, \tag{6}$$

where $c_v = 712 \text{ J/(kg} \cdot \text{K)}$ and

$$m = \frac{p_1 V_1 M}{R T_1} = \frac{10^5 \text{ Pa} \cdot 0.024 \text{ m}^3 \cdot 29 \cdot 10^{-3} \, \frac{\text{kg}}{\text{mol}}}{8.31 \, \frac{\text{J}}{\text{mol} \cdot \text{K}} \cdot 300 \text{ K}} = 0.02792 \text{ kg} = 27.92 \text{ g}.$$

Substituting these into (6) gives the following for the change in internal energy:

$$\Delta E = 712 \, \frac{\text{J}}{\text{kg} \cdot \text{K}} \cdot 0.02792 \text{ kg} \cdot 60 \text{ K} = 1192.7 \text{ J}.$$

2. By determining the mass of the gas from density at 273 K and atmospheric pressure:

$$p_0 = \frac{m}{V} \cdot \frac{R T_0}{M} = \varrho_0 \cdot \frac{R T_0}{M} = \varrho \cdot \frac{R T_1}{M},$$

as the initial pressure p_1 of the gas is equal to the atmospheric pressure p_0. From this

$$\varrho = \varrho_0 \cdot \frac{T_0}{T_1}.$$

This is substituted into the expression $m = \varrho \cdot V_1$:

$$m = \varrho_0 \cdot \frac{T_0}{T_1} \cdot V_1 = 1.29 \, \frac{\text{kg}}{\text{m}^3} \cdot \frac{273 \text{ K}}{300 \text{ K}} \cdot 0.024 \text{ m}^3 = 0.0281 \text{ kg}.$$

With these the change in internal energy is

$$\Delta U = 712 \, \frac{\text{J}}{\text{kg} \cdot \text{K}} \cdot 0.0281 \text{ kg} \cdot 60 \text{ K} = 1200.4 \text{ J}.$$

3. By determining the change in the energy directly using the degrees of freedom:

$$\Delta U = \frac{f}{2} N k \Delta T, \tag{7}$$

where $f = 5$, the product of the number of the particles and Boltzmann's constant from the state equation

$$p_1 V_1 = N k T_1$$

is:

$$N k = \frac{p_1 V_1}{T_1},$$

which is substituted into (7):

$$\Delta U = \frac{f}{2} \frac{p_1 V_1}{T_1} \cdot \Delta T = \frac{5}{2} \frac{10^5 \text{ Pa} \cdot 0.024 \text{ m}^3}{300 \text{ K}} \cdot 60 \text{ K} = 1200.0 \text{ J}.$$

4. By applying the general formula that gives the change in the internal energy:

$$\Delta U = \frac{p_2 V_2 - p_1 V_1}{y - 1} = \frac{\left(p_1 + \frac{kx}{A}\right) V_2 - p_1 V_1}{y - 1}, \tag{8}$$

with numerical values it gives

$$\Delta U = \frac{\left(10^5 \text{ Pa} + \frac{2000 \text{ N/m} \cdot 0.1 \text{ m}}{0.03 \text{ m}^2}\right)\left(0.024 \text{ m}^3 + 0.03 \text{ m}^2 \cdot 0.1 \text{ m}\right) - 10^5 \text{ Pa} \cdot 0.0024 \text{ m}^3}{1.4 - 1} =$$
$$= 1200 \text{ J}.$$

(On one hand, formula (8) gives the work done on the gas in an adiabatic change of state, but it also gives the change in the internal energy in any change of state, which can always be written as

$$\Delta U = \frac{f}{2} N k \Delta T. \tag{9}$$

If expression

$$T_2 - T_1 = \frac{p_2 V_2}{Nk} - \frac{p_1 V_1}{Nk} \tag{10}$$

is substituted in place of ΔT and

$$\frac{c_p}{c_v} = \frac{f+2}{f} = 1 + \frac{2}{f},$$

is also considered, these give

$$\frac{f}{2} = \frac{c_v}{c_p - c_v} = \frac{1}{\gamma - 1}.$$

If this and the change in temperature acquired from (10) are substituted into (9), (8) is acquired.)

With this, equation (5) gives the heat delivered by the heating filament:

$$Q = 1200 \text{ J} + 300 \text{ J} + 10 \text{ J} = 1510 \text{ J}.$$

(Those who determined mass with Method 1 received $1192 \text{ J} + 310 \text{ J} = 1502 \text{ J}$ for the energy delivered.)

Solution of Problem 206. Our data are $p_0 = 10^5$ Pa; $V_0 = 1$ m^3; $A = 0.1$ m^2; $v = 1$ cm/s.

If the temperature of the gas is constant, then its energy does not change either. According to the first law of thermodynamics

$$Q = -W.$$

Let us apply this to a short time of the process:

$$P\Delta t = pAv\Delta t,$$

where P is the heating power. From here

$$P = pAv.$$

According to the problem, the heating power should be determined as a function of time. Let us apply the gas law

$$pV = p_0 V_0,$$

where in our case

$$V = V_0 + Avt,$$

and so the pressure expressed with the variables of the process is

$$p = \frac{p_0 V_0}{V_0 + Avt},$$

and with it the power as a function of time is

$$P = \frac{p_0 V_0 Av}{V_0 + Avt}.$$

Numerically

$$P = \frac{10^5 \; \frac{\mathrm{N}}{\mathrm{m}^2} \cdot 1 \; \mathrm{m}^3 \cdot 0.1 \; \mathrm{m}^2 \cdot 10^{-2} \; \frac{\mathrm{m}}{\mathrm{s}}}{1 \; \mathrm{m}^3 + 0.1 \; \mathrm{m}^2 \cdot 10^{-2} \; \frac{\mathrm{m}}{\mathrm{s}} \cdot t} = \frac{100}{1 + 10^{-3} \; \frac{1}{\mathrm{s}} \cdot t} \; \mathrm{W}.$$

Graphically:

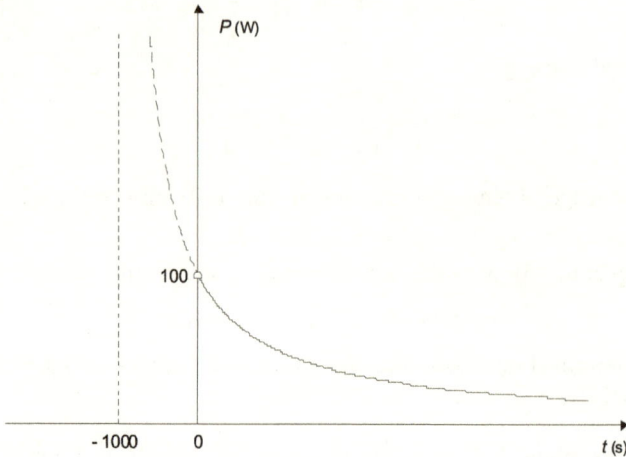

Solution of Problem 207. The first law of thermodynamics ($\Delta U = Q + W$) for small changes (where for pressure $p = $ constant can be assumed):

$$C_V n \Delta T = C n \Delta T - p \Delta V.$$

We express the molar heat capacity belonging to temperature T:

$$C(T) = C_V + \frac{1}{n} p(T) \cdot \frac{\Delta V(T)}{\Delta T}.$$

We can make use of the fact that the rate of change of $\frac{g}{2} t^2$ is gt, so the rate of change of function aT^2 is $2aT$, so

$$C(T) = C_V + \frac{1}{n} p(T) \cdot 2aT.$$

Expressing the pressure from the state equation of the ideal gas and making use of $V = aT^2$ gives

$$C(T) = C_V + \frac{1}{n} \cdot \frac{nRT}{aT^2} \cdot 2aT = C_V + 2R.$$

So the molar heat capacity is constant throughout the process and its value is $C = C_V + 2R$.

Solution of Problem 208. Let us assume that the piston is weightless (its mass is negligible). Note that the data given is quite special: on the first hand the volume of the two parts, which is half of that of the cylinder $V_1 = 44.8/2$ litre $= 22.4$ dm^3, is the molar volume of a gas at standard pressure and temperature, on the second hand each part contains 4 g of helium, which is 1 mole, and finally the gas is at standard temperature $0\ ^\circ C = 273$ K. Therefore the pressure of the gas in the two parts must be the standard pressure: $p_0 = 1.013 \cdot 10^5$ Pa $\approx 10^5$ Pa.

As the upper part is surrounded by perfect insulators, the temperature (energy) of the gas in that part can only be raised by doing work on it. The first law of thermodynamics in this case will take the form of: $Q = 0$, $\Delta U = W$.

This work is done by the piston, which is lifted up by the expanding gas in the lower part.

The equation that holds for an adiabatic compression is:

$$TV^{\gamma-1} = \text{constant},$$

where $\gamma = c_p/c_v$ or $\gamma = (f+2)/f$, where f is the degree of freedom. Using either of the above equations $\gamma = = 5/3$ so $\gamma - 1 = 2/3$.

Let us determine the final volume V_2 of the gas in the upper part, knowing that the temperature is raised from $T_1 = 273$ K to $T_2 = 409.5$ K. Using the equation for adiabatic compression:

$$273\text{ K} \cdot (22.4\text{ dm}^3)^{\frac{2}{3}} = 409.5 V_2^{\frac{2}{3}}.$$

from which

$$V_2 = 22.4\text{ dm}^3 \cdot \left(\frac{273}{409.5}\right)^{\frac{3}{2}} = 22.4\text{ dm}^3 \sqrt{\left(\frac{273}{409.5}\right)^3} = 12.19\text{ dm}^3.$$

The pressure of the gas in the upper part can be calculated using the equation of state:

$$p_2 = p_1 \frac{V_1}{T_1}\frac{T_2}{V_2} = 10^5\text{ Pa} \cdot \frac{22.4}{12.19} \cdot \frac{409.5}{273} = 2.76 \cdot 10^5\text{ Pa}.$$

The final volume of the lower part is $V_2' = 2V_1 - V_2 = 44.8$ dm$^3 - 12.19$ dm$^3 = = 32.61$ dm^3 and since the piston is weightless, the pressure in the lower part equals the pressure in the upper part, so $p_2' = 2.76 \cdot 10^5$ Pa. In the lower part, the change of state is not adiabatic, since in that case heat is given to the gas by the electric heater. The heater's energy input is given to the gas in the lower part, which transfers part of it to the upper part by doing work on it. The final temperature of the lower part is given by the equation of state:

$$T_2' = T_1 \frac{p_2' V_2'}{p_1 V_1} = 274\text{ K} \cdot \frac{2.76 \cdot 10^5 \cdot 32.61}{10^5 \cdot 22.4} = 1096.9\text{ K} = 823.9\ ^\circ C.$$

The changes in the temperature in the two parts are:

$$\Delta T_1 = T_2 - T_1 = 409.5\text{ K} - 273\text{ K} = 136.5\text{ K}$$

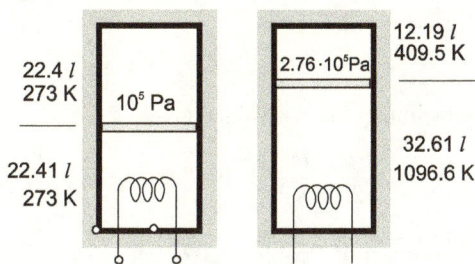

and

$$\Delta T_2 = T_2' - T_1 = 1096.9\,\mathrm{K} - 273\,\mathrm{K} = 823.9\,\mathrm{K}.$$

As the system is insulated, the heater's energy input is the sum of the changes in the energies of the two parts:

$$Q = \frac{V^2}{R} \cdot t = \Delta U_1 + \Delta U_2,$$

hence

$$t = \frac{R}{V^2}(\Delta U_1 + \Delta U_2).$$

The changes in the energy in the two parts can be written as $\Delta U_1 = c_v m \Delta T_1$ and $\Delta U_2 = c_v m \Delta T_2$, so

$$t = \frac{R}{V^2} m c_v (\Delta T_1 + \Delta T_2).$$

Substituting known values gives:

$$t = \frac{242\,\Omega}{220^2\,\mathrm{V}^2} \cdot 4 \cdot 10^{-3}\,\mathrm{kg} \cdot 3140\,\frac{\mathrm{J}}{\mathrm{kg \cdot K}}(136.5 + 823.9)\,\mathrm{K} = 60.5\,\mathrm{s} \approx 1\ \mathrm{min}.$$

Solution of Problem 209. Let p_0 and V_0 stand for the initial state variables. Let the maximum volume reached by the gas during the process be xV_0.

The efficiency of the process is

$$\eta = \frac{W_{\text{useful}}}{Q_{\text{in}}}.$$

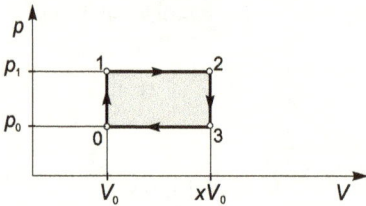

The work done by the gas (that is, the useful work) is proportional to the area enclosed by the graph of the cyclic process.

In order to calculate this, the maximum pressure should be determined. From the gas law

$$\frac{p_0 V_0}{T_0} = \frac{p_1 x V_0}{4 T_0},$$

from which

$$p_1 = \frac{4 p_0}{x}.$$

With this, the area enclosed by the graph is

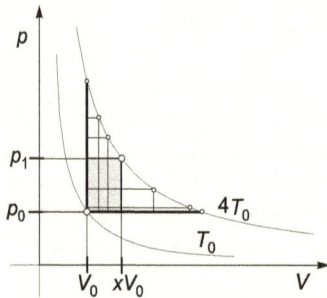

$$W_{\text{useful}} = \left(\frac{4 p_0}{x} - p_0\right)(x V_0 - V_0) =$$

$$= p_0 V_0 \left(\frac{4}{x} - 1\right)(x - 1) = \frac{p_0 V_0}{x}(4 - x)(x - 1).$$

It can be seen immediately that for the possible values of x relation $1 \le x \le 4$ holds. In the case of $x = 1$ and $x = 4$ the work done and therefore the efficiency is zero, because in these cases the rectangle representing the cyclic process degenerates into straight line segments, so both the area and the useful work become zero.

In order to determine the efficiency, the heat absorbed by the gas should be determined as well. The gas absorbs heat along segments (0-1) and (1-2). At constant volume $Q_{01} = \Delta U_1$:

$$Q_{01} = \frac{f}{2}Nk\Delta T = \frac{f}{2}\Delta pV_0 = \frac{5}{2}\left(\frac{4p_0}{x} - p_0\right)V_0 = \frac{5}{2}p_0V_0\left(\frac{4}{x} - 1\right) = \frac{5}{2}p_0V_0\frac{4-x}{x}.$$

and at constant pressure

$$Q_{12} = \Delta U_2 + p\Delta V = \frac{f}{2}p_1\Delta V + p_1\Delta V = \frac{7}{2}p_1\Delta V = \frac{7}{2}\cdot\frac{4p_0}{x}(xV_0 - V_0) =$$
$$= \frac{14}{x}p_0V_0(x-1) = 14p_0V_0\frac{x-1}{x}.$$

With these, the total heat absorbed is

$$Q_{\text{fel}} = Q_{01} + Q_{02} = \frac{5}{2}p_0V_0\frac{4-x}{x} + 14p_0V_0\frac{x-1}{x} = \frac{p_0V_0}{x}(11.5x - 4).$$

The efficiency of the process as function of x is:

$$\eta(x) = \frac{W_{\text{useful}}}{Q_{\text{in}}} = \frac{\frac{p_0V_0}{x}(4-x)(x-1)}{\frac{p_0V_0}{x}(11.5x-4)} = \frac{(4-x)(x-1)}{11.5x-4} = \frac{x^2 - 5x + 4}{4 - 11.5x} = \frac{f(x)}{g(x)}.$$

If this efficiency function is graphed and analysed in interval $1 \leq x \leq 4$ (or by means of differentiation), it can be shown that it has a maximum at $x = 1.891$. If this value is substituted back into the function, for the maximum

$$\eta_{\text{max}} = 0.1059 \approx 10.6\%$$

is acquired. (So then the volume of the gas should be increased to $V_2 = V_3 = 1.891V_0$.)
A table of values for a few values of x:

x	1	1.2	1.5	1.7	1.8	1.89	1.9
η	0	0.057	0.094	0.1035	0.105389	0.105886664	0.1058823

The efficiency function in interval a $0 \leq x \leq 10$ and in interval $1 \leq x \leq 4$ bearing physical importance:

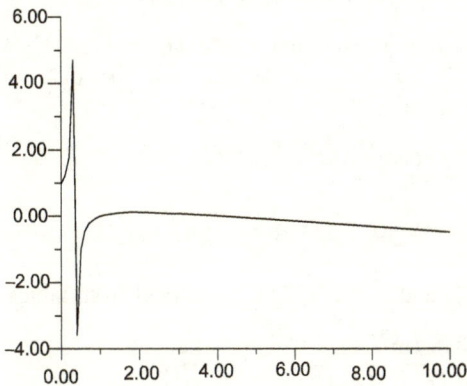

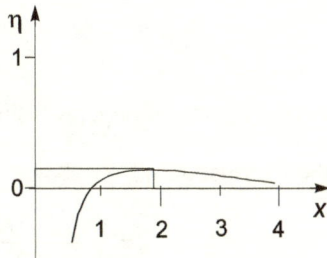

Solution using derivative. The function has an extreme value where its derivative is zero:

$$\frac{d\eta(x)}{dx} = 0.$$

According to the differentiation rule for fractional function:

$$\frac{f'(x)g(x) - f(x)g'(x)}{g^2(x)} = 0.$$

$$f(x) = x^2 - 5x + 4 \qquad \rightarrow \qquad f'(x) = 2x - 5.$$

$$g(x) = 4 - 11.5x \qquad \rightarrow \qquad g'(x) = -11.5.$$

The derivative is zero if its numerator is zero, that is, $f'(x)g(x) = g'(x)f(x)$. By using this, an equation is acquired for x:

$$(2x - 5)(4 - 11.5x) = 11.5 \cdot (x^2 - 5x + 4).$$

Reorganising:

$$11.5x^2 - 8x + 26 = 0.$$

Its solution is

$$x_{1,2} = \frac{8 \pm \sqrt{64 + 4 \cdot 11.5 \cdot 26}}{2 \cdot 11.5} = \frac{8 \pm 35.5}{23} = 1.89.$$

(x_2 cannot be negative). With this,

$$\eta = \frac{x^2 - 5x + 4}{4 - 11.5x} = \frac{1.89^2 - 5 \cdot 1.89 - 4}{4 - 11.5 \cdot 1.89} = 0.106.$$

First solution of Problem 210. From the first law of thermodynamics:

a) The process is not adiabatic since the enclosed gas absorbs heat from the 'surroundings' through the heater filament. It is isobaric because of the constant external air pressure. (There is heat transfer inwards but no heat transfer outwards.)

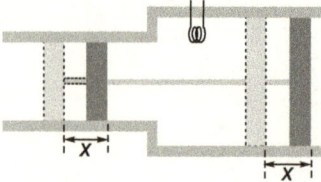

The heat absorbed is

$$Q = W_{el} = Pt = 36\,\text{W} \cdot 120\,\text{s} = 4320\,\text{J}.$$

According to the first law, $\Delta U = Q + W$, where $\Delta U = c_v m \Delta T$. In detail, with the data of the enclosed air:

$$c_v \varrho_{300} V_0 (T_1 - T_2) = Q - p_0 (A_2 - A_1)x, \qquad (1)$$

where

$$\varrho_{300} = \frac{\varrho_0}{1 + \beta \Delta T}, \qquad \text{and} \qquad V_0 = A_1 l_1 + A_2 l_2 = (A_1 + A_2)l.$$

With the information $\varrho_0 = 1.293\,\text{kg/m}^3$, and $\beta = 1/(273\,\text{K})$ obtained from tables,

$$\varrho_{300} = \frac{1.293\,\text{kg/m}^3}{1 + (300\,\text{K} - 273\,\text{K})/273\,\text{K}} = 1.176\,\frac{\text{kg}}{\text{m}^3},$$

and
$$V_0 = (10\,\mathrm{dm}^2 + 40\,\mathrm{dm}^2) \cdot 1.5\,\mathrm{dm} = 75\,\mathrm{dm}^3 = 7.5 \cdot 10^{-2}\,\mathrm{m}^3.$$

At constant pressure,
$$\frac{T_1 - T_0}{T_0} = \frac{V_1 - V_0}{V_0} = \frac{(A_2 - A_1)x}{V_0}.$$

Hence
$$T_1 - T_0 = T_0 \frac{A_2 - A_1}{V_0} x. \qquad (2)$$

(2) can be substituted into (1):
$$c_v \varrho_{300} V_0 T_0 \frac{A_2 - A_1}{V_0} x = Q - p_0 (A_2 - A_1) x.$$

With the substitution of $Q = Pt$ and rearrangement to express the displacement in question:
$$x = \frac{Pt}{(A_2 - A_1)(p_0 + c_v \varrho_{300} T_0)} =$$
$$= \frac{4320\,\mathrm{J}}{(4 \cdot 10^{-2}\,\mathrm{m}^2 - 1 \cdot 10^{-2}\,\mathrm{m}^2)\left(10^5\,\frac{\mathrm{N}}{\mathrm{m}^2} + 712\,\frac{\mathrm{J}}{\mathrm{kg \cdot K}} \cdot 1.176\,\frac{\mathrm{kg}}{\mathrm{m}^3} \cdot 300\,\mathrm{K}\right)} = 4.1\,\mathrm{cm}.$$

b) The temperature of the air in the final state is obtained from (2):
$$T_1 = T_0 \frac{(A_2 - A_1)x}{V_0} + T_0 = T_0 \frac{A_2 - A_1}{A_1 + A_2} \cdot \frac{x}{l} + T_0 =$$
$$= 300\,\mathrm{K} \cdot \frac{40\,\mathrm{dm}^2 - 10\,\mathrm{dm}^2}{10\,\mathrm{dm}^2 + 40\,\mathrm{dm}^2} \cdot \frac{4.1\,\mathrm{cm}}{15\,\mathrm{cm}} + 300\,\mathrm{K} = 349.2\,\mathrm{K}.$$

Second solution of Problem 210. From the universal gas equation:
$$p_0 V_0 = nRT_0.$$

The heat absorbed is
$$Q = c_p m \Delta T = \frac{f+2}{2} \frac{k}{m_0} m \Delta T = \frac{f+2}{2} \frac{k}{m_0} (n N_A m_0) \Delta T = \frac{f+2}{2} R n \Delta T =$$
$$= \frac{7}{2} R n \Delta T = \frac{7}{2} \frac{p_0 V_0}{T_0} \Delta T,$$

and hence the change in temperature and the final temperature are
$$\Delta T = \frac{2}{7} \frac{Q T_0}{p_0 V_0} = \frac{2 \cdot 4320\,\mathrm{J} \cdot 300\,\mathrm{K}}{7 \cdot 10^5\,\frac{\mathrm{N}}{\mathrm{m}^2} \cdot 7.5 \cdot 10^{-2}\,\mathrm{m}^2} = 49.4\,^\circ\mathrm{C},$$

and
$$T = T_0 + \Delta T = 27\,^\circ\mathrm{C} + 49.4\,^\circ\mathrm{C} = 76.4\,^\circ\mathrm{C} = 349\,\mathrm{K}.$$

Because of the constant pressure,

$$V = \frac{V_0}{T_0} \cdot T = \frac{7.5 \cdot 10^{-2} \, \text{m}^3}{300 \, \text{K}} \cdot 349 \, \text{K} = 87.37 \, \text{dm}^3,$$

and

$$\Delta V = (A_2 - A_1)x = V - V_0 = 87.34 \, \text{dm}^3 - 75 \, \text{dm}^3 = 12.34 \, \text{dm}^3.$$

Hence

$$x = \frac{\Delta V}{A_2 - A_1} = \frac{12.3 \, \text{dm}^3}{40 \, \text{dm}^2 - 10 \, \text{dm}^2} = 0.41 \, \text{dm} = 4.1 \, \text{cm}.$$

Solution of Problem 211. a) The processes that occur in the middle and rightmost compartments are adiabatic, described by the equation

$$pV^\gamma = \text{constant},$$

where $\gamma = \dfrac{c_p}{c_v} = \dfrac{0.98}{0.7} = 1.4$. Therefore, the resulting pressures can be obtained by applying the adiabatic equation of state to the initial and final states. With the use of the data in the figure, the final pressure in the rightmost (3rd) compartment is

$$p_3 = p_0 \cdot \left(\frac{V_3}{V_3'}\right)^\gamma = 20 \, \frac{\text{N}}{\text{cm}^2} \cdot \left(\frac{2}{1.5}\right)^{1.4} = 29.92 \, \frac{\text{N}}{\text{cm}^2}.$$

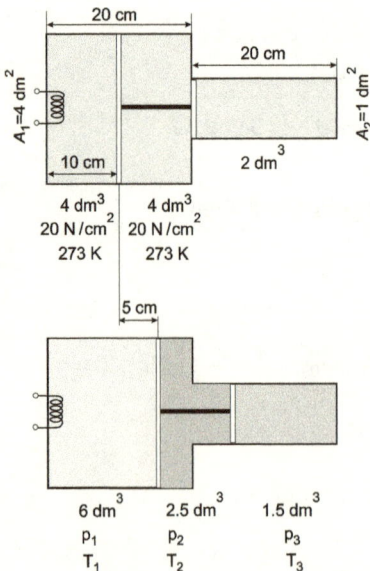

Similarly, the final pressure in the middle (2nd) compartment is

$$p_2 = 20 \, \frac{\text{N}}{\text{cm}^2} \cdot \left(\frac{4}{2.5}\right)^{1.4} = 38.62 \, \frac{\text{N}}{\text{cm}^2}.$$

The pressure in the leftmost compartment is determined from the equilibrium of the pistons, since that process is not adiabatic.

The condition for the equilibrium of the pistons is

$$\sum F = 0.$$

With the forces acting on the individual piston surfaces in detail:

$$p_1 A_1 - p_2 A_1 + p_2 A_2 - p_3 A_2 = 0.$$

Hence

$$p_1 = \frac{p_2(A_1 - A_2) + p_3 A_2}{A_1},$$

that is,

$$p_1 = \frac{38.62 \, \frac{\text{N}}{\text{cm}^2}(4-1) \cdot 10^2 \, \text{cm}^2 + 29.92 \, \frac{\text{N}}{\text{cm}^2} \cdot 10^2 \, \text{cm}^2}{4 \cdot 10^2 \, \text{cm}^2} = 36.44 \, \frac{\text{N}}{\text{cm}^2}.$$

b) Since the system does no work on the surroundings, the algebraic sum of the works done by the parts of the system on one another is 0, and the heat absorbed is equal to the change in the internal energy of the system:

$$Q = \Delta U = c_v(m_1\Delta T_1 + m_2\Delta T_2 + m_3\Delta T_3).$$

The changes in temperature are calculated from the universal gas equation:

$$\frac{p_1 V_1}{T_1} = \frac{p_1' V_1'}{T_1'}.$$

Hence the final temperature of the gas in the first compartment is

$$T_1' = T_1\frac{p_1' V_1'}{p_1 V_1} = 273\,\text{K} \cdot \frac{36.44\,\text{N/cm}^2 \cdot 6\,\text{dm}^3}{20\,\text{N/cm}^2 \cdot 4\,\text{dm}^3} = 746.11\,\text{K}.$$

Similarly,

$$T_2' = 273\,\text{K} \cdot \frac{38.62\,\text{N/cm}^2 \cdot 2.5\,\text{dm}^3}{20\,\text{N/cm}^2 \cdot 4\,\text{dm}^3} = 329.48\,\text{K},$$

and

$$T_3' = 273\,\text{K} \cdot \frac{29.92\,\text{N/cm}^2 \cdot 1.5\,\text{dm}^3}{20\,\text{N/cm}^2 \cdot 2\,\text{dm}^3} = 306.31\,\text{K}.$$

The masses of the air in the individual compartments are obtained as the product of density and volume. Since the initial pressure is twice the normal atmospheric pressure, the initial density is also doubled:

$$m_1 = V_1 2\varrho_0 = 4\,\text{dm}^3 \cdot 2 \cdot 1.3\frac{\text{g}}{\text{dm}^3} = 10.4\,\text{g},$$

$$m_2 = V_2 2\varrho_0 = 4\,\text{dm}^3 \cdot 2 \cdot 1.3\frac{\text{g}}{\text{dm}^3} = m_1 = 10.4\,\text{g},$$

$$m_3 = V_3 2\varrho_0 = 2\,\text{dm}^3 \cdot 2 \cdot 1.3\frac{\text{g}}{\text{dm}^3} = \frac{m_1}{2} = 5.2\,\text{g}.$$

The changes in temperature are

$$\Delta T_1 = T_1' - T_1 = 746.11\,\text{K} - 273\,\text{K} = 473.11\,\text{K},$$

$$\Delta T_2 = T_2' - T_2 = 329.48\,\text{K} - 273\,\text{K} = 56.48\,\text{K},$$

$$\Delta T_3 = T_3' - T_3 = 306.31\,\text{K} - 273\,\text{K} = 33.31\,\text{K}.$$

With these data, the total change in internal energy, that is, the total energy absorbed, is obtained as follows:

$$Q = \Delta U = 0.7\frac{\text{J}}{\text{g\,K}} \cdot (10.4\,\text{g} \cdot 473.11\,\text{K} + 10.4\,\text{g} \cdot 56.48\,\text{K} + 5.2\,\text{g} \cdot 33.31\,\text{K}) = 3976.7\,\text{J}.$$

Solution of Problem 212. a) Let n_1 and n_2 denote the quantities of helium and oxygen, respectively, in kilomoles, let C_{v1} and C_{v2} denote the corresponding molar specific heats, and let m be the total mass of the gas mixture. The total mass of the mixture is the sum of the masses of the components, and since $m = M \cdot n$,

$$M_1 \cdot n_1 + M_2 n_2 = m, \tag{1}$$

where M is the molar mass of the gas in kg/kmol. It follows from the first law of thermodynamics that — since the volume of the gas does not change — the change in the internal energy of the gas mixture is

$$\Delta E = (C_{v1} \cdot n_1 + C_{v2} \cdot n_2) \cdot) \Delta T = Q. \tag{2}$$

(1) and (2) expressed with numerical data:

$$4 \, \frac{\text{kg}}{\text{kmol}} \cdot n_1 + 32 \, \frac{\text{kg}}{\text{kmol}} \cdot n_2 = m, \tag{1'}$$

$$(12 \, 300 \, \frac{\text{J}}{\text{kmol} \cdot \text{K}} \cdot n_1 + 20 \, 500 \, \frac{\text{J}}{\text{kmol} \cdot \text{K}} \cdot n_2) \cdot 50 \, \text{K} = 143 \, 500 \, \text{J}. \tag{2'}$$

The solution of the simultaneous equations is

$$n_1 = 0.15 \, \text{kmol}, \quad \text{and} \quad n_2 = 0.05 \, \text{kmol},$$

that is,

$$m_{He} = M_1 n_1 = 4 \, \frac{\text{kg}}{\text{kmol}} \cdot 0.15 \, \text{kmol} = 0.6 \, \text{kg},$$

and

$$m_{O_2} = M_2 n_2 = 32 \frac{\text{kg}}{\text{kmol}} \cdot 0.05 \, \text{kmol} = 1.6 \, \text{kg}.$$

b) At constant volume,

$$\frac{p_1}{T_1} = \frac{p_2}{T_2},$$

which now means

$$\frac{p}{273 \, \text{K}} = \frac{p + 13 \, 749 \, \text{Pa}}{(273 + 50) \, \text{K}},$$

and hence

$$p = 0.75 \cdot 10^5 \, \text{Pa}.$$

c) The total quantity of gas in the container is

$$n = n_1 + n_2 = 0.15 \, \text{kmol} + 0.06 \, \text{kmol} = 0.2 \, \text{kmol}.$$

The volume of this quantity of gas at 0 °C and normal atmospheric pressure is $V_N = = n \cdot V_{\text{mol}}$, the product of molar volume and the number of moles. Now,

$$V_N = 0.2 \, \text{kmol} \cdot 22.4 \frac{\text{m}^3}{\text{kmol}} = 4.48 \, \text{m}^3.$$

The volume of the gas in question is obtained by applying Boyle's law to that state and the actual state of the gas in the container:

$$p_N V_N = pV,$$

that is,

$$1.013 \cdot 10^5 \, \text{Pa} \cdot 4.48 \, \text{m}^3 = 0.75 \cdot 10^5 \, \text{Pa} \cdot V,$$

and hence

$$V = 6.05 \, \text{m}^3.$$

Solution of Problem 213. a) The initial volume of the gas is obtained from the universal gas equation. Expressed in litres,

$$V_1 = \frac{m}{M} \frac{RT}{p_1} = \frac{2 \cdot 10^{-2} \, \text{kg}}{2 \cdot 10^{-3} \, \text{kg/mol}} \cdot \frac{8.32 \, \text{J/(mol} \cdot \text{K)} \cdot 200 \, \text{K}}{5 \cdot 10^5 \, \text{N/m}^2} = 33.24 \, \text{l}.$$

The change 1–2 is isobaric, so $V_2/V_1 = T_2/T_1$, and hence

$$V_2 = V_1 \frac{T_2}{T_1} = 33.24 \, \text{l} \cdot \frac{500 \, \text{K}}{200 \, \text{K}} = 83.1 \, \text{l}.$$

Process 2–3 is isochoric (the line segment 2–3 lies on a line passing through the origin), for which $p_3/p_2 = T_3/T_2$, and thus

$$T_3 = T_2 \frac{p_3}{p_2} = 500 \, \text{K} \cdot \frac{7}{5} = 700 \, \text{K} \qquad \text{and} \qquad V_3 = V_2 = 83.1 \, \text{l}.$$

The change 3–4 is isobaric again, so

$$V_4 = V_3 \frac{T_4}{T_3} = 83.1 \, \text{l} \cdot \frac{500 \, \text{K}}{700 \, \text{K}} = 59.36 \, \text{l}.$$

Finally, the process 4–5 is isochoric again, where $T_5 = T_1 = 200 \, \text{K}$ and $V_5 = V_4 = 59.36 \, \text{l}$. The final pressure is therefore

$$p_5 = p_4 \frac{T_5}{T_4} = 7 \cdot 10^5 \, \text{Pa} \cdot \frac{200}{500} = 2.8 \cdot 10^5 \, \text{Pa}.$$

The unknown state variables are thus determined. Now the other two diagrams can be drawn.

b) The p-V and T-V diagrams are as follows:

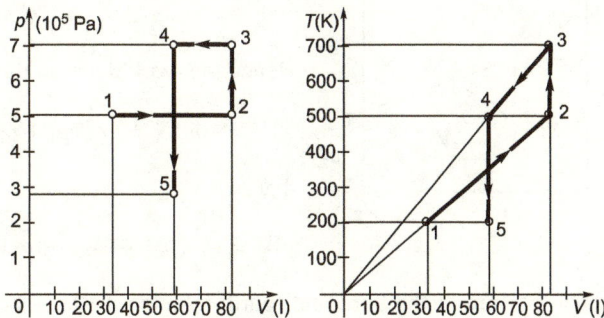

c) The work done on the gas can be calculated from the p-V diagram. Internal energy is the same at the beginning and at the end of the process since the temperatures of the gas in the initial and final states are equal. The first law of thermodynamics states $\Delta U = Q + W = 0$, thus $Q = -W$.

The work done on the gas can be determined in four stages:

$$W_{12} = -p_1(V_2 - V_1) = -5 \cdot 10^5 \, \frac{\mathrm{N}}{\mathrm{m}^2} \cdot (83.1 - 33.24) \cdot 10^{-3} \, \mathrm{m}^3 = -24930 \, \mathrm{J},$$

$$W_{23} = 0,$$

$$W_{34} = -p_3(V_4 - V_3) = -7 \cdot 10^5 \, \frac{\mathrm{N}}{\mathrm{m}^2} \cdot (59.36 - 83.1) \cdot 10^{-3} \, \mathrm{m}^3 = 16618 \, \mathrm{J},$$

$$W_{45} = 0.$$

The net work done on the gas is

$$W = W_{12} + W_{23} + W_{34} + W_{45} = -24930 \, \mathrm{J} + 0 + 16618 \, \mathrm{J} + 0 = -8312 \, \mathrm{J},$$

and the net heat absorbed is

$$Q = -W = 8312 \, \mathrm{J}.$$

Solution of Problem 214. The heat absorbed (given off) by the gas is obtained from the first law of thermodynamics. It states that $\Delta U = Q + W$, that is, the heat absorbed by the gas is $Q = \Delta U - W$. Here, the change in internal energy can be expressed in terms of the change in temperature:

$$\Delta U = nC_v(T_2 - T_1) = 0.001 \, \mathrm{mol} \cdot 20.5 \, \mathrm{J/(mol \cdot K)} \cdot (-10 \, \mathrm{K}) = -0.205 \, \mathrm{J}.$$

The work done can be determined with the help of a pressure-volume diagram.

Let p_0 denote the external air pressure, let ϱ denote the density of mercury, and let h_1 and h_2 be the initial and final heights of the mercury column. It can be seen from the diagram that the pressure of the enclosed air varies linearly with its volume.

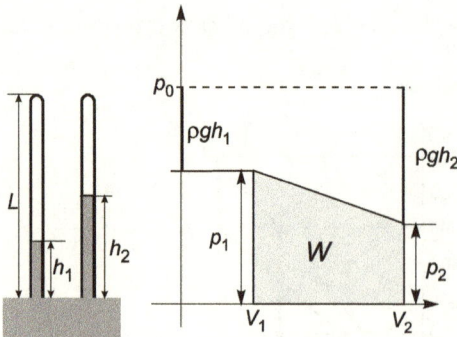

Therefore the work, represented by the area under the graph, can be calculated from the arithmetic mean of the initial and final pressures:

$$\bar{p} = (p_1 + p_2)/2.$$

Hence the work done on the gas is

$$W = -\bar{p}\Delta V = -\frac{1}{2}(p_1 + p_2) \cdot (V_2 - V_1),$$

that is,

$$W = -\frac{1}{2}(p_2V_2 - p_1V_1 + p_1V_2 - p_2V_1). \quad (1)$$

It can be shown that the sum of the third and fourth terms in the brackets is 0: Since

$$p_1V_2 = (p_0 - \varrho g h_1)(L - h_2) \cdot A,$$

and
$$p_2 V_1 = (p_0 - \varrho g h_2)(L - h_1) \cdot A,$$
with the multiplications carried out, the right-hand sides of the equations are
$$(p_0 L - p_0 h_2 - \varrho g h_1 L + \varrho g h_1 h_2) A,$$
$$(p_0 L - p_0 h_1 - \varrho g h_2 L + \varrho g h_2 h_1) A.$$

The first and last terms are the same in both expressions. It follows from the given length of the tube that the factor $\varrho g L$ in the third term is equal to p_0, which makes the second and third terms of both expressions add up to the same quantity:
$$-p_0(h_2 + h_1), \qquad -p_0(h_1 + h_2).$$

Therefore, the last two terms of (1) really cancel out.

The universal gas equation applied to the first two terms gives $p_2 V_2 = nRT_2$ and $p_1 V_1 = nRT_1$.

Hence the work done on the gas is
$$W = -\frac{1}{2} nR(T_2 - T_1) = -0.042 \, \text{J}.$$

The heat absorbed by the gas is
$$Q = \Delta U - W = nC_v(T_2 - T_1) + \frac{1}{2}(nRT_2 - nRT_1) = n(T_2 - T_1)\left(C_v + \frac{R}{2}\right) =$$
$$= 0.001 \, \text{mol} \cdot (-10 \, \text{K})\left(20.5 \, \text{J/(mol} \cdot \text{K)} + \frac{8.31 \, \text{J/(mol} \cdot \text{K)}}{2}\right) = -0.247 \, \text{J},$$

that is, the heat given off by the air is $+0.247 \, \text{J}$.

Solution of Problem 215. a) After the heating starts, the liquid membrane bulges out more and more owing to the rising temperature. This will cause its radius of curvature r to decrease. Since the pressure of the enclosed gas is in equilibrium with the external pressure plus the excess pressure of the curved liquid film:

$$p = p_0 + \frac{4\alpha}{r}.$$

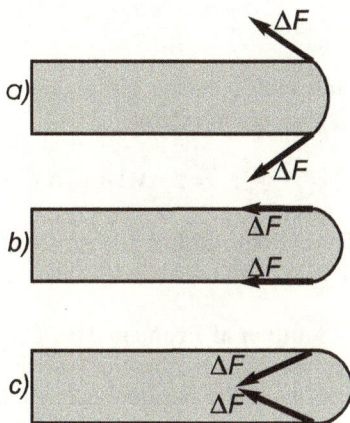

It is easy to see that the pressure increases in this stage. Figure a) shows that the smallest possible value of r is R. When that occurs, the membrane has a hemispherical shape. Therefore, the maximum pressure is
$$p_{\max} = p_0 + \frac{4\alpha}{R} = 1040 \, \text{Pa}.$$

(The same result can also be obtained without using the concept of the excess pressure of a curved liquid film. Let F denote the total force exerted by the tube on the membrane. In the situations shown by figures a) and c), $F < 4R\pi\alpha$, since F is the resultant of the lengthwise components of the forces acting on elementary arcs.

In the case b), $F = 4R\pi\alpha$, this is the maximum value of F. Since the membrane is in equilibrium,

$$pR^2\pi = F + p_0 R^2 \pi, \tag{1}$$

and hence

$$p = p_0 + \frac{F}{R^2\pi}. \tag{2}$$

With the substitution of the maximum value of F in (1), (2) gives the same result for p_{max} as obtained above.)

The temperature is calculated from the universal gas equation:

$$\frac{p_0 R^2 \pi h}{T_0} = \frac{p_{max}\left[R^2\pi h + (2/3)R^3\pi\right]}{T},$$

where $R^2\pi h$ is the volume of the cylinder and $\dfrac{2}{3}R^3\pi$ is the volume of the hemisphere. Hence,

$$T = \frac{p_{max}\left[h + (2/3)R\right]}{p_0 h}\cdot T_0 = \frac{1040\,\text{Pa}\cdot\left[25\cdot10^{-3}\,\text{m} + (2/3)\cdot5\cdot10^{-3}\,\text{m}\right]}{1000\,\text{Pa}\cdot25\cdot10^{-3}\,\text{m}}\cdot250\,\text{K} = 295\,\text{K}.$$

b) The first law of thermodynamics states $Q = \Delta U + W_{gas}$. The change in internal energy is $\Delta U = \dfrac{f}{2}Nk\Delta T$, where $Nk = \dfrac{p_0 R^2 h}{T_0}$ from the universal gas equation applied to the initial state. Therefore,

$$\Delta U = \frac{f}{2}\frac{p_0 R^2\pi h}{T_0}\cdot\Delta T = \frac{5}{2}\cdot\frac{1000\,\text{Pa}\cdot25\cdot10^{-6}\,\text{m}^2\pi\cdot25\cdot10^{-5}\,\text{m}}{250\,\text{K}\cdot(295\,\text{K}-250\,\text{K})} = 8.8\cdot10^{-4}\,\text{J}.$$

The work done by the gas is used for increasing the energy of the membrane and displacing the external air:

$$W_g = 2\alpha\Delta A + p_0\Delta V = 2\alpha(2R^2\pi - R^2\pi) + p_0\frac{2}{3}R^3\pi = 2.7\cdot10^{-4}\,\text{J}.$$

Thus, from the first law of thermodynamics, the heat absorbed is $Q = 8.8\cdot10^{-4}\,\text{J} + 2.7\cdot10^{-4}\,\text{J} = 11.5\cdot10^{-4}\,\text{J}$.

Solution of Problem 216. Let p_1, V_1, T_1. stand for the initial state variables of the enclosed gas. Furthermore, let us consider the state when the piston has moved furthest from its initial position and therefore stops for a moment. Let the state variables of the gas be p_2, V_2, T_2 then. According to the condition set in the problem:

$$V_2 = 2V_1. \tag{1}$$

The gas undergoes adiabatic change of state, and therefore:

$$p_1 V_1^\gamma = p_2 V_2^\gamma. \tag{2}$$

From equations (1) and (2)

$$\frac{p_1}{p_2} = \left(\frac{V_2}{V_1}\right)^\gamma = 2^\gamma = 2^{1.4} = 2.639. \tag{3}$$

Examining the motion of the piston between the two states in concern, according to the work-energy theorem applied to the piston:

$$W_{\text{external}} + W_{\text{gas}} = 0. \tag{4}$$

In this, the work done by the external air (considering that $\Delta V = V_1$) is

$$W_{\text{external}} = -p_k \Delta V = -p_k V_1. \tag{5}$$

As the process is adiabatic, according to the first law of thermodynamics because $Q = 0$:

$$W_{\text{gas}} = -\Delta U_{\text{gas}} = \left(\frac{f}{2}\right)(p_1 V_1 - p_2 V_2). \tag{6}$$

With this, the work-energy theorem becomes $\frac{f}{2}(p_1 V_1 - p_2 V_2) - p_{\text{ext}} V_1 = 0$. Substituting the values received from (1) and (3):

$$\frac{f}{2}\left(p_1 - \frac{2 p_1}{2.639}\right) V_1 = p_k V_1,$$

from which, after simplifying and reorganising, the unknown initial pressure is

$$p_1 = \frac{2}{f} \frac{p_{\text{ext}}}{1 - \frac{2}{2.639}} = \frac{2 \cdot 10^5 \,\text{Pa}}{5 \cdot \frac{0.639}{2.639}} = 1.652 \cdot 10^5 \,\text{Pa}.$$

From this, we can also learn that the minimum pressure of the gas was

$$p_2 = \frac{p_1}{2.939} = 0.626 \cdot 10^5 \,\text{Pa}.$$

After the process in concern the piston started to move back.

Solution of Problem 217. The speed of the piston reaches its maximum at the moment when the acceleration of the piston becomes zero, i.e. the resultant force acting on it is zero. Let m be the mass of the piston, A be the base area of the cylinder and p_0 be the atmospheric pressure. According to Newton's second law:

$$p_0 A + mg - pA = ma,$$

where p is the pressure of the gas inside the cylinder. Let p_1 be the pressure of the helium gas at the moment when the piston's acceleration becomes zero ($a = 0$). Using the above equation, p_1 can be written as:

$$p_1 = p_0 + \frac{mg}{A} = 10 \,\frac{\text{N}}{\text{cm}^2} + \frac{80 \,\text{kg} \cdot 10 \,\text{m/s}^2}{10^2 \,\text{cm}^2} = 18 \,\frac{\text{N}}{\text{cm}^2}.$$

The helium gas undergoes an adiabatic compression for which $pV^\gamma = \text{constant}$. Applying this to the initial and final states of the gas and using that the ratio of specific heats is $\gamma = c_p/c_v = 5250/3150 = 5/3$ (or with the help of the degree of freedom $\gamma = (f+2)/f = 5/3$), we get that

$$p_0 V_0^\gamma = p_1 V_1^\gamma,$$

substituting known values, we find:

$$10\,\frac{\text{N}}{\text{cm}^2} \cdot 22.4^{\frac{5}{3}}\,\text{dm}^5 = 18\,\frac{\text{N}}{\text{cm}^2} \cdot V^{\frac{5}{3}},$$

from which the final volume of helium is:

$$V = 22.4 \cdot \left(\frac{10}{18}\right)^{\frac{3}{5}}\,\text{dm}^3 = 15.74\,\text{dm}^3.$$

Let us use the equation of state to calculate the temperature of helium in is final state:

$$T_1 = T_0\,\frac{p_1 V_1}{p_0 V_0} = 273\,\text{K}\,\frac{18\,\text{N/cm}^2 \cdot 15.74\,\text{dm}^3}{10\,\text{N/cm}^2 \cdot 22.4\,\text{dm}^3} = 345\,\text{K} = 72\,^\circ\text{C}.$$

The maximum speed of the piston can be determined using the work-energy theorem:

$$\sum W = \Delta E_{\text{kin}}.$$

Let us calculate the works done by the forces acting on the piston. The distance moved by the piston until it reaches its maximum speed is:

$$s = \frac{V_1 - V_2}{A} = \frac{22.4\,\text{dm}^3 - 15.74\,\text{dm}^3}{1\,\text{dm}^2} = 6.66\,\text{dm}.$$

The work done by the atmosphere is:

$$W_{\text{atm}} = p_0(V_1 - V_2) = 10^5\,\frac{\text{N}}{\text{m}^2} \cdot (22.4 - 15.74) \cdot 10^{-3}\,\text{m}^3 = 666\,\text{J}.$$

The work done by the gravitational force is:

$$W_{\text{grav}} = mgs = mg\,\frac{V_1 - V_2}{A} = 80\,\text{kg} \cdot 10\,\frac{\text{m}}{\text{s}^2} \cdot 6.66 \cdot 10^{-1}\,\text{m} = 532.8\,\text{J}.$$

The helium gas is compressed, therefore its work will be negative (the direction of the force exerted by it and the displacement of the piston are opposite). The magnitude of this work can be found using the first law of thermodynamics:

$$\Delta U = Q + W,$$

where W is the work done on the gas. The work done by the gas is the same as the magnitude, but negative. As there is no transmission of heat during an adiabatic process, $Q = 0$, hence

$$W_{\text{He}} = -\Delta U = -c_v m_{\text{He}} \Delta T = -3150\,\frac{\text{J}}{\text{kg K}}(345\,\text{K} - 273\,\text{K}) = -907.2\,\text{J}.$$

The work-energy theorem will therefore take the form of:

$$p_0(V_1 - V_2) + mg\frac{V_1 - V_2}{A} - c_v m(T_2 - T_1) = \frac{1}{2}mv^2 - 0,$$

where v is the maximum speed reached by the piston. Solving for v, we get:

$$v = \sqrt{\frac{2p_0(V_1 - V_2)}{m} + 2g\frac{V_1 - V_2}{A} - 2c_v \frac{m_{He}}{m}(T_2 - T_1)},$$

Let us factor out $V_1 - V_2$:

$$v = \sqrt{2(V_1 - V_2)\left(\frac{p_0}{m} + \frac{g}{A}\right) - 2c_v \frac{m_{He}}{m}(T_2 - T_1)}.$$

Substituting the values of works done by the external forces, we find:

$$v = \sqrt{\frac{2}{80\,\text{kg}}(666\,\text{J} + 532.8\,\text{J} - 907.2\,\text{J})} = \sqrt{7.29\frac{\text{m}}{\text{s}^2}} = 2.7\frac{\text{m}}{\text{s}}.$$

Solution of Problem 218. a) According to the first law of thermodynamics, $\Delta E = Q + W$, from which the absorbed heat is:

$$Q = \Delta E - W = \Delta E + W_{\text{gas}}.$$

In the isobaric process the absorbed heat and the change of the internal energy are:

$$Q = c_p m \Delta T \qquad \Delta E = c_v m \Delta T.$$

Writing these into the first law, we get:

$$c_p m \Delta T = c_v m \Delta T + W_{\text{gas}}.$$

The work done by the gas is:

$$W_{\text{gas}} = (cp - cv)m\Delta T.$$

According to the statement of the problem, this work is 68% of the increase of the internal energy, therefore:

$$\frac{W_{\text{gas}}}{\Delta E} = \frac{cp - cv}{cv} = \gamma - 1 = 0.68,$$

so $\gamma = 1.68$. According to data tables, this value corresponds only to krypton, so the experiment is performed with krypton gas.

b) During the adiabatic compression the work done on the gas is:

$$W_{\text{adiab}} = \frac{p_2 V_2 - p_1 V_1}{\gamma - 1}.$$

With our data

$$36850 \text{ J} = \frac{p_3 V_3 - 24942 \text{ J}}{0.68},$$

from which

$$p_3 V_3 = 36850 \text{ J} \cdot 0.68 + 24942 \text{ J} = 50000 \text{ J}.$$

According to the ideal gas law in the final state of the adiabatic process,

$$p_3 V_3 = nRT_2$$

which means that the unknown final temperature T_2 is:

$$T_2 = \frac{p_3 V_3}{nR} = \frac{50000 \text{ J}}{10 \text{ mol} \cdot 8.314 \, \frac{\text{J}}{\text{mol} \cdot \text{K}}} = 601.395 \text{ K} \approx 601.4 \text{ K}.$$

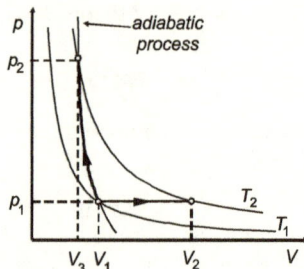

Solution of Problem 219. According to the first law of thermodynamics, $\Delta E = Q + W = Q - W_{\text{gas}}$, which means that the heat absorbed by the gas is

$$Q = \Delta E + W_{\text{gas}}. \tag{1}$$

The change of the internal energy and the work done by the gas are:

$$\Delta E = \frac{f}{2} N k \Delta T = \frac{f}{2} \frac{m}{M} R \Delta T,$$

$$W_{\text{gas}} = p \Delta V = \frac{m}{M} R \Delta T.$$

where M is the unknown molar mass of the gas. Putting these expressions into equation (1) of the absorbed heat, we get:

$$Q = \frac{f}{2} \frac{m}{M} R \Delta T + \frac{m}{M} R \Delta T = \frac{f+2}{2} \frac{m}{M} R \Delta T.$$

(We remark that the formula $Q = c_p m \Delta T$ gives the same value for the absorbed heat as the previous one.)

The heat emitted be the electric heater is

$$Q_{\text{el}} = \frac{U^2}{r} t,$$

which is only partially absorbed by the gas. The connection between the heat absorbed by the gas and the heat emitted by the heater is $Q = \eta Q_{\text{el}}$, so

$$\frac{f+2}{2} \frac{m}{M} R \Delta T = \eta \frac{U^2}{r} t.$$

From here the unknown molar mass of the gas is:

$$M = \frac{f+2}{2\eta} \cdot \frac{m}{U^2 t} \cdot r R \Delta T.$$

Numerically:

$$M = \frac{5+2}{2 \cdot 0.75} \cdot \frac{5 \text{ g}}{220^2 \text{ V}^2 \cdot 25 \text{ s}} \cdot 50 \text{ } \Omega \cdot 8.31 \frac{\text{J}}{\text{mol} \cdot \text{K}} \cdot 250 \text{ } K = 2 \frac{\text{g}}{\text{mol}},$$

which means that there is hydrogen in the container.

Solution of Problem 220. Notations, data:

$$m = m_{\text{He}} + m_{\text{H}_2} = 180 \text{ g}, \qquad W_{\text{gas}} = 56 \text{ kJ}, \qquad Q = 156 \text{ kJ}, \qquad m_{\text{H}_2} = ? \qquad \Delta T = ?$$

For the sake of simplicity, let us denote the mass of the hydrogen gas by m_1, and that of the helium gas by m_2.

According to the I. law of thermodynamics, the change of the internal energy is:

$$\Delta E = Q + W = Q - W_{\text{gas}} = 156 \text{ kJ} - 56 \text{ kJ} = 100 \text{ kJ}.$$

The expansion of the gas at constant pressure is an isobaric process.

The gas law and the expression of the internal energy are:

$$p \Delta V = (N_1 + N_2) \cdot k \Delta T \tag{1}$$

$$\Delta E = \left(\frac{f_1}{2} N_1 + \frac{f_2}{2} N_2 \right) \cdot k \Delta T \tag{2}$$

and from (1) and (2) we obtain that:

$$\Delta E = \left(\frac{f_1}{2} N_1 + \frac{f_2}{2} N_2 \right) \cdot \frac{p \Delta V}{(N_1 + N_2)} = \left(\frac{f_1}{2} N_1 + \frac{f_2}{2} N_2 \right) \cdot \frac{W_{\text{gas}}}{N_1 + N_2}.$$

It means that

$$\frac{2 \Delta E}{W_{\text{gas}}} = \frac{f_1 N_1 + f_2 N_2}{N_1 + N_2} \quad \rightarrow \quad \frac{200}{56} = \frac{5 N_1 + 3 N_2}{N_1 + N_2}.$$

Let x denote the ratio N_1 / N_2 of the number of hydrogen and helium particles. After simplifying the last equation, we get:

$$\frac{25}{7} = \frac{5x + 3}{x + 1}.$$

Solving this equation, we get:

$$25x + 25 = 35x + 21 \quad \rightarrow \quad 10x = 4,$$

thus the ratio $x = N_1 / N_2$ is: $x = 0.4$, and $N_1 = 0.4 N_2$. Now the number of particles is expressed in terms of the mass, the molar mass and Avogadro's number, and inserted into the previous equation:

$$\frac{m_1}{M_1} N_A = 0.4 \frac{m_2}{M_2} N_A, \quad \text{so} \quad m_1 = 0.4 \cdot m_2 \frac{M_1}{M_2}.$$

Writing here the numerical values of the molar masses:

$$m_1 = 0.4 \cdot m_2 \frac{2}{4} = 0.2 m_2 \quad \rightarrow \quad m_2 = 5 m_1.$$

Since $m_1 + m_2 = m$, $m_1 + 5 m_1 = 6 m_1 = m$, finally we get

$$m_1 = \frac{m}{6} = \frac{180 \text{ g}}{6} = 30 \text{ g}.$$

According to the universal gas law, the temperature change is:

$$p \Delta V = W_{\text{gas}} = \left(\frac{m_1}{M_1} + \frac{m_2}{M_2} \right) R \Delta T \quad \rightarrow \quad \Delta T = \frac{W_{\text{gas}} M_1 M_2}{R \cdot (m_1 M_2 + m_2 M_1)}.$$

Numerically:

$$\Delta T = \frac{56 \cdot 10^3 \text{ J} \cdot 2 \cdot 10^{-3} \frac{\text{kg}}{\text{mol}} \cdot 4 \cdot 10^{-3} \frac{\text{kg}}{\text{mol}}}{8.31 \frac{\text{J}}{\text{mol} \cdot \text{K}} \cdot \left(30 \cdot 10^{-3} \text{ kg} \cdot 4 \cdot 10^{-3} \frac{\text{kg}}{\text{mol}} + 150 \cdot 10^{-3} \text{ kg} \cdot 2 \cdot 10^{-3} \frac{\text{kg}}{\text{mol}} \right)} =$$

$$= 128.4 \text{ K}.$$

Solution of Problem 221. Let V_0 and p_0 as well as $y V_0$ and $x p_0$ denote the volume and pressure of the gas at the beginning as well as at the end of the process, respectively. It follows immediately from the conditions of the problem that the total heat transferred into the system equals the initial internal energy of the gas, which is:

$$E = \frac{3}{2} p_0 V_0,$$

since helium is an noble gas with three thermodynamical degrees of freedom. So the total heat transferred into the system is:

$$Q = \frac{3}{2} p_0 V_0.$$

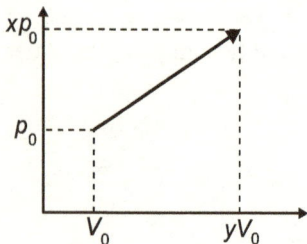

The work done by the gas in the process investigated is equal to the area of the trapezium under the graph in the pressure–volume plane:

$$W = \frac{p_0 + x p_0}{2} (y V_0 - V_0) = \frac{1}{2} p_0 V_0 (x+1)(y-1).$$

While the change of the internal energy of the gas is:

$$\Delta E = \frac{3}{2} (x p_0 y V_0 - p_0 V_0) = \frac{3}{2} p_0 V_0 (x+1)(y-1).$$

According to the I. law of thermodynamics, the total heat transferred to the gas is:

$$Q = \Delta E + W = \frac{3}{2} p_0 V_0 (xy - 1) + \frac{1}{2} p_0 V_0 (x+1)(y-1) =$$

$$= \frac{1}{2} p_0 V_0 (3xy - 3 + xy - x + y - 1).$$

After combining the similar terms:

$$Q = \frac{1}{2} p_0 V_0 (4xy + y - x - 4).$$

But this heat, as we have seen, is equal to the initial internal energy of the gas:

$$\frac{3}{2} p_0 V_0 = \frac{1}{2} p_0 V_0 (4xy + y - x - 4).$$

From this equation we get y as a function of x:

$$3 = 4xy + y - x - 4 \;\rightarrow\; 7 = (4x + 1)y - x \;\rightarrow\; y = \frac{x+7}{4x+1}.$$

In the problem we are interested in, the maximal possible volume changes. Thus we have to find the maximal value of y. This can be done by analysing the form of the above determined function. To do this, let us rewrite the function in a different form. First we multiply both the numerator and the denominator of the fraction by 4, then we eliminate x from the numerator by separating the integer part and the remainder of the division:

$$y = \frac{x+7}{4x+1} = \frac{4x+28}{4(4x+1)} = \frac{4x+1+27}{4(4x+1)} = \frac{1}{4} + \frac{27}{4(4x+1)} = \frac{1}{4}\left(1 + \frac{27}{4x+1}\right).$$

It is easy to see that the function is strictly decreasing in the physically reasonable region $x \geq 0$, so the maximal y value corresponds to $x = 0$, i.e.: $y(0) = 7$.

Thus the volume of the gas can increase at most by the ratio of 7, i.e., $V_{max} = 7V_0$. Furthermore, in this case the graph of the process in the $p - V$ plane is a line segment with negative slope, which 'reaches' the zero pressure at the volume $7V_0$. (Of course, in reality the pressure only approaches zero.)

During a part of this process the gas absorbs, during another part the gas releases heat, but the total heat transferred to the gas is certainly positive. During this process the gas does not double its internal energy; in fact, at the end of the process the internal energy tends to zero.

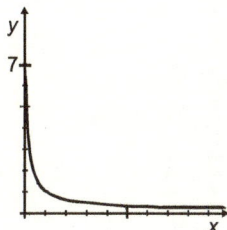

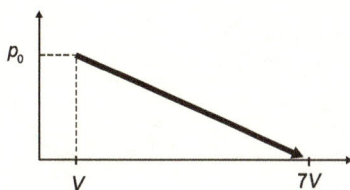

Solution of Problem 222. Let us apply the work-energy theorem to the motion between the points A and B:

$$-mg \cdot 2R \cdot \sin\alpha + kQ^2 \left(\frac{1}{2R \cdot \sin\frac{\alpha}{2}} - \frac{1}{2R \cdot \cos\frac{\alpha}{2}} \right) = \frac{1}{2}mv^2.$$

(1)

At point B (in the time instant of the tension force disappearing but still in the orbit of radius R), the resultant of the radial forces is

$$mg\sin\alpha - \frac{kQ^2}{\left(2R\cos\frac{\alpha}{2}\right)^2} \cdot \cos\frac{\alpha}{2} = \frac{mv^2}{R}.$$

(2)

The charge in question is obtained by multiplying equation (1) by 2, equation (2) by R, subtracting them and rearranging:

$$Q = \sqrt{\frac{5 \cdot mgR^2 \sin\alpha}{k\left(\frac{1}{\sin\frac{\alpha}{2}} - \frac{3}{4\cos\frac{\alpha}{2}}\right)}} = \sqrt{\frac{5 \cdot 10^{-3}\,\text{kg} \cdot 9.81\,\text{m/s}^2 \cdot 10\,\text{m}^2 \sin 60°}{9 \cdot 10^9\,\frac{\text{Nm}^2}{\text{C}^2}\left(\frac{1}{\sin 30°} - \frac{3}{4\cos 30°}\right)}} = 2.04 \cdot 10^{-7}\,\text{C}.$$

Chapter 8

Electrostatics Solutions

8.1 Electrostatics

Solution of Problem 223. Because of the equal masses of the balls and the symmetry of the opposite forces, the displacements of the balls are also symmetric. Thus after releasing the balls at their extreme positions both threads make an angle $\beta/2$ with the vertical, where β is the angle between the two threads.

According to the work-energy theorem, the sum of the works done by the forces acting on the balls is equal to the change of the kinetic energy of the system. Since at the initial and final (extreme) position the balls are at rest, their kinetic energy is zero, thus

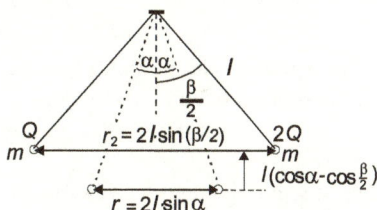

$$k \cdot 2Q^2 \left(\frac{1}{2l\sin\alpha} - \frac{1}{2l\sin\frac{\beta}{2}} \right) - 2mgl \left(\cos\alpha - \cos\frac{\beta}{2} \right) = 0.$$

From here the smaller charge is:

$$Q = \sqrt{ \frac{2mgl\left(\cos\alpha - \cos\frac{\beta}{2}\right)}{2Q^2\left(\frac{1}{2l\sin\alpha} - \frac{1}{2l\sin\frac{\beta}{2}}\right)} } = \sqrt{ \frac{2mgl^2\left(\cos\alpha - \cos\frac{\beta}{2}\right) \cdot \sin\frac{\beta}{2}\sin\alpha}{k \cdot \left(\sin\frac{\beta}{2} - \sin\alpha\right)} }.$$

Inserting the numerical values, we get:

$$Q = \sqrt{ \frac{2 \cdot 10^{-4} \text{ kg} \cdot 9.81 \frac{\text{m}}{\text{s}^2} \cdot 0.09 \text{ m}^3 \left(\cos 20° - \cos 42°\right) \cdot \sin 42° \cdot \sin 20°}{9 \cdot 10^9 \frac{\text{Nm}^2}{\text{C}^2} \left(\sin 42° - \sin 20°\right)} } = 5.2 \cdot 10^{-8}\text{C}.$$

The bigger charge is $2Q = 10.4 \cdot 10^{-8}$ C, of course.

Solution of Problem 224. Let us use an inertial reference frame attached to the centre of mass of the two particles. The above described motion is possible if in this reference frame the two particles perform a uniform circular motion around their centre of mass. (Viewing this motion from other, 'moving' inertial reference frames, the speeds of the particles would not be constant.) The centripetal force needed to maintain the uniform circular motion is produced by the Coulomb force. (The gravitational force is by many orders of magnitude smaller, so it is negligible.) Since the two particles revolve around the common centre of mass, their angular velocities are the same.

By the definition of the centre of mass,

$$\frac{m_1}{m_2} = \frac{r_2}{r_1}.$$

Furthermore, the distance of the particles is constant,

$$r_1 + r_2 = d.$$

This distance d is divided by the centre of mass at the ratio m_1/m_2, therefore:

$$r_1 = \frac{d}{m_1 + m_2} m_2 = \frac{1.5 \text{ cm}}{6 \cdot 10^{-12} \text{ kg} + 1.2 \cdot 10^{-11} \text{ kg}} \cdot 1.2 \cdot 10^{-11} \text{ kg} = 1 \text{ cm},$$

and

$$r_2 = d - r_1 = 1.5 \text{ cm} - 1 \text{ cm} = 0.5 \text{ cm}.$$

The speed of the particles can be determined from Newton's second law. Writing it for the first particle:

$$k\frac{Q_1 Q_2}{d^2} = m_1 r_1 \omega^2.$$

It means that the angular velocity is:

$$\omega = \sqrt{k\frac{Q_1 Q_2}{d^2 m_1 r_1}} = \sqrt{9 \cdot 10^9 \frac{\text{Nm}^2}{\text{C}^2} \cdot \frac{(2.43 \cdot 10^{-13})^2 \text{ C}^2}{1.5^2 \cdot 10^{-4} \text{ m}^2 \cdot 6 \cdot 10^{-12} \text{ kg} \cdot 10^{-2} \text{ m}}} = 6.274 \frac{1}{\text{s}}.$$

The speed of the first particle is:

$$v_1 = r_1 \omega = 10^{-2} \text{ m} \cdot 6.274 \frac{1}{\text{s}} \approx 0.063 \frac{\text{m}}{\text{s}} = 6.34 \frac{\text{cm}}{\text{s}},$$

and the speed of the second one, orbiting half radius, is:

$$v_2 = 0.5 v_1 = 3.17 \frac{\text{cm}}{\text{s}}.$$

Solution of Problem 225. a) According to the centre of mass theorem, in the lack of external force the two objects move in such a way that their centre of mass remains at rest in the inertial reference frame. So the two specks of dust meet at their centre of mass. This position has to be determined. Let us give the distance of the centre of mass from the first speck of mass m_1.

Let the origin of the coordinate system be at the centre of mass. The formula for the position of the centre of mass yields that:

$$0 = \frac{m_1 x_1 + m_2 x_2}{m_1 + m_2} = \frac{m_1 x_1 + [-m_2(d_1 - x_1)]}{m_1 + m_2},$$

from which

$$m_1 x_1 = m_2 d_1 - m_2 x_1 \quad \to \quad x_1 = \frac{m_2}{m_1 + m_2} d_1 = \frac{1.3}{1.7 + 1.3} \cdot 6 \text{ cm} = 2.6 \text{ cm}.$$

So the two specks of dust will meet 2.6 cm far from the initial position of the first speck of mass m_1 (and consequently 3.4 cm far from the initial position of the other speck).

b) To answer the question we have to use the conservation law of energy and of linear momentum. According to the first law, the initial electric potential energy equals the sum of the kinetic and potential energies at the distance d_2:

$$E_{\text{pot}_1} = E_{\text{pot}_2} + E_{\text{kin}_1} + E_{\text{kin}_2},$$

or, in details:

$$k\frac{Q_1Q_2}{d_1} = k\frac{Q_1Q_2}{d_2} + \frac{1}{2}m_1v_1^2 + \frac{1}{2}m_2v_2^2. \tag{1}$$

The sum of the momentum of the specks remains zero in the process, so:

$$m_1v_1 + m_2v_2 = 0.$$

From here

$$v_2 = \frac{m_1}{m_2}v_1.$$

Writing it into equation (1), and rearranging the terms, we get:

$$2kQ_1Q_2\left(\frac{1}{d_1} - \frac{1}{d_2}\right) = m_1v_1^2 + m_2\left(\frac{m_1}{m_2}v_1\right)^2 = \frac{m_1m_2 + m_1^2}{m_2}v_1^2.$$

After some calculation the following is obtained for the speed of the first speck:

$$v_1 = \sqrt{\frac{2kQ_1Q_2m_2}{m_1(m_1+m_2)} \cdot \frac{d_1 - d_2}{d_1d_2}} =$$

$$= \sqrt{\frac{2\cdot9\cdot10^9\ \frac{\text{Nm}^2}{\text{C}^2}\cdot10^{-9}\ \text{C}\cdot5\cdot10^{-9}\ \text{C}\cdot1.3\cdot10^{-11}\ \text{kg}}{1.7\cdot10^{-11}\ \text{kg}(1.7\cdot10^{-11}\ \text{kg}+1.3\cdot10^{-11}\ \text{kg})} \cdot \frac{0.06\ \text{m}-0.01\ \text{m}}{0.06\ \text{m}\cdot0.01\ \text{m}}} = 437\ \frac{\text{m}}{\text{s}}.$$

The other speed can be obtained either by exchanging the indices in this formula, or by using the formula for v_2 derived from the momentum conservation law. The result is:

$$v_2 = -\frac{m_1}{m_2}v_1 = -\frac{1.7}{1.3}437\ \frac{\text{m}}{\text{s}} = -572\ \frac{\text{m}}{\text{s}}.$$

(The negative sign means that if the positive x axis of the coordinate system is pointing in the direction of the velocity of the first speck, then the second speck moves in opposite direction to the x axis.)

The speed of approach of the two objects is just their relative speed, which is:

$$v_{\text{rel}_{12}} = v_1 - v_2 = 437\ \frac{\text{m}}{\text{s}} - \left(-572\ \frac{\text{m}}{\text{s}}\right) = 1009\ \frac{\text{m}}{\text{s}}.$$

(This is the speed of the first speck relative to the second one. Of course, the speed of the second one relative to the first speck is the opposite:

$$v_{\text{rel}_{21}} = v_2 - v_1 = \left(-572\ \frac{\text{m}}{\text{s}}\right) - 437\ \frac{\text{m}}{\text{s}} = -1009\ \frac{\text{m}}{\text{s}}.$$

The question was asking the magnitude of the speed of approach, which is the absolute value of either of these relative speeds.)

Solution of Problem 226. The problem is highly theoretical since it is impossible to concentrate such a large charge on such a small object. The order of magnitude of the radius of a spherical particle with a mass of one thousandth of a gram may be about 1 mm. That would result in an order of magnitude of 10^{10} V for the potential and 10^{13} V/m for the electric field at the surface, which is impossible. Let us assume, however, that it is still possible, and solve the problem.

The particle has to cover a vertical distance of $y = d/2$, and the initial value of its vertical speed is zero. Since the field is uniform, the acceleration will be constant and thus the distance covered is

$$y = \frac{d}{2} = \frac{1}{2}at^2.$$

Hence the time of flight is

$$t = \sqrt{d/a}.$$

From Newton's second law, the acceleration is

$$a = \frac{F_{el}}{m} = \frac{QE}{m} = \frac{QV}{md}.$$

Horizontal speed is constant between the plates. Expressed in terms of the distance to be covered and the time of flight, it is

$$v_x = v = \frac{h}{t} = \frac{h}{\sqrt{d/a}} = h\sqrt{\frac{a}{d}} = h\sqrt{\frac{QV}{md^2}} = \frac{h}{d}\sqrt{\frac{QV}{m}}.$$

Numerically:

$$v = \frac{12\,\text{cm}}{3\,\text{cm}}\sqrt{\frac{4 \cdot 10^{-3}\,\text{C} \cdot 60000\,\text{V}}{5 \cdot 10^{-6}\,\text{kg}}} = 27712.8\,\frac{\text{m}}{\text{s}}.$$

Solution of Problem 227. Let the electron arrive at velocity v at an angle of incidence α and leave at velocity u at an angle of refraction β. Just as between the meshes, only a force perpendicular to the meshes acts on the particles, their velocity component parallel with the mesh does not change: $v\sin\alpha = u\sin\beta$. According to the work–kinetic energy theorem

$$\frac{1}{2}mu^2 - \frac{1}{2}mv^2 = Vq.$$

From the two equations through transformations $\dfrac{\sin\alpha}{\sin\beta} = \sqrt{1 + \dfrac{2Uq}{mv^2}}$. Since ratio $\sin\alpha/\sin\beta$ is independent of the angle of incidence, it has the same value for every electron.

From the definition of the refractive index $n = \sqrt{1 + \frac{2Uq}{mv^2}} = 1.42$.

Solution of Problem 228. Electrons on the edge of the beam travel with a velocity $v_1 = \sqrt{2eV_0/m}$ whose direction forms an angle $\alpha/2$ with the centre-line when reaching the first lattice.

The component v_{1x} of velocity v_1 that is parallel to the lattice remains unchanged, while the perpendicular component v_{1y} should decrease to such an extent that the angle of direction of the velocity changes from $\alpha/2$ to α. The equations describing the change of the angle are:

$$\sin\alpha = \frac{v_{1x}}{v_2}, \qquad \sin\frac{\alpha}{2} = \frac{v_{1x}}{v_1},$$

hence

$$\frac{v_2}{v_1} = \frac{\sin\frac{\alpha}{2}}{\sin\alpha} = \frac{\sin\frac{\alpha}{2}}{2\sin\frac{\alpha}{2}\cos\frac{\alpha}{2}} = \frac{1}{2\cos\frac{\alpha}{2}}.$$

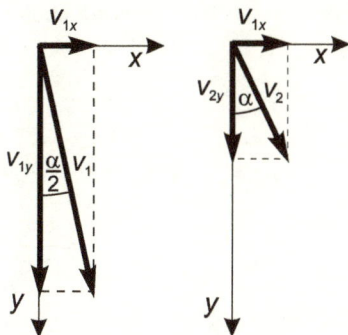

The potential difference between the lattices should decrease the velocity from v_1 to v_2. According to the work-kinetic energy theorem:

$$eV = \frac{1}{2}mv_2^2 - \frac{1}{2}mv_1^2,$$

from which the potential difference between the lattices is:

$$V = \frac{m}{2e}(v_2^2 - v_1^2) = \frac{mv_1^2}{2e}\left[\left(\frac{v_2}{v_1}\right)^2 - 1\right] = V_0\left(\frac{1}{4\cos^2\frac{\alpha}{2}} - 1\right) =$$

$$= 60000\,\text{V}\left(\frac{1}{4\cos^2 15°} - 1\right) = -43923\,\text{V}$$

This is the potential of the second lattice relative to the first (the charge of the electron is negative).

Solution of Problem 229. a) Due to the nature of force (central and repulsive) acting on the moving charge, its path can only be a hyperbola.

According to the work-kinetic energy theorem, the work done by the electric field is equal to the change in the particle's kinetic energy. As the particle's initial position is at infinity, the work done by the electric field is the negative of the particle's potential energy at the point of its closest approach, thus:

$$-k\cdot\frac{qQ}{r} = \frac{1}{2}mv^2 - \frac{1}{2}mv_0^2, \tag{1}$$

where r is the smallest separation and $k = 9\cdot10^9\,\text{Nm}^2/\text{C}$.

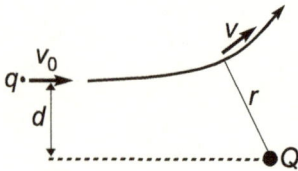

As the force acting on the moving particle is central, the angular momentum of this particle defined with respect to point Q is constant. Assuming that the mass is constant, the equation simplifies to:

$$d \cdot v_0 = r \cdot v. \tag{2}$$

Solving equation (2) for v and substituting it into equation (1), we obtain:

$$\frac{mv_0^2}{2} \cdot r^2 - kqQ \cdot r - \frac{mv_0^2 d^2}{2} = 0. \tag{3}$$

The solution of the equation is:

$$r = \frac{kqQ}{mv_0^2} + \sqrt{\left(\frac{qQk}{mv_0^2}\right)^2 + d^2}$$

Substituting known values gives:

$$r = \frac{9 \cdot 10^9 \, \frac{\text{N m}^2}{\text{C}^2} \cdot 10^{-7} \, \text{C} \cdot 10^{-5} \, \text{C}}{10^{-5} \, \text{kg} \cdot 4 \cdot 10^4 \, \frac{\text{m}^2}{\text{s}^2}} + \sqrt{\left(\frac{9 \cdot 10^9 \, \frac{\text{N m}^2}{\text{C}^2} \cdot 10^{-7} \, \text{C} \cdot 10^{-5} \, \text{C}}{10^{-5} \, \text{kg} \cdot 4 \cdot 10^4 \, \frac{\text{m}^2}{\text{s}^2}}\right)^2 + 0.01 \, \text{m}^2} =$$

$$= 0.125 \, \text{m}.$$

Using this result, we get that the minimum value of the velocity of the moving particle is:

$$v = \frac{d}{r} \cdot v_0 = \frac{0.1 \, \text{m}}{0.125 \, \text{m}} \cdot 200 \, \frac{\text{m}}{\text{s}} = 160 \, \frac{\text{m}}{\text{s}}.$$

b) Let point A be the vertex of the hyperbola, which is its closest point to the fixed charge.

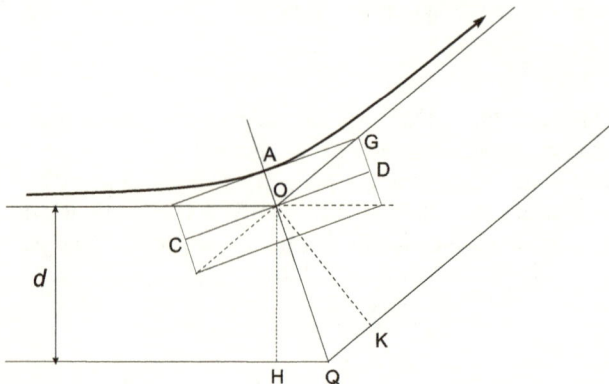

Let point O be the centre of the hyperbola, which lies on segment AQ. This is the point where the lines of directions of the moving particle's initial and final velocities (or the asymptotes) intersect each other. Distances OA and OQ are the length of the semitransverse axis and focal distance of the hyperbola respectively. Triangles OHQ and OGA are congruent, therefore $OD = OH = d$ is the semiconjugate axis of the hyperbola. The focal length can be expressed as $OQ = \sqrt{AO^2 + d^2}$, while the smallest separation (r) is given by the formula $AO + \sqrt{AO^2 + d^2}$. Therefore in case of an arbitrary initial speed v_0, the semiconjugate axis of the hyperbola is d, while its semitransverse axis is:

$$OA = \frac{kqQ}{mv_0^2}.$$

The asymptotes of the hyperbola will be perpendicular to each other if the semiconjugate and semitransverse axes are equal:

$$d = \frac{kqQ}{mv_0^2} = \frac{9 \cdot 10^9 \, \frac{\mathrm{N\,m^2}}{\mathrm{C^2}} \cdot 10^{-7} \, \mathrm{C} \cdot 10^{-15} \, \mathrm{C}}{10^{-5} \, \mathrm{kg} \cdot 4 \cdot 10^4 \, \frac{\mathrm{m^2}}{\mathrm{s^2}}} = 0.0225 \, \mathrm{m}.$$

If now distance d is changed to its new value, equation (3) gives $r = 0.05432$ m for the smallest separation and equation (2) gives $v = 82.842$ m/s for the final velocity of the moving particle.

Solution of Problem 230. When the anode current starts, the energy of the photon is equal to the work function:

$$\phi = hf = 6.63 \cdot 10^{-34} \, \mathrm{Js} \cdot 3 \cdot 10^{14} \, \frac{1}{\mathrm{s}} \approx 2 \cdot 10^{-19} \, \mathrm{J}.$$

In the second case the frequency of the applied light is:

$$f = \frac{c}{\lambda} = \frac{3 \cdot 10^8 \, \frac{\mathrm{m}}{\mathrm{s}}}{425 \cdot 10^{-9} \, \mathrm{m}} = 7 \cdot 10^{14} \, \frac{1}{\mathrm{s}}.$$

The kinetic energy of the electrons leaving the cathode:

$$hf = \phi + E_{\mathrm{kin}} \quad \rightarrow \quad E_{\mathrm{kin}} = hf - \phi,$$

with numerical values

$$E_{\mathrm{kin}} = 6.63 \cdot 10^{-34} \, \mathrm{Js} \cdot 7 \cdot 10^{14} \, \frac{1}{\mathrm{s}} - 2 \cdot 10^{-19} \, \mathrm{J} =$$

$$= 4.641 \cdot 10^{-19} \, \mathrm{JJ} - 2 \cdot 10^{-19} \, \mathrm{J} = 2.641 \cdot 10^{-19} \, \mathrm{J}.$$

While the electrons emerge from the cathode and move to the anode, the cathode gains positive charge and the anode gains negative charge, this way a 'counter-field' is created, which stops the electrons before they reach the anode after a sufficiently long time. The counter-voltage created across the capacitor can be measured between the cathode and the anode as well. This electric field does eV of work per electron to increase the potential energy of the electrons, which according to the work–kinetic energy theorem ($W = \Delta E_{\text{kin}}$) is equal to the change in the kinetic energy of the electron:

$$eV = 0 - E_{\text{m}},$$

with numerical values:

$$-1.6 \cdot 10^{-19} \ \text{C} \cdot V = -2.641 \cdot 10^{-19} \ \text{J},$$

from here, the potential of the cathode relative to the anode is:

$$V = \frac{-2.641 \cdot 10^{-19} \ \text{J}}{-1.6 \cdot 10^{-19} \ \text{C}} = 1.65 \ \text{V}.$$

The charge on the capacitor is

$$Q = CV = 10^{-9} \ \text{F} \cdot 1.65 \ \text{V} = 1.65 \cdot 10^{-12} \ \text{C}.$$

The number of electrons on the capacitor is

$$n = \frac{Q}{e} = \frac{-1.65 \cdot 10^{-12} \ \text{C}}{-1.6 \cdot 10^{-19} \ \text{C}} = 1.03 \cdot 10^{7}.$$

(The inherent capacitance of the photocell is neglected.)

Solution of Problem 231. Due to the symmetry of the arrangement, we can consider only one of the two pendulums. (Because of the equal masses, the position of the two threads is symmetric with respect to the reflection against a vertical line passing through the suspension point.) Let us write down the conditions for the equilibrium of forces acting for example on the left sphere, in horizontal as well as in vertical direction.

When the spheres are submerged into paraffin, the following forces are acting on the spheres:

the force due to gravity, the buoyant force, the Coulomb force and the force exerted by the thread. (We assume that the paraffin tank is large enough, so that the effect of the surface polarization charges can be neglected, and we also suppose that the threads have negligible width.) According to the figure, the force balance equations are:

in horizontal direction:

$$\frac{1}{4\pi\varepsilon_0\varepsilon_r} \cdot \frac{Q^2}{4l^2\sin^2\alpha_P} - K_P\sin\alpha_P = 0,$$

in vertical direction::

$$\varrho V g - \varrho_P g V - K_P\cos\alpha_P = 0.$$

Rearranging the first equation and dividing it with the second one, we obtain that:

$$\frac{Q^2}{16\pi\varepsilon_0\varepsilon_r l^2(\varrho - \varrho_P)\cdot Vg\cdot\sin^2\alpha_P} = \tan\alpha_P \tag{1}$$

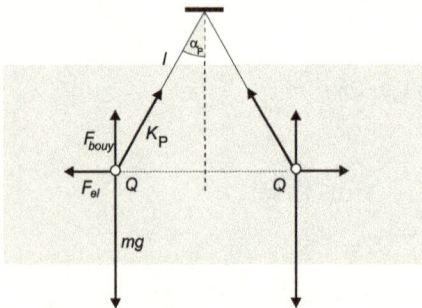

Without paraffin the structure of the first equation does not change, but since in the air (or practically, in vacuum) $\varepsilon_r = 1$, the relative permittivity can be omitted, and different letters should be used for the angle and for the force of the thread. In the second equation the buoyant force is omitted, so in the air the force balance equations are:
in horizontal direction:

$$\frac{1}{4\pi\varepsilon_0} \cdot \frac{Q^2}{4l^2 \sin^2 \alpha_A} - K_A \sin \alpha_A = 0,$$

in vertical direction:

$$\varrho V g - K_A \cos \alpha_A = 0.$$

Again rearranging the equations and taking their quotient, we get that:

$$\frac{Q^2}{16\pi\varepsilon_0 l^2 \varrho V g \cdot \sin^2 \alpha_A} = \tan \alpha_A. \tag{2}$$

Dividing the two equations (1) and (2) for the tangents of the angles in paraffin and in air, after cancellation, we obtain:

$$\frac{\tan \alpha_A}{\tan \alpha_P} = \frac{Q^2}{16\pi\varepsilon_0 l^2 \varrho V g \cdot \sin^2 \alpha_A} \cdot \frac{16\pi\varepsilon_0 \varepsilon_r l^2 (\varrho - \varrho_P) \cdot V g \cdot \sin^2 \alpha_P}{Q^2} =$$

$$= \frac{\varepsilon_r (\varrho - \varrho_P) \cdot \sin^2 \alpha_P}{\varrho \cdot \sin^2 \alpha_A}.$$

Multiplying this equation with the denominator of the right hand side:

$$\varrho \cdot \frac{\tan \alpha_A}{\tan \alpha_P} \sin^2 \alpha_A = \varepsilon_r \varrho \cdot \sin^2 \alpha_P - \varepsilon_r \varrho_P \cdot \sin^2 \alpha_P.$$

We collect the terms containing the unknown density to the left hand side of the equation, and use the distributive law of multiplication:

$$\left(\frac{\tan \alpha_A}{\tan \alpha_P} \sin^2 \alpha_A - \varepsilon_r \sin^2 \alpha_P \right) \cdot \varrho = -\varepsilon_r \varrho_P \cdot \sin^2 \alpha_P.$$

Finally, expressing the density of the spheres, we get:

$$\varrho = \varrho_P \cdot \frac{\varepsilon_r \sin^2 \alpha_P}{\varepsilon_r \sin^2 \alpha_P - \frac{\tan \alpha_A}{\tan \alpha_P} \sin^2 \alpha_A} =$$

$$= 800 \ \frac{\text{kg}}{\text{m}^3} \cdot \frac{2 \cdot \sin^2 30°}{2 \cdot \sin^2 30° - \frac{\tan 35°}{\tan 30°} \sin^2 35°} = 3960.3 \ \frac{\text{kg}}{\text{m}^3}.$$

Solution of Problem 232. If time is measured from the start of the motion, in time t the insulator slab penetrates to a distance of

$$x = \frac{a_0}{2} t^2$$

from the place of entry. At this time, the plates practically form two capacitors connected in parallel: one with area cx and capacitance C_1, which is filled by the insulator and another one with area $c(c-x)$ and capacitance C_2, which is filled with air. Their capacitances are

$$C_1 = \frac{\varepsilon_0 \varepsilon_r cx}{d} \quad \text{and} \quad C_2 = \frac{\varepsilon_0 c(c-x)}{d}.$$

The equivalent capacitance and the charge collected on the plates as function of time are

$$C = C_1 + C_2 = \frac{\varepsilon_0 c}{d}[c + (\varepsilon_r - 1)x] = \frac{\varepsilon_0 c}{d}\left[c + (\varepsilon_r - 1)\frac{a_0}{2}t^2\right],$$

and

$$Q = \frac{\varepsilon_0 c}{d}\left[c + (\varepsilon_r - 1)\frac{a_0}{2}t^2\right]U = \frac{\varepsilon_0 c^2}{d}U + \frac{\varepsilon_0(\varepsilon_r - 1)ca_0 U}{2d}\cdot t^2,$$

respectively. From the same train of thought it can be seen that as the insulator penetrates between the plates by Δx, the charge of the capacitor changes by

$$\Delta Q = \Delta C U = \left(\frac{\varepsilon_0 \varepsilon_r c\Delta x}{d} - \frac{\varepsilon_0 c\Delta x}{d}\right)U = \frac{\varepsilon_0(\varepsilon_r - 1)cU}{d}\Delta x.$$

This charge is delivered by the emf source, so the current in the wires leading to the capacitor is

$$i = \frac{\Delta Q}{\Delta t} = \frac{\varepsilon_0(\varepsilon_r - 1)cU}{d}\cdot\frac{\Delta x}{\Delta t} = \frac{\varepsilon_0(\varepsilon_r - 1)cU}{d}\cdot v = \frac{\varepsilon_0(\varepsilon_r - 1)cU}{d}a_0 t,$$

with numerical values

$$i = \frac{8.85\cdot 10^{-12}\,\frac{\text{A s}}{\text{V m}}\cdot(101-1)\cdot 200\,\text{mm}\cdot 2\frac{\text{m}}{\text{s}^2}\cdot 100\,\text{V}}{2\,\text{mm}}\cdot t = 1.77\cdot 10^{-5}\frac{\text{A}}{\text{s}}\cdot t,$$

that is, the current increases linearly from zero.

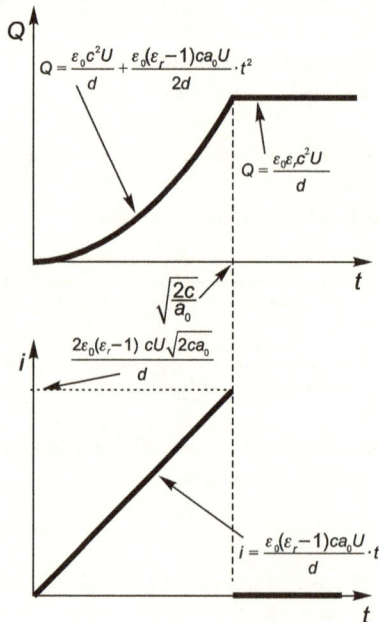

When the insulator fills the space between the plates completely, the capacitance of the capacitor does not change any more, the charge on the plates remains constant as well, the charging current ceases. This happens at time instant

$$t = \sqrt{\frac{2c}{a_0}} = \sqrt{\frac{2 \cdot 0.2\,\text{m}}{2\frac{\text{m}}{\text{s}^2}}} = 0.447\,\text{s}.$$

Until this moment the charge on the plates and the current are monotonously increasing in time, so they reach their maximum value exactly at this moment:

$$Q_{\text{max}} = \frac{\varepsilon_0 \varepsilon_{\text{r}} c^2 U}{d} = \frac{8.85 \cdot 10^{-12}\frac{\text{As}}{\text{Vm}} \cdot 101 \cdot (0.2\,\text{m})^2 \cdot 100\,\text{V}}{2 \cdot 10^{-3}\,\text{m}} = 1.79\mu\,\text{C}.$$

$$i_{\text{max}} = \frac{\varepsilon_0 (\varepsilon_{\text{r}} - 1) c U \sqrt{2ca_0}}{d} =$$

$$= \frac{8.85 \cdot 10^{-12}\frac{\text{As}}{\text{Vm}} \cdot (101 - 1) \cdot 0.2\,\text{m} \cdot 100\,\text{V} \sqrt{2 \cdot 0.2\,\text{m} \cdot 2\frac{\text{m}}{\text{s}^2}}}{2 \cdot 10^{-3}\,\text{m}} = 7.92\mu\,\text{A}.$$

Solution of Problem 233. The given data guarantee that the insulating plate can be considered in both directions as infinitely large since the distance of the sphere d is much less than the size of the square L. It means that with a good approximation the electric field of the plate is homogeneous in the investigated region. Using this (well-founded) assumption, the electric field of the charged plate can easily be determined with the help of Gauss' law (Maxwell's I. equation).

Gauss' law states that

$$\oint_A E \Delta A \cos\alpha = \frac{1}{\varepsilon_0} \sum_V Q.$$

Applying it to a thin rectangular box around the plate (and neglecting the inhomogeneity of the electric field at the lateral faces of the box), the constant E can be carried out of the sum, $\cos\alpha = 1$ and the surface area of the box is

$$\oint_A \Delta A = 2A = 2L^2.$$

Expressing this area with the distance d, and writing it, along with the total charge of the square plate, into Gauss' law, we get that:

$$E2 \cdot (100d)^2 = \frac{1}{\varepsilon_0} 100Q.$$

This electric field is perpendicular to the plate, so the components of the electric field vector, expressed in terms of the charge of the sphere Q and the distance d are:

$$E_x^{\text{plate}} = 5 \cdot 10^{-3} \frac{Q}{\varepsilon_0 d^2}, \qquad E_y^{\text{plate}} = 0, \qquad E_z^{\text{plate}} = 0.$$

Now let us investigate the electric field near the sphere. The electric field of the charged sphere inside the sphere is zero. Outside of the sphere, however, the electric field is similar to the field of a point charge Q placed at the centre of the sphere. In addition, the homogeneous electric field of the square plate penetrates into the insulating sphere so the net electric field inside the sphere is:

$$E_x = 5 \cdot 10^{-3} \frac{Q}{\varepsilon_0 d^2}, \ E_y = 0, \ E_z = 0.$$

At the given point outside the sphere the net electric field is obtained by superposing the field of the plate and that of the sphere, according to the figure.

(In the figure the lengths of the electric field vectors are not properly scaled, since in reality at the investigated point the field due to the plate is 22 times smaller than the field of the sphere. The directions, however, are properly indicated.)

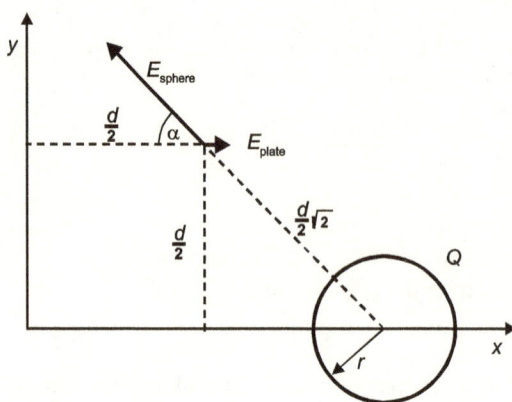

The electric field due to the (uniformly distributed) charge Q on the sphere at the point $\left(\frac{d}{2}, \frac{d}{2}, 0\right)$ is:

$$E_{\text{sphere}} = \frac{1}{4\pi\varepsilon_0} \cdot \frac{Q}{\left(\frac{d}{2}\sqrt{2}\right)^2} = \frac{Q}{2\pi\varepsilon_0 d^2} = 0.159 \frac{Q}{\varepsilon_0 d^2}.$$

The components of the net electric field are:

$$E_x = E_x^{\text{plate}} - E_x^{\text{sphere}} \cos 45° = 5 \cdot 10^{-3} \frac{Q}{\varepsilon_0 d^2} - 0.159 \frac{Q}{\varepsilon_0 d^2} \cos 45° = -0.107 \frac{Q}{\varepsilon_0 d^2},$$

$$E_y = E_y^{\text{sphere}} \sin 45° = 0.159 \frac{Q}{\varepsilon_0 d^2} \sin 45° = 0.113 \frac{Q}{\varepsilon_0 d^2}.$$

The magnitude of the net electric field is:

$$E = \sqrt{E_x^2 + E_y^2} = 0.156 \frac{Q}{\varepsilon_0 d^2},$$

and its angle relative to the x axis is:

$$\varphi = \text{arctg}\, \frac{E_y}{E_x} = \text{arctg}\, \frac{0.113}{0.107} = 46.6°.$$

Solution of Problem 234. Originally the potential differences across the capacitors are

$$V_A = V_B = \frac{V}{2},$$

their charges are

$$Q_A = Q_B = \frac{CV}{2},\tag{1}$$

and their energies are

$$W_A = W_B = \frac{1}{2}\frac{Q^2}{C} = \frac{1}{8}CV^2.\tag{2}$$

a) Let us move the plates of capacitor B. Then $C_B = C/2$. The voltage of the battery does not change but charge moves from the plates into the battery. The charges on capacitors connected in series are obviously equal, let Q' stand for this new charge. With this used for potential differences, the following relationship is acquired:

$$V = V_A + V_B = \frac{Q'}{C} + \frac{Q'}{C/2},$$

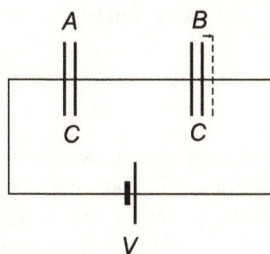

from which the magnitude of the new charge can be determined:

$$Q' = \frac{CV}{3},\tag{3}$$

The new energies are

$$W'_A = \frac{1}{2}\frac{Q'^2}{C} = \frac{1}{18}CV^2,\tag{4}$$

$$W'_B = \frac{1}{2}\frac{Q'^2}{C/2} = \frac{1}{9}CV^2.\tag{5}$$

Based on (2), (4) and (5), the changes in the energies of the capacitors are

$$\Delta W'_A = W'_A - W_A = \frac{1}{18}CV^2 - \frac{1}{8}CV^2 = -\frac{5}{72}CV^2,$$

$$\Delta W'_B = W'_B - W_B = \frac{1}{9}CV^2 - \frac{1}{8}CV^2 = -\frac{1}{72}CV^2.$$

Based on (1) and (3), the change in the energy of the battery is

$$\Delta W'_{\text{bat}} = -V\Delta Q_{\text{cap}} = V(Q - Q') = \frac{1}{2}CV^2 - \frac{1}{3}CV^2 = \frac{1}{6}CV^2.$$

The change in the energy of the system is

$$\Delta W'_{\text{system}} = \Delta W_{\text{bat}} + \Delta W'_A + \Delta W'_B = \left(\frac{1}{6} - \frac{1}{72} - \frac{5}{72}\right)CV^2 = \frac{1}{12}CV^2.$$

So the total energy of the system increased.

The change in the energy of the system is

$$\Delta W = -\Delta W_{\text{system}} = -\frac{1}{12}CV^2.$$

The work that was required to increase the separation of the plates of the capacitor was done at the expense of this energy.

[Remark: This can be understood by considering the following:

The work done by us is the work done by a changing force, because in the case of capacitor B both the charge and the potential difference across it change. So the work is given by an integral.

The work done by us is

$$W = \int_{d}^{2d} F \mathrm{d}x,$$

where F is the magnitude of the force between the plates and x is the relevant separation of the plates, which changes from d to $2d$. The electrostatic force that acts on the plates of the capacitors – as we know – is half of the product of the resultant electric field and the charge on the disc:

$$F = \frac{1}{2}QE,$$

where based on Gauss' law, the magnitude of the electric field is

$$E = \frac{1}{\varepsilon_0} \cdot \frac{Q}{A}.$$

(Due to the constant velocity) the force exerted by us in the direction of displacement on the plate of capacitor B that is pulled by us has the same magnitude as the electrostatic force that acts on it:

$$F_B = \frac{1}{2}Q_B \cdot \frac{1}{\varepsilon_0} \frac{Q_B}{A} = \frac{1}{2}Q_B^2 \cdot \frac{1}{\varepsilon_0 A} = \frac{1}{2} \frac{C_B^2 V_B^2}{\varepsilon_0 A} \tag{I.}$$

When the separation between the plates of capacitor B is increased, both its capacity and the potential difference across it change. Let us describe this two-variable function as a one-variable function of the distance between the plates. Let x stand for the changing distance between the plates of the capacitor. With it, the capacitance of capacitor B is:

$$C_B = \frac{\varepsilon_0 A}{x}.$$

The (changing) charges on the two capacitors connected in series are equal, so the potential differences across them are

$$V_A = \frac{Q}{C_A} \quad \text{and} \quad V_B = \frac{Q}{C_B}.$$

Their ratio is

$$\frac{V_A}{V_B} = \frac{C_B}{C_A}, \quad \text{that is,} \quad V_A = V_B \frac{C_B}{C_A}.$$

The sum of the two potential differences is constant and is equal to the voltage of the battery

$$V = V_A + V_B = V_B \frac{C_B}{C_A} + V_B = V_B \frac{C_A + C_B}{C_A}.$$

From this the changing potential difference across capacitor B expressed with the constant voltage across the battery is

$$V_B = V \frac{C_A}{C_A + C_B} = V \frac{1}{1 + C_B/C_A} = V \frac{1}{1 + \frac{\varepsilon_0 A}{x} \cdot \frac{d}{\varepsilon_0 A}} = V \frac{1}{1 + \frac{d}{x}} = V \frac{x}{x + d}. \qquad \text{(II.)}$$

With it the force pulling the plate of capacitor B as function of x based on (I.) and (II.) is

$$F_B = \frac{1}{2} \frac{C_B^2}{\varepsilon_0 A} \cdot \frac{V^2 x^2}{(x+d)^2} = \frac{1}{2} \frac{\varepsilon_0^2 A^2}{\varepsilon_0 A \cdot x^2} \cdot \frac{V^2 x^2}{(x+d)^2} = \frac{1}{2} \varepsilon_0 A \frac{V^2}{(x+d)^2}.$$

The work done by us is the integral of force as function of displacement:

$$W = \int\limits_{d}^{2d} F_B \mathrm{d}x = \frac{1}{2} \varepsilon_0 A V^2 \int\limits_{d}^{2d} \frac{\mathrm{d}x}{(x+d)^2}.$$

The integration is carried out with the following substitution: $(x+d) = z$ and $\mathrm{d}x = \mathrm{d}z$. Then the integral becomes

$$\int \frac{\mathrm{d}z}{z^2} = -\frac{1}{z} = -\frac{1}{x+d}.$$

Using this, our work is

$$W = \frac{1}{2} \varepsilon_0 A V^2 \left[-\frac{1}{x+d} \right]_d^{2d} = \frac{1}{2} \varepsilon_0 A V^2 \left[-\frac{1}{x+2d} - \left(-\frac{1}{x+d} \right) \right] =$$

$$= \frac{1}{2} \varepsilon_0 A V^2 \left(\frac{1}{2d} - \frac{1}{3d} \right) = \frac{1}{2} \frac{\varepsilon_0 A}{d} V^2 \frac{3-2}{6} = \frac{1}{12} \frac{\varepsilon_0 A}{d} V^2 = \frac{1}{12} C V^2,$$

as we have already stated.]

    b) Let us insert an insulator into capacitor A. Then according to the given condition $C_A = 2C$. For potential differences:

$$V = \frac{Q''}{2C} + \frac{Q''}{C}, \qquad \text{from which} \qquad Q'' = \frac{2}{3} CV.$$

The energies of the capacitors are

$$W_A'' = \frac{1}{2} \frac{Q''^2}{2C} = \frac{1}{9} C V^2.$$

$$W_B'' = \frac{1}{2} \frac{Q''^2}{C} = \frac{2}{9} C V^2,$$

the changes in the energies of the capacitors are

$$\Delta W_A'' = W_A'' - W_A = -\frac{1}{72}CV^2,$$

$$\Delta W_B'' = W_B'' - W_B = \frac{7}{72}CV^2,$$

the change in the energy of the battery is

$$\Delta W_{\text{bat}}'' = V(Q - Q'') = -\frac{1}{6}CV^2,$$

the change in the energy of the system is

$$\Delta W_{\text{system}}'' = \left(-\frac{1}{72} + \frac{7}{72} - \frac{1}{6}\right)CV^2 = -\frac{1}{12}CV^2.$$

The capacitor pulls the insulator in and in the meantime gives $\frac{1}{12}CV^2$ energy to it (which for example in the case of motion with friction is given to the surroundings as heat).

Solution of Problem 235. a) Let us assume that the area of the plates (A) is much greater than the separation (d), i.e. $A \gg d^2$, which means that the electric field between the plates is uniform. Let d be the separation of the plates of the capacitor, V be the potential difference provided by the battery, E be the initial electric field strength in the capacitor. In the initial state, the relation between the potential difference and the field strength is given by the equation:

$$E = \frac{V}{d}.$$

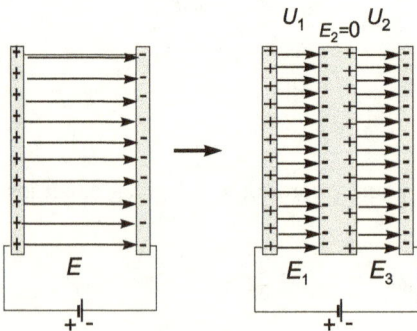

In the fist case the two plates placed inside the capacitor behave like a solid metal block of width $d/3$. Due to the induced charge on the connected plates, the electric field E_2 between them is zero. Since the potential difference provided by the battery remains constant, we have:

$$V = V_1 + V_2 = E_1\frac{d}{3} + E_3\frac{d}{3} = Ed,$$

which yields

$$E_1 + E_3 = 3E. \tag{1}$$

The electric flux between the left and right pair of plates is the same due to the symmetry of the situation:

$$\Psi_1 = \Psi_3,$$

hence

$$E_1 A = E_3 A,$$

thus

$$E_1 = E_3. \tag{2}$$

Substituting equation (2) into equation (1):

$$E_3 + E_3 = 2E_3 = 3E,$$

so the electric field strength in question is:

$$E_1 = E_3 = \frac{3}{2}E = \frac{3}{2} \cdot 600 \,\text{V/m} = 900 \,\text{V/m}.$$

b) This case is much more complicated. Let Q_1, Q_2, Q_3, Q_4, Q_5 and Q_6 be the charges on the surfaces of the plates as shown. Let E_1, E_2 and E_3 be the electric field strengths between the pair of plates moving from left to right. Applying Maxwell's third equation (Faraday's law) to loop $ABCDA$ shown in the figure, we get:

$$\oint \sum V = 0,$$

hence

$$E_2 \frac{d}{2} + E_3 \frac{d}{2} = Ed, \tag{3}$$

since the potential difference provided by the battery, that was Ed initially, remains constant. This yields

$$E_2 + E_3 = 2E, \tag{3a}$$

where E is the initial field strength inside the capacitor.

The additional two plates are connected by a wire, therefore they are equipotential, so the potential differences between the second plate and either the first or the third one is the same. This means that:

$$E_1 \frac{d}{2} = E_2 \frac{d}{2}, \tag{4}$$

hence — considering the directions of the fields — the relation between the electric field vectors is:

$$E_1 = -E_2. \tag{4a}$$

Applying the conservation of charge to the additional two plates, we obtain:

$$Q_1 + Q_4 + Q_5 = 0. \tag{5}$$

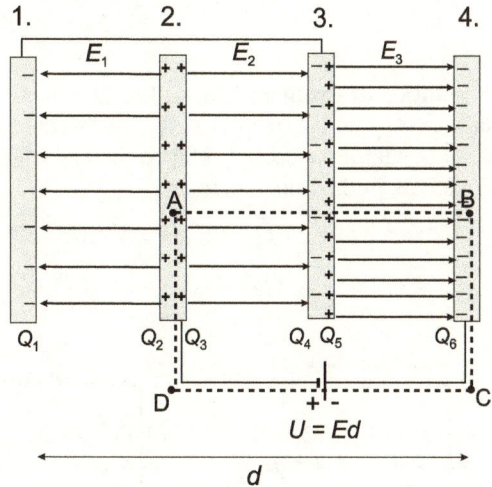

As $|E_1| = |E_2|$, the flux through Q_1 equals the flux through Q_2, hence:

$$E_1 A = E_2 A,$$

so

$$\frac{1}{\varepsilon_0} Q_1 = \frac{1}{\varepsilon_0} Q_4, \tag{6}$$

thus

$$Q_1 = Q_4. \tag{6a}$$

Inserting this into equation (5), we have:

$$2Q_4 + Q_5 = 0,$$

and therefore

$$2Q_4 = -Q_5. \tag{7}$$

The flux through Q_5 is given by:

$$\Psi_3 = E_3 A = \frac{1}{\varepsilon_0} Q_5 = -\frac{1}{\varepsilon_0} 2Q_4 = 2 \cdot \left(-\frac{1}{\varepsilon_0} Q_4\right) = 2 \cdot E_2 A,$$

which yields:

$$E_3 = 2E_2.$$

Inserting this into equation (3a), we get:

$$E_2 + 2E_2 = 2E,$$

thus the field strengths in question are:

$$E_2 = \frac{2}{3} E = \frac{2}{3} \cdot 600 \frac{V}{m} = 400 \frac{V}{m}, \quad \text{and} \quad E_3 = 2E_2 = 2 \cdot 400 \frac{V}{m} = 800 \frac{V}{m},$$

and

$$E_1 = -400 \frac{V}{m}.$$

Solution of Problem 236. a) Let Q denote the absolute value of charge, let data with subscripts 1 and 2, respectively, refer to the capacitors on the left and on the right, and let data with no subscript refer to the capacitor dropped onto them. The charges of the capacitors in the initial state are

$$Q_1 = C_1 V_1 = 2 \cdot 10^{-6} \, \mu F \cdot 150 \, V = 3 \cdot 10^{-4} \, C,$$

$$Q_2 = C_2 V_2 = 3 \cdot 10^{-6} \, \mu F \cdot 120 \, V = 3.6 \cdot 10^{-4} \, C.$$

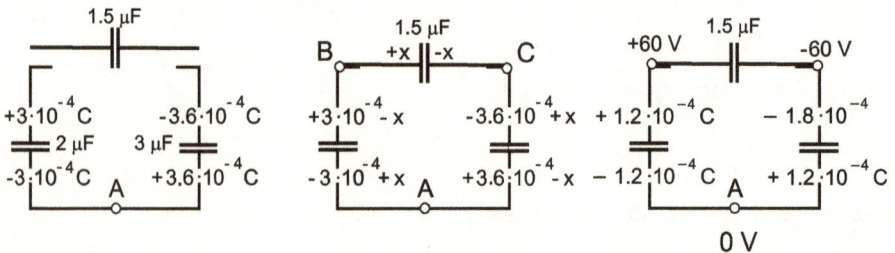

Let x be the charge on the dropped capacitor when it has connected to the free ends of the other two capacitors. The total charge of each of the three conductors containing the points marked A, B and C in the figure stays constant since they are insulated from one another. Thus the charge on the upper plate of capacitor 1 is $Q_1 - x$, the charge on its lower plate is $-Q_1 + x$, the charge on the upper plate of capacitor 2 is $-Q_2 + x$, and the charge on its lower plate is $Q_2 - x$.

The potential difference of point B relative to point A, as calculated across the capacitor (1) on the left, is

$$V_{BA} = V_1 = \frac{Q_1'}{C_1} = \frac{3 \cdot 10^{-4} - x}{2 \cdot 10^{-6}} \text{ V},$$

and the same potential difference calculated through the other two capacitors, that is, along the path BCA is

$$V_{BCA} = V_{BC} + V_{CA} = V + V_2 = \frac{x}{C} + \frac{-Q_2}{C_2} = \frac{x}{1.5 \cdot 10^{-6} \text{ F}} - \frac{3.6 \cdot 10^{-4} \text{ C} - x}{3 \cdot 10^{-6} \text{ F}}.$$

Since the electrostatic field is conservative, these two voltages are equal:

$$\frac{3 \cdot 10^{-4} \text{ C} - x}{2 \cdot 10^{-6} \text{ F}} = \frac{x}{1.5 \cdot 10^{-6} \text{ F}} - \frac{3.6 \cdot 10^{-4} \text{ C} - x}{3 \cdot 10^{-6} \text{ F}}.$$

Multiplied by the common denominator $6 \cdot 10^{-6} \text{F}$:

$$9 \cdot 10^{-4} \text{ C} - 3x = 4x - 7.2 \cdot 10^{-4} \text{ C} - 2x,$$

and hence the charge of the dropped capacitor is

$$x = \frac{16.2 \text{ C}}{9} = 1.8 \cdot 10^{-4} \text{ C}.$$

x can be used to determine the potential difference across each capacitor:

$$V_1 = V_{AB} = \frac{3 \cdot 10^{-4} \text{ C} - 1.8 \cdot 10^{-4} \text{ C}}{2 \cdot 10^{-6} \text{ F}} = +60 \text{ V}.$$

$$V_2 = V_{CA} = \frac{-3.6 \cdot 10^{-4} \text{ C} + 1.8 \cdot 10^{-4} \text{ C}}{3 \cdot 10^{-6} \text{ F}} = -60 \text{ V},$$

and the potential difference of the capacitor dropped onto them is

$$V = V_{BC} = \frac{1.8 \cdot 10^{-4} \text{ C}}{1.5 \cdot 10^{-6} \text{ F}} = +120 \text{ V}.$$

b) It is easy to see that the amount of charge passing through the point A is the charge lost by capacitor 2 and gained by capacitor 1, that is,

$$\Delta Q = x = 1.8 \cdot 10^{-4} \text{ coulombs}$$

passed from 2 to 1, which means towards the left.

Solution of Problem 237. It is known that on the surface of the Earth, whose radius is R, mass is M and density is ϱ, the gravitational acceleration can be given in the following form:

$$g = G\frac{M}{R^2} = G\frac{\varrho 4R^3\pi}{3R^2} = \frac{4}{3}G\varrho R\pi. \tag{1}$$

In order to solve the problem, we should determine the magnitude of gravitational acceleration on a disc with a very large radius, a thickness of H and a density of ϱ_m (far from the rim of the disc). We succeed relatively easily if we make use of the analogy between the force laws of electrostatic and gravitational interaction.

The electrostatic force acting on a point-like, stationary electric charge and the gravitational force acting between point-like bodies are of similar nature:

$$\mathbf{F} = -G\frac{m_1 m_2}{r^3}\cdot\mathbf{r}, \qquad \text{and} \qquad \mathbf{F} = k\frac{q_1 q_2}{r^3}\cdot\mathbf{r},$$

where $k = 1/4\pi\varepsilon_0$. It can be seen that the corresponding quantities are m mass ('gravitational charge') and q electric charge, G gravitational constant and $1/4\pi\varepsilon_0$ and $g = F/m$ gravitational acceleration and $E = F/q$ electric field. Therefore, if we determine the electric field of a disc of infinite radius and homogeneous charge density outside the disc, then through the substitution of the corresponding quantities we also get the gravitational acceleration in the case of a mass distribution having a similar geometry.

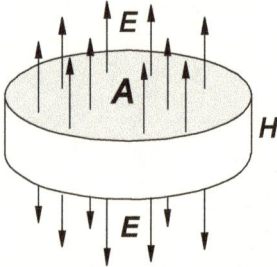

The electric equivalent is determined using Gauss' law:

$$N_E = \frac{1}{\varepsilon_0}\sum q,$$

where the electric 'source intensity' $N_E = E2A$. If the electric charge density is ϱ_q, then the total charge enclosed by a closed measuring surface is $\sum q = \varrho_q AH$, so

$$2EA = \frac{1}{\varepsilon_0}\varrho_q AH,$$

from which the electric field is

$$E = \frac{1}{\varepsilon_0}\cdot\frac{\varrho_q H}{2}. \tag{2}$$

So the gravitational acceleration gained from (2) through the replacement of the corresponding quantities is

$$g = 2\pi G\frac{\varrho_m H}{2}.$$

This should be equal to the gravitational acceleration that is measured on the surface of the Earth regarded to be uniform, which based on (1) is

$$g_{\text{sphere}} = g_{\text{disc}} = G\frac{4R\pi\varrho_m}{3} = 4\pi\frac{\varrho_m H}{2},$$

from which the thickness of the disc of the 'flat Earth' is

$$H = \frac{2}{3}R = \frac{2}{3} \cdot 6370\,\text{km} = 4250\,\text{km}.$$

Solution of Problem 238. Consider a whole cylinder of uniform volume charge density first. The electric field as a function of the distance from the axis inside the cylinder can be determined from Gauss' law, which states

$$\oint_A E \Delta A = \frac{1}{\varepsilon_0} \sum_V \varrho \Delta V.$$

Using symmetry considerations, it is easy to find a closed surface that the field lines normally intersect everywhere, and on which the intersections are distributed uniformly. Thus the division of the surface into small elements and the adding up of their contributions can both be avoided. Let us apply Gauss'law to the test surface of cylindrical symmetry with height h and radius x:

$$E \cdot 2x\pi \cdot h = \frac{1}{\varepsilon_0} \varrho x^2 \pi h,$$

where $2x\pi \cdot h = A$ is the area of the test surface (without the bases of the test cylinder, since those are not intersected by any field lines), and $x^2 \pi \cdot h = V$ is the volume bounded by the surface. The product of the volume and the charge density is the total charge surrounded by the surface, and the left-hand side of the equation is the total electric flux crossing the surface. Thus the magnitude of the electric field inside the cylinder is expressed in terms of the distance from the axis as follows:

$$E = \frac{\varrho}{2\varepsilon_0} x,$$

that is, the electric field increases linearly with the radius, and its direction is radial.

From the electrical point of view, the effect of the bore in the solid cylinder could also be achieved without cutting out a narrower cylinder: Instead, that part could be given a charge density equal and opposite to that of the original cylinder, to make the resultant charge zero in that part of the volume. Then the electric field in the bore can be obtained as the superposition of the electric fields of the two cylinders of parallel axes ($\vec{E} = \vec{E}_1 + \vec{E}_2$). With the notations of the figure:

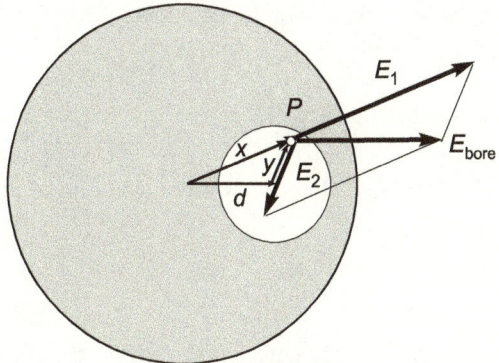

$$\vec{E}_{\text{bore}} = \frac{\varrho}{2\varepsilon_0} \cdot \vec{x} - \frac{\varrho}{2\varepsilon_0} \cdot \vec{y} = \frac{\varrho}{2\varepsilon_0} (\vec{x} - \vec{y}).$$

Notice that the vector difference $\vec{x} - \vec{y}$ is equal to the vector $\vec{d}$ connecting the axes of the two cylinders, therefore the electric field vector is parallel to $\vec{d}$ everywhere in the bore, that is, the electric field is uniform in the bore:

$$\vec{E}_{\text{bore}} = \frac{\varrho}{2\varepsilon_0} \cdot \vec{d}.$$

It is worth noting that this is not only true for a cylinder. The field is also uniform in a spherical cavity inside a sphere. It follows from the electric field being proportional to the radius, which is true in a uniformly charged sphere, too.

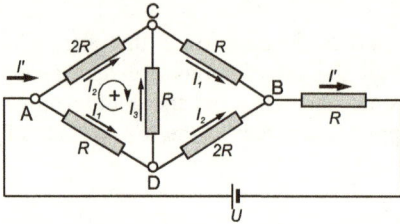

Solution of Problem 239. Suppose that the internal resistance of the voltage supply is negligible, thus the terminal voltage across the voltage supply is independent of the load. In the first case the potential at points C and D are equal, thus the resistor between these points can be taken out without changing the equivalent resistance of the system, or points C and D can even be shortcircuited. Thus the equivalent resistance of the resistors between points A and B is equal to the equivalent resistance of two resistors, both having resistances of $2R$, which are connected in parallel, which is R. This is connected in series with another resistor of resistance R, thus the equivalent resistance of the system is $2R$, and applying Ohm's law the current in the main branch is

$$I = \frac{V}{2R}.$$

If the resistances of the two diagonally opposite resistors are doubled, the symmetry which made the potential at points C and D equal is ceased thus current will flow in the bridge as well. Using the notations of the figure Kirchhoff's loop rule for the indicated loop is the following:

$$2RI_2 - RI_1 - RI_3 = 0,$$

and cancelling R:

$$2I_2 - I_1 - I_3 = 0.$$

Kirchhoff's junction rule for the junctions at points A and D are:

$$I' - I_1 - I_2 = 0$$

and

$$I_1 - I_2 - I_3 = 0.$$

the solution of the equation system for the currents in the branches:

$$I_1 = \frac{3}{5}I', \qquad I_2 = \frac{2}{5}I', \qquad I_3 = \frac{1}{5}I'.$$

Thus the voltage between the points A and B is:

$$2RI_2 + RI_1 = \frac{7}{5}RI'.$$

the equivalent resistance between the points A and B is: $R_{AB} = \frac{7}{5}R$, which is connected in series with a resistor of resistance R, thus the equivalent resistance of the whole circuit is: $R_e = \frac{7}{5}R + R = \frac{12}{5}R$, therefore the current in the second case is:

$$I' = \frac{5V}{12R}.$$

The asked ratio of the currents is:

$$\frac{I'}{I} = \frac{5}{6}.$$

8.2 Direct current

Solution of Problem 240. The figure shows the direction of the changes in potentials of the batteries, which are given. The circuit has three branches, and the currents in these branches I_1, I_2, and I are unknown. The directions of the currents can be drawn arbitrarily. They are denoted by arrows and are all directed towards junction B, for example. Thus when applying the junction rule, all of them will be written with a positive sign. In the circuit there are two independent loops and one independent junction. (If the number of junctions is n then the number of independent junctions is $n-1$. The loops are independent if there exists at least one branch in each loop which isn't any other loops.) If Kirchoff's laws are applied to these loops, the three unknowns can be determined. When setting up the loop rule, the change in the potentials of the batteries are taken as positive, as long as their direction is the same as the chosen direction of the traverse of the loop.

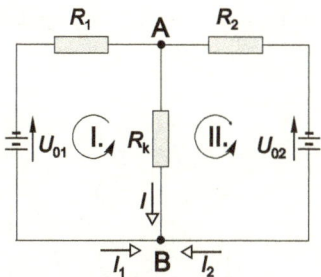

The loop rule applied for the loops and the junction rule applied for point B are the following:

$$-U_{01} + I_1 R_1 - I R_k = 0, \tag{1}$$
$$U_{02} - I_2 R_2 + I R_k = 0, \tag{2}$$
$$I_1 + I_2 + I = 0. \tag{3}$$

expressing I_1 from (1), and I_2 from (2) and writing them into (3) the following result is gained for I:

$$I = -\frac{U_{01}R_2 + U_{02}R_1}{R_k(R_1 + R_2) + R_1 R_2} = -6.142\,\text{A}.$$

In the main branch (through the load) the current flows opposite to the direction indicated by the arrow. The terminal voltage across the batteries connected in parallel (the voltage across the external resistance) is:

$$U_k = IR_k = -12.284\,\text{V}.$$

The currents that flow in the branches of the batteries are:

$$I_1 = \frac{IR_k + U_{01}}{R_1} = \frac{-12.284\,\text{V} + 12.6\,\text{V}}{0.05\,\Omega} = 6.32\,\text{A}$$

and

$$I_2 = -I - I_1 = 6.142\,\text{A} - 6.32\,\text{A} = -0.178\,\text{A}.$$

The current flows from the higher potential towards the lower potential in the battery, which has a smaller electromotive force caused by the other battery, which has a greater electromotive force.

Solution of Problem 241. For the sake of better understanding, let us draw three figures for the three cases. When the switch is in position 11', let the currents going through resistors R_1 and R_2 in branch ADB (the lower one) be I_1 and I_2, respectively, and in the upper branch — because the resistances of the opposite resistors are the same — I_1' and I_2'. Let us use the notations of the figure.

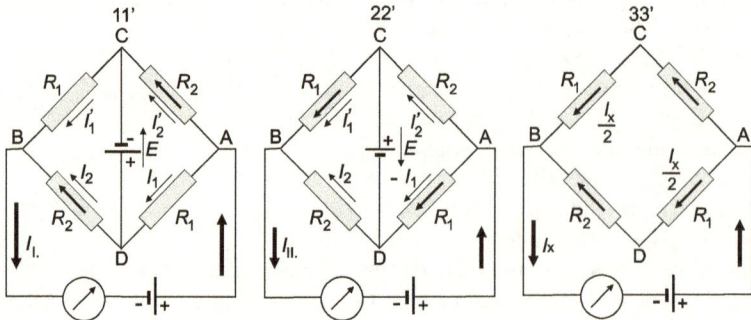

Let us apply the loop rule for the two small loops ($ACDA$ and $CBDC$) and the junction rule for junctions A and B.

$$I_2' R_2 - E - I_1 R_1 = 0,$$
$$I_1' R_1 - I_2 R_2 + E = 0,$$
$$I_I = I_1 + I_2' = I_2 + I_1'.$$

Adding the first two equations and taking out the resistances we gain:

$$(I_2' - I_2)R_2 + (I_1' - I_1)R_1 = 0.$$

From the junction rule the difference between the currents through the resistors which have equal resistances:

$$I_2' - I_2 = I_1' - I_1.$$

Substituting this into the previous equation the following interesting result is gained:

$$(I_2' - I_2)R_2 + (I_2' - I_2)R_1 = 0,$$

so

$$(I_2' - I_2)(R_1 + R_2) = 0,$$

because neither R_1, nor R_2 is zero:

$$I_2' - I_2 = 0, \quad \text{so} \quad I_2' = I_2.$$

similarly it can be derived that $I_1' = I_1$.

Using our results let us apply the loop rule for loop $ACBXYA$, and for loop $ACDA$. Assume that the emf of the two batteries are equal.

$$R_2 I_2 + R_1 I_1 - E = 0,$$

$$R_2 I_2 - E - R_1 I_1 = 0.$$

The solution of this equation system for the currents is:

$$I_1 = 0, \quad I_2 = \frac{E}{R_2}.$$

From this the current through R_2 is $I_2 = I_I = 6\,\text{A}$.

The current flows through the 'route' $ACDBXYA$ and there is no current through the resistors whose resistance is R_1. The value of the resistance of R_2 is:

$$R_2 = \frac{E}{I_I}.$$

When the switch is in position $22'$, the polarity of the battery is swapped (this is the same as if we swapped the resistors R_1 and R_2 when the switch is in position 11') so similarly to the previous case, now the current flows only through the resistors whose resistances are R_1, so $I_2 = E/R_1 = 3\,\text{A}$. There is no current through the resistors R_2 and:

$$R_1 = \frac{E}{I_{II}}.$$

When the switch is in position $33'$ the current in each branch is $I_x/2$. According to the loop rule which is applied to any of the loops containing the battery:

$$\frac{I_x}{2}(R_1 + R_2) - E = 0,$$

from which the asked current is: — using the results gained for the resistances —:

$$I_x = \frac{2E}{\frac{E}{I_{II}} + \frac{E}{I_I}} = \frac{2I_I I_{II}}{I_I + I_{II}} = \frac{2 \cdot 3 \cdot 6}{3 + 6}\,\text{A} = 4\,\text{A}.$$

Solution of Problem 242. This circuit is an example of an unbalanced Wheatstone bridge. Let us solve this problem using Kirchoff's laws.

a) In general the loop rule states that for any loop:

$$\sum_{\text{loop}} V = 0.$$

Traversing the upper loop in the counterclockwise direction (using the directions of currents shown in the figure), we find:

$$I_1 R_0 + I_2 R_0 + I_3 R_0 = 0,$$

which yields

$$I_3 = -I_1 - I_2 = -2.5\,\text{A} - (-1.5\,\text{A}) = -1\,\text{A},$$

Thus the third ammeter reads $1\,\text{A}$, and the direction of the current in that branch is opposite the direction of traverse, so it flows from point D to C.

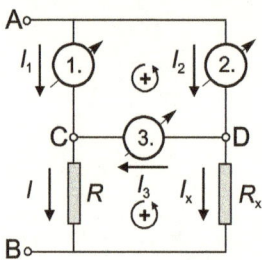

b) In this part our task is to express I_3 as a function of resistance R_x. We have 6 unknowns (the currents in the 5 branches and resistance R), which should be determined using the potential difference between points A and B and the four known resistances. Let us use Kirchoff's laws again: equations (1) and (2) are junction rules ($\sum_{junction} I = 0$) applied at points D and C respectively, while equations (3), (4) and (5) are loop rules ($\sum_{\text{loop}} V = 0$) applied to the upper and lower loops and finally to loop $ADBA$.

Resistance R can easily be calculated using the data given in part a), but let us work with it now as if it was a parameter. Using the directions shown in the figure and working with the magnitudes of currents, we obtain:

$$I_2 = I_3 + I_x \tag{1}$$
$$I = I_1 + I_3 \tag{2}$$
$$I_1 R_0 = I_2 R_0 + I_3 R_0 \tag{3}$$
$$I_x R_x = I_3 R_0 + I R \tag{4}$$
$$V = I_2 R_0 + I_x R_x. \tag{5}$$

Let us solve the system of equations step by step. Let us simplify equation (3) by R_0 and substitute I_2 from equation (1) into equations (3) and (5):

$$I = I_1 + I_3 \tag{2}$$
$$I_1 = I_3 + I_x + I_3 \tag{3'}$$
$$I_x R_x = I_3 R_0 + I R \tag{4}$$
$$V = I_3 R_0 + I_x R_0 + I_x R_x \tag{5'}$$

This way we reduced the number of equations to four. Let us now insert equation (2) into equation (4):

$$I_1 = 2I_3 + I_x \tag{3''}$$

$$I_x R_x = I_3 R_0 + I_1 R + I_3 R. \tag{4'}$$

$$V = I_3 R_0 + I_x R_0 + I_x R_x \tag{5'}$$

Substituting equation (3") into equation (4'), we reduce the number of unknowns to two:

$$I_x R_x = I_3 R_0 + 2I_3 R + I_x R + I_3 R \tag{4''}$$

$$V = I_3 R_0 + I_x R_0 + I_x R_x \tag{5'}$$

Let us now solve equation (5') for I_x ::

$$I_x = \frac{V - I_3 R_0}{R_0 + R_x},$$

inserting this into equation $(4'')$, we have:

$$\frac{V - I_3 R_0}{R_0 + R_x} R_x = I_3 (R_0 + 3R) + \frac{V - I_3 R_0}{R_0 + R_x} R.$$

Multiplying the equation by the denominator gives:

$$R_x V - R_0 R_x I_3 = R_0^2 I_3 + R_0 R_x I_3 + 3R_0 R I_3 + 3RR_x I_3 + RV - R_0 RI_3.$$

This is a linear equation for I_3. After some algebra, we find:

$$V(R_x - R) = 2R_0 R_x I_3 + 2R_0 R I_3 + 3RR_x I_3 + R_0^2 I_3 =$$

$$= (2R_0 R_x + 2R_0 R + 3RR_x + R_0^2)I_3 = [(2R_0 + 3R)R_x + R_0(R_0 + 2R)] \cdot I_3,$$

which yields

$$I_3 = \frac{V(R_x - R)}{(2R_0 + 3R)R_x + R_0(R_0 + 2R)}.$$

If the value of R is calculated, we get the required $I_3(R_x)$ function. R can be found using the data given in the fist part. The potential difference between points A and C is:

$$V_{AC} = R_0 I_1 = 2\,\Omega \cdot 2.5\,\text{A} = 5\,\text{V}$$

so the potential difference across resistance R must be:

$$V_R = V - V_{AC} = 19\,\text{V} - 5\,\text{V} = 14\,\text{V}$$

As the current in the branch of R is

$$I_R = I_1 + I_3 = 2.5\,\text{A} + 1\,\text{A} = 3.5\,\text{A}$$

the value of R turns out to be $R = V_R/I = 14\,\text{V}/3.5\,\text{A} = 4\,\Omega$. Thus current I_3 can be expressed in terms of R_x as:

$$I_3 = \frac{19\,\text{V}(R_x - 4\,\Omega)}{(2 \cdot 2\,\Omega - 3 \cdot 4\,\Omega)R_x + 2\,\Omega(2\,\Omega + 2 \cdot 4\,\Omega)} = \frac{19\,\text{V}R_x - 76\,\text{V} \cdot \Omega}{16\,\Omega \cdot R_x + 20\,\Omega^2}.$$

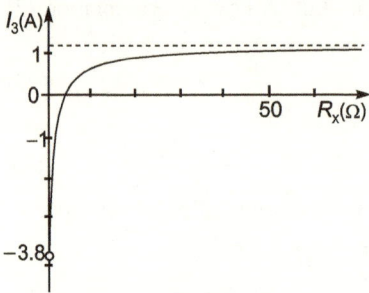

The graph of the function is a hyperbola. Its special points are: at $R_x = 0$ $I_3 = -3.8\,\text{A}$; at $R_x = 4\,\Omega$ $I_3 = 0$; at $R_x = 32\,\Omega$ $I_3 = 1\,\text{A}$; if $R_x \to \infty$, I_3 tends to $19/16 = 1.1875\,\text{A}$.

Solution of Problem 243. From the first measurements we know that the three resistances are equal (R).

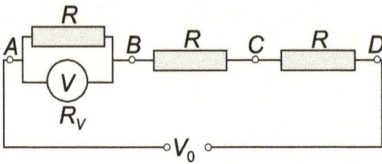

Let R_V stand for the internal resistance of the voltmeter. Then the potential differences between point pairs AB, BC, CD are divided in the ratio of the resistances measured between these points. (See the figure). From this, the potential difference between point pair AB is

$$V_{AB} = \frac{U_0}{\frac{R \cdot R_V}{R + R_V} + 2R} \cdot \frac{R \cdot R_V}{R + R_V}.$$

After simplifying and reorganising, the parametric equation for the potential difference, which was measured to be 20 V is

$$V_{AB} = \frac{V_0 \cdot R_V}{2R + 3R_V}.$$

If the voltmeter is connected between points A and C, the above mentioned proportional part can be calculated from the following formula:

$$V_{AC} = \frac{V_0}{\frac{2R \cdot R_V}{2R + R_V} + R} \cdot \frac{2R \cdot R_V}{2R + R_V},$$

after simplifying, this surprisingly results in exactly twice of value V_{AC}:

$$V_{AC} = 2 \cdot \frac{V_0 \cdot R_V}{2R + 3R_V} = 2V_{AB} = 40 \text{ V}.$$

As $R_b \approx 0$,

$$V_{AD} = V_0 = 62 \text{ V},$$

which is not three times V_{AB}!

Solution of Problem 244. In the case of a closed switch, after a sufficient time the capacitor is charged completely and then no current flows through it. In this state the potential difference across it is

$$V_C = \frac{V_0}{R_1 + R_{23}} \cdot R_{23},$$

where R_{23} is the equivalent resistance of resistances R_2 and R_3 connected in parallel:

$$R_{23} = \frac{R_2 R_3}{R_2 + R_3}.$$

Substituting the value of R_{23} into the equation:

$$V_C = V_0 \frac{R_2 R_3}{R_1 R_2 + R_1 R_3 + R_2 R_3}.$$

and the charge on the capacitor is

$$Q_C = C V_0 \frac{R_2 R_3}{R_1 R_2 + R_1 R_3 + R_2 R_3}. \tag{1}$$

After the switch is opened, the capacitor discharges through resistors R_2 and R_3. Currents i_2 and i_3 flowing through the resistors decrease continuously but their ratio remains constant:

$$\frac{i_3}{i_2} = \frac{\frac{V_C}{R_3}}{\frac{V_C}{R_2}} = \frac{R_2}{R_3}.$$

The constant ratio of the currents also gives the ratio of the charges carried by them:

$$\frac{Q_3}{Q_2} = \frac{R_2}{R_3}, \tag{2}$$

where Q_2 and Q_3 stand for the charges flowing through resistors R_2 and R_3, respectively. The sum of Q_2 and Q_3 is obviously Q_e:

$$Q_2 + Q_3 = Q_e. \tag{3}$$

Based on (2) and (3), it can be stated that in the discharge process charge Q_e flowing out of the capacitor is distributed between the discharging resistors in inverse ratio to the ratio of resistances R_2 and R_3.

Making use of this fact:

$$Q_3 = \frac{Q_C}{R_2 + R_3} R_2,$$

or based on (1)

$$Q_3 = C V_0 \frac{R_2 R_3}{R_1 R_2 + R_1 R_3 + R_2 R_3} \cdot \frac{R_2}{R_2 + R_3}. \tag{4}$$

a) Based on this, the results in the case of $R_3 = 400\ \Omega$ are

$$R_{23} = 80\ \Omega, \quad V_C = 4\ \text{V}, \quad Q_C = 200\ \mu\text{C}, \quad Q_3 = 40\ \mu\text{C}.$$

b) In this case, the expression for Q_3 given in (4) is regarded as a function of R_3. Let the R stand for the identical values of R_1 and R_2. Then (4) can be written in the form

$$Q_3 = C V_0 \frac{R R_3}{(R + 2 R_3)(R + R_3)},$$

or in a more suitable form

$$Q_3 = CV_0 R \cdot \frac{1}{2R_3 + \frac{R^2}{R_3} + 3R}.$$

Regarding the denominator as function of R_3, it can be seen that the denominator has a minimum, which results in the maximum of Q_3. Based on the inequality between the arithmetic and geometric means (taking into consideration the terms of the denominator that contain the variable):

$$\frac{2R_3 + \frac{R^2}{R_3}}{2} \geq \sqrt{2R_3 \cdot \frac{R^2}{R_3}},$$

that is,

$$\frac{2R_3 + \frac{R^2}{R_3}}{2} \geq R\sqrt{2}.$$

The left side (the arithmetic mean) is the smallest when the two terms are equal, that is, when

$$2R_3 = \frac{R^2}{R_3},$$

from which $R_3 = \frac{\sqrt{2}}{2}R$. The value of the denominator has a minimum here because the third, constant term does not influence the place of the extreme value.

So after the switch is opened, the maximum discharging charge flows through resistor R_3 if its value is

$$R_3 = \frac{\sqrt{2}}{2}R = 70.71\ \Omega,$$

and based on (4), the maximum charge that flows through it is

$$Q_{3\max} = \frac{CV_0}{2\sqrt{2}+3} = \frac{5 \cdot 10^{-5}\ \text{F} \cdot 9\ \text{V}}{2\sqrt{2}+3} = 77.2\ \mu\text{C}.$$

Solution of Problem 245. Let us connect s cells in a series in one chain. Then the equivalent no-load voltage of one chain is

$$V_{01} = sV_0$$

and the equivalent internal resistance is

$$R_1 = sR.$$

Then $k = N/s$ chains are created. ($s = 1, 2, 3, \dots, N$.) The equivalent internal resistance of the battery acquired by connecting the chains in parallel is

$$R_i = \frac{R_1}{k} = \frac{sR}{N/s} = s^2 \frac{R}{N}.$$

If the consumer whose resistance is optimal for maximum power output is connected to the battery, then its resistance is equal to the internal resistance of the battery, so

$$R_c = R_i = s^2 \frac{R}{N}.$$

The power output on the consumer is always

$$P = I^2 R_c.$$

By substituting our results into the relationship we acquire

$$P = \left(\frac{sV_0}{2\frac{s^2 R}{N}} \right)^2 \cdot \frac{s^2 R}{N} = \frac{V_0^2 N}{4R}.$$

The final result does not contain s, which means that the power output on a consumer whose resistance is optimal is the same in each case, independently of the value of s, that is, the arrangement of our battery.

With numerical values

$$P_{\max} = \frac{12^2 \text{ V}^2 \cdot 64}{4 \cdot 2\Omega} = 1152 \text{ W}.$$

Solution of Problem 246. Three different circuits can be made as shown in the figures a), b), and c). The first is when a part of the variable resistor and the resistor are connected in series, the second is a potential divider (potentiometer), and the third is when the two parts of the variable resistor are connected in parallel and this is connected in series to the resistor.

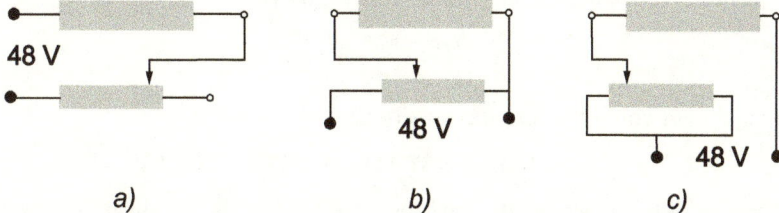

a)   b)   c)

Data: $R_R = R = 100$ Ω, $P_R = 2$ W, $0 \le r_{Var} \le r = 1000$ Ω, $P_{Var} = 15$ W, $U = 48$ V. In order to make it easier to figure out the circuits, let us denote the resistor in the circuit with the symbol of a lamp.

a) The key of the solution is to find out the maximum current through the resistor and the variable resistor. This limits the voltage across the resistor. The maximum current through the resistor is:

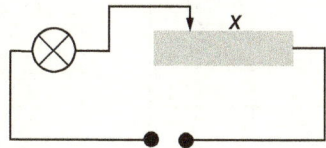

$$I_{R_{\max}} = \sqrt{P_R/R_R} = \sqrt{2\,\text{W}/100\,\Omega} = 0.1414 \text{ A},$$

the maximum current through the variable resistor:

$$I_{Var_{\max}} = \sqrt{P_{Var}/r} = \sqrt{15\,\text{W}/1000\,\Omega} = 0.1225 \text{ A}.$$

In case of a series connection the maximum current which can flow through that part of the variable resistor which is connected, and whose resistance is x, (so through the resistor as well,) is 0.1225 A, thus the maximum voltage across the resistor is:

$$U_{R_{max}} = I_{Var_{max}} R = 12.25 \text{ V}$$

The voltage is minimum if the whole variable resistor is connected into the circuit, (in this case the current decreases) which is allowed:

$$U_{R_{min}} = I_{min} R = \frac{U}{R + r_{max}} R = \frac{48 \text{ V}}{1100 \, \Omega} \cdot 100 \, \Omega = 4.364 \text{ V}.$$

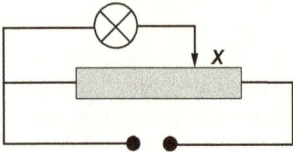

b) When the variable resistor is used as a potential divider, then part x of the variable resistor is connected in series to the rest of the variable resistor $r - x$ and the resistor R which are connected in parallel, thus the current through the system is limited by the current through part x:

$$I_{Var_{max}} = \frac{U}{x + \frac{(r-x)R}{r-x+R}}.$$

This leads to a quadratic equation:

$$I_{Var_{max}} x^2 - (U + I_{Var_{max}} r)x + U(r + R) - I_{Var_{max}} rR = 0.$$

Substituting the given data the solution will be $x = 304.4 \, \Omega$, thus the resistance of that part which is connected in parallel to the resistor is $r - x = 695.6 \, \Omega$.

The equivalent resistance of the parallel connection is:

$$R_e = \frac{R(r - x)}{R + r - x} = 87.43 \, \Omega,$$

thus the maximum voltage across the resistor is:

$$U_{R_{max}} = R_e I_{Var_{max}} = 87.43 \, \Omega \cdot 0.1225 \text{ A} = 10.71 \text{ V}.$$

The minimum voltage across the resistor in this case is 0, since the resistor is shortcircuited if the pointer is put to the left extreme position.

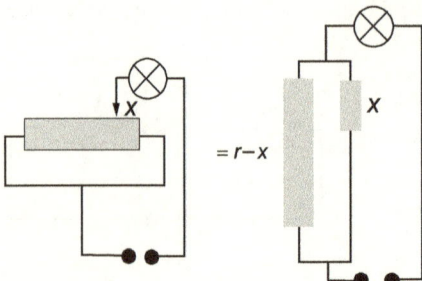

c) In the third case, the two parts of the variable resistor are connected in parallel and this is connected in series to the resistor. If the pointer of the variable resistor is placed to the middle and is moved towards the right or the left, a symmetrical change in the current will result. When the pointer is in the middle position, the half of the maximum current of the resistor flows through each part of the variable resistor, which is smaller than the maximum current through the variable resistor, so the current is limited by the resistor. Thus the maximum current in the circuit is $I_{max} = I_{R_{max}} = 0.1414$ A and the maximum voltage across the resistor is $U_{R_{max}} = I_{R_{max}} R = 14.14/V$. When the current is the maximum, the pointer splits the variable resistors into two parts for which:

$$U_{Var} = I_{R_{max}} \frac{(r-x)x}{r-x+x},$$

where $U_{Var} = U - U_R = 48\,\text{V} - 14.14\,\text{V} = 33.86\,\text{V}$. so the equation to be solved is the following:

$$I_{max}x^2 + I_{max}x + U_{Var}r = 0,$$

substituting the data this is :

$$0.1414x^2 - 141.4x + 33860 = 0,$$

Both solutions of the quadratic equation are solutions of the problem:

$$x_1 = 602.65\,\Omega \qquad \text{and} \qquad x_2 = 397.35\,\Omega.$$

If the pointer is pushed further away than four-tenths or six-tenths of the total length, then the current through the resistor will be more than the allowed maximum (and also it will exceed the allowed maximum through the shorter part of the variable resistor). Because of the symmetry, the maximum of the resistance of the variable resistor — thus the minimum of the voltage across the resistor — occurs if the pointer is in the middle position. In this case the equivalent resistance of the variable resistor is $R_{Var} = r/4 = 250\,\Omega$, and the voltage across the resistor is

$$U_{R_{min}} = \frac{U}{R + R_{Var}} R = \frac{48\,\text{V}}{100\,\Omega + 250\,\Omega} \cdot 100\,\Omega = 13.71\,\text{V}.$$

Summarizing the results, the voltages across the resistor in case of a), b), and c) are the following:

a) $$4.364\,\text{V} \le U_R \le 12.25\,\text{V},$$

b) $$0 \le U_R \le 10.71\,\text{V},$$

c) $$13.71\,\text{V} \le U_R \le 14.14\,\text{V}.$$

Solution of Problem 247. a) If R_m is the resistance of the multiplier and R_{int} is the internal resistance of the meter, then:

$$R_m = (n-1)R_{int}. \tag{1}$$

If R_s is the resistance of the shunt, then:

$$R_s = \frac{R_{int}}{n-1}. \tag{2}$$

Multiplying equation (1) by equation (2) gives:

$$R_m R_s = R_{int}^2,$$

which means that the internal resistance of the meter is the geometrical mean of the resistances of the multiplier and shunt:

$$R_{int} = \sqrt{R_m R_s} = \sqrt{3\,\Omega \cdot 27\,\Omega} = \sqrt{81\,\Omega^2} = 9\,\Omega.$$

b) The power dissipated by the moving-coil can be written in terms of the current and resistance as:

$$P = I^2 R_{int},$$

which yields:

$$I = \sqrt{\frac{P}{R_{int}}} = \sqrt{\frac{P}{\sqrt{R_m R_s}}} = \sqrt{\frac{9 \cdot 10^{-4}\,\text{W}}{9\,\Omega}} = 10^{-2}\,\text{A} = 10\,\text{m A}.$$

The voltage across the moving-coil is given by:

$$V = \frac{P}{I} = \sqrt{P R_{int}} = \sqrt{P \sqrt{R_m R_s}}.$$

Inserting given data, we find

$$V = \frac{9 \cdot 10^{-4}\,\text{W}}{10^{-2}\,\text{A}} = 9 \cdot 10^{-2}\,\text{V} = 90\,\text{m V}.$$

Solution of Problem 248. Let x stand for the resistance of the part of the variable resistance that falls between the left end of the resistor and the slide. The two resistor parts separated by the slide are connected in parallel in the circuit. The current created can be calculated from the electromotive force and the equivalent resistance:

$$I = \frac{V_0}{R_e} = \frac{V_0}{R_0 + \frac{x(R-x)}{x+R-x}} = \frac{V_0 \cdot R}{R_0 R + x(R-x)}.$$

The denominator of the fraction is a quadratic function: $-x^2 + Rx + RR_0$. Its maximum — compared to function $ax^2 + bx + c$ — is at $-b/2a$, that is, in our case at $R/2$. Then the value of the denominator is maximum, the value of the fraction and therefore current are minimum, its value is

$$I_{min} = \frac{V_0 R}{R R_0 + \frac{R}{2}\left(R - \frac{R}{2}\right)} = \frac{4V_0}{4R_0 + R}. \tag{1}$$

As according to the problem

$$R > \frac{4R_0}{3},$$

substituting the value $4R_0/3$, a value smaller than R in place of R in (1) gives a value greater than the one received in (1):

$$I_{min} = \frac{4V_0}{4R_0 + R} < \frac{4V_0}{4R_0 + \frac{4R_0}{3}} = \frac{3}{4}\frac{V_0}{R_0}. \tag{2}$$

On the other hand, the maximum current occurs when the slide is at one of the endpoints of the variable resistance, because then it is shorted, its 'included' resistance is zero (short-circuit current). Its value is

$$I_{max} = \frac{V_0}{R_0}.$$

Substituting it into (2), it is really true that

$$I_{min} < \frac{3}{4} \cdot I_{max}.$$

The minimum and maximum currents are

$$I_{min} = \frac{4V_0}{4R_0 + R}, \quad \text{and} \quad I_{max} = \frac{V_0}{R_0},$$

respectively.

Solution of Problem 249. The circuit diagram is shown in the figure.

If the motor rotates, the magnetic field of the stator induces an electromotive force in the conductors of the armature. Let $\mathcal{E}$ stand for the potential difference induced in the rotor as generator and IR stand for the potential difference across the ohmic resistor.

According to Kirchhoff's law:

$$U - \mathcal{E} - IR = 0.$$

From this, $\mathcal{E} = U - IR$ is the voltage of the motor, which should be taken into consideration for mechanical power.

The power of the motor is:

$$P = I\mathcal{E} = I(U - IR).$$

This is a quadratic function for I:

$$P = -RI^2 + UI.$$

This function may have a maximum at '$-b/2a$'. So the current belonging to the maximum power is

$$I = \frac{-U}{-2R} = \frac{U}{2R}.$$

With this, the maximum power of the motor can be calculated:

$$P_{max} = -R \cdot \left(\frac{U}{2R}\right)^2 + U \cdot \frac{U}{2R} = \frac{U^2}{4R}.$$

With numerical values:

$$P_{max} = \frac{220^2}{4 \cdot 62} W = 195.16 \text{ W}.$$

The mechanical power output of the motor cannot be more than this, meaning it cannot produce a mechanical power of 200 W.

Solution of Problem 250. First we determine the equivalent resistance of the infinite chain of internal resistances shown below. Let r_x be the equivalent resistance of the

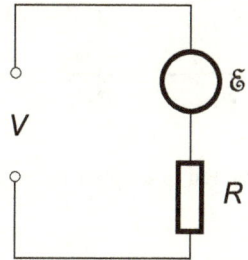

chain between points A and B. If one more recurring section is connected before the chain, the net resistance of the new chain will be r_{x+1}. Since two resistors are connected in series and one in parallel to r_x, the net resistance of the new chain can be calculated as:

$$\frac{1}{r} + \frac{1}{2r+r_x} = \frac{1}{r_{x+1}}. \tag{1}$$

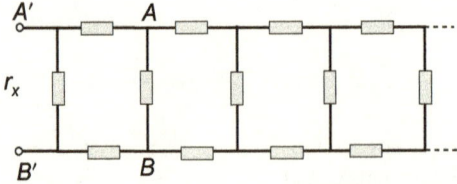

The key to the solution is to recognize that adding one more section to an infinite chain does not change the chain and its resultant resistance, hence $r_{x+1} = r_x$. Isolating r_{x+1} from equation (1) and then substituting $r_{x+1} = r_x$, we obtain:

$$\frac{(2r+r_x)r}{r+2r+r_x} = r_x,$$

which is a quadratic equation for r_x:

$$r_x^2 + 2rr_x - 2r^2 = 0.$$

The solution of this equation gives the equivalent internal resistance in question, which is:

$$r_x = r(\sqrt{3}-1). \tag{2}$$

Let us now investigate what happens if two batteries of different emf are connected in parallel. Let ε be the resultant emf of the arrangement, which in other words is the no-load potential difference across points A and B. Although no load is connected across the terminals (A and B), there is still a current (i) flowing in the closed loop. Applying Kirchoff's loop rule to the loops containing points A and B and either of the two batteries, we get:

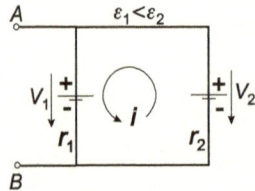

$$\varepsilon = \varepsilon_2 - ir_2,$$

$$\varepsilon = \varepsilon_1 + ir_1.$$

The solution of the system of equations gives the resultant emf of the two batteries:

$$\varepsilon = \frac{\varepsilon_1 r_2 + \varepsilon_2 r_1}{r_1 + r_2}. \tag{3}$$

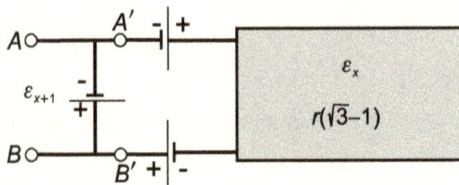

Let us now investigate the infinite chain of batteries. Let ε_x be the equivalent emf of the chain, whose equivalent resistance according to equation (2) is $r_x = r(\sqrt{3}+1)$. First let us connect two batteries in series to the chain. The resultant emf across points $A' - B'$ is now:

$$\varepsilon_2 = 2\varepsilon + \varepsilon_x,$$

and the net resistance according to equation (2) is:

$$r_2 = 2r + r(\sqrt{3}-1) = r(\sqrt{3}+1).$$

Let us then connect one more battery (of emf $\varepsilon = \varepsilon_1$ and internal resistance $r = r_1$) across points $A' - B'$. According to the formula obtained for the resultant emf of two batteries connected in parallel [see equation (3)], the resultant emf of this new arrangement is:

$$\varepsilon_{x+1} = \frac{\varepsilon r(\sqrt{3}+1) + (2\varepsilon + \varepsilon_x)r}{r + r(\sqrt{3}+1)} = \frac{\varepsilon(\sqrt{3}+3) + \varepsilon_x}{\sqrt{3}+2}.$$

Since adding one more recurring section to the infinite chain does not change its equivalent emf, we can substitute $\varepsilon_{x+1} = \varepsilon_x$:

$$\varepsilon_x = \frac{\varepsilon(3+\sqrt{3}) + \varepsilon_x}{\sqrt{3}+2}.$$

The solution of this equation gives the equivalent emf of the infinite chain, which is:

$$\varepsilon_x = \sqrt{3}\varepsilon.$$

Solution of Problem 251. a) If the condition set in part a) of the problem can be satisfied, then it is also true in cases $n = 0$ and $n = 1$, so the equivalent resistance measured between points A and B is the same in these two cases. Based on the figure

$$R_x = R_1 + \frac{R_2 R_x}{R_2 + R_x}, \qquad (1)$$

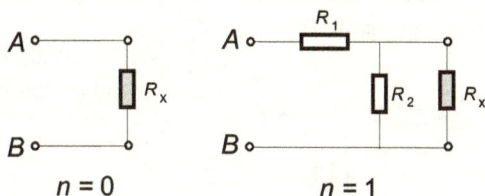

multiplying by the denominator:

$$R_x R_2 + R_x^2 = R_1 R_2 + R_1 R_x + R_2 R_x.$$

The rearranged form of the quadratic equation is

$$R_x^2 - R_1 R_x - R_1 R_2 = 0,$$

its solution is

$$R_x = \frac{R_1 + \sqrt{R_1^2 + 4R_1 R_2}}{2} = \frac{1\Omega + \sqrt{1\Omega^2 + 4 \cdot 1\Omega \cdot 6\Omega}}{2} = 3\Omega.$$

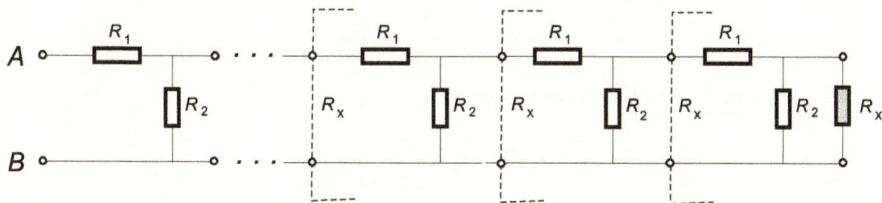

We have to examine whether in the case of $R_x = 3\Omega$ it is really true that R_{AB} is independent from the number of included quadrupoles. Let us consider the last quadrupole and resistor R_x terminating it. Based on condition (1), their equivalent is R_x. But then the quadrupole before the last one is also terminated by a resistance R_x, which means that the equivalent resistance is R_x again.

The procedure can be repeated until we reach the first quadrupole. This is terminated by a circuit part with an equivalent resistance R_x again, so the equivalent resistance between points A and B is R_x independently of the number of included quadrupoles.

b) The potential difference across resistor R_x is the potential difference across the last element now. For this, we have to determine the current flowing through resistor R_x.

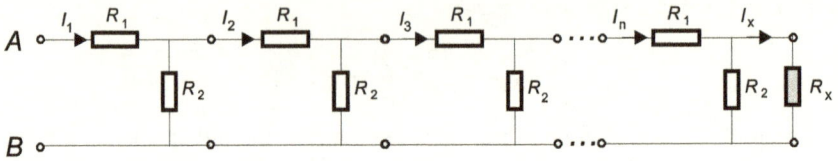

The current flowing through the first resistor R_1 is $I_1 = U_{AB}/R_{AB} = 1$ A, because $U_{AB} = 3$ V and $R_{AB} = 3\ \Omega$.

For this reason, let us consider an arbitrary quadrupole (e.g. in position j). Let I_j stand for the current flowing through resistor R_1 and I_{j+1} for the current flowing through resistor R_x.

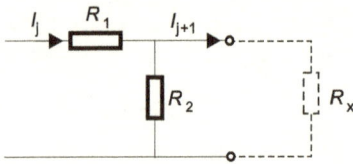

With these notations, for the current flowing through resistor R_x based on the circuit diagram: from the loop law

$$\frac{I_{j+1}}{I_2} = \frac{R_2}{R_x}$$

and from the junction law

$$I_{j+1} + I_2 = I_j.$$

The value of I_2 is expressed from the ratio:

$$I_2 = I_{j+1}\frac{R_x}{R_2}.$$

This is substituted into the junction law:

$$I_{j+1} + I_{j+1}\frac{R_x}{R_2} = I_j.$$

From this, the current flowing through resistor R_x is

$$I_{j+1} = I_j\frac{R_2}{R_x + R_2}.$$

Using these, the following relationships are acquired:

$$I_2 = I_1 \frac{R_2}{R_2 + R_x},$$

$$I_3 = I_2 \frac{R_2}{R_2 + R_x} = I_1 \cdot \left(\frac{R_2}{R_2 + R_x}\right)^2$$

$$\vdots$$

$$I_n = I_1 \cdot \left(\frac{R_2}{R_2 + R_x}\right)^{n-1}$$

$$I_x = I_1 \cdot \left(\frac{R_2}{R_2 + R_x}\right)^n = 1\ \text{A} \cdot \left(\frac{2}{3}\right)^{21} = 2.00485 \cdot 10^{-4}\ \text{A}.$$

With this, the potential difference across the terminating resistor R_x is

$$U_x = R_x I_x = 3\Omega \cdot 2.00485 \cdot 10^{-4}\ \text{A} = 0.6015\ \text{mV}$$

Solution of Problem 252. The capacitance of the metal sphere with respect to infinity, where the potential is zero, can be calculated such that the charge on the sphere, Q, is divided by the potential at the surface of the sphere, having a charge of Q. Due to the symmetry of the sphere, the distribution of the charge on the sphere is uniform, which creates a central electric field whose field lines are perpendicular to the surface of the sphere, thus outside the sphere they are drawn as if they came from the centre of the sphere. Therefore the potential at the surface of the sphere is the same as the potential at a distance of r from a pointlike charge of Q placed into the centre of the sphere, which is:

$$V = \frac{1}{4\pi\varepsilon_0} \cdot \frac{Q}{r}.$$

thus the capacitance of the sphere of radius r is

$$C = 4\pi\varepsilon_0 r.$$

If the potential difference between the ends of the wires is V, then at each touch the sphere carries a charge of $Q_1 = CV = 4\pi\varepsilon_0 r V$, thus during a time t the amount of charge carried between the ends of the wires is $Q = ntQ_1$, where according to the data $n = 54\ 1/\text{min} = 0.9\ 1/\text{s}$. Thus the average current is

$$I = \frac{Q}{t} = nQ_1 = n4\pi\varepsilon_0 r V,$$

and applying Ohm's law the resistance can be calculated as:

$$R = \frac{V}{I} = \frac{1}{n4\pi\varepsilon_0 r} = \frac{1}{0.9\ \text{s}^{-1} 4\pi 8.85 \cdot 10^{-12}\ \frac{\text{As}}{\text{Vm}} \cdot 0.01\ \text{m}} \approx 10^{12} \Omega.$$

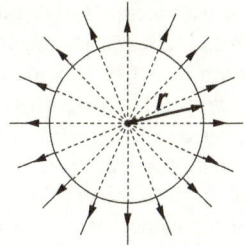

(We supposed that direct current was applied, and the potential at the end of one of the wires is equal to the potential of a point at infinity.)

Solution of Problem 253. The original resistance of the wire is $R = 2Lr = 4\ \Omega$. If the conducting path is an ideal shortcircuit, then connecting the wires at B does not effect the measurement at A, thus the total resistance of the pair of wires of segment AX would be gained. Similarly, the measurement at B would give the total resistance of the pair of wires of segment XB, thus the sum of these resistances would give the original, known resistance of the cable. Because the sum of the two measured data is greater than this ($R_1 + R_2 > Lr$), we can conclude that the conducting path is not an ideal shortcircuit, but instead has has some resistance R.

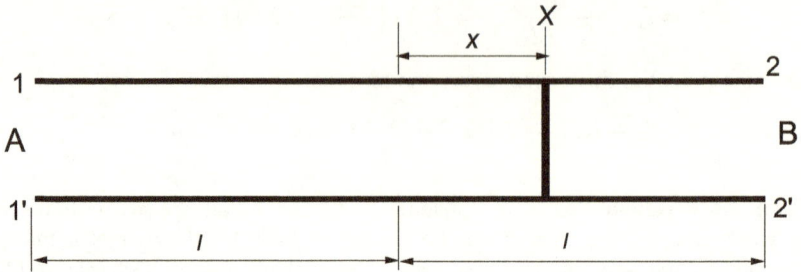

In case of the first measurement, R is connected in parallel to the two wires of length XB and this is connected in series with two wires of length AX. In case of the second measurement, R is connected in parallel with the two wires of length AX. For the two, known, equivalent resistances two equations can be set up from which the two unknowns (R and for example AX) can be determined. Though the equation system is very difficult to solve if the unknown of the equation system which characterize the position of the conducting path is chosen to be simply $x = AX$. The solution of the equation system is easier if half of the length of the cable $l = L/2$ is introduced, and the position of the conducting path is characterized by the distance x between the midpoint of the cable and the short.

With this the two equations are:

$$R_1 = 2(l + x)r + \frac{2(l - x)rR}{2(l - x)r + R},$$

$$R_2 = 2(l - x)r + \frac{2(l + x)rR}{2(l + x)r + R}.$$

After eliminating the denominators, and taking out one equation from the other the variable R can be calculated quite easily, and substituting it back into one of the equations a quadratic equation can be gained for x.

$$r(R_1 - R_2) \cdot x^2 + [R_1 R_2 - 2lr(R_1 + R_2)] \cdot x + l^2 r(R_1 - R_2) = 0.$$

the solution of this equation which makes sense is:

$$x = \frac{2lr(R_1 + R_2) - R_1 R_2 \sqrt{R_1^2 R_2^2 - 4lr R_1 R_2(R_1 + R_2 - 4lr)}}{2r(R_1 - R_2)}.$$

Substituting the data of the problem the result is $x = 50$ metres, thus the short is at three-quarters of the cable measured from A. The resistance of the conducting path is $R = 3$ ohms.

Chapter 9

Magnetism Solutions

9.1 Magnetic field

Solution of Problem 254. a) The figure shows that the chloride ions passing through both diaphragms A_1 and A_2 move along a straight line. This is possible only for those particles which travel at a specific speed, since for other speeds the orbits are curved arcs in the electric and magnetic field. Thus the first part of the device, with perpendicular electric and magnetic fields, is a 'velocity filter', which selects from the dispersed speed distribution of the ion beam a specific velocity value. Thus after the diaphragm A_2 we have to deal with only one speed value.

After the second diaphragm A_2 we have pure magnetic field, and the ions enter this region with a velocity perpendicular to the field. Here, they perform uniform circular motion until they hit the photo plate. The magnetic Lorentz force is equal to the centripetal force, and since the relevant vectors are perpendicular, the equation of motion is:

$$Bev = \frac{mv^2}{r}.$$

For the two isotopes with different masses the radii are:

$$r_1 = \frac{m_1 v}{Be}, \text{ and } r_2 = \frac{m_2 v}{Be}.$$

The difference of these radii is:

$$\Delta r = r_2 - r_1 = \frac{v}{Be}(m_2 - m_1)$$

Using the geometric fact that $\Delta x = 2\Delta r$,

$$v = \frac{Be\Delta r}{(m_2 - m_1)} = \frac{Be\Delta x}{2 \cdot (m_2 - m_1)} = \frac{2 \cdot 10^{-2} T \cdot 1.6 \cdot 10^{-19} \text{ C} \cdot 4 \cdot 10^{-2} \text{ m}}{2 \cdot 2 \cdot 1.67 \cdot 10^{-27} \text{ kg}} = 1.92 \cdot 10^4 \frac{\text{m}}{\text{s}}.$$

b) Only those particles pass through the velocity filter, for which the magnetic and electric forces compensate each other, i.e., have equal magnitudes and opposite directions:

$$eE = Bev.$$

Consequently, the magnitude of the electric field is:

$$E = Bv = 2 \cdot 10^{-2} \frac{\text{Vs}}{\text{m}^2} \cdot 1.92 \cdot 10^4 \frac{\text{m}}{\text{s}} = 384 \frac{\text{V}}{\text{m}}.$$

The electric field is homogeneous, and in the arrangement of the figure it is directed horizontally from left to right.

Solution of Problem 255. The speed of the electron is obtained from the work-energy theorem:

$$e\Delta V = \frac{1}{2}mv^2.$$

Hence

$$v = \sqrt{2\frac{e}{m}\Delta V} = \sqrt{2 \cdot \frac{1.6 \cdot 10^{-19}\,\text{C}}{9 \cdot 10^{-31}\,\text{kg}} \cdot 800\,\text{V}} = 1.686 \cdot 10^7\,\frac{\text{m}}{\text{s}}.$$

The electron is acted on by the magnetic Lorentz force:

$$\vec{F} = e\vec{v} \times \vec{B}.$$

(Since the lines of magnetic induction and the lines of magnetic field intensity have the same direction in vacuum, we can consider field lines the same as lines of magnetic induction.) The vectorial product is perpendicular to both $\vec{v}$ and $\vec{B}$, so the force will not change the magnitude of the velocity, and therefore the magnitude of the force vector also stays constant: $F = evB\sin\alpha$. Since the force has no component parallel to $\vec{B}$, the motion of the electron in the direction of the field lines is uniform, while the projection of its motion on a plane perpendicular to the field lines is uniform circular. The radius of its orbit can be determined by setting the Lorentz force equal to the centripetal force:

$$evB\sin\alpha = \frac{mv^2\sin^2\alpha}{r}.$$

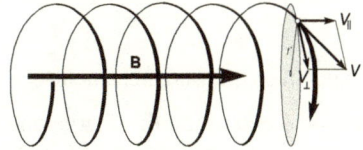

Hence

$$r = \frac{mv\sin\alpha}{eB}.$$

Thus the trajectory of the electron is a helix with its axis parallel to the field lines. In a reference frame moving along with the electron at a parallel speed of $v_\parallel = v\cos\alpha$, the electron is moving in a circular orbit at a tangential speed of $v_\perp = v\sin\alpha$, and its orbital period is

$$T = \frac{2r\pi}{v_\perp} = \frac{2\pi mv\sin\alpha}{eBv\sin\alpha} = \frac{2\pi m}{eB} =$$

$$= \frac{2\pi \cdot 9 \cdot 10^{-31}\,\text{kg}}{1.6 \cdot 10^{-19}\,\text{C} \cdot 0.02\,\text{T}} = 1.767 \cdot 10^{-9}\,\text{s},$$

independently of the initial direction of the velocity of the electron.

Travelling at a speed of $v_\| = v\cos\alpha$, it covers the distance L in a time of $t = \dfrac{L}{v\cos\alpha}$, which has to be an integer multiple of the orbital period T to satisfy the requirement of the problem:

$$t = \frac{L}{v\cos\alpha} = n \cdot \frac{2\pi m}{eB},$$

and hence

$$\cos\alpha = \frac{1}{n} \cdot \frac{BeL}{2\pi m v} = \frac{1}{n} \cdot \frac{0.02\ \text{T} \cdot 1.6 \cdot 10^{-19}\ \text{C} \cdot 0.1\ \text{m}}{2\pi \cdot 9 \cdot 10^{-31}\ \text{kg} \cdot 1.686 \cdot 10^7\ \frac{\text{m}}{\text{s}}} = \frac{3.356}{n}.$$

$0 \le \cos\alpha \le 1$ for non-negative angles, and n is a positive integer. In addition to the trivial case of $\alpha = 0$, this may only occur if at least 4 complete revolutions are made, for:

$$n_1 = 4, \quad \cos\alpha = \frac{3.356}{4} = 0.8395 \rightarrow \quad \alpha_1 = 32.91°,$$

$$n_2 = 5, \quad \cos\alpha = \frac{3.356}{5} = 0.6716 \rightarrow \quad \alpha_2 = 47.81°, \text{ etc.}$$

First solution of Problem 256. In formula booklets, it can be found that the magnetic induction due to a pointlike charge of Q undergoing uniform circular motion of radius r and of speed v at the centre of the circle is:

$$B = \frac{\mu_0}{4\pi} \cdot \frac{Qv}{r^2}.$$

From this, the magnetic field can be calculated as $H = \dfrac{B}{\mu_0}$. The only task which is left is to determine the charge and the speed of the sphere. The charge on the sphere is $Q = CV$, where $C = 4\pi\varepsilon_0 R$, is the capacitance of the isolated sphere. The potential of the sphere is calculated with respect to infinity. Thus

$$Q = 4\pi\varepsilon_0 R \cdot V.$$

The speed of the sphere is $v = r\omega = r2\pi n$, where n is the number of revolutions. Therefore the asked magnetic field is:

$$H = \frac{1}{4\pi} \cdot \frac{4\pi\varepsilon_0 R \cdot r2\pi n \cdot V}{r^2} = \frac{2\pi\varepsilon_0 RnV}{r} =$$

$$= \frac{2\pi \cdot 8.85 \cdot 10^{-12}\frac{\text{As}}{\text{Vm}} \cdot 0.01\ \text{m} \cdot \frac{18000}{60}\frac{1}{\text{s}} \cdot 900\ \text{V}}{0.3\ \text{m}} = 5 \cdot 10^{-7}\ \frac{\text{A}}{\text{m}}.$$

Second solution of Problem 256. The problem can be solved by using the note at the end of the problem about the circular current-carrying wire. We have to determine the magnitude of that current which is equivalent to the charge moving along a circular path. This can be found if we calculate how many times the charge crosses the cross section of the circular path in a unit of time, which should be multiplied by the magnitude of the charge in order to get the equivalent current.

The sphere passes one cross section $\dfrac{18000}{60} = 300$ 1/s times during one second, thus the equivalent current is $I = nQ$. If the value of $Q = CV = 4\pi\varepsilon_0 RV$ and the equivalent current are substituted into the given formula then:

$$H = \frac{I}{2r} = \frac{n2\pi\varepsilon_0 RV}{r} = 5\cdot 10^{-7}\,\text{A/m}$$

is gained.

Solution of Problem 257. Let us use the following notations for the data given: $\dfrac{N}{l} = 2000\ \dfrac{1}{\text{m}}$, $r_1 = 5$ cm, $B_1 = 4\cdot 10^{-4}$ T, $B =?$

Let us assume that the coil carries an electric current I. Because of the symmetry of the arrangement, the magnetic field produced by the coil outside the solenoid is similar to that of a straight, current-carrying wire, as it is shown in the figure on page 474. Let us apply Maxwell's second law to a circle of radius $r_1 = 5$ cm, whose plane is perpendicular to the axis of the solenoid. Since the surface of the circle is crossed by the current I, the strength of the magnetic field at the distance r_1 from the axis is:

$$B_1 = \mu_0 \frac{I}{2r_1\pi},$$

which means that the current in the coil is:

$$I = \frac{2r_1\pi B_1}{\mu_0}.$$

Inside the long solenoid this current produces a magnetic field:

$$B = \mu_0 \frac{IN}{l},$$

thus the strength of the magnetic field inside the solenoid is:

$$B = \mu_0 \frac{2r_1\pi B_1}{\mu_0} \cdot \frac{N}{l} = 2r_1\pi B_1 \frac{N}{l} = 2\cdot 5\cdot 10^{-2}\ \text{m}\cdot\pi\cdot 4\cdot 10^{-4}\ \text{T}\cdot 2000 = 0.251\ \text{T}.$$

If the coil is wound in two layers, and in the second layer the turns are placed in opposite direction along the solenoid, then the net magnetic field outside the solenoid is zero, since in the direction of the axis of the solenoid the currents flowing in the two layers cancel each other. (Inside the coil the magnetic field remains the same.) If, however, after finishing one layer of turns, the wire is carried back to the beginning of the solenoid, and the second layer is placed in the same direction along the solenoid, then the net current through the plane perpendicular to the axis of the solenoid is again I, so outside the coil the magnetic field is B_1, as in the first case.

If the turns of the successive layers are placed back and forth along the coil, as convenient, then for even number of layers the net magnetic field outside is zero, while for odd number of layers it is B_1, provided that the current and the density of turns are the same.

The direction of the magnetic field inside the solenoid, is always perpendicular to the field outside it.

Solution of Problem 258. Let us denote the given data by: $\dfrac{N}{l} = 2000\ \dfrac{1}{\mathrm{m}}$, $r_1 = 5$ cm, $B = 0.251$ T, $I = 40$ A.

First we determine the magnetic field produced by the solenoid at the distance of 5 cm from its axis. Then it is easy to calculate the Lorentz force of this field acting on the wire. The opposite of this force (reaction force) is exerted on the solenoid.

Since the strength of the homogeneous magnetic field inside the coil is B, the electric current in the solenoid is:

$$I_{\mathrm{sol}} = \frac{Bl}{\mu_0 N}$$

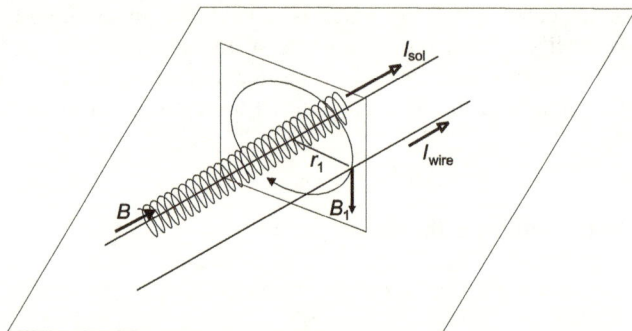

Because of the symmetry of the arrangement, the magnetic field produced by the coil outside the solenoid is similar to that of a straight, current-carrying wire, as it is shown in the figure. Let us apply Maxwell's second law to a circle of radius $r_1 = 5$ cm, whose plane is perpendicular to the axis of the solenoid. Since the surface of the circle is crossed by the current I, the strength of the magnetic field at the distance r_1 from the axis is:

$$B_1 = \mu_0 \frac{I_{\mathrm{sol}}}{2 r_1 \pi}.$$

This magnetic field can be considered homogeneous in the region of the thin wire, so the magnetic Lorentz force exerted on the length l of the wire is:

$$F = B_1 I_{\mathrm{wire}} l.$$

In details:

$$F = B_1 I_{\mathrm{wire}} l = \mu_0 \frac{I_{\mathrm{sol}}}{2 r_1 \pi} I_{\mathrm{wire}} l = \mu_0 \frac{Bl}{\mu_0 N} \frac{I_{\mathrm{wire}}}{2 r_1 \pi} l = \frac{B l^2 I_{\mathrm{wire}}}{2 r_1 \pi N}.$$

It means that the Lorentz force exerted on the length $l = 1$ m of the solenoid is:

$$F = \frac{0.251\ \frac{\mathrm{Vs}}{\mathrm{m}^2} \cdot 1\ \mathrm{m}^2 \cdot 40\ \mathrm{A}}{2 \cdot 0.05\ \mathrm{m} \cdot \pi \cdot 2000} = 16\ \mathrm{mN} = 1.6 \cdot 10^{-2}\ \mathrm{N}.$$

Remarks:

1. If the coil is wound in two layers, and in the second layer the turns are placed in opposite direction along the solenoid, then the net magnetic field outside the solenoid is zero, since in the direction of the axis of the solenoid the currents flowing in the two layers cancel each other. If, however, after finishing one layer of turns, the wire is carried back to the beginning of the solenoid, and the second layer is placed in the same direction along the solenoid, then the net current through the plane perpendicular to the axis of the solenoid is again I, so outside the coil the magnetic field is B_1, as in the first case.

2. If the turns of the successive layers are placed back and forth along the coil, as convenient, then for even number of layers the net magnetic field outside is zero, while for odd number of layers it is B_1, provided that the current and the density of turns are the same.

3. The direction of the magnetic field inside the solenoid is always perpendicular to the field outside it.

4. If the winding of the coil is bifilar, i.e., in the second layer the turns are wound in opposite sense, backwards along the solenoid (with the same density), then the magnetic field is zero inside as well as outside the solenoid.

Solution of Problem 259. The force acting on a particle of charge Q that moves with a velocity of v in a magnetic field is given by the formula:

$$\vec{F} = Q\vec{v} \times \vec{B} \tag{1}$$

This force is perpendicular to both the velocity and the magnetic field, so as in the present case the magnetic field is uniform and horizontal, the ball will move along a curve in a vertical plane perpendicular to the field lines. Since the force is perpendicular to the velocity, it can only change its direction and not its magnitude (i.e. this force can not do work), therefore the conservation of energy holds in this case:

$$mgh = \frac{1}{2}mv^2$$

thus

$$v = \sqrt{2gh}. \tag{2}$$

First let us investigate the x component of the motion. The reference frame shown in the figure is defined such that its horizontal axis x and vertical axis y are both perpendicular to the magnetic field and the origin is the initial position of the ball. The velocity, force and acceleration vectors can be resolved into horizontal and vertical components.

Newton's second law applied to the horizontal components states:

$$F_x = ma_x,$$

where $F_x = F\sin\alpha$, and α is the angle formed by the force and the vertical.

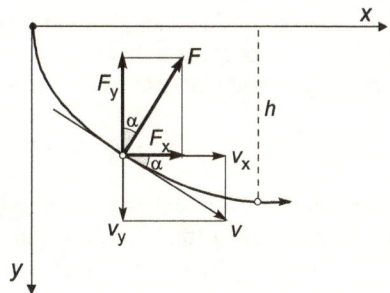

As in our case $\vec{v}$ is perpendicular to $\vec{B}$, the magnitude of the magnetic force will be $F = QvB$, which is now substituted into the previous equation to get:

$$QvB\sin\alpha = ma_x. \tag{3}$$

Note that in equation (3) $v\sin\alpha = v_y$, which is the y coordinate of velocity. Assuming that acceleration is the time derivative of velocity and velocity is the time derivative of displacement, we obtain:

$$QB \cdot \frac{dy}{dt} = m \cdot \frac{dv_x}{dt}.$$

Integrating this leads us to:

$$QB \int_0^h dy = m \cdot \int_0^v dv_x, \tag{4}$$

where the integration limits of depth are chosen to be 0 and h and the corresponding values 0 and $v_x = v$ are the limits of velocity. We assumed that the x coordinate of velocity reaches its maximum at the deepest point of the path, since that is the point where the velocity of the ball becomes horizontal. After integration equation (4) becomes:

$$QBh = mv.$$

Substituting v from equation (2), we find:

$$QBh = m\sqrt{2gh}.$$

From which the deepest point's y coordinate is ($y_{max} = h$):

$$h = \frac{2m^2 g}{Q^2 B^2} = \frac{2 \cdot (0.003 \cdot 10^{-3}\,\text{kg})^2 \cdot 9.81\,\text{m/s}^2}{(5 \cdot 10^{-5}\,\text{C})^2 \cdot (0.4\,\text{T})^2} = 0.441\,\text{m}.$$

This is the depth in which the velocity of the ball reaches its maximum, so:

$$v_{max} = \sqrt{2gh} = \frac{2mg}{QB} = \frac{2 \cdot 0.003 \cdot 10^{-3}\,\text{kg} \cdot 9.81\,\frac{\text{m}}{\text{s}^2}}{5 \cdot 10^{-5}\,\text{C} \cdot 0.4\,\text{T}} = 2.94\,\frac{\text{m}}{\text{s}}.$$

Remarks: 1. The data given in this problem are unreal. The radius of a ball of mass 0.003 g cannot be less than a few millimeters, because if it was charged to $5 \cdot 10^{-5}$ C, the electric potential near to the surface of the ball would be approximately of magnitude

$$V = 9 \cdot 10^9 \frac{5 \cdot 10^{-5}}{10^{-6}}\,V = 4.5 \cdot 10^{11}\,V$$

Therefore it is impossible to charge this ball to the given magnitude, as electric sparks would be emitted (that discharge the ball) well before reaching the required charge.

2. The path of the falling ball is a cycloid. Integrating equation (4) to an upper limit of y gives:

$$QBy = mv_x,$$

which means that the horizontal component of velocity is in direct proportion to the depth (i.e. the y coordinate). We will show that the same relation exists between the horizontal component of velocity and y coordinate of an arbitrary point on a circle rolling along the x axis with constant speed. Let a circle of radius r roll without slipping along the x axis as shown. Let its constant angular velocity be ω. The coordinates of a point on the rolling circle can be written as:

$$x = r\varphi - r\sin\varphi,$$

$$y = r - r\cos\varphi.$$

If the circle rolls with a constant angular velocity, $\varphi = \omega t$, so:

$$x = r\omega t - r\sin\omega t,$$

$$y = r - r\cos\omega t = r(1 - \cos\omega t).$$

The x component of velocity is the time derivative of the x coordinate, so:

$$v_x = \frac{\mathrm{d}x}{\mathrm{d}t} = \omega r - \omega r\cos\omega t = \omega r(1 - \cos\omega t) = \omega y.$$

This shows that the horizontal component of the velocity is indeed in direct proportion to the y coordinate. Therefore we have shown that the path of the ball dropped in a uniform magnetic field is a cycloid.

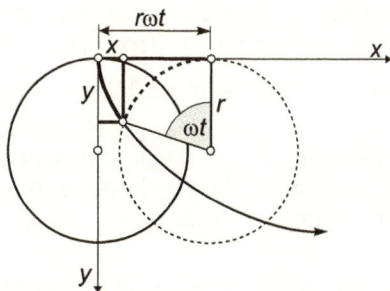

9.2 Induction (motional emf)

Solution of Problem 260. Since the metal rod is moving in magnetic field, electromotive force is induced in it. This starts an electric current, and the capacitor gradually loaded with electric charge. The instantaneous current is determined by the induced electromotive force and the voltage across the capacitor, according to Ohm's law:

$$Ri(t) = \mathcal{E}_{\mathrm{ind}}(t) - U_C,$$

so

$$Ri(t) = BLv(t) - \frac{Q(t)}{C}.$$

According to Lenz's law, the magnetic force acting on the rod, which is carrying electric current, works against the motion, so the speed of the rod decreases, although there is no friction nor air resistance. The rod decelerates as long as there is current flowing in the circle, so as long as the voltage of the capacitor does not balance the induced electromotive force. After this, the speed of the rod remains constant:

$$BLv_{\min} = \frac{Q_{\max}}{C}. \tag{1}$$

According to the impulse-momentum theorem, the (infinitesimal) change of the momentum of the rod is equal to the impulse, i.e. the product of the force and the (short) time of its action:

$$m\Delta v = F\Delta t.$$

In our case only the magnetic Lorentz force is acting on the rod, thus for a short time the following is true:

$$m\Delta v_n = -BLi\Delta t.$$

(The negative sign is due to Lenz's law; the Lorentz force decreases the speed of the rod.)

But the product $i\Delta t$ is just the infinitesimal charge flowed across the circuit and accumulated in the capacitor during this (short) time interval. So the change of the charge of the capacitor is:

$$i\Delta t = \Delta Q,$$

so combining the previous equations for the investigated short time interval we get that:

$$m\Delta v_n = -BL\Delta Q_n.$$

Let us divide the whole motion into infinitesimal intervals, and let us sum up these equations written for each small interval. We get that

$$m\sum_n \Delta v_n = -BL\sum_n \Delta Q_n,$$

so

$$m(v_{\min} - v_0) = -BLQ_{\max}. \tag{2}$$

Expressing $Q_{\max}$ from equation (1),

$$Q_{\max} = CBLv_{\min},$$

and writing it into equation (2),

$$mv_{\min} - mv_0 = -BLCBLv_{\min} = -B^2L^2Cv_{\min},$$

we get that the final constant speed of the rod is:

$$v_{\min} = \frac{mv_0}{m + (BL)^2 C}.$$

Solution of Problem 261. The electromotive force induced in the moving wire creates electric current in the two stationary frames which are connected to the wire at its two ends, whose currents are opposite to each other. The current in the moving wire is determined only by the resistance of the ammeter R, thus the value of the current is:

$$I = \frac{1}{R} \cdot Blv.$$

478

The two loops which are connected to the two ends of the wire, which behaves as the current source, are connected in parallel. The currents in the loops are not infinite even though their resistances are considered zero, because the resistance of the ammeter in the moving wire restricts these currents as well. Kirchhoff's junction rule holds true, according to which

$$I = I_1 + I_2.$$

Even though the resistances of the loops are negligible with respect to the resistance of the ammeter, their resistance with respect to each other is not negligible, thus the currents that run through them are determined by the ratio of their resistances. For the sake of simplicity, let us assume that the wire of the frame is made of the same material and have the same diameter everywhere.

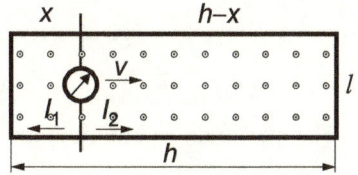

The resistances of both U-shaped loops change depending on the instantaneous position of the moving wire, therefore the currents running through them also depend on the position (thus the elapsed time) of the moving wire. The resistance of each loop using the notations of the figure are:

$$R_1 = \varrho \frac{2x+l}{A} \qquad \text{and} \qquad R_2 = \varrho \frac{2(h-x)+l}{A}.$$

According to Kirchhoff's loop rule, the currents in the two branches are inversely proportional to these resistances:

$$\frac{I_1}{I_2} = \frac{R_2}{R_1} = \frac{2(h-x)+l}{2x+l} \qquad \text{and} \qquad I_1 + I_2 = \frac{Blv}{R}.$$

Expressing I_2 from this and substituting back into the former equation the currents in the two branches are:

$$I_1 = \frac{2(h-x)+l}{2(l+h)} \cdot \frac{Blv}{R},$$

$$I_2 = \frac{l+2x}{2(l+h)} \cdot \frac{Blv}{R}.$$

The currents in the two branches change oppositely, and the current in each branch vary linearly with the displacement x (or with the time t) $I_1 = a - bx$, or $I_1 = a - bvt$ and $I_2 = a' + b'x$, or $I_2 = a' + b'vt$ which is

$$I_1 = \frac{2h+l}{2(h+l)} \cdot \frac{Blv}{R} - \frac{2Blv}{2(h+l)R} \cdot x, \quad \text{or} \quad I_1 = \frac{2h+l}{2(h+l)} \cdot \frac{Blv}{R} - \frac{2Blv^2}{2(h+l)R} \cdot t$$

and

$$I_2 = \frac{l}{2(h+l)} \cdot \frac{Blv}{R} + \frac{2Blv}{2(h+l)R} \cdot x, \quad \text{or} \quad I_2 = \frac{l}{2(h+l)} \cdot \frac{Blv}{R} + \frac{2Blv^2}{2(h+l)R} \cdot t.$$

When the direction of the motion of the wire changes, the direction of both currents change. The figure shows how the currents change with the time.

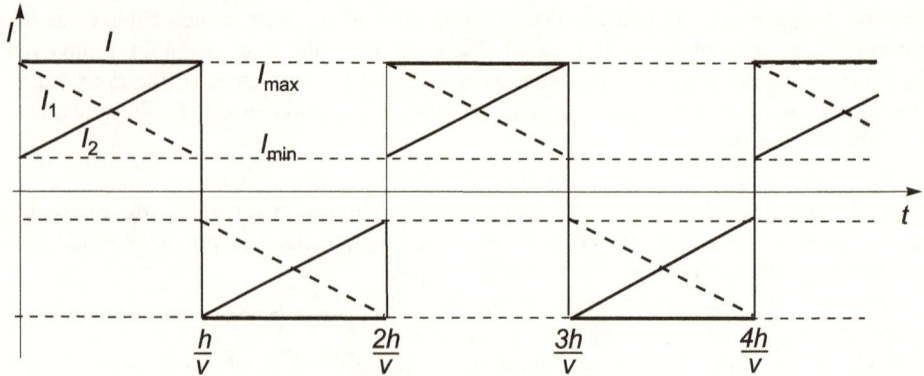

The maximum and minimum values of the currents are:

$$I_{1_{\max}} = I_{2_{\max}} = \frac{2h+l}{2(h+l)} \cdot \frac{Blv}{R},$$

$$I_{1_{\min}} = I_{2_{\min}} = \frac{l}{2(h+l)} \cdot \frac{Blv}{R}.$$

Let us consider an example. Let the resistance of the meter be $R = 1\Omega$, the length of the moving wire be $l = 0.25\,\mathrm{m}$, its speed be $v = 2\,\mathrm{m/s}$, the length of the parallel wires be $h = 1\,\mathrm{m}$, and the magnetic induction be $B = 0.8\,\mathrm{T}$. Calculating with these data:

$$I_1 = 0.36\ \mathrm{A} - 0.32\ \frac{\mathrm{A}}{\mathrm{m}} \cdot x = 0.36\ \mathrm{A} - 0.64\ \frac{\mathrm{A}}{\mathrm{s}} \cdot t,$$

$$I_2 = 0.04\ \mathrm{A} + 0.32\ \frac{\mathrm{A}}{\mathrm{m}} \cdot x = 0.36\ \mathrm{A} + 0.64\ \frac{\mathrm{A}}{\mathrm{s}} \cdot t,$$

$$I_{1_{\max}} = I_{2_{\min}} = 0.36\ \mathrm{A},$$

$$I_{1_{\min}} = I_{2_{\max}} = 0.04\ \mathrm{A}.$$

Solution of Problem 262. a) One key to the solution is that the resistance of the frame is negligible. This means that inside the frame the electric field is zero (in macroscopical sense), because otherwise an infinitely large current would flow. Let us apply Maxwell's second law along the frame:

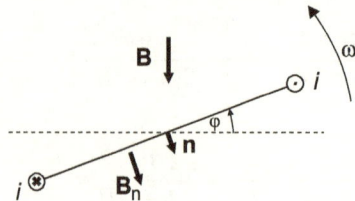

$$\oint \vec{E}\Delta\vec{s} = -\frac{\Delta\Phi}{\Delta t} = 0.$$

So the total magnetic flux surrounded by the frame cannot change during the motion. As the initial flux was $\Phi = B.A$, it should have the same value in any position of the frame.

In a position characterised by angle φ, the flux of the frame originates partly from the field with induction B ($B \cdot A \cdot \cos\varphi$), partly from the magnetic field created by the current induced in the frame ($L \cdot i$). So the total flux is

$$B \cdot A \cdot \cos\varphi + L \cdot i.$$

But because of the constant value of the flux

$$B \cdot A = B \cdot A \cdot \cos\varphi + L \cdot i.$$

From this the current is

$$i = \frac{B \cdot A}{L}(1 - \cos\varphi).$$

The current has maximum when $\cos\varphi = -1$, that is, when $\varphi = \pi$:

$$i_{max} = \frac{2B \cdot A}{L}.$$

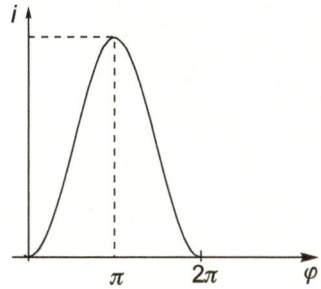

Remark: The relationship $i_{max} \cdot L = 2B \cdot A$ at $\varphi = \pi$ is reasonable, because the flux that originates from the external field is $-B \cdot A$ (due to the turning of the frame), so the 'own' flux should be $+2B \cdot A$ if the total flux remains $+B \cdot A$.

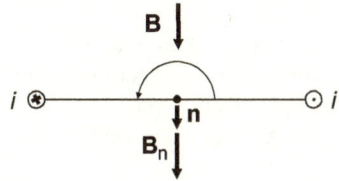

b) During the motion, the frame experiences a turning moment:

$$M(\varphi) = -B \cdot A \cdot i \cdot \sin\varphi.$$

Using the relationship for current, the turning moment can be written in the following form:

$$M(\varphi) = -\frac{(B \cdot A)^2}{L} \cdot \sin\varphi(1 - \cos\varphi).$$

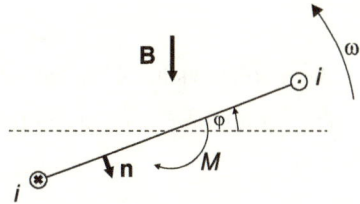

By examining the turning moment, it can be seen that until an angular displacement of $180°$ the turning moment slows down the frame and after that it helps the rotation. So it can be stated that position $\varphi = \pi$ is the 'standstill position' if the frame reaches this position (instable equilibrium position) then it turns over.

The extremes of this expression can be acquired to an arbitrary accuracy by drawing the graph of the function and calculating a few substitution values using a calculator. Drawing the graph is simple if we make use of the identity

$$\sin\varphi(1 - \cos\varphi) = \sin\varphi - \sin\varphi\cos\varphi = \sin\varphi - \frac{1}{2}\sin 2\varphi.$$

So functions $\sin\varphi$ and $-\frac{1}{2}\sin 2\varphi$ should be added and then reflected about the φ axis:

481

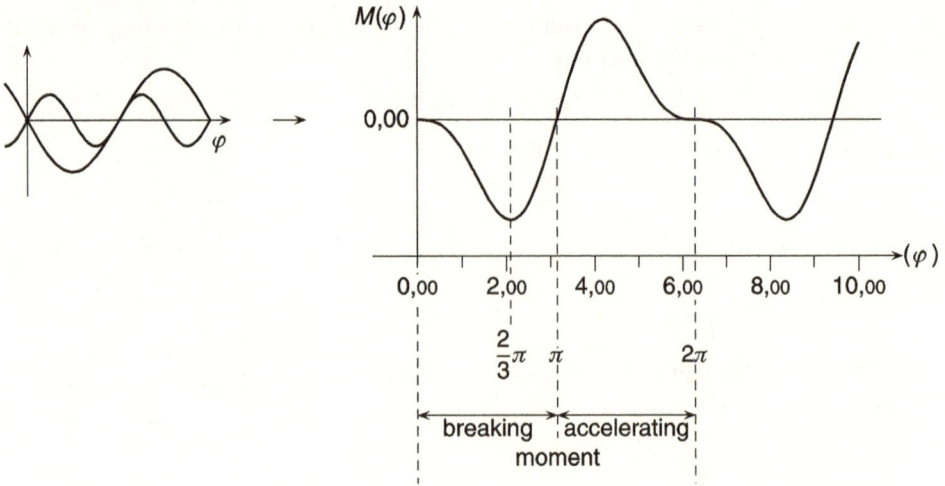

It can be seen that the 'maximum breaking moment' arises at the place of the minimum of the function. By examining the graph, it is clear that this place is an angular position smaller than π and greater than $\pi/2$.

Let us substitute $100°$ first:

$$-(\sin 100° - 0.5 \cdot \sin 200°) = -1.15581,$$

At $110°$:

$$-(\sin 110° - 0.5 \cdot \sin 220°) = -1.26108,$$

so the absolute value of the substitution value of the function increases.

The substitution value of the function at $150°$ is

$$-(\sin 150° - 0.5 \cdot \sin 300°) = -0.93301,$$

so the absolute value of the substitution value decreases again. Let us examine the function around $120°$.

$$-(\sin 120° - 0.5 \cdot \sin 240°) = -1.299038.$$

Its absolute value is the greatest so far. Let us check the value of the function at $121°$ and at $119°$.

$$-(\sin 121° - 0.5 \cdot \sin 242°) = -1.298641097,$$

and

$$-(\sin 119° - 0.5 \cdot \sin 238°) = -1.298643755.$$

Both values are smaller in absolute value than the absolute value belonging to $120°$, so we can state with great confidence that we have determined the requested angular position with an error less than $2/120 = 1.6\%$.

Remark. The extreme value of the function can be found using derivative as well. The place of the minimum is given by the solution of equation $\dfrac{dM}{d\varphi}=0$. The equation leads to the quadratic equation

$$2\cdot\cos^2\varphi-\cos\varphi-1=0,$$

whose solution is

$$\cos\varphi=-\frac{1}{2},\qquad \text{that is,}\qquad \varphi=\frac{2\pi}{3}\ \text{rad}=120°.$$

Solution of Problem 263. The system described above is the model of a unipolar induction generator, i.e. a generator which produces DC current by electromagnetic induction.

The conduction electrons in the disc move on a circular path due to the rotation, therefore the magnetic deflecting force (or Lorentz force) makes them move in the radial direction building up a potential difference between the shaft and the perimeter of the disc. If resistor R is connected across the shaft and the perimeter of the disc, a current will flow in the circuit. The conduction electrons will drift outwards, and since now their velocities have a radial component as well, the Lorentz force will act on them in a direction opposite the rotation, which makes the disc decelerate (Lenz's law). The deceleration caused by the torque of this Lorentz force is proportional to the current flowing in the radial direction, which is proportional to the potential difference existing between the centre and the perimeter of the disc. Since this potential difference depends upon the angular velocity of the rotation, the disc will accelerate until the magnitude of the torque of Lorentz force reaches the magnitude of the torque caused by mass m.

Let us first determine the potential difference induced between the shaft and the perimeter of the disc, and then express the current flowing in the circuit. The second step is then to determine the net torque of the forces acting on the current flowing in the radial direction, which then should be made equal to the torque of mass m.

To find the potential difference between the centre and the perimeter of the disc, let us consider a metal rod rotating about one of its ends in a plane perpendicular to the uniform magnetic field. The potential difference induced between the ends of the rod can be written as the sum of the potential differences $\Delta V=B\Delta lr\omega$ induced in the elements of the rod. If the rod is divided into n equal parts of length $\Delta l=l/n$, the sum can be written as:

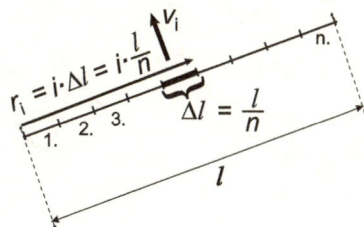

$$V=\sum_{i=1}^{n}\Delta V_i=\sum_{i=1}^{n}B\Delta lv_i=\sum_{i=1}^{n}B\cdot\frac{l}{n}\cdot r_i\omega=\sum_{i=1}^{n}B\cdot\frac{l}{n}\cdot i\cdot\frac{l}{n}\cdot\omega,$$

where $r_i=i\cdot\dfrac{l}{n}$ is the distance of the ith element from the rotation axis, or in other words it is the radius of its circular path. If this radius is multiplied by the angular velocity, we get the velocity of the given element ($v_i = r_i\omega$), which is perpendicular to the magnetic field.

Factoring out the constants, we find:

$$V = B\frac{l^2}{n^2}\omega \sum_{i=1}^{n} i = B\frac{l^2}{n^2}\omega\frac{1+n}{2}n = B\frac{l^2}{n^2}\omega(\frac{n}{2} + \frac{n^2}{2}) = Bl^2\omega\left[\frac{1}{2n} + \frac{1}{2}\right].$$

If n tends to infinity (which means that the rod is divided into smaller and smaller parts), the first term in the bracket tends to zero, while the second remains constant. Hence the potential difference between the two ends of the rod is:

$$V = \frac{Bl^2\omega}{2}.$$

The rotating disc can be handled as if it were an infinite number of rods connected in parallel. The potential difference induced between the centre and perimeter of the disc can therefore be determined as the net potential difference produced by identical batteries connected in parallel, which is:

$$V = \frac{Br^2\omega}{2}.$$

The current flowing in the circuit due to this potential difference is:

$$I = \frac{V}{R} = \frac{Br^2\omega}{2R}.$$

This current is a stream of conduction electrons moving along complicated paths from the shaft to the perimeter. In spite of the complicated paths of the electrons, the Lorentz force acting on the current can be calculated as if the current was flowing along a straight line in the radial direction.

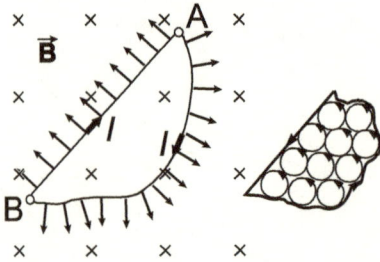

To prove this, let us consider a wire connecting points A and B that has an arbitrary shape in the plane perpendicular to the magnetic field. Let us then connect points A and B with a straight wire as well, thus producing a closed loop as shown. If current I flows in the loop, the magnetic field exerts forces on each segment of the loop. The resultant of these forces which are all in the plane of the loop must be zero, or otherwise the loop would start to move in the plane determined by itself, which is impossible. (Or let us investigate what happens if the current in the original loop is substituted by small circular current loops in which the direction and magnitude of the currents are the same as that in the original loop. Inside the original loop, where the small loops adjoin, the forces that are the same in magnitude but opposite in direction cancel each other. Therefore all we need to consider is the current on the perimeter of the small loops, which is the same as the current in the original loop. Since the small loops are all perpendicular to the magnetic field, there is no magnetic force acting on them, therefore the net force for the whole system of loops is zero as well. Knowing that the net force inside the original loop is zero, we can conclude that the resultant force acting on the original loop must be zero as well.

It can be useful to prove our statement for a special case that can easily be generalized. Let us consider a semi-circular wire in the plane perpendicular to the magnetic field and also a straight wire that connects the ends of the semicircle. Let us assume that the same current flows in each of the two wires. The semi-circular wire can be approximated by an open polygon whose sides are all equal and have a length of Δl.

The magnetic forces (Lorentz forces) acting on each side of the polygon have the same magnitude, which is:

$$\Delta F = BI\Delta l$$

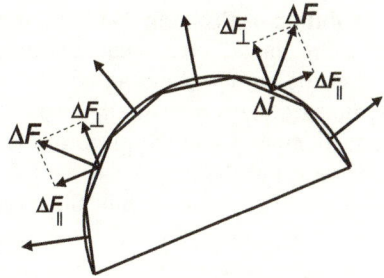

Let us resolve these forces into components that are parallel and perpendicular to the straight wire (or the diameter of the semi-circle). Due to the symmetry, the resultant of the parallel force components must be zero. The magnitudes of the perpendicular components can be written as

$$\Delta F_\perp = BI\Delta l \sin\alpha,$$

where α is the angle which the given side of the polygon forms with the line of the diameter. Note that $\Delta l \sin\alpha$ is the length of the orthogonal projection of the given side to the diameter, therefore the sum of these expressions gives the length of the diameter itself. Thus the sum of the perpendicular components of forces equals the force acting on the straight wire:

$$\sum_{i=1}^{n} BI\Delta l_i \sin\alpha_i = BI \sum_{i=1}^{n} \Delta l_i \sin\alpha_i = BIl_{AB} = BI2r.$$

Hence we proved that the magnetic force acting on a current carrying wire between points A and B is independent of the shape of the wire and equals $F = BIl_{AB}$. Applying this to our case, we get that the resultant of the forces acting on the current, which is produced by electrons moving along arbitrary paths from the shaft to the perimeter of the disc, equals a force that would act on a current of the same magnitude flowing straight along the radius of the disc. Thus the force acting on the current in the disc is $F = BIr$.

Substituting the expression for the magnitude of the current, we obtain:

$$F = \frac{B^2 r^3 \omega}{2R}.$$

This force is distributed evenly along radius r (since $I = $ constant), therefore it can be substituted by a force that acts at a distance of $r/2$ from the centre of the disc. The torque of this force about the shaft is:

$$M = F\frac{r}{2}.$$

The angular velocity of the disc increases until this torque reaches the magnitude of the torque produced by mass m and their net torque becomes zero:

$$\frac{B^2 r^3 \omega}{2R} \cdot \frac{r}{2} - mg\varrho = 0,$$

which yields

$$\omega = \frac{4mg\varrho R}{B^2 r^4} = 100 \text{ s}^{-1}.$$

Solution of Problem 264. The straight wire accelerates to a speed at which the torque of the magnetic force is equal to the torque of the drag force.

Let the current flow out of the axle towards the two ends of the wire. Due to the symmetry, the currents in the two branches are equal, its value is $I/2$. Let the magnetic induction point into the plane of the figure. In this case the wire rotates anticlockwise. The torque of the drag force $k_1 v^2$ is $k_1 v^2 l/2$. The speed in terms of the angular speed of the wire is $v = \omega l/2$ thus the torque in terms of the angular speed is:

$$M = \frac{k_1 \omega^2 l^3}{8}.$$

The magnetic field exerts a force of

$$F_1 = B \cdot \frac{I}{2} \cdot \frac{l}{2}$$

on one half of the wire, the length of which is $l/2$ (independently of its motion). Because this force is distributed evenly, its resultant is in the midpoint of the half-wire, thus its torque calculated for the axle is:

$$M_1 = F_1 \frac{l}{4} = B \cdot \frac{I}{2} \cdot \frac{l}{2} \cdot \frac{l}{4}.$$

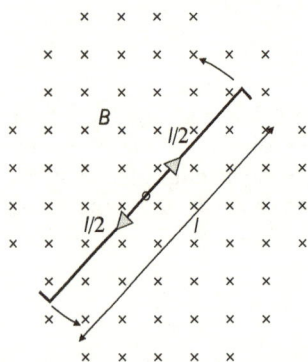

The torque exerted on the whole wire is:

$$M = 2M_1 = \frac{BIl^2}{8}.$$

From the equation of the torque of the drag force and the magnetic force we gain:

$$\frac{k_1 \omega^2 l^3}{8} = \frac{BIl^2}{8}.$$

From this the asked angular speed is:

$$\omega = \sqrt{\frac{BI}{k_1 l}}.$$

Substituting the given data: $\omega = 12.65 \, \frac{1}{\text{s}}$, and the number of revolutions is $n = 2.013 \, \frac{1}{\text{s}}$.

The ohmic resistance of the wire system connected to the power supply is zero everywhere, thus there is no voltage across any of the elements, which is generated from the power supply. The voltage between the axle and the mercury tank is the electromotive force generated by the motional induction. If the wire is perpendicular to the magnetic induction and the direction of the motion is perpendicular to both the the wire and the magnetic induction, the magnitude of the induced emf is:

$$\varepsilon = Blv,$$

where l is the length of the wire, v is its speed. The voltage between points which are a unit length apart has the same magnitude as that of the electric field, which is generated by the induced charges. Its magnitude is:

$$E = Bv.$$

It can be seen that in the case of the rotating straight wire the electric field along the wire is uniformly increasing with the distance r measured from the axle. The total voltage can be calculated as a sum:

$$V = \sum \Delta V = \sum E\Delta l = \sum Bv\Delta l,$$

where the speed as a function of the angular speed is $v = \omega \cdot r$. Substituting this into the formula of the induced voltage:

$$V = \sum B\omega r\Delta l,$$

Factorizing this sum:

$$V = B\omega \sum r\Delta l.$$

The value of the sum is more punctual if the Δl distances, into which the wire is divided, are smaller. Let $\Delta l = \dfrac{l}{n}$, in this case the radius of the i-th segment is $r_i = i \cdot \dfrac{l}{n}$, and the voltage across this segment is $\Delta V_i = B\omega r_i \Delta l$ thus the total voltage is:

$$V = B\omega \sum i \cdot \frac{l}{n} \cdot \frac{l}{n}.$$

Taking out the factor l/n:

$$B\omega \frac{l^2}{n^2}(1+2+3+\ldots+i+\ldots+n),$$

where in the bracket there is the sum of the first n natural numbers. Using the formula of the sum of the first n elements of an arithmetic sequence, the voltage is:

$$B\omega \frac{l^2}{n^2} \cdot \frac{n(n+1)}{2} = B\omega l^2 \left(\frac{n^2+n}{2n^2} \right) = \frac{B\omega l^2}{2} \left(1 + \frac{1}{n} \right).$$

If the length of the segments is decreased, so n tends to infinity the second term in the bracket tends to zero, thus the voltage between the ends of a wire which is rotated about one of its ends is:

$$V = \frac{B\omega l^2}{2}.$$

In our case we have two wires of length $l/2$, which are connected in parallel and across which the voltage is the same as the induced voltage in only one of them:

$$V = \frac{B\omega l^2}{8}.$$

Substituting the data: $V = 3.16 \cdot 10^{-3}$ V.

Solution of Problem 265. Based on the direction of rotation, there are two cases to distinguish: 1. $\vec{B}$ and $\vec{\omega}$ point in opposite directions, 2. $\vec{B}$ and $\vec{\omega}$ point in the same direction.

Case 1: $\vec{B}$ and $\vec{\omega}$ are oppositely directed:

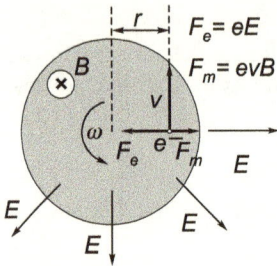

In the figure, the induction vector points towards the page and the angular velocity vector points away from the page. The figure shows the (relevant) forces acting on a particular electron when the constant electron density has already set. (There may be fluctuations.) These forces are the magnetic Lorentz-force and the electric force owing to the field of the separated charges. The Lorentz-force now points radially outwards. Since the electron accelerates towards the centre of the circular path, the electric force must act towards the centre. Thus the electric field vector points radially outwards.

The net force (expressed in terms of the magnitudes of the vectors) provides the centripetal force:

$$Ee - er\omega B = mr\omega^2. \tag{1}$$

Hence the magnitude of the electric field is

$$E = \frac{(e\omega B + m\omega^2)}{e} \cdot r. \tag{2}$$

What charge distribution is responsible for the electric field expressed in (2)?

It is known that the magnitude of the electric field in the interior of a long straight cylinder of uniform volume charge density is:

$$E = \frac{\varrho}{2\varepsilon_0} \cdot r, \tag{3}$$

and in the case of positive charge density it points radially outwards, that is, it has the same structure as the electric field established in our rotating cylinder. (With a difference worth mentioning: in the rotating metal cylinder, the result will be accurate for a short cylinder too, since that is the only distribution of the electric field that can provide the force distribution required by the stationary state of rigid rotation). This leads to the conclusion that the charge density inside the rotating cylinder is uniform. The magnitude of that charge distribution is obtained from (2) and (3):

$$\varrho = \frac{2\varepsilon_0\omega(eB + m\omega)}{e}. \tag{4}$$

The whole cylinder is neutral, its interior is positively charged, the corresponding negative charge is situated on the outer surface.

Case 2: $\vec{B}$ and $\vec{\omega}$ point in the same direction. Then the magnetic Lorentz-force points towards the centre of the circle. In that case, three subcases may occur, depending on the speed of the rotation:

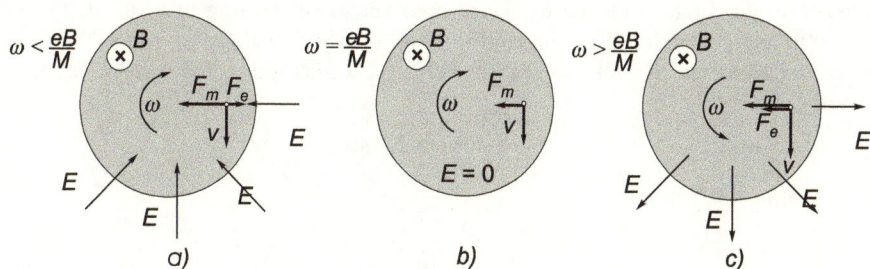

a)   b)   c)

(a) $$mr\omega^2 < er\omega B \quad \rightarrow \quad \omega < \frac{eB}{m},$$

then the electric force is outwards and the electric field vector $\vec{E}$ points towards the axis of the cylinder, the electric charge density is negative. The outer surface of the cylinder is positively charged.

(b) $$mr\omega^2 = er\omega B \quad \rightarrow \quad \omega = \frac{eB}{m},$$

then the Lorentz-force alone can keep the electrons in orbit, there is no electric field, charge density is zero. This provides the answer to question b).

(c) $$mr\omega^2 > er\omega B \quad \rightarrow \quad \omega > \frac{eB}{m},$$

then the electric force points towards the centre of the circle and the electric field vector $\vec{E}$ is radially outwards, the electric charge density is positive. The outer surface of the cylinder carries a negative charge.

In the cases a) and c), the equations of the motion and the magnitudes of the electric field and the charge density are as follows:

$$mr\omega^2 - er\omega B - eE, \qquad mr\omega^2 = er\omega B + eE,$$

$$E = \frac{e\omega B - m\omega^2}{e} \cdot r, \qquad E = \frac{m\omega^2 - e\omega B}{e} \cdot r,$$

$$\varrho = \frac{2\varepsilon_0 \omega(eB - m\omega)}{e}, \qquad \varrho = \frac{2\varepsilon_0 \omega(m\omega - eB)}{e}.$$

Solution of Problem 266. Let us resolve the induction of the magnetic field of the Earth into vertical and horizontal components. The vertical component does not induce electromotive force (loop emf) in the ring, because its flux is always zero. Let B stand for the horizontal component. If the ring rotates at angular velocity ω, its magnetic flux is

$$\Phi = r^2 \pi B \cos \omega t,$$

where ωt is the angle enclosed by the normal vector of the ring and vector $\vec{B}$. The electromotive force induced in the ring — based on the analogy of simple harmonic motion (relationship rate of change of velocity–acceleration; see simple harmonic motion) — is:

$$\mathcal{E} = -\frac{\Delta \Phi}{\Delta t} = r^2 \pi B \omega \sin \omega t.$$

The current in the ring is

$$I = \frac{\mathcal{E}}{R} = \frac{r^2 \pi B \omega}{R} \sin \omega t,$$

where R is the resistance of the ring. Let B_O stand for the induction of the magnetic field induced by the current in the centre of the ring. Its magnitude is:

$$B_O = \mu_0 \frac{I}{2r} = \mu_0 \frac{r^2 \pi B \omega}{2rR} \sin \omega t = \mu_0 \frac{r \pi B \omega}{2R} \sin \omega t.$$

The direction of magnetic induction B_O is perpendicular to the plane of the ring and rotates with it. Let us resolve vector B_O into components parallel with and perpendicular to the horizontal induction B of the magnetic field of the Earth. The magnitude of the parallel component is:

$$B_O^p = \mu_0 \frac{r \pi B \omega}{2R} \sin \omega t \cdot \cos \omega t = \mu_0 \frac{r \pi B \omega}{4R} \sin(2\omega t).$$

So the mean of the parallel component is zero in time. The magnitude of the perpendicular component is:

$$B_O^m = \mu_0 \frac{r \pi B \omega}{2R} \sin^2 \omega t.$$

Its mean in time (similarly to the root mean square value of a sinusoidal current) is

$$\langle B_O^m \rangle = \mu_0 \frac{r \pi B \omega}{4R}.$$

This mean induction diverts the magnetic ring from the direction of the magnetic field of the Earth.

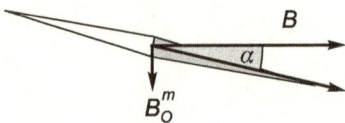

The magnetic needle points in the direction of the resultant of B and B^m. Let α stand for the angle of this diversion. Then

$$\tan \alpha = \frac{\langle B_O^m \rangle}{B} = \mu_0 \frac{r \pi \omega}{4R} = \mu_0 \frac{2r \pi^2 n}{4R} = \mu_0 \frac{r \pi^2 f}{2R},$$

where n stands for the number of revolutions of the ring.

Let us realize that the angle of the diversion of the magnetic needle does not depend on the magnitude of the induction of the magnetic field of the Earth, the only important thing is that the magnetic field of the Earth has a non-zero horizontal component. Furthermore, the above relationship gives the average value of the diversion. It is possible that the magnetic needle oscillates a little bit around its new equilibrium position.

The numerical value of the electric resistance of the ring is:

$$R = \mu_0 \frac{\pi^2 r f}{2 \cdot \tan \alpha} = \frac{4\pi \cdot 10^{-7} \frac{V s}{A m} \cdot \pi^2 \cdot 0.1\,\mathrm{m} \cdot 10\,\mathrm{s}^{-1}}{2 \cdot \tan 2^o} = 1.78 \cdot 10^{-4}\,\Omega \approx 0.18\,\mathrm{m}\Omega.$$

Solution of Problem 267. a) The change in magnetic flux induces an emf, which generates a current:

$$\mathcal{E} = \frac{\Delta \Phi}{\Delta t} = RI, \quad \text{where} \quad \Phi = B_z \cdot r_0^2 \pi + LI.$$

Since the resistance of the ring is $R = 0$, the net emf should also be zero: $\mathcal{E} = 0$, thus the magnetic flux Φ is constant:

$$\Phi = B_0(1 - \alpha z) r_0^2 \pi + LI = \text{constant.} \tag{1}$$

With the initial conditions ($z = 0$, $I = 0$) considered, the constant flux is

$$\Phi = B_0 r_0^2 \pi. \tag{2}$$

b) The current flowing in the ring can be expressed from the equations (1) and (2):

$$I = \frac{1}{L} B_0 \alpha r_0^2 \pi z. \tag{3}$$

The external magnetic field exerts forces on the current elements of the current-carrying ring. The resultant force is

$$F_z = -B_r \cdot I(z) \cdot 2 r_0 \pi = -B_0 \beta r_0 \cdot \frac{B_0 \alpha r_0^2 \pi}{L} \cdot 2 r_0 \pi \cdot z = -kz.$$

Newton's second law applied to the ring gives the equation

$$m a_z = F_z - mg = -kz - mg, \tag{4}$$

where

$$k = \frac{2 B_0^2 \alpha \beta r_0^4 \pi^2}{L},$$

thus the ring will oscillate harmonically.

With the initial conditions considered, the motion of the ring is described by the equation

$$z(t) = A(\cos \omega t - 1), \tag{5}$$

where the angular frquency is

$$\omega = \sqrt{\frac{k}{m}} = \pi r_0^2 B_0 \sqrt{\frac{2\alpha\beta}{mL}}.$$

The equilibrium position ($a_z = 0$) and the amplitude A are obtained from equation (4):

$$z_0 = -A = -\frac{mg}{k} = -\frac{mgL}{2B_0^2 \alpha\beta r_0^2 \pi^2}, \tag{6}$$

that is,

$$\omega = \pi \cdot 0.5^2 \cdot 10^{-4}\,\mathrm{m}^2 \cdot 0.01 \frac{\mathrm{V\,s}}{\mathrm{m}^2} \sqrt{\frac{2 \cdot 32\,\mathrm{m}^{-1} \cdot 16\,\mathrm{m}^{-1}}{50 \cdot 10^{-6}\,\mathrm{kg} \cdot 1.3 \cdot 10^{-8}\,\mathrm{Vs/A}}} = 31.2\frac{1}{\mathrm{s}}$$

and

$$A = \frac{50 \cdot 10^{-6}\,\mathrm{kg} \cdot 9.8\,\mathrm{m/s}^2 \cdot 1.3 \cdot 10^{-8}\,\mathrm{Vs/A}}{2 \cdot 0.01^2\,\mathrm{V}^2\,\mathrm{s}^2/\mathrm{m}^4 \cdot 32\,\mathrm{m}^{-1} \cdot 16\,\mathrm{m}^{-1} \cdot 0.5^4 \cdot 10^{-8}\pi^2} = 1\,\mathrm{cm}.$$

c) The current in terms of time is obtained by substituting the expression (5) into the equation (3):

$$I(t) = \frac{B_0 \alpha r_0^2 \pi}{L} \cdot A(\cos\omega t - 1).$$

With the expression (6) of the amplitude:

$$I(t) = \frac{mg}{2\pi r_0^2 B_0 \beta}(\cos\omega t - 1),$$

and hence the maximum value of the current is

$$I_{\max} = \frac{2mg}{\pi r_0^2 B_0 \beta} = I_{\max} = \frac{2 \cdot 50 \cdot 10^{-6}\,\mathrm{kg} \cdot 9.8\,\mathrm{m/s}^2}{2\pi \cdot 0.5^2 \cdot 10^{-4} \cdot 0.01\,\mathrm{V\,s/m}^2 \cdot 16\,\mathrm{m}^{-1}} = 39\,\mathrm{A}.$$

9.3 Induction (transformer emf)

Solution of Problem 268. a) According to Ohm's law,

$$I = \frac{V}{R} = \frac{V}{\varrho l / A} = \frac{VA}{\varrho l},$$

where

$$\frac{V}{l} = E$$

is the electric field in the conductor. Thus the current is

$$I = \frac{1}{\varrho} E A,$$

and the current density, suitable for describing the phenomenon locally, is

$$j = \frac{I}{A} = \frac{nevA}{A} = nev = \frac{1}{\varrho} E,$$

where n is the number of conduction electrons per unit volume, e is the elementary charge, v is the drift speed in question and A is the cross-sectional area of the conductor. Hence

$$v = \frac{1}{ne\varrho} E. \tag{1}$$

According to the law of induction, the change of the magnetic field creates an electric field around the changing flux, which is present inside the metal ring, too. The magnitude of the electric field at a distance r from the axis is

$$E = \frac{1}{2r\pi} \frac{\Delta \Phi}{\Delta t} = \frac{1}{2r\pi} \frac{\Delta B \cdot R_i^2 \pi}{\Delta t} = \frac{1}{2} \frac{\Delta B}{\Delta t} \frac{R_i^2}{r}, \tag{2}$$

it is inversely proportional to the distance from the axis.

This electric field generates a current in the ring. The speed of the electrons constituting the current is obtained from (1) and (2):

$$v = \frac{R_i^2}{2\varrho ne} \frac{\Delta B}{\Delta t} \frac{1}{r} = c_1 \cdot \frac{1}{r},$$

and their angular speed is

$$\omega = \frac{v}{r} = \frac{R_i^2}{2\varrho ne} \frac{\Delta B}{\Delta t} \frac{1}{r^2} = c_1 \cdot \frac{1}{r^2}.$$

b) Question b) can be answered with a similar reasoning. According to Maxwell's law, the total electromotive force around a closed curve is proportional to the rate of change of the flux through it. Because of symmetry, the total emf can be expressed for a circular electric field line:

$$E 2r\pi = \frac{\Delta B}{\Delta t} r^2 \pi,$$

and hence the electric field is directly proportional to the radius:

$$E = \frac{1}{2}\frac{\Delta B}{\Delta t}r,$$

and the drift speed of the electrons obtained from (1) is

$$v = \frac{1}{2\varrho ne} \cdot \frac{\Delta B}{\Delta t} \cdot r = c_2 \cdot r.$$

Their angular speed is

$$\omega = \frac{v}{r} = \frac{1}{2\varrho ne}\frac{\Delta B}{\Delta t} = c_2,$$

which is a constant independent of the radius.

The task is to determine the coefficients c_1 and c_2. The data is taken from tables. The molar mass of copper is $M = 0.0635$ kg/mol, its density is $d = 8960$ kg/m^3, its resistivity is $\varrho = 1.78 \cdot 10^{-8}$ Ω m, and the elementary charge is $e = 1.6 \cdot 10^{-19}$ C. Hence, (with the assumption of one conduction electron per copper atom on average,) the number of conduction electrons per unit volume is

$$n = \frac{N}{V} = \frac{m}{M}N_A\frac{1}{V} = \frac{N_A d}{M}.$$

With the substitution of the data, the drift speed in case a) is

$$v = \frac{MR_b^2}{2\varrho N_A de}\frac{\Delta B}{\Delta t}\frac{1}{r},$$

and numerically:

$$c_1 = \frac{0.0635\,\text{kg/mol}\cdot 25\cdot 10^{-4}\,\text{m}^2\cdot 0.2\,\text{T}}{2\cdot 1.78\cdot 10^{-8}\,\Omega\,\text{m}\cdot 8960\frac{\text{kg}}{\text{m}^3}\cdot 6\cdot 10^{23}/\text{mol}\cdot 1.6\cdot 10^{-19}\,\text{C}\cdot 2\,\text{s}} = 1.037\cdot 10^{-6}\frac{\text{m}^2}{\text{s}}.$$

Thus

$$v = 1.037\cdot 10^{-6}\frac{\text{m}^2}{\text{s}}\cdot\frac{1}{r}.$$

(At the middle radius, that only means a speed of $v = 1.728 \cdot 10^{-5}$ m/s!)

In the angular speed, the coefficient of $\frac{1}{r^2}$ is the same.

The coefficient in case b) is obtained if the previous value is divided by R_i^2, that is,

$$c_2 = \frac{1.037\frac{\text{m}^2}{\text{s}}\cdot 10^{-6}}{25\cdot 10^{-4}\,\text{m}^2} = 4.148\cdot 10^{-4}\frac{1}{\text{s}}.$$

Thus the speed and angular speed are now

$$v = 4.148\cdot 10^{-4}\frac{1}{\text{s}}\cdot r \qquad \text{and} \qquad \omega = 4.148\cdot 10^{-4}\frac{1}{\text{s}}.$$

The graphs below represent the variation of the speed as a function of the radius in each case:

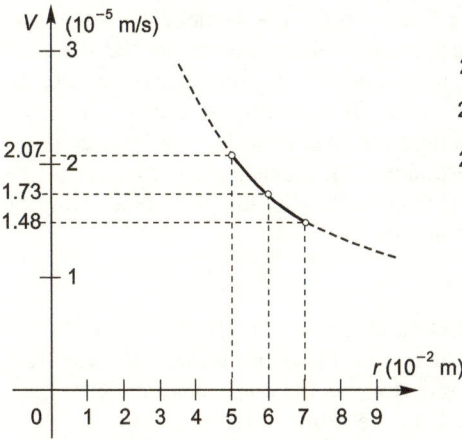

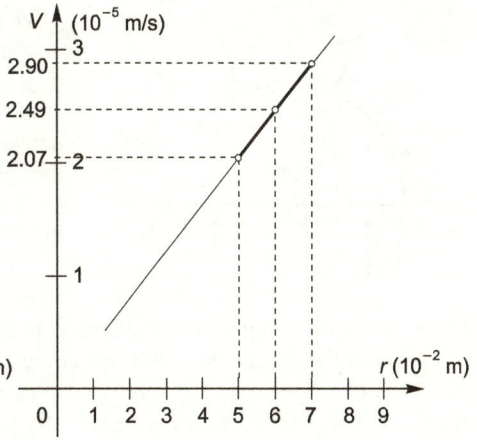

First solution of Problem 269. The magnetic field changing in time induces an electric field that enters the metallic ring and starts a current in it. On this already current-bearing conductor (whose induction increases in time), a magnetic Lorentz force acts from the same field, which is perpendicular to both the induction lines and the conducting ring, and because of the direction of the induced current points in the direction of the centre of the ring, so it strives to crash the ring. Therefore it creates tensile stress in the ring. (If the ring were in a magnetic field whose induction decreases in time, the force would strive to burst the ring.) We have to determine this force.

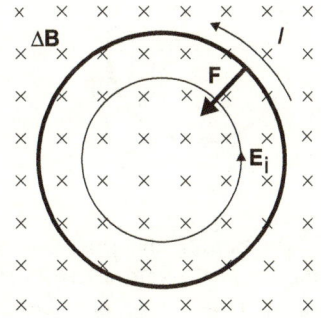

As the field changes uniformly in time, the induced electric field and so the loop emf is constant in time, self induction has no part in the process.

The magnitude of the current induced in the conducting ring of resistance r is (applying Ohm's law to our case)

$$I = \frac{U_0}{r} = \frac{\Delta\Phi}{\Delta t \cdot r} = \frac{\Delta B R^2 \pi}{\Delta t \cdot \varrho \frac{2R\pi}{A}} = \frac{\Delta B}{\Delta t} \cdot \frac{RA}{2\varrho}.$$

The simplest way to calculate the created tensile stress is by determining the resultant magnetic field acting on a semicircle and dividing this by twice the cross-sectional area of the wire.

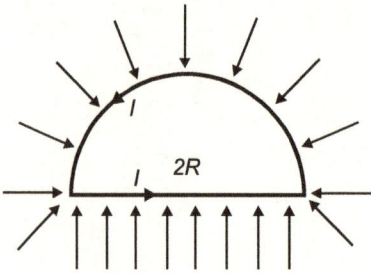

The force acting on a semicircle is obviously as much as the force acting on the $2R$ diameter of a current-bearing wire that consists of a semicircle and its diameter, because in the homogeneous field the conductor does not accelerate, so the resultant of the magnetic Lorentz force acting on it should be 0. With this, the force acting on the semicircle is

$$F = B_1 I 2R,$$

where B_1 is the magnitude of magnetic induction at time instant t_1.

Similar to the endpoints of the semicircle, the forces pulling one semicircle away from the other, or in our case pushing one semicircle towards the other, are parallel to each other, and thus one cross-section gets only half of the resultant force:

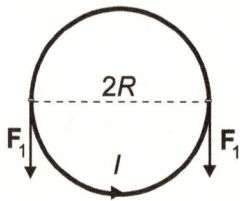

$$F_1 = \frac{F}{2} = B_1 I R,$$

where

$$B_1 = \frac{\Delta B}{\Delta t} \cdot t_1 = \frac{B_{\max}}{2},$$

so the tensile stress created by the magnetic Lorentz force is

$$\sigma = \frac{F_1}{A} = \frac{1}{A} \frac{B_{\max}}{2} \frac{\Delta B}{\Delta t} \frac{RA}{2\varrho} \cdot R = \frac{B_{\max}}{4\varrho} R^2 \frac{\Delta B}{\Delta t}.$$

By turning the ring, we ensure that besides the compressive stress produced by the magnetic field a tensile stress also appears, which — given a suitable number of revolutions — can compensate for each other. This is why the experiment would not work in a magnetic field with decreasing induction, when the magnetic field would be of tensile nature as well (in the ring the direction of the current would turn but the direction of vector **B** would remain the same, so the direction of the magnetic Lorentz force would also turn).

The mechanical stress can be determined through two different trains of thought:

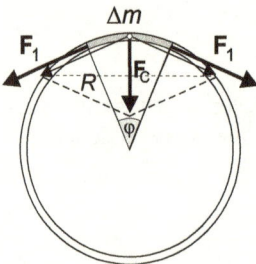

I. The magnitude of the centripetal force acting on a small piece of mass $\Delta m = dAR\varphi$ of a ring rotated around an axis that passes through its centre and is perpendicular to its plane is

$$F_C = dAR\varphi \cdot R\omega^2$$

(where d is the density of the material of the ring), if this small mass element is forced to undergo uniform circular motion. This force is exerted by the neighbouring parts in touch with the given part (through elastic interaction) as shown in the figure.

The central angle $\Delta\varphi$ is also equal to the angle enclosed by the force vectors pulling the element in the two directions (they are angles with perpendicular arms), so their resultant (the centripetal force acting on the mass element) is

$$2F_1 \sin\frac{\varphi}{2} = dAR^2 \varphi\omega^2,$$

from which the pulling force is

$$F_1 = dAR^2\omega^2 \frac{\frac{\varphi}{2}}{\sin\frac{\varphi}{2}}.$$

The smaller the segment of length $\Delta l = R\varphi$, the more accurately we can calculate the force acting on a small bit with mass Δm (because then the direction of the centripetal forces acting on the ends of the bit of the ring differ less and less). It is known that $\frac{\sin\alpha}{\alpha} \to 1$ if $\alpha \to 0$, so

$$F_1 = dAR^2\omega^2,$$

and the tensile stress is

$$\sigma = \frac{F_1}{A} = dR^2\omega^2.$$

From the required equality of the two tensile stresses that arise due to two different reasons and act in the opposite direction, the required angular speed can be determined:

$$dR^2\omega^2 = \frac{B_{\max}}{4\varrho} \cdot R^2 \cdot \frac{\Delta B}{\Delta t},$$

from which the angular speed is

$$\omega = \frac{1}{2}\sqrt{\frac{B_{\max}}{d\varrho} \cdot \frac{\Delta B}{\Delta t}} = 0.5 \cdot \sqrt{\frac{2\,\frac{\mathrm{Vs}}{\mathrm{m}^2}}{8.96\cdot 10^3\ \mathrm{kg/m^3}\cdot 1.78\cdot 10^{-8}\ \Omega\mathrm{m}} \cdot \frac{2\,\frac{\mathrm{Vs}}{\mathrm{m}^2}}{0.2\ \mathrm{s}}} = 177\ \frac{1}{\mathrm{s}},$$

and the corresponding number of revolutions is

$$n = \frac{\omega}{2\pi} = 28.17\ \frac{1}{\mathrm{s}}.$$

II. The tensile stress can be determined in an elementary way using the following train of thought as well:

The mass elements of the rotated copper ring would move apart from each other if no elastic (tangential) contracting force acted between them. Its magnitude — as we have already seen — should be

$$F_1 = dAR^2\omega^2.$$

This can also be seen if we examine a closed cylinder of radius R and height h, which is placed into a pressurized environment. The compressive force produced by this external pressure corresponds to the centripetal force that is required for circular motion.

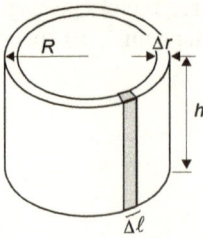

What is this pressure?

Let us imagine that we cut a segment of arc Δl and height h out of the nappe of the cylinder. The centripetal force acting on it is $\Delta m R \omega^2$, in detail:

$$\Delta F_C = \Delta l \Delta r h d R \omega^2.$$

Let us find the pressure that would cause the same effect:

$$\Delta l \Delta r h d R \omega^2 = p \Delta l h,$$

from which

$$p = \Delta r d R \omega^2.$$

This pressure can be used for the proof.

Let us imagine a closed cylinder of radius R, semicircular base, height h in the pressurized environment determined now. The resultant force on the semicylinder caused by the pressure should have the same magnitude as the force acting on the rectangle with area $2Rh$, because the cylinder does not accelerate despite the external forces acting on it. So the magnitude of this force is

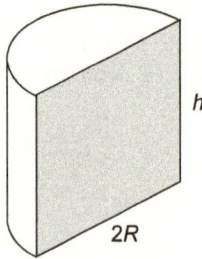

$$F = p2Rh,$$

that is, based on the above

$$F = \Delta r d R \omega^2 \cdot 2Rh,$$

and the tensile stress produced in cross section $A = \Delta r h$ is

$$\sigma = \frac{F/2}{A} = d R^2 \omega^2,$$

which we wanted to prove.

Second solution of Problem 269. We could also start from the assumption that there is no tensile stress in the ring, if the magnetic Lorentz force acting on an arbitrary tiny mass element of it provides exactly the normal force required for the circular track of radius R (because then the ring can be divided into mechanically independent circular arc segments, its parts would remain in the track of radius R, the shape of the ring would not change even in the absence of tensile stress).

Let Δm stand for the mass of a sufficiently small arc element of the copper ring; the equation of its motion is (only radial force acts):

$$B \cdot i \cdot \Delta l = \Delta m R \omega^2.$$

Dividing by Δl results in the appearance of linear mass density, which can be calculated from the total mass and the circumference:

$$B \cdot i = \frac{\Delta m}{\Delta l} \cdot R \omega^2 = \frac{m}{2R\pi} R \omega^2 = \frac{m \omega^2}{2\pi}.$$

Substituting the values of instantaneous induction and instantaneous current:

$$\frac{\Delta B}{\Delta t} \cdot t \cdot \frac{U_{ind}}{r} = \frac{m\omega^2}{2\pi}.$$

The induced potential difference and the resistance of the ring can be determined from the data. By calculating these, the left side of the equation gains the form

$$\frac{\Delta B}{\Delta t} \cdot t \cdot \frac{\frac{\Delta \Phi}{\Delta t}}{\varrho \cdot \frac{2R\pi}{A}} = \frac{\Delta B}{\Delta t} \cdot t \cdot \frac{\frac{\Delta B \cdot R^2 \pi}{\Delta t}}{\varrho \cdot \frac{2R\pi}{A}} = \left(\frac{\Delta B}{\Delta t}\right)^2 \cdot t \cdot \frac{RA}{2\varrho}.$$

With this, our equation of motion becomes

$$\left(\frac{\Delta B}{\Delta t}\right)^2 \cdot t \cdot \frac{RA}{2\varrho} = \frac{m\omega^2}{2\pi}.$$

The mass of the copper ring expressed with its volume and density d is $m = d \cdot 2R\pi \cdot A$, by substituting this into our equation, it becomes

$$\left(\frac{\Delta B}{\Delta t}\right)^2 \cdot t \cdot \frac{RA}{2\varrho} = \frac{d \cdot 2R\pi \cdot A \cdot \omega^2}{2\pi} = dRA\omega^2.$$

From this, the requested angular speed independently of the radius and the width of the ring is

$$\omega = \frac{\Delta B}{\Delta t} \sqrt{\frac{t}{2\varrho d}} = \frac{2 \text{ Vs/m}^2}{0.2 \text{ s}} \sqrt{\frac{0.1 \text{ s}}{2 \cdot 1.78 \cdot 10^{-8} \ \Omega\text{m} \cdot 8.96 \cdot 10^3 \text{ kg/m}^3}} = 177 \ \frac{1}{\text{s}}.$$

Solution of Problem 270. a) The changing magnetic field induces a non-conservative electric field, which results in currents flowing in the conducting loops placed in the field. The currents in the individual branches can be determined by using Maxwell's second law (that is, Kirchhoff's loop rule) and applying Maxwell's first law (that is, Kirchhoff's junction rule) to one of the branch points.

To keep track of algebraic signs, let us assign directions to currents and voltages. Let us move around the loops in the positive direction, and assume that current flows from A to B in the shorter arc and through the meter, while it flows fom B to A in the longer arc.

Let ε_1 denote the emf induced in the smaller loop (I.) and let ε_2 be the emf induced in the larger loop (II.). Let A_1 and A_2 denote the areas of the smaller and greater loops respectively. It follows from Maxwell's law that

$$\varepsilon_1 = \frac{\Delta B}{\Delta t} \cdot A_1 \quad \text{and} \quad \varepsilon_2 = \frac{\Delta B}{\Delta t} \cdot A_2.$$

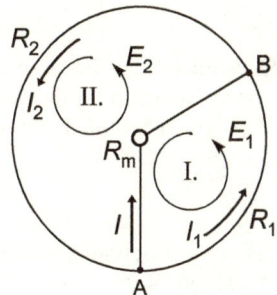

Applied to the Ohmic loops I. and II.:

$$\oint_{I.} V = \varepsilon_1, \quad \text{and} \quad \oint_{II.} V = \varepsilon_2.$$

In detail, using the assumed directions of currents:

$$I_1 R_1 - I R_m = \frac{\Delta B}{\Delta t} \cdot A_1, \quad \text{and} \quad I_2 R_2 + I R_m = \frac{\Delta B}{\Delta t} \cdot A_2.$$

Hence I_1 and I_2 are

$$I_1 = \frac{\Delta B}{\Delta t} \cdot \frac{A_1}{R_1} + I \cdot \frac{R_m}{R_1}, \tag{1}$$

$$I_2 = \frac{\Delta B}{\Delta t} \cdot \frac{A_2}{R_2} - I \cdot \frac{R_m}{R_2}. \tag{2}$$

According to Kirchhoff's junction rule applied to point A,

$$I_2 = I + I_1. \tag{3}$$

If (1) and (2) are substituted in (3), an equation is obtained with the single unknown being the current flowing through the meter:

$$\frac{\Delta B}{\Delta t} \cdot \frac{A_2}{R_2} - I \cdot \frac{R_m}{R_2} = I + \frac{\Delta B}{\Delta t} \cdot \frac{A_1}{R_1} + I \cdot \frac{R_m}{R_1}.$$

Rearranged:

$$\frac{\Delta B}{\Delta t} \cdot \left(\frac{A_2}{R_2} - \frac{A_1}{R_1} \right) = I \left(\frac{R_m}{R_2} + 1 + \frac{R_m}{R_1} \right).$$

Hence, by finding the common denominator and simplifying, the following expression is obtained for the current in question:

$$I = \frac{\Delta B}{\Delta t} \cdot \frac{A_2 R_1 - A_1 R_2}{R_m (R_1 + R_2) + R_1 R_2}. \tag{4}$$

Numerically, expressed in terms of the resistance R_m of the meter:

$$I = 0.4 \frac{V}{m^2} \cdot \frac{0.2\,m^2 \cdot 5\,\Omega - 0.1\,m^2 \cdot 2\,\Omega}{R_m \cdot 7\,\Omega + 10\,\Omega^2} = \frac{0.32\,V}{7 \cdot R_m + 10\,\Omega}.$$

Question a) can be answered if the given value of $0.5\,\Omega$ is substituted for R_m. To answer question b), the voltage across the meter needs to be expressed and the value of $R_m = \infty$ substituted. Thus, in the a) the meter reads a current of

$$I = \frac{0.32}{7 \cdot 0.5 + 10}\,A = 0.0237\,A.$$

It is instructive to determine the currents I_1 and I_2 flowing in the arcs $A1B$ and $A2B$, too. If the value (4) of I is substituted in (1) and (2) and a common denominator is applied, the following expressions are obtained:

$$I_1 = \frac{\Delta B}{\Delta t} \cdot \frac{A_1 [R_m (R_1 + R_2) + R_1 R_2] + A_2 R_1 R_m - A_1 R_2 R_m}{[R_m (R_1 + R_2) + R_1 R_2] R_1}.$$

The term $A_1 R_m R_2$ cancels out and then the numerator and denominator can both be divided by R_1. Thus the parametric expression of I_1 simplifies to

$$I_1 = \frac{\Delta B}{\Delta t} \cdot \frac{(A_1 + A_2)R_m + A_1 R_2}{R_m R_1 + R_m R_2 + R_1 R_2}. \tag{5}$$

By symmetry considerations, a similar expression is obtained for I_2 by simply interchanging indices:

$$I_2 = \frac{\Delta B}{\Delta t} \cdot \frac{(A_1 + A_2)R_m + A_2 R_1}{R_m R_1 + R_m R_2 + R_1 R_2}. \tag{6}$$

Numerically:

$$I_1 = 0.4 \frac{V}{m^2} \cdot \frac{0.3\,m^2 \cdot 0.5\,\Omega + 0.1\,m^2 \cdot 2\,\Omega}{0.5\,\Omega \cdot 5\,\Omega + 0.5\,\Omega \cdot 2\,\Omega + 5\,\Omega \cdot 2\,\Omega} =$$

$$= 0.4 \cdot \frac{0.15 + 0.2}{13.5}\,A = \frac{0.14}{13.5}\,A = 0.01037\,A = 10.37\,mA,$$

and

$$I_2 = 0.4 \cdot \frac{0.3 \cdot 0.5 + 0.2 \cdot 5}{13.5}\,A = 0.4 \cdot \frac{0.15 + 1}{13.5}\,A = \frac{0.46}{13.5}\,A = 0.03407\,A = 34.07\,mA.$$

Clearly, the result will be the same if I_1 is added to I:

$$I_2 = 0.0237\,A + 0.01037\,A = 0.03407\,A.$$

b) The voltmeter being ideal means that no current flows through it. However, the expressions obtained in a) remain valid, and they can be used as they are. If the current I flowing through the meter is multiplied by the resistance R_m of the meter, the reading of the voltmeter is obtained. The value of I is taken from (4):

$$V = I R_m = \frac{\Delta B}{\Delta t} \cdot \frac{A_2 R_1 - A_1 R_2}{R_m R_1 + R_m R_2 + R_1 R_2} \cdot R_m = \frac{0.32\,V}{7 R_m + 10\,\Omega} \cdot R_m.$$

To determine the limit of this expression as $R_m \to \infty$, the numerator and denominator are both divided by the resistance R_m of the meter:

$$V = \frac{0.32\,V}{7 + 10\,\Omega/R_m} \to \frac{0.32\,V}{7} = 0.0457\,V,$$

since for a large enough resistance of the meter, the term $10\,\Omega/R_m$ becomes negligible next to 7. Mathematically, $10/R_m \to 0$ as $R_m \to \infty$.

Thus the value obtained is the voltage measured between the points A and B.

The current is now the same in both arcs (they are conductors connected in series). The value of the current is obtained by substituting the value $R_m = \infty$ into either (5) or (6) after dividing both the numerator and the denominator by R_m:

$$I_1 = I_2 = \frac{\Delta B}{\Delta t} \cdot \frac{(A_1 + A_2) + \frac{A_1 R_2}{R_m}}{R_1 + R_2 + \frac{R_1 R_2}{R_m}} \to \frac{\Delta B}{\Delta t} \cdot \frac{A_1 + A_2}{R_1 + R_2}.$$

Numerically:

$$I_1 = I_2 = 0.4 \frac{V}{m^2} \cdot \frac{0.3\,m^2}{7\,\Omega} = 0.01714\,A = 17.14\,mA.$$

Solution of Problem 271. If the uniformly changing magnetic field was present everywhere inside the big cylinder, then, because of the symmetry of the arrangement, the field lines of the induced electric field would be concentric circles in the plane perpendicular to the axis, and the electric field at a distance r from the axis $(r \leq R)$ could be easily calculated from Maxwell's law of induction:

$$\sum_{\text{closed}} E \Delta s \cos \alpha = \frac{\Delta \Phi}{\Delta t}.$$

Applying the law for a circle of radius r, the constant magnitude of the electric field can be carried out of the sum, and $\cos \alpha = 1$, so:

$$E \sum_{\text{closed}} \Delta s = E 2 r \pi = \frac{\Delta B r^2 \pi}{\Delta t}, \tag{1}$$

where

$$B r^2 \pi = BA = \Phi,$$

is the magnetic flux inside the circle. Thus, from equation (1) the induced electric field at the distance r from the axis has the magnitude:

$$E = \frac{r}{2} \cdot \frac{\Delta B}{\Delta t}. \tag{2}$$

Now let us consider the magnetic field in the problem as the superposition of two uniformly changing magnetic fields (produced separately by appropriate coils):

– a homogeneous, uniformly changing magnetic field $\vec{B}(t)$, which is present everywhere inside the big cylinder,

– and a magnetic field $-\vec{B}(t)$, which is present only inside the small cylinder.

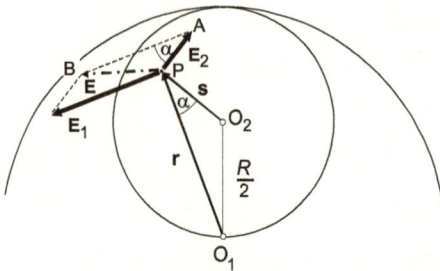

In a perpendicular cross section of the cylinders, let O_1 be the centre of the big, and O_2 be that of the small cylinder, and consider a point P inside the small cylinder, which is at a distance r from O_1 and at a distance s from O_2. Let $\mathbf{r}$ and $\mathbf{s}$ denote the vectors from the centres to P. (See the figure.) Then the induced net electric field $\mathbf{E}$ at P is the superposition of the two electric fields induced separately by the two magnetic fields: $\mathbf{E} = \mathbf{E}_1 + \mathbf{E}_2$, where, by equation (2),

$$E_1 = \frac{1}{2} \cdot \frac{\Delta B}{\Delta t} r \qquad \text{due to the change of } B(t)$$

$$E_2 = \frac{1}{2} \cdot \frac{\Delta B}{\Delta t} s \qquad \text{due to the change of } -B(t).$$

Since $\mathbf{E}_1 \perp \mathbf{r}$ and $\mathbf{E}_2 \perp \mathbf{s}$, the angles α are equal in the triangles $O_2 P O_1$ and PAB.

On the other hand, the ratios of the sides forming the angle α are also equal,

$$\frac{E_1}{E_2} = \frac{r}{s},$$

thus the two triangles are similar. Using this fact, the net induced electric field is:

$$\frac{BP}{AB} = \frac{E}{E_1} = \frac{O_1O_2}{O_1P} = \frac{R}{2r} = \text{constant}.$$

Numerically,

$$E = E_1 \frac{R}{2r} = \frac{R}{4} \frac{\Delta B}{\Delta t} = \frac{0.1\ \text{m}}{4} \cdot 80 \ \frac{\text{V}}{\text{m}^2} = 2.0 \ \frac{\text{V}}{\text{m}}.$$

Since two sides of the similar triangles are pairwise perpendicular to each other, the third sides are also perpendicular,

$$\mathbf{E} \perp O_1O_2,$$

so the electric field induced inside the small cylinder is homogeneous.

(We remark that the fact that the magnitude of the electric field is constant in a region where the magnetic field vanishes (or static), implies that the electric field is homogeneous there. This can be deduced from Maxwell's second law. If the magnitude of the electric field is constant, then the field lines have the same spacial 'density', and they form a system of parallel straight lines. Otherwise we could find a closed circle along which $\Sigma E \Delta r \cos \alpha$ would not be zero, which is impossible if the magnetic flux is not changing. This means that the electric field is homogeneous.)

Solution of Problem 272. a) Let us determine the flux surrounded by the circular track as function of time. As the induction changes along the radius, the area of the circle is divided into small regions in which the magnetic field can be regarded as homogeneous. For this purpose, let us take a circular ring of radius r and a width $\Delta r \ll r$ whose flux is:

$$\Delta \Phi = B(r,t) \cdot 2r\pi \cdot \Delta r.$$

According to the condition given in the problem

$$\Delta \Phi = \frac{E_0}{r} t \cdot 2\pi r \Delta r.$$

Let us sum up the elementary fluxes:

$$\Phi(t) = \sum \Delta \Phi = 2\pi E_0 t \sum_i \Delta r_i = 2\pi E_0 tR,$$

that is,

$$\Phi(t) = 2\pi E_0 Rt. \tag{1}$$

Due to the cylindrical symmetry of the situation, the induced electric field created also has cylindrical symmetry, so considering (1), the electric field at the place of the bead is

$$E(R) = \frac{1}{2\pi R} \cdot \frac{\Delta \Phi}{\Delta t} = \frac{1}{2\pi R} \cdot \frac{2\pi R E_0 \Delta t}{\Delta t} = E_0. \tag{2}$$

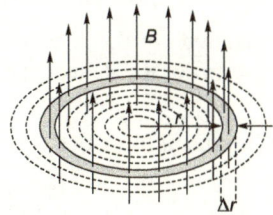

503

The bead experiences a constant electric field in the direction of the tangent, so according to (2), its velocity as function of time is

$$v(t) = \frac{E_0 q}{m} \cdot t. \tag{3}$$

b) Applying the fundamental law of dynamics in radial direction:

$$qvB + N = m\frac{v^2}{R},$$

where N is the normal force exerted by the track. Using (3), its magnitude is

$$N = m\frac{v^2}{R} - qvB = \frac{m}{R} \cdot \frac{E_0^2 q^2 t^2}{m^2} - q \cdot \frac{E_0 q}{m} t \cdot \frac{E_0 t}{R} = 0.$$

There is no force between the bead and the ring in a magnetic field of such structure $N = 0$, that is, the track does not exert a radial normal force and thus does not have to be there. (The principle of the betatron particle accelerator.)

Solution of Problem 273. The acceleration of the electron equals the product of the induced electric field and the charge to mass ratio of the electron. The electric field can be determined from Faraday's law of induction:

$$\sum^{\circ} E\Delta s \cos\alpha = -\frac{\Delta\Phi}{\Delta t}.$$

If the summation is carried out along the circumference of the circle of radius r_A, then $\cos\alpha = 1$ everywhere and the magnitude of the electric field is also constant, and thus, with magnitudes considered only,

$$E \cdot 2r_A \pi = \frac{\Delta\Phi}{\Delta t}.$$

Hence the electric field at the starting point of the electron is $E_A = \frac{1}{2r_A\pi}\frac{\Delta\Phi}{\Delta t}$. The magnitude of the change in flux inducing the electric field is $\Delta\Phi = A\Delta B$. Expressed in terms of the data of the coil:

$$\Delta\Phi = R^2\pi\Delta B.$$

With this information, the acceleration of the electron is

$$a = \frac{F}{m} = \frac{eE}{m} = \frac{e \cdot \frac{1}{2r_A\pi}\frac{\Delta\Phi}{\Delta t}}{m} = \frac{eR^2\pi\Delta B}{m2r_A\pi\Delta t} = \frac{e}{m}\frac{R^2\Delta B}{2r_A\Delta t} =$$

$$a = \frac{1.6\cdot10^{-19}\,\text{A}\,\text{s}\cdot4\cdot10^{-4}\,\text{m}^2\cdot0.8\,\text{Vs/m}^2}{9.1\cdot10^{-31}\,\text{kg}\cdot2\cdot3\cdot10^{-2}\,\text{m}\cdot10^{-1}\,\text{s}} \approx 9.38\cdot10^9\,\frac{\text{m}}{\text{s}^2}.$$

b) The speed of the electron is determined by the induced electric field. The difficulties are due to the electron 'drifting off' the electric field line that passes through point A. Neither the path of the electron nor the values of the electric field along the path can be calculated by elementary methods.

Although the electric field is now constant, it is not conservative, and therefore no potential or potential difference can be defined in it. However, the total emf $\displaystyle\oint E\Delta s$ is zero for any closed cuve that does not surround a changing flux. Thus, if the actual path of the electron is completed to a closed curve such that it does dot surround a changing flux and the work done by the electric field is easy to calculate in the additional segments of the closed curve, then it provides an elementary method to obtain the work done on the electron along the actual path, too.

The figure shows a possible closed curve of that kind: it consists of the actual electron path, a circular arc subtending the same angle and centred at the axis of the coil, and a radial line segment. The work done by the electric field along the arc AB' is

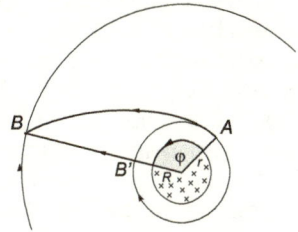

$$W_{\text{el}} = F\cdot s = eEr_A\varphi = e\frac{1}{2r_A\pi}\frac{\Delta\Phi}{\Delta t}\cdot r_A\varphi =$$

$$= e\frac{1}{2r_A\pi}\frac{R^2\pi\Delta B}{\Delta t}r_A\varphi = \frac{eR^2\varphi\Delta B}{2\Delta t},$$

independently of the distance r_A of the starting point A from the axis. The work done by the electric field along the radial line segment BB' is zero since the electric field vector is perpendicular to the displacement. Therefore the actual work done on the electron along the path AB is equal to the W_{el} above.

Hence the speed of the electron is obtained from the work-energy theorem ($W_{\text{el}} = mv^2/2$, with the assumption that it travels in vacuum):

$$v = \sqrt{\frac{2W_{\text{el}}}{m}} = \sqrt{\frac{e}{m}\frac{R^2\Delta B}{\Delta t}\varphi} = \sqrt{\frac{1.6\cdot10^{-19}\,\text{A s}\cdot4\cdot10^{-4}\,\text{m}^2\cdot0.8\frac{\text{V s}}{\text{m}^2}}{9.1\cdot10^{-31}\,\text{kg}\cdot10^{-1}\,\text{s}}\cdot\frac{2\pi}{3}} \approx 34.3\frac{\text{km}}{\text{s}}.$$

Remark: The result can also be obtained by considering the formula for the speed of the uniformly accelerated circular motion of the electron along the arc AB':

$$v = \sqrt{2as} = \sqrt{2\frac{eE}{m}r\varphi} = \sqrt{\frac{eR^2\Delta B}{m\Delta t}\varphi},$$

since the magnitude of the electric field E is constant along the arc and its direction is tangential, so the electron will move along the arc with uniformly changing speed.

Solution of Problem 274. A moving electron is affected by both magnetic and electric fields. We should investigate the fields that are present in the centre of the circle at the time instants in question and the direction of the electric field and magnetic induction vectors that characterise these.

When no magnetic field is present ($I_a = 0$), only the changing magnetic flux creates (a stationary) electric field, which accelerates the electron with a force of $\vec{F} = e\vec{E}$ (regardless of its velocity condition). When there is current in the coil again (e.g. at time instant $t_1 = 0.6$ s), a magnetic field is also present in the centre of the circle, which acts with a force of $\vec{F} = e\vec{v} \times \vec{B}$ on the electron; this force is perpendicular to the previous force. Therefore we should determine the magnitude of the electric field and the induction of the magnetic field in the centre of the central circle of the coil at the given moment.

a) When the current is zero, only electric field is present. Within the thin iron wire a so-called toroidal magnetic field is created, whose flux density can be considered constant for the whole cross-section, because the 3.6-mm diameter of the iron wire can be neglected relative to the 200-mm diameter of the circle. This thin magnetic flux tube acts like the thin current-bearing wire in the creation of the magnetic field, therefore the (non-stationary) electric field created by the magnetic flux element can be described in the same way as the magnetic field created by the current element, with a law that corresponds to the Biot–Savart law. All one needs to do is determine which quantities correspond to each other in the two processes. The corresponding quantities are given by the circuital law and the law of induction.

In the case of a straight conductor for one induction line

$$B2r\pi = \mu_0 I \qquad \rightarrow \qquad B = \frac{\mu_0}{2\pi}\frac{I}{r},$$

in the case of a straight thin coil (flux tube)

$$E2r\pi = -\frac{\Delta\Phi}{\Delta t} \qquad \rightarrow \qquad E = -\frac{1}{2r\pi}\frac{\Delta\Phi}{\Delta t}.$$

From these, it is obvious that the quantity corresponding to $\mu_0 I$ in the Biot–Savart law is $\dfrac{\Delta\Phi}{\Delta t}$. With this, the two types of Biot–Savart law are

$$\Delta B = \frac{\mu_0}{4\pi}\frac{I\Delta l}{r^2}\sin\alpha, \qquad \text{and} \qquad \Delta E = \frac{1}{4\pi}\frac{\Delta\Phi}{\Delta t}\frac{\Delta l}{r^2}\sin\alpha.$$

In the centre of the circle the resultant electric field can be determined through the known summation:

$$E = \sum\Delta E = \sum\frac{1}{4\pi}\frac{\Delta\Phi}{\Delta t}\frac{\Delta l}{r^2}\sin\alpha = \frac{1}{4\pi}\frac{\Delta\Phi}{\Delta t}\frac{1}{r^2}\sum\Delta l\sin 90°,$$

where $\sum\Delta l = 2r\pi$ is the circumference of the circle. From this, after simplifying by $2r\pi$ the following expression is acquired for the electric field in the centre of the circle:

$$E = \frac{1}{2r}\frac{\Delta\Phi}{\Delta t},$$

which is constant due to the condition given in the problem.

In case a) $B = 0$ but $\dfrac{\Delta B}{\Delta t} \neq 0$ both outside the toroidal coil (including the centre of the circular coil) and inside the coil. (The hysteresis of the soft-iron wire can be neglected, therefore even if remanent magnetism exists at the moment in question, the rate of change of remanent magnetism, which determines the electric field, can be approximated well with the rate of change of magnetism that belongs to zero induction of the first magnetizing curve, which is proportional to the rate of change of current.)

The change of magnetic flux in the iron wire is

$$\Delta \Phi = \Delta B A = \mu_0 \mu_r \frac{\Delta I N}{2R\pi} \cdot A.$$

If this is substituted into the law analogous with the Biot–Savart law, the acceleration of the electron is acquired:

$$a = \frac{eE}{m} = \frac{1}{2}\mu_0 \mu_r \frac{N A \Delta I}{2R^2 \pi \Delta t} \frac{e}{m} = 0.0008 \left(\frac{\text{kgm}}{\text{Cs}^2}\right)\frac{e}{m} =$$
$$= 140659340.7 \frac{\text{m}}{\text{s}^2} \approx 1.41 \cdot 10^8 \frac{\text{m}}{\text{s}^2},$$

and its direction is perpendicular to the plane of the circle.

b) At $t_1 = 0.6\,$s the magnetic field, which is created by the current that flows in the copper wire, is present again. The value of current 0.1 s after becoming zero is $I_1 = 0.2 I_{\max} = 2\,$A. This current — although it flows in the circular coil — creates exactly the same magnetic field in the centre of the central circle of the toroid as a single thin circular conductor placed along the central circle that bears the same current. The induction of this field is perpendicular to the plane of the circle and the

magnetic Lorentz force produced by it is perpendicular to both $\vec{B}$ and $\vec{v}$, therefore it acts in the plane of the circle, therefore it is perpendicular to $\vec{E}$ as well. The resultant acceleration can be acquired from the Pythagorean theorem.

$$a_{\text{mag}} = \frac{F_{\text{mag}}}{m} = \frac{e}{m}v\mu_0\frac{I_1}{2R} =$$
$$= 0.0012566 \left(\frac{\text{kgm}}{\text{Cs}^2}\right)\frac{e}{m} = 220947176 \text{ m/s}^2 \approx 2.21 \cdot 10^8 \text{ m/s}^2.$$

The total acceleration of the electron is

$$a = \sqrt{a_{\text{mag}}^2 + a_{\text{el}}^2} = \frac{e}{m}\sqrt{(12.6 \cdot 10^{-4})^2 + (8 \cdot 10^{-4})^2} \frac{\text{kg m}}{\text{C s}^2} =$$
$$= 0.0014925 \left(\frac{\text{kgm}}{\text{Cs}^2}\right)\frac{e}{m} = 262420159.4 \text{ m/s}^2 \approx 2.624 \cdot 10^8 \text{ m/s}^2.$$

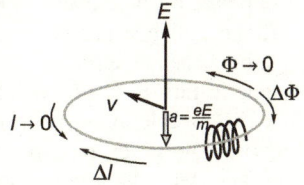

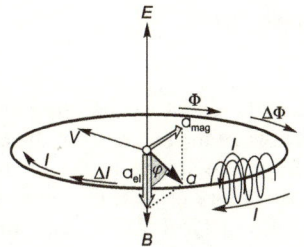

507

The direction of the acceleration encloses an angle of

$$\varphi = \arctan \frac{|\vec{v} \times \vec{B}|}{E} = \arctan \frac{0.001266}{0.0008} = 57.7°$$

with the axis.

Remark: Some would think that the iron wire that fills the inside of the coil – being a a conductor that surrounds a changing flux – would produce a current whose direction is opposite to the current in the coil and therefore decreases its magnetic field.

If the coil bearing the iron wire is not only bent into a circle but is also soldered together, then a circular conductor that surrounds the (inhomogeneously distributed) magnetic flux is acquired indeed, but this — even if calculated with the homogenous flux that is calculated from the maximum induction measured along the centre line of the toroid — gives an upper limit of less than one thousandth for the current of the iron wire and the induction created by it.

9.4 Alternating current

Solution of Problem 275. If the initial charge of the loaded sphere is Q, then its potential is:

$$U_0 = \frac{Q}{4\pi \varepsilon_0 R}.$$

The potential of the other sphere is initially zero. Since there is a potential difference between the two ends of the coil, an electric current is produced, i.e. charge is transferred from one sphere to the other. From this, it is clear that the system investigated is an oscillatory circuit, the spheres acting as capacitors.

In an ideal LC circuit undamped harmonic oscillations are produced, i.e. first all charges go from one plate of the capacitor to the other, and then all charges go back to the first plate without loss. (We investigate only one period of the oscillation, and neglect the losses due to Joule–heat and dipole electromagnetic radiation.)

What is the capacitance of the 'substituting capacitor' consisting of the spheres? (We have to take into consideration that the total charge of the plates is not zero.) The answer is given by the following reasoning: Let us consider the charge Q on the first sphere as the sum of charges $Q/2$ and $Q/2$, and let us regard the charge 0 on the second sphere as the sum of charges $Q/2$ and $-Q/2$. The potential difference due to the equal $Q/2$ charges on both spheres is zero, while the voltage due to the opposite charges $Q/2$ and $-Q/2$ on the two spheres is $U_{\max} = U_0$. So the charge of the substituting capacitor is $Q/2$, and its voltage is U_0, thus its capacitance is:

$$C = \frac{Q/2}{U_0} = 2\pi \varepsilon_0 R.$$

It means that the period of the oscillatory circuit is:

$$T = 2\pi \sqrt{LC} = 2\pi \sqrt{2\pi \varepsilon_0 R}.$$

After this time, the charges on the spheres become equal to their initial values. When the charge of the first sphere is $Q/2$, the charge of the second sphere is $Q/2$ as well, so the voltage across the coil is zero, and the time elapsed until this state is a quarter of the period:

$$t = \frac{T}{4} = \frac{\pi}{2}\sqrt{2\pi\varepsilon_0 LR}.$$

Solution of Problem 276. a) The potential difference applied to the combination is divided between the two capacitors in the ratio of their resistances. Thus the potential difference across the first capacitor is:

$$V_1 = \frac{V}{R_1 + R_2} \cdot R_1 = \frac{220\,\mathrm{V}}{1 \cdot 10^9 + 4 \cdot 10^9} \cdot 1 \cdot 10^9 = \frac{220}{5}\,\mathrm{V} = 44\,\mathrm{V},$$

while the potential difference across the second capacitor is:

$$V_2 = V - V_1 = 220\,\mathrm{V} - 44\,\mathrm{V} = 176\,\mathrm{V} > 170\,\mathrm{V},$$

which means that the second capacitor breaks down.

b) If a potential difference is applied to a capacitor, there will always be a current (I_R) due to the ohmic conductivity of the capacitor. At the same time there is a charging current (I_C) flowing through the capacitor due to the same potential difference. Therefore the capacitor can be substituted by an ideal capacitor that is connected in parallel to the ohmic resistance of the capacitor.

The potential difference across the capacitors are in proportion to their net impedances (Z). If components are connected in parallel, their conductivities are added together as vectors, so according to Pythagoras' theorem the net conductivity of the combination is:

$$Y = \sqrt{G^2 + B^2},$$

where Y is the net conductivity, $G = 1/R$ is the ohmic conductivity and $B = 1/X_C$ is the capacitive conductivity. The net impedance of the combination is $Z = 1/Y$. The net conductivity of the first capacitor is therefore:

$$Y_1 = \sqrt{\left(\frac{1}{R_1}\right)^2 + (\omega C_1)^2} = \frac{\sqrt{1 + (R_1 \omega C_1)^2}}{R_1}$$

while for its impedance, we get:

$$Z_1 = \frac{1}{Y_1} = \frac{R_1}{\sqrt{1 + (R_1 \omega C_1)^2}}.$$

Let us divide both the numerator and the denominator by R_1:

$$Z_1 = \frac{1}{\sqrt{1/R_1^2 + (\omega C_1)^2}}.$$

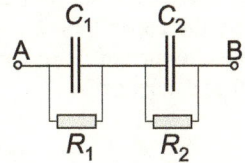

The capacitive conductance $B_1 = \omega C_1$ of the capacitor is much greater than its ohmic conductance $1/R_1$. Assuming the frequency to be $\nu = 50$ Hz, we find:

$$B_1 = 2\pi\nu \cdot C_1 = 314.16\,\text{s}^{-1} \cdot 10 \cdot 10^{-6}\,\text{F} = 3.1416 \cdot 10^{-3}\,\Omega^{-1},$$

similarly

$$B_2 = 314.16\,\text{s}^{-1} \cdot 12.5 \cdot 10^{-6}\,\text{F} = 3.927 \cdot 10^{-3}\,\Omega^{-1},$$

while the ohmic conductivities are:

$$\frac{1}{R_1} = \frac{1}{10^9\,\Omega} = 10^{-9}\,\Omega^{-1},$$

$$\frac{1}{R_2} = \frac{1}{4 \cdot 10^9\,\Omega} = 0.25 \cdot 10^{-9}\,\Omega^{-1}.$$

This means that the ohmic conductivity is six orders of magnitude less than the capacitive conductivity, so the ohmic conductivity is negligible, which holds even more to its square:

$$\frac{1}{10^{18}\,\Omega^2} = 10^{-18}\,\Omega^{-2} \ll 3.14^2 \cdot 10^{-6}\,\Omega^{-2}.$$

Therefore the net impedances of the capacitors are equal to their capacitive resistances, because:

$$Z_1 \approx \frac{1}{\sqrt{0 + (\omega C_1)^2}} = \frac{1}{\omega C_1} = X_{C_1}.$$

Similarly the net impedance of the second capacitor is equal to its capacitive resistance. As the capacitors are connected in series, their potential differences are in the ratio of their impedances or capacitive resistances, therefore the potential difference across the first capacitor is:

$$V_1 = \frac{X_1}{X_1 + X_2}V = \frac{1/C_1}{1/C_1 + 1/C_2}V = \frac{1/10}{1/10 + 1/12.5} \cdot 220\,\text{V} = 122.2\,\text{V},$$

similarly the potential difference across the second capacitor is:

$$V_2 = \frac{1/12.5}{1/10 + 1/12.5} \cdot 220\,\text{V} = 97.8\,\text{V}.$$

(The potential difference across the first capacitor is greater than the one across the second, which is opposite to the situation in the first case.)

If we want to find out whether the capacitors will break down or not, we need to calculate the maximum values of their potential differences. These are:

$$V_{1_{max}} = \sqrt{2}V_1 = \sqrt{2} \cdot 122.2\,\text{V} = 172.8\,\text{V} > 130\,\text{V},$$

$$V_{2_{max}} = \sqrt{2}V_2 = \sqrt{2} \cdot 97.8\,\text{V} = 138.3\,\text{V} < 170\,\text{V},$$

therefore in this case the capacitor of capacitance C_1 breaks down.

Solution of Problem 277. a) As the current lags behind the voltage, the circuit is of inductive nature. The phase angle is $\varphi = \pi/4 \mathrm{rad} = 45°$.

The impedance is

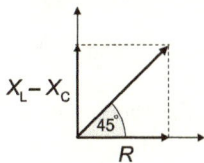

$$Z = \frac{V_{rms}}{I_{rms}} = \frac{V_{max}}{I_{max}} = \frac{200\,\mathrm{V}}{7.07\,\mathrm{A}} = 28.29\,\Omega.$$

The ohmic resistance is:

$$R = Z \cdot \cos 45° = 28.29\,\Omega \cdot \cos 45° = 20\,\Omega.$$

From the isosceles right-angled triangle:

$$X_L - X_C = R, \qquad \text{,that is,} \qquad \omega L - \frac{1}{\omega C} = R.$$

From this

$$C = \frac{1}{\omega(\omega L - R)} = \frac{1}{628\,\mathrm{s}^{-1} \cdot (628 \cdot 0.143 - 20)\,\Omega} = 22.81\,\mu\mathrm{F}.$$

b) The maximum potential difference across the coil is $V_{L_{max}} = I_{max} X_L$, so the maximum potential difference across the coil is

$$V_{L_{max}} = I_{max} \cdot \omega L = 7.07\,\mathrm{A} \cdot 628\,\mathrm{s}^{-1} \cdot 0.143\,\mathrm{H} = 634.91\,\mathrm{V}.$$

As the potential difference across the coil is ahead of the voltage V in the circuit by $\pi/4$, the potential difference across the coil as function of time is

$$V_L = 634.91\,\mathrm{V} \sin\left(628\,\frac{1}{\mathrm{s}} \cdot t + \frac{\pi}{4}\right).$$

The maximum potential difference across the capacitor is

$$V_{C_{max}} = I_{max} X_C = I_{max} \frac{1}{\omega C} = \frac{7.07\,\mathrm{A}}{628\,\mathrm{s}^{-1} \cdot 22.8 \cdot 10^{-6}\,\mathrm{F}} = 493.77\,\mathrm{V},$$

and as the potential difference across the capacitor lags behind the terminal voltage by $3\pi/4$, the potential difference as function of time is

$$V_C = 493.77\,\mathrm{V} \cdot \sin\left(628\frac{1}{\mathrm{s}} \cdot t + 3\frac{\pi}{4}\right).$$

Solution of Problem 278. According to the statement of the problem, the impedance of the circuit is independent of the resistance of the Ohmic resistor. Let us find out the necessary condition of this.

We illustrate the currents and voltages through and across the individual electric components by rotating vectors. To draw an adequate diagram, we use the following facts:

1. The part RC and the coil are connected in parallel, thus the voltage across the coil and the voltage of the generator are the same. ($U_{RC} = U_L = U$.)

2. The current of the coil (I_L) has a delay of $90°$ with respect to the voltage.

3. Let φ denote the phase shift between the current (I_{RC}) through R, C and the voltage of the generator (U_{RC})! It is known that the current leads the voltage.

4. The voltage across the Ohmic resistor (U_R) is in phase with the current (I_{RC}) of the RC branch.

5. The voltage (U_C) across the capacitor lags the current (I_{RC}) by a phase shift of $90°$.

6. The total voltage U_{RC} across the resistor R and capacitor C is the vector sum of the voltages U_R and U_C.

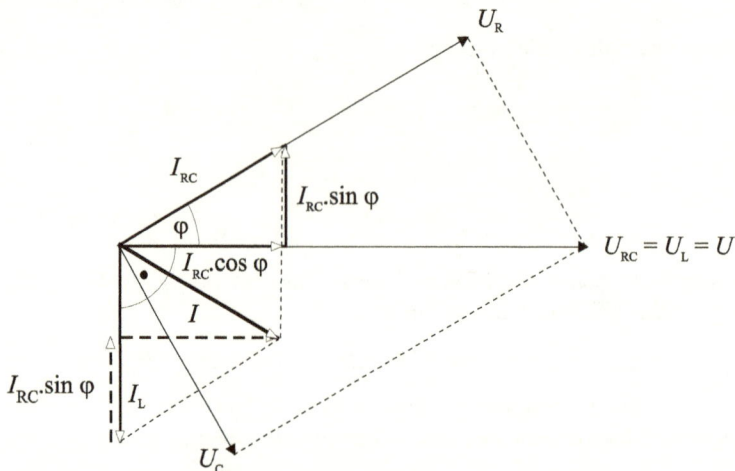

The (rotating) vector representing the current (I) of the main branch is the sum of the (rotating) vectors representing the current (I_{RC}) through RC and the current (I_L) through the coil. According to the figure (splitting the vector I_{RC} to components and adding the vector I_L):

$$I^2 = (I_L - I_{RC}\sin\varphi)^2 + I_{RC}\cos^2\varphi,$$

or equivalently

$$I^2 = I_L^2 + I_{RC}^2 - 2I_L I_{RC}\sin\varphi. \tag{1}$$

From the theory of AC circuits it is known that:

$$I = \frac{U}{Z}; \quad I_L = \frac{U}{X_L}; \quad I_{RC} = \frac{U}{\sqrt{R^2 + X_C^2}}; \quad \sin\varphi = \frac{X_C}{\sqrt{R^2 + X_C^2}}.$$

Substituting these formulas into equation (1), the following is obtained for the impedance:

$$\frac{1}{Z^2} = \frac{1}{X_L^2} + \frac{1}{R^2 + X_C^2} - \frac{2X_C}{X_L(R^2 + X_C^2)},$$

or in a simpler form:

$$\frac{1}{Z^2} = \frac{1}{X_L^2} + \frac{X_L - 2X_C}{X_L(R^2 + X_C^2)}.$$

It can be seen that if $X_L = 2X_C$ then the second term on the right hand side equals zero, thus in this case the total impedance is independent of the Ohmic resistance: $Z = X_L$. The frequency corresponding to this case is determined by the equation

$$Lw = \frac{2}{Cw},$$

from which

$$w = \sqrt{\frac{2}{LC}} = 1000 \text{ Hz},$$

and finally the frequency is:

$$\nu = \frac{w}{2\pi} = 159.2 \text{ Hz}.$$

Solution of Problem 279. a) The inductive reactance is $X_L = Lw = 628\Omega$, the capacitive reactance is $X_C = 1/Cw = 0.636\Omega$. The voltages across the inductor and capacitor are in opposite phases, and they also have different magnitudes. Thus their sum may only be zero if each of them is zero.

At the given time instant, the current increases the voltage on the capacitor, so it must be a time instant in the first quarter period of the graph. Let x denote the time interval in question.

The voltage and current of the capacitor as functions of time are

$$V_C = V_{C_0} \cdot \sin wt,$$

and

$$I = I_0 \cdot \cos wt.$$

Their ratio is

$$\frac{V_C}{I} = X_C \cdot \tan wt,$$

that is,

$$1 = 0.636 \cdot \tan\left(314\,\frac{1}{s}t\right).$$

Hence $t = 0.0032\,s$ and

$$x = \frac{T}{2} - t = \frac{0.02\,s}{2} - 0.0032\,s = 0.0068\,s. \tag{1}$$

b) The voltage on the coil has a constant value of

$$V_L = L \cdot \frac{\Delta I}{\Delta t} = 2\text{ H} \cdot 0.8\frac{A}{s} = 1.6\text{ V}.$$

Since the current decreases, V_L is opposite in polarity to the voltage on the capacitor. The capacitor needs to be charged further to increase its voltage by $\Delta V = 0.6$ V,

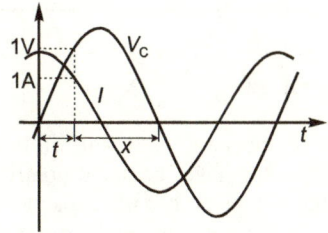

so that the resultant voltage is zero. That takes an extra charge of $\Delta Q = C\Delta V = = 5 \cdot 10^{-3}$ F $\cdot 0.6$ V $= 0.003$ C supplied by the current. Since the mean current during the time interval t is

$$I_{mean} = \frac{1\,\text{A} + (1\,\text{A} - 0.8\,\text{A}\,\text{s}^{-1} \cdot t)}{2} = 1\,\text{A} - 0.4\frac{\text{A}}{\text{s}} \cdot t,$$

and

$$I_{mean} \cdot t = \Delta Q,$$

the equation

$$(1\,\text{A} - 0.4\frac{\text{A}}{\text{s}} \cdot t)t = 0.003\,\text{C}$$

is obtained. By rearrangement, the equation for the time in seconds is

$$0.4t^2 - t + 0.003 = 0.$$

The solution is

$$t = 0.003\,\text{s}.$$

c) In the case of a sinusoidal current, the roles of the quantities t and x above are interchanged:

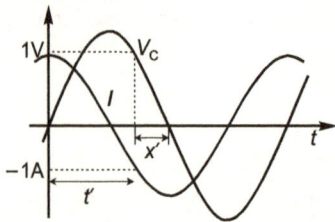

In (1), let x' be the new time interval in question. Now $t' = 0.0068$ (the value of x above), and

$$t' = \frac{T}{2} - x'.$$

Hence

$$x' = \frac{T}{2} - t' = 0.01\,\text{s} - 0.0068\,\text{s} = 0.0032\,\text{s}.$$

In the case of a uniformly decreasing current, the voltages on the inductor and capacitor have the same polarity. Thus the resultant voltage may only become zero if the voltage across the capacitor changes from $+1$ V to -1.6 V.
That takes a charge transfer of

$$Q = 5 \cdot 10^{-3}\,\text{F} \cdot (1 + 1.6)V = 0.013\,\text{C}.$$

With the mean current during the time interval $t = x''$ required:

$$I_{mean} \cdot x'' = \frac{1\,\text{A} + 1\,\text{A} - 0.8\,\text{A}\,\text{s}^{-1} \cdot x''}{2} \cdot x'' = 0.013\,\text{C}.$$

Rearranged:

$$0.4x''^2 - x'' + 0.013 = 0$$

for the time in seconds. Hence

$$x'' = 0.013\,\text{s}.$$

(This is shorter than the time 1.25 s of the current vanishing altogether.)

Solution of Problem 280. We can assume that the box contains ohmic resistors, capacitors and inductors, which may occur in an infinite number of combinations. Let us find the simplest case (that is, an equivalent combination that contains a single element of each kind). Since the impedance has a minimum, the capacitor and inductor should be connected in series. According to the table, the impedance is not zero at the resonant frequency, so there must be an ohmic resistor in the combination, too. The resultant impedance of a resistance R, inductance L and capacitance C connected in series is:

$$Z = \sqrt{R^2 + \left(\omega L - \frac{1}{\omega C}\right)^2} = \sqrt{R^2 + \left(\frac{1 - \omega^2 LC}{\omega C}\right)^2}.$$

There are three unknowns that can be determined from three appropriate equations. The table contains more than enough pairs of corresponding values that could be used to set up three equations. That solution, however, would involve long and inconvenient calculations. Instead, with a little insight, we can easily get very good approximate values.

It is known that $Z = R$ at resonance. According to the table, the minimum impedance is about $25\,\Omega$. This provides an estimate for the ohmic resistance.

For very low frequencies, it is enough to consider the reactance of the capacitor, inductive reactance is negligible:

$$Z^2 = R^2 + \frac{1}{(\omega C)^2}.$$

Hence

$$C = \frac{1}{\omega\sqrt{Z^2 - R^2}},$$

that is,

$$C = \frac{1}{20\,\mathrm{s}^{-1}\sqrt{782^2\,\Omega^2 - 25^2\,\Omega^2}} = 63.97\,\mu\mathrm{F}.$$

For very high frequencies, on the other hand, it is the capacitive reactance that can be neglected, it is enough to consider inductive reactance:

$$Z^2 = R^2 + (\omega L)^2, \qquad \text{and hence} \qquad L = \frac{1}{\omega}\sqrt{L^2 - R^2},$$

that is, with the large-frequency data of the table,

$$L = \frac{1}{5000\,\mathrm{s}^{-1}} \cdot \sqrt{792^2 - 25^2} = 0.1583\,\mathrm{H}.$$

(Note that approximately the same values are obtained if even the ohmic resistances are ignored in the extreme cases, that is, the equation

$$782\,\Omega = \frac{1}{20\,\mathrm{s}^{-1}C}$$

is solved for capacitance: the result is $C = 63.93\,\mu\mathrm{F}$, and the equation

$$792\,\Omega = 5000\,\mathrm{s}^{-1}L$$

is solved for inductance: the result is $L = 0.1584\,\mathrm{H}$.)

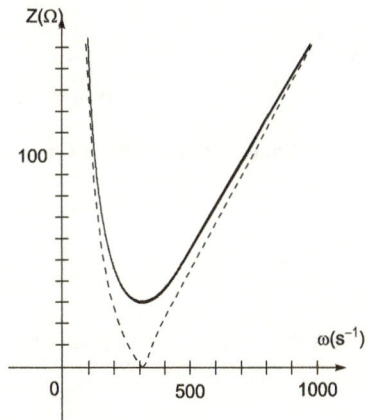

Solution of Problem 281. In a given instant, the magnitude of current between points (a, b, c and d) is the same. The emf of the generator is the sum of the potential differences across these segments. Note that the RMS voltages should be added as vectors, since it is an AC circuit.

Our first task is to investigate the circuit when the angular frequency of the AC generator is ω. Since the RMS current is $I = 1$ mA and $R = 5$ kΩ, the RMS voltage across points $a-b$ must be $V_{ab} = 5$ V, thus $V_{bd} = 0$. This means that there is a resonance between points b and d.

Since $b-c$ is capacitive the parallel LC circuit between $c-d$ must be inductive, hence:

$$\omega L < \frac{1}{\omega C}.$$

The net impedance between points c and d can be calculated as:

$$Z = \frac{1}{\frac{1}{X_L} - \frac{1}{X_C}} = \frac{X_L \cdot X_C}{X_C - X_L},$$

thus

$$X_{cd} = \frac{(\omega L) \cdot (1/\omega C)}{(1/\omega C) - \omega L} = \frac{L/C}{(1/\omega C) - \omega L}. \tag{1}$$

The resonance condition in this case is:

$$X_{C_{b,c}} = X_{c,d},$$

hence

$$\frac{L/C}{(1/\omega C) - \omega L} - \frac{1}{\omega C} = 0.$$

From this equation we obtain that the original angular frequency is:

$$\omega^2 = \frac{1}{2LC}.$$

The RMS voltage across points b and c can be calculated using the reading of the voltmeter:

$$V_{ac}^2 = V_{ab}^2 + V_{bc}^2,$$

substituting given data, we find:

$$(13\,\text{V})^2 = (5\,\text{V})^2 + V_{bc}^2,$$

which yields

$$V_{bc} = 12\,\text{V}.$$

Using our results above, we can determine the capacitive reactance of the capacitor in the first case (when the angular frequency is ω):

$$X_C = X_{bc} = \frac{V_{bc}}{I} = \frac{12\,\text{V}}{0.001\,\text{A}} = 12\,\text{k}\Omega; \tag{2}$$

while the inductive reactance of the coil is:

$$X_L = \omega L = \frac{1}{2\omega C} = 6\,\text{k}\Omega. \tag{3}$$

Let us now find out what happens if the angular frequency is changed to $\omega/\sqrt{2}$. The inductive reactance should by divided by $\sqrt{2}$ while the capacitive reactance should be multiplied by $\sqrt{2}$ to get their new values. Thus, according to equation (1), the net impedance of the parallel LC circuit between points c and d will be:

$$\frac{(6\,\text{k}\Omega/\sqrt{2}) \cdot 12\,\text{k}\Omega \cdot \sqrt{2}}{12\,\text{k}\Omega \cdot \sqrt{2} - (6\,\text{k}\Omega/\sqrt{2})} = 4\sqrt{2}\,\text{k}\Omega,$$

being an inductive type of impedance. The net impedance between points b and d is:

$$X_{bd} = X_C - X_{cd} = 12\sqrt{2}\,\text{k}\Omega - 4\sqrt{2}\,\text{k}\Omega = 8\sqrt{2}\,\text{k}\Omega$$

being a capacitive type of impedance.

The net impedance between points a and d can be calculated as:

$$Z_{ad} = \sqrt{R^2 + X_{bd}^2} = \sqrt{(5\,\text{k}\Omega)^2 + (8\sqrt{2}\,\text{k}\Omega)^2} = \sqrt{153}\,\text{k}\Omega = 12.37\,\text{k}\Omega.$$

Therefore the ammeter in the second case reads:

$$I = \frac{V_{gen}}{Z} = \frac{5\,\text{V}}{12.37\,\text{k}\Omega} = 0.404\ \text{mA}.$$

The net impedance between points a and c is:

$$X_{ac} = \sqrt{R^2 + X_C^2} = \sqrt{(5\,\text{k}\Omega)^2 + (12\sqrt{2}\,\text{k}\Omega)^2} = \sqrt{313}\,\text{k}\Omega = 17.69\,\text{k}\Omega.$$

Therefore in the second case the reading of the voltmeter (which is the RMS voltage across these two points) will be:

$$V_{ac} = X_{ac} \cdot I = 17.68\,\text{k}\Omega \cdot 0.404\ \text{mA} = 7.15\,\text{V}.$$

Solution of Problem 282. The parts in the two branches that are above points P and Q should have the same net impedances and phase differences. In the left branch, where elements are connected in parallel, the current leads the potential difference by φ, whose tangent is:

$$\tan\varphi = \frac{R}{X_{C_e}} = \frac{R\omega C}{2},$$

in the right branch, where elements are connected in series:

$$\tan\varphi = \frac{X_C}{R_x} = \frac{1/\omega C}{R_x}.$$

Assuming that the right-hand sides of the equations are equal, we obtain:

$$\frac{R\omega C}{2} = \frac{1}{\omega C R_x}.$$

from which the angular frequency of the alternating potential difference is:

$$\omega = \frac{1}{C} \cdot \sqrt{\frac{2}{RR_x}}.$$ (1)

Assuming that the impedances in the two branches are the same, we get:

$$\frac{1}{\sqrt{\left(\frac{\omega C}{2}\right)^2 + \frac{1}{R^2}}} = \sqrt{\left(\frac{1}{\omega C}\right)^2 + R_x^2}.$$ (2)

We have a system of equations for ω and R_x. Substituting the angular frequency from the first equation into the second, we gain a quadratic equation for the unknown resistance:

$$4R_x^2 + 4RR_x - 3R^2 = 0,$$

whose solution is:

$$R_x = \frac{R}{2} = 0.5\,\text{k}\Omega,$$

from which the angular frequency is:

$$\omega = \frac{2}{CR} = 1000\ \text{s}^{-1},$$

and thus the frequency of the alternating potential difference is:

$$n = \frac{\omega}{2\pi} = 159.2\ \text{s}^{-1}.$$

Solution of Problem 283. Let us assume that the internal resistance of the AC network is negligible. The DC potential differences supplied by the cells and the AC potential difference supplied by the network are superimposed. The DC voltmeter cannot follow the AC potential difference because of its high frequency, therefore its reading is not affected by the AC network. As the internal resistance of the AC network is zero, the circuit in the first case behaves as if it was shorted as shown. In this case the coils do not affect the reading of the DC voltmeter.

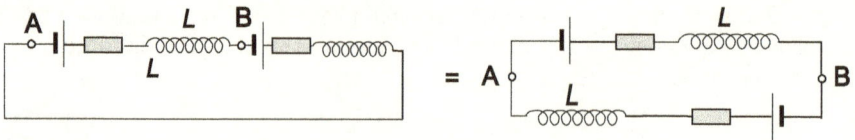

Since the DC voltmeter reads $V_{AB} = 0$, the potential differences accross the internal resistances should be equal to the respective emfs of the cells. (The problem can only be solved if the resistances of the coils are taken to be 0.)

The potential difference across points A and B is zero in both the upper and lower branch of the circuit, therefore:

$$V_{AB} = IR_1 - \mathcal{E}_1 = 0 \quad \rightarrow \quad IR_1 = \mathcal{E}_1,$$

$$V_{AB} = IR_2 - \mathcal{E}_2 = 0 \quad \rightarrow \quad IR_2 = \mathcal{E}_2,$$

hence

$$\frac{R_2}{R_1} = \frac{\mathcal{E}_2}{\mathcal{E}_1} = \frac{100\,\text{V}}{50\,\text{V}} = 2,$$

therefore $R_2 = 2R_1$. The reading of the DC voltmeter was used to find the ratio of the internal resistances of the cells. Let us now connect an AC voltmeter across points A and B.

The phase constant in an RL circuit is given by the formula:

$$\tan\varphi = \frac{X_L}{R},$$

substituting known values, we find:

$$\tan 45° = 1 = \frac{2\omega L}{R_1 + R_2} = \frac{2\omega L}{R_1 + 2R_1},$$

which yields $R_1 = 2\omega L/3$ and $R_2 = 2R_1 = 4\omega L/3$. The net impedance of the circuit is:

$$Z = \sqrt{(R_1 + R_2)^2 + (2\omega L)^2} = \sqrt{(6\omega L/3)^2 + (2\omega L)^2} = 2\sqrt{2}\omega L.$$

The AC component of the current has an RMS value of:

$$I = \frac{V}{Z} = \frac{V}{2\sqrt{2}\omega L}.$$

The impedance between points A and B can be calculated as:

$$Z_{AB} = \sqrt{R_1^2 + (\omega L)^2} = \sqrt{\frac{4}{9}(\omega L)^2 + (\omega L)^2} = \frac{\sqrt{13}}{3} \cdot \omega L,$$

therefore the potential difference across these two points (or across the terminals of the AC voltmeter) is:

$$V_{AB} = IZ_{AB} = \frac{V}{2\sqrt{2}\omega L} \cdot \frac{\sqrt{13}}{3} \cdot \omega L = \frac{\sqrt{26}}{12} \cdot V =$$

$$= 0.425V = 0.425 \cdot 220\,\text{V} = 93.5\,\text{V}.$$

Chapter 10

Optics Solutions

Solution of Problem 284. Using batteries the problem has no solution. Though we can use AC voltage supplies whose maximum voltages are equal, there is a 120° phase difference between them. In practice we can use two identical transformers, their primary coils have to be connected to two different phases of a three-phase generator, and then the secondary coils have to be connected in series. The voltage across one of the secondary coils is the same as the voltage across the two secondary coils connected in series.

Solution of Problem 285. Let us determine the quantities typical for the four layers. The distances travelled by light are:

$$\overline{A_1B_2} = \frac{b}{\sin\alpha_1}, \qquad \overline{A_2B_3} = \frac{b}{\sin\alpha_2}, \qquad \overline{A_3B_4} = \frac{b}{\sin\alpha_3}.$$

The speeds of light in the different plates are:

$$c_1 = \frac{c}{n_1}, \qquad c_2 = \frac{c}{n_2}, \qquad c_3 = \frac{c}{n_3}.$$

The elapsed times that are equal can be written as:

$$t = \frac{\overline{A_1B_2}}{c_1} = \frac{n_1}{c}\frac{b}{\sin\alpha_1} = \frac{\overline{A_2B_3}}{c_2} = \frac{n_2}{c}\frac{b}{\sin\alpha_2} = \frac{\overline{A_3B_4}}{c_3} = \frac{n_3}{c}\frac{b}{\sin\alpha_3}.$$

Snell's law states that:

$$\frac{\sin\alpha}{\sin\beta} = \frac{c_1}{c_2} = \frac{c}{n_1}\cdot\frac{n_2}{c} = \frac{n_2}{n_1},$$

assuming that in the case of the critical angle $\sin\beta = 1$, we get:

$$\sin\alpha_1 = \frac{n_2}{n_1}, \qquad \sin\alpha_2 = \frac{n_3}{n_2}, \qquad \sin\alpha_3 = \frac{n_4}{n_3}.$$

Substituting these into the expressions for the elapsed times and simplifying by b/c, we get:

$$\frac{n_1^2}{n_2} = \frac{n_2^2}{n_3} = \frac{n_3^2}{n_4} = C \text{ constant.}$$

As the first two refractive indices are given, c can be determined:

$$C = \frac{2.7^2}{2.43} = 3.$$

The remaining two refractive indices are therefore:

$$n_3 = \frac{n_2^2}{k} = \frac{2.43^2}{3} = 1.968,$$

$$n_4 = \frac{n_3^2}{k} = \frac{1.968^2}{3} = 1.291.$$

To be able to calculate the thicknesses of the layers, we need to determine the angles of incidence first. These are:

$$\sin \alpha_1 = \frac{n_2}{n_1} = \frac{2.43}{2.7} = 0.9 \quad \rightarrow \quad \alpha_1 = 64.16°$$

$$\sin \alpha_2 = \frac{n_3}{n_2} = \frac{1.968}{2.43} = 0.81 \quad \rightarrow \quad \alpha_2 = 54.1°$$

$$\sin \alpha_3 = \frac{n_4}{n_3} = \frac{1.291}{1.968} = 0.656 \quad \rightarrow \quad \alpha_3 = 41°$$

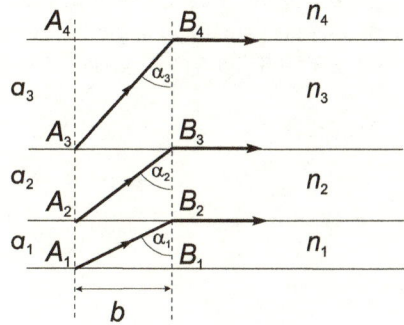

The thickness of the bottom layer can be written as:

$$a_1 = b \cdot \cot \alpha_1 =$$

$$= b \frac{\sqrt{1 - \sin^2 \alpha_1}}{\sin \alpha_1} = b \frac{\sqrt{1 - n_2^2/n_1^2}}{n_2/n_1} = b \frac{\sqrt{n_1^2 - n_2^2}}{n_2},$$

substituting known values, we find:

$$a_1 = 10 \, \text{mm} \cdot \frac{\sqrt{2.7^2 - 2.43^2}}{2.432} = 4.82 \, \text{mm}.$$

Similarly:

$$a_2 = b \frac{\sqrt{n_2^2 - n_3^2}}{n_3} = 10 \, \text{mm} \frac{\sqrt{2.43^2 - 1.968^2}}{1.968} = 7.24 \, \text{mm},$$

$$a_3 = b \frac{\sqrt{n_3^2 - n_4^2}}{n_4} = 10 \, \text{mm} \frac{\sqrt{1.986^2 - 1.291^2}}{1.291} = 11.51 \, \text{mm}.$$

Remark: This problem is a simplified model of fibre-optics. In fibres used for transmitting information, it is essential that light rays entering the fibre in different directions should arrive simultaneously independent of their distances travelled. It can be done if the refractive index in the fibre decreases in proportion to the distance from the axis squared. The technology for making such fibres has already been developed.

Solution of Problem 286. This problem can only be solved by making certain assumptions. A light ray that is refracted at the boundary, which means that part of it leaves the system, also has a part that is reflected. Due to the symmetry of the sphere, however, this part will reach the boundary again under the same angle of incidence and part of it will leave the system again. Therefore, all light rays that are refracted at the boundary for the first time will sooner or later leave the system. These light rays form a double cone in the inside of the shell, whose cone angle 2φ is determined only by the critical angle at the glass-air boundary. Note that this reasoning neglects the phenomenon of absorption loss that happens during reflections even in materials that are permeable to light and which causes the warming-up of the system. After stating these assumptions, let us start solving the problem.

Let us follow back the way of the light ray that leaves the outer surface of the glass shell at point C with an angle of refraction $\beta_2 = 90°$. In this case the angle of incidence at the glass-air boundary α_2 is the critical angle, so:

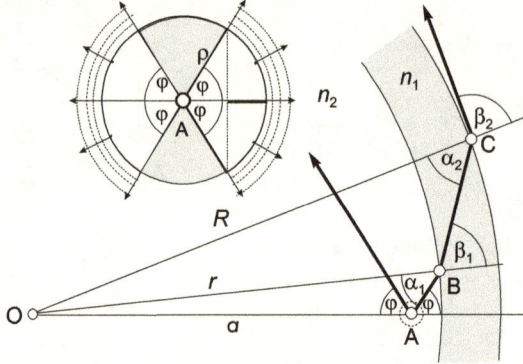

$$\sin\alpha_2 = \frac{1}{n_2}$$

The angle of refraction at the carbon disulphide-glass boundary β_1 can be determined applying the Sine-law to triangle OBC:

$$\frac{\sin\beta_1}{\sin\alpha_2} = \frac{R}{r},$$

so:

$$\sin\beta_1 = \frac{R}{r}\sin\alpha_2 = \frac{1}{n_2}\cdot\frac{R}{r}.$$

Applying the law of refraction to point B, we find:

$$\frac{\sin\alpha_1}{\sin\beta_1} = \frac{n_2}{n_1},$$

hence

$$\sin\alpha_1 = \frac{n_2}{n_1}\cdot\sin\beta_2 = \frac{1}{n_1}\cdot\frac{R}{r}.$$

Finally, the angle formed by the light ray and the radius at point A is given by the Sine-law applied to triangle OAB:

$$\frac{\sin\varphi}{\sin\alpha_1} = \frac{r}{a},$$

from which we get:

$$\sin\varphi = \frac{r}{a}\sin\alpha_1 = \frac{1}{n_1}\cdot\frac{R}{a}.$$

The same result is obtained if we examine the light rays going in the opposite direction, therefore it can be stated that only the light rays that are emitted inside the double cone with cone angle 2φ leave the system. Note the interesting fact that the result is independent of both the refractive index of the glass and the inner radius of the shell.

To calculate the percent of the energy that leaves the system let the source of light be the centre of an imaginary sphere with radius ϱ. Inside this sphere the energy flow is the same in all directions, therefore the area of the spherical caps determined by the double cone divided by the area of the sphere gives the percent of energy in question.

The height of the spherical caps is $\varrho - \varrho\cos\varphi$, so the total area of the two caps is given by: $2\cdot 2\pi\varrho(\varrho - \varrho\cos\varphi)$, while the area of the sphere is $4\pi\varrho^2$. The ratio of energy that leaves the system is therefore:

$$\frac{4\pi\varrho^2(1-\cos\varphi)}{4\pi\varrho^2} = 1 - \cos\varphi.$$

Substituting our result for half the cone angle:

$$\cos\varphi = \cos\arcsin\frac{1}{n_1}\cdot\frac{R}{a} = \cos\arcsin\frac{1}{1.6}\cdot\frac{7.5}{6} = 0.6242,$$

from which we have

$$\varphi = 51.35°.$$

Giving the leaving energy in percentage:

$$\frac{E_{\text{leaving}}}{E_{\text{total}}} = 1 - \cos 51.35° = 0.375 = 37.5\%.$$

Solution of Problem 287. The whole half-space can be seen if the rays which come from the solid angle of a 2π steradian enter into the core of the optical fibre. The boundary case is when the ray at the most extreme position enters into the medium of refractive index n_1 from the medium whose refractive index is n_3, sweeping their boundary. (Of course the information transmitted by these extreme rays is very dim.) The angle of refraction of the rays which enter from the half-space is between 0 and the critical angle of total internal reflection α_c, thus the extreme rays must satisfy the following condition:

$$\frac{\sin 90°}{\sin\alpha_c} = \frac{n_1}{n_3}.$$

In order not to have much loss, the rays inside the fibre must be reflected at the cladding, and thus for the

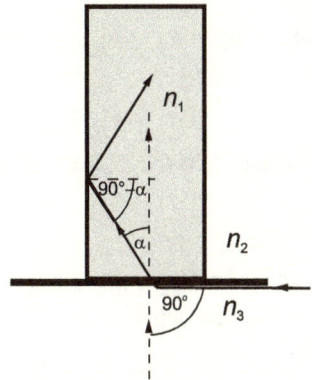

extreme ray the following condition must be satisfied at the boundary of the two media of refractive indices n_1-n_2:

$$\frac{\sin 90°}{\sin(90° - \alpha)} = \frac{n_1}{n_2}.$$

Because $\sin 90° = 1$ and $\sin(90° - \alpha) = \cos \alpha$, thus $\sin \alpha = n_3/n_1$ and $\cos \alpha = n_2/n_1$. From the equation system α can easily be eliminated:

$$\left(\frac{n_3}{n_1}\right)^2 + \left(\frac{n_2}{n_1}\right)^2 = \sin^2 \alpha + \cos^2 \alpha = 1.$$

Ordering the equation n_1 is:

$$n_1^2 = n_2^2 + n_3^2, \quad \text{and} \quad n_1 = \sqrt{n_2^2 + n_3^2}.$$

The solution of the problem is: $n_1 \geq \sqrt{n_2^2 + n_3^2}$. Let us notice that the result is symmetrical for n_2 and n_3, thus theoretically the role of two materials can be swapped.

The asked refractive indices in cases a) and b) are:

$$n_1 = \sqrt{1+1} = \sqrt{2} \approx 1.41, \quad \text{and} \quad n_1' = \sqrt{1 + \frac{16}{9}} = \frac{5}{3} \approx 1.67.$$

Solution of Problem 288. Let us denote the distance between the first lens and the object by x. According to the thin lens formula,

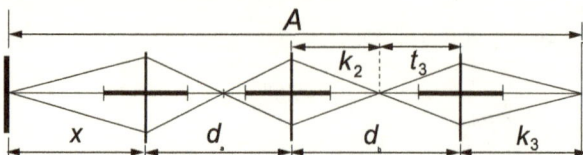

$$\frac{1}{x} + \frac{1}{k_1} = \frac{1}{f},$$

where k_1 is the distance between the lens and its image. Expressing it, we get:

$$k_1 = \frac{xf}{x - f}.$$

It means that the distance of this image from the second lens is

$$t_2 = d_a - k_1 = d_a - \frac{xf}{x - f}.$$

This real image is the object for the second lens, and its image is produced at the distance k_2 from the lens:

$$k_2 = \frac{t_2 f}{t_2 - f} = \frac{f[d_a - xf/(x - f)]}{d_a - f - xf/(x - f)}.$$

The distance of this image from the third lens is $d_b - k_2$. The image produced by the third lens is at the distance

$$k_3 = \frac{t_3 f}{t_3 - f} = \frac{(d_b - k_2)f}{d_b - f - k_2}$$

from the third lens.

The distance A between the object and the screen is simply the sum of the lengths x, d_a, d_b and k_3:

$$A = x + d_a + d_b + \frac{(d_b - k_2)f}{d_b - k_2 - f}.$$

Inserting here k_2 from one of the previous equations, after a lengthy but straightforward calculation, we get that

$$A = d_a + d_b + \frac{[d_a d_b - 2(d_a + d_b)f + 3f^2]x^2 + f^2(d_a - d_b)x + f^2[(d_a + d_b)f - d_a d_b]}{[d_a d_b - 2(d_a + d_b)f + 3f^2]x + f[d_a f - (d_a - f)(d_b - f)]}.$$

According to the statement of the problem, the above expression of A is independent of x. It is possible only if all the multipliers of x are zero. Let us investigate these terms one by one. The multiplier of x in the numerator has to vanish, so

$$f^2(d_a - d_b) = 0.$$

Consequently $d_a = d_b$, so the three lenses are placed at equal distances from each other. Let us denote this common distance by d. With this notation the formula for A has a simpler form:

$$A = 2d + \frac{[d^2 - 4fd + 3f^2]x^2 + f^2 d[2f - d]}{[d^2 - 4fd + 3f^2]x + f[-f^2 + 3df - d^2]}.$$

The multiplier of x^2 in the numerator and that of x in the denominator are the same, so there is only one further requirement:

$$d^2 - 4fd + 3f^2 = 0.$$

This is a quadratic equation for d (since f is a given parameter), whose solution is

$$d_{1,2} = \frac{4f \pm \sqrt{16f^2 - 12f^2}}{2} = 2f \pm f,$$

thus

$$d_1 = 3f, \quad \text{and} \quad d_2 = f.$$

Writing these values back into the formula for the distance A between the object and the screen, we obtain two different solutions:

$$A_1 = 2d + \frac{f^2 d(2f - d)}{f(-f^2 + 3df - d^2)} = 2 \cdot 3f + \frac{f^2 3f(2f - 3f)}{f(-f^2 + 3 \cdot 3f^2 - 9f^2)} = 9f,$$

and

$$A_2 = 2f + \frac{f^2 f(2f - f)}{f(-f^2 + 3f^2 - f^2)} = 3f.$$

Thus the requirements of the problem can be satisfied in two different ways. In the first case the distance between the lenses is three times their focal length, and the object–screen distance is nine times the focal length.

In the second case the distance between the lenses is equal to their focal length, and the object–screen distance is three times the focal length.

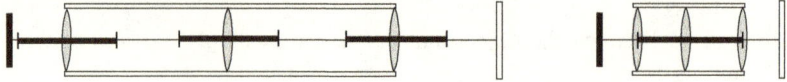

Solution of Problem 289. The last datum, which is the absolute value of the focal length of the eyepiece, implies that definitely two solutions are expected to be given for the problem. Let us examine first when the focal length is positive, so the eyepiece is a converging lens of Keplerian telescope.

The image of very distant objects formed by the astronomical telescope is diminished, but the angle subtended by the object is increased. Observing an object through a telescope means three optical devices are needed: the objective (object lens) of the telescope which has a big diameter, the ocular (eyepiece) which has small focal length and the lens of the eye of the observer. During the observation, the eye is 'accommodated to infinity', which means that the observer adjusts their eyes such that the image of an infinitely distant object is 'sharp', so the image of an infinitely far object (which is very far from the observer) is formed on the retina. In this case the eye forms an image from the rays which come from the object and which are parallel. The rays which pass through the eyepiece of the Keplerian telescope will be parallel if it passes the focus of the eyepiece which is on the side of the objective so that the light-rays, which travel from a distant object and which are parallel, will travel in the above described way as long as the eyepiece and the objective have a common principal axis and their foci coincide. In this case the image formed by the objective is in the focal plane of the object lens, and this image behaves as a real object of the eyepiece. If the two foci coincide, then a sharp image can only be gained if the observer's eye is accommodated to infinity. Placing the screen there, a blurred image will be formed on the screen since the parallel rays do not meet. But if the eyepiece is moved into the right direction and by the appropriate amount, we may gain converging rays, which form a sharp image on the screen. Our task is to determine the displacement of the eyepiece.

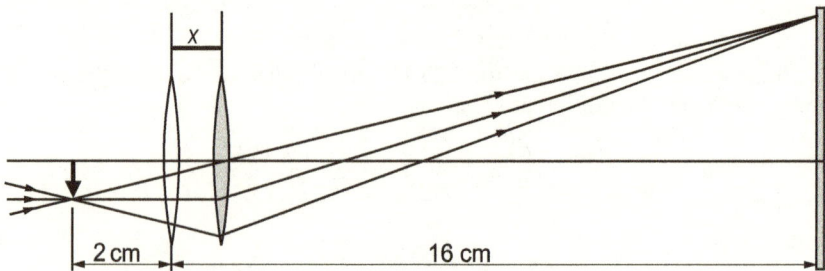

If the ocular is moved further from the objective, the real image formed by the objective is further from the eyepiece than the focus of the eyepiece, thus the eyepice also forms a real image. Let us substitute the numerical values of the given data into the thin lens equation, all data are measured in centimetres. In this case the object distance is $t = 2 + x$, the image distance is $k = 16 - x$, and the focal length is $f = 2$. The lens equation is :

$$\frac{1}{t} + \frac{1}{k} = \frac{1}{f}$$

substituting the data

$$\frac{1}{2+x} + \frac{1}{16-x} = \frac{1}{2}.$$

Ordering the equation:

$$x^2 - 14x + 4 = 0.$$

This equation has two solutions: $x = 7 \pm 3 \cdot \sqrt{5}$, thus $x_1 = 0.28$ cm and $x_2 = 13.72$ cm. This latter one —though the solution of the problem — cannot be used in practice, because if the lens moved along such a long distance the image would be very small.

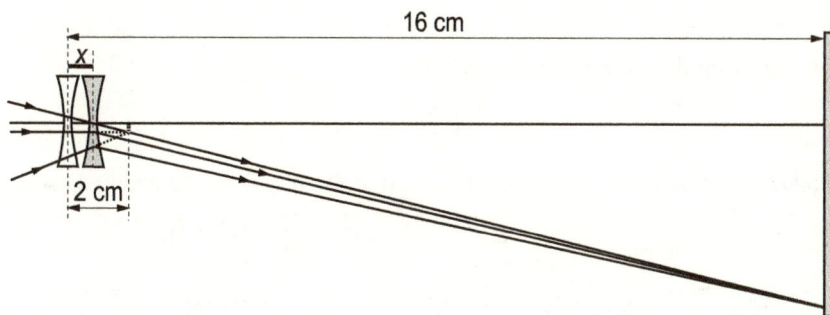

The image of the Sun can also be formed by the Galilean telescope in which there is a diverging lens as an eyepiece allowing it to have a virtual focus and giving it a negative focal length. The ocular is placed in the way of the converging beam of light, and travels through the objective before they meet at one point. Thus the rays become parallel (so the observer can look with his eyes adjusted to infinity) although the angle between the rays and the principal axis is greater than it would be without the diverging lens. Moving the eyepiece with the appropriate distance of x, converging rays can be produced again, so a real image is formed on the screen which is at a finite distance from the telescope. Again the eyepiece must be moved outwards, so that the image formed by the objective is at the focus of the objective (without the eyepiece) which will be between the eyepiece and the focus of the eyepiece at a distance of 2 cm $- x$, measured from the eyepiece. This will thus be the virtual object of the eyepiece. The object distance is 16 cm $- x$ again. The thin lens equation (considering that the object distance of a virtual object and the focal length of a diverging lens are negative) is the following:

$$\frac{1}{-(2-x)} + \frac{1}{16-x} = \frac{1}{-2}.$$

After ordering the equation:

$$x^2 - 18x + 4 = 0.$$

The solutions are: $x = 9 \pm \sqrt{77}$, so seemingly, we have discovered two solutions again. $x_1 = 17.77$ cm and $x_2 = 0.22$ cm. But the solution of the problem is only the $x = 0.22$ cm, because 17.77 cm > 16 cm, thus the lens should have been placed behind the screen, which would make it impossible to form an image.

Solution of Problem 290. A so-called Galilean telescope is to be built, which would create an upright image. This is why the middle lens is needed in order to turn the upside-down image back. The first image of the object, which is at infinity, is formed at the focus of the objective of focal length f_1. The next image is formed in front of the eyepiece at a distance of f_3 from it, which is its focal length. Since the length of the tube is d, the distance which remains for the sum of the object distance and the image distance of the middle lens, $o+i$ is equal to $d - f_1 - f_3$. So

$$o + i = d - f_1 - f_3.$$

The lens equation for the middle lens is:

$$\frac{1}{o} + \frac{1}{k} = \frac{1}{f_2}.$$

The equation system leads to a quadratic equation for o and i. The solutions will be:

$$o = \frac{d - f_1 - f_3 - \sqrt{(d - f_1 - f_3)(d - f_1 - f_3 - 4f_2)}}{2},$$

$$i = \frac{d - f_1 - f_3 + \sqrt{(d - f_1 - f_3)(d - f_1 - f_3 - 4f_2)}}{2}.$$

The angular magnification of the middle lens is f_1/o, the angular magnification of the eyepiece is i/f_3, thus the total angular magnification is:

$$N = \frac{f_1}{o} \cdot \frac{i}{f_3} = \frac{f_1}{f_3} o.$$

using the values of i and o:

$$N = \frac{f_1}{f_3} \cdot \frac{1 + \sqrt{1 - 4f_2/(d - f_1 - f_3)}}{1 - \sqrt{1 - 4f_2/(d - f_1 - f_3)}}.$$

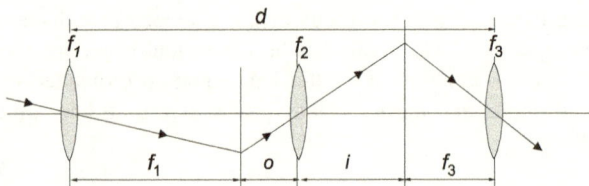

The greatest magnification can be gained by varying the order of the lenses, since the data (d, f_1, f_2, f_3) are fixed. (From the formula of the magnification it can be seen that the magnification is the greatest if d is the longest possible value.) So for the different orders of lenses the magnifications must be calculated. So obviously the lens of focal length $f_1 = 90$ cm will be the objective and the whole length of the tube $d = 150$ cm must be used. The following results can be calculated:

f_1	f_2	f_3	o	i	N
90 cm	8 cm	10 cm	10 cm	40 cm	36 cm
90 cm	10 cm	8 cm	13.5 cm	38.5 cm	32.06 cm.

It can be seen that the magnification is the greatest if the middle lens is the one which has a focal length of 8 cm, and the eyepiece is the lens of focal length 10 cm.

Solution of Problem 291. The focal length of both lenses is $f = 1/D = 1/2$ m, thus the two lenses are at the foci of each other. Because of the special data, the formation of the image can easily be described.

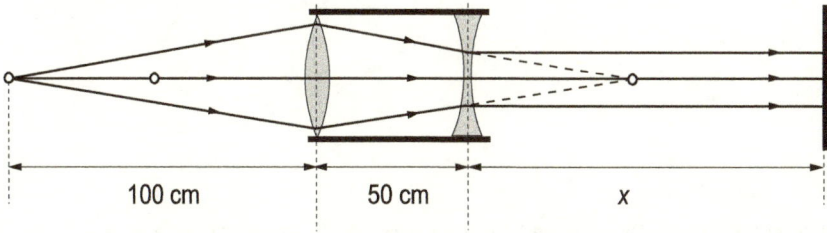

Let us place a pointlike light source towards the axis at a distance of 100 cm from the converging lens. According to the given data, this object is at a distance of twice the focal length and so its image would also be formed at a distance of twice the focal length on the other side of the lens. This means, due to the special data, that the object will be 50 cm from the diverging lens, and thus at its focus. Because the beam which travels towards the focus of the diverging lens is refracted parallel to the axis of the lens, the mirror, which is placed perpendicularly to the axis, will reflect the beam along itself independently of the distance x. Because the way of light is reversible, the beam will travel back to the original position from where it was emanated, forming a pointlike image.

Now let us place a small object above the axis perpendicularly to the axis. Its image will be located where the image of its point on the axis is formed. Because the magnification is $M = I/O = p/i$, and in the case of the first lens the image and object distances are equal, and since the system only reflects back the image to that side of the converging lens where the object is at the same distance from the lens, the magnification is 1, meaning that the object and the image are the same size. Therefore the image is real, inverted and has the same size as the object.

Solution of Problem 292. Ths light cone that passes the circular hole and the light cone that is formed from the beam refracted by the rest of the lens must meet exactly at the wall. Let us denote the radius of the bright circle formed on the wall with h, the radius of the hole on the lens with r and the radius of the lens with $R = 2r$. The distance between the light-source and the lens is the object distance o.

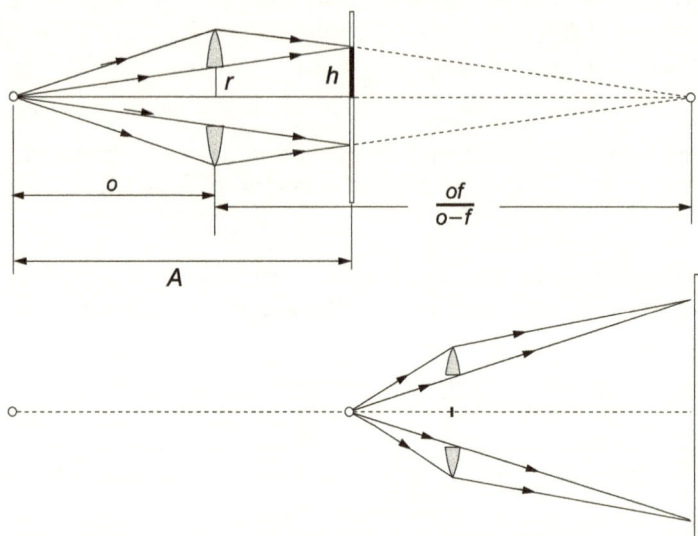

The distance between the lens and the image of the light-source is: $i = \dfrac{of}{o-f}$.

From the similar triangles:

$$\frac{h}{r} = \frac{A}{o} \quad \text{and} \quad \frac{h}{R} = \frac{h}{2r} = \frac{o+i-A}{i} = \frac{o+\frac{of}{o-f}-A}{\frac{of}{o-f}}.$$

from the first equation $\dfrac{h}{r}$ can be substituted and the following quadratic equation can be gained for o:

$$2o^2 - 2Ao + af = 0.$$

Its solutions are:

$$o = \frac{A}{2} \pm \frac{1}{2}\sqrt{A(A-2f)}.$$

In our case the following two solutions are gained for the possible positions of the light-source: $o_1 = 6\,\text{cm}$ and $o_2 = 3\,\text{cm}$. In the first case, the lens must be placed $6\,\text{cm}$ from the light source. The second solution is also a correct solution, though in this case the image is virtual. (A trivial solution is the $o = 0$.)

The problem can only be solved if $A > 2f$.

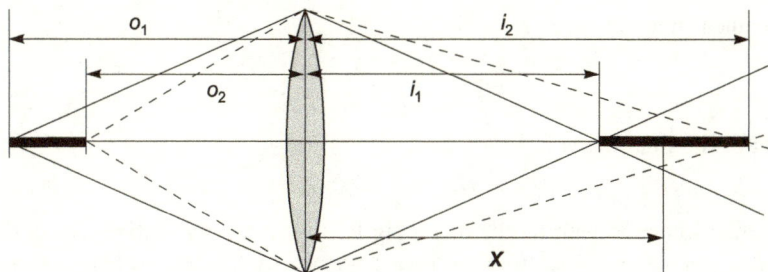

Solution of Problem 293. The images of the points of the light tube are on the principal axis. Let the required position of the screen be at a distance of x from the lens and let the diameter of the light spot be $2r$ in that position. The images of the ends of the tubes are at distances o_1 and o_2 from the lens are formed at distances:

$$i_1 = \frac{o_1 f}{o_1 - f}, \qquad i_2 = \frac{o_2 f}{o_2 - f}.$$

Assuming that the ratios of corresponding sides are equal in similar triangles, we obtain:

$$\frac{r}{x - i_1} = \frac{R}{i_1}, \qquad \frac{r}{i_2 - x} = \frac{R}{i_2}.$$

Solving the system of equations for x and r, we find:

$$x = \frac{2 i_1 i_2}{i_1 + i_2}, \qquad r = R \cdot \frac{i_2 - i_1}{i_2 + i_1}.$$

Substituting the image distances calculated above, we get:

$$x = \frac{2 o_1 o_2 f}{2 o_1 o_2 - (o_1 + o_2) f}, \qquad r = R \cdot \frac{(o_1 - o_2) f}{2 o_1 o_2 - (o_1 + o_2) f}.$$

The length of the image of the light tube is:

$$l_i = i_2 - i_1 = \frac{(o_1 - o_2) f^2}{(o_2 - f)(o_1 - f)} = \frac{l f^2}{(o_1 - f)(o_2 - f)},$$

where l is the length of the light tube.

Substituting given data, we find $x = 96$ cm, $r = 0.4$ cm, $l_i = 40$ cm. Note that the minimum value of the radius of the image is 4 mm, which is quite impossible for a light tube, whose radius is at least about 2 cm. This means that a single wire filament should be used in this experiment instead of the light tube.

Solution of Problem 294. Let us follow the way the images are formed by the lenses and the mirror. The virtual image formed by the diverging lens has an image distance of:

$$i_1 = \frac{o_1 f_1}{o_1 - f_1} = \frac{-4 \cdot 4}{4 - (-4)} \, \mathrm{dm} = -2 \, \mathrm{dm}.$$

Since the linear magnification is

$$m_1 = \frac{H_{i1}}{H_{o1}} = \frac{i_1}{o_1} = \frac{1}{2},$$

the height of the first image is

$$H_{i1} = \frac{x}{2} = H_{o2}.$$

This virtual image is seen by the diverging lens as an object with an object distance of $o_2 = f_2 + |i_1| = 6\,\mathrm{dm}$, therefore the image formed by the second lens has an image distance of

$$i_2 = \frac{o_2 f_2}{o_2 - f_2} = \frac{6 \cdot 4}{6 - 4}\,\mathrm{dm} = 12\,\mathrm{dm}.$$

The linear magnification of the second lens is:

$$m_2 = \frac{i_2}{o_2} = \frac{12}{6} = 2.$$

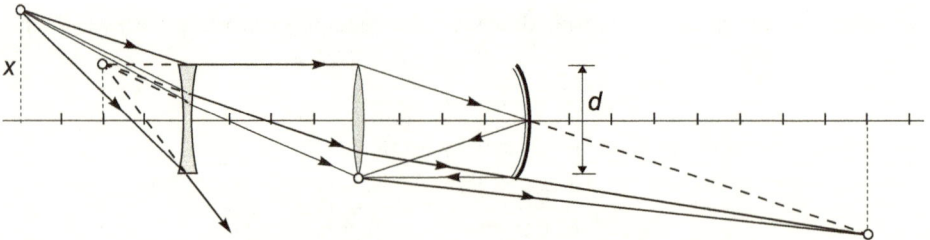

Hence the height of the second image is $H_{i2} = m_2 H_{o2} = m_2 H_{i1} = 2H_{i1} = x = H_{o3}$.

The second image is seen by the concave mirror as a virtual object being at a distance of $o_3 = f_3 - i_2 = -8\,\mathrm{dm}$, therefore the image is formed at:

$$i_3 = \frac{o_3 f_3}{o_3 - f_3} = \frac{-8 \cdot 8}{-8 - 8} = \frac{-64}{-16} = 4\,\mathrm{dm}.$$

This is a real image and since the linear magnification of the mirror is:

$$m_3 = \frac{i_3}{o_3} = -\frac{1}{2},$$

the height of the final image is $H_{i3} = m_3 H_{o3} = \frac{x}{2}$.

Note that the final image is formed in the plane of the converging lens, therefore the image can only be captured on a screen if its height is greater than the radius of the lens. This happens when x is greater than d, therefore the first condition for the perpendicular displacement is $d < x$. If x is increased further than 1.5 d, the rays will all pass under the concave mirror, and there will be no image formation. Therefore the solution of the problem is:

$$d < x < 1.5\,d.$$

* 9 7 8 0 8 5 7 2 8 4 0 2 0 *